I0435136

United States
Department of
Agriculture

Forest Service

Pacific Southwest
Research Station

General Technical
Report
PSW-GTR-240

November 2012

USDA

Proceedings of the Fourth International Workshop on the Genetics of Host-Parasite Interactions in Forestry: Disease and Insect Resistance in Forest Trees

July 31 to August 5, 2011 – Eugene, Oregon, USA

Disclaimer

Papers were provided by the authors in camera-ready form for printing. Authors are responsible for the content and accuracy. Opinions expressed may not necessarily reflect the position of the U.S. Department of Agriculture.

The use of trade or firm names in this publication is for reader information and does not imply endorsement by the U.S. Department of Agriculture of any product or service.

Pesticide Precautionary Statement

This publication reports research involving pesticides. It does not contain recommendations for their use, nor does it imply that the uses discussed here have been registered. All uses of pesticides must be registered by appropriate state or federal agencies, or both, before they can be recommended.

CAUTION: Pesticides can be injurious to humans, domestic animals, desirable plants, and fish or other wildlife if they are not applied properly. Use all pesticides selectively and carefully. Follow recommended practices for the disposal of surplus pesticides and pesticide containers

Technical Coordinators

Richard A. Sniezko is center geneticist, U.S. Department of Agriculture Forest Service, Dorena Genetic Resource Center, 34963 Shoreview Road, Cottage Grove, OR 97424 (e-mail address: rsniezko@fs.fed.us).

Alvin D. Yanchuk is senior scientist, British Columbia Ministry of Forests, Lands and Natural Resource Operations, Tree Improvement Branch, PO Box 9518, Stn Prov Govt, Victoria, BC, V8W9C2, Canada (e-mail address: Alvin.Yanchuk@gov.bc.ca).

John T. Kliejunas is regional forest pathologist (retired), U.S. Department of Agriculture Forest Service, Pacific Southwest Region, 1323 Club Drive, Vallejo, CA 94592-1110   (e-mail address: Kliejunas@comcast.net).

Katharine M. Palmieri is public information officer, California Oak Mortality Task Force, 163 Mulford Hall, University of California, Berkeley, CA 94720-3114   (e-mail address: kpalmieri@berkeley.edu).

Janice M. Alexander is sudden oak death outreach specialist, University of California, Cooperative Extension, Suite 150-B, 1682 Novato Blvd, Novato CA 94947   (e-mail address: jalexander@ucdavis.edu).

Susan J. Frankel is plant pathologist, U.S. Department of Agriculture Forest Service, Pacific Southwest Research Station, 800 Buchanan Street, West Annex Building, Albany, CA 94710   (e-mail address: sfrankel@fs.fed.us).

Proceedings of the Fourth International Workshop on the Genetics of Host-Parasite Interactions in Forestry: Disease and Insect Resistance in Forest Trees

July 31 to August 5, 2011 – Eugene, Oregon, USA

Richard A. Sniezko, Alvin D. Yanchuk, John T. Kliejunas,

Katharine M. Palmieri, Janice M. Alexander, and Susan J. Frankel

Technical Coordinators

U.S. Department of Agriculture, Forest Service
Pacific Southwest Research Station
Albany, CA
General Technical Report PSW-GTR-240
October 2012

Conference Sponsors

International Union of Forest Research Organizations (IUFRO):
- Working Party 7.03.11 Resistance to Insects
- Working Party 2.02.15 Breeding and Genetic Resources of Five-Needle Pines

USDA Forest Service:
- Western Wildland Environmental Threat Assessment Center (WWETAC)
- Eastern Forest Environmental Threat Assessment Center (EFETAC)
- Pacific Northwest Region, Forest Health Protection & Genetic Resource Programs
- Pacific Northwest Research Station (PNW)
- Pacific Southwest Research Station (PSW)

King Estate Winery
University of California Cooperative Extension
California Oak Mortality Task Force, California Forest Pest Council
Futuragene
Starker Forests

Cover illustration: The Elders, Sugar Pine in the Morning by Dean Davis.

Technical Committee

Richard Sniezko, USDA Forest Service, Dorena Genetic Resource Center, USA

Alvin Yanchuk, British Columbia Ministry of Forests and Range, Canada

Dan Herms, Ohio State University, USA

Everett Hansen, Oregon State University, USA

Jeff Stone, Oregon State University, USA

Anna Schoettle, USDA Forest Service, Rocky Mountain Research Station, USA

Susan Frankel, USDA Forest Service, Pacific Southwest Research Station, USA

Dana Nelson, USDA Forest Service, Southern Research Station, USA

Fred Hebard, The American Chestnut Foundation, USA

Acelino Couto Alfenas, Universidade Federal de Viçosa, Brazil

Arnaud Dowkiw, French National Institute for Agricultural Research (INRA Orléans), France

Luis Sampedro, Centro de Investigación Forestal de Lourizán at Galicia, Spain

Alberto Santini, Istituto per le Protezione delle Piante – National Research Council (CNR), Italy

Charles G. "Terry" Shaw, USDA Forest Service, Western Wildland Environmental Threat
   Assessment Center, USA

Dan Quiring, University of New Brunswick, Canada

Fred Hain, North Carolina State University, USA

Brian Stanton, GreenWood Resources, Inc., USA

Bohun B. Kinloch, USDA Forest Service, Pacific Southwest Research Station,
      Institute of Forest Genetics (retired), USA

Fikret Isik, Research Associate Professor of Quantitative Genetics, NCSU Cooperative Tree
      Improvement Program, North Carolina State University, Raleigh, North Carolina, USA

Local Organizing Committee

Richard Sniezko, USDA Forest Service, Dorena Genetic Resource Center, OR - Workshop Chair

Katie Palmieri, University of California, Berkeley; California Oak Mortality Task Force

Janice Alexander, University of California, Cooperative Extension, Marin County,
      California Oak Mortality Task Force

Susan Frankel, USDA Forest Service, Pacific Southwest Research Station, CA

Angelia Kegley, USDA Forest Service, Dorena Genetic Resource Center, OR

Sunny Lucas, USDA Forest Service, Dorena Genetic Resource Center, OR

Michael Crawford, USDI Bureau of Land Management, OR

Larry Johnston, USDI Bureau of Land Management, OR

Abstract

Sniezko, R.A.; Yanchuk, A.D.; Kliejunas, J.T.; Palmieri, K.M.; Alexander, J.M.; Frankel, S.J. 2012.
Proceedings of the Fourth International Workshop on the Genetics of Host-Parasite Interactions in Forestry: Disease and Insect Resistance in Forest Trees. General Technical Report PSW-GTR-240. Albany, CA: U.S. Department of Agriculture, Forest Service, Pacific Southwest Research Station. 372 p.

The Fourth International Workshop on the Genetics of Host-Parasite Interactions in Forestry: Disease and Insect Resistance in Forest Trees provided a forum for research and management options and successes which have occurred over the last 30 years (the previous workshop was held in 1980 in Wageningen, The Netherlands). Eighty-eight submissions from oral and poster presentations at the 2011 workshop held in Eugene, Oregon provide a worldwide, comprehensive update on many aspects of research and operational programs on genetic resistance to forest insects and diseases. Topics of concern to natural forest systems and intensively managed forests are discussed, including resistance mechanisms, durability of resistance, ecology and evolutionary biology of resistance and tolerance, pathogen evolution, molecular tools, short-term screening assays for resistance and status of several applied forest tree resistance programs.

Key words: forest disease and insect resistance, evolutionary biology, climate change, durable resistance

Contents

Preface

Native and non-native pathogens, insects and animals continue to have serious negative impacts on forest ecosystems and planted forests worldwide. Climate change will alter host-pest relationships and may increase detrimental impacts from many biotic agents. Genetic variation in resistance within tree species is a key element to maintaining forest health. It is the primary natural method of tree defense and utilizing genetic resistance is one of the few viable management options available to combat the adverse impacts of pests. Resistance research programs, including resistance breeding, are vital since they increase the efficiency in utilizing genetic variation to restore forest health when mortality becomes unacceptably high. Resistance research and breeding has been underway in some forest tree species for over 50 years.

The Fourth International Workshop on the Genetics of Host-Parasite Interactions in Forestry: Disease and Insect Resistance in Forest Trees was convened to serve as the first major international gathering of researchers and technical specialists on this topic in the past 30 years. These Proceedings provide an update on many resistance programs at different stages throughout the world, with added insights and program examples from researchers in horticulture, plant genetics and evolutionary biology. Key past meetings that inspired this workshop, include:

> **Breeding Pest-Resistant Trees. 1964.** University Park, Pennsylvania, USA.
> **Biology of Rust Resistance in Forest Trees. 1969.** Moscow, Idaho, USA.
> **Resistance to Diseases and Pests in Forest Trees. 1980.** Wageningen, The Netherlands.
>
> Other related conferences:
> **Breeding Insect and Disease Resistant Forest Trees. 1982.** Eugene, Oregon, USA.
> **Mechanisms and Deployment of Resistance in Trees to Insects. 2000.** Iguassu Falls, Brazil.

An informal survey by the Food and Agriculture Organization of the United Nations (FAO 2008) provides a snapshot of the level of world-wide activity in pest resistance breeding (http://www.fao.org/forestry/26445/en/). In a recent review (Sniezko 2006), an update on four operational disease-resistance programs in the United States is presented. This Proceedings provides a much more comprehensive update. With climate change and continued invasion by non-native pathogens and insects, the contributions of resistance breeding to planted forests and natural ecosystems are needed more than ever. Long-term public support for these programs is essential to the success of these applied programs.

The purpose of this workshop was to advance progress in genetic resistance programs by fostering collaboration between scientists from throughout the world, and to provide an update to the forest community on resistance in forest trees. Updates on current status, issues and future plans for applied resistance programs, as well as research information and tools to fast-track the development and use of resistance in trees were presented and discussed. Presentations on the efforts in annual crops, as well as tree crops such as hazelnut (*Corylus avellana*) and rubber (*Hevea brasiliensis*), helped increase the breadth of understanding of the potential of genetic resistance in forest trees. The inclusion of topics in evolutionary biology broadened our perspectives. The conference field trip provided an opportunity to visit USDA Forest Service and USDI Bureau of Land Management facilities in Oregon to see some of the applied operational resistance programs that have been underway for decades, notably the white pine blister rust resistance work with *Pinus monticola*, *P. lambertiana*, *P. albicaulis*, *P. flexilis*, *P. strobiformis* and *P. aristata*; the *Phytophthora lateralis* resistance program for *Chamaecyparis lawsoniana* ; and to see operational seed orchards of *Pseudotsuga menziesii*.

There are many people and groups to thank for the success of this workshop. The technical committee and local organizing committees provided essential inputs on planning and logistics. The generous support of the sponsors made possible the inclusion of some of the invited speakers. The early encouragement of Jerry Beatty and Charles G. Shaw and sponsorship of the USDA Forest Service, Western Wildland

Environmental Threat Assessment Center provided the impetus to undertake organization of this meeting. The IUFRO Working Parties 7.03.11 (Resistance to insects) and 7.02.15 (Breeding and genetic resources of five-needle pines) provided scientific sponsorship. Volunteers Rob Mutch and Wesley Clark organized and implemented the live webcast of this meeting – providing the opportunity for those unable to attend to see and hear the presentations and discussions (http:ucanr.org/sites/tree_resistance_2011conference). A special thanks to the USDA Forest Service, Pacific Southwest Research Station for production of this Proceedings, and also my co-technical editors Susan Frankel, Katie Palmieri, Janice Alexander, John Kliejunas and Alvin Yanchuk, whose many hours made both the conference and proceedings come to fruition. Lastly, I would like to thank all of the presenters, moderators and other participants, who took time out of very busy schedules to participate in the workshop and share their work.

It is my hope that the 2011 workshop will provide impetus for a continued dialog – initial planning is underway for a possible follow-up meeting in 2015 in France. For further information and to stay engaged in this topic, subscribe to the Pest Resistance in Trees (Insect or pathogen resistance) mailing list at www.fs.usda.gov/goto/r6/dorena. Stay tuned!

RICHARD A. SNIEZKO

Coordinator, IUFRO Working Party 2.02.15 – Breeding and genetic resources of five-needle pines

http://www.iufro.org/science/divisions/division-2/20000/20200/20215/

Center Geneticist

USDA Forest Service - Dorena Genetic Resource Center

34963 Shoreview Road, Cottage Grove, Oregon, U.S.A.

July 31, 2012

Literature Cited

FAO. 2008. Selection and breeding for insect and disease resistance. www.fao.org/forestry/26445 (31 July 2012).

Sniezko, R.A. 2006. Resistance breeding against nonnative pathogens in forest trees — current successes in North America. Canadian Journal of Plant Pathology. 28: S270–S279.

Participants in the Fourth International Workshop on the Genetics of Host-Parasite Interactions in Forestry Disease and Insect Resistance in Forest Trees held July 31 to August 5, 2011 in Eugene, Oregon USA. (Photo: Rob Mutch)

Mechanisms of Resistance to Pests and Pathogens

Weevil resistant Sitka spruce genotype 898 stands tall amidst weevil damaged trees at the Pacific Forestry Centre in Victoria, BC.
(Photo: Justin Whitehill)

Tree Breeding for Pest Resistance for the Next 50 Years: the Search for Cross Resistance?

Alvin D. Yanchuk[1]

Abstract

Research activities aimed at developing resistance to pests (insect, pathogens, mammals) in forest trees can be documented back over 5 decades. While a substantial body of research has been published on resistances in forest trees, not much of this work has made its way into applied tree improvement programs. There are several reasons for this, e.g.: (i) a new or interesting incursion is noticed, and studies are developed that work on materials not related to a breeding program; (ii) adequate infection or artificial inoculation techniques are too expensive and a large enough population cannot be screened; and (iii) the genetic gain in resistance may not be silviculturally useful or effective. However, a few notable exceptions are present, and important lessons should be taken from our experiences over the last 50 years.

What has changed recently is the concern that pest and disease occurrences (with notable outbreaks) are increasing and are likely to continue to increase. Moreover, it might be difficult to know what particular disease or pest may become the new threat, particularly with climate change and the increased movement of goods around the world leading to the introduction of exotic pests. We can go about tree breeding, in a re-active approach, as we have for the past 50 years, hoping that a genetic option can be developed within one cycle of selection and testing; however, it is not uncommon for this to take a decade or more. At some point soon, funding agencies and managers will start asking how useful is pest resistance breeding as a strategic and viable option for future forest health and biosecurity programs. The other approach may be that we more aggressively look for situations of cross resistance against future 'classes of threats' rather than the traditional 'one-tree/one-pest' program(s) of the past. The risk we face here is that some pests (diseases in particular) will be quite host or genotype specific and we may provide no additional protection to future crops. While this is a risk, it seems that, particularly with a growing body of research showing that cross resistance is present, breeding trees which may have more 'durable' forms of resistance is probably a timely endeavor in forest tree breeding. At the very least, it should be seriously considered in particular programs.

[1] British Columbia Ministry of Forests, Lands and Natural Resources Operations, Tree Improvement Branch, 727 Fisgard Street, Victoria, BC Canada. V8W 9C1.
Corresponding author: alvin.yanchuk@gov.bc.ca.

Multiple Resistances Against Diseases and Insects in a Breeding Population of *Pinus pinaster*

Alejandro Solla,[1] María Vivas,[1] Elena Cubera,[1] Luis Sampedro,[2] Xoaquín Moreira,[2] Esther Merlo,[3] Raúl de la Mata,[4] and Rafael Zas[4]

Abstract

The different plant defenses existing within a given taxon have been commonly assumed to trade-off among each other because of both evolutionary and physiological reasons. The higher the efficiency of a single defensive trait, the lower selective pressure for other redundant defenses expected. On the other hand, production of multiple defenses might be constrained by the resources required for maintaining, at a time, increased growth and reproductive rates. However, different defensive traits do not need to always be redundant, and plants require the combination of multiple defenses to cope with all possible damages. This is particularly true in the case of forest trees, because their large size and long-life span make them targets for a wide range of enemies. Theory predicts that trees tend to evolve generalized defenses that are effective against a wide array of herbivores and pathogens, but empirical evidences of multiple resistances are lacking.

Objectives were to (1) compile data from several independent experiments of the same genetic material and explore whether resistances to an array of different pests and diseases were genetically related; (2) determine to what extent resistances are genetically related with quantitative defensive traits; (3) check for possible trade-offs between resistances and other fitness-related traits, such as growth and cone production; and (4) identify genotypes with multiple resistances to be used for breeding. Plant material consisted of *Pinus pinaster* Aiton open-pollinated families from 39 maternal-plus trees of northwest Spain and control seedlings from unimproved material. The pathogens tested included *Fusarium oxysporum*, *F. circinatum*, and *Armillaria ostoyae*. The insects tested were *Thaumetopoea pithyocampa*, *Dioryctria sylvestrella*, and *Hylobious abietis*. Susceptibility to water stress was also assessed. Defensive traits included constitutive and induced levels of diterpene content, total phenolics, condensed tannins, starch, and soluble sugars. Inducibility of defenses was determined as the difference of the concentration of a given compound between methyl jasmonate(MeJA)-treated plants and untreated plants, i.e., the induced levels minus the constitutive levels. Resistances to diseases, insects, and water stress were normalized, and the relationships between these parameters together with the defensive traits were examined by Pearson's correlations.

Heritability values of *P. pinaster* were high enough to allow the studied pathogens and pests to be individually reduced through appropriate genetic strategies. However, breeding *P. pinaster* for resistance to a particular pathogen would enhance its susceptibility to another pathogen or pest. Although resistances to fungal pathogens were correlated with resistance to water stress, the Spanish breeding population of *P. pinaster* was not simultaneously resistant to a wide range of potential enemies. Moreover, all plus families were generally more susceptible than the unimproved control family. No trade-offs between resistances and plant growth or cone production was observed. Families showing multiple resistances were those showing low inducibility. Lack of multiple resistances appears to be the norm in this pine species, and would not be easily used for breeding.

[1] Universidad de Extremadura, Virgen del Puerto 2, 10600 Plasencia, Spain.
[2] Centro de Investigación Forestal de Lourizán, Apdo 127, 36080 Pontevedra, Spain.
[3] CIS Madeira, Avenida de Galicia, 32901 San Cibrao das Viñas, Ourense, Spain.
[4] Misión Biológica de Galicia, CSIC, Carballeira 8, 36143 Pontevedra, Spain.
Corresponding author: rzas@cesga.es.

Endophyte Mediated Plant-Herbivore Interactions or Cross Resistance to Fungi and Insect Herbivores

Kari Saikkonen[1] and Marjo Helander[2]

Abstract

Endophytic fungi are generally considered to be plant mutualists that protect the host plant from pathogens and herbivores. Defensive mutualism appears to hold true particularly for seed-transmitted, alkaloid producing, grass endophytes. However, we propose that the mutualistic nature of plant-endophyte interactions via enhanced plant resistance to pathogens and herbivores should be reconsidered when focusing on woody plants.

We compared phenotypic and genetic frequency correlations for two endophytic fungal genera (*Fusicladium* and *Melanconium*) and birch rust (*Melampsoridium betulinum*) with the performance of six invertebrate herbivores growing on the same half sib progenies of mountain birch *Betula pubescens* Ehrh. ssp. *czerepanovii* (N. I. Orlova) Hämet-Ahti in two environments over a 3-year period. We found little support for causal association between fungal frequencies and performance of herbivore species. Instead, genetic correlations, particularly between autumnal moth (*Epirrita autumnata*) and birch rust, suggest that herbivore performance may be affected by (1) genetic differences in birch quality for fungi and herbivores, or (2) genetic differences in responses to environmental conditions. Genetic analysis of *Venturia ditricha* (anamorph *Fusicladium betulae*) revealed that (1) birch genotypes and environment influence the probability of infection by particular endophyte genotypes, (2) genetic variation correlated negatively with infection frequencies of the fungus, and (3) the susceptibility of the birch to a particular endophyte genotype may change when environmental conditions are changed (environment-host genotype interaction).

Furthermore, statistical perusal of endophyte literature revealed clear contrasts between grass and tree endophytes. Grass endophytes appear to provide support for the hypothesis of defensive mutualism, whereas variability appears to be the nature of the tree endophyte mediated plant herbivore interactions.

We propose that: (1) the performance of endophytes, pathogens, and herbivores may be responses to genetically determined plant qualities rather than interconnected associations; (2) the observed genetic correlation structure may have importance for evolution of birch resistance to fungi and herbivores (e.g., negative correlation between birch resistance to rust fungus and autumnal moth may constrain birch population from reaching optimal species-specific resistance); this should be considered also in forest tree improvement attempting to overcome pests and pathogens; and (3) more knowledge about multispecies coevolution is necessary to fully understand bilateral interactions between plants and the organisms living on them.

[1] MTT Agrifood Research Finland, Plant Production Research, 31600 Jokioinen, Finland.
[2] Section of Ecology, Department of Biology, University of Turku, 20014 Turku, Finland.
Corresponding author: kari.saikkonen@mtt.fi.

Insertion Site Selection and Feeding of the Hemlock Woolly Adelgid: Implications for Host-Plant Resistance

K.L.F. Oten,[1] A.C. Cohen,[1] and F.P. Hain[1]

The hemlock woolly adelgid (HWA), *Adelges tsugae* (Hemiptera: Adelgidae), is an invasive forest pest that threatens the existence of eastern hemlock (*Tsuga canadensis* (L.) Carr.) and Carolina hemlock (*T. caroliniana* Engelm.) in the eastern United States. It is a small, aphid-like insect with piercing-sucking mouthparts that it uses to penetrate its host plant and feed off the xylem ray parenchyma cells (Young et al. 1995). The hemlock woolly adelgid is native to eastern Asia and northwestern North America where it feeds on, but does not kill, its host (Annand 1924, Havill et al. 2006). The mechanism of resistance and/or tolerance is unknown. The invasive population in the eastern United States was first detected near Richmond, Virginia in 1951 (Gouger 1971, Souto et al. 1996). The range of HWA in the east has since spread through the range of hemlocks, now affecting 18 states (USDA FS 2011). The mortality caused by HWA to eastern and Carolina hemlocks is tremendous. Approximately 80 to 90 percent of infested hemlocks native to the eastern United States have already vanished as a result of this exotic insect (Hale 2004, Townsend and Rieske-Kinney 2006). Moreover, the production of hemlocks for the ornamental industry, valued at $34 million between Tennessee and North Carolina alone, has been virtually eliminated (Bentz et al. 2002).

Following initial infestation, a susceptible hemlock declines in health, evident by needle drop, bud abortion, and inhibition of new growth (McClure 1991). A healthy hemlock dies in as few as 4 years, but may survive beyond 10 (McClure 1987, 1991). In its native range, HWA is described as a minor pest and almost never kills its host (Bentz et al. 2002, Furniss and Carolin 1977, Keen 1938). For years, it was believed that eastern and Carolina hemlocks were entirely and exclusively susceptible to HWA. However, in the wake of widespread mortality, anecdotal evidence suggested surviving individuals or stands of eastern and Carolina hemlocks may be less susceptible. This has since been corroborated by research, and distinct populations have been selected and continue to be pursued as putatively resistant to HWA (Caswell et al. 2008, Ingwell and Preisser 2010, Kaur 2009, Oten et al. 2011). In addition, Carolina hemlock has been identified as less susceptible to HWA than eastern hemlock (Jetton et al. 2008, Oten 2011).

The purpose of this research is to investigate host-plant selection and host use of HWA to further understand mechanisms of resistance that occurs both inter- and intra-specifically. Understanding this may facilitate progress toward a resistant hemlock by identifying characteristics that can be identified among individuals in natural stands for selection and/or to screen within a breeding program.

The crawler stage of HWA is the first stage and thus the host-seeking stage of the insect. Crawlers lack wings and compound eyes; consequently, transportation between host trees is entirely passive. Dispersal occurs either by crawling to nearby branches, wind, phoresy on macro-vertebrates (e.g., birds, deer), or by human movement of infested stock (Butin et al. 2007, McClure 1990). Therefore, habitat and host location, the initial two steps in host-plant selection by phytophagous insects (Bernays and Chapman 1994), does not occur as part of the host selection behaviors of HWA. Using scanning electron microscopy (SEM), we studied the sensilla of HWA crawlers because it is this stage that must accurately determine feeding sites on hemlocks. The distal segment of the HWA labium possesses two fields of sensilla, including six long subapical sensilla trichodea and five shorter apical labial sensilla trichodea. Two apical sensilla are observed touching the stylet bundle in some

[1] North Carolina State University, Raleigh, NC 27695.
Corresponding author: klfelder@ncsu.edu.

images and are hypothesized to play a role in sensing the orientation and/or movement of the stylets during insertion site selection. In aphids, stylet penetration is initially based on substrate color and texture and chemoreception occurs after short probing of the host plant and internal gustation (Ibbotson and Kennedy 1959, Miles 1958, Powell et al. 2006). Given their biological similarities to aphids, we theorize that HWA use a similar host acceptance tool, and probes the plant briefly, sensing its host with internal contact chemoreceptors. However, this research should be extended to substantiate this conjecture. HWA tarsi are two-segmented and bear a claw on the distal end. A long pair of knobbed setae and four pairs of shorter, spatulate setae are observed. Such setae are present in other adelgids: a pair in the pine leaf adelgid (*Pineus pinifoliae*) and three per tarsus in the spruce gall adelgid (*Adelges lariciatus*). However, the authors of these studies did not speculate about the function of the setae (Cumming 1968, Underwood 1955). We suggest they may be involved in adhesion based on casual visual observations of surface contact during inverted walking and the morphological similarity to the adhesive tenant hairs of some springtails (Blottner and Eisenbeis 1984). In comparison to the sessile adults, antennae of the same generation crawlers are well-developed and elongated. The scape and pedicel each have a pair of trichoid sensilla, seated in a pit and lacking an observable pore at its tip, indicating they likely function as mechanoreceptors. The flagellum has a long terminal sensillum and four secondary sensilla at the distal end. A sensorium lays subapically on the posterior edge of the flagellum and is surrounded by a cuticular fringe that may aid in keeping foreign particles out. The sensorium is likely analogous to the primary rhinaria of chemoreceptory function in aphids and is referred to by Stoetzel (1998) in alate female Adelgidae.

Using whole-body homogenate of HWA, general protease enzyme activity was assayed using the EnzChek® protease assay kit (Invitrogen, Eugene, OR). Trypsin-like activity in HWA was present, although lower than in *Lygus lineolaris*, which was used as a positive control. The kinetic for HWA enzymatic activity reached its asymptote at 30 minutes, whereas the *L. lineolaris* comparison continued to increase after more than 1 hour (fig. 1).

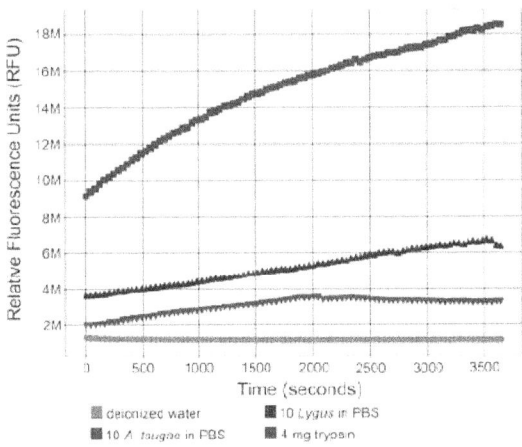

Figure 1—Enzyme kinetics of trypsin-like assay.

Although this enzyme could be present in the salivary gland complex, midgut, or hemolymph of the insect, its occurrence is nevertheless revealing of the feeding habits of HWA. Generally, the presence or absence of specific enzymes is indicative of a consumer's ability to digest plant or prey materials (Agusti and Cohen 2000; Baptist 1941; Cohen 1990, 1998). The presence of trypsin-like enzyme activity in HWA confirms the ability of HWA to digest protein rather than depending upon free amino acids as is the case for sap-feeding insects such as aphids. If used extra-orally by HWA (i.e., injected into their host plant) the enzyme may be used to digest structural proteins of the plant that are otherwise insoluble (Hori 1971). In addition, the presence of protease may have implications for host response and host-plant resistance. The wound-response pathway, which may be triggered by the feeding of herbivorous insects, is one of these responses that may induce protease inhibitor genes

(Dietrich et al. 1999). The systemic response of hemlock to HWA feeding, which is currently uncharacterized, implicates HWA feeding in inducing the systemic response (Radville et al. 2011, Walker-Lane 2009). The response could be triggered by mechanical wounding or physiological elicitors in the saliva. Future research should focus on this interaction to understand if HWA is triggering the wound-response pathway in hemlocks via mechanical or salivary wounding and the differences in the response between susceptible and resistant hemlocks.

Physical characteristics of hemlock surfaces were observed using low-temperature SEM to document differences and how they may relate to resistance. There were differences in trichome density, placement, and length on the species studied, but they did not relate to the degree of susceptibility to HWA and are likely not involved in host selection or resistance. Cuticle thicknesses were compared for various locations on the pulvinus: at the HWA stylet bundle insertion point, at the side of the needle where the HWA settles, and on the outside of the needle (fig. 2). We compared thicknesses to determine if cuticle was related to insertion site selection. Based on preliminary observations, there appears to be a slight trend. The cuticle thickness at the point on stylet insertion appears to be thinner than the other two locations on the pulvinus that were measured. Although this needs to be investigated more thoroughly, including a statistical analysis, this suggests that the specificity for stylet bundle insertion of HWA may be a result of accessibility to host tissues.

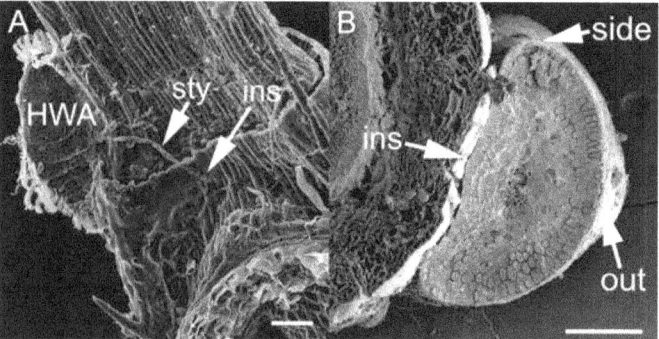

Figure 2—A) Settled hemlock woolly adelgid (HWA), showing adaxial side of the needle and pulvinus. HWA, hemlock woolly adelgid; ins, insertion point; sty, stylet bundle. Scale, 100 µm. B) Locations measured on pulvini for cuticle thickness. ins, insertion point; out, outside. Scale, 200 µm.

Understanding the interactions between HWA and naïve hemlocks in the eastern United States furthers our understanding of mechanisms involved in host-plant selection and resistance, aiding the progress towards a hemlock resistant to HWA. Ideally, a resistant hemlock will be a component of an integrated pest management program to control populations of HWA in the eastern United States, allowing ecosystem restoration and restoring the hemlock ornamental industry.

Literature Cited

Agusti, N.; Cohen, A.C. 2000. *Lygus hesperus* and *L. lineolaris* (Meniptera: Miridae), phytophages, zoophages, or omnivores: evidence of feeding adaptations suggested by the salivary and midgut digestive enzymes. Journal of Entomological Science. 35: 176–186.

Annand, P.N. 1924. A new species of *Adelges* (Hemiptera: Phylloxeridae). The Pan-Pacific Entomologist. 1: 79–82.

Baptist, B.A. 1941. The morphology and physiology of the salivary glands of Hemiptera-Heteroptera. Quarterly Journal of Microscopical Science. 83: 91–139.

Bentz, S.E.; Riedel, L.G.H.; Pooler, M.R.; Townsend, A.M. 2002. Hybridization and self-compatibility in controlled pollinations of eastern North American and Asian hemlock (*Tsuga*) species. Journal of Arboriculture. 28(4): 200–205.

Bernays, E.A.; Chapman, R.F. 1994. Host-plant selection by phytophagous insects. New York: Chapman and Hall. 312 p.

Blottner, D.; Eisenbeis, G. 1984. Ultrastructure of long tibiotarsal spatula-hairs in *Tomocerus flavescens* (Collembola: Tomoceridae). Annales de la Société Royale Zoologique de Belgique. 114: 51–57.

Butin, E.; Preisser, E.; Elkinton, J. 2007. Factors affecting settlement rate of the hemlock woolly adelgid, Adelges *tsugae*, on eastern hemlock, *Tsuga canadensis*. Agricultural and Forest Entomology. 9: 215–219.

Caswell, T.; Casagrande, R.; Maynard, B.; Preisser, E. 2008. Production and evaluation of eastern hemlocks potentially resistant to the hemlock woolly adelgid. In: Onken, B., Rheardon, R., eds. Fourth symposium on the hemlock woolly adelgid in the eastern United States. FHTET-2008-01. Morgantown, WV: U.S. Department of Agriculture, Forest Service, Forest Health Protection: 124–134.

Cohen, A.C. 1990. Feeding adaptations of some predaceous Hemiptera. Annals of the Entomological Society of America. 83(6): 1215–1223.

Cohen, A.C. 1998. Feeding biology of the silverleaf whitefly (Homoptera: Aleyrodidae). Chinese Journal of Entomology. 18: 65–82.

Cumming, M.E.P. 1968. The life history and morphology of *Adelges lariciatus* (Homoptera: Phylloxeridae). Canadian Entomologist. 100(2): 113–126.

Dietrich, R.A.; Lawton, K.; Friedrich, L. [et al.]. 1999. Induced plant defense responses: scientific and commercial development possibilities. In: Chadwick, D.J.; Goode, J.A., eds. Insect-plant interactions and induced plant defence. Chichester, England: Wiley: 205–216.

Furniss, R.L.; Carolin, V.M. 1977. Western forest insects. Miscellaneous Publication 1339. Washington, DC: U.S. Department of Agriculture, Forest Service, Government Printing Office.

Gouger, R.J. 1971. Control of *Adelges tsugae* on hemlock in Pennsylvania. Scientific Tree Topics. 3: 1–9.

Hale, F.A. 2004. The hemlock woolly adelgid: a threat to hemlock in Tennessee. SP503-G. Knoxville: The University of Tennessee, Agricultural Extension Service.

Havill, N.P.; Montgomery, M.E.; Yu, G.; Shiyake, S.; Caccone, A. 2006. Mitochondrial DNA from hemlock woolly adelgid (Hemiptera: Adelgidae) suggests cryptic speciation and pinpoints the source of the introduction to eastern North America. Annals of the Entomological Society of America. 99(2): 195–203.

Hori, K. 1971. Studies on the feeding habits of *Lygus disponsi* Linnavuori (Hemiptera: Miridae) and the injury to its host plants. I. Histological observations of the injury. Applied Entomology and Zoology. 6: 84–90.

Ibbotson, A.; Kennedy, J.S. 1959. Interaction between walking and probing in *Aphis fabae*. Journal of Experimental Biology. 36: 377–390.

Ingwell, L.L.; Preisser, E.L. 2010. Using citizen science programs to identify host resistance in pest-invaded forests. Conservation Biology. 25(1): 182–188.

Jetton, R.M.; Hain, F.P.; Dvorak, W.S.; Frampton, J. 2008. Infestation rate of hemlock woolly adelgid (Hemiptera: Adelgidae) among three North American hemlock (*Tsuga*) species following artificial inoculation. Journal of Entomological Science. 43(4): 438–442.

Kaur, N. 2009. Developing artificial rearing techniques for hemlock woolly adelgid, *Adelges tsugae* and balsam woolly adelgid, *Adelges piceae*; artificial infestation and epicuticular wax study of Carolina hemlock, *Tsuga caroliniana*, provenances. Raleigh, NC: North Carolina State University. 118 p. M.S. thesis.

Keen, F.P. 1938. Insect enemies of western forests. Misc. Pub. 273. Washington, DC: U.S. Department of Agriculture, Forest Service.

McClure, M.S. 1987. Biology and control of hemlock woolly adelgid. Bull. 851. New Haven: Connecticut Agricultural Station.

McClure, M.S. 1990. Role of wind, birds, deer, and humans in dispersal of hemlock woolly adelgid (Homoptera: Adelgidae). Environmental Entomology. 19(1): 36–43.

McClure, M.S. 1991. Density-dependent feedback and population cycles in *Adelges tsugae* (Homoptera: Adelgidae) on *Tsuga canadensis*. Environmental Entomology. 20(1): 258–264.

Miles, P.W. 1958. Contact chemoreception in some Heteroptera, including chemoreception internal to the stylet food canal. Journal of Insect Physiology. 2(4): 338–347.

9

Oten, K.L.F. 2011. Host-plant selection by the hemlock woolly adelgid, *Adelges tsugae* Annand: sensory systems and feeding behavior in relation to physical and chemical host-plant characteristics. Raleigh, NC: North Carolina State University. 259 p. Ph.D. dissertation.

Oten, K.L.F.; Walker-Lane, L.N.; Jetton, R.M. [et al.]. 2011. Developing hemlocks resistant to the hemlock woolly adelgid. http://www.threatenedforests.com/research/wp-content/uploads/2011/08/NAFIWC-2011.pdf. (11 August 2011).

Powell, G.; Tosh, C.R.; Hardie, J. 2006. Host plant selection by aphids: behavioral, evolutionary, and applied perspectives. Annual Review of Entomology. 51: 309–330.

Radville, L.; Chaves, A.; Preisser, E.L. 2011. Variation in plant defense against invasive herbivores: evidence for a hypersensitive response in eastern hemlocks (*Tsuga canadensis*). Journal of Chemical Ecology. 37: 592–597.

Souto, D.; Luther, T.; Chianese, B. 1996. Past and current status of HWA in eastern and Carolina hemlock stands. In: Salom, S.M.; Tignor, T.C.; Reardon, R.C., eds. Proceedings of the first hemlock woolly adelgid review. Morgantown, WV: U.S. Department of Agriculture, Forest Service: 9–15.

Stoetzel, M.B. 1998. Antennal and other characters useful in identification of the Aphidoidea (Homoptera). Proceedings of the Entomological Society of Washington. 100(3): 588–593.

Townsend, L.; Rieske-Kinney, L. 2006. Meeting the threat of the hemlock woolly adelgid. ENTFACT-452.Lexington: University of Kentucky. Cooperative Extension Service.

Underwood, G.R. 1955. The external morphology of the five forms of *Pineus pinifoliae* (Fitch) (Homoptera: Phylloxeridae). Canadian Entomologist. 87(5): 201–209.

U.S. Department of Agriculture, Forest Service [USDA FS]. 2011. Counties with established HWA populations 2010. http://na.fs fed.us/fhp/hwa/maps/2010.pdf. (24 August 2011).

Walker-Lane, L.N. 2009. The effect of hemlock woolly adelgid infestation on water relations of Carolina and eastern hemlock. Raleigh, NC: North Carolina State University. 61 p. M.S. thesis.

Young, R.F.; Shields, K.S.; Berlyn, G.P. 1995. Hemlock woolly adelgid (Homoptera: Adelgidae): stylet bundle insertion and feeding sites. Annals of the Entomological Society of America. 88(6): 827–835.

Genetic Basis of Resistance in *Eucalyptus* spp. Pathosystems

Acelino Couto Alfenas,[1]Lúcio Mauro da Silva Guimarães,[1]and Marcos Deon Vilela de Resende[2]

Introduction

Eucalyptus is the most widely planted hardwood crop in world-wide tropical and subtropical regions because of its high growth rate, broad adaptability, and multipurpose wood properties. Until the 1970s, the *Eucalyptus* plantations in Brazil were practically disease free. However, plantations have continued to expand into warmer and more humid areas that are more favorable to pathogen infection. Furthermore, the use of high-yielding genotypes with unknown disease resistance, the implementation of clonal forestry, and the introduction of new management techniques have favored the emergence of disease epidemics in recent decades. Presently, prominent diseases such as rust (*Puccinia psidii*), Ceratocystis wilt (*Ceratocystis fimbriata*), and canker (*Chrysoporthe cubensis*) are the most damaging diseases in *Eucalyptus* plantations. During recent years, we have conducted a series of inoculation experiments with controlled-crossed progenies to better understand the genetic basis of resistance for the prominent *Eucalyptus* pathosystems.

Eucalyptus x Puccinia psidii Pathosystem

Under favorable conditions, *Puccinia psidii* infects juvenile organs of the plant, either in the nursery or field. Rust infection can reduce tree growth and lead to loss of apical dominance. In highly susceptible genotypes, rust can also induce malformations of the affected organs, necrosis, hypertrophy, mini-cankers, and death of growing tips (Alfenas et al. 2009, Coutinho et al. 1998, Glen et al. 2007). The wide inter- and intra-specific genetic variability for rust resistance allows selection of resistant clones, progenies, or species for planting (Carvalho et al. 1998, Xavier et al. 2007). *Eucalyptus grandis* (Hill) Maiden is one of the most planted eucalypt species, but it is also among the most susceptible species. Thus, rust is currently the most damaging disease to eucalypt plantations in tropical regions because of the wide use of *E. grandis* (Zauza et al. 2010).In contrast, species such as *E. pellita* F. Muell. can be considered an important reservoir of genes for rust resistance (Guimarães et al. 2010b). Resistance to rust is predominately expressed by a hypersensitive reaction (HR) (Xavier 2002), which is a common type of response triggered when plants that contain resistance genes (R genes) are challenged by pathogens that contain avirulence genes (Avr genes).

In 2003, a major gene for rust resistance, *Ppr*-1, was identified in a control pollinated family of *E. grandis* and mapped near the $AT9_{917}$ RAPD marker (Junghans et al. 2003). The locus *Ppr*-1 was positioned on a microsatellite reference genetic map for *Eucalyptus* on the linkage group 3 (Mamani et al. 2010). Additionally, its position was validated by association genetics in one related and two unrelated background families. These results are consistent with the hypothesis that *Ppr*-1 controls a large proportion of the variation for rust resistance in *E. grandis*. However, in recent studies, analyses of several inter-specific families, displaying different segregation patterns for rust resistance, provided additional evidence that the genetic control of rust resistance in *Eucalyptus* is more complex

[1]Departamento de Fitopatologia/BIOAGRO, Universidade Federal de Viçosa (UFV), 36570-000, Viçosa, MG, Brazil.
[2]Embrapa Florestas. Current address: Departamento de Engenharia Florestal, Universidade Federal de Viçosa, 36570-000, Viçosa, MG, Brazil.
Corresponding author: aalfenas@ufv.br.

and includes quantitative resistance traits (Alves et al. 2012).The recognition that both additive and non-additive genetic variation (epistasis) are important contributors to rust resistance in eucalypts reveals the complexity of this host-pathogen interaction and helps explain the success that breeding has achieved in selecting rust-resistant clones, where the additive and non-additive effects are readily captured.

Eucalyptus x Ceratocystis fimbriata Pathosystem

Due to its lethal nature, broad host range, and wide geographical distribution, Ceratocystis wilt caused by *Ceratocystis fimbriata* is currently one of the most important diseases of eucalyptus plantations in Brazil (Alfenas et al. 2009).Genetic variability for resistance to Ceratocystis wilt in *Eucalyptus* genotypes was confirmed by Zauza et al. (2004). Subsequently, Rosado et al. (2010) studied Ceratocystis wilt resistance by stem inoculations of *E. grandis* and *E. urophylla* S. T. Blake genotypes, and estimated the heritability and gains of selection in families derived from controlled interspecific crosses. In both species, some genotypes were highly resistant and others highly susceptible to Ceratocystis wilt. Estimates of individual narrow (50 percent) and broad (59 percent) sense heritability suggested a high degree of genetic control and low allelic dominance of the trait. A genetic gain inlesion size up to -74.4 percent was obtained from selection ofthe 50 best clones in the evaluated families.

Continuing the studies with this pathosystem, Rosado (2009) built a microsatellite genetic map for the inter-specific, full-sibling family DGxUGL [(*E. grandis x E. dunnii* Maiden) x (*E. urophylla x E. globulus*)] (127 individuals) and detected five QTLs for Ceratocystis wilt resistance. Marker analysis showed that five markers located in the linkage groups 1, 3, 5, 8, and 10 were associated with significant quantitative effects on resistance with heritabilities ranging from 9.6 to 34.2.

Eucalyptus x Chrysoporthe cubensis Pathosystem

The existence of inter- and intra-specific genetic variability for canker resistance in eucalypts (Alfenas et al. 1983, Ferreira et al. 1978), together with the development of large-scale cloning in the 1980s, has led to the control of the disease through the selection and cloning of resistant genotypes (Alfenas et al. 2009). Recently, Guimarães et al. (2010a) evaluated resistance in *E. grandis* and *E. urophylla* trees, as well as in individuals from progenies derived from controlled crosses between the trees. Six-month-old plants were inoculated, and xylem and bark lesions were measured at 8 months post-inoculation. The results demonstrated that xylem lesions are strong indicators for the selection of resistant clones. The phenotypic analyses indicated the existence of high genetic variability for resistance in both species. Individual narrow and broad sense heritability estimates were 17 percent and 81 percent, respectively, suggesting that canker resistance is quantitative and highly dependent on dominance and epistasis.

Due to the wide genetic variation for canker resistance in *E. grandis* and *E. urophylla*, the introduction of resistant parent trees into ongoing breeding programs may increase the chances of obtaining disease-resistant clones at the end of the selection program. The results of our study also reinforce the need for using artificial inoculation with *C. cubensis*, when selecting pathogen-resistant parent trees and progenies of *Eucalyptus* spp. Furthermore, these studies also demonstrate the importance of cloning resistant genotypes for disease control.

Breeding for Disease Resistance

Plantations of clones or elite-resistant varieties represent the most efficient strategy for disease control. Currently, most Brazilian commercial eucalyptus clones are based on inter-specific hybrids (Assis and Resende 2011). However, artificial inoculations have shown that 80 percent of these clones are susceptible to at least one important disease. In contrast to canker resistance, most eucalypt breeding programs have not targeted rust and Ceratocystis wilt resistance until recently. Rust and Ceratocystis wilt resistance has usually been assessed in the final stages of clonal trials, and susceptible clones are recommended for areas with no history of epidemics or simply discarded. With the expansion of clonal plantations, epidemics have become more frequent. As a result, several tropical breeding programs now specifically include rust and Ceratocystis wilt resistance as a selection criterion.

Since forestry breeding programs are usually medium to long term in duration, it is essential to have disease-resistant parents. Thus, before the formation of a breeding orchard, it is recommended that the resistant parental materials are thoroughly evaluated and selected. Moreover, one should also evaluate the resistance clones selected in the breeding program. This evaluation should be performed after the selection of promising clones prior to implementation of expanded clonal trials.

In reciprocal recurrent selection (RRS), evaluation of eucalyptus rust resistance should be made in the hybrid progeny before selection of parents for recombination, submitting all the families to mass inoculation of the pathogen under controlled conditions. Only the parents of families with resistant plants must be recombined and thus participate in the RRS. A new screening test must be performed in pure progeny test, selecting only plants that are resistant to rust (fig. 1). Evaluation of resistance to Ceratocystis wilt and canker, which require clonal replicates, should be performed in progeny tests of pure species. Resistant plants should be selected for the new breeding orchard (fig. 1).

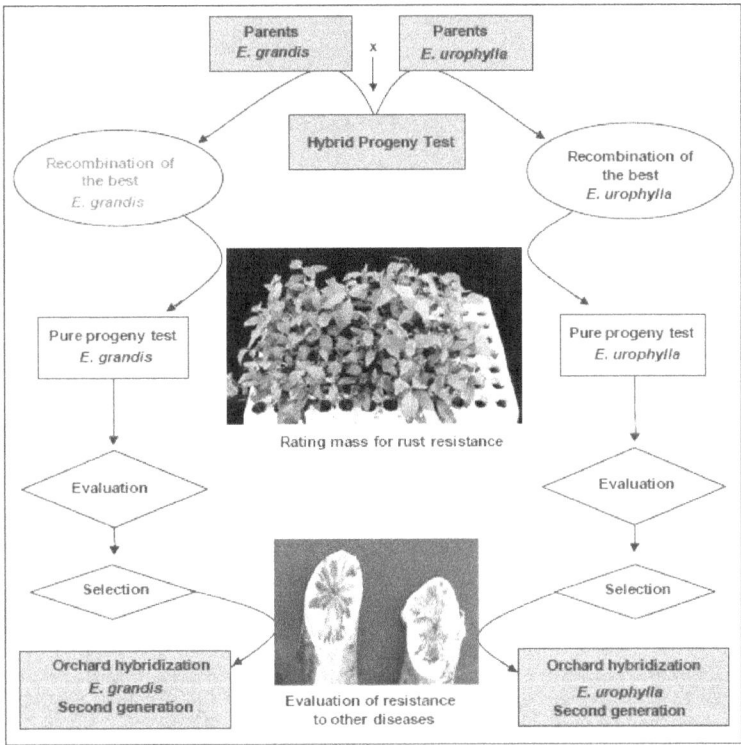

Figure 1— Stages of the breeding program in the reciprocal recurrent selection, in which assessments should be performed for disease resistance.

In addition to determining when disease resistance of the clones will be evaluated during the breeding program, other issues should be considered: (i) reliable inoculation protocols are needed for disease-resistance evaluations; (ii) determining the genetic basis and the mode of inheritance of disease resistance is an essential step to obtaining disease-resistant plant material for the breeding program; (iii) the introgression of genes from different *Eucalyptus* species has been suggested to broaden the genetic basis of commercial clones for resistance to the main diseases; and (iv) a better understanding of the population genetic structures of the pathogens is needed to determine the role of pathogen variability in disease resistance that is targeted by the breeding strategies.

Acknowledgments

We would like to thank Dr. Ned Klopfeintein (USDA Forest Service, USA) and Mee-Sook Kim (Kaokmin University, Seoul, Korea)for kindly reviewing the text and to CNPq, Fapemig, Suzano Papel, and Celulose, Fibria, Veracel, Jari Celulose, Cenibra, Plantar, and Vale for supporting our research line on disease resistance of tree species.

Literature Cited

Alfenas, A.C.; Jeng, R.; Hubbes. M. 1983. Virulence of *Cryphonectria cubensis* on *Eucalyptus* species differing in resistance. European Journal of Forest Pathology.13: 197–205.

Alfenas, A.C.; Zauza, E.A.V.; Maffia, R.G.; Assis, T.F. 2009. Clonagem e doenças do Eucalipto. Viçosa. Editora UFV. 2ª edição. 500p.

Alves, A.A.; Rosado, C.C.G.; Faria, D.A.; Guimarães, L.M.G.; Lau, D.; Brommonschenkel, S.H.; Grattapaglia, D.; Alfenas, A.C. 2012. Genetic mapping provides evidence for the role of additive and non-additive QTLs in the response of inter-specific hybrids of *Eucalyptus* to *Puccinia psidii* rust infection. Euphytica. 183: 27–38.

Assis, T.F.; Resende, M.D.V. 2011. Genetic improvement of forest tree species. Crop Breeding and Applied Biotechnology. S1: 44–49.

Carvalho, A.D.O.; Alfenas, A.C.; Maffia, L.A.; Carmo, M.G.F. 1998. Resistance of *Eucalyptus* species, progenies and provenances to *Puccinia psidii*. Pesquisa Agropecuária Brasileira. 33: 139–147.

Coutinho, T.A.; Wingfield, M.J.; Alfenas, A.C.; Crous, P.W. 1998. Eucalyptus rust: a disease with the potential for serious international implications. Plant Disease. 82: 819–825.

Ferreira, F.A.; Alfenas, A.C.; Freitas, A.L. 1978. Determinação da resistência de 16 procedências de *Eucalyptus* ao cancro do eucalipto causado por *Diaporthe cubensis* Bruner, no Vale do Rio Doce, MG. Revista Árvore. 2: 110–129.

Glen, M.; Alfenas, A.C.; Zauza, E.A.V.; Wingfield, M.J.; Mohammed, C. 2007. *Puccinia psidii*: a threat to the Australian environment and economy - a review. Australasian Plant Pathology. 36: 1–16.

Guimarães, L.M.S.; Resende, M.D.V.; Lau, D.; Rosse, L.N.; Alves, A.A.; Alfenas, A.C. 2010a. Genetic control of *Eucalyptus urophylla* and *E. grandis* resistance to canker caused by *Chrysoporthe cubensis*. Genetics and Molecular Biology. 33: 525–531.

Guimarães, L.M.S.;Titon, M.; Lau, D.; Rosse, L.; Oliveira, L.S.S.; Rosado, C.C.G.; Christo, G.G.O.; Alfenas, A.C. 2010b. *Eucalyptus pellita* as a source of resistance to rust, Ceratocystis wilt and leaf blight. Crop Breeding and Applied Biotechnology. 10: 124–131.

Junghans, D.T.; Alfenas, A.C.; Brommonschenkel, S.H.; Oda, S.; Mello, E.J.; Grattapaglia, D. 2003. Resistance to rust (*Puccinia psidii* Winter) in *Eucalyptus*: mode of inheritance and mapping of a major gene with RAPD markers. Theoretical and Applied Genetics. 108: 175–180.

Mamani, E.M.C.; Bueno, N.W.; Faria, D.A.; Guimarães, L.M.S.; Lau, D.; Alfenas, A.C.; Grattapaglia, D. 2010. Positioning of the major locus for *Puccinia psidii* rust resistance (Ppr1) on the *Eucalyptus* reference map and its validation across unrelated pedigrees.Tree Genetics & Genomes 6: 953–962.

Rosado, C.G.C. 2009. Genética da resistência à murcha de ceratocystis (*Ceratocystis fimbriata*) em *Eucalyptus* spp. Viçosa, MG: UFV. Dissertação de MestradoemGenética e Melhoramento.

Rosado, C.C.G.; Guimarães, L.M.S.; Titon, M.; Lau, D.; Rosse, L.; Resende, M.D.V.; Alfenas, A.C. 2010. Resistance to ceratocystis wilt (*Ceratocystis fimbriata*) in parents and progênies of *Eucalyptus grandis* x *E. urophylla*. Silvae Genetica. 59: 99–106.

Xavier, A.A. 2002. Histoptologia da interação*Puccinia psidii* e virulência de isolados do patógeno em espécies de Myrtaceae. Viçosa, MG: UFV.Tese de Doutorado em Fitopatologia.

Xavier, A.A.; Sanfuentes, E.V.; Junghans, D.T.; Alfenas, A.C. 2007. Resistência de *Eucalyptus globulus* e *Eucalyptus nitens* à ferrugem (*Puccinia psidii*). Revista Árvore. 31(4): 7317–7335.

Zauza, E.A.V.; Alfenas, A.C.; Harrington, T.C.; Mizubuti, E.S.; Silva, J.F. 2004. Resistance of *Eucalyptus* clones to *Ceratocystis fimbriata*. Plant Disease. 88: 758–760.

Zauza, E.A.V.; Alfenas, A.C.; Old, K.; Couto, M.M.F.; Graça, R.N.; Maffia, LA. 2010. Myrtacea especies resistance to rust caused by *Puccinia psidii*. Australasian Plant Pathology. 39: 406–411.

Genetic Variation of Lodgepole Pine Physical and Chemical Defenses Associated With Each Step in Host Selection Behavior Sequence by Mountain Pine Beetle

Kimberly F. Wallin,[1,2,3] Daniel S. Ott,[1,2] and Alvin D. Yanchuk[2,4]

Abiotic and biotic stressors exert selective pressures on plants, and over evolutionary time lead to the development of specialized adaptations and specific responses to stresses (Safranyik and Carroll 2006, Wallin and Raffa 2002). In this way, the environment in which plants evolve shapes their life cycles, range, growth, reproduction, and defenses. Insects and diseases are particularly potent plant stressors. Insect herbivores exert pressure on plants by feeding on plant parts and using them to reproduce by forming galls and cysts. Some insect species carry mutualistic pathogens on their bodies, which exert pressure on plants in the form of disease.

The model system of mountain pine beetle *Dendroctonus ponderosae* (Coleoptera: Scolytidae (Curculionidae)) (MPB), in association with the blue stain fungus *Ophiostoma clavigerum* (*Grossimania clavigera*), attacking lodgepole pine *Pinus contorta* Douglas ex Louden var. *latifolia* Engelm. ex S. Watson trees is an example of how selective pressures construct changes in co-evolution and trade-offs between defenses. In the process of identifying traits, it is important to understand where and when during attack defensive traits arise within trees.

Colonization behavior by the MPB can be broken into several steps. The process begins when adult beetles emerge from their natal host and begin their dispersal flight in search of a suitable host. The mass attack of a tree by MPB is a dynamic process that involves both host chemical cues and pheromone compounds. Prior to, and during colonization, attacking beetles detect volatile secondary metabolites, such as kairomonal cues, to locate suitable hosts. Upon landing on a host tree, the female will either attempt to colonize the tree, or after testing the tree for levels of secondary metabolites or nutrients, she will leave in search of a more suitable host tree. When a female accepts and enters a host tree, she excavates a nuptial chamber and begins forming an egg gallery. At this time, the female begins producing aggregation pheromone that attracts other female beetles to the tree as well as males for mating. Due to the co- evolved association between MPB and its host tree species, the female MPB is able to use host chemicals as precursors for pheromone production. The MPB completes development within the host tree and must locate a new host upon emerging as an adult.

The first and primary line of physical and chemical-based defense that a tree employs is the physical exudation of oleoresin (resin) (Wainhouse et al. 1990). Oleoresin is a complex blend of water, nutrients, terpenoids (Martin et al. 2002), and phenolics. If tree resin volume and pressure are high during colonization, their attempt to enter the tree against the resin flow will be physically halted (Raffa and Berryman 1983, Ruel et al. 1998, Wallin and Raffa 1999). High volume of resin can expel an insect or fungal spores from a wound or bind and contain insects or pathogens (Franceschi et al. 2005, Phillips and Croteau 1999). Constitutive oleoresin is stored in resin ducts; however, induced resin can also be produced in other locations, known as traumatic resin ducts, following wounding by an insect or pathogen (Martin et al. 2002, Phillips and Croteau 1999). The primary terpenoids found in conifer oleoresin are monoterpenes, sesquiterpenes, and diterpenes. Monoterpenes are composed of

[1] University of Vermont, The Rubenstein School of Environment and Natural Resources, Burlington, VT 05405.
[2] University of Northern British Columbia, Prince George, B.C. Canada.
[3] USDA Forest Service, 705 Spear Street, South Burlington, VT 05404.
[4] British Columbia Forest Service, Victoria, B.C. Canada.
Corresponding author: kwallin@uvm.edu.

two isoprene units; sesquiterpenes are composed of three isoprene units; and di-terpenes are composed of four isoprene units. Various side groups can/may be present, and terpenoids are often oxygenated. Terpenoids constitute a major class of secondary metabolites in conifer oleoresin; they play an important role in the relationship between conifers, insects, and pathogens. They may deter insect feeding or affect fungal growth; be induced to change in abundance in response to wounding; be precursors for pheromone components used in insect communication; and affect insect and fungal reproductive success. Raffa and Berryman (1987) found induced monoterpenes to be a major factor in tree resistance to mountain pine beetle colonization.

The type and quantity of compounds in the oleoresin of plants influence herbivory (Zangerl and Berenbaum 2004). These same compounds or a combination thereof also affect pathogens that attack plant systems. Herbivores may be deterred or killed because of an inability to overcome these resin toxins or physical defenses (Raffa and Berryman 1983). Pathogens may be compartmentalized and contained within the tree, unable to spread. The mode of toxicity of a particular resin secondary metabolite to an invading pest varies. Some terpenoids interfere with insect digestion, while others affect insect reproduction, decreasing fecundity or future fitness. Secondary metabolites may also interfere with disease processes; for instance, some terpenoids inhibit germination of spores or growth of fungi (Klepzig et al. 1996, Six and Klepzig 2004).

The third line of defense for lodgepole pine is through its secondary metabolites, including terpenoids (Franceschi et al. 2005). Constitutive terpenoids may be enough to overwhelm attacking beetles. If the constitutive defenses are not successful, induced terpenoids are produced and may stop the bark beetle and its associated fungi. These tree chemicals can be very toxic to the mountain pine beetle (Klepzig et al. 1996, Raffa and Smalley 1995, Reid and Robb 1999). Quantifying the relationships between concentrations of host compounds at the early phase of host colonization is an important step toward understanding how variability of host responses impacts the success of MPB attacks. This information will be used to improve indices of tree resistance and relate specific host properties to survival of MPB outbreaks. Studies have already demonstrated that the composition and/or concentration of monoterpenes in either constitutive or induced tissue can be linked to the likelihood of host mortality to subcortical complexes (Nebeker et al. 1992, Raffa and Berryman 1982).

While resin flow and tree chemistry affect MPB progression throughout its life cycle in the tree, a tree also responds to the fungi by allocating carbon-based defenses to the site in an attempt to stop the growth of the fungi (Krokene et al. 2000). The tree defense strategy against blue stain fungus is apparent as a dark, resinous lesion on the phloem and xylem (Raffa and Berryman 1983, Wallin and Raffa 2001), which may compartmentalize and stop fungal growth. When this occurs, the tree successfully halts the colonization attempt by the individual beetle or pair of beetles and their associated fungi.

The goal of this research was to quantify responses during outbreak using replicated study plots of 20-year-old lodgepole pine, which provided the opportunity to calculate heritabilities and correlate MPB behaviors and tree responses during colonization sequence. The trees used in this research were open pollinated, so the mother of each tree and her provenance are clearly known. Known pedigree of progeny will allow the comparison of defense-related phenotypical differences across a broad range of lodgepole pine families. An understanding of the heritability of defenses in lodgepole pines will provide guidance to tree breeders as they seek to develop more resistant strains of pines for planting future forests.

The current outbreak of MPB has killed about 15 million ha of lodgepole pine in British Columbia. This is of great concern to the entire forestry industry and provided a framework to study genetic variation of lodgepole pine defense mechanisms against MPB. Based on a previous study, we selected 45 open-pollinated families from a population of 180 families, with the number of trees per family ranging from 16 to 26 (for a total of 887 trees) across two sites. During the summer of 2006, we quantified chemical and physical defensive responses to simulated attack by the MPB fungal complex. These responses included: physical exudation of resin, host compartmentalization response to fungal inoculation, and constitutive and induced terpenoids. During the summer and fall of 2007, we further assessed tree height, DBH (diameter at breast height, about 1.4 m), bark texture, tree mortality; and MPB presence, attack density, reproduction, and brood development, as well as the presence of hypersensitivity reactions by the tree to MPB.

Our data suggests variation in terpenoid makeup pre- and post- induction of simulated MPB attack is significantly different between families. Traits in lodgepole pine that affect MPB colonization and tree mortality also vary among families. Estimates show many host tree traits that affect the MPB life cycle are significantly heritable. We calculated family mean correlations of traits with significant heritabilities. Results suggest that several specific lodgepole pine tree defenses are heritable. Some constitutive (pre- induction) terpenes were negatively correlated with family mean mortality. The frequencies of induced reactions were negatively correlated with MPB gallery production, reproduction, and brood development. These results may provide future direction for management groups trying to manage MPB outbreaks in lodgepole pine stands.

Acknowledgments

This work was funded by a British Columbia Forest Service grant to K. F. Wallin and A. D. Yanchuk, with support from Oregon State University, the University of Vermont, and the USDA Forest Service to K. F. Wallin. The authors thank laboratory and field crews for their assistance.

Literature Cited

Franceschi, V.R.; Krokene, P.; Christiansen, E.; Krekling, T. 2005. Anatomical and chemical defenses of conifer bark against bark beetles and other pests. New Phytologist. 167: 353–376.

Klepzig, K.D.; Smalley, E.B.; Raffa, K.F. 1996. Combined chemical defenses against an insect-fungal complex. Journal of Chemical Ecology. 22: 1367–1388.

Krokene, P.; Solheim, H.; Langstrom, B. 2000. Fungal infection and mechanical wounding induce disease resistance in Scots pine. European Journal of Plant Pathology. 106: 537–541.

Martin, D.; Tholl, D.; Gershenzon, J.; Bohlmann, J. 2002. Methyl jasmonate induces traumatic resin ducts, terpenoid resin biosynthesis, and terpenoid accumulation in developing xylem of Norway spruce stems. Plant Physiology. 129: 1003–1018.

Nebeker, T.E.; Hodges, J.D.; Blanche, C.A.; Honea, C.R.; Tisdale, R.A. 1992. Variation in the constitutive defensive system in loblolly pine in relation to bark beetle attack. Forest Science. 38: 457–466.

Phillips, M.A.; Croteau, R.B. 1999. Resin-based defenses in conifers. Trends in Plant Science. 4: 184–190.

Raffa, K.F.; Berryman, A.A. 1982. Physiological differences between lodgepole pines resistant and susceptible to the mountain pine beetle and associated microorganisms. Environmental Entomology. 11: 486–492.

Raffa, K.F.; Berryman, A.A. 1983. The role of host plant resistance in the colonization behavior and ecology of bark beetles (Coleoptera: Scolytidae). Ecological Monographs. 53: 27–49.

Raffa, K.F.; Berryman, A.A. 1987. Interacting selective pressures in conifer-bark beetle systems: A basis for reciprocal adaptations? American Naturalist. 129: 234–262.

Raffa, K.F.; Smalley, E.B. 1995. Interaction of pre-attack and induced monoterpene concentrations in host conifer defense against bark beetle-fungal complexes. Oecologia. 102: 285–295.

Reid, M.L.; Robb, T. 1999. Death of vigorous trees benefits bark beetles. Oecologia. 120: 555–562.

Ruel, J.J.; Ayres, M.P.; Lorio, P.L. Jr. 1998. Loblolly pine responds to mechanical wounding with increased resin flow. Canadian Journal of Forest Resources. 28: 596–602.

Safranyik, L. and Carroll, A. L. 2006. The biology and epidemiology of the mountain pine beetle in lodgepole pine forests. Natural Resources of. Canada.1-66.

Six, D.L.; Klepzig, K.D. 2004. *Dendroctonus* bark beetles as model systems for studies on symbiosis. Symbiosis. 37: 1–26.

Wainhouse, D.; Cross, D.J.; Howell, R.S. 1990. The role of lignin as a defense against the spruce bark beetle *Dendroctonus micans*: effect on larvae and adults. Oecologia. 85: 257–265.

Wallin, K.F.; Raffa, K F. 1999. Altered constitutive and inducible phloem monoterpenes following natural defoliation of jack pine: implications to host mediated interguild interactions and plant defense theories. Journal of Chemical Ecology. 25: 861–880.

Wallin, K.F.; Raffa, K.F. 2001. Effects of folivory on subcortical plant defenses: Can defense theories predict interguild processes? Ecology. 82: 1387–1400.

Wallin, K.F.; Raffa, K.F. 2002. Density-mediated responses of bark beetles to host allelochemicals: a link between individual behaviour and population dynamics. Ecological Entomology. 27: 484–492.

Zangerl, A.R.; Berenbaum, M.R. 2004. Genetic variation in primary metabolites of *Pastinaca sativa*; Can herbivores act as selective agents? Journal of Chemical Ecology. 30: 1985–2002.

Stilbenes as Constitutive and Induced Protection Compounds in Scots Pine (*Pinus sylvestris* L.)

Anni Harju[1] and Martti Venäläinen[1]

Abstract

The goals of our studies are to describe the natural variation in the concentration of constitutive heartwood extractives; estimate the genetic parameters related to heartwood characteristics; determine whether there is a genetic connection between constitutive and inducible production of stilbenes; and, together with technical experts, to develop fast and reliable techniques to quantify stilbenes from wood samples and determine whether there are rapid ways to utilize the existing variation in silviculture. We are also collaborating with molecular geneticists to find the markers for pine stilbene biosynthesis that could be used in early selection.

The study material includes three generations of Scots pine (*Pinus sylvestris* L.): the first generation consists of grafted clones in seed orchards; their half-sib progenies growing in about 40-year-old progeny trials are the second generation; and the third generation includes seedlings in a nursery. The first and the second generations provide heartwood samples for stilbene analysis and the third generation has been used to study mechanical induction of stilbenes. Moreover, after heartwood samples from a large natural stand have been surveyed for stilbenes and total phenolics (end of 2012), we will be ready to make experiments on their seedling progenies and their biotic challengers.

We hypothesize that trees having strong inducible defense ability against biotic and abiotic stresses in their living tissues may also have high concentration of stilbenes in their heartwood when they mature. Such trees would be optimal to cultivate as timber with natural stilbene impregnation. One vision with practical importance is the exploitation of the genetic variation in stilbene production for the improvement of Scots pine regeneration material. For the evaluation of the possibilities and strategies to improve Scots pine trees to produce more durable heartwood, we need to estimate the interaction between genotype and environment as well as the genetic correlation between quality and growth traits.

Key words: *Pinus sylvestris*, stilbenes, protection compounds

Introduction

Because of its natural characteristics, Scots pine (*Pinus sylvestris* L.) heartwood is an important timber resource in Nordic countries, the potential of which is currently not fully utilized. Due to its high content of durability providing extractives, Scots pine heartwood timber has been used in construction where high decay resistance was required. Today, after more than 100 years of using super effective pressure treated wood, the interest on the natural durability of Scots pine (*Pinus Sylvestris* L.) heartwood has increased due to the legal restrictions on the use of wood preservation chemicals. Natural decay resistance is a special and important wood quality trait of Scots pine heartwood; however, it is very laborious to measure and study.

Heartwood is dead tissue, where extractives such as stilbenes have accumulated constitutively under developmental inevitability. It has an important role in living trees (Taylor et al. 2002), and its features continue to be important when heartwood serves as construction material. One of the most

[1] The Finnish Forest Research Institute, Punkaharju Unit, Finlandiantie 18, FI-58450 Punkaharju, Finland.
Corresponding author: anni.harju@metla.fi.

important goals of our studies has been to find indirect ways to grade heartwood material according to its natural decay resistance. Based on previous studies, it is evident that the concentration of extractives is an important factor in giving natural decay resistance to heartwood (Scheffer and Cowling 1966). Besides resin acids (Harju et al. 2002), stilbenes pinosylvin (PS) and its monomethyl ether (PSM) are the most important extractives in Scots pine heartwood (Venäläinen et al. 2004). Laboratory decay tests with the brown-rot fungus *Coniophora puteana* (strain BAM Ebw. 15) of heartwood material have shown a strong negative correlation between the concentration of stilbenes and total phenolics for mass loss (Harju and Venäläinen 2006, Heijari et al. 2005, Leinonen et al. 2008). The result suggests that quantifying stilbenes or total phenolics might be used as an indirect measure of natural decay resistance.

The living tissues in the trunk of Scots pine—namely the sapwood, phloem, and the cambium located between them—are constitutively protected on the outside by the bark and on the inside by the heartwood (Franceschi et al. 2005). However, attacks by damaging agents such as insects and their fungal associates trigger additional defensive responses in the form of induced production of secondary compounds and changes in wood anatomy (Lieutier et al. 1989, Nagy et al. 2005, Raffa et al. 2005).

Scots pine seedlings have been shown to produce stilbenes in various types of tissue in response to different kinds of stress factors, such as ultraviolet light (Schoeppner and Kindl 1979), ozone (Rosemann et al. 1991), and infection by fungi (Bonello et al. 1993, Gehlert et al. 1990). In intact sapwood, stilbenes do not occur in detectable amounts. However, even the mere mechanical wounding of Scots pine sapwood (Nilsson et al. 2002) induces the production of chemical defenses. The discolored sapwood induced by mechanical wounding has a similar high-performance liquid chromatography (HPLC) chromatogram as natural heartwood (Nilsson et al. 2002).

In this paper we describe the natural variation in the concentration of constitutive heartwood extractives and present estimates for the genetic parameters related to heartwood characteristics in Scots pine. We have used mechanical wounding to induce production of secondary compounds in the sapwood of 3-year-old seedlings and we present genetic parameters for some chemical and growth traits from that experiment.

Methods and Materials

Heartwood Studies

Study material consisted of two progeny trials with identical half-sib progenies, 53 of which were included in this study (10 trees/progeny). The first 5.4 ha progeny trial area is in Leppävirta (62°25'N, 27°45'E) and the second 5.5 ha area in Savonranta (62°15'N, 29°00'E), both in eastern Finland. The trees were 43 and 45 years old, respectively, at the time of the increment core sampling of heartwood The original design for both trials was 12 randomized blocks, with three rows of three trees per plot, at a spacing of 2 × 2 m (equivalent to 2,500 trees/ha).

The diameter at breast height (DBH) was measured, and 5 mm increment cores were drilled radially through the stem at about breast height in Savonranta, and in Leppävirta at about 90 cm. The pith-including cores were placed in plastic tubes and stored in darkness at -20 °C. The boundary between the sapwood and heartwood was marked on the increment cores under UV light, and the radius of the heartwood was measured from both sides of the pith. From each increment core, sections covering annual rings five to eight counted from the pith were separated from both sides of the pith. The aim was to obtain heartwood annual rings with the same cambial age. One section was used for the Folin–Ciocalteu (FC) assay to measure the concentration of total phenolics, and the other section was used for gas chromatography – mass spectrometry (GC–MS) analysis of stilbenes. The heartwood samples for the chemical analyses were oven dried at 60 °C for 24 h, weighed, and stored in a desiccator prior to grinding with an analytical mill (Kinematica). The milled samples were stored in darkness in sealed test tubes and glass bottles at -20 °C.

Mechanical Wounding of the Seedlings

The seeds were collected in October 2000 from 18 unrelated trees from a progeny trial in Mäkrä (Kerimäki, Mäkrä, 61°50'N, 29°23'E), the heartwood of which had earlier been studied (Harju et al. 2003, Tiitta et al. 2003, Venäläinen et al. 2004). Seeds from each known mother tree comprised a half-sib family, where the fathers originated from an unknown stochastic pollen pool. The seedlings were grown for 3 years in a greenhouse at the Punkaharju Research Unit (61°48'N, 29°19'E) of the Finnish Forest Research Institute.

A total of 10 seedlings from each half-sib family were wounded on April 2004, when elongation of the buds of the seedlings had just begun. Ten seedlings of each family were left unwounded as controls. When wounding, about 10 holes were drilled through the stem with a 2.5 mm drill at intervals of about 2 cm along the 2002 internode (2-year-old segment of the stem). After about 3 months of growth, the wounded internodes were cut apart, the bark and phloem removed, and the internodes frozen at -20°C. Similar sections were cut from the control seedlings. A longitudinal 5 mm section from above and below each wound hole was sampled (fig. 1). The samples were prepared for chemical analysis using the same methods as used for the increment cores. The analysis of stilbenes, resin acids, and lignans in the seedlings was carried out in accordance with the procedure for stilbenes described in Karppanen et al. (2007). More details of the experiment are found in Harju et al. (2009).

 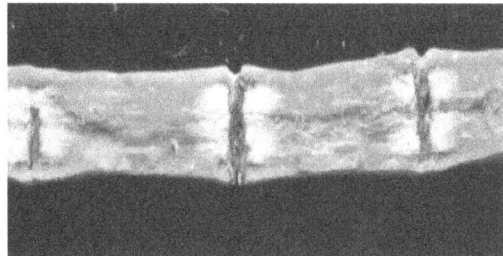

Figure 1—(left) Wounding of a 3-year-old Scots pine seedling by drilling holes through the stem, and (right) longitudinal section of the wounded stem under UV light (wavelength 313 nm). The brightly fluorescent areas of the stem were sampled for chemical analysis.

Analysis of Stilbenes and Total Phenolics

The gas chromatography-mass spectrometry (GC–MS) analysis of stilbenes was carried out as described by Karppanen et al. (2007). However, slight changes were made to the procedure. For a detailed description of the accelerated GC–MS analysis used in the study, please contact Tarja Tapanila (tarja.tapanila@metla.fi). The Folin–Ciocalteu assay for measuring total phenolics is described in Harju and Venäläinen (2006). The absorptivity was measured after 20 to 90 min at 735 nm against a mixture containing all reagents except the sample. Tannic acid (Merck; 1.59446.0010) was used as a standard. Therefore, the results are expressed as milligram tannic acid equivalents (TAE) per gram of dry mass of wood.

Estimation of Genetic Parameters

Heritabilities were estimated using the formula $\hat{h}^2 = 4\hat{\sigma}_f^2 / (\hat{\sigma}_f^2 + \hat{\sigma}_e^2)$. True half-sibs and unrelated parents were assumed. Variance components were estimated using a model, where block effects were regarded as fixed and family effects as random effects. The model did not include interaction effect. A mixed procedure of Statistical Package for Social Sciences (SPSS) system with restricted maximum likelihood (REML) technique (SPSS Inc. 2006) was used to estimate the variance components. Genetic correlation between the traits in the same environment (Leppävirta) was estimated as $r_A = \text{cov}_{xy} / (\text{Var}_x \text{Var}_y)^{0.5}$ and the genetic correlation between the two environments was estimated applying the formula 22.8 in Lynch and Walsh (1998).

Results and Discussion

Heartwood Studies

For the grading of existing timber or for tree improvement it is important to know the distribution of the stilbene concentration and the concentration of total phenolics in the heartwood among the trees within a single stand. In all the materials studied, the distribution was slightly skewed to the right, which is typical for many biological distributions.

We estimated heritability for some chemical and growth variables (table 1). Quantification of stilbenes is continuing for the progeny trial Savonranta. To date, the results show that for heartwood stilbenes and total phenolics, the prospects of breeding are really promising compared to other traits studied. The heritabilities were quite similar, but the coefficients of additive genetic variation were about half of the ones estimated by Fries et al. (2000) from a full-sib Scots pine progeny trial of about the same age as the trials in our study.

Table 1—Estimates for heritability in narrow sense and the coefficient of additive genetic variation (CV$_A$) for the chemical and growth characteristics of Scots pine

	Heritability (CV$_A$%)		
	Leppävirta		Savonranta
	2003	**2009**	**2010**
PS[a]		0.67 (35)[c]	
PSM		0.41 (33)[c]	
PS + PSM		0.56 (33)[c]	
Total phenolics	0.71 (33)[b]	0.52 (26)[c]	0.54 (31)
Density	0.60 (6)	0.58 (7)[c]	0.26 (6)
DBH	0.15 (6)	0.28 (8)[c]	0.12 (5)
Heartwood proportion	0.23 (16)	0.16 (13)[c]	0.16 (11)

[a] PS = pinosylvin, PSM = pinosylvin monomethyl ether.
[b] Harju and Venäläinen (2006).
[c] Partanen et al. (2011).

Genetic correlation between the two environments (Leppävirta and Savonranta), which are located about 100 km from each other, were ≥ 0.80 for the concentration of total phenolics, density, DBH, and the proportion of heartwood. There were evident rank changes between the sites among the families, but there were many families that held their rank position in both environments.

For the progeny trial in Leppävirta, it was possible to estimate the genetic correlation between the measured traits. For the extractives mentioned in table 1, the genetic correlations were ≥ 0.75. Genetic correlation between the concentration of extractives and the proportion of heartwood was around 0.20. Heartwood density and DBH had a negative genetic correlation of -0.35, and they both had unfavorable negative genetic correlation with the concentration of extractives varying from -0.06 to -0.33. However these negative genetic correlations could be handled during the thinning of the actual production stands by cutting the largest trees, which produce the poorest quality of wood.

Induced Stilbenes in Seedlings

In our study, besides the increased amount of resin acids (from the average of 3.4 mg/g in control seedlings to the average of 71.9 mg/g in wounded seedlings), typical heartwood compounds PS and PSM were found (fig. 2) from the brightly fluorescing areas of the mechanically wounded seedlings (Harju et al. 2009). Two lignans, nortrachelogenin (NTG) and matairesinol (MR), typical for Scots pine knot wood (Holmbom et al. 2003), were found as well (fig. 2).

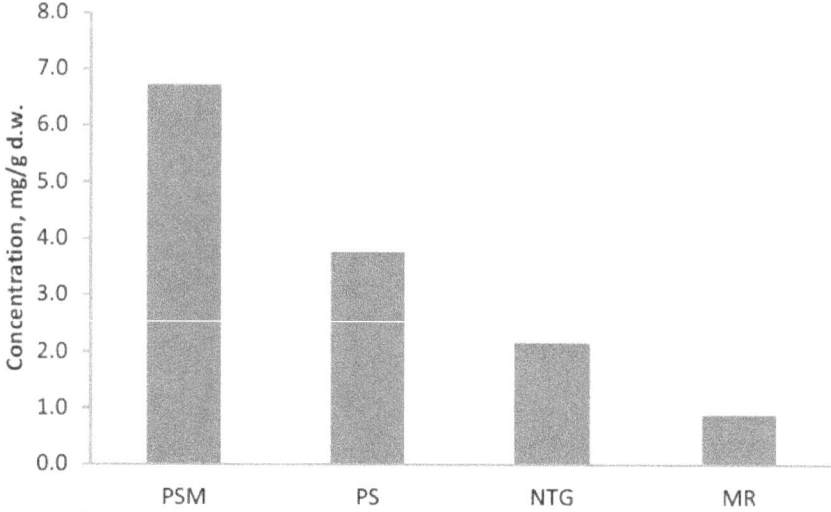

Figure 2—Average concentration of pinosylvin , pinosylvin monomethyl ether , nortrachelogenin , and matairesinol found from the brightly fluorescing areas of the mechanically wounded seedlings.

We were especially interested in quantifying the variation among the seedlings and in the proportion of the heritable variation in response to the wounding. Except for the concentration of PSM and resin acids, the heritabilities in the narrow sense were surprisingly high for all the traits that were measured (table 2). The coefficient of additive genetic variation was higher for the chemical than for the growth traits.

Table 2—Estimates for the heritability in narrow sense ($\hat{h}^2$) and the coefficient of additive genetic variation (CV$_A$) for growth and chemical traits induced by mechanical wounding of 3-year-old seedlings (Harju et al. 2009)

Variable	n	Heritability in narrow sense, $\hat{h}^2$ (SE)	Coefficient of additive genetic variation, CV$_A$, %
PS[a]	175	0.71 (0.36)	29
PSM	176	0.35 (0.25)	15
NTG	175	0.73 (0.37)	37
MR	171	1.03 (0.46)	52
Sum of resin acids	176	0.31 (0.24)	21
Height	180	0.84 (0.40)	10
Diameter of the sampled section[b], mm	180	0.64 (0.34)	8

[a] PS = pinosylvin; PSM = pinosylvin monomethyl ether; NTG = nortrachelogenin; MR = matairesinol.
n = the number of seedlings. Number of half-sib families was 18.
[b] Measured from the middle of the section.

In this material, there was no phenotypic correlation between the growth traits and the concentration of extractives. Because of the small number of studied families, it was not possible to estimate genetic correlation. However, correlation of family means was estimated. Except for resin acids, the family mean correlation between chemical and growth traits was negative, varying from -0.22 to -0.39 and did not differ statistically significantly from zero (n = 18). For resin acids, the correlation was positive, but did not differ statistically significantly from zero (Harju et al. 2009).

If mechanical wounding of the seedlings induces a reaction related to the extractive composition of their mother's heartwood, then wounding could be utilized in developing an early testing method in the breeding of durable Scots pine heartwood. Thus, we also estimated heritability from the regression of the offspring mean values based on their mothers, i.e., regression of the induced concentration of extractives in the xylem of the seedlings on the concentration of extractives in the heartwood of their mothers. The heritability value for PS was 0.31, which suggests that there might be a positive connection between the constitutive and inducible synthesis of PS (Harju et al. 2009).

We are now interested in the role of induced production of stilbenes for tree survival and we are looking for proper research tools to approach the topic. In terms of tree breeding, it would be profitable if the constitutive and induced resistance could be selected for simultaneously.

Acknowledgments

We greatly appreciate the contribution of the personnel in the Finnish Forest Research Institute for the research described in this paper. This study was financed by the Finnish Forest Research Institute and by Tekes (the Finnish Funding Agency for Technology and Innovation) as part of the EffTech (Intelligent and Resource-Efficient Production Technologies) and EffFibre (Value through Intensive and Efficient Fibre Supply) research programs of the Forestcluster ltd.

Literature Cited

Bonello, P.; Heller, W.; Sandermann, H. Jr. 1993. Ozone effects on root-disease susceptibility and defence responses in mycorrhizal and non-mycorrhizal seedlings of Scots pine (*Pinus sylvestris* L.). New Phytologist. 124: 653–663.

Franceschi, V.R.; Krokene, P.; Christiansen, E.; Krekling, T. 2005. Anatomical and chemical defenses of conifer bark against bark beetles and other pests. New Phytologist. 167: 353–376.

Fries, A.; Ericsson, T.; Gref, R. 2000. High heritability of wood extractives in *Pinus sylvestris* progeny tests. Canadian Journal of Forest Research. 30: 1707–1713.

Gehlert, R.; Schöppner, A.; Kindl, H. 1990. Stilbene synthase from seedlings of *Pinus sylvestris*: purification and induction in response to fungal infection. Molecular Plant-Microbe Interactions. 3: 444–449.

Harju, A.M.; Anttonen, S.; Viitanen, H.; Kainulainen, P.; Saranpää, P.; Vapaavuori, E. 2003. Chemical factors affecting brown-rot decay resistance of Scots pine heartwood. Trees. 17: 263–268.

Harju, A.M.; Kainulainen, P.; Venäläinen, M.; Tiitta, M.; Viitanen, H. 2002. Differences in resin acid concentration between brown-rot resistant and susceptible Scots pine heartwood. Holzforschung. 56: 479–486.

Harju, A.M.; Venäläinen, M. 2006. Measuring the decay resistance of Scots pine heartwood indirectly by the Folin-Ciocalteu assay. Canadian Journal of Forest Research. 36: 1797–1804.

Harju, A.M.; Venäläinen, M.; Saranpää, P.; Laakso, T. 2009. Mechanical wounding of the Scots pine seedlings results in stilbene and lignan biosynthesis. Tree Physiology. 29(1): 19–25.

Heijari, J.; Nerg, A.M.; Kaakinen, S.; Vapaavuori; E.; Raitio, H.; Levula, T.; Viitanen, H.; Holopainen, J.K.; Kainulainen, P. 2005. Resistance of Scots pine wood to brown-rot fungi after long-term forest fertilization. Trees. 19: 728–734.

Holmbom, B.; Eckerman, C.; Eklund, P.; Hemming, J.; Nisula, L.; Reunanen, M.; Sjöholm, R.; Sundberg, A.; Sundberg, K.; Willför, S. 2003. Knots in trees - a new rich source of lignans. Phytochemistry Reviews. 2: 331–340.

Karppanen, O.; Venäläinen, M.; Harju, A.M.; Willför, S.; Pietarinen, S.; Laakso, T.; Kainulainen, P. 2007. Knotwood as a window to the indirect measurement of the decay resistance of Scots pine heartwood. Holzforschung. 61: 600–604.

Leinonen, A.; Harju, A.M.; Venäläinen, M.; Saranpää, P.; Laakso, T. 2008. FT-NIR spectroscopy in predicting the decay resistance related characteristics of solid Scots pine (*Pinus sylvestris* L.) heartwood. Holzforschung. 62: 284–288.

Lieutier, F.; Cheniclet, C.; Garcia, J. 1989. Comparison of the defense reactions of *Pinus pinaster* and *Pinus sylvestris* to attacks by two bark beetles (Coleoptera: Scolytidae) and their associated fungi. Environmental Entomology. 18: 228–234.

Lynch, M.; Walsh, B. 1998. Genetics and analysis of quantitative traits. Sunderland, MA: Sinauer Associates, Inc.

Nagy, N.E.; Krokene, P.; Solheim, H. 2005. Anatomical-based defense responses of Scots pine (*Pinus sylvestris* L.) stems to two fungal pathogens. Tree Physiology. 26: 159–167.

Nilsson, M.; Wikman, S.; Eklund, L. 2002. Induction of discolored wood in Scots pine (*Pinus sylvestris*). Tree Physiology. 22: 331–338.

Partanen, J.; Harju, A.M.; Venäläinen, M.; Kärkkäinen, K. 2011. Highly heritable heartwood properties of Scots pine: possibilities for selective seed harvest in seed orchards. Canadian Journal of Forest Research. 41(10): 1993–2000.

Raffa, K.F.; Aukema, B.H.; Erbilgin, N.; Klepzig, K.D.; Wallin, K.F. 2005. Interactions among conifer terpenoids and bark beetles across multiple levels of scale: an attempt to understand links between population patterns and physiological processes. In: Romero, J., ed. Chemical ecology and phytochemistry of forest ecosystems. Proceedings of the Phytochemical Society of North America. Recent Advances in Phytochemistry. 39: 79–118.

Rosemann, D.; Heller, W.; Sandermann, H., Jr. 1991. Biochemical plant responses to ozone II. Induction of stilbene biosynthesis in Scots pine (*Pinus sylvestris* L.) seedlings. Plant Physiology. 97: 1280–1286.

Scheffer, T.C.; Cowling, E. 1966. Natural resistance of wood to microbial deterioration. Annual Review of Phytopathology. 4: 147–170.

Schoeppner, A.; Kindl, H. 1979. Stilbene synthase (pinosylvine synthase) and its induction by ultraviolet light. FEBS Letters. 108: 349–352.

SPSS Inc. 2006. SPSS 14.0.2. for Windows. Chicago: SPSS Inc.

Taylor, A.M.; Gartner, B.L.; Morrell, J.J. 2002. Heartwood formation and natural durability – a review. Wood and Fiber Science. 34(4): 587–611.

Tiitta, M.; Kainulainen, P.; Harju, A.M.; Venäläinen, M.; Manninen, A.M.; Vuorinen, M.; Viitanen, H. 2003. Comparing the effect of chemical and physical properties on complex electrical impedance of Scots pine wood. Holzforschung. 57: 433-–439.

Venäläinen, M.; Harju, A.M.; Saranpää, P.; Kainulainen, P.; Tiitta, M.; Velling, P. 2004. The concentration of phenolics in brown-rot decay resistant and susceptible Scots pine heartwood. Wood Science and Technology. 38: 109–118.

Simultaneous Laurel Wilt Disease Biology and Resistance Research

Jason A. Smith[1] and Randy C. Ploetz[2]

Abstract

Laurel wilt (LW) is a devastating, emerging disease of native and non-native members of the Lauraceae family in the southeastern United States. Currently, the fungal pathogen (*Raffaelea lauricola*) and its vector (*Xyleborus glabratus*) are found in Alabama, Florida, Georgia, Mississippi, and North and South Carolina. The wilt is decimating native stands of redbay (*Persea borbonia* (L.) Spreng.), and causing significant damage to planted and native sassafras (*Sassafras albidum* (Nutt.) Nees) and avocado (*Persea americana* Mill.). Research has addressed significant knowledge gaps that exist for the biology and management of this disease. To date, effective fungicidal management of LW has been limited to the expensive, preventive treatment of high-value landscape trees with systemic fungicides. Long-term management in landscape and avocado plantings may rely on a combination of sanitation practices and the use of disease-resistant germplasm. The susceptibility/tolerance of different taxa and avocado germplasm has been assessed in artificial inoculation work in the field. Host range experiments have assessed the response of 35 taxa in the Annonaceae, Fagaceae, Lauraceae, Magnoliaceae, Moraceae, and Sapindaceae, which include known hosts of the vector in southeast Asia and their relatives. In general, members of the Lauraceae that are native to the southeastern United States have been most susceptible, whereas those in the family from Asia and in other families have been resistant. Forty-one cultivars of avocado, representing the three races of the species (Guatemalan, West Indian, and Mexican) and hybrids thereof, have been screened for disease response. Unfortunately, West Indian cultivars that predominate in Florida have been most susceptible. Host-pathogen interactions have been examined in greenhouse and field studies. Results from this work indicate that: (i) systemic colonization by the pathogen, without apparent internal or external symptom development, occurs in some hosts; (ii) wilting is associated with reduced hydraulic conductivity in the xylem; (iii) vascular dysfunction results from host responses, not occlusion of vessels by the pathogen; and (iv) the pathogen does not produce wilt-inducing toxins. In ongoing research, greater understandings are sought for how susceptible and tolerant/resistant host plants respond to this disease.

[1] School of Forest Resources and Conservation, University of Florida, Gainesville, Florida 32611.
[2] Tropical Research and Education Center, Homestead, Florida 33031.
Corresponding author: jasons@ufl.edu.

Breeding for Resistance in a Changing Environment - Durable Resistance: Hopes, Pitfalls, and Management Strategies

Plantings of sugar pine (*Pinus lambertiana*) started in 1998 at Happy Camp, CA for white pine blister rust resistance testing.
(Photo: Deems Burton).

Breeding Poplars With Durable Resistance to *Melampsora larici-populina* Leaf Rust: A Multidisciplinary Approach to Understand and Delay Pathogen Adaptation

A. Dowkiw,[1] V. Jorge,[1] M. Villar,[1] E. Voisin,[1] V. Guérin,[1] P. Faivre-Rampant,[2] A. Bresson,[2] F. Bitton,[2] S. Duplessis,[3] P. Frey,[3] B. Petre,[3] C. Guinet,[3] C. Xhaard,[3] B. Fabre,[3] F. Halkett,[3] C. Plomion,[4] C. Lalanne,[4] and C. Bastien[1]

Introduction

During the last decades, European poplar breeders learned the hard way that *Melampsora larici-populina* (commonly abbreviated as *Mlp*, fig. 1) has an impressive adaptive potential (McDonald and Linde 2002). This fungal pathogen defeated all the deployed cultivars carrying qualitative (i.e., complete) resistances inherited from the American eastern black cottonwood *Populus deltoides* Bartram ex Marsh. in less time than needed to grow a poplar tree.

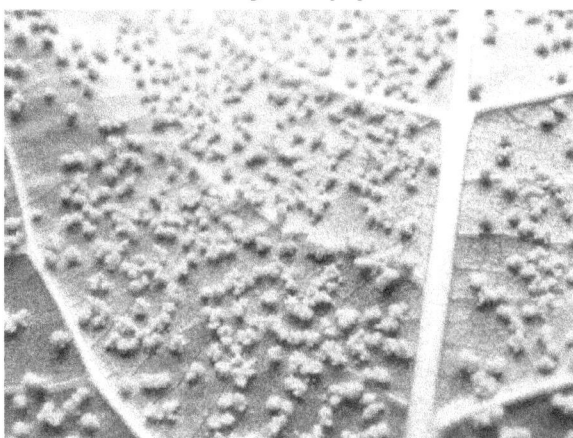

Figure 1—Sporulating *Melampsora larici-populina* uredinia on the abaxial side of a *Populus deltoides x P. nigra* cv 'Robusta' poplar leaf. (Photo by A. Dowkiw)

Populus deltoides is a key species for poplar breeding and growing in Europe. As an illustration, 90 percent of the cultivars sold by nurseries to growers in 2009 in France were interspecific hybrids of two types: *P. deltoides x P. trichocarpa* (i.e., interamerican hybrids) or *P. deltoides x P. nigra* (i.e., Euramerican hybrids, *P. nigra* being a European species) (French Ministry of Agriculture – DGPATT – 2009 national statistics of forest reproductive material sales). Of the three parental species involved, *P. deltoides* is the only one where we ever found qualitative resistances to *Mlp*. Moreover, hybrid vigor (i.e., positive heterosis for growth traits) is generally high in these cultivars. Unfortunately, most of the hybrid material deployed over the last 30 years exhibited high rust susceptibility once their one or two major resistance genes inherited from *P. deltoides* were defeated.

[1] INRA, UR0588 AGPF, 45075 Orléans Cedex 2, France.
[2] INRA, UMR1165 URGV, 91057 Evry Cedex, France.
[3] INRA UMR1136 IAM, 54280 Champenoux, France.
[4] INRA, UMR1202 BIOGECO, 33612 Cestas Cedex, France.
Corresponding author: arnaud.dowkiw@orleans.inra.fr.

The present situation is as follows: (i) all of the 44 clones found in the French registry of poplar cultivars, except two cultivars involving the non-host species *P. alba*, are susceptible to *Mlp*, and (ii) from 1990 to 2004, the proportion of immune clones in the *P. deltoides* breeding material grown in the nursery of INRA Orléans decreased from 45 percent to 2 percent (fig. 2).

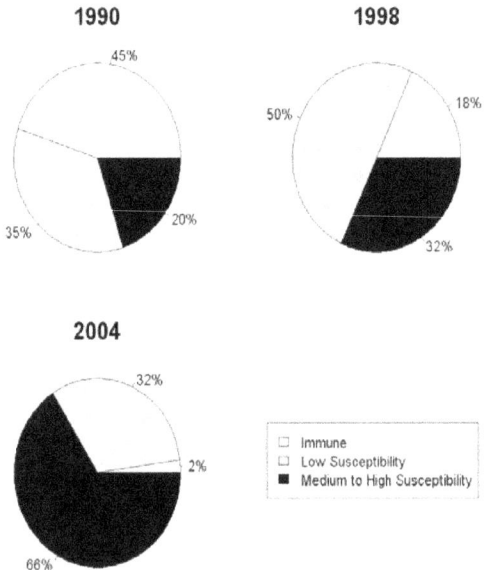

Figure 2—Evolution of *Mlp* rust susceptibility from 1990 to 2004 in a breeding collection of 545 *P. deltoides* clones evaluated under natural rust infection at the Institut National de la Recherche Agronomique in Orléans, France.

Breeding for quantitative resistance (QR) was considered a reasonable option as it is often described as an a priori for a more durable strategy. Although significant genetic variability was found for slow rusting traits in laboratory inoculation experiments and for field resistance under natural rust pressure in the three considered poplar species and their hybrids (Dowkiw et al. 2003, Lefèvre et al. 1994, Lefèvre et al. 1998, Pinon 1992, Pichot and Teissier du Cros 1993), three major results raised doubts on this optimistic point of view. First, elucidating the genetic determinism of QR in *P. deltoides x P. trichocarpa* hybrid progenies essentially yielded a few loci with major effects (Dowkiw and Bastien 2004) while small effect QTLs were either rare or hard to detect and often exhibited strain specificity (Jorge et al. 2005, fig. 3a). Second, quantitative and qualitative resistances did not appear to be completely independent as most identified defeated qualitative resistances inherited from *P. deltoides* happened to have statistical (possibly residual) effects on QR against virulent strains of the pathogen (Dowkiw and Bastien 2007, fig. 4). Third, *Mlp* strains able to completely defeat a major QR factor inherited from *P. richocarpa* have been identified before any commercial deployment of this resistance factor (Dowkiw et al. 2010).

Based on these considerations, poplar breeders and pathologists developed a broad holistic approach to understand the factors governing the durability of resistance, from genes to landscape, in order to conceive new breeding and deployment strategies.

Functional Genomics of the Poplar-*Mlp* Interaction

Following Eenink (1976), we believe that "the stability (i.e., the durability) of resistance is determined by the genetics of host-parasite relationships and not by the genetics of resistance. Quantity as well as quality of resistance and pathogenicity genes may be important. Monogenic and polygenic resistances can be stable or unstable." Consequently, many efforts are made to elucidate the functions of both qualitative and quantitative resistances and plant and rust geneticists try to bring the knowledge about the host-pathogen interaction at the same level for both protagonists.

Because genes with strong effects are the easiest ones to study and to follow among pedigrees, an integrated approach combining quantitative genetics, transcriptomics, and proteomics was conducted on three major loci: R_1 and *Mer*, two qualitative resistances inherited from *P. deltoides* defeated by virulences 1 and 7 of the pathogen, respectively, and R_{US}, a major QR factor inherited from *P. trichocarpa* with strong effect on uredinia size. R_{US} and R_1 were identified at INRA (Dowkiw and Bastien 2004) whereas *Mer* was identified by a Belgian team (Cervera et al. 1996). All outputs from this combined approach led to the same conclusion of similarities between qualitative and quantitative resistances.

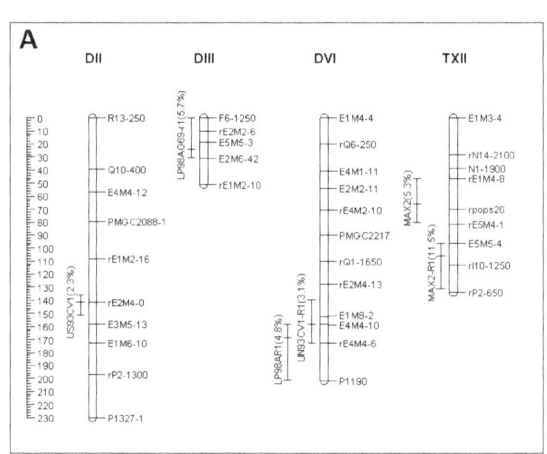

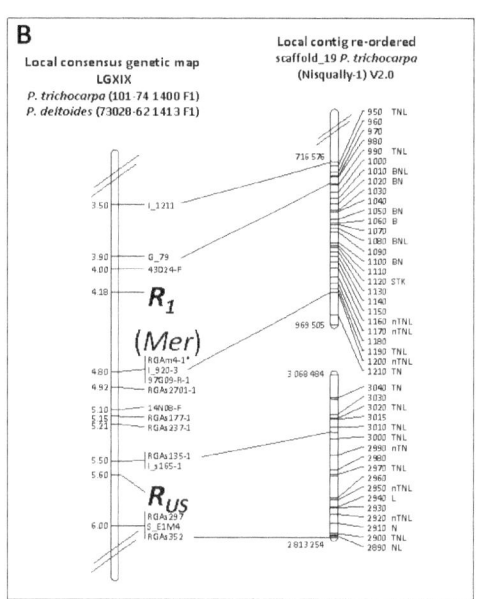

Figure 3—*Mlp* resistance loci described in the litterature (Bresson et al. 2011, Cervera et al. 1996, Cervera et al. 2001, Jorge et al. 2005, Lescot et al. 2004): **A**: Minor QTLs described in Jorge et al. (2005) and detected in *P. deltoides* (D) and *P. trichocarpa* (T) after inoculation in controlled conditions with 7 *Mlp* strains followed by QR assessments (UN: uredinia size; LP: latent period; UN: uredinia number) or after natural rust infection in the field (MAX). Numbers in parentheses represent the percentage of clonal variance explained by each QTL. See Jorge et al. (2005) for further details. **B**: Localization of three major resistance factors on a consensus genetic map and alignment on the *P. trichocarpa* genome sequence for chromosome 19 (v2.0). Genetic distances in cM are indicated on the left of the linkage groups. The gene models are designated by their number without the prefix POPTR_0019s. Resistance gene analog domains are abbreviated as follows: B for BEAF and DREF DNA-binding finger (BED), L for leucine-rich repeat (LRR), n for nuclear localization sequence (NLS), N for nucleotide-binding site (NBS) and T for Toll interleukin 1 receptor (TIR). STK stands for serine threonine kinase. Position of the *Mer* locus (Cervera et al. 2001) is deduced from marker RGAm4-1 designed from a *P. deltoides* BAC sequence developed for positional cloning of *Mer* (Lescot et al. 2004). For marker details, see Bresson et al. (2011).

Although R_{US} maps to a clearly distinct area, all three loci map on the same chromosome (XIX, fig. 3b) which happens to be particularly rich in NBS-LRR resistance gene analogs (Kohler et al. 2008).

A combined transcriptomic and proteomic approach has been carried out in two contrasted groups of poplar half-sib genotypes possessing the resistant R_{US} allele (i.e., heterozygous $R_{US}r_{US}$ genotypes) or deprived from it (i.e., $r_{US}r_{US}$ genotypes) to determine molecular markers associated to the R_{US}-mediated QR. Interestingly, whereas almost no genes were induced at 2 and 4 days after inoculation

GENERAL TECHNICAL REPORT PSW-GTR-240

in the $r_{US}r_{US}$ bulk compared to mock-inoculated leaves, the $R_{US}r_{US}$ bulk was characterized by a strong induction of many marker genes typically associated to qualitative resistance (Rinaldi et al. 2007), suggesting a delay in defense reaction activation for QR. Several of these "marker" genes were confirmed by proteomic and by RTqPCR expression profiling (e.g., thaumatin-like protein, glutathione *S*-transferase).

Uredinia size

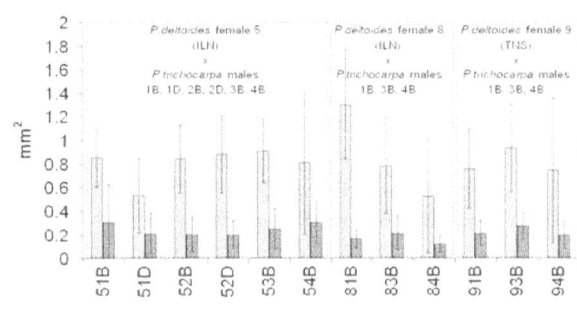

Latent period

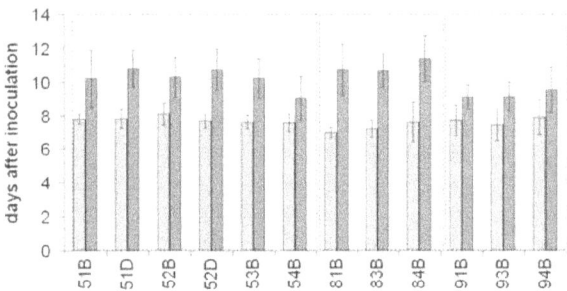

Uredinia number

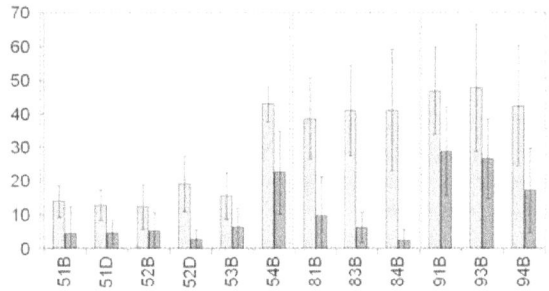

Figure 4—Family means (+/- associated standard errors) for three epidemiological components in 12 *P. deltoides* x *P. trichocarpa* F_1 families involving three distinct *P. deltoides* mothers of different origins (ILN, TNS) after leaf-disk inoculation with an *Mlp* strain able to sporulate in presence of any complete resistance factor inherited from *P. deltoides* segregating in this material. For each family, a distinction is made between genotypes carrying such qualitative resistance factor (in black) and genotypes lacking it (in grey). Presence of segregating qualitative resistance factors was revealed using incompatible stains of the pathogen. See Dowkiw and Bastien (2007) for further details.

Regarding the genetics of the pathogen's side of the interaction, not much is known yet, even on the genetic determinism of virulence (i.e., the pathogen's matching piece to qualitative resistance). One reason is that progenies are difficult to obtain due to the heteroecious life cycle of the pathogen (i.e., the need to perform its sexual stage on a different host plant, here larch) and to its strict biotrophic status. However, recent sequencing of the *Mlp* genome opens the way for new genomics tools and makes the popular rust interaction a model pathosystem for forest pathology (Duplessis et al. 2011a). Most pathogenicity effectors described so far in fungal biotrophic pathogen encode small cysteine-rich secreted proteins (SSP) (Stergiopoulos and de Wit 2009). The *Mlp* genome contains a total of 1,184 SSP-encoding genes, which are mostly specific to this rust fungus (i.e., no homologs are found in other fungi, including the wheat stem rust; Duplessis et al. 2011b). More than 50 percent of these SSP genes are expressed during the successful colonization of poplar leaves representing candidate pathogenicity factors (Duplessis et al. 2011b; Hacquard et al., in press)

Thinking at Larger Scales

One of the reasons for the rapid spread of newly adapted strains of *Mlp* lies within the spatial and temporal organization of host diversity over the country. Poplar is a perennial host that is essentially cultivated as monoclonal stands, and less than 10 cultivars are being significantly used by growers. In this context, we investigated to what extent the population genetic structure of *Mlp* can be impacted by the deployment of resistant poplar cultivars over the country.

Since 1982, the interamerican hybrid poplar cv. 'Beaupré' carrying the rust resistance gene *Mer* was broadly planted in France and remained immune for 12 years, but once overcome by virulence 7 of the pathogen, severe rust outbreaks occurred (Xhaard et al. 2011). Using both phenotypic (i.e., virulence profiles) and genotypic (i.e., microsatellites) markers, we showed that *Mlp* isolates carrying virulence 7 were widely distributed all across France and displayed a specific genetic signature consistent with a history of selection and drastic demographic changes resulting from the resistance breakdown (Xhaard et al. 2011, fig. 5). This study illustrates how poplar cultivation has influenced the spatial and genetic structure of the pathogen, and has led to the spread of virulence alleles in most pathogen populations. As a consequence, resistance management should certainly be thought about at a continental scale in order to maximize its sustainability (McDonald and Linde 2002).

Alternative Breeding Strategies

Urged by growers to deliver new cultivars, breeders explore multiple (possibly combinable), very pragmatic, strategies to delay pathogen adaptation.

Pure *P. deltoides* genotypes, although defeated, always show much lower field susceptibility to the pathogen in our nursery in Orléans than their interspecific hybrid progenies. This may result from favorable gene associations that happen to be broken in these hybrids. Constitutive resistance traits related to leaf anatomical characteristics may be particularly affected by hybridization with *P. trichocarpa* and *P. nigra*. As a short-term solution, pure *P. deltoides* cultivars selected for productivity in northern climatic conditions under traditional cultivation practices will be released in 2013. They all carry defeated qualitative resistances but repeatedly showed high QR levels under natural rust infections. Backcrossing interamerican F_1 hybrids to the *P. deltoides* species is also being considered.

Medium-term solutions will rely on a more careful exploration of the genetic variability available in the European species *P. nigra* that co-evolved with the pathogen and on the simultaneous release of several unrelated cultivars to generate host diversity at regional scale. A collection of 2,300 *P. nigra* genotypes, most of them originating from different French natural populations, but also from Italy, Germany, and the Netherlands, have recently been screened for rust resistance under natural and controlled infection. Additional breeding traits like avoidance and tolerance (i.e., the ability to maintain growth despite being susceptible to the disease) are also being evaluated using fungicide treated *vs.* untreated field experiments.

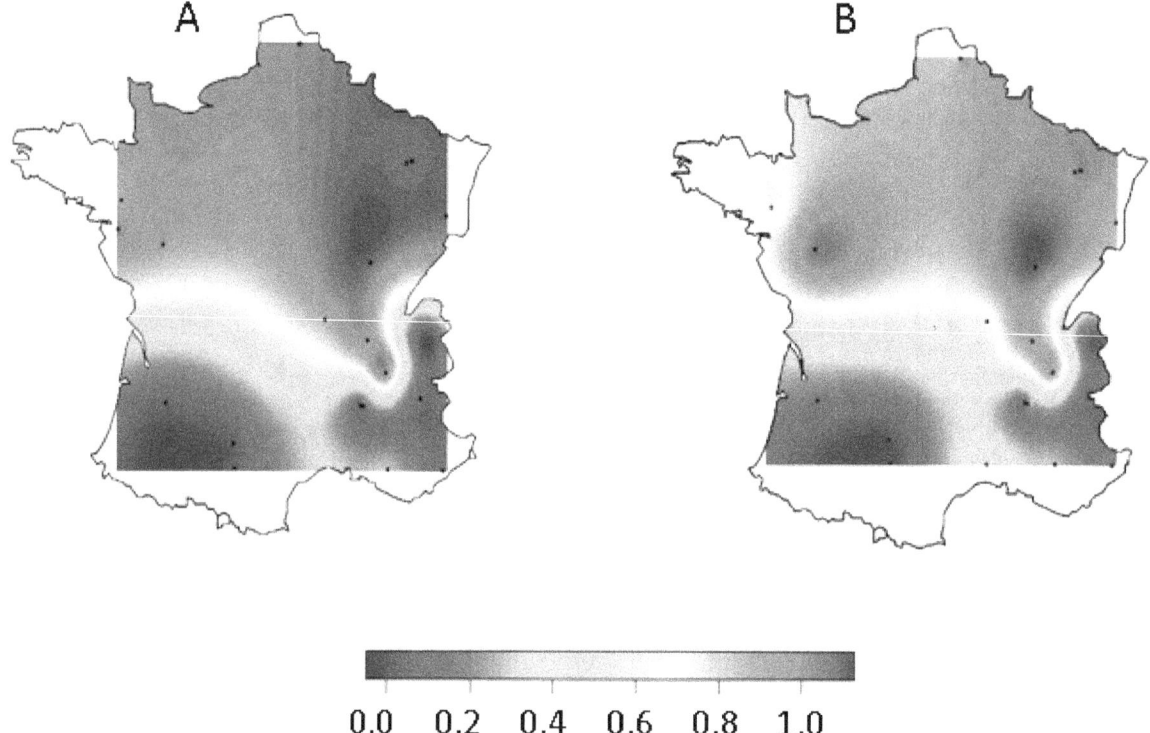

Figure 5—Spatial interpolations for the frequency of *Mlp* strains. A: belonging to the "cultivated" genetic group (i.e., "group 1" in Xhaard *et al.* 2011), and B: possessing virulence 7.

Acknowledgments

The research on genetic variation for rust resistance in the *Populus* host species received funding from the European Community's Seventh Framework Program (FP7/ 2007-2013) under the grant agreement n 211868 (Noveltree Project), from INRA under the ECOGER Program (AIP 00295-298, INTERPOPGER Project) and from the French Ministry of Agriculture under grant agreements GIS n E05/08 and E05/09. The research on population genetics of *Mlp* was supported by INRA under the ECOGER Program (AIP 00295-298, INTERPOPGER Project), the Agence Nationale de la Recherche (ANR 07/BDIV-003, EMERFUNDIS Project), and INRA (projet innovant EFPA). S.D. was supported by junior scientist grants from INRA and Région Lorraine. Physical mapping of the resistance factors was supported by INRA and the French Bureau des Ressources Génétiques (BRG). C.X. and A.B. were supported by PhD fellowships from the French Ministry of Education and Research (MESR). B.P. and C.G were supported by joint PhD fellowships from INRA and Région Lorraine. We would like to thank Axelle Andrieux, Béranger Bertin, Christine Géhin, I. Le Clainche, and the INRA Orléans Experimental Unit GBFOR for their technical help.

Literature Cited

Barres, B.; Halkett, F.; Dutech, C.; Andrieux, A.; Pinon, J.; Frey, P. 2008. Genetic structure of the poplar rust fungus *Melampsora larici-populina*: evidence for isolation by distance in Europe and recent founder effects overseas. Infection Genetics and Evolution. 8(5): 577–587.

Bresson, A.; Jorge, V.; Dowkiw, A.; Guerin, V.; Bourgait, I.; Tuskan, G.A.; Schmutz, J.; Chalhoub, B.; Bastien, C.; Rampant, P.F. 2011. Qualitative and quantitative resistances to leaf rust finely mapped within two nucleotide-binding site leucine-rich repeat (NBS-LRR)-rich genomic regions of chromosome 19 in poplar. New Phytologist. 192(1): 151–163.

Cervera, M.T.; Gusmao, J.; Steenackers, M.; Peleman, J.; Storme, V.; Vanden Broeck, A.; Van Montagu, M.; Boerjan, W. 1996. Identification of AFLP molecular markers for resistance against *Melampsora larici-populina* in *Populus*. Theoretical and Applied Genetics. 93: 733–737.

Cervera, M.T.; Storme, V.; Ivens, B.; Gusmão, J.; Liu, B.H.; Hostyn, V.; Van Slycken, J.; Van Montagu, M.; Boerjan, W. 2001. Dense genetic linkage maps of three populus species (*Populus deltoides*, *P. nigra* and *P. trichocarpa*) based on AFLP and microsatellite markers. Genetics. 158: 787–809.

Dowkiw, A.; Bastien, C. 2004. Characterization of two major genetic factors controlling quantitative resistance to *Melampsora larici-populina* leaf rust in hybrid poplars: strain specificity, field expression, combined effects, and relationship with a defeated qualitative resistance gene. Phytopathology. 94(12): 1358–1367.

Dowkiw, A.; Bastien, C. 2007. Presence of defeated qualitative resistance genes frequently has major impact on quantitative resistance to *Melampsora larici-populina* leaf rust in *P. xinteramericana* hybrid poplars. Tree Genetics and Genomes. 3(3): 261–274.

Dowkiw, A.; Husson, C.; Frey, P.; Pinon, J.; Bastien, C. 2003. Partial resistance to *Melampsora larici-populina* leaf rust in hybrid poplars: genetic variability in inoculated excised leaf disk bioassay and relationship with complete resistance. Phytopathology. 93(4): 421–427.

Dowkiw, A.; Voisin, E.; Bastien, C. 2010. Potential of Eurasian poplar rust to overcome a major quantitative resistance factor. Plant Pathology. 59: 523–534.

Duplessis, S.; Cuomo, C.A.; Lin, Y.C.; Aerts, A.; Tisserant, E.; Veneault-Fourrey, C.; Joly, D.L.; Hacquard, S.; Amselem, J.; Cantarel, B.L.; Chiu, R.; Coutinho, P.M.; Feau, N.; Field, M.; Frey, P.; Gelhaye, E.; Goldberg, J.; Grabherr, M.G.; Kodira, C.D.; Kohler, A.; Kues, U.; Lindquist, E.A.; Lucas, S.M.; Mago, R.; Mauceli, E.; Morin, E.; Murat, C.; Pangilinan, J.L.; Park, R.; Pearson, M.; Quesneville, H.; Rouhier, N.; Sakthikumar, S.; Salamov, A.A.; Schmutz, J.; Selles, B.; Shapiro, H.; Tanguay, P.; Tuskan, G.A.; Henrissat, B.; Van de Peer, Y.; Rouze, P.; Ellis, J.G.; Dodds, P.N.; Schein, J.E.; Zhong, S.B.; Hamelin, R.C.; Grigoriev, I.V.; Szabo, L.J.; Martin, F. 2011a. Obligate biotrophy features unraveled by the genomic analysis of rust fungi. Proceedings of the National Academy of Sciences of the United States of America. 108(22): 9166–9171.

Duplessis, S.; Hacquard, S.; Delaruelle, C.; Tisserant, E.; Frey, P.; Martin, F.; Kohler, A. 2011b. *Melampsora larici-populina* transcript profiling during germination and timecourse infection of poplar leaves reveals dynamic expression patterns associated with virulence and biotrophy. Molecular plant-microbe interactions : MPMI. 24: 808–818.

Eenink, A.H. 1976. Genetics of host-parasite relationships and uniform and differential resistance. Netherlands Journal of Plant Pathology. 82: 133–145.

Hacquard, S.; Joly, D.L.; Lin, Y.C.; Tisserant, E.; Feau, N.; Delaruelle, C.; Legué, V.; Kohler, A.; Tanguay, P.; Petre, B.; Frey, P.; Van de Peer, Y.; Rouzé, P.; Martin, F.; Hamelin, R.C.; Duplessis, S. [In press]. A comprehensive analysis of genes encoding small secreted proteins identifies candidate effectors in *Melampsora larici-populina* (poplar leaf rust). Molecular Plant-Microbe Interactions.

Jorge, V.; Dowkiw, A.; Faivre-Rampant, P.; Bastien, C. 2005. Genetic architecture of qualitative and quantitative *Melampsora larici-populina* leaf rust resistance in hybrid poplar: genetic mapping and QTL detection. New Phytologist. 167(1): 113–127.

Kohler, A.; Rinaldi, C.; Duplessis, S.; Baucher, M.; Geelen, D.; Duchaussoy, F.; Meyers, B.C.; Boerjan, W.; Martin, F. 2008. Genome-wide identification of NBS resistance genes in *Populus trichocarpa*. Plant Molecular Biology. 66: 619–636.

Lefèvre, F.; Goué-Mourier, M.C.; Faivre-Rampant, P.; Villar, M. 1998. A single gene cluster controls incompatibility and partial resistance to various *Melampsora larici-populina* races in hybrid poplars. Phytopathology. 88(2): 156–163.

Lefèvre, F.; Pichot, C.; Pinon, J. 1994. Intra- and interspecific inheritance of some components of the resistance to leaf rust (*Melampsora larici-populina* Kleb.) in poplars. Theoretical and Applied Genetics. 88: 501–507.

Lescot, M.; Rombauts, S.; Zhang, J.; Aubourg, S.; Mathe, C.; Jansson, S.; Rouze, P.; Boerjan, W. 2004. Annotation of a 95-kb *Populus deltoides* genomic sequence reveals a disease resistance gene cluster and novel class I and class II transposable elements. Theoretical and Applied Genetics. 109(1): 10–22.

McDonald, B.A.; Linde, C. 2002. Pathogen population genetics, evolutionary potential, and durable resistance. Annual Review of Phytopathology. 40: 349–379.

Pichot, C.; Teissier du Cros, E. 1993. Susceptibility of *P.deltoides* Bartr. to *Melampsora larici-populina* and *M.allii-populina*. Silvae Genetica. 42: 4–5.

Pinon, J. 1992. Variability in the genus *Populus* in sensitivity to *Melampsora* rusts. Silvae Genetica. 41(1): 25–34.

Rinaldi, C.; Kohler, A.; Frey, P.; Duchaussoy, F.; Ningre, N.; Couloux, A.; Wincker, P.; Le Thiec, D.; Fluch, S.; Martin, F.; Duplessis, S. 2007. Transcript profiling of poplar leaves upon infection with compatible and incompatible strains of the foliar rust *Melampsora larici-populina*. Plant Physiology. 144: 347–366.

Stergiopoulos, I.; de Wit, P. 2009. Fungal effector proteins. Annual Review of Phytopathology. 47: 233–263.

Xhaard, C.; Fabre, B.; Andrieux, A.; Gladieux, P.; Barrès, B.; Frey, P.; Halkett, F. 2011. The genetic structure of the plant pathogenic fungus *Melampsora larici-populina* on its wild host is extensively impacted by host domestication. Molecular Ecology. 20: 2739–2755.

Developing Hazelnuts (*Corylus* spp.) With Durable Resistance to Eastern Filbert Blight Caused by *Anisogramma anomala*

Thomas J. Molnar,[1] John Capik,[1] Clayton W. Leadbetter,[1] Ning Zhang,[1] Guohong Cai,[1] and Bradley I. Hillman[1]

Abstract

Eastern filbert blight (EFB) is a devastating fungal disease of European hazelnut, *Corylus avellana* L., and is considered to be the primary reason hazelnuts have not been developed as a commercial crop in the eastern United States. The pathogen, *Anisogramma anomala*, is native to a wide area east of the Rocky Mountains, where it is harbored by the wild hazelnut *C. americana* Marshall. While *C. americana* is tolerant of the disease, EFB causes stem cankers, dieback, and death of *C. avellana*, the hazelnut of commerce. The absence of EFB, along with a mild climate, allowed for the development of a commercial hazelnut industry in the Pacific Northwest (PNW), which thrived for nearly a century. However, despite quarantine efforts, EFB was discovered in Washington in the late 1960s and has spread throughout the Willamette Valley of Oregon, where 99 percent of the United States crop is produced, causing significant economic losses. To combat this disease, a major investment in research and breeding was made by Oregon State University (OSU), the U.S. Department of Agriculture, and the Oregon hazelnut industry. Over the last 30 years, these efforts have resulted in the development of a better understanding of *A. anomala* as well as effective disease management protocols and improved resistant cultivars, leading to a recent revival of the industry.

Building on advances made in Oregon, a hazelnut research and genetic improvement program was initiated at Rutgers University in New Jersey in 1996. Realizing the major limiting factor to production of commercial-quality hazelnuts in this region was EFB, the initial focus was to evaluate known sources of resistance to the disease in both *C. avellana* and other *Corylus* species, along with investigating pathogenic variation of the fungus, which was unknown at the time. In support of this work, close collaboration was developed with the OSU hazelnut program to evaluate their plant material when exposed to *A. anomala* isolates originating from across its native range; it is believed a limited diversity of the fungus is present in the PNW due to its occurrence likely having arisen from a single point introduction. In addition, wide germplasm collections were made in Europe to search for novel sources of resistance and to identify plants expressing other traits important in the eastern United States, such as cold hardiness and nuts that fall free from the husk at maturity. Concurrent with this work, controlled hybridizations were made annually to incorporate genes for EFB resistance from a diversity of backgrounds with the superior nut quality and yield expressed by OSU cultivars and breeding selections. Today, over 25,000 hazelnut seedlings are under evaluation in greenhouses and field nurseries at Rutgers.

An overview of the objectives and progress to date of the Rutgers breeding program were provided, including resistance screening protocols, findings on the pathogenic variation of *A. anomala*, the identification of novel sources of resistance, and the development of molecular biology tools to assess genetic diversity and population structure of the pathogen and to assist in its early detection for disease management and efficient breeding.

[1] Plant Biology and Pathology Department, Rutgers University, New Brunswick, NJ 08901.
Corresponding author: molnar@aesop.rutgers.edu.

Breeding for Growth Improvement and Resistance to Multiple Pests in *Thuja plicata*

John H. Russell[1] and Alvin D. Yanchuk[1]

Introduction

Western redcedar (*Thuja plicata* Donn ex D. Don), a member of the Cupressaceae, is an important commercial species in British Columbia (BC) and the Pacific Northwest (PNW), which is prized for its heartwood and its performance as a naturally durable outdoor building material. Although a genetic improvement program has been ongoing for only 15 years in BC, substantial progress has been made owing in part to its unique genetic and biological properties. These include early precious flowering and short generations (Russell and Ferguson 2008), the ability to self with minimal inbreeding depression (Russell et al. 2003), and ease of vegetative propagation and clonal deployment.

Initial population improvement focused on growth and adaptability as well as heartwood durability—an important wood quality trait for second growth western redcedar. The heartwood of this species contains secondary extractives implicated in rot resistance to a number of fungal species (Daniels and Russell 2007, Maclean and Gardner 1956). Tropolones are a group of extractives that are present in relatively small concentrations, but are highly fungitoxic to a suite of fungal rot species in living trees. These extractives are readily leached out of wood in service, but lignans, another group of secondary compounds (e.g., plicatic acid) are not. Lignans are mildly fungitoxic as compared to the tropolones, but are in greater concentrations in the heartwood (Morris and Sterling 2010). Individual tropolone and lignin compounds have moderate to high heritibilities (h^2_{ns} = 0.25 to 0.58) and additive coefficients of variability (CV_{add} >68 percent) (Russell and Daniels 2010).

In addition to fungal rots, black-tailed deer (*Odocoileus hemionus columbianus*) and cedar leaf blight (*Didymascella thujina*) have increasingly caused western redcedar plantation failures and reduced growth, and resulted in longer times to reach free to grow status. Black-tailed deer have been shown to avoid browsing trees that are high in volatile foliage monoterpenes (Kimball et al. 2012, Vourc'h et al. 2002). Similar to heartwood secondary extractives, foliage monoterpenes have moderate to high heritibilities (h^2_{ns} = 0.48 to 0.60) and additive coefficients of variability (CV_{add} 24 to 66 percent) (Russell, unpublished data)

Cedar leaf blight (CLB) occurs throughout western redcedar's range, but is especially virulent in humid, warm environments typical of the highly productive maritime ecosystems for western redcedar (Kope and Trotter 1998). There is significant genetic variation in resistance to CLB across moderately to heavily infected sites (h^2_{ns}=0.18; CV_{add}=14 percent) (Russell et al, 2007) and this variation is strongly correlated to population-origin climate with parents from wetter, milder sites having greater resistance.

As climates change and pests, known and unknown, become more abundant, breeding strategies need to adapt to better accommodate shifts in environmental stresses. Developing breeding populations that are resilient to multiple pests, as well as maintaining adaptability and growth, is imperative to ensure current and future forest health.

[1] Research Scientists, Forest Genetics, British Columbia Forest Service, Canada.
Corresponding author: John.Russell@gov.bc.ca.

Initial Population Improvement

Western redcedar has been under domestication since the late 1990s. Two main populations were used for initial selections and breeding: 1) 1,000 wildstand parent trees selected from throughout the species coastal range from northern California to northern BC, and grafted into clonebanks at Cowichan Lake Research Station (CLRS), and 2) BC range-wide provenance trials with open-pollinated family structure. The four main traits described above had the following improvement to date:

1) Growth and CLB resistance. The above wildstand parent trees were polycrossed with a common 20 parent mix, and progeny established in 45 field tests across seven annual series throughout BC between 2000 and 2008. Top breeding value parents for predicted volume production at 60 years varied from 18 to 35 percent, over wildstand seedlots based on 7 to 10 year heights. On individual sites highly infected with CLB, an increase in the disease impacted height and diameter growth significantly with genetic correlations from -0.58 to -0.88 at age 10 years (fig. 1); however, type B genetic correlations between CLB and height on sites with no CLB are not significantly different from zero. Backward selections that are both CLB resistant and high volume producers have been established in a breeding orchard and are currently being mated using partial diallels with assortative mating. Approximately 350 full-sib families have been completed to date with an anticipated 700 families in total when completed.

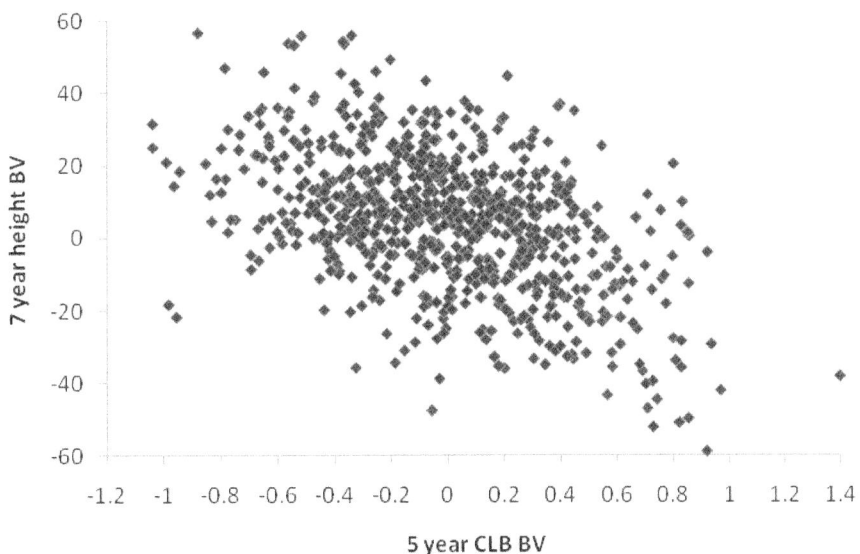

Figure 1—Relationship between western redcedar parental breeding values (BV) for cedar leaf blight (CLB) and height at a British Columbia maritime low elevation test site. Positive CLB BVs indicate susceptibility.

2) Heartwood rot-resistant population. Approximately 350 of the wildstand parent trees were old enough (20 years) to estimate heartwood extractives. Inner and outer heartwood from these trees have been profiled for tropolones (implicated in resistance of living heartwood) and lignans (responsible for durability of wood in service) using multiple ramets from clonebanks and seed orchard trees. Sixty backward selections have been made based on total thujaplicins and plicatic acid. These backward selections are currently in a breeding orchard for advanced generation breeding.

3) Deer browse-resistant population. All 1,000 wildstand parent trees were profiled for individual monoterpene compounds using foliage from multiple ramets in clone banks and seed orchards. In addition, foliar monoterpenes were estimated from 2,200 open-pollinated progeny from the range-wide provenance trial mentioned above, at age 6 years. Approximately 120 clonal and forward selections were made from both populations based on deer browse intensity and total monoterpenes. These parents were bred using partial diallels with assortative mating including selfs. Approximately 400 families were sown and forward selections made based on total foliage monoterpenes from one-year-old seedlings in the greenhouse (target age for deer browse resistance). First generation selections averaged around 35,000 ppm total monoterpenes and second generation selections averaged over 75,000 ppm. These forward selections are established in a breeding orchard and are currently available for 3rd generation breeding.

Advanced Population Improvement

Our objective for western redcedar is to develop a durable advanced generation breeding population with potential cross resistance. Developing breeding populations that are resilient to multiple pests may not only give protection against the current target pests, but potentially against future unknown ones. Selections for both increased volume production and CLB resistance are readily achieved for deployment on sites that have CLB, which is currently the majority of productive western redcedar forests. Genetic correlations between secondary extractives in the foliage and growth rate (fig. 2), and secondary extractives in heartwood and foliage (fig. 3), although not strong, are positively low to moderate. This is a simplistic measure and assessment of complex chemical pathways, but it does give us a potential indication that there is minimal competition in chemical resources between foliage and heartwood extractives. We have no information on CLB resistance mechanisms at this time, but as in many leaf disease studies, foliar monoterpenes have played a significant role (e.g., Wallis et al. 2011).

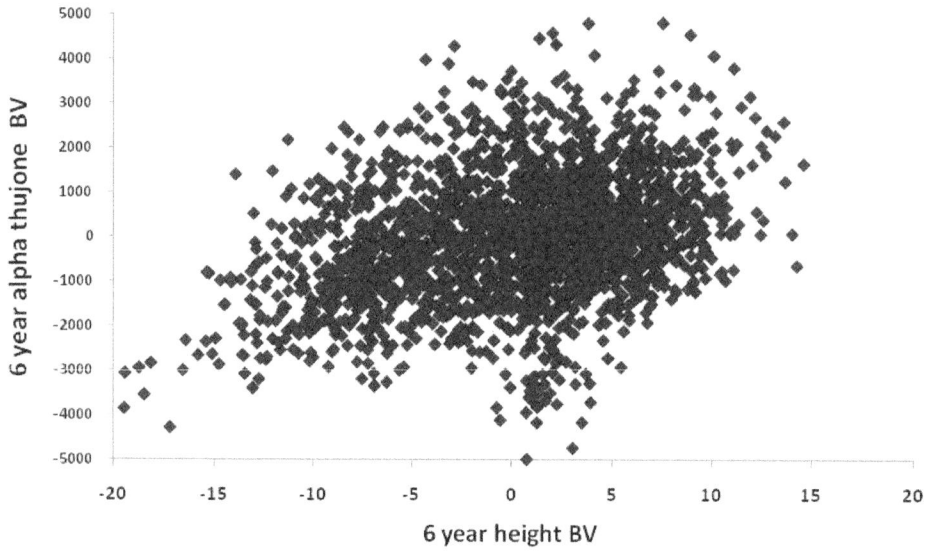

Figure 2—Relationship between western redcedar breeding values (BV) for foliage monoterpene and growth in a BC coastal open-pollinated progeny trial.

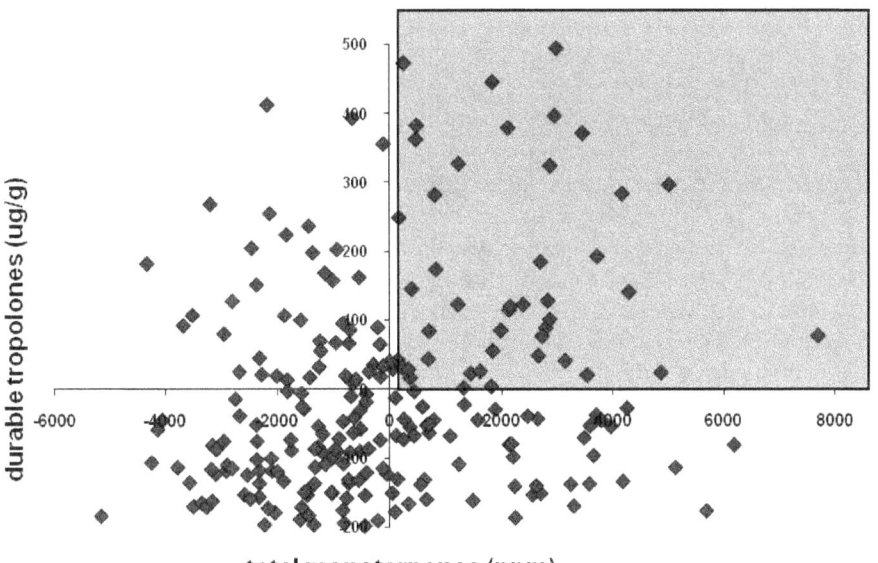

total monoterpenes (ppm)

Figure 3—Relationship between western redcedar clonal values for foliar monoterpenes and heartwood tropolones in a 20-year-old clonal trial (blue box = independent culling).

Advanced generation breeding strategy will involve breeding groups by traits and matings performed within and between groups using partial diallels (fig. 4) with assortative mating within groups.

	Growth			CLB			Foliage terpenes			Hdwd extractives		
Growth	X	X	X	X	X		X	X		X	X	
		X	X		X			X			X	
			X									
CLB				X	X	X	X	X		X	X	
					X	X		X			X	
						X						
Foliage terpeness							X	X	X	X	X	
								X	X		X	
									X			
Hdwd extractives										X	X	X
											X	X
												X

Figure 4—Western redcedar advanced generation breeding strategy for multiple pests and growth.

This new population will be tested in environments conducive to the respective stresses. Because of the partial confounding of population with selection objectives in the first generation of screening, we expect it would be beneficial to do further field testing in each of the growth/CLB and the deer resistance populations prior to make final selections for advanced generation breeding population.

For the growth/CLB selections, advanced generation full-sib matings from backward selections have already been done. Seed from these families will be grown in the nursery and tested for foliar monoterpenes at age one year. The top selections for total monoterpenes will then be cloned and tested for growth/CLB in short-term tests. For the deer resistance population, families from second generation breeding have already been tested for foliar monoterpenes and forward selections cloned for production hedges. These clones will be established in short-term tests in environments conducive to good growth and cedar leaf blight infection. Clones from both of these additional trials will be selected based on the respective target traits for the advanced generation durable breeding population.

The final population (Ne~100) will be composed of: 1) 50 third generation forward selections from the deer resistant population further clonally selected for growth and CLB resistance; 2) 50 first generation parental selections based on clonal values for total heartwood extractive content with independent culling for the other target traits; and 3) 50 second generation forward selections for volume further selected for deer resistance. Currently, mechanisms for CLB resistance are unknown, but being researched. It may be appropriate to make additional CLB selections based on future potential resistance mechanisms.

Literature Cited

Daniels, B.; Russell, J.H. 2007. Analysis of western redcedar (*Thuja plicata* Donn) heartwood components by HPLC as a possible screening tool for trees with enhanced natural durability. Journal of Chromatographic Science. 45(5): 281–285.

Kimball, B.A.; Russell, J.H.; Ott, P. 2012. Phytochemical variation within a single plant species influences foraging behavior of deer. Oikos. 121: 743–751.

Kope, H.H.; Trotter, D. 1998. The use of degree days to establish biological events for *Didymascella thujina*, a foliar fungal leaf blight of *Thuja plicata* seedlings. Proceedings of the 7th International Congress of Plant Pathology. Oxford, UK: Elsevier.

Maclean, H; Gardner, J.A.F. 1956. Distribution of fungicidal extractives (thujaplicin and water-soluble phenols) in western red cedar heartwood. Forest Products Journal. 6(12): 510–516.

Morris, P.I; Stirling, R. 2011. Western redcedar extractives associated with durability in ground contact. Wood Science and Technology. DOI: 10.1007/s00226-011-0459-2.

Russell, J.H.; Burdon, R.B.; Yanchuk, A.D. 2003. Inbreeding depression and variance structures for height and adaptation in self- and outcross *Thuja plicata* families in varying environments. Forest Genetics. 10(3): 171-184.

Russell, J.H.; Daniels, B. 2010. Variation in western redcedar heartwood extractives. In: Harrington, C., (ed.). A tale of two cedars – international symposium on western redcedar and yellow-cedar. Gen. Tech. Rep. PNW-GTR-828. Portland, OR: U.S. Department of Agriculture, Forest Service, Pacific Northwest Research Station: 83–86.

Russell, J.H.; Ferguson, C.F. 2008. Preliminary results from five generations of a western redcedar (*Thuja* plicata) selection study with self mating. Tree Genetics and Genomes. 4(3): 509–518.

Russell, J.H.; Kopes, H.; Ades, P.; Collinson, H. 2007. Genetic variation in *Didymascella thujina* resistance of *Thuja plicata*. Canadian Journal of Forest Research. 37(10): 1978–1986.

Vourc'h, G.; Russell, J.H.; Martin, J.L. 2002. Linking deer browsing and terpene production among genetic identities in *Chamaecyparis nootkatensis* and *Thuja plicata* (Cupressaceae). Journal of Heredity. 93(5): 370–376.

Wallis, C.M.; Huber, D.P.W.; Lewis. K.D. 2011. Ecosystem, location and climate effects on foliar secondary metabolites of lodgepole populations from central British Columbia. Journal of Chemical Ecology. 37: 607–621.

The New Zealand Douglas-fir Breeding Program: Proposed Adjustments for a Changing Climate

Heidi Dungey,[1] Charlie Low,[1] Mark Miller,[1] Kane Fleet,[1] and Alvin D. Yanchuk[1]

Abstract

Genetic improvement of Douglas-fir (*Pseudotsuga menziesii* (Mirb.) Franco) in New Zealand was initiated in 1955 with large provenance trials established in the late 1950s. These trials showed that material of Oregon and Californian origin was growing faster than other provenances. Additional collections were made to further evaluate provenance performance from these two areas, and in 1996 additional trials were established at four low-altitude sites across New Zealand.

Genotype ×environment (GxE) interaction between these sites was found to be important for diameter at breast height (DBH), less important for stem straightness and malformation, and not important for outerwood acoustic velocity (a surrogate for wood stiffness). Heritabilities were low to moderate for all growth traits, and very low for malformation. Heritability for Swiss needle cast caused by *Phaeocryptopus gaeumannii*, measured as needle retention, was moderate at one site (0.37) with a high infection rate, and was likely a major factor creating GxE interactions for growth among sites. The heritability of wood acoustic velocity was moderate to high at individual sites (0.26 to 0.74) and across sites (0.49). Individual-trait selection revealed the potential for good genetic gains to be made when selecting the top 20 families for diameter growth (an average of 10.7 percent), straightness (an average of 11.5 percent), and acoustic velocity (an average of 7.0 percent).

When we examined how gains were distributed when selecting for needle retention and/or DBH, we found that selecting for needle cast at the affected site did not compromise DBH gains at that site. Selecting for genotypes with low needle cast at the affected site did, however, effect gains for DBH estimated across all sites and would not be an ideal scenario. In order to maximize gains across the current Douglas-fir growing estate, a division of growing sites between those affected by needle cast and those not affected would seem sensible, particularly given recent work into climate change scenarios indicating that Swiss needle cast will become more important in the South Island and even more destructive in the North Island of New Zealand. We therefore suggest addressing differences in site through the development of separate deployment populations.

[1] Scion, Te Papa Tipu Innovation Park, 49 Sala Street, Private Bag 3020, Rotorua, 3046, New Zealand.
Corresponding author: Heidi.Dungey@scionresearch.com.

White Pine Blister Rust Resistance Research in Minnesota and Wisconsin

Andrew David,[1] Paul Berrang,[2] and Carrie Pike[3]

Abstract

The exotic fungus *Cronartium ribicola* causes the disease white pine blister rust on five-needled pines throughout North America. Although the effects of this disease are perhaps better known on pines in the western portion of the continent, the disease has also impacted regeneration and growth of eastern white pine (*Pinus strobus* L.), especially in the upper Great Lakes region of Minnesota, Wisconsin, Michigan, and Ontario. This paper summarizes some of the early white pine blister rust research in Minnesota and Wisconsin, particularly the Moose Fence site near Tofte, Minnesota, the consistently high resistance level of genotype P327, and how the Minnesota Tree Improvement Cooperative (MTIC) housed at the University of Minnesota and the USDA Forest Service Oconto River Seed Orchard (ORSO) are working together to advance the state of blister rust resistance in eastern white pine.

Introduction

At the turn of the 20th century, the exotic fungus *Cronartium ribicola* was brought to North America on seedling stock imported from Europe. Although there were multiple introductions across the continent, the results were similar; five-needled pines could become infected and die wherever the fungus entered an ecosystem that contained these pines and *Ribes* species that could act as an alternate host (Van Arsdel and Geils 2011). Forest pathologists came to recognize the life cycle of *Cronartium ribicola* or white pine blister rust in its new environment and combating the disease took on a two-pronged approach. One option was to physically remove individual *Ribes* plants. This method was cumbersome as it required a large, committed workforce to survey vast acreages on a repeated basis. The second option was to search for genetic resistance to the new disease in the native population.

One of the first plant pathologists to search for and find eastern white pine trees with putative resistance to white pine blister rust was A.J. Riker at the University of Wisconsin. By the mid-1930s, Riker recognized that, while most young white pines were susceptible to the new disease, there were rare individuals (roughly 1 in 400) that remained healthy. In the late 1930s, he identified 163 young white pine trees in Wisconsin that exhibited no external signs of infection despite coexisting with *Ribes* and the blister rust fungus for at least 15 to 20 years (Riker and Kouba 1940). In the early 1940s, Riker and his team artificially inoculated the progeny of these trees in a nursery setting and found differences between the offspring of selected and unselected trees (Riker et al. 1943). Although not complete resistance, this research was among the earliest evidence of natural occurring genetic resistance in eastern white pine and it offered hope that a genetic basis for full resistance was possible. These results also spawned the development of an active rust research group in the Lake States that included Cliff and Isabel Ahlgren at the Quetico-Superior Wilderness Research Foundation, Bob Patton at the University of Wisconsin, and Gene Van Arsdel also of the University of Wisconsin and U.S. Department of Agriculture, Forest Service (USDA FS), as well as many more

[1] Department of Forest Resources, University of Minnesota, North Central Research and Outreach Center, 1861 Highway 169 East, Grand Rapids, MN 55744.
[2] USDA Forest Service, 626 E. Wisconsin Avenue, Milwaukee, WI 53202.
[3] Department of Forest Resources, University of Minnesota, Cloquet Forestry Center, 175 University Avenue, Cloquet, MN 55720.
Corresponding author: adavid@umn.edu.

applied state and federal employees. The methodology established by Riker also set a precedent for the rust screening efforts by the USDA FS in Wisconsin and in the western states.

However, the efforts of these researchers notwithstanding, a high level of heritable resistance remained elusive in eastern white pine. Unlike the western five-needled pines where outdoor nursery screening techniques identified a stably inherited source of major gene resistance (MGR), time and time again eastern white pine researchers found increased levels of resistance, but not complete resistance. Due to the apparent lack of MGR in eastern white pine, researchers began to see the need for a large-scale, long-term experiment that would expose the most promising genotypes to a high level of fungal inoculum. Such an experiment, if allowed to continue long enough, would create a population of eastern white pine with a higher than average level of genetic resistance.

Moose Fence Planting Near Tofte, Minnesota

In the 1960s, Cliff and Isabelle Ahlgren proposed a large-scale, long-term experiment and began collecting cones from putative rust resistant white pine along the north shore of Lake Superior and in the Boundary Waters Canoe Area Wilderness. By the late 1960s, the Quetico-Superior Wilderness Research Foundation, the USDA FS, and the University of Minnesota had entered into an agreement to establish an eastern white pine blister rust disease garden trial in a high blister rust risk area. The goals of the project were to provide a source of eastern white pine with higher than average rust resistance that could be used as a source of seed for reforestation purposes, and could serve as a source of advanced generation breeding material. This idea came to fruition when a total of 43,176 open pollinated 3-year-old eastern white pine seedlings from 873 families were planted in two stages (1972 and 1974) at a site near Tofte, Minnesota. The 873 mother trees came from 22 sites in two general areas in northern Minnesota: the Boundary Waters Canoe Area Wilderness and the north shore of Lake Superior, with a 23rd site in northern Wisconsin (Merrill et al. 1984). The 8.9 ha "Moose Fence" site was fenced to keep out moose (*Alces alces*) (hence the name) and interplanted with various *Ribes* species, the obligate alternate host, to increase the spore load and the chance for disease incidence.

In the fall of 1984, after these seedlings had spent 11 or 13 years in the field (14 or 16 years from seed), each tree in the 10 tree row plots was scored for survival and evidence of previous infection by white pine blister rust. The results of this initial screening indicated that overall survival ranged from 38 percent (1972 planting) to 41 percent (1974 planting). The frequency of seedlings with no evidence of previous infection was very low at 1.0 percent and 0.5 percent (1972 and 1974 respectively). Furthermore, in the 1972 cohort, the two best families had 14 percent non-infected seedlings while the two best families in the 1974 cohort had a 6 percent non-infected rate. This information suggested two things: the frequency of uninfected individuals occurred at a very low frequency in the natural population, and the data do not support the existence of a major gene for resistance (MGR) among the maternal parents (Merrill et al. 1984).

Subsequent to the 1984 assessment, surviving trees were evaluated for vigor and rust and 888 non-infected trees with high vigor were selected and permanently tagged with aluminum tags on nylon rope tied at the base of a lower branch. These 888 non-infected trees represented 2.1 percent of the total number of seedlings planted and were two to four times higher than the estimate of non-infected seedlings from the 1984 assessment. This difference is likely the result of stringent initial scoring in 1984 which used the terminology, "no evidence of previous infection" before a seedling was considered non-infected. This would have resulted in seedlings with marks on stems or branches (potential hail or insect damage) being left out of the non-infected category. Additionally, when the trees were tagged, their larger size relative to the 1984 scoring undoubtedly made visualization of the entire bole and all stems more difficult, potentially resulting in missed infections.

After the 1993 growing season, at approximately 20 years of age, the tagged trees at the Moose Fence site were scored for survival, vigor, and evidence of rust. Rust incidence was scored on a 1 to 4 scale, with 4 representing a tree free of rust, 3 a tree with inactive canker(s), 2 a tree with active canker(s), and 1 indicating a tree dead from rust. Vigor was scored on a 1 to 4 scale with 4 being the most vigorous and 1 representing dead. Only 802 of the 888 tagged trees could be found because, at roughly 20 years of age, a combination of factors were rendering the monumentation in the planting difficult to use. The serpentine layout of the 10 tree family plots, small size of the aluminum stakes, considerable mortality, and non-linear rows due to 1.5 m by 1.5 m spacing on shallow, rocky soils, all contributed to making navigation in the plantation extremely difficult. Of the 86 missing trees, 67 were never found, while 19 trees were found in future assessments. These 67 lost trees represent trees that either died or lost their tags due to breakage or self-pruning of their lower branches where the aluminum tags were attached. Results of this 1993 scoring indicated that 747 (93.1 percent) of the 802 assessed trees were uninfected while 4.6 percent had inactive cankers and 2.2 percent had active cankers. There were no dead trees among the 802 assessed (table 1), although there may have been dead trees among the 67 that could not be found.

Table 1—Number of select eastern white pine trees by rust score category (4 = uninfected, 3 = inactive canker(s), 2 = active canker(s), 1 = dead) and average rust score at the 20, 30, and 37 year assessments[a]

| Year | Age | Rust Score | | | | Not found | Rust score | |
		4	3	2	1		Average	N =
<1993	11-19 years	888						888
1993	20 years	747	37	18	0	86	3.9	802
2003	30 years	516	191	95	0	0	3.5	802
2010	37 years	442	55	255	47	3	3.1	802
2003	30 years	552	194	97	0	0	3.5	843
2010	37 years	465	59	266	48	5	3.1	843

[a] 888 trees were initially selected and tagged sometime between 1984 and 1993 of which only 802 could be found in 1993. The 843 trees in 2003 and 2010 represent the 802 tagged trees plus the inclusion of 32 uninfected trees likely among the 86 lost trees in 1993 and 9 trees found from the original 888.

Prior to the 30 year assessment in 2003, an additional 32 non-infected trees (rust score = 4) were tagged permanently with numbers from 900 to 931. These trees were most likely from the group of 67 trees that had lost their original tags prior to the 1993 assessment. The remaining 35 trees from the group of 67 were unaccounted for and were either infected and not tagged or died of unknown causes, most likely blister rust. The 2003 assessment recorded rust scores on the same 1 to 4 scale for 843 trees (table 1). The percentage of uninfected trees dropped approximately one-third between age 20 and age 30. Despite this drop in the average health of the population, it should be noted that the majority dropped just one classification, while approximately 70 trees dropped two classifications. None of the tagged individuals died between the 20 and 30 year assessments.

Despite the lack of mortality among tagged trees, by age 30 it was obvious that blister rust was actively working in the planting. Large, standing dead trees could be seen throughout the plantation while other trees had fantastically contorted trunks due to multiple cankers. The frequency of tagged trees in the plantation appeared to be increasing over time as non-tagged trees died at a faster rate. Surprisingly, some trees that appeared to be growing vigorously were infected, but had not been tagged. Presumably these trees were infected before the tags were put on the original 888 uninfected trees. Therefore, these vigorous but infected trees had existed with the disease longer than any of the selected tagged trees and, borrowing the parlance from western North American breeding programs, we began to think of these trees as potential "slow rusters".

In 2010, a complete census of the plantation was performed, placing the remaining live trees into one of three categories: 1) previously tagged, 2) not previously tagged, with cankers but appearing healthy, and 3) not previously tagged, with cankers and appearing unhealthy and/or likely to die within the next year. The census results indicated that there were a total of 1,274 trees alive after 37 years, a survival rate of 2.9 percent. The 1,274 surviving trees were categorized as follows: 794 were previously tagged, 346 had cankers but appeared otherwise healthy, and 134 were cankered, appeared unhealthy, and/or were likely to die within the next year (table 2).

Table 2—Thirty-seven year census results for the Moose Fence eastern white pine blister rust trial near Tofte, Minnesota

Category	Description	Number alive
1	Previously selected	794
2	Possible slow-rusting genotypes	346
3	Severely cankered or likely to die within 1 year	134
Total		1,274

After the 2010 census, all the category 1 trees and the best of the category 2 trees were evaluated for vigor (very good, good, fair, poor), rust score (1 to 4 scale as previous), the number and type of cankers (round or linear), presence or absence of callus at the canker edge, and the percentage of the stem alive at the most infected point. This process identified 114 trees (84 category 1 trees and 30 category 2 trees) that are considered potential slow rusters and will be followed over time. Of these 114 potential slow rusters, 52 were selected based on percent bole alive (> 80 percent), with preference given to linear vs. round cankers, two or fewer cankers, rust score = 3, and the subjective "this looks like a good slow ruster". All selections had callus formation around the canker edges. Scions from these 52 trees were collected and grafted in 2011 and were outplanted in spring 2012. These 52 trees represent 43 category 1 trees and 9 category 2 trees.

The trial at Tofte has provided some very valuable long-term research results. It is obvious from the rust score numbers in table 1 that a wave of mortality is working through the tagged trees. Because most of these trees are dying due to cankers that are located within 3.0 m of the ground (personal observation), we know that these trees were at least 3.0 m tall before they were infected. Since it is taking at least 10 to 20 years for them to die from blister rust, there is a period of time where the tree is still functional while the pathogen is a) moving through the branch towards the bole or b) latent in the branch and/or bole. As the remaining trees have few lower branches to become infected and the incidence of blister rust infection is partially ontologically controlled (Patton 1961), we expect that the rate of new infections will decrease in the future. The health of currently infected trees, whether the infection is latent or not, is expected to decrease over time. The census indicated that after 37 years, 2.9 percent of the trees were still alive, although that is expected to drop to 2.6 percent by the 40th year in the field as the category 3 trees succumb to the disease. In retrospect, this 2.6 percent survival rate is remarkable considering there is no evidence for MGR in the population, the trial was established in a high blister rust risk area, and *Ribes* spp. were interplanted among the seedlings.

By comparing survival rates between selected trees and the population as a whole it is clear that early selection for uninfected trees with high vigor during the second decade was successful in this population. The initial census of the trial (Merrill et al. 1984) indicated total survival was approximately 40 percent at 12 years. After 37 years, total survival was down to 2.9 percent with the selected trees representing 62.3 percent of the survivors. Furthermore, the fact that the selected trees had an 89.4 percent survival rate (794 of 888 trees) at age 37 and that 52.7 percent of the selected trees (468 of 888) were still considered uninfected roughly 20 years after selection, is additional evidence that early selection was effective in this population.

After close to 40 years of constant selection under real world conditions, it is clear that the Moose Fence planting has tremendous practical value. The remaining trees represent the largest genetically diverse source of potentially resistant eastern white pine anywhere in North America and most likely the world. As such, Moose Fence is a unique site that provides locally adapted seed and genotypes with increased genetic resistance to white pine blister rust that can be used for reforestation purposes and advanced generation breeding.

The Genotype P327

The Moose Fence planting at Tofte is not the only source of genetic material being used in Minnesota or Wisconsin. Dr. Patton at the University of Wisconsin oversaw a large white pine blister rust selection and screening program. He and his team scoured woods and plantings throughout Minnesota, Wisconsin, and Michigan for potential rust resistant trees and tested their scion and open pollinated progeny at several locations throughout Wisconsin. The most famous of these Patton selections is P327 which was identified in a planting of unknown origin outside of Duluth, Minnesota. Because P327 is consistently one of the last families to reach 25 percent, 50 percent, and 75 percent mortality levels in greenhouse screening trials, it is often used as a positive control.

Jurgens et al. (2003) used histological techniques to identify a potential mechanism of resistance among a portion of open pollinated P327 seedlings. Using various stains he was able to differentiate the fungal mycelium from mesophyll cells as the hyphae moved into and through the needle of infected white pine seedlings. Figure 1 compares infected needles from progeny of P327 and a susceptible control H109. What is clear from the figure is that mesophyll cells in P327 collapse just ahead of the fungal hyphae slowing down the spread of the fungus which requires live cell tissue to survive. Conversely, needles of the very susceptible H109 are packed with mycelium allowing the hyphae to progress through the needles to twigs and branches.

More recent research (Smith et al. 2006) has shed some light on stomatal status in P327. Environmental scanning electron microscopy (eSEM) images demonstrate that needles of P327 have occluded stomates (fig. 2). These occlusions were shown to be similar to the waxes that envelope the needles and are hypothesized to act as a physical barrier that prevents fungal hyphae from entering the needles. In theory, the more susceptible clones like H111 lack occluded stomates, allowing blister rust hyphae an opportunity to enter the needles following spore germination on the needle surface.

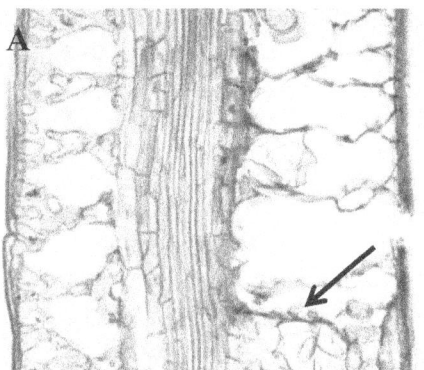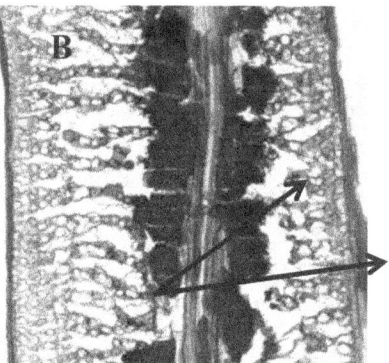

Figure 1—Needle sections stained with periodic acid-Schiff's reagent reveal (A) lysed mesophyll cells ahead of blister rust hyphae in an open pollinated seedling of P327, and (B) densely packed mycelium surrounding the vascular bundle in an open pollinated seedling of the more susceptible H109.

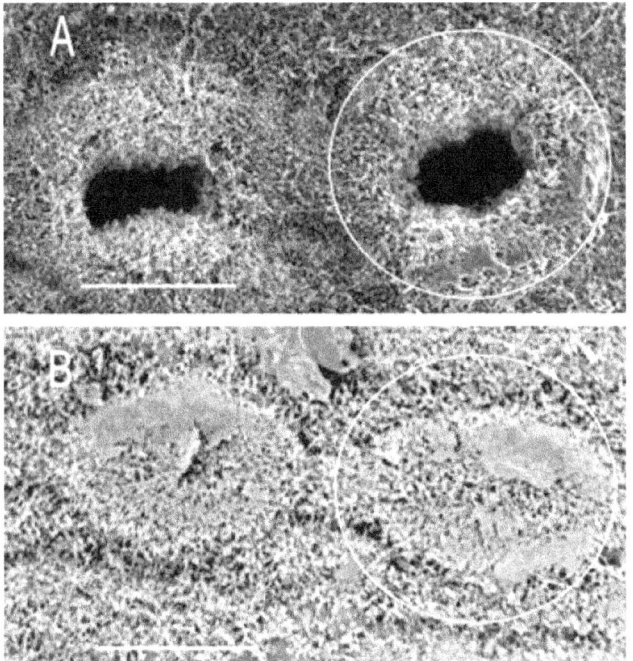

Figure 2—Environmental scanning electron microscopy image of secondary needles showing (A) open stomates in susceptible H111, and (B) wax occluded stomates in more resistant P327.

USDA Forest Service Oconto River Seed Orchard

The USDA FS's Oconto River Seed Orchard (ORSO) near Langlade, Wisconsin serves as the source of seed for white pine regeneration efforts in Region 9. The bulk of this seed comes from an interim seed orchard comprised of 30 Heimberger and five Patton selections. Future plans call for the establishment of at least one new clonal seed orchard of local origin where the increased resistance to white pine blister rust is well documented. At ORSO there is also a grafted clone bank (roughly 1,200 selections) from northern Minnesota, northern Wisconsin, and the upper peninsula of Michigan. Clonal material of non-infected and slow rusting Tofte genotypes has been kept separate to facilitate tracking known origins.

One of ORSO's mandates is to screen for blister rust resistant white pine. This is accomplished using an indoor system that was refined (starting in 2004) using suggestions from Paul Zambino (research pathologist; formerly at the USDA FS Rocky Mountain Forest Research Station). A typical example would use open pollinated seedlings with a mixture of primary and secondary needles from mother trees in the orchards or clone bank and expose them to blister rust spores at a spore load of approximately 10,000 spores/cm^2. The seedlings are sown in the greenhouse in February or March and inoculated in November of the first year. In May of the second year they are scored for percent of seedlings with foliar symptoms and the severity of symptoms before being placed outside. In mid-summer of the second year, the seedlings are scored for the percent of seedlings with stem cankers and their severity. Ideal families would have many seedlings with foliar symptoms, indicating exposure and initial infection, but a decided lack of stem symptoms indicating some level of resistance. The seedlings are followed for an additional 2 to 3 years while they are evaluated for evidence of resistance mechanisms, although at this time there is no formal, definitive end to the evaluation period. Initial work has shown that the 10,000 spores/cm^2 appears to provide sufficient inoculum to produce foliar symptoms across all families without killing all seedlings. The 10,000 spores/cm^2 level also demonstrates a definite dosage effect associated with susceptible and resistant families. In the most recent results ORSO has identified four to five additional genotypes out of 34 tested that show promise for elevated levels of blister rust resistance.

University of Minnesota's Tree Improvement Cooperative

The Minnesota Tree Improvement Cooperative (MTIC) is based on the industry-governmental organization-university model and is headquartered at the University's Cloquet Forestry Center. It is comprised of 14 full members and six supporting members who focus their efforts on five conifer species native to Minnesota, including white pine. The MTIC's white pine program has been active since the mid-1980s. Among the cooperators with full membership, there are five 1st generation clonal seed orchards totaling 3.4 ha. These seed orchards are comprised of genotypes selected by earlier researchers for increased blister rust resistance in nursery and early field trials. Sources include: USFS ORSO, University of Wisconsin, and the Quetico-Superior Wilderness Research Foundation. The MTIC has been collecting open pollinated cones from individuals in these seed orchards and at Tofte in anticipation of establishing a progeny trial in 2014.

The MTIC also manages two other long-term white pine plantings. One site, the Moose Fence trial mentioned earlier, is jointly managed with the USDA FS, Superior National Forest, Tofte Ranger District while the second planting is a white pine breeding arboretum located at the Cloquet Forestry Center in Cloquet, Minnesota. As of August 2011, the white pine breeding arboretum has three ramets each of 214 Tofte genotypes and 94 non-Tofte genotypes; primarily selections from Minnesota and Wisconsin. In the spring of 2012, grafts of the 52 potential slow rusting genotypes from Tofte were planted at Grimsbo Field, increasing the total to over 350 individual genotypes in the breeding program. Current plans are to breed these selections both for testing increased resistance using the ORSO method and to establish more traditional field based progeny tests.

In summary, MTIC and ORSO have programs that have benefited from previous white pine blister rust research. As a result of this early work, both organizations have been able to establish seed orchards and provide their stakeholders with eastern white pine seed for reforestation needs. Early selections such as P327, which consistently produces progeny that outlive other families in blister rust screening trials, have formed the bulk of this early research. However, recognition is growing that, to support white pine reforestation efforts across Minnesota and Wisconsin, there is a need for locally adapted germplasm of known origin and more genetic diversity than existed in the early selections. The value of the Moose Fence site at Tofte is that over the past 40 years there has been active selection for increased blister rust resistance in a population that is genetically diverse and adapted to growing conditions that are found in northern Minnesota and northern Wisconsin. As a result, both the MTIC and ORSO have been working cooperatively to critically evaluate individual trees within Moose Fence and determine the genetic value of both uninfected and slow rusting phenotypes.

Acknowledgments

The authors thank Jim Blanchard, Kathy Haiby, Egon Humenberger, Sam Krueger, Carrie Sweeney, Jim Warren, and Keith Webb for assistance in the field at Moose Fence; Jim Warren specifically for the GIS map of Moose Fence selections; and Bro Kinloch for thoughtful comments in the field on identifying slow rusting phenotypes. Recognition and thanks also to Minnesota Tree Improvement Cooperative, University of Minnesota Agricultural Experiment Station, University of Minnesota Department of Forestry, USDA Forest Service Gene Conservation Program, USDA Forest Service Region 9, and the Hubachek Wilderness Research Foundation (formerly the Quetico-Superior Wilderness Research Foundation) for previous and continued support of research to decrease the impact of white pine blister rust on eastern white pine. This manuscript was improved through the thoughtful comments of Thomas Saielli and Joseph Zeleznik.

Literature Cited

Merrill, R.E.; Mohn, C.A.; Ahlgren, C.E. 1984. Survival and white pine blister rust infection in a Minnesota white pine screening study. Misc. Journal Series Article No. 2049. St. Paul, MN: Univ. Minn. Ag. Exp. Station. 13 p.

Patton, R.F. 1961. The effect of age upon susceptibility of eastern white pine to infection by *Cronartium ribicola*. Phytopathology. 51: 429–434.

Jurgens, J.A.; Blanchette, R.A.; Zambino, P.J.; David, A.J. 2003. Histology of white pine blister rust in needles of resistant and susceptible eastern white pine. Plant Disease. 87(9): 1026–1030.

Riker, A.J.; Kouba, T.F. 1940. White pine selected in blister rust areas. Phytopathology. 30(1): 20.

Riker, A.J.; Kouba, T.F.; Brener, W.H.; Byam, L.E. 1943. White pine selections tested for resistance to blister rust. Journal of Forestry. 41(10): 753–760.

Smith, J.A.; Blanchette, R.A.; Burnes, T.A.; Gillman, J.H.; David, A.J. 2006. Epicuticular wax and white pine blister rust resistance in resistant and susceptible selections of eastern white pine (*Pinus strobus*). Phytopathology. 96(2): 171–177.

Van Arsdel, E.P.; Geils, B.W. 2011. Blister rust in North America: what we have not learned in the past 100 years. In: Fairweather, M., comp. Proceedings of the 58th Annual Western International Forest Disease Work Conference. Flagstaff, AZ: U.S. Department of Agriculture, Forest Service, Forest Health Protection.

Phenotypic Evidence Suggests a Possible Major-Gene Element to Weevil Resistance in Sitka Spruce

John N. King,[1,] René I. Alfaro,[2] Peter Ott,[1] and Lara vanAkker[2]

Abstract

The weevil resistance breeding program against the white pine weevil, *Pissodes strobi* Peck (Coleoptera: Curculionidae), particularly for Sitka spruce (*Picea sitchensis* (Bong.) Carr), is arguably one of the most successful pest resistance breeding programs for plantation forest species, and it has done a lot to rehabilitate this important western conifer. Nearly all planting stock currently comes from this breeding program and so far the resistance seems effective, durable, and stable. We have used this program to also study causes behind this resistance, including: various hindrance mechanisms including induced and constitutive resin cells, sclereid or stone cells, and terpene defenses. All of them appear factors in resistance, but none singly is strongly predictive to resistance - the strongest are sclereid cells. All of these factors are in their nature complex, multifaceted, and appear to offer some partial solution that is likely controlled by complex multigenic systems. We do note, however, that we have very strongly expressed and complete resistance in some individuals. This and some preliminary data investigation indicates that there may also be a major gene element in our observed resistance. Such elements are well described against rusts and other pathogens in forestry, but are also well described for insects and nematodes in crop breeding. Particularly interesting is the Hessian fly in wheat which has a similar life strategy to the weevil. We describe here the elements that suggest this conjecture and how we might go about proving this. Understanding the genetic elements behind this observed resistance has implications for the overall strength and durability to resistance against the white pine weevil.

Keywords: *Pissodes strobi*, white pine weevil, Sitka spruce, resistance breeding program

Introduction and Background

White pine weevil (*Pissodes strobi* Peck) is one of the most devastating pests of young spruce (*Picea* spp.) and pines (*Pinus* spp.) in North America. The weevil is a native insect that occurs across Canada and the northern United States. In eastern North America, it is a major pest of eastern white pine (*Pinus strobus* L.) and introduced Norway spruce (*Picea abies* (L.) Karst.), but in the west it mainly attacks spruce species; Sitka spruce (*Picea sitchensis* (Bong.) Carr.) is particularly susceptible. Adult weevils lay eggs in the bark on tree leaders, emerging larvae mine down under the bark, consuming the phloem, severing the cambial layer, girdling and eventually killing the leader. Damage is so severe that young plantation trees often become stunted and bushy as terminal leaders are repeatedly killed and young trees fail to achieve apical dominance. Because of the weevil, Sitka spruce has been avoided as a re-forestation species in many parts of its former range.

A resistance breeding program initiated in the early 1990s is relatively unique for insect pests in forest trees, but it has been successful and has done a lot to rehabilitate this important western conifer (Alfaro and King these proceedings, King and Alfaro 2009). Nearly all planting stock currently

---

[1] British Columbia Ministry of Forests and Range, Research Branch, P.O. Box 9519, Stn. Prov. Govt., Victoria, British Columbia, Canada V8W 9C2.
[2] Natural Resources Canada, Canadian Forest Service, Pacific Forestry Centre, 506 W. Burnside Rd., Victoria, British Columbia, Canada V8Z 1M5.
Corresponding author: King forgen@gmail.com.

comes from this breeding program and, to date, the resistance seems effective, durable, and stable. We have also used this program as a case study for mechanisms of resistance in conifers against shoot infesting insects (Alfaro et al. 2002). To date, various hindrance mechanisms including: induced and constitutive resin cells, sclereid or stone cells; and terpene defenses have been studied (Alfaro 1995, Alfaro et al. 1997, King et al. 2011, McKay-Byun et al. 2006, Robert et al. 2010). All of these appear factors in resistance, but none singly is strongly predictive to resistance - the strongest to date appears to be sclereid or lignified stone cell (King et al. 2011). All of these factors are in their nature complex, multifaceted, and appear to offer some partial solution that is most likely controlled by complex multigenic sytems. We do note, however, that we have very strongly expressed, complete, or total resistance in some individuals.

Major gene, or R-gene, resistance is characterized as "total resistance" and is well documented for pathogens in forest trees (Kinloch et al. 2007, Kubisiak et al. 2005), but is also well characterized for insects in many crop plants, especially phloem feeding insects such as is the white pine weevil (examples include aphids, leaf hoppers, and fly larvae). Particularly interesting are the midges, such as the Hessian fly in wheat, which, as a phloem feeder (Harris et al. 2003), has a similar life strategy to the weevil.

In this paper, we review the evidence to date for the hypothesis of "total resistance" in the spruce - insect pest system. We present features associated with this type of resistance and describe what we know about these highly resistant individuals. We suggest methods of confirming this type of resistance and discuss the implications of deploying major gene resistance.

Marked Distribution of Resistance in Native Populations

Early provenance trials indicated strong geographic regions of resistance: the hybrid area of northwest British Columbia and two provenance sources within the high hazard region of southwest British Columbia (Haney and Big Qualicum) (Ying 1991). Screening included clonal selections of individuals from these two provenances as well as a series of open-pollinated (OP) collections from this high-hazard region (King and Alfaro 2009). Results from the first of these OP series indicated weevil resistance was not widely distributed through this region, but had a marked area of resistance close to the original provenances (King et al. 2004). Figure 1 incorporates results from all four of the OP family series trials and graphically demonstrates the distribution of naturally occurring resistance found in the high-hazard zone of southwest British Columbia. The dots indicate provenance sources where trees were sampled in this region. Three to 30 trees per source were included (with over 500 families screened overall) – the relative resistance of these sources is shown by color coding with red expressing higher resistance and blue susceptible. The strongly defined resistance boundaries for the Fraser Valley (Haney) and East Vancouver Island (Big Qualicum) regions are evident. They transition over relatively short distances to susceptible regions to the north (Salmon River and Amor de Cosmos, North Vancouver Island), and south (Duncan and Saanich, South Vancouver Island, and Puget Sound, Washington).

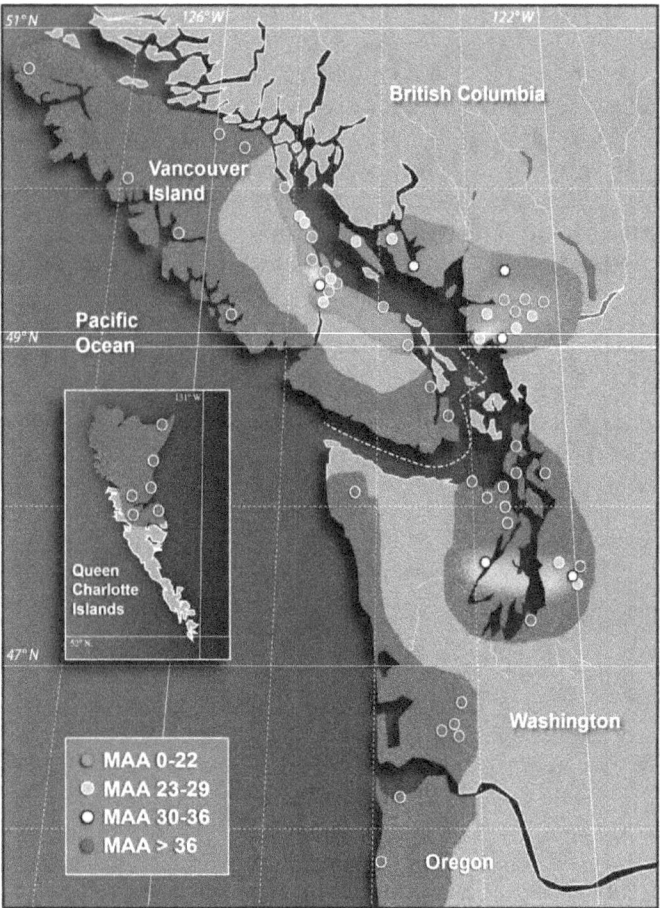

Figure 1—Resistant provenances by mean annual attack (MAA) level and zones of high and low natural resistance; MAA is expressed as a percentage. The resistant region is shown in red, the susceptible region in blue shades (intermediate in yellow).

The strong geographic demarcation noted is also demonstrated clearly by the plots of the frequency distributions based on families from the first OP series families that most widely sampled this high-hazard zone (King et al. 2004). In fig. 2, the distribution f_0 represents the hypothesis that there is one underlying distribution within the high-hazard zone (broad-based resistance). The trendline, f_R, represents the families from the resistant Big Qualicum sources, and f_S represents families from other sources within the high-hazard zone, but outside the resistant (red) region described in fig. 1. The trendline, f_C, represents the combined distribution of f_R and f_S, and fits significantly better than the single distribution f_0, with a likelihood ratio statistic of 42.5 (P <0.0001). Mean annual attack rates of the Haida Gwaii (Queen Charlotte Islands) families used also in this first OP series range from 0.28 to 0.40 (the archipelago is free of the weevil), the resistant Big Qualicum families (range 0.05 to 0.23) did not overlap at all.

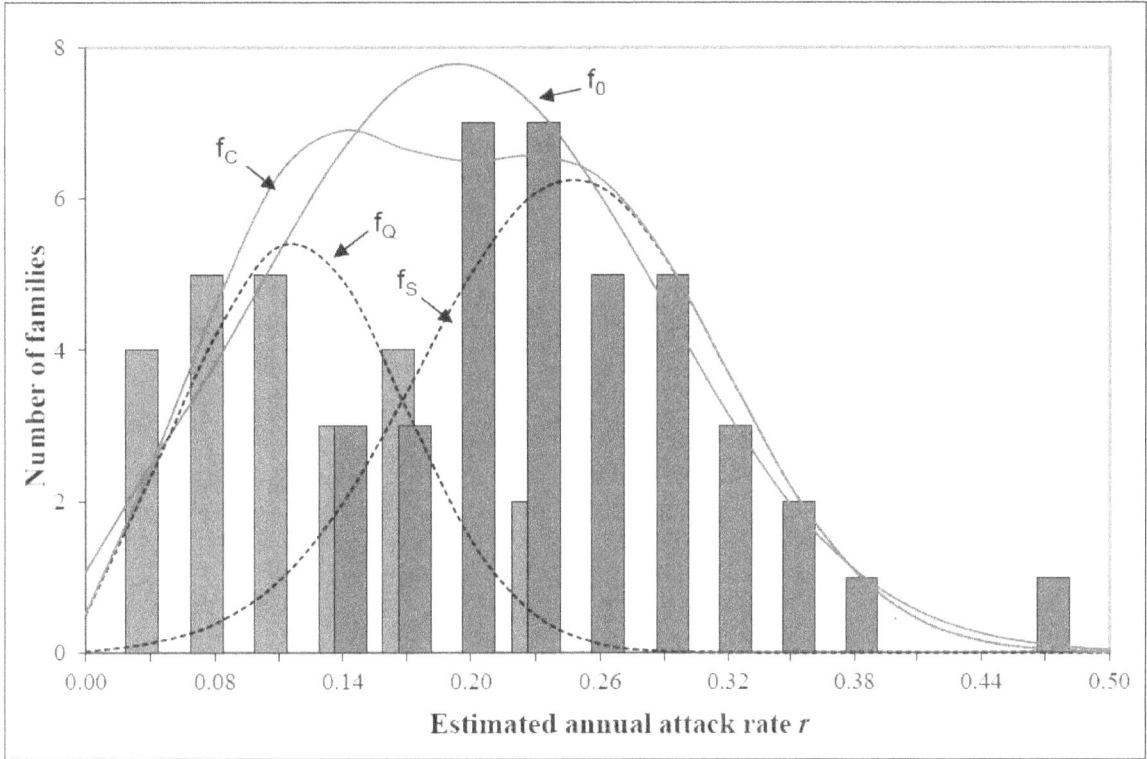

Figure 2—Frequency distributions of weevil attack. f_0 represents the null hypothesis that high-hazard mean families belong to one distribution. f_q depicts families from the high resistant Big Qualicum source (fig. 1). f_s depicts families from the other sources in the high hazard zone. f_c shows the combined frequency distribution (f_q + f_s). Bars show frequency of actual data points – the red shaded are those for f_q and blue for f_s.

Observation of Segregation within Families

Besides analyzing the distribution of family means within the high-hazard zone, within family segregation can also offer insights. Simple statistical evaluation techniques to detect segregation within families have been widely used especially in human and animal genetics (Fain 1978, Uimari et al. 1996). Such techniques have recently also been used in forest trees (Zeng and Li 2003). These tests assume that the presence of major genes with large effects will inflate the variance within the families in which the genes are segregating. This segregation may also cause non-normality of the phenotypic data, producing significant skewness and/or kurtosis. One method to explore this within-family phenotypic effect is to regress the offspring variance on the sib or family means (Fain 1978). With no inbreeding there should be no relationship between the family variance and its phenotypic value in traits influenced by many genes with small effects. When a character is controlled by genes with large effects, individuals with the most extreme phenotypes are likely to be homozygotes (extreme means and low variance), whereas intermediate phenotypes are likely to be heterozygotes (intermediate means and high variance). This quadratic (concave down) relationship can be described by a polynomial regression of offspring variance on phenotypic value:

$$\mathrm{var}(z_i) = \beta_0 + \beta_1 z_i + \beta_2 z_i^2 \tag{1}$$

Where var (z_i) is the phenotypic variance within the ith offspring family, and z_i is the family mean (Fain 1978).

This analysis is designed for continuous normally distributed data, and although major gene segregation will distort the normal distribution, this test is considered robust to non-normality of the data. Our data (the number of attacked leaders divided by number of years of observation) follows more correctly a Poisson distribution, characterized by a single parameter where the variance equals the mean. Specific study of this variance requires a generalization, so an overdispersed Poisson distribution (McCullagh and Nelder 1989) was fitted to the 20 observations within each family. Under this distribution, the expected number of attacked leaders per observation is $E(X_i) = rt_i$ where x_i denotes the number of attacked leaders over t_i years for the ith plot, and r denotes the annual attack rate for the family. The variance is $Var(X_i) = \phi \cdot rt_i$, where ϕ represents an overdispersion parameter – the degree to which the nominal Poisson variance should be inflated or deflated as dictated by the data (i.e., $\phi = 1$ indicates no overdispersion). The scaled residual deviance was used to estimate ϕ.

Results from fitting the Fain model to the estimated Poisson parameters $\hat{r}$ and $\hat{\phi}$ are shown in fig. 3 for the resistant Big Qualicum families. Figure 3 shows a good, significant curvilinear fit ($R^2 = 0.63$, n = 23) to the quadratic term in the model (P <0.0001). This same model fit poorly to the susceptible families ($R^2 = 0.37$, n = 44), and the quadratic term was not significant (P = 0.5389). Using simply the average attack rate and (log) variance as in Equation (1) instead of the Poisson distribution, a curvilinear regression was also highly significant for the Big Qualicum families ($R^2 = 0.86$, P <0.0001 for the quadratic term), and the susceptible families again fit poorly ($R^2 = 0.02$ and P = 0.5377 for the quadratic term).

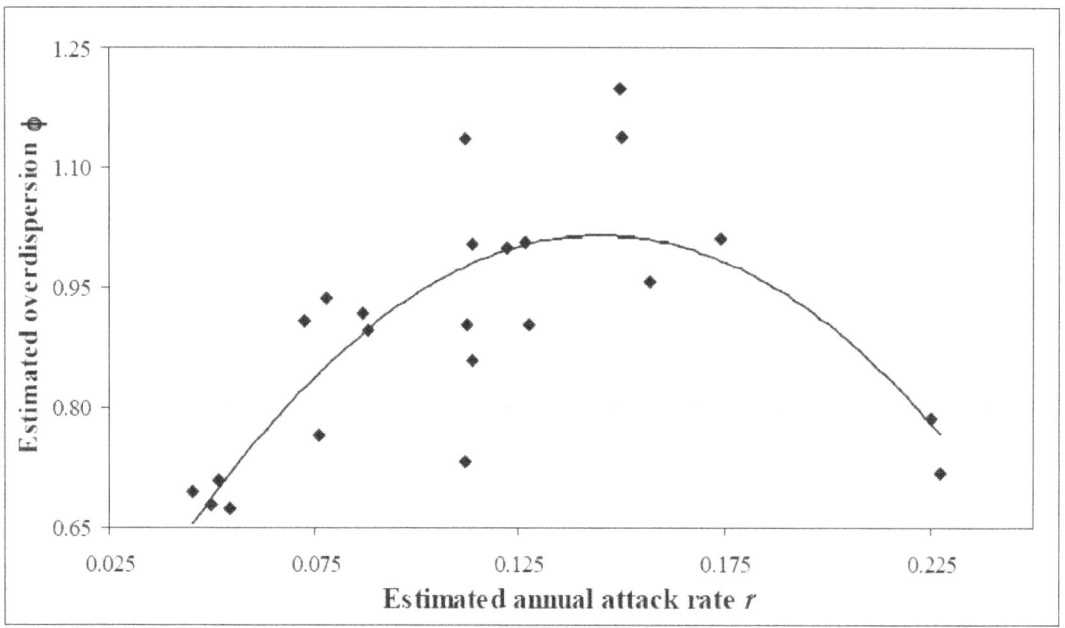

Figure 3—Plot of Big Qualicum families and fitted quadratic (Fain 1978) model ($R^2 = 0.63$, n = 23). Overdispersion and annual attack rate are estimated from an overdispersed Poisson distribution.

Studies of Strongly Expressed Phenotypic Resistant Individuals

A series of studies focused on gaining insight into weevil resistance has been conducted on one particular tree, parent clone 898, since this highly resistant individual was first noticed at the Sayward

(Bigtree Creek) trial (Alfaro and Ying 1990, King and Alfaro 2009). This individual has been clonally replicated in many field trials, archives, and nursery experiments. Over a decade of observations have been made in screening trials containing close to 100 898 clonal ramets, and in this time only two trees of this clone have been noted to have leader kill – this compared to observations of leader kill in 100 percent of individuals, many times repeatedly, in many other clones (King and Alfaro 2009). In addition to being weevil resistant, the 898 clone is easily identified in a plantation by its exceptional growth form. Its vigorous growth produces long, straight internodes that typically cause the tree to stand out among its neighbors and make it highly desirable for forestry (fig. 4).

Figure 4—Clonal blocks of 898 (and other immune clone 1210) with susceptible seedlots in foreground. At this site (Hisnit – King and Alfaro 2009) under very heavy attack, not a single 898 individual was successfully attacked.

In efforts to gain insight into the resistance strategy of the 898 clone, feeding and oviposition behavior have been observed through caging experiments over the years (fig. 5). Where weevils had a choice, they preferred not to colonize 898. However, when caged on ramets of clone 898, weevils preferred not to feed on the leader, but rather on the one-year-old internode. Again, in caged (no choice) experiments, gravid females would lay eggs that hatched, but the larvae died at first instar and females that were not gravid did not produce eggs (Tony Ibaraki, personal communication).

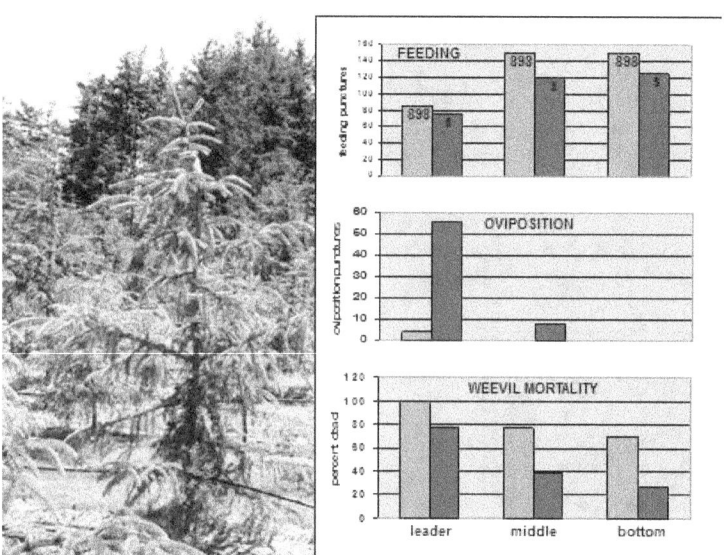

Figure 5—Weevil caging studies showing some of the results of forced caging in different positions on the crown.

Studies of the resin canal systems of Sitka spruce revealed 898 has high bark constitutive resin cell density as well as high sclereid cell density, but most of the trees from the resistant region (East Vancouver Island – Big Qualicum or Fraser Valley – Haney) show this compared to individuals from the more susceptible regions. Interestingly, although 898 is high for both of these traits it is not 'off the chart' (King et al. 2011) which suggests other mechanisms may also be present. The traumatic resin response in Sitka spruce has not been thoroughly explored. However, observations to date indicate that this trait does not seem to be as well expressed in Sitka spruce as it is in white spruce (O'Neill et al. 2002). This perhaps accounts for the particular susceptibility of Sitka spruce and why it acts in such an unstable manner to this endemic pest. Our work to date on traumatic resin with 898 was inconclusive.

Various biochemical studies have been made of 898, but none so far have shown anything unique for this clone (McKay-Byun et al. 2006, Robert et al. 2010). One interesting hypothesis is that the resistant 898 clone inhibits the expression of the vitellogenin gene in weevils after they feed. Vitellogenin is an egg-yolk protein precursor necessary for the maturation of eggs in reproductively active female weevils (Leal et al. 1997). Weevils that fed on resistant ortets or cuttings of the 898 clone had fewer eggs form in their ovaries, and ovaries of *P. strobi* females that fed on this clone were less likely to mature. Levels of ovarian growth and expression of the vitellogenin gene were also reduced in weevils that fed on severed leaders of the resistant 898 clone relative to those that fed on severed leaders of a susceptible family (Sahota et al. 2001). However, as we noted earlier, gravid females can successfully lay eggs in 898, although they would not prefer it.

It needs to be noted that 898 is not the only 'highly resistant' or immune individual, but it has been the most extensively studied. An F_1 generation breeding program was instituted (King and Alfaro 2009) and some preliminary investigation has begun. Seven of the ten most resistant crosses in the F_1 generation had 898 as either parent (Moreira et al. 2012). A full segregation analysis has yet to be conducted on the F_1 generation, but it should be noted that these trials, primarily made with resistant x resistant crosses, have far fewer attacks, thus the difficulty with getting robust screening compared to the 1st generation OP trials. It is also possible at this time to get to a backcross generation – this would really help us to confirm the segregation – which should be unambiguous compared to either the F_1 or OP generation.

Major Gene Resistance in Other Plant – Insect Systems

Some of the best documented insect resistance systems involving *R* genes are gall midges (Cecidomyiidae) in both wheat and rice. Harris et al. (2003) detailed the genetic and biochemical interactions between gall midge *avr* genes and plant *R* genes. In the wheat-Hessian fly system, close to 30 major genes in the host interact with various biotypes of the pest that display virulence to specific *R* genes in typical gene-for-gene fashion (Ratcliffe and Hatchett 1997). Although antibiosis appears to be the primary mechanism, often leading to the death of the first-instar larvae within a few days of establishment, the nature of this antibiosis is only beginning to be understood. Although hypersensitive responses (HR) have been reported in this system (Grover 1995) this may not be the only or even key defense response to these piercing/sucking type of insects (Kaloshian 2004). Harris et al. (2006) investigated with detailed microscopy the compatibility interactions between larvae and plant. In the compatible interaction in these gall-forming insects, a virulent larva promotes gall formation in the host. This gall does not have any noticeable macroscopic structure, but is defined as aberrant tissue structure resulting from stimulation from a foreign organism, in this case the fly larva (Harris et al. 2003). It had been proposed that injection of salivary substances by the larvae during the first instar might be part of the attack process (Hatchett et al. 1990, Ollerston et al. 1990) and piercing marks by larva mandibles were indicated in the microscopy investigation (Harris et al. 2006). It is hypothesized that *avr* gene products from the larva are secreted into epidermal cells and activate a galling process (Harris et al. 2003). Part of the ensuing aberrant tissue structure (in this compatible interaction) is enhanced protein synthesis combined with breakdown of cell walls – the cells rupturing with 'nutritive tissue' providing the larva with a diet rich in soluble amino acids and sugars (Harris et al. 2006). The virulence genes that aid the larva in successfully attacking a susceptible plant would act as avirulence genes in a plant defended by *R* genes (incompatible reaction) (Harris et al. 2003). In fact, it appears the interaction of *R* gene product and *avr* effectors can involve complex recognition and response interactions (Kaloshian 2004). In a defended plant this gall-induced nutritive tissue is not formed and the larva starves. It has been noted that when virulent and non-virulent biotypes colonize the same plant the nutritive tissue can be enough to also sustain the non-virulent larvae (Grover et al. 1989) which has implications for fitness and survival in the evolution of fly virulence (Harris et al. 2003).

This type of galling response, associated with nutritive tissue has been noted in many plant defense responses to insects (Rohfritsch 1992). There is also a phenotypic difference in the expression of these incompatible reactions between resistant genotypes (Harris et al. 2003). Classic HR may also be observed as part of a gall midge attack (e.g., *Salix viminalis* to the gall midge *Dasineura marginemtorquens* (Ollerston et al. 2002). But there appears to be substantial variability in the manifestation of *R*-gene mediated plant defenses in host-insect interactions. HR may be a feature but not always and different forms of limitation to phloem feeding have been observed (Kaloshian 2004).

Summary and Conclusions

There are important hallmarks of large genetic effects for resistance to the weevil: marked geographic distribution, and some evidence of within family segregation. This does not necessarily indicate classic major gene or R- gene resistance and it could be explained by relatively few genes controlling the hindrance traits, resin canals, and sclereid cells already investigated. Also, the induced or traumatic resin cell investigation that appears so effective in interior spruce has so far not been managed in Sitka spruce. Genotypes showing 'total resistance' in Sitka spruce with respect to the white pine weevil and indication of life-history parallels with similar phloem feeding insects – e.g. the starvation of first instar larvae manifested in R-gene defense in the Hessian fly, clearly though point to the need for follow-up investigations. Although investigative work to date has concentrated on one particular cloned individual – other individuals have been identified but as yet have not been followed through in such detail. F_1 breeding has been carried out with these individuals (resistant x resistant,

resistant x susceptible, susceptible x susceptible) (Moreira et al. 2012) and it would be very feasible to make backcross segregating lines (with clonal emblings). Developing such segregating lines would certainly help in any further investigation and would set up a good experimental population in further understanding the phenotypic and biochemical natures of this resistance. Molecular genetic surveys based on linked molecular markers could also help in identifying the genetic architecture underlying resistant phenotypes. The molecular and proteomic signatures for R-gene resistance can be also be identified (Liu et al 2004) and structured experimental populations and structured experimental pedigrees would help in this investigation.

Although the genetic variation governing plant-insect interactions is usually observed as continuously variable, and most likely controlled by the segregation of multigenic quantitative trait loci, this does not preclude major genes as important mechanisms of resistance. Certainly for phloem feeding insects that attack crop plants, R genes are widely used as key plant defense mechanisms. We do know that long term stable and manageable resistance is possible by the nature of the resistance we see in white spruce in Eastern North America, where it is not a major problem and acts more like a classic endemic system. An understanding of the genetics behind this resistance is necessary to assess the durability and effectiveness of the resistance found so far in Sitka spruce.

Acknowledgments

We acknowledge the many people who have worked on this weevil resistance program over the decades in the British Columbia Forest Service, Canadian Forest Service, University of British Columbia, and Simon Fraser University; and the Forest Industries and Forest Genetics Council. We would like to thank Ward Strong and Alvin Yanchuk of the British Columbia Forest Service and Timothy Sexton of the University of British Columbia for their thoughtful reviews, and Richard Sniezko and organizers of this conference for providing a place to publish this valuable information.

Literature Cited

Alfaro, R.I. 1995. An induced defense reaction in white spruce to attack by the white pine weevil, *Pissodes strobi*. Canadian Journal of Forest Research. 25: 1725–1730.

Alfaro, R.I.; Ying, C.C. 1990. Levels of Sitka spruce weevil, *Pissodes strobi* (Peck), damage among Sitka spruce provenances and families near Sayward, British Columbia (Canada). The Canadian Entomologist. 122: 607–616.

Alfaro, R.I.; He, F.; Tomlin, E.; Kiss, G.K. 1997. Resistance of white spruce to the white pine weevil related to resin canal density. Canadian Journal of Botany. 75: 568–573.

Alfaro, R.I.; Borden, J.H.; King, J.N.; Tomlin, E.S.; McIntosh, R.L.; Bohlmann, J. 2002. Mechanisms of resistance in conifers against shoot infesting insects: the case of the white pine weevil *Pissodes strobi* (Peck) (Coleoptera: Curculionidae). In: Wagner, M.R.; Clancy, K.M.; Lieutier, F.; Paine, T.D., eds. Mechanisms and deployment of resistance in trees to insects. Dordrecht, The Netherlands: Kluwer Academic Publishers: 101–126.

Fain, P.R. 1978. Characteristics of simple sibship variance tests for the detection of major loci and application to height, weight and spatial performance. Annals of Human Genetics. 42: 109 120.

Grover, P. 1995. Hypersensitive response of wheat to the Hessian fly. Entomologia Experimentalis et Applicata. 74: 283–294.

Grover, P.; Shukle, R.H.; Foster, J.E. 1989. Interactions of Hessian fly (Diptera: Cecidomyiidae) biotypes on resistant wheat. Environmental Entomology. 18: 687–690.

Harris, M.O.; Freeman, T.P.; Rohfritsch, O.; Anderson, K.G.; Payne, S.A.; Moore, J.A. 2006. Virulent Hessian fly (Diptera: Cecidomyiidae) larvae induced nutritive tissue during compatible interactions with wheat. Annals of the Entomological Society of America. 99(2): 305–306.

Harris, M.O.; Stuart, J.J.; Mohan, M.; Nair, S.; Lamb, R.J.; Rohfritsch, O. 2003. Grasses and gall midges: plant defense and insect adaptation. Annual Review of Entomology. 48: 549–577.

Hatchett, J.H.; Kreitner, G.L.; Elzinga, R.J. 1990. Larval mouthparts and feeding mechanisms of the Hessian fly (Diptera: Cecidomyiidae). Annals of the Entomological Society of America. 83: 1137–1147.

Kaloshian, I. 2004. Gene-for-gene disease resistance: bridging insect pests and pathogen defense. Journal of Chemical Ecology. 30: 2419–2438.

King, J.N.; Alfaro, R.I. 2009. Developing Sitka spruce populations for resistance to the white pine weevil: summary of research and breeding program. Tech. Rep. 050. Victoria, BC: B.C. Ministry of Forests and Range, Forest Science Program. www.for.gov.bc.ca/hfd/pubs/Docs/Tr/Tr050.htm. (28 April, 2012).

King, J.N.; Alfaro, R.I.; Cartwright, C. 2004. Genetic resistance of Sitka spruce (*Picea sitchensis*) populations to the white pine weevil (*Pissodes strobi*): distribution of resistance. Forestry. 77: 269–278.

King, J.N.; Alfaro, R.I.; Grau Lopez, M.; vanAkker, L. 2011. Resistance of Sitka Spruce (*Picea sitchensis* (Bong.) Carr.) to white pine weevil (*Pissodes strobi* Peck): characterizing resistant populations for bark defense mechanisms. Forestry 84(1): 83–91.

Kinloch, B.B. Jr.; Davis, D.A.; Burton, D. 2007. Resistance and virulence interactions between two white pine species and blister rust in a 30-year field trial. Tree Genetics & Genomes. 4: 65–74.

Kubisiak, T.L.; Amerson, H.V.; Nelson, C.D. 2005. Genetic interaction of the fusiform rust fungus with resistance gene *Fr1* in loblolly pine. Phytopathology. 95: 376–380.

Leal, I.; White, E.E.; Sahota, T.S.; Manville, J.F. 1997. Differential expression of the vitellogenin gene in the spruce terminal weevil feeding on resistant versus susceptible hosts. Insect Biochemistry and Molecular Biology. 27(6): 569–575.

Liu, J.J.; Hunt, R.S.; Ekramoddoullah, A.K.M. 2004. Recent insights into western white pine genetic resistance to white pine blister rust. Recent Research in Development, Biotechnology, and Bioengineering. 6: 65–76.

McCullagh, P.; Nelder, J. 1989. Generalized linear models, Second Edition. Boca Raton, Florida: Chapman & Hall/CRC. 532 p.

McKay-Byun, A.; Godard, K.A.; Toudefallah, M; Martin, D.M.; Alfaro, R.I.; King, J.N.; Bohlmann, J.; Plant, A.L. 2006. Wound-induced terpene synthase gene expression in Sitka spruce that exhibit resistance or susceptibility to attack by the white pine weevil. Plant Physiology. 104: 1009–1021.

Moreira, X.; Alfaro, R.I.; King, J.N. 2012. Constitutive defenses and damage in Sitka spruce progeny obtained from crosses between white pine weevil resistant and susceptible parents. Forestry. 85(1): 79–86.

Ollerstam, O.; Rohfritsch, O.; Hoglund, S.; Larsson, S. 2002. A rapid hypersensitive response associated with resistance in willow *Salix viminalis* against the gall midge *Dasineura marginemtorquens*. Entomologia Experimentalis et Applicata. 102: 153–162.

Ollerston, H.; Kreitner, G.L.; Elzinga, R.J. 1990. Larval mouthparts and feeding mechanisms of the Hessian fly (Diptera: Cecidomyiidae). Annals of the Entomological Society of America. 83: 1137–1147.

O'Neill, G.A.; Aitken, S.N; King, J.N.; Alfaro, R.I. 2002. Geographic variation in resin canal defences in seedlings from the Sitka × white spruce introgression zone. Canadian Journal of Forest Research. 32: 390–400.

Ratcliffe, R.H.; Hatchett, J.H. 1997. Biology and genetics of the Hessian fly and resistance in wheat. In: Bondari, K., ed. New developments in entomology. Trivandurm, India: Research Signpost: 47–56.

Rohfritsch, O. 1992. Patterns in gall development. In: Shorthouse, J.; Rohfritsch, O., eds. Biology of insect-induced galls. New York: Oxford University Press: 60–86.

Robert, J.A.; Madilao, L.L.; White, J.; Yanchuk, A.; King, J.N.; Bohlmann, J. 2010. Terpenoid metabolite profiling in Sitka spruce identifies association of dehydroabietic acid, (+)-3-carene and terpinolene with resistance against the white pine weevil. Botany 88(9): 810–820.

Sahota, T.S.; Manville, J.F.; Hollmann, J.; Leal, I.; Ibaraki, A.; White, E.E. 2001. Resistance against *Pissodes strobi* (Coleoptera: Curculionidae) in severed leaders and in water-soluble bark extract of *Picea sitchensis* (Pinaceae): evidence for a post-ingestive mode of action. Canadian Entomologist. 133: 315-323.

Uimari, P.; Kennedy, B.W.; Dekkers, C.M. 1996. Power and sensitivity of some simple tests for detection of major genes in outbred populations. Journal of Animal Breeding and Genetics. 113: 17–28.

Ying, C.C. 1991. Genetic resistance to the white pine weevil in Sitka spruce. Res. Note No. 196. Victoria, B.C.: British Columbia Ministry of Forests. 17 p.

Zeng, W.; Li., B. 2003. Simple tests for detecting segregation of major genes with phenotypic data from a diallel mating. Forest Science. 49: 268–278.

Operational Program to Develop *Phytophthora lateralis*-Resistant Populations of Port-Orford-cedar (*Chamaecyparis lawsoniana*)

R.A. Sniezko,[1] J. Hamlin,[2] and E.M. Hansen[3]

Abstract

Port-Orford-cedar (*Chamaecyparis lawsoniana* (A. Murr.) Parl.) (POC) is a long-lived conifer native to northwestern California and southwestern Oregon. It has been widely used in horticulture in both western North America and elsewhere. The accidental introduction of the non-native pathogen *Phytophthora lateralis* into North America and Europe has raised concerns about the future viability of POC in some forest ecosystems, in managed forests, and in horticultural settings. Fortunately, some level of natural genetic resistance to *P. lateralis* exists in POC. Utilizing this genetic resistance in reforestation and restoration of POC offers considerable benefits without the negative side-effects of alternatives. In 1997, the USDA Forest Service and USDI Bureau of Land Management began a large operational program to develop populations of POC with genetic resistance to *P. lateralis*. With essential ongoing pathology support from Oregon State University, this resistance program has advanced rapidly. The program goal includes developing orchards for production of resistant seed, while maintaining genetic variation and adaptability within the species. Using classical selection and testing techniques, over 12,600 initial field selections have been made, resistance screening protocols refined, 13 breeding zones delineated, field trials established, eight seed orchards started, and resistant seed produced and being used for some breeding zones. Early, short-term testing in the greenhouse of orchard seedlots shows a 30 percent or higher survival than woods-run seedlots. In greenhouse testing, survival among individual susceptible and resistant families varies from 0 to 100 percent, and at least two types of resistance are apparent. Field trials have been established and early results are encouraging, but much longer monitoring is needed to examine a full range of sites for efficacy and durability of resistance under different environments and a changing climate. The recent finding of *P. lateralis* in Europe and Taiwan warrants further investigation into the pathogenicity of these isolates on resistant POC. The biology of POC and the concerted efforts of all those involved have made this fast moving resistance program one of the few involving non-native pathogens to produce seed for restoration and reforestation. Planting the less susceptible seedlings will increase the frequency of resistance in areas affected by *P. lateralis* and help to establish a new balance in affected ecosystems.

Key words: Port-Orford-cedar, *Chamaecyparis lawsoniana*, *Phytophthora lateralis*, resistance program

Introduction

Port-Orford-cedar (*Chamaecyparis lawsoniana* (A. Murr.) Parl.) (POC) is a large, long-lived conifer species native to southwestern Oregon and northwestern California (figs. 1 and 2) (Betlejewski et al. 2011; USDA FS and USDI BLM 2003, 2004; Zobel et al. 1985). It has also been widely utilized in urban plantings in North America, Europe, and elsewhere, where it is often called Lawson's cypress. However, the introduction of a root disease, caused by the non-native pathogen *Phytophthora lateralis* (Tucker and Milbrath), in North America and Europe has caused high mortality in some forest ecosystems and has limited POC's use in forest plantings and in horticulture (Betlejewski et al. 2011, Casavan et al. 2003, Robin et al. 2011, Sansford 2011, Zobel et al. 1985). *Phytophthora lateralis* is spread primarily via water and soil. All sizes and ages of POC can be killed by *P. lateralis*. POC is the only species in North America currently known to be highly susceptible to *P.*

---

[1] USDA Forest Service, Dorena Genetic Resource Center, Cottage Grove, Oregon.
[2] USDA Forest Service, Umpqua National Forest, Roseburg, Oregon.
[3] Oregon State University, Department of Botany and Plant Pathology, Corvallis, Oregon.
Corresponding author: rsniezko@fs.fed.us.

lateralis, although Pacific yew (*Taxus brevifolia* Nutt.) is occasionally killed (DeNitto and Kliejunas 1991).

Figure 1—Port-Orford-cedar (a) tree in urban area, (b) large, healthy tree in southern Oregon, (c) dead trees in forest along a creek in southwest Oregon, (d) dead and dying trees along Highway 101 in southwest Oregon, (e) resistant parent tree (510015) surrounded by dead Port-Orford-cedar. (Photo credits: Richard Sniezko, a to d; Chuck Frank, e)

The native range of POC encompasses lands managed by many governmental and private organizations and individuals. In this region, POC occurs widely on lands managed by the USDA Forest Service (USFS) and USDI Bureau of Land Management (BLM). The USFS and BLM have implemented an integrated strategy to manage POC ecosystems on their lands in the presence of *P. lateralis*, including: measures to exclude the pathogen from areas not yet affected, sanitation of some infested areas, and minimizing planting sites of highest hazard, such as wet, low-lying areas (Betlejewski et al. 2011, USDA FS 2004, 2006; USDI BLM 2004). However, genetic resistance is a species' natural line of defense against potentially damaging biotic and abiotic agents, and resistance to *P. lateralis* is necessary to retain POC in some ecosystems and to help ensure its continued use in managed forests and horticulture. Fortunately, early work examining possible genetic resistance in POC (Hansen et al. 1989, Sniezko et al. 2003) showed enough promise to begin an operational program to develop resistant populations of POC. The production of seed from seed orchards containing genetically-resistant parents offers land managers the opportunity to continue to use POC in reforestation and restoration. Until recently, however, few operational programs have been undertaken to develop genetic resistance to a non-native pathogen and even fewer are currently producing resistant seed (FAO 2008, Sniezko 2006). In this paper, we provide an update on the substantial progress made since 1997 in the *P. lateralis* resistance program for Port-Orford-cedar.

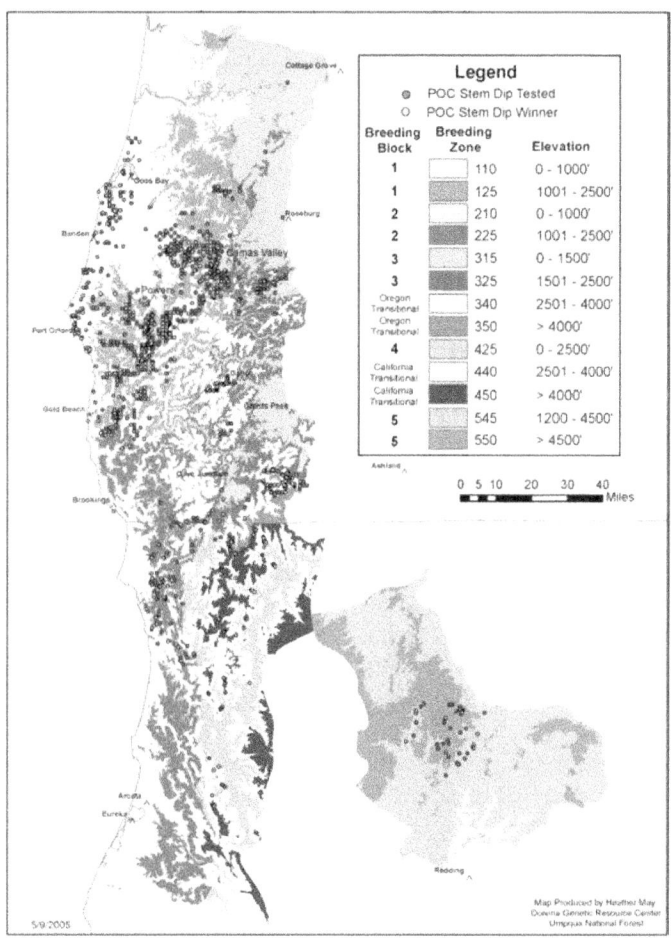

Figure 2—Map showing the 13 breeding zones in the natural range of Port-Orford-cedar and the geographic distribution of field selections being tested for *Phytophthora lateralis* resistance.

Overview

The USFS and BLM program to develop populations of Port-Orford-cedar with genetic resistance to *P. lateralis* expanded to an operational level in 1997. Earlier work at Oregon State University (OSU) and by the USFS and BLM focused on confirming the presence of genetic resistance, selecting the first several hundred candidate trees displaying reduced susceptibility, refining screening techniques for resistance, and developing tree improvement protocols necessary to implement an operational program for this species. The USFS provides overall design for the resistance program and oversees most operational phases, including coordination of field trial establishment, control pollinations for breeding to enhance resistance, data analysis, and seed orchard development for producing resistant seed for reforestation and restoration. Oregon State University provides essential pathology support, including work on biology of the pathogen as well as establishment and monitoring short-term resistance screening trials. The USFS and BLM provide genetics expertise, funding and personnel for the resistance program, sites for field trials, and have identified most of the field selections. The BLM has established and maintains a gene conservation clone bank. Other federal, state, and private cooperators have supported the program by providing tree selections for resistance testing and sites for field trials. Summaries of genetic and resistance work in the operational program through to 2001 are reported elsewhere (Kitzmiller et al. 2003, Sniezko 2004; Sniezko and Hansen 2000, 2003; Sniezko et al. 2003), but significant updates on delineation of breeding zones, seed orchard development, seed availability, testing protocols, and understanding of resistance have occurred over the intervening 10 years.

Integrated Strategy

Developing populations of POC with resistance to *P. lateralis* will be key to increasing success in reforestation and restoration efforts. At this stage, to help maximize the progress in disease resistance, the POC program has focused only on genetic resistance and has not selected for increased growth rate or other traits that may be of interest in reforestation.

POC is a long-lived species that spans very diverse environments (e.g., soils, climate) (Zobel et al. 1985). It is therefore essential to include both genetic diversity and adaptability considerations in the implementation of the resistance program to ensure resulting seedlings will be adapted to current conditions, as well as to buffer the species against a changing climate and other possible insect or pathogen problems.

To help ensure adaptability of future reforestation and restoration plantings, the natural range of POC is currently divided into five breeding blocks, and a total of 13 breeding zones (fig. 2). A breeding block designates the geographic area that envelops a number of breeding zones. The preliminary breeding blocks and zones serve to guide seed transfer and associated breeding activities, where genetic reproductive materials (such as seed, seedlings, and cuttings) are procured or produced in a breeding program, and then subsequently deployed (seeded or planted). The preliminary breeding blocks and zones were updated in 2005 by the BLM and USFS, and were delineated on the basis of various short-term and long-term studies and data. Breeding zones are represented by an elevation band within a respective breeding block. Further analyses of existing long-term common garden studies (fig. 3) that supplement the earlier analysis of 7-year-old data by Kitzmiller (2006), or other future studies, will be used to refine the breeding blocks/zones over time. Seedlots may also be delineated in the future within any respective breeding zone on the basis of source soil type. The tree species occurs on both ultramafic (serpentine) and other soil types (Zobel et al. 1985). A number of plant species have differentially adapted to these distinct soil types (Linhart 1995), but the degree to which POC is specifically adapted is not known.

Since 1997, over 12,600 field selections have been made to help maintain genetic diversity during the subsequent testing and selection process for parents for the seed orchards and for future breeding. Many of the selections have been made in areas where mortality from *P. lateralis* is evident, while others represent random selections in areas not yet impacted. Selections have been made throughout the range of POC, with more selections in the areas where the species is more prominent (fig. 2). Field selections are tested in several steps for resistance (Hansen et al., Methods for screening Port-Orford-cedar for resistance to *Phytophthora lateralis*, these proceedings; Sniezko et al. 2003) with the final selections placed in seed orchards or breeding orchards. Based on their rating in the stem dip test, approximately 10 percent of the original field selections have been retained for further resistance evaluation using a root dip testing method (Hansen et al., Methods for screening Port-Orford-cedar for resistance to *Phytophthora lateralis,* these proceedings; Sniezko et al. 2003). The root dip testing of much of this subset of parental selections (or their progenies) has been completed. Results from this test are used to determine which materials are placed into orchards and used for breeding.

Figure 3—Port-Orford-cedar: (a) measuring height in 2011 in1996 POC provenance trial in northern California; (b) different color and form for multiple copies of two different parent trees in the Tyrrell clone bank; (c) clone bank. (Photo credits: Chuck Frank, a; Richard Sniezko, b and c)

In general, the disease-resistance program involves a sequence of steps to identify resistant parent trees and to propagate those parent trees in seed orchards to provide seed for reforestation and restoration (fig. 4). In the first cycle of selection and testing, candidate parent trees are selected from forest stands within the range of POC (fig. 2). These selections are tested for resistance in short-term tests (for methods, see Hansen et al., Methods for screening Port-Orford-cedar for resistance to *Phytophthora lateralis*, these proceedings; Sniezko et al. 2003) and resistant parents or progeny are retained for orchard development and breeding. Control crosses (selfs and outcrosses) are used to generate progenies for testing resistance and for further selection to increase resistance. A project to examine the genetic diversity within the orchard populations using molecular markers is underway.

Resistance Testing

Efficient, short-term resistance testing is a key step in any operational resistance program. It permits the rapid identification of parent trees to be included in the production orchards or for further breeding. Several short-term tests have been used (Hansen et al., Methods for screening Port-Orford-cedar for resistance to *Phytophthora lateralis*, these proceedings; Sniezko et al. 2003), but a greenhouse root dip test of seedling families or of rooted cuttings of parent trees provides the most information on resistance. The seedling test is preferred over that of rooted cuttings of older parent trees which sometimes give anomalous results. The root dip testing of seedlings can identify differences in survival among families with qualitative resistance, as well as differences in time of mortality among families and the substantial within-in family variation in resistance when quantitative resistance is present (Sniezko 2004). In the POC program, these differences became much more apparent beginning with the 2005 testing, when the duration of the assessment period for the root dip test was expanded from less than a year to up to 3 years.

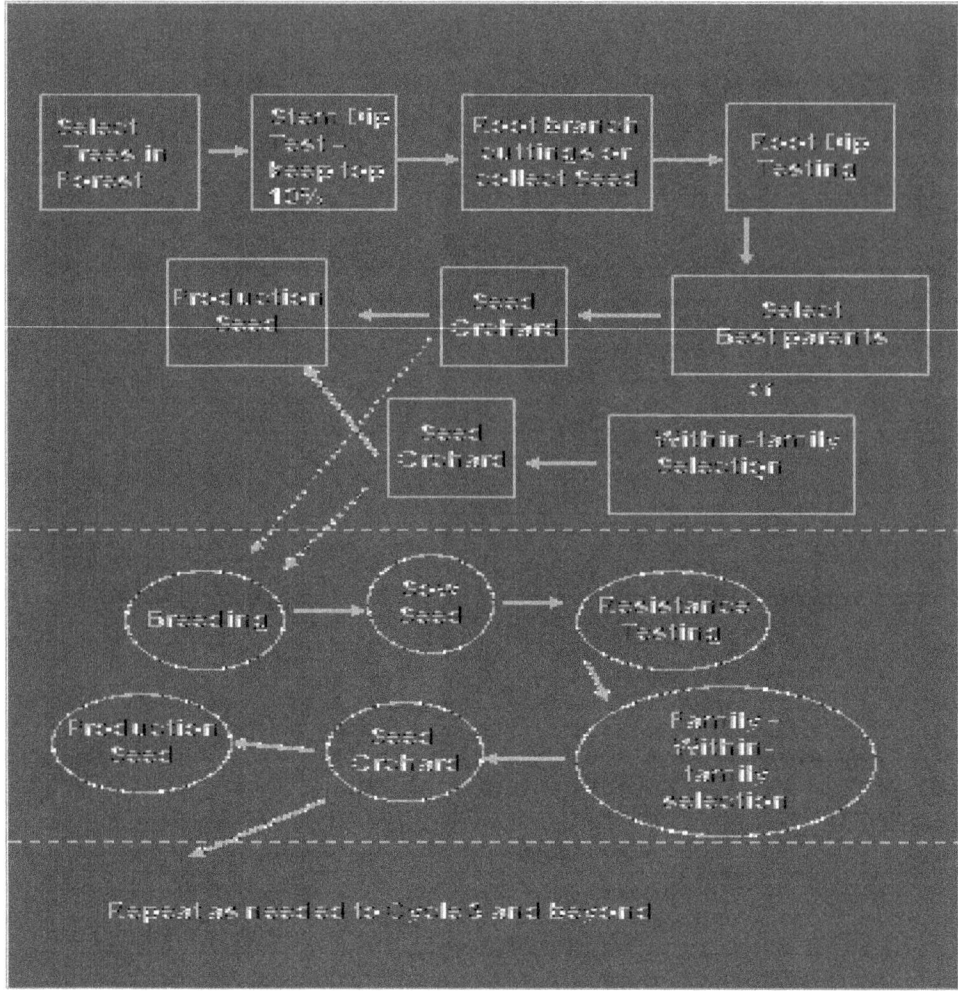

Figure 4—Selection and breeding cycles for developing *Phytophthora lateralis* resistant populations of Port-Orford-cedar for reforestation and restoration.

Both wind-pollinated (especially if collected from forest stands) and control-crossed families are used in the root dip testing. Many POC are somewhat self-fertile (Sniezko et al. 2003), and self-pollinated families have been used routinely for resistance testing in the last few years. In the short-term root dip test, families can vary in survival from 0 to 100 percent (fig. 5) (Sniezko 2004). One or more high-susceptible controls are normally included to provide a baseline to compare all families. The susceptible control families usually reach 100 percent mortality in 100 to 150 days after artificial inoculation (fig. 5). Current efforts are primarily focused on finishing the root dip resistance testing of the forest selections and adding these parents (or their progenies) to the orchards. Other efforts include increasing resistance through breeding, gaining further understanding of the types of resistance and their inheritance, and examining the level of genetic resistance present in wind-pollinated seedlots from the orchards.

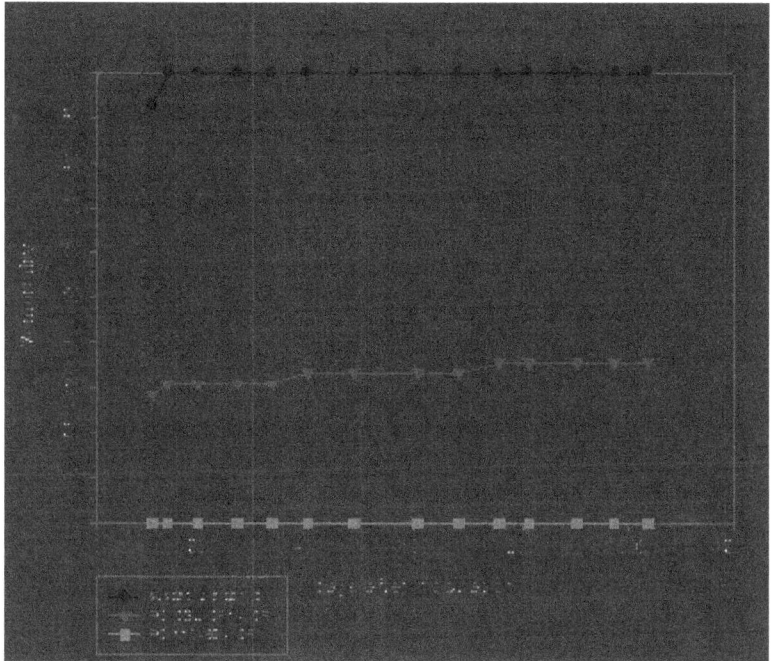

Figure 5—Percent mortality in root dip testing for a susceptible control Port-Orford-cedar family and two resistant families.

The greenhouse root dip test has provided a relatively quick assay to identify resistance in POC. In the root dip test, it appears that at least two types of resistance are present, a qualitative one that identifies some families with high survival (fig. 5) and a quantitative one in which there is often very wide variation within a family for the rate of progress of *P. lateralis* in reaching the root collar (Sniezko, unpublished data). Expansion of the assessment period of the root dip test in 2005 from approximately 9 months to up to 3 years more clearly identifies those families with qualitative resistance, quantitative resistance, or both. Families with each type of resistance are now under field test. Breeding to combine resistances is also underway.

Research on a small subset of resistant and susceptible families from the operational program was undertaken to examine the underlying nature of the resistance in POC Symptom development on resistant trees included cell wall thickening, cell collapse, and deposition of electron-dense materials around hyphae; all reactions consistent with a hypersensitive response in the host (Oh and Hansen 2007, Oh et al. 2006). Further work to discern the number of resistance mechanisms, their inheritance, the underlying nature of resistance, and its durability is warranted.

Durability of Resistance

Genetic variability within North American isolates of *P. lateralis* is small, likely due to a genetic bottleneck from the original introduction of this pathogen from elsewhere (Goheen et al. 2003), and this may bode well for durability of resistance. Recorded survival for a decade or more of many of the initial field selections in areas of high *P. lateralis*-caused mortality is encouraging (fig. 1e). These trees could serve as permanent plots to help monitor resistance. In addition to the root dip testing, short-term testing using raised beds infested with *P. lateralis* has been used to test resistance (Hansen et al., this proceedings). No change in efficacy of resistance is apparent in continued use of these raised beds for more than a decade (Sniezko, unpublished data). However, the relatively recent findings of *P. lateralis* in Europe (Sansford 2011) and Taiwan (Brasier et al. 2010, Webber et al. 2011) raise concerns about potential increased pathogenicity from new introductions or the evolutionary potential of current isolates. Testing the efficacy of POC resistance to these different isolates is planned.

Long-term field testing of a subset of the resistant selections is essential to assay resistance under a variety of field conditions as well as to continue to monitor durability of resistance. An extensive set of field trials have been established, and early results from the first ones are encouraging (Sniezko et al. 2006; Sniezko et al., Nine Year Survival of 16 *Phytophthora lateralis* resistant and susceptible Port-Orford-cedar families in a southern Oregon field trial, these proceedings). However, it is essential that these trials continue to be monitored to assess the efficacy and durability of resistance in long-lived POC.

Seed Orchards

Resistant seed can be collected from selected trees in the forest and from seed orchards. Seed orchards offer several potential advantages, including increased genetic resistance and relatively easy production of large quantities of resistant seed from a diverse array of parents. For POC, seedlings from wind-pollinated containerized seed orchards (CSOs) are the principal source of reproductive materials for reforestation and restoration (fig. 6). The biology of POC is very conducive to the use of CSOs for the production of large quantities of seed at an early age (Elliott and Sniezko 2000, Sniezko et al. 2003). Branches from resistant trees or tops clipped from 1-year-old resistant seedlings are used to produce rooted cuttings which are then placed in pots in a greenhouse orchard. The CSO technology for POC has allowed for a much shorter time interval between identification of resistant trees and operational production of seed. With the ability to induce seed cones and pollen cones, seed can be produced within 5 years of orchard establishment. For some breeding zones, resistant seed has been available since 2003. In addition, breeding POC to enhance resistance can be done within several years of identifying resistant trees. Seed orchards have been started for eight of the 13 breeding zones (table 1). In these orchards, rooted cuttings of resistant clones have been propagated

Figure 6—Containerized seed orchards at Dorena Genetic Resource Center: (a) seed orchard, (b) abundant cone production on orchard tree, (c) control pollinations. (Photo credits: Richard Sniezko)

and placed together by breeding zones in the greenhouses. The current number of parents per orchard varies from five to 115 (table 1). Ongoing priorities include screening more forest selections for potential inclusion into orchards for additional breeding zones and to increase the number of parent trees in existing orchards as well as to retest some of the early orchard selections to confirm their resistance. The utilization of containerized seed orchards allows for easy updating of orchards as resistance screening results become available. Rooted cuttings of many of the most resistant trees have also been used to establish a clone bank for long-term preservation (fig. 3).

Table 1—Number of *Phytophthora lateralis*-resistant Port-Orford-cedar parents in containerized seed orchards (CSOs) for eight breeding zones as of 2011

Breeding zone[a]	Number of parents
110	60
125	115
210	10
225	9
325	16
340	68
440	5
450	8

[a] See fig. 1 for delineation of 13 breeding zones; No CSOs for BZs 315, 350, 425, 545, 550.

The first-generation seed orchards are wind-pollinated and produce a genetically heterogeneous mix of seed with an intermediate level of resistance. A short-term greenhouse root dip trial, inoculated in 2004, of several orchard breeding zones, showed 30 percent or higher survival in many zones over woods-run seed (fig. 7) (Sniezko et al. 2005). Results from short-term tests like the greenhouse root dip test probably represent an upper limit to resistance from the current generation of orchards, and confirmation of the level under field conditions is needed. Field tests on sites of moderate to extreme disease hazard are essential to determine any limits on the use of resistance and the level of survival to be expected over time. Seedlots from several orchards have been included in recent field tests and results are pending. This field data will be essential information to guide activities of land managers interested in utilizing resistant POC. Early results from some of the first field trials using individual half-sib and full-sib families show encouraging results (Sniezko et al. 2006; Sniezko et al., Nine year survival of 16 *Phytophthora lateralis*-resistant and -susceptible Port-Orford-cedar families in a southern Oregon field trial, these proceedings), but as with any long-lived species, these trials need continued monitoring. Information on the disease hazard of sites would also be useful to managers planning on utilizing resistant POC. Until more field results are available, planting sites should be chosen carefully, avoiding the highest risk sites such as low-lying wet areas down slope from infested areas. The impact of changing climate on the spread of *P. lateralis* or the efficacy of resistance is unknown and warrants investigation. The level of genetic resistance in advanced-generation orchards should increase with breeding and subsequent testing and selection. The containerized orchards serve to meet seed needs for both the Forest Service and BLM. In addition, the Oregon Department of Forestry (ODF) has acquired resistant seed for its seed bank (Oregon Forest Tree Seed Bank) to serve the needs of other landowners. The ODF has filled requests for seed from nurseries and non-federal landowners from 2003 to 2011 (Larry Miller, Oregon Department of Forestry, personal communication). Over 3.85 kg of seed (385,000 to 452,000 seed per kg, approximately 60 percent filled seed) has been dispersed (table 2). Most of the seed need has been for the western most portions of Oregon (Breeding Zones 110 and 125, fig. 1; table 2).

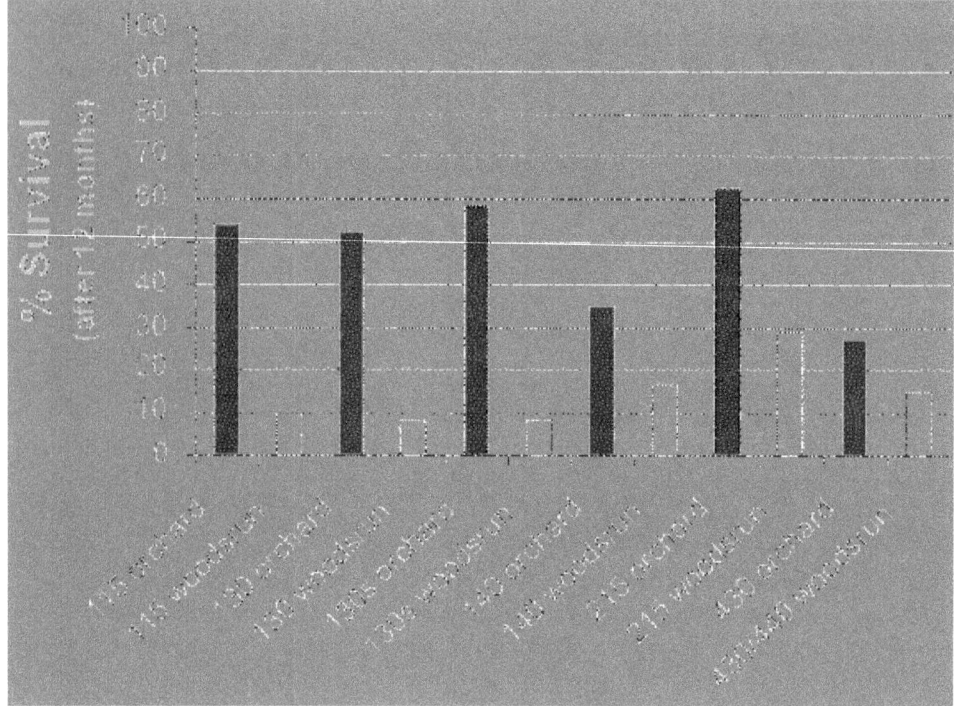

Figure 7—Port-Orford-cedar survival of orchard seedlings versus 'woodsrun' seedlings for five breeding zones (from 2000 zones) in a 2004 greenhouse root dip test for *Phytophthora lateralis* resistance.

Resistant seed is now being used by federal and non-federal land managers for reforestation and restoration (figs.8 and 9; table 2). Due to changing management practices on some federal lands, including reduced timber harvest, opportunities for using resistant POC seed in restoration and reforestation are now more limited, and the use of the highest level of resistance possible would aid efforts to retain POC in ecosystems while allowing resistance genes to spread as trees reach reproductive age. On USFS and BLM lands, plantings are often in areas that have been burned by wildfires (USDA FS 2010). Plantings on non-federal lands will facilitate more diversely managed forests, while also setting up opportunities via natural pollen and seed dispersal for increasing the spread of resistance genes to adjacent USFS or BLM lands. Increasing the frequency of genetic resistance over the landscape will help ensure that POC remains a viable component in forest ecosystems impacted by *P. lateralis*.

With the discovery of a number of POC parent trees with resistance to *P. lateralis*, there is revived interest in POC in the horticultural sector. The only option currently available, and limited in use, is grafting established cultivars onto the one resistant parent that has been made available for this purpose. However, the resistance screening of parent trees and their progenies from throughout the range of POC and crosses among them offers additional possibilities. In order to meet the different objectives for horticulture, materials should be carefully evaluated for the range of usage anticipated.

Figure 8—Volunteers from several community groups and a USDA Forest Service biologist planting 900 Port-Orford-cedar (POC) along Grayback Creek in southern Oregon in 2008. This planting project will help restore a riparian area used by salmon and steelhead and also serve as a test of resistant *P. lateralis*-resistant POC. (Photo credit: Scott Kolpak)

Figure 9—Port-Orford-cedar technical committee visiting 2011 planting of resistant POC along trail at South Slough National Estuarine Research Reserve in western Oregon. (Photo credit: Richard Sniezko)

Table 2—Seed (grams) requested by non-federal landowners[a]

| Year | Breeding Zones[b] | | | | | | | Total |
	110	115	125	130	210	215	430	
2003	-	172	-	-	-	-	-	172
2004	-	340	-	-	-	-	-	340
2005	-	458	-	254	-	-	-	712
2006	-	481	-	-	-	-	73	554
2007	-	503	-	-	-	50	-	553
2008	-	-	-	-	45	-	-	45
2009	68	-	340	-	-	-	-	408
2010	-	-	340	-	-	-	-	340
2011	386	-	340	-	-	-	-	726
Total	454	1954	1020	254	45	50	73	3,850

[a] Data provided by Larry Miller, Oregon Department of Forestry.

[b] Breeding zones were reduced and reorganized in 2005 (see fig. 1 for current zones).

Other Possible Future Activities

If funding permits, other components of the program could be refined:

(1) The seedling assay is currently the most favored, but it can take several years to fully distinguish the different types of resistance. The development of chemical biomarkers or genomic tools for selecting for resistance would help increase our understanding of resistance and its genetic control.

(2) The recent development of microsatellite markers for POC has allowed a start on further investigation of genetic variation patterns across the range of the species. This work will complement previous isozyme and common garden studies and help demarcate potential additional areas for gene conservation.

(3) Research is needed to understand the evolutionary potential of *P. lateralis* and its potential impact on durability of resistance in POC. Investigations into the genetics and pathogenicity of isolates of *P. lateralis* from outside North America will expand our knowledge base.

(4) More work is needed to understand the limits to resistance in POC, particularly mortality and any fall down in resistance on the sites of highest risk: wet, low-lying areas.

Summary

Genetic variation within a species is the key to helping it evolve and adapt to changes in its environment, even to an unexpected threat such as a non-native pathogen. In an extreme case, such as the one that occurred with Port-Orford-cedar and the introduction of *P. lateralis*, humans can help re-establish a more balanced ecological equilibrium through active measures such as a resistance selection program. Such a program harnesses natural genetic variation within POC and would not have the negative side effects that other management activities could have. The program to develop *P. lateralis* resistance in POC has made significant progress in a relatively short period of time. Aspects of the program have involved not only USFS, BLM, and OSU, but also a wide array of other land managers. It is one of few operational resistance programs to non-native pathogens to produce significant levels of seed for potential restoration and reforestation. A large number of field selections have undergone the first rounds of resistance testing, breeding zones and a large genetic base has been established, seed orchard establishment is well underway, protocols for short-term resistance testing have been refined, field trials are underway, and the planting of resistant seedlings has started. Future efforts will focus on completing the development of first-cycle orchards, breeding to increase resistance and monitoring field trials for efficacy and durability of resistance. Genetic resistance is an invaluable tool to complement other management activities that prevent or reduce the spread of *P. lateralis*.

Acknowledgments

We thank Leslie Elliott, Scott Kolpak, Heather May, Sunny Lucas, Pete Angwin, Katy Mallams, Don Goheen, Kirk Casavan, Rod Stevens, Frank Betlejewski, Joe Linn, Clinton Armstrong, Paul Reeser, Wendy Sutton, the nursery crew at Dorena GRC, and the many others for their key roles in the operational elements of the resistance program. Stable funding and key personnel support from both USFS and BLM have been key in the program development. We also thank all of the other governmental, industrial, and private landowners who have supported the program; and Pete Angwin, Steve Lee, Sunny Lucas, Larry Miller, and Greg Filip for their reviews of an earlier version of this paper.

Literature Cited

Betlejewski, F.; Goheen, D.; Angwin, P.; Sniezko, R. 2011. Port-Orford-cedar root disease. Forest insect and disease leaflet 131. Portland, OR: U.S. Department of Agriculture, Forest Service, Pacific Northwest Region. 12 p. http://www.fs.usda.gov/Internet/FSE_DOCUMENTS/stelprdb5346825.pdf. (17 January 2012).

Brasier, C.M.; Vettraino, A.M.; Chang, T.T.; Vannini, A. 2010. *P. lateralis* discovered in an old growth *Chamaecyparis* forest in Taiwan. Plant Pathology. 59: 595–603.

Casavan, K.C.; White, D.E.; Goheen, D.J.; Rose, D.L. 2003. Impacts of *Phytophthora lateralis* on Port-Orford-cedar. In: Betlejewski, F.; Casavan, K.C.; Dawson, A.; et al., eds. A range-wide assessment of Port-Orford-cedar (*Chamaecyparis lawsoniana)* on federal lands. BLM/OR/WA/PL-004/004-1792. Portland, OR: U.S. Department of Agriculture, Forest Service and U.S. Department of Interior, Bureau of Land Management: 47–60. http://www.fs.fed.us/r6/rogue-siskiyou/projects/foresthealth/poc/poc-range-wide-assess.pdf. (31 December 2011).

DeNitto, G.; Kliejunas, J.T. 1991. First report of *Phytophthora lateralis* in pacific yew (Abstract). Plant Disease. 75: 968.

Elliott, L.; Sniezko, R.A. 2000. Cone and seed production in a Port-Orford-cedar containerized orchard. In: Hansen, E.; Sutton, W., eds. Proceedings of the first international meeting on *Phytophthoras* in forest and wildland ecosystems (IUFRO Working Party 7.02.09). Corvallis, OR: Oregon State University: 105–106. http://www.iufro.org/download/file/5442/4591/70209-grantspass99_pdf/. (31 December 2011).

Food and Agriculture Organization [FAO]. 2008. Selection and breeding for insect and disease resistance. http://www.fao.org/forestry/26445. (30 December 2011).

Goheen, D.J; McWilliams, M.G.; Angwin, P.A.; Rose, D.L. 2003. *Phytophthora lateralis* and other agents that damage Port-Orford-cedar. In: Betlejewski, F.; Casavan, K.C.; Dawson, A.; et al., eds. A range-wide assessment of Port-Orford-cedar (*Chamaecyparis lawsoniana)* on federal lands. BLM/OR/WA/PL-004/004-1792. Portland, OR: U.S. Department of Agriculture, Forest Service and U.S. Department of Interior, Bureau of Land Management: 33-45. http://www.fs.fed.us/r6/rogue-siskiyou/projects/foresthealth/poc/poc-range-wide-assess.pdf. (31 December 2011).

Hansen, E.M.; Hamm, P.B.; Roth, L.F. 1989. Testing Port-Orford cedar for resistance to *Phytophthora*. Plant Disease. 73: 791–794.

Kitzmiller, J.H. 2006. Range-wide genetic variation in Port-Orford-cedar (*Chamaecyparis lawsoniana*) [A. Murr.] Parl.) III: Survival and growth in coastal and inland field test plantations. Journal of Sustainable Forestry. 23(3): 1–46.

Kitzmiller, J.; Sniezko, R.A.; Hamlin, J.E.; Stevens, R.D.; Casavan, K.C. 2003. Genetics of Port-Orford-cedar. In: Betlejewski, F.; Casavan, K.C.; Dawson, A.; et al., eds. A range-wide assessment of Port-Orford-cedar (*Chamaecyparis lawsoniana)* on federal lands. OR/WA/PL-004/004-1792: 61-74. Portland, OR. U.S. Department of Agriculture, Forest Service and U.S. Department of Interior, Bureau of Land Management. http://www.fs.fed.us/r6/rogue-siskiyou/projects/foresthealth/poc/poc-range-wide-assess.pdf. (31 December 2011).

Linhart, Y.B. 1995. Restoration, revegetation, and the importance of genetic and evolutionary perspectives. In: Roundy, Bruce A.; McArthur, E. Durant; Haley, Jennifer S.; Mann, David K., comps. Proceedings: Wildland shrub and arid land restoration symposium. Gen. Tech. Rep. INT-GTR-315. Ogden, UT: U.S.

Department of Agriculture, Forest Service, Intermountain Research Station: 271–287. http://www fs.fed.us/rm/pubs_int/int_gtr315/int_gtr315_271_287.pdf. (31 December 2011).

Oh, E.; Hansen, E.M. 2007. Histopathology of infection and colonization of Port-Orford-cedar by *Phytophthora lateralis*. Phytopathology. 97: 684–693.

Oh, E.; Hansen, E.M.; Sniezko, R.A. 2006. Port-Orford-cedar resistant to *Phytophthora lateralis.* Forest Pathology. 36: 385–394.

Robin, C.; Piou, D.; Feau, N.; Douzon, G.; Schenck, N.; Hansen, E.M. 2011. Root and aerial infections of *Chamaecyparis lawsoniana* by *Phytophthora lateralis*: a new threat for European countries. Forest Pathology. 41 (5): 417–424.

Sansford, C. 2011. A serious threat to Lawson's cypress (*Chamaecyparis lawsoniana*): *Phytophthora lateralis*. Plant disease fact sheet. Sand Hutton, York: The Food and Environment Research Agency. http://www fera.defra.gov.uk/plants/publications/documents/factsheets/phytophthoraLateralis.pdf. (19 December 2011).

Sniezko, R.A. 2004. Genetic resistance in Port-Orford-cedar to the non-native root rot pathogen *Phytophthora lateralis*: 2003 update. In: Geils, B.W., comp. Proceedings of the 51st Western International Forest Disease Work Conference. Flagstaff, AZ: U.S. Department of Agriculture, Forest Service, Rocky Mountain Research Station: 127–131. http://www fs.fed.us/foresthealth/technology/wif/proceedings/WIFDWC2003.pdf. (31 December 2011).

Sniezko, R.A. 2006. Resistance breeding against nonnative pathogens in forest trees — current successes in North America. Canadian Journal of Plant Pathology. 28: S270–S279.

Sniezko, R.A.; Hansen, E. 2000. Screening and breeding program for genetic resistance to *Phytophthora lateralis* in Port-Orford-cedar (*Chamaecyparis lawsoniana*): early results. In: Hansen, E.; Sutton, W., eds. Proceedings of the first international meeting on *Phytophthoras* in forest and wildland ecosystems (IUFRO Working Party 7.02.09). Corvallis, OR: Oregon State University: 91–94. http://www.iufro.org/download/file/5442/4591/70209-grantspass99_pdf/ (31 December 2011).

Sniezko, R.A.; Hansen, E. 2003. Breeding Port-Orford-cedar for resistance to *Phytophthora lateralis*: current status & considerations for developing durable resistance. In: McComb, J.A.; Hardy, G.E.; Tommerup, I.C., eds. Proceedings: *Phytophthora* in forests and natural ecosystems: second international IUFRO working party 7.02.09 Meeting., Murdoch, WA, Australia: Murdoch University Print: 197–201.

Sniezko, R.A.; Kitzmiller, J.; Elliott, L.J.; Hamlin, J.E. 2003. Breeding for resistance to *Phytophthora lateralis*. In: Betlejewski, F.; Casavan, K.C.; Dawson, A.; et al., eds. A range-wide assessment of Port-Orford-cedar (*Chamaecyparis lawsoniana)* on federal lands. . BLM/OR/WA/PL-004/004-1792. Portland, OR: U.S. Department of Agriculture, Forest Service and U.S. Department of Interior, Bureau of Land Management: 75–89. http://www fs.fed.us/r6/rogue-siskiyou/projects/foresthealth/poc/poc-range-wide-assess.pdf. (31 December 2011).

Sniezko, R.A.; Kolpak, S.E.; Hansen, E.M.; Goheen, D.J.; Elliott, L.J.; Angwin, P.A. 2006. Field survival of *Phytophthora lateralis* resistant and susceptible Port-Orford-cedar families. In: Brasier, C.; Jung, T.; Osswald, W., eds. Progress in research on *Phytophthora* diseases of forest trees: Proceedings of the third international IUFRO working party S07.02.09. Farnham, UK: Forest Research: 104–108.

Sniezko, R.A.; Mylecraine, K.; Kolpak, S.; Reeser, P.; Hansen, E. 2005. Genetic resistance in Port-Orford-cedar to *Phytophthora lateralis*: survival of seedlings from first orchard seed in greenhouse testing. In: Guyon, J.C., comp. 2006. Proceedings of the 53rd Western International Forest Disease Work Conference. Ogden, UT; U.S. Department of Agriculture, Forest Service, Intermountain Region: 158. http://www fs fed.us/foresthealth/technology/wif/proceedings/wifdwc2005.pdf. (31 December 2011).

U.S. Department of Agriculture, Forest Service [USDA FS]. 2004. Record of decision and land and resource management plan amendment for management of Port-Orford-cedar in southwest Oregon, Siskiyou National Forest. Medford, OR: Rogue River-Siskiyou National Forest. 62 p. http://www fs.usda.gov/Internet/FSE_DOCUMENTS/stelprdb5316520.pdf. (31 December 2011).

U.S. Department of Agriculture, Forest Service [USDA FS]. 2006. Managing for healthy Port-Orford-cedar in the Pacific Southwest Region. 19 p. www.fs.usda.gov/Internet/FSE_DOCUMENTS/stelprdb5332563.pdf. (21 January 2012).

U.S. Department of Agriculture, Forest Service [USDA FS]. 2010. Reforesting burned areas with Port-Orford-cedar using genetically resistant planting stock in post-fire reforestation efforts. 1p. http://www.fs.fed.us/r5/spf/fhp/wbbi/POC%20Success%20story%202010--Siskiyou%20Fire%20Reforestation.pdf. (20 January 2012).

U.S. Department of Agriculture, Forest Service; U.S. Department of Interior, Bureau of Land Management [USDA FS and USDI BLM]. 2003. A Range-wide assessment of Port-Orford-Cedar (*Chamaecyparis lawsoniana*) on federal lands. Portland, OR: BLM Oregon/Washington State Office. 182 p. http://www.fs.usda.gov/Internet/FSE_DOCUMENTS/stelprdb5316517.pdf . (31 December 2011).

U.S. Department of Agriculture, Forest Service; U.S. Department of Interior, Bureau of Land Management [USDA FS and USDI BLM]. 2004. Final supplemental environmental impact statement – Management of Port-Orford-cedar in southwest Oregon. Portland. OR. 485p. http://www.fs.usda.gov/detail/rogue-siskiyou/landmanagement/resourcemanagement/?cid=stelprdb5316256. (31 December 2011).

U.S. Department of Interior, Bureau of Land Management [USDI BLM]. 2004. Record of decision and land and resource management plan amendment for management of Port-Orford-cedar in southwest Oregon, Coos Bay, Medford, and Roseburg Districts. Portland, OR: BLM: 64 p. http://www.fs.usda.gov/Internet/FSE_DOCUMENTS/stelprdb5316518.pdf. (31 December 2011).

Webber, J.F.; Vettraino, A.M.; Chang, T.T.; Bellgard, S.; Brasier, C.M.; Vannini, A. 2011. Isolation of *Phytophthora lateralis* from *Chamaecyparis* foliage in Taiwan. Forest Pathology. doi: 10.1111/j.1439-0329.2011.00729.x.

Zobel, D.B.; Roth, L.F.; Hawk, G.M. 1985. Ecology, pathology, and management of Port-Orford-cedar (*Chamaecyparis lawsoniana*). Gen. Tech. Rep. PNW-184. Portland, OR; U.S. Department of Agriculture, Forest Service, Pacific Northwest Forest and Range Experiment Station. 161 p. http://www.fs.fed.us/pnw/pubs/pnw_gtr184.pdf. (31 December 2011).

Strong Partial Resistance to White Pine Blister Rust in Sugar Pine

Bohun B. Kinloch, Jr.,[1] Deems Burton,[2] Dean A. Davis,[2] Robert D. Westfall,[3] Joan Dunlap,[4] and Detlev Vogler[1]

Abstract

Quantitative resistance to white pine blister rust in 128 controlled- and open-pollinated sugar pine families was evaluated in a "disease garden", where alternate host *Ribes* bushes were interplanted among test progenies. Overall infection was severe (88%), but with great variation among and within families: a 30-fold range in numbers of infections per tree, and a 10- fold range in trees with completely inactive, or aborted infections. Inheritance of these partial resistances was strong, with significant amounts of both additive and non-additive genetic variance evident. They will be most useful in combination with major gene resistance (MGR) by reducing the probability of infections virulent to MGR.

Key words: *Cronartium ribicola*, *Pinus lambertiana*, partial resistance

Introduction

Sugar pine (*Pinus lambertiana* Dougl.), one of the most susceptible of white pines to white pine blister rust (*Cronartium ribicola*), has a major gene (*Cr1*) that confers virtual immunity to the disease, but is vulnerable to specific virulence from a complementary gene (*vcr1*) in the pathogen. Partial resistance (PR; also known as slow rusting, SR) is a suite of traits that reduces the amount and rate of infection through lowered receptivity to infection and incompatibility reactions in the host when infections do occur. Partial resistance has been shown to be effective and durable to blister rust in white pines (King et al. 2010, Kinloch et al. 2008). Combining the two types of resistance in synthetic lines could be mutually reinforcing by sanitizing all inoculum lacking *vcr1* with *Cr1* and by reducing the probability of infection by *vcr1* with PR.

Methods

To assess the degree and inheritance of PR, 128 sugar pine progenies with different pedigrees were exposed to the pathogen in a plantation at Happy Camp (HC) in northern California. Happy Camp has been used since 1958 as the principal site for breeding, testing, and evaluating sugar pine and other white pines by the Genetic Resources Unit of the Pacific Southwest Region, USDA Forest Service, with the objective of developing durable resistance to blister rust. Here, resistant parent selections were grafted in a clone bank and interbred when reproductively mature, and different cohorts of test progenies established every year. Seedlings are naturally challenged by blister rust inoculum (enhanced by interplanting alternate host *Ribes* sp. among pines in the test plots). Surviving seedlings are allowed to remain in place indefinitely, and many reach reproductive maturity. Although many parent trees were known to carry *Cr1*, this gene was effectively neutralized by the overwhelming prevalence of *vcr1* inoculum on the site, allowing other kinds of resistance to express.

Test progenies consisted of four main groups: 1) a full-sib and half-sib matrix of 75 families controlled-pollinated (CP) among select parents; 2) 14 families of the same select parents that were wind or open-pollinated (OP) by the ambient pollen cloud on the site (_xW(HC)); 3) 33 families from

[1] Institute of Forest Genetics, Pacific Southwest Research Station, Albany, CA and Placerville, CA.
[2] Genetics Resource Unit, USDA FS Pacific Southwest Region, Klamath National Forest, Yreka, CA.
[3] USDA FS Pacific Southwest Research Station, Albany, CA.
[4] Genetics Resource Unit, USDA FS Pacific Southwest Region, Camino, CA.
Corresponding author: bkinloch@earthlink.net.

cone bearing parents of uncertain genotype that had survived the chronic epidemic at HC, also pollinated from pollen on site (?xW(HC); and 4) four multi-tree seed lots, each mixed and bulked from four different natural stands.

The full- and half-sib group was made from parents a) known from previous experience to transmit relatively high resistance (SR) or susceptibility (fast rusting, FR) to their offspring; b) F1s of some of the selects; and c) F1s of other trees on the site of unknown or uncertain resistance genotypes that had survived many years of the chronic epidemic. Controlled crosses were made among the 16 parents in this group in all available combinations, emphasizing known SR x SR, SR x FR, and FR x FR genotypes (see tables 1 and 2).A mixed general linear model (GLM) was used to account for repeated measurement of families. The SAS (v. 9.2) MIXED procedure was used to perform paired t-tests with the Satterthwaite adjusted degrees of freedom and the Bonferroni's level of significance adjustment.

All parents were SR phenotypes, by virtue of identified characteristics or survival under chronic high-hazard exposure to the disease. This included two that were known to produce highly susceptible (FR) offspring (i.e., were FR genotypes, though SR phenotypes). Because crowns damaged by rust rarely bear cones, adequate numbers of FR phenotypes are difficult to find.

We hoped to make enough crosses for a balanced partial diallel, but this goal was frustrated because of sugar pine's notoriously erratic reproductive behavior. Many crosses were not successful, resulting in a severely unbalanced mating design. The shortage of susceptible control genotypes was particularly conspicuous. Nevertheless, we were able to extract two factorials of unrelated seed and pollen parents from the matrix of crosses to make estimates of additive and non-additive variances.

We expected that F1 parents would generally transmit the greatest amount of SR to offspring, followed by SR parent (P1) selects. We also expected on-site pollen to have a major effect. Since this pollen derived overwhelmingly from both select SR and other parents surviving the chronic epidemic, we presumed it would carry strong resistance, especially if additive genetic variance is predominant. In effect, it would simulate pollen in a seed orchard of inter-pollinating selected parents, and allow estimates of realized heritability. Thus, we expected the open-pollinated progenies from the select SR parents would perform well; less than resistant selects, but probably somewhat better than the other 33 open-pollinated seed parents. We expected the FR crosses to depress expression of SR and we assumed the bulked seed lots would represent average susceptibility in the wild population.

Table 1—Mean number of infections per tree on sugar pine families

A) Controlled- and wind-pollinated families:

Seed	K71	K86	K44	K23	K33	K72	K14	K36	K71 x K73	K86 x K44	K71 x K44	K70 x K43	K87 x K19	K36 x K73	K16 x K17	K36 x K17	x W (HC)
K71		2.2	1.5			1.6	3.3			1.0			2.1	2.8	2.5		2.0
K86	1.2		1.3	2.4	1.1	1.7		3.2	1.7		1.1		1.0	2.0	1.2		2.2
K44																	2.0
K23	2.7				2.1												3.3
K33	2.2	1.7							2.6	1.0		1.4	2.6				4.9
K72										1.1							2.8
K14	3.6	3.3	4.1	5.9		6.1		11.8		3.1			5.4	10.2		10.2	7.2*
K36		2.7	3.9							2.8							6.3
K71 x K73	1.6	3.4				3.2		5.4									3.3
K70 x K43		1.4		1.4			2.7	3.6	4.3	0.4				2.8			2.2
K87 x K19	3.8		1.2					5.4	2.3	1.0							3.2
K36 x K73			3.3			3.0		8.3					4.2				6.1
K16 x K17				3.3	1.6			2.8		0.7	2.2	1.5	1.5	4.2			3.0
K36 x K17		2.8	2.8						5.5	1.7							4.5
Parent mean[1]	**2.3**	**2.0**	**2.7**	**2.7**	**1.7**	**3.1**	**5.8**	**5.0**	**3.3**	**1.4**	**1.6**	**1.9**	**2.7**	**4.5**	**2.2**	**4.6**	**3.5**

Half-sib mean:　3.0

Full-sib range:　0.4 - 11.8

Half-sib parent mean/W(HC) mean　r$_p$ = 0.82

x W (wild stand)

B) Group means:

	No. families in type	Seed	Pollen	Mean	Range		Rank Obs.	Rank Exp.
SR select parent	12			**1.8**	1.1	2.7	2	5
F_1 of SR select parent	9			**1.9**	1.0	3.4	3	2
F_1 survivor	20			**2.3**	1.0	3.8	5	4
FR select parent	9			**4.0**	2.7	6.1	8	8
	0			-	-	-	-	1
	8			**2.2**	0.4	5.5	4	3
	3			**3.7**	2.8	5.4	7	7
	5			**2.8**	1.5	4.2	6	6
	8			**6.1**	2.7	11.1	9	9
	1			**11.8**	-	-	**10**	10
	75			4.06			$r_p =$	0.90
	33	?	x W (HC)	5.00	2.1	10.5		
	4	Bulked mix	x W (wild)	4.79	4.2	5.6		

† includes both seed and pollen entries.

Table 2—Percent of sugar pine families with no active infections from blister rust

A) Controlled- and wind-pollinated families:

Parents:

Seed	K71	K86	K44	K23	K33	K72	K14	K36	K71 x K73	K86 x K44	K71 x K44	K70 x K43	K87 x K19	K36 x K73	K16 x K17	K36 x K17	x W (HC)
K71		41.4	54.7			35.7	17.8			73.0				44.4	30.7	28.0		23.6
K86	55.3		37.5	36.2	51.4	34.1		16.7	37.8		67.1		32.8	40.0	43.5		21.4
K44																		31.0
K23	27.0				15.8					52.1			20.6				7.7
K33	24.1	38.1							25.4	44.1		29.0					16.3
K72																	20.5
K14	26.8	16.2	9.6	8.2		6.9		0.0		23.5			12.9	0.7		1.4	6.56*
K36		20.6	13.5							41.5							14.3
K71 x K73	50.7		4.4			9.6		13.6									20.0
K70 x K43				34.0			10.5	22.0		73.2				23.5			22.4
K87 x K19			42.4					2.9	16.0	58.7							17.0
K36 x K73	20.3		17.8					6.1					8.7				7.0
K16 x K17		45.2		15.2		25.0		14.1	23.4	64.4	46.6	26.9	29.6	10.8			18.2
K36 x K17		20.3	18.1	21.3					20.0	30.8							5.1
Parent Mean[1]	37.8	36.0	24.7	26.1	31.1	22.2	11.2	15.1	22.3	51.2	56.9	32.0	26.9	17.1	30.3	18.1	16.5

Half-sib mean: 28.70

Full-sib range: 0 - 73

C-P parent mean : x W(HC) mean : $r_p =$ 0.60

* x W (wild)

B) Group means:

Legend:

	SR select parent
	F$_1$ of SR select parent
	F$_1$ survivor
	FR select parent

No. families in type	Seed	Pollen	Mean	Range	Rank Obs.	Rank Exp.
12			37.6	16 - 55	4	5
9			40.5	4 - 73	3	2
20			28.9	13 - 45	5	4
9			15.1	8 - 27	8	8
0			-	-	-	1
8			41.6	16 - 46	2	3
3			26.2	14 - 42	6	7
5			19.9	9 - 30	7	6
8			8.8	1 - 22	9	9
1			0.0	-	10	10
75			24.3		r_p =	0.95
33	?	x W (HC)	11.90	2 - 25		
4 bulk lots	Bulked mix	x W (wild)	7.7	3 - 11		

[7] includes both row and column entries

85

Progenies were established in 2006 with an average of 57 trees each in single-tree plots in 75 blocks. In all, 7,545 trees in 128 controlled- or open-pollinated families were planted and evaluated. Disease was assessed in 2010 and 2011, after overall infection was nearly complete on susceptible controls. Separate infections were counted on each seedling in 2010, usually in their incipient stages (fig. 1A), and determined to be either typical (normal) for the disease or reactive. Reactions were of two main kinds. The first, bark reactions (BRs), caused infections to abort or 'cork out' (Struckmeyer and Riker 1951), leaving a necrotic scar beneath and surrounding the infection site (fig. 1B). BRs ranged in size from "micro-" necrotic lesions surrounding the base of the infection court of the short shoot to lesions many cm long. The other reaction was a blighting (BL) of the infected shoot, from the point of infection distal to the end of the shoot (fig. 1C). Both reactions often occur on the same tree, and reactions of both types often expressed only partially: death and collapse of most diseased tissue, but with some activity remaining on the margins of the lesion (see Kinloch and Davis 1996 for further details). Trees with typical infections, or those with incomplete reactions, were classed as normal/susceptible; trees with BRs, BLs, or both were classed as reactive, but only if disease symptoms were in complete remission and the tree had no active infections (NAI).

Results

The epidemic started early, with 3 successive wave years from 2007 to 2009. By spring 2011, 88 percent of all trees were infected and 9 percent were dead from rust. Individual families ranged from 44 to 100 percent infected and 0 to 51 percent dead.

The most useful indexes of resistance were low receptivity to infection (LRI), measured by numbers of separate infections on individual trees, and the percent of trees in individual families with no active infections (percent NAI). Mean number of infections for all families (CP and OP) was 3.7 and ranged from 0.39 to 11.80. Within families, there was great variability among trees, many having no infections and ranging as high as 92. For percent NAI, the mean of all families was 22.1, and ranged from 0.0 to 81.1. Correlation between the two indexes was -0.71.

Tables 1A and 2A summarize data for numbers of infections and percent NAI, respectively, for the matrix of individual full-sib families of select parents; half-sib means of select parents; and select xW(HC) means. Part B of tables 1 and 2 compare families grouped according to parental generation (P1, F1) or parental genotype (SR, FR) with each other, and with the 33 families that were open-pollinated from the ambient pollen cloud at HC (♀xW(HC)), and the four seed lots bulked from wild stands.

Figure 1—Reactions of sugar pine seedlings to infection by blister rust. A) Typical incipient infections, susceptible phenotype; note pink discolorations, swelling at base of short shoots; four separate infections are visible, but will soon coalesce. B) Micro bark reactions on slow rusting (SR) phenotype. About 10 are visible. C) Blight reactions on SR phenotype resulting from several separate infections.

For both indexes the general ranking of the four main group means, from most resistant to most susceptible, was: the CP matrix of full/half-sib select parents > OP select parents > OP non-select parent survivors > OP bulk seed lots from wild stands. None of OP family group means were significantly different from one another (figs. 2 and 3).

The greatest variation was among individual full-sib families, which ranged (resistant to susceptible) from 0.39 to 11.8 infections/tree and from 73.0 to 0.0 percent NAI. Half-sib family means from P1 and F1 selects ranged from 1.4 to 5.8 infections/tree, and from 56.9 to 11.2 percent NAI. The 14 families from open-pollination of the P1 and F1 parents ranged from 2.0 to 7.2 infections/tree, and 31.0 to 5.1 percent NAI. Correlations between these OP families and their CP counterparts were 0.82 for infections/tree and 0.60 for percent NAI.

The nine full-sib family groups generally ranked as expected, with correlations between observed and expected values of 0.90 and 0.95 for numbers of infections and percent NAI, respectively (tables 1B and 2B). Half-sib means varied greatly, with strong resistance from families with parents K86 and/or K44 in their pedigrees, and the greatest from the F1 (K86xK44). But this performance was not always consistent; for example, K44, as pollen parent, performed relatively poorly with another F1 select (K71xK73; table 2). None of the groups was statistically different from others, with the sole exception of the single FR x FR family (K14xK36), which was significantly more susceptible than all other groups (figs. 4 and 5). The negative influence of the FR parents was pervasive: groups with FR, taken as a whole (coded red, figs. 4 and 5), were significantly different from groups lacking FR (coded black, figs. 4 and 5).

Discussion

For a species so generally susceptible to an introduced disease, sugar pines show remarkable variability in resistance to blister rust: a 30-fold range in mean numbers of infections among full-sib families, and a ten-fold range in percent of trees with no active infections (tables 1 and 2). The modest correlation (-0.71) between the two indexes indicates that they can be selected for separately or simultaneously for development of stable resistance.

Although the expression and underlying causes are different, both mechanisms are highly effective, either in reducing the probability of infection occurring (LRI) or the probability of an infection becoming lethal (percent NAI). Both are strongly inherited; several of the best select parents in this test have shown consistent performance in several previous trials (Kinloch and Davis 1996, Kinloch et al. 2008). Still, modes of inheritance remain unclear. From the two factorials, we estimated additive effects to consist of 78 and 58 percent of the total genetic variance in LRI and percent NAI, respectively, but both estimates have large standard errors of the estimated means. In a related pathosystem, Isik et al. (2003) estimated that epistatic effects were nearly equal to additive effects for resistance to fusiform rust in loblolly pine, and we have observed that certain sugar pine parents (e.g., K71, K36) sometimes exhibit specific rather than general combining abilities to blister rust resistance (Kinloch and Davis 1996, Kinloch et al. 2008). Although most quantitative genetic traits are additive, partial resistance to disease can be controlled by specific interactions with pathogens (Krenz et al. 2008) or even gene-for-gene interactions (Antonovics et al. 2011).

The lack of a stronger effect of on-site pollen (_xW(HC)) on progeny performance was contrary to expectations, implying that pollen from the ambient cloud at HC does not carry particularly strong or abundant genes for SR that combine additively. Neither of the two open-pollinated groups, select xW(HC) or ? xW(HC), were significantly different from controls represented by the four bulk seed lots from natural stands or from each other (figs. 2 and 3). Seed parents of the ? xW(HC) group, on the other hand, showed wide variation in resistance (tables 1B and 2B). Taken together, the data suggests that both additive and non-additive effects are important in controlling resistance.

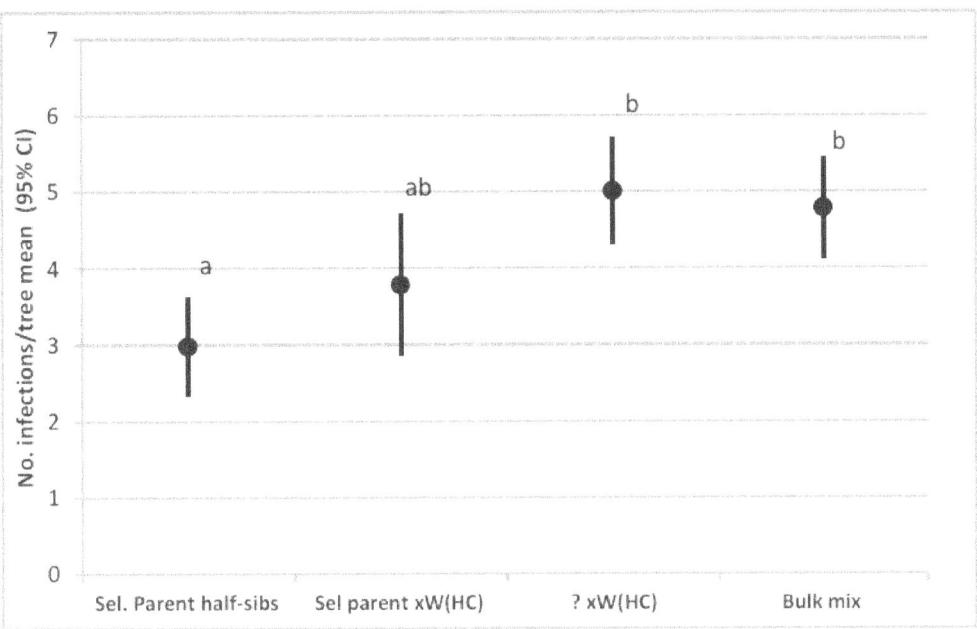

Figure 2—Means and 95 percent confidence intervals for numbers of infections/family in four main open-pollinated groups of sugar pine progenies. Groups with the same letter are not statistically different; the six pairwise comparisons were tested using a Bonferoni's adjusted-a=.05/60.0082to attain an experimentwise error rate a=0.05.

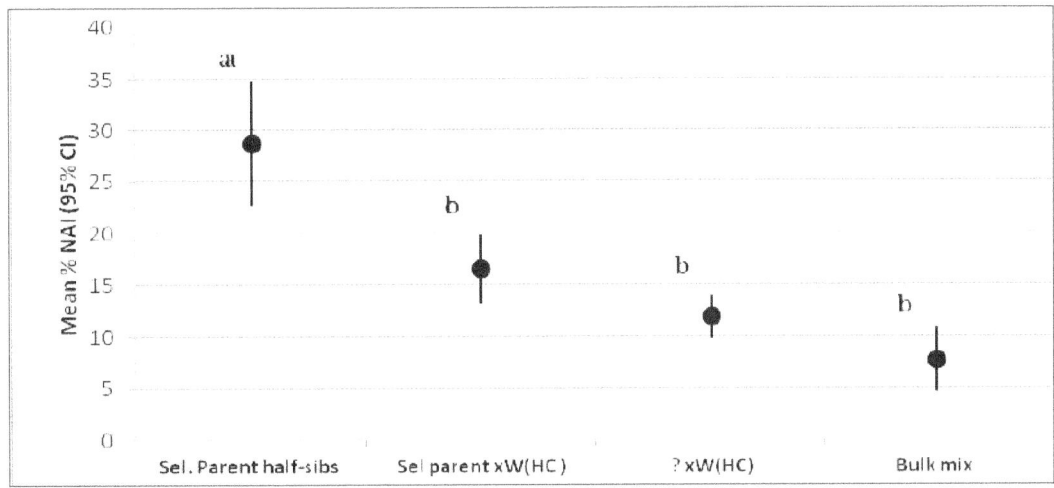

Figure 3—Means and 95 percent confidence intervals for percentage of trees with no active infections/family (percent NAI) in four main open-pollinated groups of sugar pine progenies. Groups with the same letter are not statistically different; the six pairwise comparisons were tested using a Bonferoni's adjusted-a=.05/6=0.0082 to attain an experimentwise error rate a=0.05.

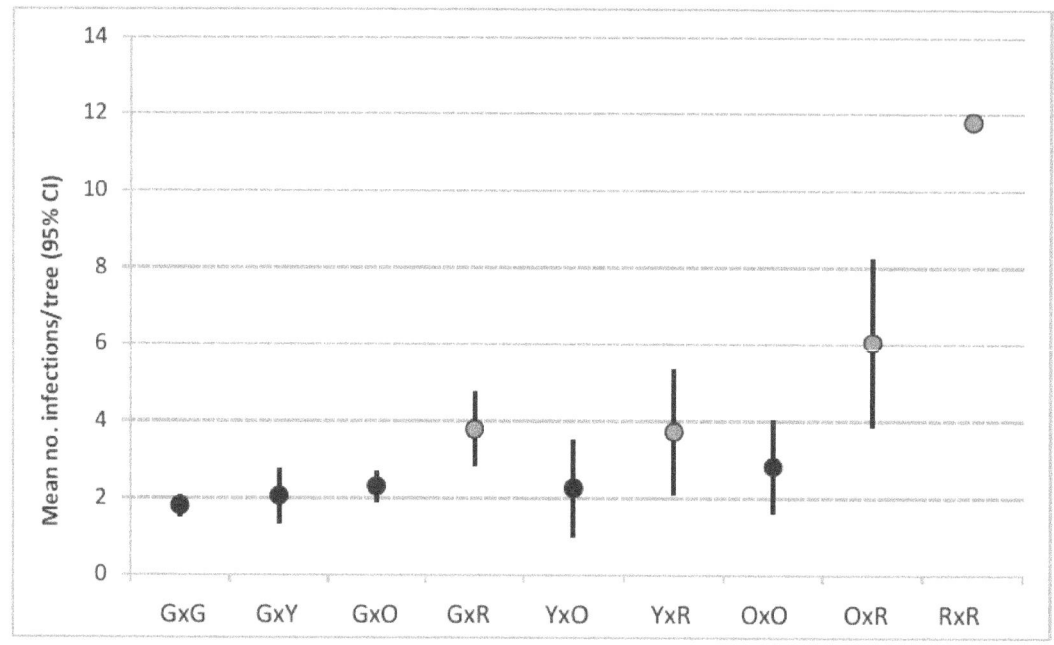

Figure 4—Means and 95 percent confidence intervals for numbers of infections/family in nine full-sib groups of sugar pine progenies. (cf., table 1 or 2 for group color codes. The mean of the groups in red is significantly different than the mean of groups in black).

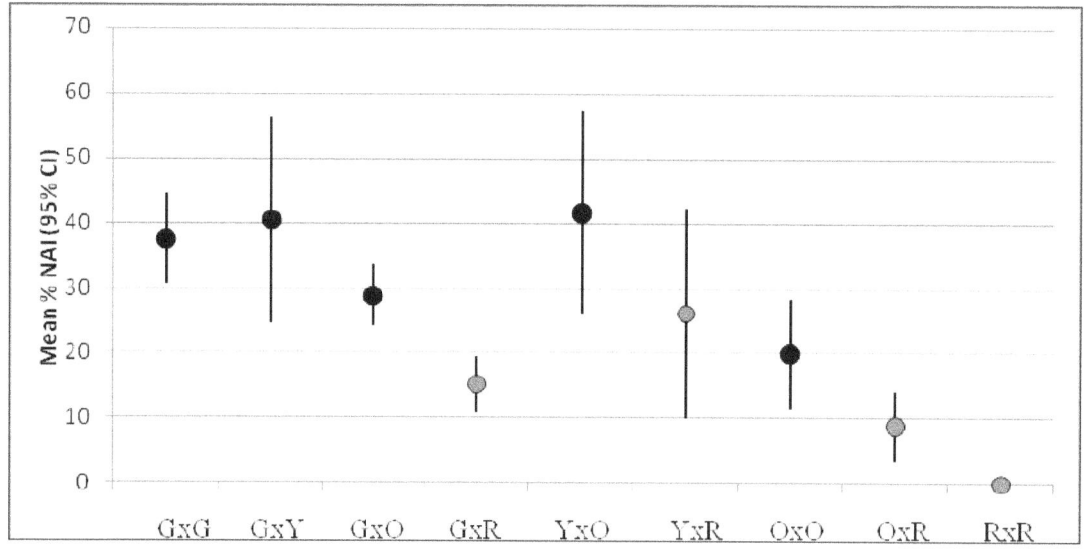

Figure 5—Means and 95 percent confidence intervals for percentage of trees with no active infections/family (percent NAI) in nine full-sib groups of sugar pine progenies. (cf., table 1 or 2 for group color codes. The mean of the groups in red is significantly different than the mean of groups in black).

Regardless of the type of inheritance of PR, there is increasing consensus that major resistance genes are more effective when deployed in a background containing quantitative resistance traits (Brun et al. 2010, Wulff et al. 2011). Quantitative resistance genes can work additively with R genes, prolonging their durability, probably through reduction in pathogen effective population size and especially the number of virulent mutants that could be selected by R-genes (McDonald, 2010). Accordingly, the highest value of PR in breeding sugar pine is to protect Cr1 from vcr1 in synthetic populations with combined pedigrees. Cr1 will protect against all ambient inoculum except that containing vcr1. Concentrated PR genes will sanitize a great proportion of incoming inoculum, reducing the probability of vcr1, which is rare in natural populations, from becoming epidemic (Kinloch and Davis 1996, Kinloch et al. 2008). The prospect of developing more durable resistance in sugar pine is good.

Acknowledgments

We thank John Gleason and Sara Wilson for assistance with field assessments, Sylvia Mori for statistical advice, and Nancy Gillette for helpful suggestions on an earlier draft.

Literature Cited

Antonovics, J.; Thrall, P.H.; Burdon, J.J; Laine, A.L. 2011. Partial resistance in the *Linum-Melampsora* host-pathogen system: Does partial resistance make the red queen run slower? Evolution. 65: 512–522.

Brun, H.; Chèvre, A.M.; Fitt, B.D.; Powers, S.; Besnard, A.L.; Ermel, M.; Huteau, V.; Marquer, B.; Eber, F.; Renard, M.; Andrivon, D. 2010. Quantitative resistance increases the durability of qualitative resistance to *Leptosphaeria maculans* in *Brassica napus*. New Phytologist. 185: 285–299.

Isik, F.; Li, B.; Frampton, J. 2003. Estimates of additive, dominance and epistatic genetic variances from a clonally replicated test of loblolly pine. Forest Science. 49: 77–88.

King, J.N.; David, A.; Noshad, D.; Smith, J. 2010. A review of genetic approaches to the management of blister rust in white pines. Forest Pathology. 40: 292–313.

Kinloch, B.B., Jr.; Davis, D. 1996. Mechanisms and inheritance of resistance to blister rust in sugar pine. In: Kinloch, B.B., Jr.; Marosy, M; Huddleston, M., eds. Sugar pine: status, values, and roles in ecosystems: proceedings of a symposium presented by the California sugar pine management committee. Publication 3362. Davis, CA: University of California, Division of Agriculture and Natural Resources: 125–132.

Kinloch, B.B., Jr.; Davis, D.A; Burton, D. 2008. Resistance and virulence interactions between two white pine species and blister rust in a 30-year field trial. Tree Genetics & Genomes. 4: 65–74.

Krenz, J.E.; Sackett, K.E.; Mundt, C.C. 2008. Specificity of incomplete resistance to *Mycosphaerella graminicola* in wheat. Phytopathology. 98: 555–561.

McDonald, B. 2010. How can we achieve durable disease resistance in agricultural ecosystems? New Phytologist. 185: 3–5.

Struckmeyer, E.B.; Riker, A.J.R. 1951. Wound periderm formation in white pine trees resistant to blister rust. Phytopathology. 41: 276–281.

Wulff, B.B.H.; Horvath, D.M.; Ward, E.R. 2011. Improving immunity in crops: new tactics in an old game. Current Opinion in Plant Biology. 14: 468–476.

An Investigation into Western White Pine Partial Resistance Against the Rust Pathogen *Cronartium ribicola* Using In Vitro Screening Method

D. Noshad[1] and J.N. King[1]

Abstract

Cronartium ribicola is one of the most destructive forest pathogens of North American white pines. The pathogen infects pine trees through their stomata, colonizes the stem, and produces stem cankers the following growing season. In this research, we collected samples from different white pine populations across Canada and the United States to develop an efficient ex vitro and in vitro screening method for phenotype expression of western white pine (*Pinus monticola* Douglas ex D. Don) following inoculation with *C. ribicola.* A major group of partial resistant plants in British Columbia, described as difficult-to-infect (DI), presented significant resistance in our field trials. We developed a disease assessment index, based on both in vitro and ex vitro techniques, to evaluate specific reactions to the pathogen of the DI plants. A disease progression index (DPI) for each category has been established. *Ribes* leaves from 2-year-old plants have been successfully cultured and maintained on the half-strength Murashige and Skoog (MS) medium supplemented with $0.02\mu M$ NAA+$0.1\mu M$ IBA. These in vitro inoculated leaves produced urediospores after 2 weeks and teliospores after 6 weeks in culture. The preliminary results from our DI screening experiments indicated a significant difference in the number of successful infections between DI and control populations. Further morphological investigation into the mechanism(s) responsible for these variations with electron microscopy revealed a considerable difference in the morphology of stomata. Also, the amount of epicuticular wax on the stomata of the resistant populations was significantly higher than the control plants. These adaptations could provide a greater structural defense system against white pine blister rust.

[1] BC Forest Service, PO Box 9519, Stn Prov Govt, Victoria, BC V8W 9C2 Canada.
Corresponding author: dnoshad@interchnage.ubc.ca.

Resistance Gene Management: Concepts and Practice

Christopher C. Mundt[1]

Abstract

There is now a very long history of genetics/breeding for disease resistance in annual crops. These efforts have resulted in conceptual advances and frustrations, as well as practical successes and failures. This talk will review this history and its relevance to the genetics of resistance in forest species. All plant breeders and pathologists are familiar with boom-and-bust cycles of single major resistance genes. Though there may be occasional situations where a single-gene approach to resistance is reasonable, most interest is in finding alternatives to this approach. This is especially true of long-lived species, for which durability of resistance becomes essential.

Combinations or "pyramids" of major genes can greatly increase durability of resistance and have provided some major success stories in annual crops. The mechanisms by which pyramids contribute durability, however, still are not entirely clear, and this is of importance to potential for success of this approach. Accumulating multiple resistances in a single genotype is complicated by epistatic effects of major genes, though both phenotypic and marker approaches can reduce this difficulty to some degree. Deploying major genes in mixed populations has been highly successful in some cases, including for some woody perennials. There is considerable variation in the epidemiological effectiveness of mixtures, however, and much is yet to be learned about the mechanisms behind this variability. Concern about selection for "superraces" in host mixtures has likely been greatly overstated, and the mechanisms by which selection for multiple virulences occur are much more complex than a simplistic evaluation of "virulence costs."

Once firmly established in a breeding program, the value of quantitative resistance (QR) is difficult to argue against. Though erosion due to pathogen adaptation may be possible, QR has a solid history of durability. Some have avoided QR because of its perceived complexity of inheritance. Research has shown, however, that QR is much less complex than initially thought. In recent years, many QTL studies have been conducted, and this information may be useful in both augmenting field selection for QR and in avoiding "Vertifolia effects" in the presence of effective major genes. A significant challenge, however, will be in identifying QTL that express in multiple genetic backgrounds of the host.

Theoretical considerations aside, the best approach to breeding for resistance also will depend strongly on availability of resistance sources and on other traits being addressed in the breeding program. Flexibility and forethought must also be used in preparing for changes in silvicultural practices, introduction of new pathogen populations, and climate change that may influence disease. Combining different approaches to resistance should increase both the epidemiological effectiveness and durability of resistance.

---

[1] Dept. of Botany and Plant Pathology, 2082 Cordley Hall, Oregon State University, Corvallis, OR 97331-2902.
Corresponding Author: mundtc@science.oregonstate.edu.

Ecology and Evolutionary Biology of Resistance and Tolerance - Natural Systems

Whitebark pine (*Pinus albicaulis*) at Crater Lake National Park in southern Oregon. (Photo: Robert Mutch)

An Overview of Ecological and Evolutionary Research on Disease in Natural Systems: An Annotated Reference List

Helen M. Alexander[1]

Background

The Fourth International Workshop on the Genetics of Host-Parasite Interactions in Forestry (July 31-August 5, 2011) included a session on "Ecology and Evolutionary Biology of Resistance and Tolerance, Natural Systems." Within this session, I gave a talk entitled "An overview of ecological and evolutionary research on disease in 'natural' systems" that reviewed research on disease that is primarily in ecology and evolutionary biology journals (as opposed to forestry and plant pathology journals). Several people requested that I provide details of the references listed in that talk, and this annotated reference list is the result.

To reduce the length of this document, I note that several of the references in my talk were cited in a recent review article (Alexander 2010). Thus, instead of writing the full reference, I have simply listed "PD" next to the names of the authors for citations included in this review.

Overview and a Brief Timeline of Studies of Disease by Ecologists/Evolutionary Biologists

Most work on plant disease has been done by plant pathologists working in agriculture or forestry. In contrast, ecologists and evolutionary biologists working in less applied settings have historically largely ignored disease (but see Haldane 1949, PD). Harper, a well-established British ecologist, was one of the first to focus attention on disease when he included a chapter on pathogens in his classic book on plant population biology (Harper 1977 PD). The 1970s and 1980s were also a time when many researchers compared disease levels in crops and wild plants (e.g., Thresh 1981 PD). Burdon's (1987 PD) book on the interactions between pathogens and the ecology and genetics of plant populations stimulated considerable work. Since the 1980s, studies of plant disease by ecologists and evolutionary biologists in natural/unmanaged systems have become increasingly common.

The reference to plant disease in "natural" systems is potentially confusing. Realistically, there are no plant communities on earth that are not in some way impacted by humans and, of course, indigenous people have always interacted with plant communities. It is useful, however, to recognize that there is a continuum of landscapes from "managed" on one hand to "unmanaged/natural" on the other hand. An example of the former is row crops in western agriculture where there is reduced plant species diversity, high uniformity within plant populations (low genetic diversity, even-age age structure, regular plant spacing), and a lack of linkage in plant dynamics from year to year (i.e., plants growing at a site are not the result of seeds produced at the site in the previous year). In contrast, unmanaged systems typically have higher species diversity, more complex structure within a plant population, and a linkage in plant dynamics from year to year. Unmanaged systems can include apparently pristine settings, but also apply equally well to disturbed environments such as roadside weed communities.

---

[1] Department of Ecology and Evolutionary Biology, University of Kansas, Lawrence, KS 66045.
halexander@ku.edu.

Overview of Talk: Studies of Disease in Relation to Plant Population Dynamics, Evolutionary Interactions Between Plants and Pathogens, Plant Community Composition, and Global Change and Ecosystem Function

Within these areas there are biases, with more research on the effects of pathogens on plants than vice versa and more emphasis on fungal pathogens than other types of pathogens.

Plant Population Dynamics

Research in this area examines how pathogen populations affect the size and spatial distribution of plant populations. A variety of approaches are used; excellent examples include experimental approaches (such as pesticide applications; Roy et al. 2011) and long-term surveys of plant and pathogen numbers (research on anther-smut disease; Antonovics 2004 PD, Antonovics et al. 1998 PD). Both of these examples also have a strong modeling component. Other examples of research in disease/plant population dynamics include:

a. Effects of disease on plant age/stage composition (Davelos and Jarosz 2004).

b. Effects of pathogens on seed populations and seed bank persistence (Beckstead et al. 2010, Eviner and Chapin 2003 PD, Meyer et al. 2007 PD).
c. Density-dependent effects of disease and the degree to which plants and plant populations can compensate for disease losses (Alexander and Mihail 2000 PD, Lively et al. 1995 PD).

d. Examining plant-pathogen interactions on landscape spatial scales; effects on plant metapopulation dynamics (Antonovics 1999 PD, Antonovics 2004 PD, Antonovics et al. 1994 PD).

e. Temporal and spatial variation in disease (19–year-study over large number of Swedish islands; Smith et al. 2011).

Other examples include: Alexander et al. 2007 PD, Antonovics 2004 PD, Antonovics et al. 1994 PD, Augspurger and Kelly 1984 PD, Carlsson et al. 1990, Carlsson-Granér and Thrall 2002 PD, Koslow and Clay 2010, Laine and Hanski 2006, Reinhart and Clay 2009, Smith et al. 2003 PD, Thrall et al. 2001 PD.

Evolutionary Interactions Between Plants and Pathogens: Genetic Variation in Resistance, Virulence, and Tolerance

Studies of genetic interactions between plants and pathogens have a long history, and were the primary focus of talks by B. Roy and J. Burdon at this conference. The references below provide examples of this kind of work: Antonovics et al. 2010, Barrett et al. 2007 PD, Barrett et al. 2009, Burdon and Thrall 2009, Burdon et al. 2002 PD, Carr et al. 2003, Carr et al. 2006, Dinoor 1977 PD, Gilbert and Parker 2010, Harry and Clarke 1986, Inglese and Paul 2006 PD, Jarosz and Burdon 1991, Koslow and Clay 2007, Laine 2004 PD, Laine et al. 2011, Roy 1993 PD, Roy and Bierzychudek 1993, Roy and Kirchner 2000 PD, Roy et al. 2000 PD, Roux et al. 2010, Simms 1993, Springer 2007 PD, Thompson and Burdon 1992 PD, Thrall et al. 2002 PD.

Of particular importance is research that links ecology and genetics; examples include:
a. Links between resistance structure and disease levels and plant dynamics: Alexander et al. 1996 PD, Thrall and Burdon 2000 PD, Thrall and Jarosz 1994 PD, Laine 2004 PD, Springer 2007 PD.

b. Passive resistance – heritable traits other than resistance genes affect field disease levels: Alexander 1989 PD, Alexander et al. 1993, Biere and Antonovics 1996 PD, Giles et al. 2006 PD.

c. Links between community ecology and population genetics/phylogeny

     1. Host shifts: Antonovics et al. 2002 PD, López-Villavicencio et al. 2005 PD, Roy 2001 PD.

2. Use of metagenomics to determine viral prevalence (70 percent and 25 percent of samples across tropical forest and prairie communities, respectively, have viral RNA): Muthukumar et al. 2009 PD, Roossinck et al. 2010.

3. Role of phylogeny in host range: Gilbert and Webb 2007 PD, Webb et al. 2006.

Plant Community Composition

Research in this area includes work examining the direct and indirect effects of pathogens on the number of plant species in an area and their relative frequency. Many of the classic studies in this area come from work in forest systems, such as research on mortality centers caused by *Phellinus weirii* in mountain hemlock forests (Hansen and Goheen 2000 PD) and work on sudden oak death in California forests (Rizzo and Garbelotto 2003 PD, Rizzo et al. 2005 PD).

Three subdisciplines of community ecology have been of major interest in recent years:
1. Interactions of pathogens with multiple hosts: apparent competition and pathogen spillover. Generalist pathogens may lead to the development of "apparent competition" where increases in pathogen populations on tolerant hosts may "spill over" and lead to increased disease on less tolerant hosts (Holt 1984 PD, Power and Mitchell 2004 PD). In addition to forestry examples (e.g., sudden oak death), another classic example of this phenomenon is work on barley yellow dwarf virus in California, where increases in virus prevalence and aphid vector numbers on exotic grasses can lead to adverse viral impacts on nearby native grasses (Malmstrom et al. 2005 PD). Recent work by Cronin et al. (2010) suggests that host physiological phenotypes may be predictive of pathogen reservoir potential.

2. Soil microbial community: feedback studies, Janzen-Connell studies. Several models and research groups have examined similar questions such as the following: Consider plant species "A:" Does the presence or high density of plant species A contribute to the development of a soil microbial community that leads to low survival for individuals of species A (but not species B, C, D, etc.)?. Such processes may be important in the maintenance of plant species diversity. Research examples include: Bagchi et al. 2010, Bever 2003 PD, Bever et al. 1997 PD, Diez et al. 2010, Holah and Alexander 1999, Klironomos 2002 PD, Mangan et al. 2010, Mills and Bever 1998 PD, Packer and Clay 2000 PD, Petermann et al. 2008 PD, Reinhardt et al. 2003 PD, Reynolds et al. 2003 PD, Swamy and Terborgh 2010, Van der Putten et al. 1993 PD. Many of the studies provide general support for the theories noted above, but there are major gaps in our knowledge. In particular, there is a tendency in previous work to treat the microbial community as a "black box" in most experiments. Further, most theory in this area focuses on specialist pathogens, yet most soil pathogens are generalists.

3. Invasion ecology and disease. A major issue in ecology and conservation biology is the unprecedented movement of species around the world due to both intentional and nonintentional introductions. One mechanism that may be important is the idea of "enemy release," where pathogens regulate plant populations in native sites, but the reduced pathogen presence or pressure in introduced sites allow for an expansion of the plant population. There is supporting evidence for this mechanism, but results are variable and can depend on the system being studied (Agrawal et al. 2005, Diez et al. 2010, Mitchell et al. 2006 PD, Mitchell et al. 2010, Parker and Gilbert 2007 PD, Reinhart et al. 2003 PD, Roy et al. 2011, van Kleunen and Fisher 2009 PD). Current work on invasion ecology and disease have focused on a) plant demography and dynamics (Chun et al. 2010, Roy et al. 2011), b) role of generalists versus specialist enemies (Halbritter et al. 2012), c) variation among species in enemy release (Blumenthal et al. 2009), and d) accumulation of pathogens on invasive plants and evolutionary responses (Diez et al. 2010, Gilbert and Parker 2010, Mitchell et al. 2010).

Global Change and Ecosystem Function

In recent years, there is increasing emphasis on how global change variables may affect pathogen populations and communities, and in turn, how pathogens may alter the functioning of ecosystems. Due to time limitations in my talk, I did not cover this area deeply. Examples of work, however, include:

a. Effects of temperature, carbon dioxide, and nutrients on plant disease: Mitchell et al. 2003 PD, Nordin et al. 1998 PD, Nordin et al. 2009, Roy et al. 2004 PD, Strengbom et al. 2002 PD, Strengbom et al. 2006, Tylianakis et al. 2008.

b. Genetic variation in pathogen populations in response to environmental change: Laine 2007 PD.

c. Effects of disease on ecosystem function: Eviner and Likens 2008 PD, Mitchell 2003 PD, Lovett et al. 2006 PD.

Conclusions

As we contemplate the future, it is important to emphasize that natural areas are increasingly fragmented and occur within a mosaic of human impacted biomes (see concept of "anthropogenic biomes," Ellis and Ramankutty 2008 PD). An area worthy of increased emphasis is studies of disease at the interface between agriculture/forestry and "natural" habitats (Burdon and Thrall 2008 PD, Fabiszewski et al. 2010 PD).

Literature Cited

As noted earlier, to save space on references, many citations above have the letters "PD" after them. This means that the full reference can be found in a recent review article in the journal Plant Disease (Alexander 2010); such PD references are not listed below.

Agrawal, A.A.; Kotanen, P.M.; Mitchell, C.E. [et al.]. 2005. Enemy release? An experiment with congeneric plant pairs and diverse above- and belowground enemies. Ecology. 86: 2979–2989.

Alexander, H.M. 2010. Disease in natural plant populations, communities, and ecosystems: insights into ecological and evolutionary processes. Plant Disease. 94: 492–503.

Alexander, H.M.; Antonovics, J.; Kelly, A.W. 1993. Genotypic variation in disease resistance – physiological resistance in relation to field disease transmission. Journal of Ecology. 81: 325–333.

Antonovics, J.; Thrall, P.H.; Burdon, J.J. [et al.]. 2010. Partial resistance in the *Linum-Melampsora* host pathogen system: does partial resistance make the red queen run slower? Evolution. 65: 512–522.

Bagchi, R.; Swinfield, T.; Gallery, R.E. [et al.]. 2010. Testing the Janzen-Connell mechanism: pathogens cause overcompensating density dependence in a tropical tree. Ecology Letters. 13: 1262–1269.

Barrett, L.G.; Thrall, P.H.; Dodds, P.N. [et al.]. 2009. Diversity and evolution of effector loci in natural populations of the plant pathogen *Melampsora lini*. Molecular Biology and Evolution. 26: 2499–2513.

Beckstead, J.; Meyer, S.E.; Connolly, B.M. [et al.]. 2010. Cheatgrass facilitates spillover of a seed bank pathogen onto native grass species. Journal of Ecology. 98: 168–177.

Blumenthal, D.; Mitchell, C.E.; Pysek, P. [et al.]. 2009. Synergy between pathogen release and resource availability in plant invasion. Proceedings of the National Academy of Sciences. 106: 7899–7904.

Burdon, J.J.; Thrall, P.H. 2009. Coevolution of plants and their pathogens in natural habitats. Science. 324: 755–756.

Carlsson, U.; Elmqvist, T.; Wennstrom, A. [et al.]. 1990. Infection by pathogens and population age of host plants. Journal of Ecology. 78: 1094–1105.

Carr, D.E.; Murphy, J.F.; Eubanks, M.D. 2003. The susceptibility and response of inbred and outbred *Mimulus guttatus* to infection by Cucumber mosaic virus. Evolutionary Ecology. 17: 85–103.

Carr, D.E.; Murphy, J.F.; Eubanks, M.D. 2006. Genetic variation and covariation for resistance and tolerance to Cucumber mosaic virus in *Mimulus guttatus* (Phrymaceae): a test for costs and constraints. Heredity. 96: 29–38.

Chun, Y.J.; van Kleunen, M.; Dawson, W. 2010. The role of enemy release, tolerance, and resistance in plant invasions: linking damage to performance. Ecology Letters. 13: 937–946.

Cronin, J.P.; Welsh, M.E.; Dekkers, M.G. [et al.]. 2010. Host physiological phenotype explains pathogen reservoir potential. Ecology Letters. 13: 1221-1232.

Davelos, A.L.; Jarosz, A.M. 2004. Demography of American chestnut populations: effects of a pathogen and a hyperparasite. Journal of Ecology. 92: 675–685.

Diez, J.M.; Dickie, I.; Edwards, G. [et al.]. 2010. Negative soil feedbacks accumulate over time for non-native plant species. Ecology Letters. 13: 803–809.

Gilbert, G.S.; Parker, I.M. 2010. Rapid evolution in a plant-pathogen interaction and the consequences for introduced host species. Evolutionary Applications. 3: 144–156.

Halbritter, A.H.; Carroll, G.C.; Güsewell, S. [et al.]. 2012. Testing assumptions of the enemy release hypothesis: generalist versus specialist enemies of the grass *Brachypodium sylvaticum*. Mycologia. 104:34–44.

Holah, J.C.; Alexander, H.M. 1999. Soil pathogenic fungi have the potential to affect the co-existence of two tallgrass prairie species. Journal of Ecology. 87: 598–608.

Harry, I.B.; Clarke, D.D. 1986. Race-specific resistance in groundsel *Senecio vulgaris* to the powdery mildew *Erysiphe fischeri*. New Phytologist. 103: 167–176.

Jarosz, A.M.; Burdon, J.J. 1991. Host-pathogen interactions in natural populations of *Linum marginale* and *Melampsora lini* II. Local and regional variation in patterns of resistance and racial structure. Evolution. 45: 1618–1627.

Koslow, J.M.; Clay, K. 2007. The mixed mating system of *Impatiens capensis* and infection by a foliar rust pathogen: patterns of resistance and fitness consequences. Evolution. 61: 2643–2654.

Koslow, J.M.; Clay, K. 2010. Spatial and temporal patterns of rust infection on jewelweed (*Impatiens capensis*). International Journal of Plant Sciences. 5: 529–537.

Laine, A.L.; Hanski, I. 2006. Large-scale spatial dynamics of a specialist plant pathogen in a fragmented landscape. Journal of Ecology. 94: 217–226.

Laine, A.L.; Burdon, J.J.; Dodds, P.N. [et al.]. 2011. Spatial variation in disease resistance: from molecules to metapopulations. Journal of Ecology. 99: 96–112.

Mangan, S.A.; Schnitzer, S.A.; Herre, E. [et al.]. 2010. Negative plant-soil feedback predicts tree-species relative abundance in a tropical forest. Nature. 466: 752–755.

Mitchell, C.E.; Blumenthal, D.; Jarosik, V. [et al.]. 2010. Controls on pathogen species richness in plants' introduced and native ranges: roles of residence time, range size, and host traits. Ecology Letters. 13: 1525–1535.

Nordin, A.; Strengbom, J.; Forsum, A. [et al.]. 2009. Complex biotic interactions drive long-term vegetation change in a nitrogen enriched boreal forest. Ecosystems. 12: 1204–1211.

Reinhart, K.O.; Clay, K. 2009. Spatial variation in soil-borne disease dynamics of a temperate tree, *Prunus serotina*. Ecology. 90: 2984–2993.

Roossinck, M.J.; Prasenjit, S.; Wiley, G.B. [et al.]. 2010. Ecogenomics: using massively parallel pyrosequencing to understand virus ecology. Molecular Ecology. 19: 81–88.

Roux, F.; Gao, L.; Bergelson, J. 2010. Impact of initial pathogen density on resistance and tolerance in a polymorphic disease resistance gene system in *Arabidopsis thaliana*. Genetics. 185: 283–291.

Roy, B.A.; Bierzychudek, P. 1993. The potential for rust infection to cause natural selection in apomictic *Arabis holboelli* (Brassicaceae). Oecologia. 95: 533–541.

Roy, B.A.; Coulson, T.; Blaser, W. [et al.]. 2011. Population regulation by enemies of the grass *Brachypodium sylvaticum*: demography in native and invaded ranges. Ecology. 92: 665–675.

Simms, E.L. 1993. Genetic variation for pathogen resistance in tall morning glory. Plant Disease. 77: 901–904.

Smith, D.L.; Ericson, L.; Burdon, J.J. 2011. Co-evolutionary hot and cold spots of selective pressure move in space and time. Journal of Ecology. 99: 634–641.

Strengbom, J.; Englund, G.; Ericson, L. 2006. Experimental scale and precipitation modify effects of nitrogen addition on a plant pathogen. Journal of Ecology. 94: 227–223.

Swamy, V.; Terborgh, J.W. 2010. Distance-responsive natural enemies strongly influence seedling establishment patterns of multiple species in an Amazonian rain forest. Journal of Ecology. 98: 1096–1107.

Tylianakis, J.M.; Didham, R.K.; Bascompte, J. [et al.]. 2008. Global change and species interactions in terrestrial ecosystems. Ecology Letters. 11: 1351–1363.

Webb, C.O.; Gilbert, G.S.; Donoghue, M.J. 2006. .Phylodiversity dependent seedling mortality, size structure, and disease in a Bornean rain forest. Ecology. 87: S123–S131.

What Do We Know About Mechanisms for Tolerating Pathogens, and Can Tolerance Be Applied to Managing Tree Diseases?

Bitty A. Roy[1]

Abstract

The terms ''resistance'' and ''tolerance'' have been used by different scientists to refer to different things, and they have often been measured (and thus operationally defined) in ways that confuse the two concepts with each other. In keeping with the emerging consensus on resistance and tolerance, the following conceptual distinction is useful: resistance refers to traits that prevent infection or limit its extent, and tolerance refers to traits that do not reduce or eliminate infection, but instead reduce or offset its fitness consequences. Thus, resistance and tolerance can both improve host fitness; resistance does so by reducing infection, whereas tolerance does so by reducing the fitness loss under infection. In this review, I will briefly set up the differences between resistance and tolerance, then discuss what we know about mechanisms for tolerance and what is known about tolerance in relation to tree diseases.

[1]Center for Ecology and Evolutionary Biology, University of Oregon, Eugene, OR.
Corresponding author: bit@uoregon.edu.

Approaches to Understanding the Impact of Life-History Features on Plant-Pathogen Co-Evolutionary Dynamics

Jeremy J. Burdon,[1] Peter H. Thrall,[1] and Adnane Nemri[1]

Abstract

Natural plant-pathogen associations are complex interactions in which the interplay of environment, host, and pathogen factors results in spatially heterogeneous ecological and epidemiological dynamics. The evolutionary patterns that result from the interaction of these factors are still relatively poorly understood. Recently, integration of the appropriate spatial and temporal context of the metapopulation has permitted an essential conceptual advance stressing the importance of these factors in evolutionary interactions. Yet, a major aspect of host and pathogen biologies that still needs considerable attention is that of the impact of particular life-history traits of both host and pathogen and how these may influence patterns of disease incidence and prevalence and the evolution of host resistance and pathogen infectivity. Here we outline the importance of both empirical comparisons and simulation modelling as a means of uncovering the full impact of host and pathogen life history traits on co-evolutionary dynamics.

Key words: empirical comparisons, simulation models, co-evolutionary dynamics

Introduction

Individual plant species frequently have wide geographic ranges that cover considerable latitude and distinctly different climatic zones. Yet, within particular regions their distribution is usually patchy and individual demes are often associated with local micro-environments showing specific moisture, temperature, and humidity regimes. Over the course of evolutionary history this mixture of broad and narrow scale environmental variation has provided a range of selective pressures across the space-time continuum. In turn this has generated a complex mosaic of genetic variation in the plant with differentiation within and among regions in a wide range of morphological (e.g., leaf shape and thickness), phenological (e.g., timing of bud-break, flowering), biochemical (e.g., lignin/terpene content), and other life-history characters (e.g., growth rate, life span, mating system). In a similar way, the biology and life-history characteristics of pathogens, particularly their responses to environmental cues, often show differentiation among and within regions. Among those traits, host specificity, transmission mode, life cycle complexity, and dispersal ability can have major influence on spread, diversity, and persistence of pathogen populations (Barrett et al. 2008a). At a broad level, these traits control the range of environments, and hence host populations in which pathogens may be found, the genetic structure of pathogen populations and, as a result, the extent to which they exert selective pressure on their host (Barrett et al. 2009).

Pathogens form associations with their hosts that cover part or all of the host's range (although, in some situations, a pathogen's range can exceed that of an individual host species if, as is the case for many necrotrophic species, they are capable of attacking/parasitizing more than one host). The epidemiological and evolutionary interaction that develops between host and pathogen in these associations is influenced by the detailed interplay of life-history differences at the individual patch and metapopulation level. Clearly, as the spatial scale of interactions expands across the full geographic distribution of the host, opportunities for differences in the nature of epidemiological outcomes occur both in different individual population associations and in different parts of the

[1] CSIRO-Plant Industry, GPO Box 1600, Canberra, ACT. 2601 Australia.
Corresponding author: jeremy.burdon@csiro.au.

overall geographic range of the interaction. Given the potential for stochastic colonization/extinction processes in partially isolated local populations and hence differences in the intensity and persistence of consequent selective pressures, this raises the possibility of the development of divergent longer-term evolutionary trajectories in different parts of the geographic range of individual host-pathogen associations.

Assessing the Impact of Host-Pathogen Life-History Features on the Epidemiological and Evolutionary Trajectory of Specific Interactions

How can we start to tease out whether or not life-history features affect the epidemiological and evolutionary trajectories of host-pathogen associations, and, if they do, the role of specific life-history characters? This would be an essential first step towards developing a more general conceptual framework. Importantly, the integration of information on host and pathogen life history has the potential to advance our predictive ability with regard to disease outbreak and emergence (Barrett et al. 2008a).

Thrall and Burdon (1997) developed a framework based on three realistic scenarios which illustrate the link between simple host and pathogen life history combinations and spatial considerations (spatial scale of associations; temporal predictability), and how these together are likely to influence the longer-term evolutionary trajectory of associations. Those scenarios recognized the existence of associations in which the scale of pathogen dispersal was likely to be (a) substantially less than that of its host (e.g., soil-borne pathogens); (b) roughly comparable with that of its host (e.g., seed borne viruses, vector-borne floral smuts); and (c) substantially greater than that of its host (e.g., wind-dispersed rusts, persistent aphid-borne viruses). Subsequently, they used simulation modelling to illustrate the importance of spatial scale and the occurrence of multiple demes showing varying degrees of interconnectedness in the longer-term ecological and evolutionary dynamics of hosts and their pathogens (Thrall and Burdon 1999, 2002).

Within pathogens themselves there is also a major life-history dichotomy between biotrophic and necrotrophic fungi. The former essentially rely on living host material for growth and, in its absence, surviving as relatively inert long-lived spores or other protected structures. Necrotrophic pathogens, on the other hand, exploit host tissue that they kill through toxin release. Unlike biotrophs, during off-season periods these pathogens may continue active growth by saprophytic exploitation of dead plant remains. This alternation between parasitic and saprophytic growth phases typically results in switches in the intensity, direction, and indeed the traits under selection – a situation that is markedly contrast to the patterns of selection experience by typical biotrophic pathogens.

Despite these differences, the most apparent way in which to assess the impact of life-history features is to characterize their influence on the epidemiology of the host-pathogen interaction and through this ultimately the reciprocal selective pressures applied by host and pathogen. The longer-term evolutionary consequences of such selective pressures are ultimately manifest in a variety of ways, but perhaps the clearest is through changes in the incidence of resistance in the host and pathogenicity in sympatric pathogen populations. Indeed, plants possess a range of different resistance mechanisms whereby they minimize their susceptibility to pathogens and the extent of damage they incur. Broadly speaking, these mechanisms can be categorized into qualitative or major gene resistance that is typically controlled by single genes with major phenotypic effects, and quantitative resistance that is usually controlled by many loci each with small phenotypic effects. In a classic genetic sense, qualitative resistance is characterized by Mendelian responses while quantitative resistance is typified by continuous variation. In real world host-pathogen systems, some plant populations may be protected against particular pathogens by one or other, or by a combination of these mechanisms.

Heuristic arguments have been developed (Burdon et al. 1996) as to the circumstances that may favor the evolution of one or other of these genetic mechanisms (largely reflecting the predictability of infection and its selective intensity), but as yet no concerted effort has been made to assess their incidence in natural systems and little is known about the selective and evolutionary forces that determine their balance. There are two clear ways in which to explore these possibilities. First, empirically through comparative investigation of situations where various combinations of host and pathogen species are assessed and contrasted, and second, through the development of simulation models that help develop a general conceptual framework for predicting outcomes in broad classes of plant-pathogen interactions.

Empirical Comparisons

In the first of these approaches, a number of combinations can be assessed. Thus:

One Host – One Pathogen; Distinctly Different Environments

Within single host-pathogen associations, correlations between parameters of pathogen dynamics (e.g., prevalence, severity, predictability) and the structure and nature of resistance occurring in contrasting host populations provide insights into the way spatio-temporal variation in selective intensity and predictability can shape host and pathogen population structure and life history features. An example of the insights provided by this sort of comparison is found in the *Populus – Melampsora* interaction occurring on the eastern and western sides of the Rocky Mountains. This interaction is one involving an annual host target (deciduous leaves) and hence one in which the pathogen tends to cycle through massive amplitudes in population size over short periods of time. Because the pathogen cannot survive on this host during the winter season, it is repeatedly forced to re-establish through migration from more benign environments or from alternate hosts. Under these circumstances, race-specific resistance genes which thwart initial entry of pathogen isolates carrying corresponding avirulence genes may provide adequate long-term resistance for the host. On the dry, cold eastern side of the Rocky Mountains in western Canada, this pattern of major gene resistance appears to predominate (Hsiang and Chastagner 1993). In contrast, west of the mountains, the more temperate winter environment means that the pathogen is constantly present, and only multigenic race non-specific resistance is found.

A similar potential direct effect of the environment on pathogen dynamics leading to varying selection pressures on associated hosts is seen in the interaction between *Avena fatua* (wild oats) and the rust fungus *Puccinia coronata* in Australia. In that situation, host and pathogen population pairs occurring in southern and northern New South Wales (NSW) respectively exhibit marked differences in the phenology of their interaction. In northern NSW, winters are warmer than further south and pathogen populations have the opportunity to develop earlier in the host's vegetative stage. As a consequence, earlier, more damaging disease epidemics are likely to ensue with the potential for greater selective impact on their hosts than in the south (Burdon et al. 1983). Consistent with this prediction, surveys reveal a marked increase in the incidence of resistance with major phenotypic effects in the more benign north.

One Host – One Pathogen; Distinctly Different Major Life History Feature Contrast

Mating system is possibly the life-history character that has the biggest single impact on populations of all organisms. It is at the core of the structure of plant populations (Barrett 2002; Barrett et al. 2008) and has been implicated as a determinant of the success of biological control programs to use insect herbivores and fungal pathogens to manage invasive weeds (Burdon and Marshall 1981). Indeed, it has long been hypothesized that differences in recombination systems provide hosts with quite different strategies for controlling their pathogens (cf., the Red Queen hypothesis; Hamilton 1980).

In some cases, lack of the opportunity for completing a full life cycle can present major impediments to the development of pathogen populations, which in turn influences the geographic distribution of resistance in host populations. For example, the rust fungus *Cronartium comptoniae* is a full-cycle heteroecious rust fungus that naturally alternates between its telial and aecial hosts (*Myrica gale* and *Pinus contorta* respectively). Where the range of these two plant species overlaps, the pathogen is also present and significant levels of resistance are found in *P. contorta* populations. However, the geographic range of *P. contorta* is considerably greater than that of *M. gale* and outside their sympatric range, the pathogen is rarely found; populations of *P. contorta* are essentially susceptible (Hunt and Van Sickle 1984).

The presence or absence of sexual recombination may also have a marked effect on pathogen populations. Evidence for this is seen in two distinct examples – one from agriculture, the other from a naturally occurring interaction. In the first case, the contrast found between populations of wheat stem rust (*P. graminis* f.sp. *tritici*) in the Pacific Northwest and the Great Plains of the United States clearly demonstrates the contribution that sexual recombination makes to population diversity. In the Pacific North West, sexual recombination occurs annually leading to the generation of an enormous number of incipient clonal lineages, each with a distinctive genotype for both neutral (isozyme) and selected (pathogenicity) traits. A sample of 427 isolates collected from that population in 1975 contained 100 distinct pathotypes (Roelfs and Groth 1980), while among a sub-sample of 92 of those isolates (Burdon and Roelfs 1985), no two isolates with the same isozyme multilocus phenotype had the same combination of avirulence genes. When the possibility of sexual recombination is removed from such an interaction, population diversity falls dramatically and the way in which this diversity is distributed also changes markedly. Thus, further east in the Great Plains, the virtual eradication of barberry (the alternate host required to complete the sexual cycle) during the late 1920s generated significant genetic changes. On a yearly average, the number of distinct pathotypes fell by more than half while those that did occur could be grouped into a number of distinct clonal lineages that differ from one another by an average of 11 virulences and various isozyme markers (Roelfs and Groth 1980; Burdon and Roelfs 1985).

A not dissimilar effect is seen in the interaction between the herbaceous perennial *Linum marginale* and an associated rust pathogen (*Melampsora lini*) where differences in the extent of sexual recombination are found between montane and plains populations of both species. In montane regions the rust pathogen is trapped in an asexual cycle (Burdon and Roberts 1995), where it undergoes severe population crashes each winter; its sympatric hosts also show a high level of selfing. In contrast, on the plains, host populations show significant levels of outcrossing (~30 percent; Burdon et al. 1999). Although their sympatric pathogen populations face a summer survival bottleneck, this is ameliorated by the pathogen's ability to survive via telia and subsequently undergo sexual recombination (Barrett et al. 2008b). Comparisons of the resistance and avirulence structure of host and pathogen populations respectively showed significant differences in the diversity of pathogen populations between the two regions and the way in which resistance genes were distributed within and among host populations.

Two Closely Related But Different Hosts – One Pathogen

While the examples above give hints of the potential impact of mating system on host and pathogen diversity, and have strength as a result of their focus on the same host and pathogen species, their value is simultaneously weakened by the lack of a common environment. In contrast, analogous examples in a common environment could be achieved by comparing patterns of resistance and pathogenicity in two closely related, co-occurring host species which differ markedly in a particular life history feature.

To our knowledge, no such comparisons have yet been made, although a number of potential species comparisons exist. One such example occurs in Australia and New Zealand where the two closely related beach strandline species *Cakile edentula* (tight inbreeder) and *C. maritima* (obligate outcrosser) are both attacked by the necrotrophic pathogen, *Alternaria brassicicola*, making this an ideal system to investigate the evolution of resistance in individual host populations with contrasting recombination constraints (Cousens and Cousens 2011). Furthermore, data already exists for the *C. maritima – A. brassicicola* component of this potential comparison that clearly demonstrates the occurrence of severe pathogen epidemics, and the existence of variation in both host resistance and pathogen pathogenicity (Oliver et al. 2001; Thrall et al. 2001) - both necessary pre-conditions for pathogens to have a detectable role in the evolution of their hosts.

A not dissimilar example is found in the work of Sicard and her colleagues (2007) who assessed evidence for local adaptation in infectivity and aggressiveness in the pathogen *Colletotrichum lindemuthianum* attacking three native Mexican populations of *Phaseolus vulgaris*. This interaction was elaborated with a second association in which the pathogen was the same and the host closely related (*P. coccineus – Colletotrichum lindemuthianum*). The two host species differed in a number of life-history features – perenniality, population size and stability, and degree of outcrossing – but, while the pathogen showed evidence of local adaptation in its interaction with the annual *P. vulgaris*, it did not when attacking the longer-lived *P. coccineus* which is also predominately out-crossing.

One Host – Two Contrasting Pathogens

Biotrophic and necrotrophic pathogens exhibit distinct differences in their relationship with their hosts, especially with respect to survival. Biotroph populations (e.g., many rusts and mildews) typically undergo periodic seasonal crashes with individual demes within a metapopulation going extinct or being subject to marked genetic drift from one year to the next. Necrotroph populations, on the other hand, are usually far less affected by environmental change as they typically can survive in a saprophytic phase on dead plant material or generate persistent infections of perennial parts of the plant. These different life history strategies have been predicted to generate different epidemiological patterns and impose distinctly different selective regimes on hosts (Burdon et al. 1996) and their pathogens. Indeed, as demonstrated in the barley scald pathogen *Rhynchosporium secalis*, selection pressures may be quite different between parasitic and saprophytic phases of the life cycle (Abang et al. 2006).

Examples of this category of host–pathogen interaction abound and could include attack by different leaf pathogens [e.g., Meadowsweet (*Filipendula ulmaria*) attacked by *Melampsora* (biotrophic rust) and *Ramularia* (necrotrophic leaf blight)] or by pathogens attacking different organs [e.g., Poplar (*Populus* spp.) attacked by *Melampsora* (leaf rust) and *Hypoxylon* (stem canker)]. Thus, in the latter comparative set of host and pathogens, depending on the environment, both race-specific and more broadly based non-specific resistance has been detected in the interaction between *Populus* and *Melampsora* (Hsiang and Chastagner 1993, Prakash and Thielges 1987; see discussion above). In contrast, once established, the interaction between *Populus* and the stem canker fungus *Hypoxylon* is protected from environmental fluctuations, and progress through the tree is primarily determined by characters which are controlled through the combined action of multiple genes (French and Manion 1975).

Simulation Modelling and Meta-Analyses

In contrast to animal host-parasite and agriculturally based plant-pathogen interactions, there has been relatively little use of theoretical models to explore aspects of the impact of life-history characters on the epidemiological or evolutionary trajectory of natural plant-pathogen associations. However, the development of a general conceptual framework is critical for understanding links between different systems. For example, much of the current general theoretical work on animal host-parasite dynamics has been based on models that differentiate between two broad classes of parasites: micro- and macroparasites (Anderson and May 1981). Not only are there qualitative dynamical differences that emerge from these models, but this work has led to the recognition that different factors must be considered for these two broad classes of host-parasite systems.

A perceived lack of comparable generalizing principles with respect to natural plant-pathogen dynamics is probably due, in part, to a combination of the great range of plant pathogens and their diverse life histories (e.g., multiple hosts, free-living stages, vectors, vertical transmission, mortality vs. fecundity effects, epidemic vs. endemic) and the fact that study of plant-pathogen interactions has tended to arise from agriculture and forestry which focused more on traditional plant pathology approaches than on the tools of population biology. However, similar to the useful sets of generalizations that have been made for animal diseases (Lockhart *et al.* 1996), it seems likely that plant pathogens can also be divided into broad categories recognizing fundamentally different effects that are likely to transcend taxonomic categories. Thus even very general comparisons between associations involving (i) systemic diseases of plants with varying degrees of vegetative reproduction (Wennström and Ericson 1992); (ii) sporulation and infection characteristics in airborne pathogens (Sache and de Vallavielle Pope 1995); (iii) pathogen dispersal scale (Thrall and Burdon 1997); or differences in host fecundity and mortality effects (Burdon 1993) all illustrate the potential for life history differences to have consequences for co-evolutionary dynamics.

Indeed, an early comparative study assessing the success of biological control programs aimed at reducing the size of invasive weed populations demonstrated that the reproductive mode of the target species was an important factor in the success of biological control with species with low or no recombination being more vulnerable to pathogens than those with high levels of recombination (Burdon and Marshall 1981). More recently, some simple comparative models have been developed to generate insights into the most appropriate types of pathogen to deploy in biological control of weeds. Using a spatially explicit simulation modelling approach built around simple single life-history difference comparisons such as whether a pathogen has its impact solely through host fecundity or host mortality, Thrall and Burdon (2004) found that even with such broad caricatures, there were profound impacts on host population size and persistence, and the potential for evolution of host resistance. Importantly, the effect of these pathogen traits was itself mediated by host traits such as longevity. Other simulation studies, supported by some data from natural plant-pathogen interactions, also predict that increasing host longevity and connectivity of host patches is likely to select for pathogen strains with lower transmission rates as well as for hosts with higher resistance (Carlsson-Granér and Thrall 2002, 2006).

Many host and pathogen life-history traits are likely to have at least some impact on the intensity of ecological and evolutionary forces affecting individual associations. However, the nature and sign of those effects is often less than intuitively obvious, especially when such interactions are considered in realistic ecological settings involving spatially patchy, small, and ephemeral host populations in which genetic drift, extinction, and re-colonization are relatively frequent occurrences. In these circumstances, simulation modelling is a very powerful means of exploring the impact of variation in key host and pathogen life history features on patterns of disease incidence and prevalence and likely changes in the intensity of selective pressures leading to evolution of variation in resistance and virulence. Overall, a simulation modelling approach, particularly one that incorporates both demographic and genetic processes, will help understanding of how interactions between host and pathogen life-histories influence:

a) pathogen invasion and spread and the degree to which dynamics are endemic vs. epidemic;
b) levels of impact on host demography and fitness;
c) conditions favoring the evolution of different genetic systems of resistance and pathogenicity;
d) the maintenance of polymorphisms; and
e) correlated life histories of hosts and pathogens that are likely to favor long-term associations.

Conclusions

Individually empirical comparisons and simulation models both have their strengths and weaknesses. While comparisons in which one or more life history traits can be held constant provide powerful clues to the interactive effects of life history characters and host spatial heterogeneity in the long-term development of co-evolutionary trajectories of specific associations, at the same time, empirical testing of the causal relationships between, and polarity of, particular life-history attributes and the structure of host and pathogen populations is always going to be very difficult. Indeed, ultimately, unless sufficient comparisons are available to allow rigorous meta-analyses to be conducted, such studies will remain open to criticism that observed patterns are due to nothing more than chance or uncontrolled variation in other key factors. Stimulation of a broader range of empirical studies on natural host-pathogen interactions and the development of rigorous meta-analyses represent clear research challenges for the immediate future.

Similarly, simulation modelling can be extremely powerful in setting up direct comparisons between specific life-history traits and in uncovering counter-intuitive interactions. However, at the same time such models also suffer from an inevitable lack of biological reality, rapidly becoming unwieldy and complex as more variables are added.

The two approaches we advocate here – empirical comparisons and simulation modelling – are essential companion components in developing a strong conceptual framework grouping pathogens with similar ecologies. Doing this will stimulate the development of theory, provide testable hypotheses for empirical studies, and place the relative differences between long-term coevolved systems, recent exotic invasions, novel emerging pathogens, and biological control programs into a generally understandable context.

Acknowledgments

This research was supported by the National Institutes of Health (NIH grant 5RO1 GM074265-01A2).

Literature Cited

Abang, M.M.; Baum, M.; Ceccarelli, S.; Grando, S.; Linde, C.C.; Yahvaoui, A.; Zhan, J.S.; McDonald, B.A. 2006. Differential selection on *Rhychosporium secalis* during parasitic and saprophytic phases in the barley scald disease cycle. Phytopathology. 96: 1214–1222.

Anderson, R.M.; May, R.M. 1991. The population dynamics of micro-parasites and their invertebrate hosts. Philosophical Transactions Royal Society of London, Series B, Biological Sciences. 291: 451–524.

Barrett, L.G.; Kniskern, J.M.; Bodenhausen, N.; Zhang, W.; Bergelson, J. 2009. Continua of specificity and virulence in plant host-pathogen interactions: causes and consequences. New Phytologist 183: 513–529.

Barrett, L.G.; Thrall, P.H.; Burdon, J.J.; Linde, C.C. 2008a. Life history determines genetic structure and evolutionary potential of host-parasite interactions. Trends in Ecology and Evolution. 23: 678–685.

Barrett, L.G.; Thrall, P.H.; Burdon, J.J.; Linde, C.C.; Nicotra, A.B. 2008b. Population structure and diversity across sexual and asexual populations of the pathogenic fungus *Melampsora lini*. Molecular Ecology. 17: 3401–3415.

Barrett, S.C.H. 2002. The evolution of plant sexual diversity. Nature Reviews: Genetics. 3: 274–284.

Barrett, S.C.H.; Colautti, R.I.; Eckert, C.G. 2008. Plant reproductive systems and evolution during biological invasion. Molecular Ecology. 17: 373–383.

Burdon, J.J. 1993. The role of parasites in plant populations and communities. In: Schulze, E.-D.; Mooney, H.A., eds. Biodiversity and ecosystem function. Berlin: Springer-Verlag: 165–179.

Burdon, J.J.; Marshall, D.R. 1981. Biological control and the reproductive mode of weeds. Journal of Applied Ecology. 18: 649–658.

Burdon, J.J.; Oates, J.D.; Marshall, D.R. 1983. Interactions between *Avena* and *Puccinia* species. I. The wild hosts: *Avena barbata* Pott ex Link, *A. fatua* L. and *A. ludoviciana* Durieu. Journal of Applied Ecology. 20: 571–585.

Burdon, J.J.; Roberts, J.K. 1995. The population genetic structure of the rust fungus *Melampsora lini* as revealed by pathogenicity, isozyme and RFLP markers. Plant Pathology. 44: 270–278.

Burdon, J.J.; Roelfs, A.P. 1985. The effect of sexual and asexual reproduction on the isozyme structure of populations of *Puccinia graminis*. Phytopathology. 75: 1068–1073.

Burdon, J.J.; Thrall, P.H.; Brown, A.H.D. 1999. Resistance and virulence structure in two *Linum marginale - Melampsora lini* host-pathogen metapopulations with different mating systems. Evolution. 53: 704–716.

Burdon, J.J.; Wennström, A.; Elmqvist. T.; Kirby, G.C. 1996. The role of race specific resistance in natural plant populations. Oikos. 76: 411–416.

Carlsson-Granér, U.; Thrall, P.H. 2002. The spatial distribution of plant populations, disease dynamics and evolution of resistance. Oikos. 97: 97–110.

Carlsson-Granér, U.; Thrall, P.H. 2006. The impact of host longevity on disease transmission: host-pathogen dynamics and the evolution of resistance. Evolutionary Ecology Research. 8: 659–675.

Cousens, R.D.; Cousens, J.M. 2011. Invasion of the New Zealand coastline by European sea-rocket (*Cakile maritima*) and American sea-rocket (*Cakile edentula*). Invasive Plant Science and Management. 4: 260–263.

French, J.R.; Manion, P.D. 1975. Variability of host and pathogen in Hypoxylon canker of aspen. Canadian Journal of Botany. 53: 2740–2744.

Hamilton, W.D. 1980. Sex versus non-sex versus parasite. Oikos. 35: 282–290.

Hsiang, T.; Chastagner, G.A. 1993. Variation in *Melampsora occidentalis* rust on poplars in the Pacific Northwest. Canadian Journal of Plant Pathology. 15: 175–181.

Hunt, R.S.; Van Sickle, G.A. 1984. Variation in susceptibility to sweet fern rust among *Pinus contorta* and *P. banksiana*. Canadian Journal of Forestry Research. 14: 672–675.

Lockhart, A.B.; Thrall, P.H.; Antonovics, J. 1996. Sexually transmitted diseases in animals: ecological and evolutionary implications. Biological Reviews of the Cambridge Philosophical Society. 71: 415–471.

Oliver, E.J.; Thrall, P.H.; Burdon, J.J.; Ash, J.E. 2001. Vertical disease transmission in the *Cakile-Alternaria* host-pathogen interaction. Australian Journal of Botany. 49: 561–569.

Prakash, C.S.; Thielges, B.A. 1987. Pathogenic variation in *Melampsora medusae* leaf rust of poplars. Euphytica. 36: 563–570.

Roelfs, A.P.; Groth, J.V. 1980. A comparison of virulence phenotypes in wheat stem rust populations reproducing sexually and asexually. Phytopathology. 70: 855–862.

Sache, I.; de Vallavielle Pope, C. 1995. Classification of airborne plant pathogens based on sporulation and infection characteristics. Canadian Journal of Botany. 73: 1186–1195.

Sicard, D.; Pennings, P.S.; Grandclément, C.; Acosta, J.; Kaltz, O.; Shykoff, J.A. 2007. Specialization and local adaptation of a fungal parasite on two host species as revealed by two fitness traits. Evolution. 61: 27–41.

Thrall, P.H.; Burdon, J.J. 1997. Host-pathogen dynamics in a metapopulation context: the ecological and evolutionary consequences of being spatial. Journal of Ecology. 85: 743–753.

Thrall, P.H.; Burdon, J.J. 1999. The spatial scale of pathogen dispersal: consequences for disease dynamics and persistence. Evolutionary Ecology Research. 1: 681–701.

Thrall, P.H.; Burdon, J.J. 2002. Evolution of gene-for-gene systems in metapopulations: the effect of spatial scale of host and pathogen dispersal. Plant Pathology. 51: 169–184.

Thrall, P.H.; Burdon, J.J. 2004. Host-pathogen life-history interactions affect biological control success. Weed Technology. 18: 1269-1274.

Thrall, P.H.; Burdon, J.J.; Bock, C.H. 2001. Short-term epidemic dynamics in the *Cakile maritima – Alternaria brassicicola* host-pathogen metapopulation association. Journal of Ecology. 89: 723–735.

Wennström, A.; Ericson, L. 1992. Environmental heterogeneity and disease transmission within clones of *Lactuca sibirica*. Journal of Ecology 80: 71–77.

Integrating Regeneration, Genetic Resistance, and Timing of Intervention for the Long-Term Sustainability of Ecosystems Challenged by Non-Native Pests – a Novel Proactive Approach

A.W. Schoettle,[1] J.G. Klutsch,[1] and R.A. Sniezko[2]

Abstract

Global trade increases the likelihood of introduction of non-native, invasive species which can threaten native species and their associated ecosystems. This has led to significant impacts to forested landscapes, including extensive tree mortality, shifts in ecosystem composition, and vulnerabilities to other stresses. With the increased appreciation of the importance of healthy ecosystems for watershed protection, wildlife habitat, and aesthetics, we present a new management approach specifically designed for the long-term sustainability of ecosystems challenged by non-native pests for continued non-timber ecosystem services. Sustaining host population resilience in the presence of a non-native pest requires maintenance of the population's recovery capacity after disturbance, adaptive capacity over time, and multi-generational persistence. Therefore, the management approach must incorporate a long-term and evolutionary perspective which also incorporates continued adaptation to climate change. Management to promote self-sustaining host populations to support ecosystem processes and services can be implemented (1) in degraded ecosystems as reactive restoration management or (2) in threatened ecosystems not yet impacted as proactive intervention. When threatened ecosystems can be identified, we can choose to act proactively by gathering baseline genetic and ecological characteristics of the species and ecosystems to design timely interventions to increase resilience. Such a proactive approach herein referred to as the Proactive Strategy, can be contemplated for any threat that is anticipated to impact critical ecosystems. In this paper, we use the white pine blister rust – high elevation pine pathosystem as an example application. Genetic resistance is an essential management tool for both restoration and proactive management, yet the Proactive Strategy can also manipulate the timing of (1) resistance deployment and (2) landscape management of the mosaic of stand age class structures. These two additional tools provide further opportunities to sustain the host population and genetic diversity and mitigate the development of impacts over time. Populations having little disease resistance may need to be enhanced by direct planting. However, in other cases, manipulation of the age-class structure of stands across the landscape in populations in which heritable resistance is present at high enough frequency, can facilitate selection and accelerate the evolution of resistance after the pathogen eventually invades. Therefore, management that generates a mosaic of patches of different stand ages across a landscape can effectively generate patches with different rates of selection upon white pine blister rust invasion, thereby mitigating the effect of mortality in any one cohort or stand on overall ecosystem function of the greater landscape. Positioning ecosystems for greater resilience before invasion may avert impaired ecosystem conditions after invasion, when ecosystem services would be compromised, and reduce the need for later restoration. Regeneration is a stabilizing factor in populations; how and when it is managed in coordination with gene frequencies for resistance will play an important role in the establishment of a new sustainable condition for the host population and its ecosystems in the presence of a non-native pest.

Key words: genetic resistance, disease impacts, proactive strategy, *Cronartium ribicola*, invasive species

Proactive vs. Reactive Strategy

Global trade increases the likelihood of introduction of non-native, invasive species which can threaten native species and their associated ecosystems. This has led to significant forested landscape

[1] USDA Forest Service, Rocky Mountain Research Station, Fort Collins, CO.
[2] USDA Forest Service, Dorena Genetic Resource Center, Cottage Grove, OR.
Corresponding author: aschoettle@fs.fed.us.

impacts, including extensive tree mortality, shifts in ecosystem composition, and vulnerabilities to other stresses.

Until recently, the use of genetic resistance to mitigate disease impacts in forest trees was focused primarily on plantation species, principally because of their obvious economic importance and the cost involved. However, as invasive species continue to decimate ecosystems beyond the traditionally managed forests, there is now an ever-increasing appreciation of the importance of sustaining healthy ecosystems that provide services such as snow capture, watershed protection, wildlife habitat, and aesthetics. As with the plantation species, there will be a cost involved, but we suggest that in some cases, it may be time to consider novel approaches specifically designed for the long-term sustainability of ecosystems challenged by non-native pests for continued non-timber ecosystem services. We present a proactive strategy that offers options for addressing a potential problem early and focuses on sustaining healthy ecosystems in the presence of an invasive species.

In some cases, non-native species spread slowly enough through a host species range to allow early-affected ecosystems to be studied and to identify threatened, but not-yet-impacted, ecosystems. For threatened ecosystems, we have a choice between acting proactively to increase resilience of the threatened ecosystem or waiting until it is degraded before doing restoration management (fig. 1). If ecosystems have been invaded and are already heavily impacted by a non-native species, the Restoration Strategy pathway (upper pathway, fig. 1) is the only option for restoring ecosystem function. In ecosystems threatened, but not yet heavily impacted by a non-native species, the Proactive Strategy (lower pathway, fig. 1) can be followed to minimize impaired ecosystem conditions and sustain ecosystem function during naturalization of the pest.

Both approaches have uncertainty. While genetic resistance is an essential management tool for both, the Proactive Strategy can also manipulate the timing of resistance deployment and the mosaic of stand age-class structures across the landscape to utilize natural processes to further support resilience over time. These two additional tools provide further opportunities to sustain populations and genetic diversity and mitigate the development of impacts over time (Schoettle and Sniezko 2007). Additional opportunities of the Proactive Strategy include (1) gathering baseline genetic and ecological characteristics of the species and intact ecosystems, including the frequency of resistance to the non-native invader; (2) minimizing genetic bottlenecks through gene conservation and management efforts; (3) timing interventions relative to invasion for optimal benefit; and (4) manipulating natural processes to promote further intervention effectiveness.

Proactive Strategy approaches can be developed for many ecosystems challenged by invasive organisms, climate change, or other anthropogenic stress. For the purposes of this paper, the discussion will focus on its application to invasions by *Cronartium ribicola*, the non-native pathogen that causes white pine blister rust (WPBR), in North American five-needle pine (Family Pinaceae, Genus *Pinus*, Subgenus *Strobus*) ecosystems. The fungus was introduced to North America in the early 1900s and continues to spread. All of the North American five-needle pines have at least low frequencies of genetic resistance, yet high mortality is unavoidable (Sniezko et al. 2011a). The southern Rocky Mountains and Great Basin are currently at the expansion front for WPBR in the western United States. These landscapes are susceptible to invasion, and microclimate analyses suggest that invasion of the pathogen over time is inevitable (Howell et al. 2006). This paper provides an overview of some of the key elements of the Strategy and highlights some measures currently being implemented (e.g. gene conservation, screening seedling progenies for genetic resistance, stand dynamics studies, and modeling) as an integrated program in the southern Rocky Mountains.

The rust disease has caused high mortality in five-needle pine species in the northern Rocky Mountains (Tomback and Achuff 2010). The western white pine (*Pinus monticola* Douglas ex D. Don) timber industry collapsed and the incidence of this species is now a small fraction of its historic occurrence (Fins et al. 2001). As a consequence of WPBR, mountain pine beetle, and climate change pressures, whitebark pine (*Pinus albicaulis* Engelm.), a non-timber species, has recently been listed as a candidate species for endangered status under the Endangered Species Act in the United States, and is listed along with limber pine (*Pinus flexilis* James) as Endangered under the Alberta Wildlife Act in Canada. With early intervention, we can position the threatened populations of five-needle pines so that they do not follow the same trajectory as whitebark pine.

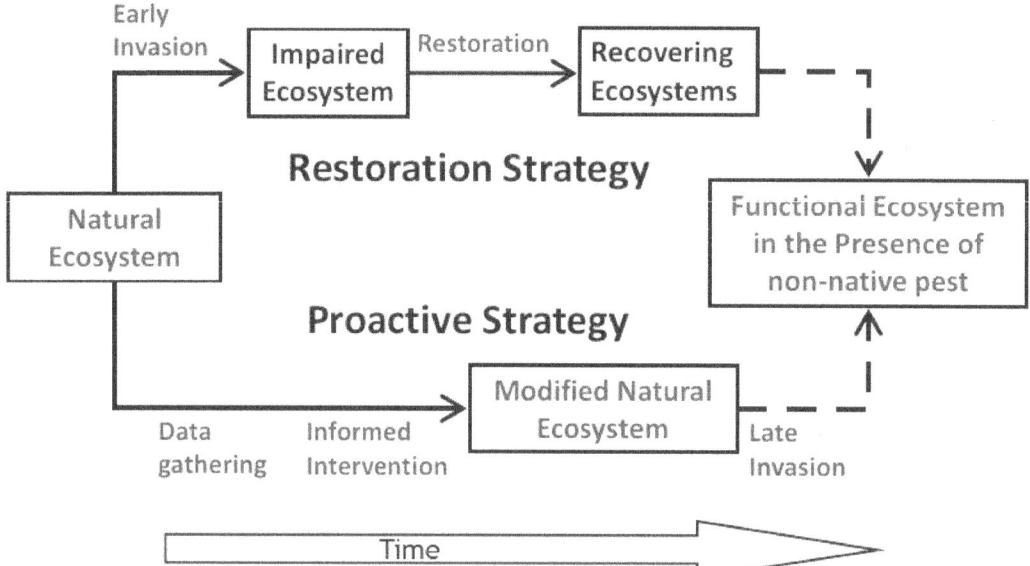

Figure 1—A schematic of pathways for facilitating transitions from native ecosystems threatened by a non-native species to functional ecosystems where the invader is present.

Shifting to an Evolutionary Perspective

Historically, the context for management of genetic resources to mitigate disease impacts has been plantation forestry. However, the management goals for non-timber species differ from those for species for extracting timber resources. Restoration efforts for timber species focus primarily on managing tree growth to merchantable size and are supported by intensive resistance breeding programs (e.g., Kearns et al. 2012, Schwandt et al. 2010). Five-needle pines that are not timber resources, but are important components of natural ecosystems, such as whitebark, limber, and Rocky Mountain bristlecone (*Pinus aristata* Engelm.) pines, and in some areas western white pine, provide ecosystem services (e.g., watershed protection and wildlife habitat) that depend not just on the health of the pines, but the overall ecosystem (Schoettle 2004, Tomback and Achuff 2010). These pines and their ecosystems are traditionally not managed and are in remote, high-elevation areas, including wilderness. They are also considered foundation and keystone species and are often the only tree species that can tolerate the extreme environmental conditions at treeline. As a consequence, other species are not available to replace the trees' ecological functions, should the five-needle pines be lost from the ecosystem (Tomback et al. 2011). The management goal for these ecosystems is promotion of self-sustaining pine populations in the presence of WPBR and other stresses to support ecosystems processes and services (Keane and Schoettle 2011, Schoettle and Sniezko 2007). Therefore, success is evaluated on multi-generation outcomes of the treated landscape in contrast to the stand-based, generation-by-generation, outcomes for plantation forestry.

Sustaining population resilience requires maintenance of populations' (1) recovery capacity after disturbance, (2) genetic diversity to support adaptive capacity over time, and (3) multi-generational persistence. Therefore, the management approach must incorporate a long-term and evolutionary perspective which also incorporates adaptation to climate change. Maintaining a functioning regeneration cycle is essential as it is the engine that supports post-disturbance recovery and enables selected traits to accumulate within populations (fig. 2 – solid narrow arrows). Unfortunately for the high-elevation, non-timber five-needle pines, generation time is very long. The species are not prolific seed producers and establishment of seedlings after disturbance is protracted in the harsh high-elevation habitats and is constrained by competition by other species on more moderate sites (e.g., Coop and Schoettle 2009). Once established, high-elevation five-needle pine seedlings mature very slowly and only begin to produce full cone crops after 100 years under natural conditions. The mature trees can be long-lived, commonly reaching ages of 1,000 years. These species are tolerant of stresses under which they have evolved, but are not well equipped, without additional regeneration opportunities, for rapid adaptation to novel stresses such as those imposed by the introduction of *C. ribicola* in a changing climate.

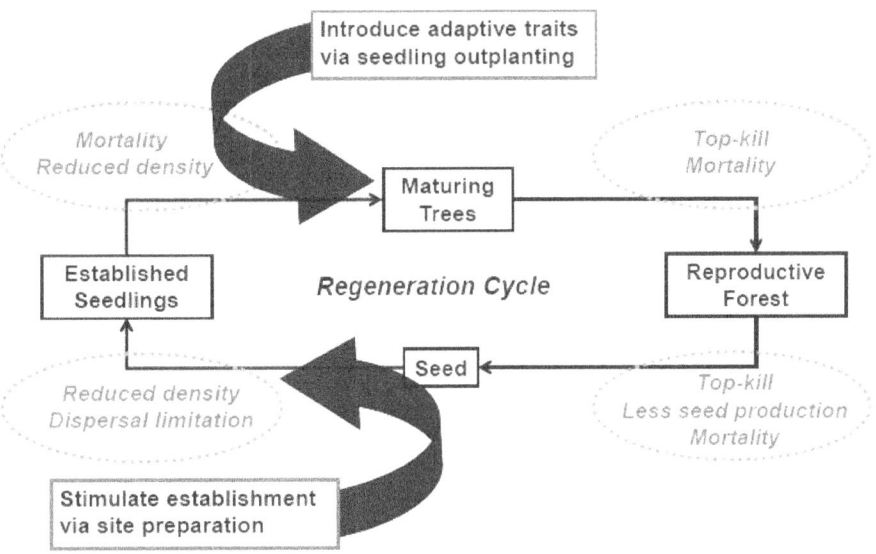

Figure 2—Flow diagram of the forest regeneration cycle and the points of interaction with white pine blister rust and management. White pine blister rust can cause impacts (ovals) at all life stage. Broad arrows depict intervention options for increasing blister rust resistance and population resiliency. (Redrawn from Schoettle et al. 2009)

Managing Host Demography to Offset Disease-Caused Mortality

In some cases, the regeneration cycle can be managed to increase the resilience of the host population to mortality from non-native disease even without genetic disease resistance. *Cronartium ribicola* impacts the regeneration cycle of the pines at each life stage: rapidly killing young seedlings, reducing cone production in infected mature trees, and later causing mature tree mortality (fig. 2 – ovals) (Schoettle and Sniezko 2007). At locations where infection is high, the number of survivors may be insufficient to sustain populations. Maintaining a functioning regeneration cycle requires trees from multiple age classes distributed across landscapes.

Using a population infection model parameterized for high–elevation, five-needle pines and WPBR, Field et al. (2012) reveal that pine populations with high seedling recruitment are sustainable under moderate levels of WPBR infection (table 1). In contrast, in a situation where regeneration is suppressed by inter-specific competition, the model predicts that WPBR-caused mortality and inter-specific competition further depress regeneration and the population enters a downward spiral. Alternatively, if regeneration is stimulated by removing inter-specific competing trees prior to rust invasion, the population remains sustainable under the same infection conditions. The greater the regeneration capacity of a population, the greater is its recovery ability and tolerance of the population to mortality under moderate disease pressure. Therefore, management to promote regeneration in low to moderate rust hazard sites will contribute to populations' resilience upon *C. ribicola* invasion (fig. 2 – lower broad arrow). Under conditions of greater infection, regeneration can slow, but not offset, population decline (table 1). These model runs are conservative as they do not include other important disturbance agents such as bark beetles that further compromise the population and impose demographic imbalances by selectively reducing mature cohorts at their peak of fecundity.

Table 1—Model predictions of population projections for three high-elevation, five-needle pine populations[a]

Competition	Zero Infection Probability		Mod. Infection Probability		High Infection Probability	
	MA	TotPop	MA	TotPop	MA	TotPop
None	354	624	171	815	70	165
High	200	354	59	145	38	60
High → Low	404	472	176	746	42	99

[a] The initial stage structure for the no inter-specific competition and high inter-specific competition are at equilibrium densities (trees per hectare at zero infection probability) and the initial conditions for the high to low competition condition are equilibrium five-needle pine densities with inter-specific competition and then competitors are removed at time zero. White pine blister rust is introduced (except for the "zero infection probability" case) at time zero, and projections are for 200 years. The density (per hectare) predictions include mature adults (MA), total population (TotPop) at 200 years. See Field et al. (2012) for more details. Data adapted from Field et al. (2012).

The ability of a population to respond to site manipulation for increased seedling establishment is time dependent in the rust-pine pathosystem. Because WPBR kills trees of all ages, and therefore directly impacts the pine regeneration cycle, intervention to increase seedling establishment is best accomplished before or during the early stages of WPBR invasion. Attempts to stimulate regeneration in whitebark pine forests heavily impacted by WPBR have failed to produce established seedlings, even after more than a decade (Keane and Parsons 2010). Therefore, this intervention option is a tool unique to the Proactive Strategy.

The model suggests that management of regeneration can favorably affect the outcome of a population under low to moderate rust hazard conditions. We know regeneration capacity varies among habitats (Coop and Schoettle 2009). Integrating this understanding into risk and hazard models can provide further guidance for the spatial design and prioritization of treatment areas and improved outcome projections. Regeneration capacity information can be gained through field surveys and studies of healthy ecosystems and is much more difficult to ascertain in ecosystems already impaired by disease.

Managing the Regeneration Cycle for Increased Disease Resistance

Due to the harsh sites that high-elevation, five-needle pines occupy, protracted regeneration dynamics on those sites, and persistence of introduced pathogens, management of demographic structure and distribution alone will not sustain all pine populations in the presence of WPBR. Reducing the effect of disease on survival and fecundity by increasing heritable disease resistance is essential to sustaining many of these populations and ecosystems services. Fortunately, some level of natural genetic resistance to this non-native pathogen is present in each North American five-needle pine species, and many trials are underway to discern geographic patterns of resistance and identify parent trees and populations for protection and from which seed collections can be made (Schoettle et al. 2011b; Sniezko et al. 2007, 2011a). Ultimately, we need to increase the frequencies of resistance genes over landscapes to help establish a new equilibrium from which pine species and associated ecosystems will have the best opportunity to exist and function in the face of the permanent residence of *C. ribicola*. We can also learn from studying ecosystems where the disease is native. Resistance, life history traits and disturbance dynamics of white pine species that have co-evolved with *C. ribicola*, such as in Russia and other parts of Asia, provide optimism as well as insights into possible equilibrium population outcomes for North American species.

Early deployment of genetic resistance through artificial regeneration and stimulating natural regeneration to facilitate selection of genetic resistance are key tools for preparing a threatened landscape for invasion (Schoettle and Sniezko 2007). The natural frequency of resistance will determine if supplemental resistance is required through outplanting (fig. 2 – upper broad arrow) or if the natural frequency of resistance can be increased sufficiently via natural regeneration (fig. 2 – lower broad arrow).

Benefits of Estimating Baseline Resistance Frequencies

Estimates of disease resistance frequencies and their geographic distributions in threatened native pine populations provide valuable information for designing, prioritizing, and evaluating proactive management options. Similar to assessing variation in regeneration capacity, estimating the frequencies of disease resistance in the host populations is best accomplished in non-invaded populations where sampling is not biased by disease-caused tree mortality or reduced cone production. Likewise, collections of seed, pollen, buds/scion, and DNA in intact ecosystems offer opportunities for gene conservation of the full genetic diversity of the host before it is reduced by the disease.

Information on resistance mechanisms and their frequencies helps identify the populations that are least and most susceptible to disease-caused mortality. For example, the proportion of seedlings from different seedlots collected from healthy populations of Rocky Mountain bristlecone pine that were disease-free 3 years after heavy artificial inoculation with *C. ribicola* ranged from 17 to 60 percent, demonstrating both high levels of natural resistance and high variability across the range of this host species (Schoettle et al. 2011b). In combination with mapping disease risk and regeneration potential of the site, the types and geographic distribution of genetic resistance can be used to prioritize and implement proactive management options (Schoettle et al. 2011a). North American white pine species show a number of types of resistance to WPBR (Hoff and McDonald 1980, Kegley and Sniezko 2004, Kinloch and Davis 1996, Kinloch and Dupper 2002, Kinloch et al. 2003, Sniezko and Kegley 2003, Sniezko et al. 2007, 2008). Early identification of areas with simply-inherited resistance mechanisms (e.g., R genes) versus those with complex polygenic inheritance also offers insight into resistance durability which should be included in management planning.

Supplementing Resistance Through Artificial Regeneration

If resistant stock is planted in a mosaic across the landscape before or at the time of WPBR invasion, young resistant trees will be maturing as older, diseased trees are dying (Schoettle and Sniezko 2007). Not only would these resistant trees be providing ecosystem services in the eventually disease-impacted landscape, they would also provide pollen, and eventually seed, for the flow of resistance genes to neighboring native populations. Therefore, the earlier resistant seedlings can be planted before WPBR invasion the shorter the window of time the recovery capacity (i.e., ability to produce sufficient seed to regenerate) of the overall population is compromised upon invasion. Planting also offers opportunity to provide 'assisted migration' if needed to help counter-balance the projected impacts of climate change. With a proactive deployment of genetic resistance, the amount of time that ecosystem services are at risk for interruption by the disease is reduced.

Development of disease-resistant planting material for proactive deployment requires (1) transport of seed from resistant parent trees identified from distant areas already impacted by the disease or (2) identification of resistant seedtrees in local, healthy host populations. In populations already invaded, seeds are traditionally collected from individual trees that appear disease-free or have less severe disease symptoms than most of the other trees in the population. The progeny from these putatively resistant trees are then screened for heritable resistance under controlled conditions and further tested under natural growing conditions (Sniezko et al. 2011a). In combination with genecological studies, the consequences of seed movement (i.e., using non-local seed sources) can be evaluated and appropriate seed sources identified. The development of seed orchards is one option to maximize the level of, and availability of, resistant seed. However, because maturation of high-elevation, five-needle pines is slow, orchards will not provide seed in the near future. For immediate and near future needs, the only option is to utilize seed collections from parent trees in natural ecosystems. To identify resistant seed trees in populations not yet invaded by the pathogen, pre-selection of seed trees for putative resistance traits is not possible, so trees are essentially random samples from the population. This may appear to be inefficient compared to identifying putatively resistant seedtrees in impacted areas; however the benefits of early resistance identification and deployment for sustained ecosystem benefits could be substantial and warrant the extra effort. Fortunately, rust screening facilities can evaluate progenies from 100s to 1,000s of parent trees in a relatively short time. With proper sampling, these studies also offer added significant benefits for gene conservation and providing estimates of the baseline population frequencies of disease resistance, allowing a forecast of the likely direct impacts of the disease before it happens and enabling managers to make more informed decisions (see above; Schoettle et al. 2011b,Sniezko et al. 2011a, 2011b).

In the southern Rocky Mountains, genetic resistance to WPBR has been identified in healthy limber pine and Rocky Mountain bristlecone pine populations (Schoettle et al. 2011b) and summaries of the geographic distribution of some resistances are underway. Screening studies allow us to discern (1) if there is resistance, (2) what level of resistance is present, and (3) how it is distributed over landscapes. They also provide some first ideas on how resistance might be inherited (which influences strategies) and how many types of resistance are present and whether they would be durable under different sets of circumstances. This provides a foundation for further work on the underlying mechanisms and the genes involved. This early detection of resistance has enabled *in situ* protection of WPBR-resistant seed trees and populations from the recent mountain pine beetle (*Dendroctonus ponderosae*) epidemic, collection of resistant seed stocks for outplanting and gene conservation, and refinement of management plans (Schoettle et al. 2011a).

Facilitating Selection for Resistance Through Landscape Management

Planting resistant stock will be needed in populations with little disease resistance. However, in populations in which heritable resistance is present at high enough frequency, manipulation of the age class structure of stands across the landscape can facilitate selection and therefore accelerate the evolution of resistance throughout the population once WPBR invades (Schoettle and Sniezko 2007). After infection with WPBR, young trees are killed more quickly than older, larger trees, so selection for resistance proceeds more rapidly in younger cohorts. The model of Field et al. (2012) demonstrates high mortality of young seedlings even when all age cohorts have the same probability of infection (see fig. 11 in Field et al. 2012). When an R gene for WPBR resistance is incorporated into the model, it shows accelerated increase in the allele frequency in younger cohorts (Schoettle et al., unpublished information). Consequently, selection against susceptible genotypes (i.e., disease-caused mortality) will occur more rapidly in young stands than older stands. Therefore, management that generates a mosaic of patches of different stand ages across a landscape can effectively generate patches with different rates of selection upon WPBR invasion, thereby mitigating the effect of mortality in any one cohort or stand on overall ecosystem function of the greater landscape.

A landscape of diverse age class structures will also reduce the susceptibility of the populations to future impacts by mountain pine beetle. Likewise, in other host-pest systems, a diversified host age-class structure may affect not only the distribution of mortality, but also susceptibility to infection or infestation by those pests that preferentially infest one host age or size over another. The scale of the landscape, the patch sizes, and the portion of the landscape that is managed can be adjusted to optimize gene flow and management objectives. At a minimum, establishment of some refugia populations with resistance and genetic diversity would serve as progenitors of future generations and re-establishment. The landscape perspective can help manage the effects of mortality and retain overall population resilience and ecosystem services.

Continued Management to Promote Further Adaptive Capacity

Whether the genetic resistance was in the native population or added via artificial regeneration, maintaining a diverse mosaic of stand structures across the landscape will sustain the benefits of initial interventions, facilitate further adaptation to changing climate conditions, and reduce susceptibility to mountain pine beetle impacts. Future estimates of resistance frequencies in populations can be compared to original baseline resistance frequencies to assess management efficacy and detect changes in durability of resistance. Likewise, changes in environmental condition with climate change may also affect the expression or efficacy of resistance.

The introduction of a non-native pathogen changes many dynamics for host species (McDonald et al. 2005). The disturbance regime to best promote adaptation to this novel stress is not likely to be the same as the historic pattern for the species (Coop and Schoettle 2011); monitoring and research is needed on these new landscapes as they develop to optimize the mosaic for adaptation and sustainability of the pine and ultimately naturalization of the rust.

Applying the Proactive Strategy – Southern Rockies Example

In 2008, the USDA Forest Service Rocky Mountain Research Station (RMRS), Rocky Mountain National Park (RMNP), USDA Forest Service, Rocky Mountain Region Forest Health Management, several National Forest districts, and USDA Forest Service Dorena Genetic Resource Center initiated an application of the Proactive Strategy to conserve and develop management plans for limber pine in Rocky Mountain National Park and northern Colorado. Approximately 42,000 ha of limber pine occur in this area. Most are threatened and not yet impacted by WPBR.

The objectives of the cooperative program to conserve and sustain limber pine on the northern Colorado landscape are five-fold: (1) protect limber pine from the mountain pine beetle epidemic so seed collections can immediately be made for WPBR resistance tests, genetic conservation, and research; (2) screen seedlings for WPBR resistance to determine the frequency of resistance across the landscape and to identify resistant parent trees and populations for further seed collections; (3) estimate population differentiation along the elevation and latitudinal gradient to refine seed transfer guidelines; (4) survey forest health, biotic damage incidence, regeneration capacity, and advanced regeneration condition to project persistence of these populations after MPB invasion; and (5) prepare proactive management plans for northern Colorado. The program is described in detail by Schoettle et al. (2011a).

The Northern Colorado Limber Pine Conservation Program contributes site-specific scientific data and tools for decision making about the need for and/or trade-offs of intervention to promote sustainability of limber pine populations in the presence of multiple stressors (WPBR and mountain pine beetle). Some of the information, tools, and activities, such as estimating rust resistance frequency, understanding natural regeneration dynamics, and capturing the pine's full genetic diversity via seed collections, can only be taken advantage of in healthy forests that have not yet had their processes disrupted by these stressors. Common garden studies are also underway to refine seed transfer guidelines. The early availability of information facilitates justification and direction for interventions if prescribed and permits the inclusion of science-based information in prioritizing sites for strategic planning. It also provides the opportunity for early implementation of some management options, such as stimulating regeneration in populations with high frequencies of rust resistance, that are best implemented when those forests are still healthy. Gathering and using this information before the loss of ecosystem functions allows land managers the widest range of management options to sustain limber pine populations and mitigate future impacts in these ecologically important ecosystems.

The Proactive Strategy framework can be adapted for other five-needle pine species threatened by WPBR and/or mountain pine beetle and possibly for other pathosystems. It is currently also being applied in Rocky Mountain bristlecone pine and Great Basin bristlecone pine (*Pinus longaeva* D.K. Bailey) ecosystems and is being adopted for some remaining healthy whitebark pine ecosystems. An intensive location-based program, such as that implemented in northern Colorado, is especially appropriate for administrative units that want to use local genotypes as much as possible, such as national parks. Understanding the interaction of the species' life history traits and ecology with resistance mechanisms will highlight factors that limit the species' sustainability in the presence of the pathogen. Focusing timely management on maintaining genetic diversity and a functional regeneration cycle will promote sustained adaptive capacity and ecosystem resiliency. Early intervention activities also allow better potential maintenance of overall genetic diversity within the species which provides the foundation for the species to continue to evolve in a changing environment.

Summary

Managing threatened populations and ecosystems that are not yet impacted by a non-native pest can position the population or ecosystem for greater resilience. The Proactive Strategy is especially appropriate for long-lived, slow-maturing species. Utilization of genetic tools in conjunction with timely management of natural demographic processes can facilitate the transition of the native ecosystems to a new and sustainable condition in the presence of the introduced pest. Early research on healthy populations enables regeneration capacity and disease resistance frequencies and their geographic distributions to be estimated, enabling more accurate forecasting of impacts and providing valuable information for designing, prioritizing, and evaluating management options. Early intervention allows management to (1) increase regeneration to increase genetic combinations and offset disease-caused mortality; (2) deploy resistance in a temporal and spatial array to promote population persistence and gene flow; (3) diversify the age class structures on the landscape to affect selection rates, mitigate impacts of mortality, and promote further adaptive capacity; and (4) preserve genetic diversity with in situ and ex situ conservation. Positioning the ecosystems for greater resilience before invasion may avoid the impaired ecosystem condition after invasion when ecosystem services are compromised and reduce the likelihood of the need for restoration later. Information learned while conducting the Proactive Strategy can likewise help inform restoration efforts in impacted ecosystems. Effective implementation of the strategy requires a concerted effort by researchers, forest health professionals, and land managers working together.

The existing genetic management programs (including development of disease resistance) for the timber species provide infrastructure and a solid foundation of knowledge about genetic disease resistance and management from which to more efficiently build management plans for ecosystems that deliver essential ecosystem services. Building on this foundation and shifting from a stand-based plantation perspective to a landscape evolutionary perspective requires considerations, and provides opportunities for managing host demographics and timing of intervention to achieve multi-generational sustainability of populations that can maintain ecosystem functions. Regeneration is a stabilizing factor and is an important factor in determining if a new sustainable condition is established or the population spirals into decline in the presence of the disease.

Gathering information in threatened, but not-yet-impacted, ecosystems also allows time to explore the interactions of life-history traits of the host with (1) pathogen infection, (2) regeneration capacity, (3) heritable resistance, (4) cost of infection on survival and fecundity, and (5) transitory population dynamics (Field et al. 2012). All of these factors affect the outcome of invasion on the populations, and through modeling, insights can be gained to optimize the type and timing of management interventions for the best outcomes. Co-evolution dynamics between the host and pest are also important to consider when implementing either proactive or restoration approaches. As we learn more about these interactions for specific pathosystems and develop silvicultural prescriptions to manipulate regeneration dynamics, it will enable us to further address these and other key questions: (1) What frequency of resistance(s) is enough to sustain a population under an array of conditions? (2) What spatial arrangement of structural and genetic diversity on the landscape is best to optimize selection, regeneration, gene flow, and adaptive capacity for long-term host population sustainability? (3) When during the invasion process does intervention achieve optimal ecological effectiveness? (4) What will be the characteristics of the new population condition and how will it behave in relation to natural disturbances after pathogen naturalization? (5) What are the public preferences and economic and ecological trade-offs of different management options implemented at different times during the invasion process?

The recent national-level directive on the management of invasive species across aquatic and terrestrial areas of the U.S. National Forest System (U.S. Department of Agriculture, Forest Service 2011) includes an aspiration to sustain healthy native ecosystems through proactive detection and mitigation of ecosystems threatened or impacted by non-native species. High-elevation pine forests, under the threat of multiple stressors, serve as an excellent flagship to lead the paradigm shift away from crisis management and toward proactive management for ecosystem resilience. The Proactive Strategy is a novel approach to providing information and technologies to make informed decisions to better sustain mountaintop ecosystems. The components of the strategy are also amendable to other biotic and abiotic agents that will impact forest ecosystems.

Acknowledgments

We would like to thank Mike Antolin, Stu Field, Kelly Burns, Jeff Connor, Betsy Goodrich, Angelia Kegley, Bill Jacobi, Jonathan Coop, and Phyllis Pineda-Bovin for their collaborations and many discussions regarding this topic. We also thank Paul Zambino and John King for their helpful reviews of an earlier version of this manuscript.

Literature Cited

Coop, J.D.; Schoettle, A.W. 2009. Regeneration of Rocky Mountain bristlecone pine (*Pinus aristata*) and limber pine (*Pinus flexilis*) three decades after stand-replacing fires. Forest Ecology and Management. 257: 893–903.

Coop, J.D.; Schoettle, A.W. 2011. Fire and high-elevation, five-needle pine (*Pinus aristata* & *P. flexilis*) ecosystems in the southern Rocky Mountains: What do we know? In: Keane, R.E.; Tomback, D.F.; Murray, M.P.; Smith, C.M., eds. The future of high-elevation, five-needle white pines in western North America: proceedings of the high five symposium. Proc. RMRS-P-63. Fort Collins, CO: U.S. Department of Agriculture, Forest Service, Rocky Mountain Research Station: 164–175. http://www.fs.fed.us/rm/pubs/rmrs_p063/rmrs_p063_164_173.pdf. (03 May 2012).

Field, S.G.; Schoettle, A.W.; Klutsch, J.G.; Tavener, S.J.; Antolin, M.F. 2012. Demographic projection of high-elevation white pines infected with white pine blister rust: a nonlinear disease model. Ecological Applications. 22: 166–183.

Fins, L.; Byler, J.; Ferguson, D.; Harvey, A.; Mahalovich, M.F.; McDonald, G.; Miller, D.; Schwandt, J.; Zach, A. 2001. Return of the giants: restoring white pine ecosystems by breeding and aggressive planting of blister rust-resistant white pines. Station Bulletin 72. Moscow, ID: University of Idaho, College of Natural Resources. 20 p. http://www.fs.fed.us/rm/pubs_other/rmrs_2001_fins_l001.pdf . (02 May 2012).

Hoff, R.J.; McDonald, G.I. 1980. Improving rust-resistant strains of inland western white pine. Res. Pap. INT-245. Ogden, UT: U.S. Department of Agriculture, Forest Service, Intermountain Forest and Range Experiment Station. 13 p.

Howell, B.; Burns, K.S.; Kearns, H.S.; Witcosky, J.J.; Cross, F. 2006. Biological evaluation of a model for predicting presence of white pine blister rust in Colorado based on climatic variable and susceptible white pine species distribution. Biological Evaluation. R2-06-04. Lakewood, CO: U.S. Department of Agriculture, Forest Service, Rocky Mountain Region, Renewable Resources. 15 p.

Keane, R.E.; Parsons, R.A. 2010. A management guide to ecosystem restoration treatments: the whitebark pine forests of the northern Rocky Mountains. Gen. Tech. Rep. RMRS-GTR-232. Fort Collins, CO: U.S. Department of Agriculture, Forest Service, Rocky Mountain Research Station. 133 p.

Keane, R.E.; Schoettle, A.W. 2011. Plenary paper: Strategies, tools, and challenges for sustaining and restoring high elevation five-needle white pine forests in western North America. In: Keane, R.E.; Tomback, D.F.; Murray, M.P.; Smith, C.M., eds. The future of high-elevation, five-needle white pines in western North America: proceedings of the high five symposium. Proc. RMRS-P-63. Fort Collins, CO: U.S. Department of Agriculture, Forest Service, Rocky Mountain Research Station: 276–294. http://www fs.fed.us/rm/pubs/rmrs_p063/rmrs_p063_276_294.pdf. (03 May 2012).

Kearns, H.S.J.; Ferguson, B.A.; Schwandt, J.W. 2012. Performance of rust-resistant western white pine in operational plantations in northern Idaho: 1995-2006. Report 12-03. Missoula, MT: U.S. Department of Agriculture, Forest Service, Forest Health Protection, Northern Region.

Kegley, A.J.; Sniezko, R.A. 2004. Variation in blister rust resistance among 226 *Pinus monticola* and 217 *P. lambertiana* seedling families in the Pacific Northwest. In: Sniezko, RA; Samman, S.; Schlarbaum, S.E.; Kriebel, H.B., eds. Breeding and genetic resources of five-needle pines: growth, adaptability and pest resistance. Proceedings RMRS-P-32. Fort Collins, CO: U.S. Department of Agriculture, Forest Service, Rocky Mountain Research Station: 209–226. http://www.fs fed.us/rm/pubs/rmrs_p032 html. (05 May 2012).

Kinloch, B.B., Jr.; Davis, D.A. 1996. Mechanisms and inheritance of resistance to blister rust in sugar pine. In: Kinloch, B.B., Jr.; Marosy, M.; Huddleston, M.E., eds. Sugar pine: status, values, and roles in ecosystems. Davis, CA: University of California, Division of Agriculture and Natural Resources: 125–132.

Kinloch, B.B., Jr.; Dupper, G.E. 2002. Genetic specificity in the white pine-blister rust pathosystem. Phytopathology. 92: 278–280.

Kinloch, B.B., Jr.; Sniezko, R.A.; Dupper, G.E. 2003. Origin and distribution of Cr2, a gene for resistance to white pine blister rust in natural populations of western white pine. Phytopathology. 93: 691–694.

McDonald, G.I.; Zambino, P.J.; Klopfenstein, N.B. 2005. Naturalization of host-dependent microbes after introduction into terrestrial ecosystems: Evolutionary epidemiology of white pine blister rust. In: Lundquist, J.E.; Hamelin, R.C., eds. From molecules to ecosystems - forest pathology in the era of genes and landscapes. St. Paul, MN: American Phytopathological Society Press: 41–57.

Schoettle, A.W. 2004. Ecological roles of five-needle pines in Colorado: potential consequences of their loss. In: Sniezko, R.A.; Samman, A.S.; Schlarbaum, S.E.; Kriebel, H.B., eds. Breeding and genetic resources of five-needle pines: growth, adaptability, and pest resistance. RMRS-P-32. Ft. Collins, CO: U.S. Department of Agriculture, Forest Service, Rocky Mountain Research Station: 124–135. http://www fs.fed.us/rm/pubs/rmrs_p032/rmrs_p032_124_135.pdf. (05 May 2012).

Schoettle, A.W.; Goodrich, B.A.; Klutsch, J.G.; Burns, K.S.; Costello, S.; Sniezko, R.A.; Connor, J. 2011a. The proactive strategy for sustaining five-needle pine populations: an example of its implementation in the southern Rocky Mountains. In: Keane, R.E.; Tomback, D.F.; Murray, M.P.; Smith, C.M., eds. The future of high-elevation, five-needle white pines in western North America: Proceedings of the high five symposium. RMRS-P-63. Fort Collins, CO: U.S. Department of Agriculture, Forest Service, Rocky Mountain Research Station: 323-334. http://www.fs.fed.us/rm/pubs/rmrs_p063/rmrs_p063_323_334.pdf. (05 May 2012).

Schoettle, A.W.; Sniezko, R.A. 2007. Preparing the landscape for invasion – proactive intervention to mitigate impacts of a non-native pathogen. Journal of Forest Research. 12: 327–336. http://www.springerlink.com/content/9v91t44278w74430/. (05 May 2012).

Schoettle, A.W.; Sniezko, R.A.; Burns, K.S. 2009. Sustaining *Pinus flexilis* ecosystems of the southern Rocky Mountains (USA) in the presence of *Cronartium ribicola* and *Dendroctonus ponderosae* in a changing climate. In: Noshad, D.; Noh, E.; King, J.; Sniezko, R., eds. Breeding and genetic resources of five-needle pines conference, iufro working party 2.02.15. Yangyang, Republic of Korea: Korea Forest Research Institute: 63–65. http://www.iufro.org/publications/proceedings/proceedings-meetings-2008/. (05 May 2012).

Schoettle, A.W.; Sniezko, R.A.; Kegley, A.; Burns, K.S. 2011b. Preliminary overview of the first extensive rust resistance screening tests of *Pinus flexilis* and *Pinus aristata*. In: Keane, R.E.; Tomback, D.F.; Murray, M.P.; Smith, C.M., eds. The future of high-elevation, five-needle white pines in western North America: proceedings of the high five symposium. Fort Collins, CO: U.S. Department of Agriculture, Forest Service, Rocky Mountain Research Station: 265–269. http://www.fs.fed.us/rm/pubs/rmrs_p063/rmrs_p063_265_269.pdf. (05 May 2012).

Sniezko, R.A.; Kegley, A.J. 2003. Blister rust resistance experience in Oregon/Washington: evolving perspectives. In: Stone, J.; Maffei, H., comps. 50th Annual Western International Forest Disease Work Conference. Bend, OR: U.S. Department of Agriculture, Forest Service, Central Oregon Forest Insect and Disease Service Center: 111–119.

Sniezko, R.A.; Kegley, A.J.; Danchok, R.S.; Long, S. 2007. Variation in resistance to white pine blister rust among 43 whitebark pine families from Oregon and Washington—early results and implications for conservation. In: Goheen, E.M.; Sniezko, R.A., tech. coords. Whitebark pine: a Pacific Coast perspective. R6-NR-FHP-2007-01. Portland, OR: U.S. Department of Agriculture, Forest Service, Pacific Northwest Region: 82–97. http://www fs fed.us/r6/nr/fid/wbpine/papers/2007-wbp-wpbr-resist-sniezko.pdf. (05 May 2012).

Sniezko, R.A.; Kegley, A.J.; Danchok, R. 2008. White pine blister rust resistance in North American, Asian, and European species – results from artificial inoculation trials in Oregon. Annals of Forest Research. 51: 53–66. http://www.e-afr.org. (05 May 2012).

Sniezko, R.A.; Mahalovich, M.F.; Schoettle, A.W.; Vogler, D.R. 2011a. Plenary paper: Past and current investigations of the genetic resistance to *Cronartium ribicola* in high-elevation five-needle pines. In: Keane, R.E.; Tomback, D.F.; Murray, M.P.; Smith, C.M., eds. The future of high-elevation, five-needle white pines in western North America: Proceedings of the high five symposium. RMRS-P-63. Fort Collins, CO: U.S. Department of Agriculture, Forest Service, Rocky Mountain Research Station: 246–264. http://www fs.fed.us/rm/pubs/rmrs_p063/rmrs_p063_246_264.pdf. (05 May 2012).

Sniezko, R.A.; Schoettle, A.W.; Dunlap, J.; Vogler, D.; Conklin, D.; Bower, A.; Jensen, C.; Mangold, R.; Daoust, D.; Man, G. 2011b. *Ex situ* gene conservation in high elevation white pine species in the United States-a beginning. In: Keane, R.E.; Tomback, D.F.; Murray, M.P.; Smith, C.M., eds. The future of high-elevation, five-needle white pines in Western North America: Proceedings of the high five symposium. RMRS-P-63. Fort Collins, CO: U.S. Department of Agriculture, Forest Service, Rocky Mountain Research Station: 147–149. http://www fs fed.us/rm/pubs/rmrs_p063/rmrs_p063_147_149.pdf. (05 May 2012).

Schwandt, J.W.; Lockman, I.B.; Kliejunas, J.T.; Muir, J.A. 2010. Current health issues and management strategies for white pines in the western United States and Canada. Forest Pathology. 40: 226–250.

Tomback, D.F.; Achuff, P. 2010. Blister rust and western forest biodiversity: ecology, values and outlook for white pines. Forest Pathology. 40: 186–225.

Tomback, D.F.; Achuff, P.; Schoettle, A.W.; Schwandt, J.W.; Mastrogiuseppe, R.J. 2011. Plenary paper: The magnificent high-elevation five-needle white pines: ecological roles and future outlook. In: Keane, R.E.; Tomback, D.F.; Murray, M.P.; Smith, C.M., eds. The future of high-elevation, five-needle white pines in western North America: Proceedings of the high five symposium. RMRS-P-63. Fort Collins, CO: U.S. Department of Agriculture, Forest Service, Rocky Mountain Research Station: 228. http://www.fs.fed.us/rm/pubs/rmrs_p063/rmrs_p063_002_028.pdf. (05 May 2012).

U.S. Department of Agriculture, Forest Service. 2011. National forest system invasive species management policy. Federal Register. Vol. 76 (233): 75860-75866.

Plant Compensatory Growth in Aspen Seedlings: The Role of Frequency and Intensity of Herbivory and Resource Availability

Nadir Erbilgin,[1] David A. Galvez,[2] and Bin Zhang[3]

Abstract

Plant ecologists have debated the mechanisms used by plants to cope with the impact of herbivore damage for more than a century. During that time, plant resistance mechanisms, which reduce the amount of herbivore damage before and during herbivory, have received most of the attention, while plant tolerance mechanisms, which may minimize the impacts of damage after herbivory, have been less studied. The aim of this presentation is to bring the topic of plant compensatory responses, especially compensatory growth, to the front of research in plant ecology and plant-herbivore interactions. We conducted a greenhouse experiment to evaluate how carbon sink-source relationships and compensatory plant growth operate under different intensities and frequencies of simulated defoliation of aspen seedlings, with or without N-enriched media. We found large variations in plant responses, ranging from undercompensatory to overcompensatory growth, depending on the resource availability and defoliation intensity and frequency. We developed a new predictive model, the Frequency and Intensity of Herbivory and Resource Availability (FIRA), based on carbon sink-source relationships. Our model incorporates the interactions between frequency and intensity of herbivory and resource availability as modulators of plant compensatory responses. We concluded by discussing the results of this and earlier studies in the context of the FIRA model, and elaborated the intricate relationship between resource availability and compensatory growth following herbivory.

[1] University of Alberta, Department of Renewable Resources, 4-42 ESB, Edmonton, Alberta, T6G2E3, Canada.
[2] University of Alberta, Edmonton, Alberta, Canada.
[3] Southwest University, Chongqing, P.R. China.
Corresponding author: erbilgin@ualberta.ca.

Trade-Offs Between Induced and Constitutive Resistance in Two Pine Species: Secondary Chemistry, Effective Antiherbivore-Resistance, and Effect of Nutrient Availability

Luis Sampedro,[1] Xoaquín Moreira,[2] and Rafael Zas[2]

Abstract

Constitutive chemical defenses, always expressed in the plants, and plastic defensive responses, those mobilized in response to plant injury or other cues or herbivory risk, differ in their benefits in terms of fitness for long-lived plants. Induced defenses are considered to be less expensive than constitutive preformed defenses since the cost is realized only when required. Plant defense theory predicts that, as secondary metabolism is costly for the plant, presenting effective levels of constitutive defenses and the ability of expressing efficient inducible defenses by a plant are two resource-related attributes that are not likely to be maximized at the same time. Furthermore, selective pressure favoring the expression of induced responses is likely to be lower in those lineages well defended constitutively, as they would be less subjected to herbivore attacks. A negative, non-spurious genetic correlation between constitutive and inducible defenses illustrates this classical trade-off. The existence of these evolutionary conflicts has been suggested often in the literature and sometimes reported for angiosperms, but rarely in conifers and not yet in pine trees. Besides, the emergence of this genetic constraint could be hidden by environmental factors affecting growth potential, such as nutrient availability.

In this paper we present the results from three independent experiments aimed to explore the existence of this trade-off in 2-year-old seedlings of Maritime pine (*Pinus pinaster* Aiton) and Monterey pine (*P. radiata* D. Don), native from similar climate regions in Europe and North America. We used 22 mM methyl-jasmonate (MJ), a fitohormone involved in the biosynthetic pathways of chemical defenses, to induce pine defensive responses. In the first experiment, we analyzed the secondary chemistry of constitutive (control) and MJ-induced *P. pinaster* seedlings belonging to 18 half-sib families from the Atlantic population of Galicia (northwest Spain). One month after induction, we performed an *in vivo* feeding bioassay with a generalist insect herbivore (the large pine weevil, *Hylobius abietis*) to check how the expressed defenses reflected the ability to resist the attack. In the second experiment, we reproduced the same design with 34 half-sib families belonging to *P. radiata*. In the third experiment, we analyzed this trade-off in a wider collection of *P. pinaster* genetic entries (33 half-sib families) grown either in low- or in high-phosphorus availability, to test if this trade-off could be dependent on environmental context. We explored the existence of trade-offs regressing the difference in mean resistance levels between experimentally MJ-induced individuals and control individuals from a given family (induced-control) against the family means of control treatment. Correlations were checked not to be spurious by means of Monte-Carlo analysis.

We identified, in both species, strong negative genetic correlations between induced and constitutive concentrations of total polyphenolics, resin content, and effective resistance against weevil and caterpillar damage, with R^2 ranging from 0.38 to 0.80 (all relationships significant at $P < 0.001$). Negative genetic correlations observed under complete fertilization in *P. pinaster* appeared to be likely spurious, providing evidence that this trade-off is context dependent.

[1]Centro de Investigación Forestal de Lourizán – UA MBG-CSIC, Apdo 127, 36080 Pontevedra, Galicia, Spain.
[2]Misión Biológica de Galicia, MBG-CSIC, Apdo. 28, 36080 Pontevedra, Galicia, Spain.
Corresponding author: lsampe@uvigo.es.

Host Preference of the Vector Beetle, Host Resistance, and Expanding Patterns of Japanese Oak Wilt in a Stand

Kazuyoshi Futai,[1] Hiroaki Kiku,[1] Hong-ye Qi,[1] Hagus Tarn,[1] Yuko Takeuchi,[1] and Michimasa Yamasaki[2]

Introduction

Since the early 1980s, an epidemic forest disease, Japanese Oak Wilt (JOW), has been spreading from coastal areas along the Sea of Japan to the interior of Honshu island and has been devastating huge areas of forests by killing an enormous number of oak trees in urban fringe mountains, gardens, and parks. The disease is caused by a fungus, *Raffaelea quercivora,* and is spread by the vector beetle, *Platypus quercivorus* (Coleoptera: Platypodidae). On the thorax of female *P. quercivorus,* are several holes, so called mycangia, where several species of yeasts are kept as the beetles' food. Together with such yeasts, the pathogenic fungus *R. quercivora* exists in the mycangia and is thereby transferred to the next tree. The spreading pattern of this disease is, therefore, determined by the searching and host preference behavior of the vector beetle. To control epidemic spreading of JOW, it is essential to understand the spread dynamics of JOW in infected trees. The object of this study was to analyze the spread dynamics of JOW in infected trees in relation to the host selection behavior of vector beetles in a stand.

Materials and Methods

Study Site

We have been studying the spreading pattern of this disease at a nearby low elevation mountain (109 m, 35°01′N, 135°47′E) in Kyoto city. The experimental site established at the mountain in the spring of 2009 is 1.36 ha and involved 288 living oak trees (*Quercus serrata* Murray) with DBH ranging from 10 to 90 cm.

Categorization of Host Damage

Based on the quality of frass produced from beetle tunnels, the density of beetle attacks (= number of entrance holes per given area of trunk surface), exudates from the trunks, and symptoms (alive or killed, and if killed, which year it was killed), we diagnosed the damage of each tree and classified the different levels of damage into seven categories (Cat.) (table 1).

Spatial Relationships Between Two Categories of Trees

To examine if the trees attacked by *P. quercivorus* in a given year influenced the occurrence of newly attacked trees in the following year, we analyzed the overlap between the trees attacked in 2009 and those newly attacked in 2010 using Iwao's m-m* method (Iwao 1977). When the individuals

[1] Laboratory of terrestrial microbial ecology, Graduate school of Agriculture, Kyoto University, Sakyo-ku, 606-8502, Kyoto, Japan.
[2] Laboratory of forest biology, Graduate school of Agriculture, Kyoto University, Sakyo-ku, 606-8502, Kyoto, Japan. Corresponding author: futai@kais.kyoto-u.ac.jp.

Table 1—Categorization of host trees based on their damage history

Boring attack in		Condition in	Category
2009	2010	October 2010	(Cat.)
+	+	Alive	I
+	+	Dead	II
+	-	Alive	III
+	-	Dead	IV
-	+	Alive	V
-	+	Dead	VI
-	-	Alive	VII

belonging to species X and Y are distributed over the same space, the mean crowding on sp. X by sp. Y can be given by

$$\overset{*}{m}_{XY} = \sum_{j=1}^{Q} x_{Xj}\, x_{Yj} \Big/ \sum_{j=1}^{Q} x_{Xj}$$

and mean crowding on sp. Y by sp. X by

where x_{Xj} and x_{Yj} are the numbers of individuals of sp. X and sp. Y in the j quadrat respectively, and Q is the total number of quadrats contained in the whole area. The mean crowding within each species is denoted by

$$\overset{*}{m}_{X} = \sum_{j=1}^{Q} x_{Xj}(x_{Xj}-1) \Big/ \sum_{j=1}^{Q} x_{Xj} \qquad \overset{*}{m}_{Y} = \sum_{j=1}^{Q} x_{Yj}(x_{Yj}-1) \Big/ \sum_{j=1}^{Q} x_{Yj}$$

and

Then, as a measure of the degree of spatial correlation or the degree of overlapping relative to the independent distributions, we have

$$\omega_{(+)} = \sqrt{\frac{\overset{*}{m}_{XY}\,\overset{*}{m}_{YX} - m_X m_Y}{(\overset{*}{m}_X + 1)(\overset{*}{m}_Y + 1) - m_X m_Y}} \qquad \omega_{(-)} = \sqrt{\frac{\overset{*}{m}_{XY}}{m_X}\,\frac{\overset{*}{m}_{YX}}{m_Y}} - 1$$

or

where the value ω changes from its maximum of +1 for complete overlapping, to the minimum of -1 for complete exclusion. In this method, we calculated the ω value as an index of spatial overlapping of two categories of trees while changing the unit size from 25 m^2 to 625 m^2 (Iwao 1972).

The Densities of Beetle Holes on the Stems of Host Trees

To estimate the number of beetles visiting each host tree, the densities of beetle holes on the host stems were compared among five categories of trees. We also examined the density of beetle holes in relation to the distance from the trees of Category III.

Results and Discussion

Disease Spreading in the Stand

There were 288 trees in the spring of 2009. Then in June and July 2009, 177 trees were attacked; 111 trees remained without attack. Among the 177 trees attacked, only 10 trees were killed and the remaining 167 trees survived. In the following year, 2010, 113 (67.7 percent) of 167 trees that survived the 2009 attack were re-attacked, while the other 54 trees avoided the attack.

Among 111 trees that avoided the attack in 2009, 103 trees (92.8 percent) were newly attacked in 2010. So, only 8 trees remained free from *Platypus* attack over 2 successive years. Thus, the probability of being attacked in 2010 was markedly lower in the trees that had survived the attack in 2009 (67.7 percent) than those not attacked in 2009 (92.8 percent).

Spatial Relationships Between Two Categories of Trees

As shown in fig. 1, the distribution of a group of trees (Category III) that had survived beetle attack in 2009 and avoided the attack of 2010 did not overlap the distribution of the trees newly attacked in 2010 (Category V, VI). On the other hand, the distribution of Category I trees that had survived the attack in 2009 and were reattacked in 2010 overlapped the trees that were newly attacked in 2010. Iwao's m-m* analysis revealed that the trees newly attacked in 2010 (Category V, VI) were spatially segregated from the trees of Category III at the quadrat sizes of 100 m^2 and 225 m^2 (fig. 2). Thus, beetles of *P. quercivorus* seem to be repelled from the trees of Category III, and are thereby segregated from the trees newly attacked in 2010.

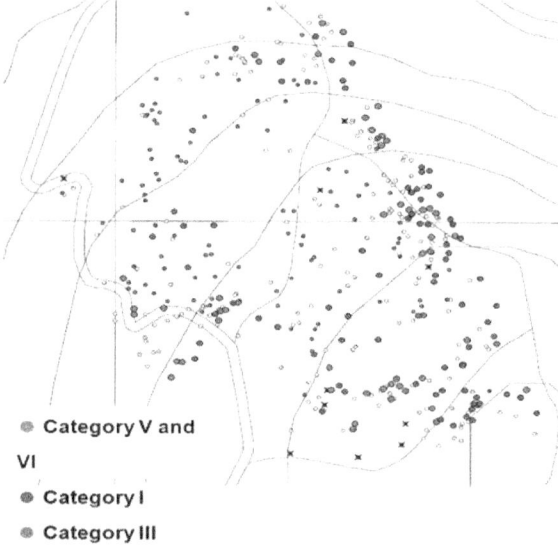

Category V and
VI
Category I
Category III

Figure 1—Distribution of the trees newly attacked in 2010 (Category V and VI) and those that had survived beetle attack in 2009 and were re-attacked (Category I) or avoided the attack (Category III) in 2010.

The Densities of Beetle Holes

As shown in fig. 3, the density of beetle holes on the surviving trees, such as those in Cat. I and III, were significantly lower than those on the stems of dead trees (Cat. II and VI). This suggests that the density of boring attack affects host survivability. More importantly, *Platypus* beetles seem to select host trees, preferring the trees of Cat.II and VI, while seeming to be repelled by the trees of Cat. I and III.

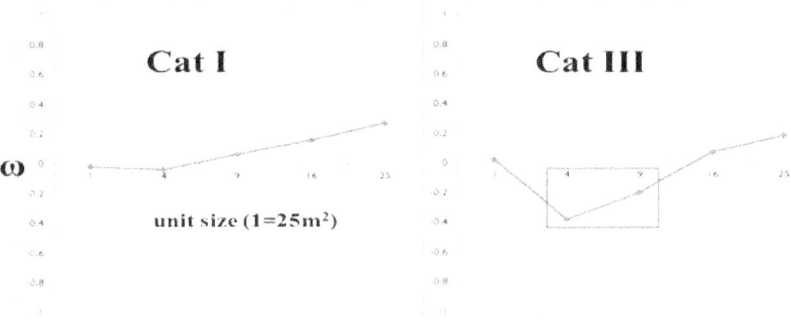

Figure 2—Spatial overlapping between the trees newly attacked in 2010 (Category V, VI) and the trees that had survived beetle attack in 2009 and were re-attacked (Category I) or avoided the attack (Category III) in 2010.

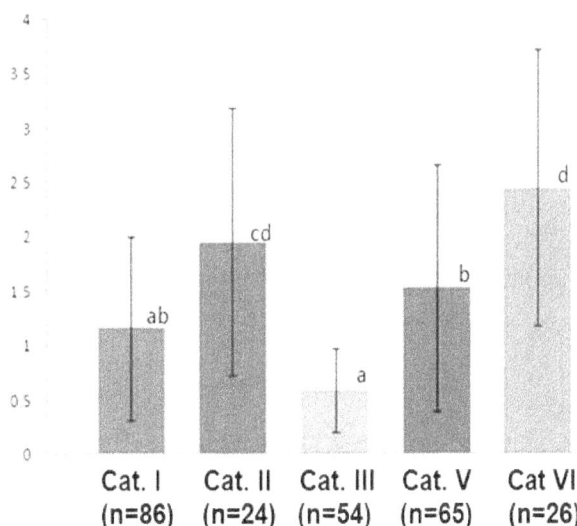

Figure 3—The density of beetle holes made on the stems of five categories of trees. For categories see table 1.

We also examined the density of beetle attack in relation to the distance from the trees of Category III, and found that the density of beetle attack was lower within a 5 m radius around the trees of Category III than that of the outer area, suggesting the lower flight frequency in the vicinity of the Category III trees. The trees that exuded sap were mainly found among the trees surviving the beetle attack in 2009, such as those in Category I and III.

From these findings we hypothesize that there are some differences in resistance against the attack of *P. quercivorus* beetle among oak trees in a stand. Resistant trees may survive the first attack of the beetle and then release some repellent from the trunk and thereby escape the following attack.

Acknowledgments

We thank Dr. H. Barclay, a visiting professor from Pacific Forestry Centre, Victoria, BC, Canada, for critical reading of the manuscript and linguistic correction.

Literature Cited

Iwao, S. 1972. Application of m-m* method to the analysis of spatial patterns by changing the quadrat size. Researches on Population Ecology. 14: 97–128.

Iwao, S. 1977. Analysis of spatial association between two species based on the interspecies mean crowding. Researches on Population Ecology. 18: 243–260.

The Effect of Hemlock Woolly Adelgid Infestation on Water Relations of Carolina and Eastern Hemlock

Laura Rivera,[1] JC Domec,[1] John Frampton,[1] Fred Hain,[1] John King,[1] and Ben Smith[1]

Abstract

In North America, hemlock woolly adelgid (HWA; *Adelges tsugae*) is an exotic insect pest from Asia that is causing rapid decline of native eastern hemlock (*Tsuga canadensis* (L.) Carr.) and Carolina hemlock (*Tsuga caroliniana* Engelm.) populations. The exact physiological mechanisms that cause tree decline and mortality are not known, despite substantial research efforts on ecological impacts and potential control measures of HWA. Eastern and Carolina hemlock may be reacting to infestation in a manner similar to the response of Fraser fir (*Abies fraseri* (Pursh.) Poir.) to infestation by balsam woolly adelgid (BWA; *Adelges picea*). It is known that Fraser fir produces abnormal xylem in response to BWA feeding. This abnormal xylem obstructs water movement within the trees, causing Fraser fir to die of water stress.

In this study, water relations within 15 eastern and Carolina hemlock were evaluated to determine if infestation by HWA was causing water stress. Water potential, carbon-13 isotope ratio, stem conductivity, and stomatal conductance measurements were conducted on samples derived from those trees. In addition, branch samples were analyzed for possible wood anatomy alterations as a result of infestation. Pre-dawn branch water potential measurements were more negative in infested hemlock than in non-infested trees. Carbon isotope ratios of the branches were more positive for infested trees, while stomatal conductance was lower in infested trees. These results indicate that infested eastern and Carolina hemlock are experiencing drought-like symptoms. Wood anatomy of the branches provided evidence that infested hemlocks are experiencing abnormal wood production in the xylem, including lower earlywood to latewood ratios and increased frequency of false rings. The significant reduction in conducting sapwood area, terminal branch growth, and leaf area in infested trees were sufficient to influence sap flux and whole-tree water use.

[1] North Carolina State University, Raleigh, NC.
Corresponding author: bcsmith6@ncsu.edu.

Genotype x Environment Interaction and Growth Stability of Several Elm Clones Resistant to Dutch Elm Disease

Alberto Santini,[1] Francesco Pecori,[1] Alessia L. Pepori,[1] and Luisa Ghelardini[1]

Abstract

The elm breeding program carried out in Italy at the Institute of Plant Protection - Consiglio Nazionale delle Ricercje (CNR) during the last 40 years aimed to develop Dutch elm disease (DED)-resistant elm selections specific to the Mediterranean environment. The need for genotypes adapted to Mediterranean conditions was evident from the poor performance of the Dutch elm clones in the hot and dry areas of central Italy, and the opportunity to breed better adapted hybrids was offered by the favorable adaptation in Italy of the Siberian elm (*Ulmus pumila* L.), a species that does not thrive in central Europe and the Netherlands. For this reason, a base of valuable individuals of native elms was bred with several accessions of Asian elm species that proved to easily acclimate to different conditions in the Mediterranean region. As a result, four resistant hybrid elms have been patented and released to the market, and many experimentally tested DED-resistant elm hybrids of different parentage are under evaluation to be released in the near future.

Conventionally, hybrid elm clones obtained within DED resistance breeding programs were selected to meet requirements for use as ornamentals. However, it has been long and commonly observed that these clones may show hybrid vigour and enhanced growth. Nowadays, DED-resistant hybrid elm clones, which have been released to the market or are under evaluation for an upcoming release, are numerous enough to be considered for timber production or short rotation coppice (SRC). But experimental testing of the growth performances of these clones in different environments is still lacking. Here, growth and stability of performance of several DED-resistant hybrid elm clones planted at three experimental sites with contrasting environmental conditions in Italy were studied. Height and diameter were measured yearly from 2001 to 2009, and the mean yearly increments after plant establishment were calculated. The study revealed a general good growth performance of the majority of the clones with mean height increments above 1 m per year, and an excellent growth performance of some genotypes. Analysis of variance showed significant effects of clone, site, and clone x site interaction, for both height and diameter increments. Stability analysis of diameter and height increments was performed using two parametric (Coefficient of variation, CV percent and Wricke's Ecovalence, W^2) and two non-parametric (Hühn's $S_i(1)$ and $S_i(2)$) indexes. According to all indexes, two clones showed superior and stable growth. These clones may be suitable for planting in a range of environments. In addition, several other clones had high growth in general or at a particular site. The results support our belief that these elm clones could be successfully used for timber and biomass production, and provide new knowledge for an informed choice of the most suitable genotypes.

[1] Istituto per la Protezione delle Piante – C.N.R Via Madonna del Piano, 10 50019 Sesto fiorentino, Italy. Corresponding author:a.santini@ipp.cnr.it.

Rapid Evolution of Introduced Tree Pathogens Via Episodic Selection and Horizontal Gene Transfer

Clive Brasier[1]

Episodic and Routine Selection

Routine selection is simply defined as "the ecological constraints experienced by an endemic organism that favor a relatively stable but fluctuating population structure over time." Its antithesis is episodic selection, defined as "any sudden ecological disturbance likely to lead to a significant alteration in a species' population structure" (Brasier 1986, 1995). In plant pathogens, examples of episodic selection are common in the context of modern anthropogenically driven disturbance conditions such as sudden exposure to crop monoculture or to a new fungicide, host, or vector; or sudden introduction into a new biogeographic zone; an increasingly frequent event because of increasing international trade in plants.

The introduction of pathogens into new biogeographic zones is the concern of the present paper. Such an introduction is a major episodic selection event for any organism, let alone a plant pathogen. It can result in sudden release from many of the routine selection constraints experienced in the endemic environment; and sudden exposure to new constraints such as new hosts, substrates, competitors, parasites, phylogenetic relatives, vectors, and microclimates (Brasier 1995). For this reason, every introduced pathogen is an uncontrolled, open-ended experiment in evolution (Brasier 2008).

In populations of outcrossing (heterothallic) pathogens, two significant evolutionary processes can occur as a result of introduction-mediated episodic selection. One is the emergence of highly fitted clones, examples being the clones of the Dutch elm disease pathogens *Ophiostoma ulmi* and *O. novo-ulmi* that spread across Eurasia and North America between 1910 to1930 and 1940 to 1990 respectively (Brasier 1996, Brasier and Kirk 2000, Brasier et al. 2004a, Mitchell and Brasier 1994). If the episodic selection conditions are maintained over the longer term, this process could ultimately lead to clonal speciation (Brasier 1995). The second process, and again the particular concern of this paper, is rapid evolution via interspecific hybridization.

Interspecific Hybridization Between Introduced and Resident Pathogens

Novel contact between phylogenetically related introduced and resident pathogens will often result in their direct ecological competition for resources. It also provides an opportunity for rapid evolution via the transfer of genes between the residents and the immigrants (Brasier 2000b). Sympatric fungi, like animals, are likely to exhibit strong genetic or behavioral barriers to inter-specific gene flow as a result of prior co-evolution. Allopatric fungi, arising in geographical isolation, may not have evolved such barriers. Today, many previously allopatric fungal pathogens are being brought into contact by man, especially through inappropriate plant imports (Brasier 2008). Figure 1 shows an increase in major tree disease events in the United Kingdom since the mid-1990s, some 25 years after the arrival of *O. novo-ulmi*. Many of these new events are caused by introduced pathogens.

[1]Forest Research, Alice Holt Lodge, Farnham, Surrey, GU10 4LH, U.K.
Corresponding author: clive.brasier@forestry.gsi.gov.uk.

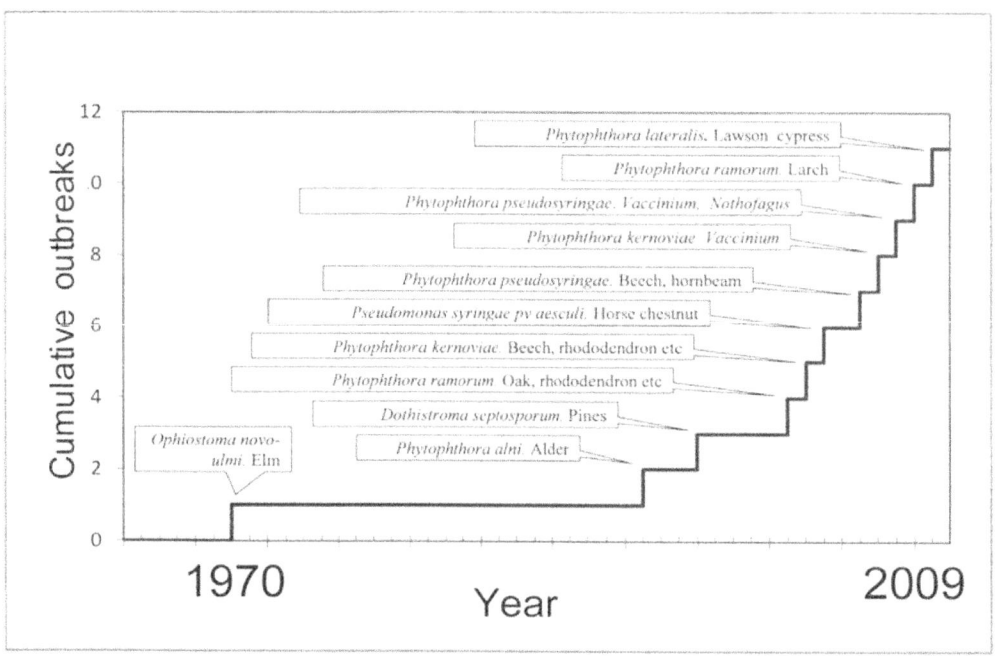

Figure 1—Cumulative major tree disease outbreaks in the United Kingdom since 1970. (Courtesy of Sandra Denman, Forest Research, UK)

A variety of factors will influence whether or not contact between two previously geographically isolated pathogens will result in hybridization (Brasier 1995, 2000b). These include their level of reproductive isolation (both pre-zygotic and post- zygotic); the degree of niche contact between them (fig. 2); and the genetic and ecological conditions that will determine whether any hybrids can survive in the presence of the parent species. Often, hybrids will need to be fitter than one or both parents to become established. Modern conditions of anthropogenically driven environmental disturbance are more likely to favor the successful establishment of hybrids. In horticultural nurseries, which these days can be infested with non-native pathogens, unusual combinations of introduced and resident pathogens may be brought together. The plants themselves may be stressed by the watering and chemical regimes and therefore susceptible to pathogens and hybrids that would not normally colonize them under natural conditions (Brasier 2008). Plantations of non-native trees may also be more susceptible to infection because they are growing 'off site,' i.e., under sub-optimal conditions.

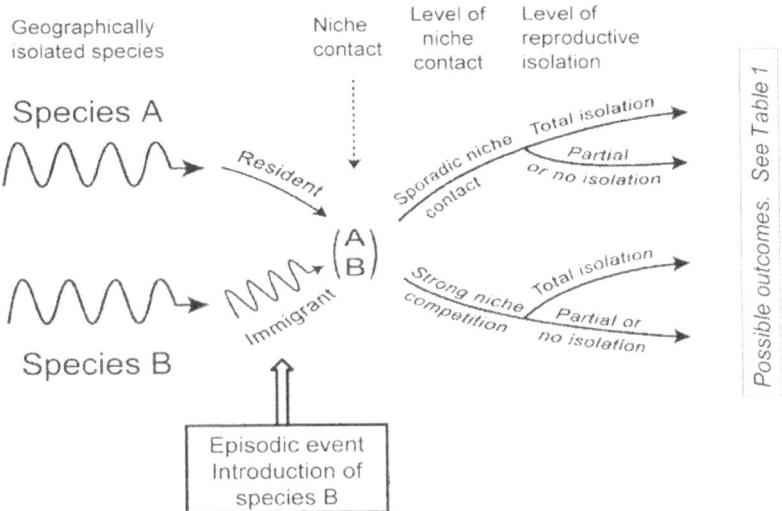

Figure 2—Genetical and environmental constraints on emergence of species hybrids in fungal pathogens. Adapted from Brasier (1995).

There are many possible outcomes to fungal interspecific hybridization, as shown in table 1. These range from the acquisition of a few nuclear genes or cytoplasmic elements to the emergence of a new organism that contains the genomes of both parents. Either way, with fungal pathogens there is a risk that the resulting genetic modification will be damaging to the natural environment. Before 1990, examples of hybridization between fungal pathogens were very rare. Recently, striking examples have occurred in all the major fungal groups, and most especially among tree pathogens. Several of the more prominent examples will now be discussed. A basic knowledge of the biology of the organisms will be assumed.

Table 1—Possible outcomes of contact between two previously geographically isolated pathogens (see fig. 2)[a].

- No change: no ecological displacement and no interspecific gene transfer.

- Introgression: acquisition and fixation of genes (also viruses, plasmids) by one or both parent species. Example: *Ophiostoma ulmi* x *O. novo-ulmi*.

- Extinction of the ecologically 'weaker' species via competition.

- Extinction of the 'weaker' species and genetic modification of the other species via introgression. Example: *Ophiostoma ulmi* x *O. novo-ulmi*.

- Emergence of a hybrid swarm: free recombination between two species resulting in many genotypes. Optimal phenotypes may emerge via natural selection. Examples: the *Ophiostoma novo-ulmi* subspecies hybrids; *Heterobasidion annosum* x *H. irregulare*; *Melampsora occidentalis* x *M. medusae*.

- Emergence of an allodiploid or allotetreploid hybrid species: a hybrid with the chromosome compliments of both parents. May be stable or give rise to further new heteroploid forms via haploidisation or diploidisation. Example: *Phytophthora alni*, subspecies *alni*.

[a]Adapted from Brasier (1995). The examples given are described in the main text.

Emerging Hybrids in the Dutch Elm Disease Pathogens (Ascomycetes)

The intercontinental spread of Dutch elm disease in the last century resulted in two massive pandemics on elms across the Northern Hemisphere (fig. 3). It has also provided classic examples of hybridization operating at two different taxonomic levels with two very different outcomes: introgression and full genetic recombination.

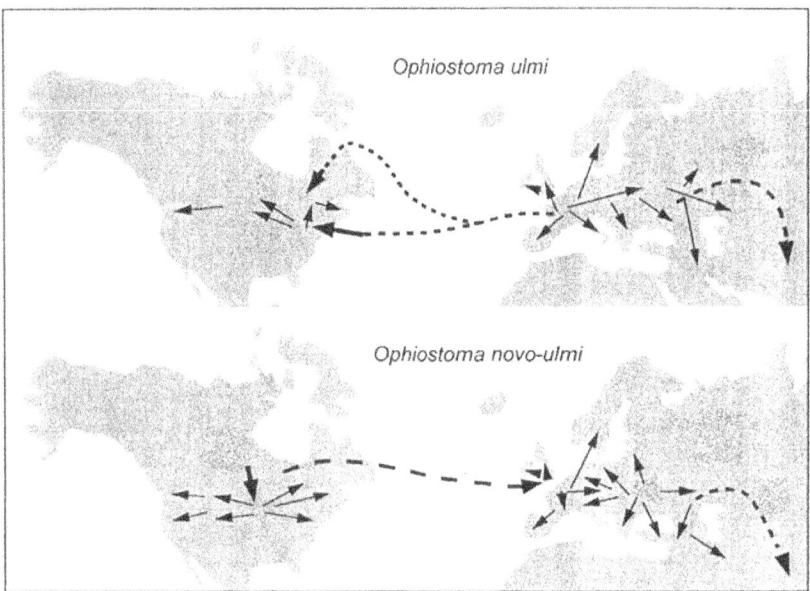

Figure 3—Spread of the pathogens *Ophiostoma ulmi* and *O. novo-ulmi* in the two pandemics of Dutch elm disease. Adapted from Brasier (2001).

At the species level, *Ophiostoma novo-ulmi*, responsible for the current second pandemic of Dutch elm disease beginning in the 1940s, has been displacing *O. ulmi*, responsible for the first pandemic in the 1920s to 40s (fig. 3). The two species are rather differently adapted, *O. novo ulmi* being an aggressive pathogen that grows fastest at ~ 22 °C; *O. ulmi* being a weaker pathogen that grows fastest at ~28 °C. Their molecular profiles indicate they are anciently divergent. The geographic origin of *O. novo-ulmi* remains unknown, but *O. ulmi* may have come from Japan. During the replacement of *O. ulmi* by *O. novo-ulmi* across Eurasia, a series of remarkable evolutionary events has occurred. These can be summarized as follows:

1. When *O. novo-ulmi* arrived in Europe (coming from east and west, fig. 3) the resident *O. ulmi* population was highly variable both phenotypically and genetically. Whereas *O. novo-ulmi* initially spread as frontal clones of a single vegetative compatibility (*vic*) type and only a single sexual mating type: *Mat-2*. Hence these frontal clones could not undergo sexual reproduction.

2. *O. novo-ulmi* and *O. ulmi* occupied the same ecological niche, coming into close physical contact in the breeding galleries of the vector beetles in diseased elm bark.

3. *O. novo-ulmi* and *O. ulmi* are only partially reproductively isolated (at both pre-zygotic and post-zygotic levels), probably due to their having evolved allopatrically. Hybrids formed between them via sexual crosses. These hybrids were highly unfit and transient, but they provided a genetic bridge between *O. ulmi* and *O. novo-ulmi*, probably via backcrosses.

4. Debilitating dsRNA viruses also spread from *O. ulmi* into the *O. novo-ulmi* frontal *vic* clones, again as a result of their close contact in the bark phase. The build-up of these viruses considerably lowered the fitness of *O. novo-ulmi* and therefore 'threatened' its survival.

136

5. Simultaneously, *O. novo-ulmi* populations acquired the 'missing' *Mat*-1 mating type allele and new *vic* alleles from *O. ulmi* via introgression from the hybrids.

6. As a result the *O. novo-ulmi* population rapidly diversified into many new *vic* types via sexual recombination (crosses between *Mat*-1 and *Mat*-2 types).*O. novo-ulmi* also acquired other *O. ulmi* genes such as pathogenicity and cell surface hydrophobin genes at this time.

7. Virus spread in the *O. novo-ulmi* population was suppressed by a sudden increase in the diversity of its *vic* types.

8. *O. ulmi* rapidly became extinct in any one location, declining at circa 10 percent per annum. It could not compete with the more aggressive, faster growing *O. novo-ulmi*.

9. *O. novo-ulmi* 'retained' the novel *Mat*-1 and *vic* genes by fixation but 'discarded' other *O. ulmi* DNA that rendered it less fit, such as *O. ulmi* pathogenicity genes. Figure 4 shows the strong negative impact of small amounts of *O. ulmi* DNA on the fitness of emerging *O. novo-ulmi* introgressants.

10. Some key references: Brasier 1986, 1988, 1996, 2000a; Brasier and Kirk 2000; Brasieret al. 1998, 2004a; Buck et al.2002; Et Touil et al. 1999; Masuya et al. 2009; Paoletti et al. 2006; Pipe et al. 2000, 2001. For further references see www.forestry.gov.uk/fr/infd-8mraqc.

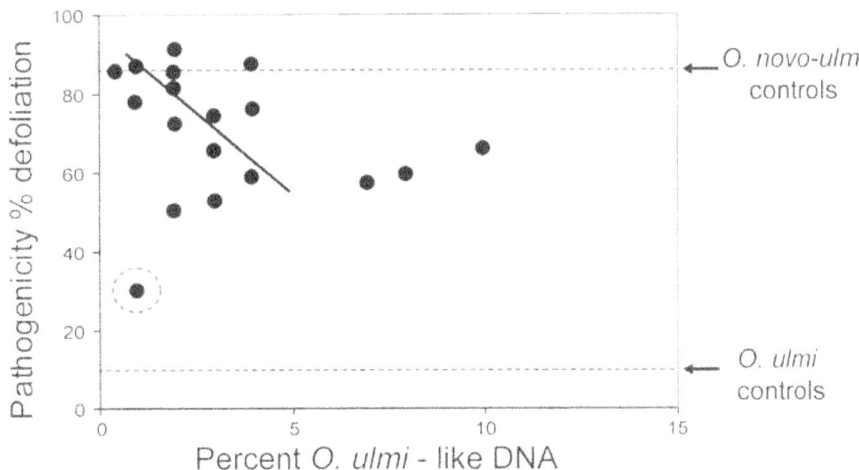

Figure 4—Influence of introgressed *Ophiostoma ulmi* DNA on fitness (pathogenicity) of *O. novo-ulmi* isolates. Note that small amounts (2 to 4 percent) of introgressed DNA have a major effect on fitness. (M.Paolettii, C.M. Brasier, and K.W. Buck, unpublished data)

The *O. novo-ulmi* x *O. ulmi* interaction illustrates most of the main variables that influence the outcome of interspecific hybridization (see fig. 2). It also shows how complex, rapid, and dynamic the underlying evolutionary events can be. *Ophiostoma ulmi* was replaced because it could not compete either with the invading *O. novo-ulmi* or with the ensuing introgressants. Strong selection pressure exerted by the deleterious viruses probably favored the survival of the introgressants over the original *O. novo-ulmi* genotypes. It is somewhat ironic that the viruses as well as the *Mat*-1 and *vic* genes were probably acquired by *O. novo-ulmi* from *O. ulmi* via somatic or sexual fusion—rather like a sexually transmitted disease. Also, that in Eurasia and North America today *O. novo-ulmi* now carries *O. ulmi* genes almost by definition, much as *Homo sapiens* now carries the DNA of *H. neanderthalensis*. *Ophiostoma novo-ulmi* is no longer the same organism that it was when it was first introduced into Eurasia and North America around 70 years ago (fig. 3).

But that is far from the end of the matter. Another remarkable hybridization event is now occurring. *Ophiostoma novo-ulmi* actually spread across the northern hemisphere as two subspecies named *americana* and *novo-ulmi* (fig. 5). These differ in colony development, perithecial (sexual fruit body) morphology, mean pathogenicity, and molecular profiles (Brasier and Kirk 2001). During the

1980s, the distributions of the two subspecies began to overlap along a zone running approximately from southern Sweden to southern Italy, with an outlier in southern Ireland (fig. 6). In this zone they have come into strong niche contact in the galleries of the vector beetles.

There is also only a weak pre-zygotic mating barrier between the two subspecies and their sexual progeny are highly fit. Fully recombinant hybrid swarms have begun to appear, probably involving many further backcrosses and intercrosses (Brasier and Kirk 2010). A recent study has shown that 30 years on the surviving hybrids in the overlap zones are still very genetically heterogeneous, but now exhibit the colony and pathogenicity characteristics of subspecies *americana* and the perithecial characteristics of *O. novo-ulmi* (C.M. Brasier, unpublished). Evidently a new phenotype of *O. novo-ulmi* is emerging from the hybrid swarms under natural selection. *Ophiostoma novo-ulmi* is undergoing yet another evolutionary transformation. If this new phenotype stabilizes and becomes widespread it will need to be formally taxonomically recognized.

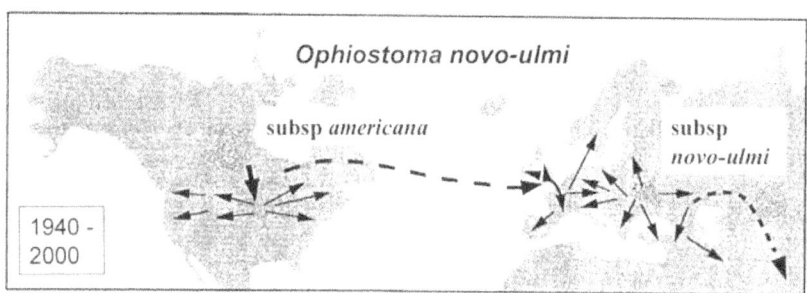

Figure 5—Spread of the two *Ophiostoma novo-ulmi* subspecies. Note their recent overlap in western Europe. Adapted from Brasier (2001).

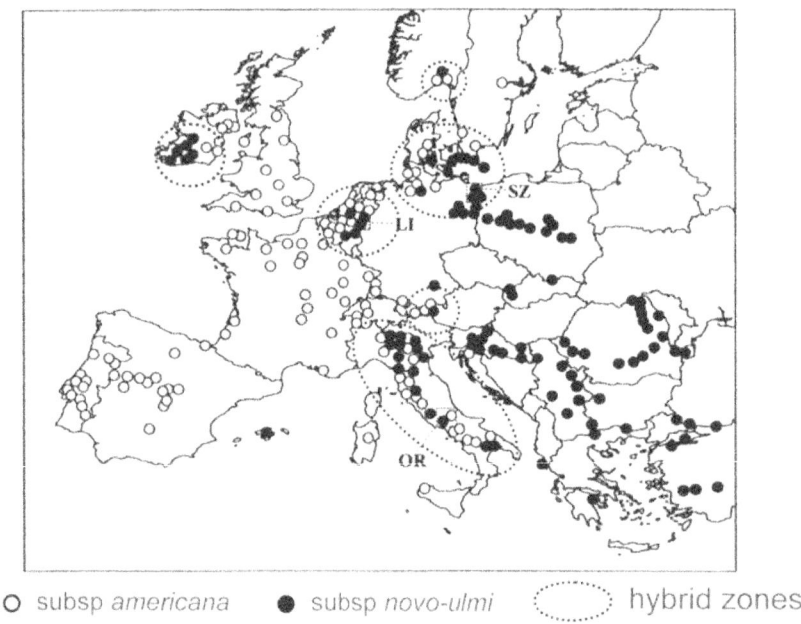

Figure 6—Known distribution of the two *Ophiostoma novo-ulmi* subspecies in 1995 (omitting central Asia), showing potential hybrid zones. Adapted from Brasier and Kirk (2010) and based on >2,500 field samples collected by the author.

Emerging Hybrids in *Melampsora, Heterobasidion,* and *Phytophthora* (Basidiomycetes and Oomycetes)

In the Pacific Northwest of North America, hybrids have recently appeared between the resident Basidiomycete rust pathogen *Melampsora occidentalis* and the introduced *M. medusae*. *Melampsora occidentalis* occurs naturally on the leaves of the local *Populus trichocarpa* in the Columbia Valley. *Melampsora medusae* is endemic on *P. deltoides* in the southeastern United States. A swarm of hybrid rust genotypes and morphotypes ('*M.* x *columbiana*') has emerged as a result of backcrosses and intercrosses between the two species on *P. trichocarpa* (Newcombe et al.2000, Newcombe et al. 2001). The hybrids show abundant pathogenic variation and commercially produced *P. trichocarpa* x *P. deltoids* clones are vulnerable to this variation. It is noteworthy that screening using host differentials carrying known resistance genes using *M.* x *columbiana* hybrids has led to the discovery of three new genes for rust resistance in poplar. The long-term evolutionary potential of these hybrids is presently unclear.

In the economically important conifer root rot Basidiomycete *Heterobasidion*, a wide range of hybrids and introgressants between the resident *H. annosum* and the introduced North American *H. irregulare* have recently appeared on native pines in the Castel Porziano region of southwest Italy (Gonthier and Garbelotto 2011, Gonthier et al. 2007). Both species specialize in attacking pines. *Heterobasidion irregulare* may have been imported into the area on pine packing material during the Second World War (M. Garbelotto, professor, University of California, Berkeley, personal communication). In this case it is especially noteworthy that the hybridization process has included the evolution of novel alleles via intralocus recombination. Introgression is mostly occurring unilaterally from the resident to the introduced species. Currently it also appears to be occurring randomly—by population expansion rather than natural selection—but again, the long-term evolutionary potential of this development is unclear.

In the well-known Oomycete genus *Phytophthora*, a very aggressive new hybrid species, *P. alni*, has emerged on alder in Europe, possibly as a result of a recent hybridization event in a European nursery. *Phytophthoras* are diploid in the vegetative state but the common hybrid form, *P. alni* subspecies *alni*, is a near allotetreploid (i.e., with two sets of chromosomes, one from each parent). It appears to be sexually sterile (probably due to pairing failures at first meiotic division) and its genome, such as its rDNA ITS region profile, is apparently still evolving (Brasier 2003, Brasier and Kirk 2001, Brasier et al. 1999, Brasier et al. 2004b, Delcan and Brasier 2001). *Phytophthora alni* subspecies *alni* is causing serious damage to native riparian alders, especially *A. glutinosa*, along rivers in France, Germany, and the United Kingdom (Gibbs et al. 2003, Jung and Blashke 2004) and has now spread to at least 15 neighboring countries.

The 'parents' of *P. alni* subspecies *alni* were originally suggested to be taxa close to *P. cambivora* and *P. fragariae* (Brasier et al. 1999). New evidence suggests otherwise. Two additional phenotypically and genetically unique forms of *P. alni* also occur in Europe, but at low frequency: *P. alni* subspecies *uniformis* and *P. alni* subspecies *multiformis* (Brasier et al. 2004b). Both are only weak pathogens on alder (Brasier and Kirk 2000). Since these forms had chromosome compliments closer to diploid they were originally suggested to be genetic breakdown products of the allotetreploid *P. alni* subspecies *alni*. The new evidence, from additional molecular profiling, indicates that these two forms are most probably the parents of *P. alni* subspecies *alni* (Ioos et al. 2006, 2007a, 2007b). This event has therefore resulted in a hybrid that is much more aggressive than either parent. *Phytophthora alni* subspecies *multiformis* may itself be a product of a reticulation event.

Conclusions

The five examples provided illustrate most of the theoretical outcomes of interspecific hybridization between fungal pathogens, ranging from genetically modified pathogens to new pathogen species (table 1). Similar examples are being reported increasingly in the literature. An increase in the introduction of plant pathogens into new biogeographic areas (by the plant trade and other agencies)—episodic selection events—coupled with increasing environmental disturbance, is leading to an increase in rapid pathogen evolution via interspecific hybridization.

At present we may be recording only the 'tip of the iceberg': hybridization events associated with more overt disease episodes such as epidemics. More subtle events—such as the introgression of one or two loci into organisms currently viewed only as a minor threat—are perhaps less likely to be recorded unless they lead to a significant change in pathogen behavior.

Interspecific hybridization between pathogens, whether overt or subtle, must now be considered a major genetic risk issue, not only for the biosecurity of our forests and natural ecosystems, but also for tree disease resistance breeding programs. It adds another element of uncertainty to disease control policy and to practice. How do you breed against an emerging hybrid swarm or against the risk of future horizontal gene transfer?

Unfortunately present international plant health protocol, formulated by the Food and Agriculture Organization of the United Nations (FAO) and the World Trade Organization, and operated by organizations such as the Animal and Plant Health Inspection System (APHIS) in the United States and the Standing Committee on Plant Health in the European Union, has failed to provide an acceptable level of protection against the export and import of exotic pathogens; and failed to educate the public on the issue (Brasier 2008, Stenlid et al. 2011, Webber 2010). In present circumstances, none of the world's tree populations, whether native or introduced, whether natural or the products of sophisticated tree breeding, can be considered secure.

Literature Cited

Brasier, C.M. 1986. The population biology of Dutch elm disease: its principal features and some implications for other host-pathogen systems. In: Ingram, D.S.; Williams, P.H., eds. Advances in plant pathology. Volume 5. London and New York: Academic Press: 55–118.

Brasier, C.M. 1988. Rapid changes in genetic structure of epidemic populations of *Ophiostoma ulmi*. Nature. 332: 538–541.

Brasier, C.M. 1995. Episodic selection as a force in fungal microevolution with special reference to clonal speciation and hybrid introgression. Canadian Journal of Botany. 73: 1213–1221.

Brasier, C.M. 1996. Low genetic diversity of the *Ophiostoma novo-ulmi* population in North America. Mycologia. 86: 951–964.

Brasier, C.M. 2000a. Intercontinental spread and continuing evolution of the Dutch elm disease pathogens. In: Dunne, C.P., ed. The elms: breeding, conservation and disease management. Boston: Kluwer Academic Publishers: 61–72.

Brasier, C.M. 2000b. Rise of the hybrid fungi. Nature. 405: 134–135.

Brasier, C.M. 2001. Rapid evolution of introduced plant pathogens via interspecific hybridization. Bioscience. 51: 123–133.

Brasier, C.M. 2003. The hybrid alder *Phytophthoras*: their genetic status, cultural properties pathogenicity, distribution and survival. In: Phytophthora disease of alder in Europe. Forestry Commission Bulletin 126. London: HMSO: 51–60.

Brasier, C.M. 2008. The biosecurity threat to the UK and global environment from international trade in plants. Plant Pathology. 57: 792–808.

Brasier, C.M.; Buck, K.W.; Paoletti, M.; Crawford, L.; Kirk, S.A. 2004a. Molecular analysis of evolutionary changes in populations of *Ophiostoma novo-ulmi*. In: Gil, L.; Solla, A.; Oullett, G., eds. New approaches to elm conservation. Forest Resources and Systems. 13: 93–103.

Brasier, C.M.; Kirk, S.A.; Pipe, N.; Buck, K.W. 1998. Rare hybrids in natural populations of the Dutch elm disease pathogens *Ophiostoma ulmi* and *O. novo-ulmi*. Mycological Research. 102: 45–57.

Brasier, C.M.; Kirk, S.A. 2000. Survival of clones of NAN *Ophiostoma novo-ulmi* around its probable centre of appearance in North America. Mycological Research. 104: 1322–1332.

Brasier, C.M.; Kirk, S.A. 2001. Designation of the EAN and NAN races of *Ophiostoma novo-ulmi* as subspecies. Mycological Research 105: 547–554.

Brasier, C.M.; Kirk, S.A. 2010. Rapid emergence of hybrids between the two subspecies of *Ophiostoma novo-ulmi* with a high level of pathogenic fitness. Plant Pathology. 59: 186–199.

Brasier, C.M.; Cooke, D.; Duncan, J.M. 1999. Origins of a new *Phytophthora* pathogen through interspecific hybridization. Proceedings of the National Academy of Sciences USA. 96: 58–78.

Brasier, C.M.; Kirk, S.A.; Delcan, J.; Cooke, D.E.; Jung, T.; Man in´t Veld, W.A. 2004b. *Phytophthora alni* sp. nov. and its variants: designation of emerging heteroploid hybrid pathogens spreading on *Alnus* trees. Mycological Research. 108: 1172–1184.

Buck, K.W.; Brasier, C.M.; Paoletti, M.; Crawford, L. 2002. Virus transmission and gene flow between two species of Dutch elm disease fungi, *Ophiostoma ulmi* and *O. novo-ulmi*: deleterious viruses as selective agents for gene introgression. In: Hails, R.S.; Beringer, J.E.; Godfray, H.C.J., eds. Genes in the environment. Oxford, UK: Blackwell Publishing: 26–45.

Delcan, J.; Brasier, C.M. 2001. Oospore viability and variation in zoospore and hyphal tip derivatives of the hybrid alder *Phytophthoras*. Forest Pathology. 31: 65–83.

Et Touil, A.; Brasier, C.M.; Bernier, L. 1999. Localization of a pathogenicity gene in *Ophiostoma novo-ulmi* and evidence that it may be introgressed from *O. ulmi*. Molecular Plant-Microbe Interactions. 12: 6–15.

Gibbs, J.N.; van Dijk, C.; Webber, J., eds. 2003. Phytophthora disease of alder in Europe. Forestry Commission Bulletin 126. Edinburgh: UK Forestry Commission. 82 p.

Gonthier, P.; Garbelotto, M. 2011. Amplified fragment length polymorphism and sequence analyses reveal massive gene introgression from the European fungal pathogen *Heterobasidion annosum* into its introduced congener *H. irregulare*. Molecular Ecology. 20: 2756–2770.

Gonthier, P.; Nicolotti, G.; Linzer, R.; Guglielmo, F.; Garbelotto, M. 2007. Invasion of European pine stands by a North American forest pathogen and its hybridization with a native infertile taxon. Molecular Ecology. 16: 1389–1400.

Ioos, R.; Andrieux, A.; Marçais, B.; Frey, P. 2006. Genetic characterization of the natural hybrid species *Phytophthora alni* as inferred from nuclear and mitochondrial DNA analyses. Fungal Genetics and Biology. 43: 511–529.

Ioos, R.; Panabières, F.; Industri, B.; Andrieux, A.; Frey, P. 2007a. Distribution and expression of elicitin genes in the interspecific hybrid oomycete *Phytophthora alni*. Applied and Environmental Microbiology. 73: 5587–5597.

Ioos, R.; Barres, B.; Andrieux, A.; Frey, P. 2007b. Characterization of microsatellite markers in the interspecific hybrid *Phytophthora alni* ssp. *alni*, and cross-amplification with related taxa. Molecular Ecology Notes. 7: 133–137.

Jung, T.; Blaschke, M. 2004. Phytophthora root and collar rot of alders in Bavaria: distribution, modes of spread and possible management strategies. Plant Pathology. 53: 197–208.

Masuya, H.; Brasier, C.; Ichihara, Y.; Kubono, T.; Kanzaki, N. 2009. First report of the Dutch elm disease pathogens *Ophiostoma ulmi* and *O. novo-ulmi* in Japan. Plant Pathology New Disease Reports. 20: 6.

Mitchell, A.G.; Brasier, C.M. 1994. Contrasting structure of European and North American populations of *Ophiostoma ulmi*. Mycological Research. 98: 576–582.

Newcombe, G.; Stirling, B.; Mcdonald, S.K.; Bradshaw, H.D., Jr. 2000 *Melampsora ×columbiana*, a natural hybrid of *M. medusae* and *M. occidentalis*. Mycological Research. 104: 261–274.

Newcombe, G.; Stirling, B.; Bradshaw, H.D., Jr. 2001. Abundant pathogenic variation in the new hybrid rust *Melampsora ×columbiana*. Phytopathology. 91: 981–985.

Paoletti, M.; Buck, K.W.; Brasier, C.M. 2006. Selective acquisition of novel mating type and vegetative incompatibility genes via interspecies gene transfer in the globally invading eukaryote *Ophiostoma novo-ulmi*. Molecular Ecology. 14: 249–263.

Pipe, N.D.; Brasier, C.M.; Buck, K.W. 2000. Evolutionary relationship of the Dutch elm disease fungus *Ophiostoma novo-ul*mi to other *Ophiostoma* species investigated by RFLP analysis of the rDNA region. Journal of Phytopathology-PhytopathologischeZeitschrift.148: 533–539.

Pipe, N.; Brasier, C.M.; Buck, K.W. 2001. Two natural cerato-ulmin deficient mutants of *Ophiostoma novo-ulmi*: one has an introgressed *O. ulmi* cu gene; the other has an *O. novo-ulmi* cu gene with a mutation in an intron splice concensus sequence. Molecular Plant Pathology. 1: 379–382.

Stenlid, J.; Oliva, J.; Boberg, J.B.; Hopkins, A.J.M. 2011. Emerging diseases in European forest ecosystems and responses in society. Forests. 2: 486–504.

Webber, J.F. 2010. Pest risk analysis and invasion pathways for plant pathogens. New Zealand Journal of Forestry Science. 40: S45–S56.

Dynamics of Surviving Ash (*Fraxinus* spp.) Populations in Areas Long Infested by Emerald Ash Borer (*Agrilus planipennis*)

Kathleen S. Knight,[1] Daniel Herms,[2] Reid Plumb,[3] Eileen Sawyer,[3] Daniel Spalink,[3] Elizabeth Pisarczyk,[3] Bernadette Wiggin,[3] Rachel Kappler,[3] Emily Ziegler,[3] and Karen Menard[3]

Abstract

Emerald ash borer (EAB) (*Agrilus planipennis*), an introduced wood-boring insect, has killed millions of ash (*Fraxinus* spp.) trees in the Midwest region of the United States and Canada. However, in some areas where EAB has caused almost complete mortality of mature ash trees, a small number of healthy ash trees intermingled with the dead ash trees have been discovered, sparking interest in these "lingering" ash trees. Here we present the results of surveys in 2010 and 2011 of two populations of surviving ash trees in southeast Michigan and northwest Ohio, where the vast majority of ash trees had died by 2008. A 2010 survey of ash trees ≥10 cm DBH (diameter at breast height, 1.4 m) along 10 km of floodplain forest in northwest Ohio found 2.6 percent of the ash trees were alive and 1 percent of the ash trees were healthy in an area where most of the ash trees had died by 2008. The canopy condition and EAB symptoms of these surviving trees were recorded. A repeated survey in 2011 found that most of the surviving trees that had healthy canopies in 2010 remained healthy in 2011, while trees with unhealthy canopies declined or died by 2011. In southeast Michigan, a population of living ash trees was discovered in 2010, at which time 39 trees were tagged and their canopy condition and EAB symptoms were recorded. When the trees were re-surveyed in 2011, the same pattern observed in northwest Ohio was evident: most of the trees that had healthy canopies in 2010 remained healthy in 2011, while trees with unhealthy canopies declined or had died by 2011. At both sites, some of the trees with healthy canopies show evidence of past EAB infestation, while others had no symptoms. Research is ongoing to determine whether these "lingering" ash trees express resistance or tolerance to EAB, or are simply the last to die.

Key words: emerald ash borer, *Agrilus planipennis*, *Fraxinus* spp., lingering ash

Introduction

Emerald ash borer (EAB) (*Agrilus planipennis*) has killed millions of ash trees (*Fraxinus* spp.) in North America since its accidental introduction from Asia (Poland and McCullough 2006). All eastern North American ash tree species are susceptible, including green (*F. pennsylvanica* Marsh.), white (*F. Americana* L.), black (*F. nigra* Marsh.), blue (*F. quadrangulata* Michx.), and pumpkin ash (*F. profunda* (Bush) Bush) (Anulewicz et al. 2007, Knight et al. 2010, Smith 2006). Ash stands can progress from healthy to nearly complete mortality within 5 to 7 years (Knight et al. 2010), and ash mortality now exceeds 99 percent in forested areas of southeast Michigan (Herms et al. 2009) and northwest Ohio (Knight et al. 2010). As EAB continues to spread, it threatens to devastate ash throughout its range.

The initial introduction of EAB to North America occurred in an urban area near Detroit, where planted ash trees were primarily grafted horticultural selections representing only a few genotypes.

[1] USDA Forest Service, Northern Research Station, 359 Main Rd, Delaware, OH 43015.
[2] Department of Entomology, Ohio Agricultural Research and Development Center, The Ohio State University, 1680 Madison Ave., Wooster, OH 44691.
[3] Metroparks of the Toledo Area, Toledo, OH.
Corresponding author: ksknight@fs fed.us.

No resistance to EAB was observed in these populations. Later, EAB spread into forests with greater genetic variation among trees. Healthy, living ash trees have been observed in areas infested by EAB for several years where the vast majority of ash trees have been dead for a few years; these healthy trees have been termed "lingering ash." Lingering ash trees are intermingled with dead ash trees with EAB symptoms, so it is unlikely that they are escapes. It is possible that these are simply the last trees to die, as EAB remains in these areas, but at low densities (Knight et al. 2010). It is also possible that these trees are resistant or tolerant to EAB and have either remained healthy or recovered from EAB damage.

Objectives:
1. Determine the incidence of ash survival at a site in northwest Ohio where "lingering ash" have been observed.
2. Study the population dynamics and health of surviving ash populations over time at a site in northwest Ohio and a site in southeast Michigan

Methods

Two populations of surviving ash trees, one in northwest Ohio and one in southeast Michigan (fig. 1), were surveyed in 2010 and 2011 using the method described by Smith (2006) for rating canopy condition and recording symptoms of EAB. Canopy condition was rated on a 1 to 5 scale, where 1 is a healthy tree, 5 is a dead tree, and 2 to 4 are progressive stages of thinning and dieback (fig. 2). Tree stress symptoms associated with EAB activity were recorded as present or absent. These symptoms include woodpecker holes and EAB exit holes visible on the tree trunk, splitting bark, new epicormic shoots, and basal sprouts. Each tree's trunk diameter at 1.38 m height (DBH) and the global position coordinates were also recorded. Living ash trees surveyed in 2010 were re-surveyed in 2011 using the same methods.

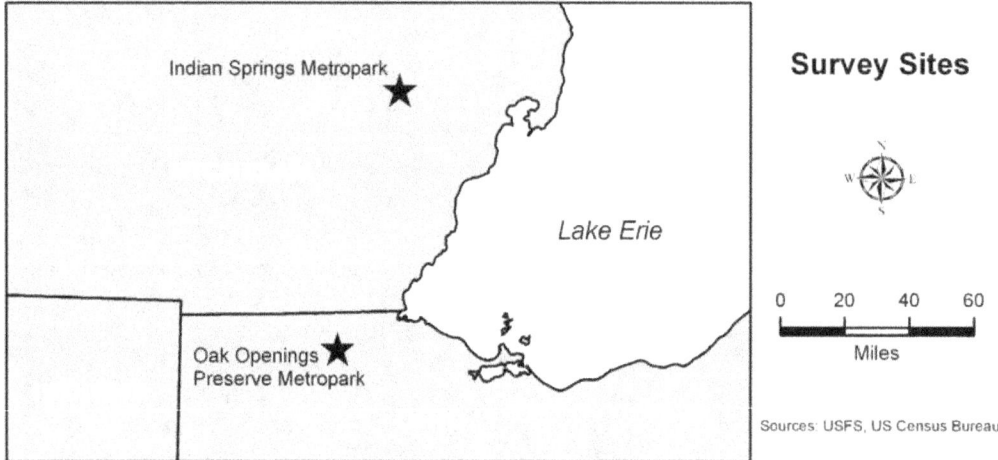

Figure 1—Study sites: Oak Openings Preserve Metropark in northwest Ohio and Indian Springs Metropark in southeast Michigan.

1   2   3   4   5

Figure 2—Photos showing ash canopy condition rating scale (Smith 2006). (Photos: D.A. Herms)

Northwest Ohio

Oak Openings Preserve Metropark, located in western Lucas County, Ohio, is a nearly 2,024 ha nature preserve in the heart of the Oak Openings region. This biologically rich region, formed at the western shore of the ancient glacial lakes Warren, Wayne, and Lundy, has extensive deposits of sand underlain by a glacial till consisting of drainage-impeding clay minerals (Brewer and Vankat 2004). Variations in sand and soil depth, pH, moisture, and elevation create a multitude of habitats ranging from sand blowouts, sand barrens, black oak savannas, wet prairies, and floodplain forests (Easterly 1976). The original floodplain forests of the early 1800s were dominated by American elm (*Ulmus americana* L.), black willow (*Salix nigra* Marsh.), green ash, sycamore (*Platanus occidentalis* L.), basswood (*Tilia americana* L.) and quaking aspen (*Populus tremuloides* Michx.), with less dominant species of silver maple (*Acer saccharinum* L.), red oak (*Quercus rubra* L.), Ohio buckeye (*Aesculus glabra* Willd.), honey locust (*Gleditsia triacanthos* L.), and hackberry (*Celtis occidentalis* L.) (Brewer and Vankat 2004). Although successive waves of drainage, urbanization, fire-suppression, farming, and lumbering have dramatically fragmented the landscape, this region nevertheless remains home to over 140 state and federally listed species (Brewer and Vankat 2004). The modern floodplain is a mix of closed-crown floodplain forest and areas of herbaceous vegetation with scattered trees.

The study area was located along the 10 km section of the Swan Creek floodplain that resides within the Oak Openings Preserve Metropark boundaries (fig. 3). The study area encompassed approximately 1 km² of the 1.23 km² 100-year floodplain. We surveyed living ash trees (foliage present) ≥10 cm DBH within 50 m of the creek, and, in addition, dead ash and other live or dead tree species in 20 plots systematically placed every 1,000 m along the length of the river. In areas where the floodplain was wider than 50 m, trees beyond 50 m were not surveyed, and in areas where the floodplain was less than 50 m wide, we surveyed to the edge of the floodplain. Additional living ash trees that were discovered in 2011 were measured and recorded as well.

The 20 plots for surveying standing dead ash trees, and other tree species, were 100 m long and 50 m wide. Plots were located within the 100-year floodplain using geographical information system in areas where the floodplain was 50 m wide and approximately 1,000 m intervals along the contour of Swan Creek. Approximately 10 percent of the length of Swan Creek was included in the plots. Information recorded on trees in these plots included DBH and global position. By 2010, many ash trees had already fallen and were difficult to tally as they washed downstream into piles during flooding. Therefore, we used the mean percentage of ash trees fallen in three sites in the Swan Creek floodplain that each had three 0.04 ha monitoring plots that were monitored yearly since 2005 to estimate the number of ash trees fallen in the floodplain.

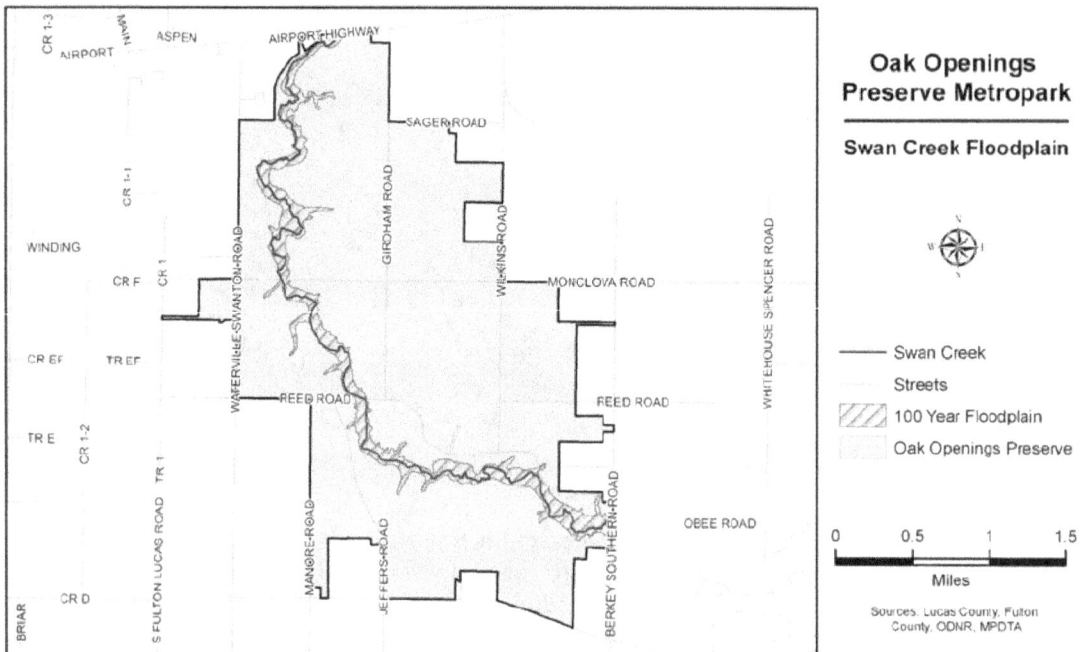

Figure 3—Swan Creek floodplain at Oak Openings Preserve Metropark, Ohio.

Southeast Michigan

Indian Springs Metropark, in Oakland County in southeast Michigan, encompasses 896 ha of wooded wetlands, upland forest, and rolling meadows. Forested areas are dominated by a diversity of mixed hardwoods. A 3-ha area with lingering ash, discovered in 2009 by Kevin Rice (Dept. of Entomology, The Ohio State University), is an upland successional area with a mix of closed canopy young forest and old fields with scattered trees dominated by herbaceous vegetation. Thirty-nine living ash trees were surveyed in 2010 and re-surveyed in 2011. The trees were selected to represent some healthy ash trees and some declining ash trees within the larger population of living ash trees at the site.

Results

Mortality Estimate

Until recently, ash was the most abundant tree species in the Swan Creek floodplain. Now, nearly all ash trees have died and the most abundant tree species is American elm (table 1). The 20 surveyed plots, representing approximately 10 percent of the floodplain within 50 m of the river, and representing 8 percent of the 100-year floodplain area, contained 858 standing dead ash trees.

Table 1—Standing trees in survey plots of Swan Creek floodplain

Species	Health	Number of trees in plots	Average DBH (cm)
American elm	Alive	864	19
Green ash	Dead	858	29
Boxelder	Alive	615	22
Silver maple	Alive	513	29
American elm	Dead	287	21
Cottonwood	Alive	237	41
Hawthorne	Alive	145	15
Boxelder	Dead	118	18
Black walnut	Alive	73	34
Green ash	Alive	53	17
White oak	Alive	43	34
Black willow	Alive	36	36
Silver maple	Dead	32	22
Red maple	Alive	30	30
Red oak	Alive	30	32
Hackberry	Alive	24	21
Black willow	Dead	18	38
Cottonwood	Dead	17	37
Mulberry	Alive	11	21
Sycamore	Alive	9	39

The three sites monitored since 2005 had a mean of 74 percent of the ash trees standing dead (including trees that were leaning and trees that were snapped above DBH) and 26 percent fallen by 2010. There was considerable variation among the three sites, ranging from 5 percent to 56 percent fallen trees, which creates considerable uncertainty in our estimates. Based on these data, we estimate that 8,580 standing dead and 3,015 fallen ash trees are within 50 m of the river, for a total of 11,595 dead ash trees. Depending on the estimate used for fallen trees, the total could range from 9,032 to 19,500 dead ash trees. These estimates are based on the following formulas:

Standing dead = 858×10 = 8,580

Fallen = (0.26×(858/0.74))×10 = 3,015

Total = 8,580 + 3,015 = 11,595.

If the rest of the floodplain is similar in tree species composition to our plots that were within 50 m of the river, we estimate that the 100-year floodplain contains 14,494 dead ash trees, of which 10,725 were standing dead and 3,769 were fallen in 2010. Depending on the estimate used for fallen trees, the total number of dead trees could range from 11,289 to 24,375. These estimates are based on the following formulas:

Standing dead = 858×(100/8) = 10,725

Fallen = (0.26×(858/0.74))×(100/8) = 3,769

Total = 10,725+3,769 = 14,494.

The 2010 survey found 299 live ash trees within 50 m of the river, representing 2.5 percent of the estimated total number of ash trees present within 50 m of the river when EAB arrived. Depending on the estimate used for fallen trees, the percent of live trees could range from 1.5 percent to 3.2 percent. Spatially, these trees were mixed with dead ash trees that had clearly died from EAB several years ago.

Surviving Ash Health in 2010 and 2011

The 2010 and 2011 data for the surviving trees in Ohio and Michigan show remarkably similar patterns. At Oak Openings in 2010, 111 ash trees were healthy (rated a 1) and 188 were in stages of decline (fig. 4). The healthy trees represented 0.9 percent of the original population, ranging from 0.6 percent to 1.2 percent depending on the estimate used for fallen trees. Of the healthy trees, 48 percent exhibited symptoms of EAB and 52 percent had no symptoms of EAB. Of the declining trees, 93 percent exhibited symptoms of EAB. At Indian Springs in 2010, 20 healthy ash trees and 19 trees in various stages of decline were selected (fig. 5). Of the healthy trees, 85 percent exhibited symptoms of EAB and 15 percent expressed no symptoms, while 100 percent of the declining trees had EAB symptoms. In 2011 at both sites, the majority of the trees that were healthy in 2010 remained healthy, while trees that were declining in 2010 continued to decline or died in 2011. The less healthy the tree was in 2010, the more likely it was to die in 2011 (table 2a and 2b).

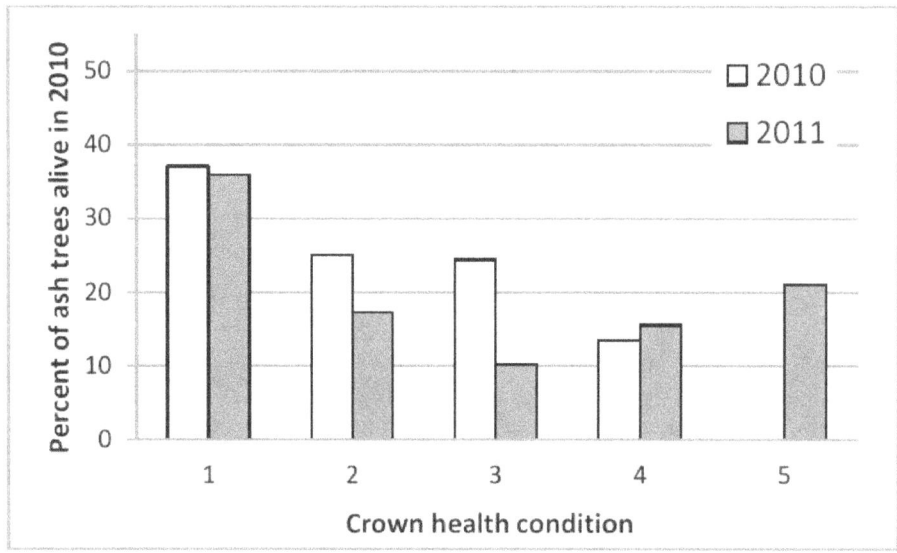

Figure 4—Ash tree health at Oak Openings.

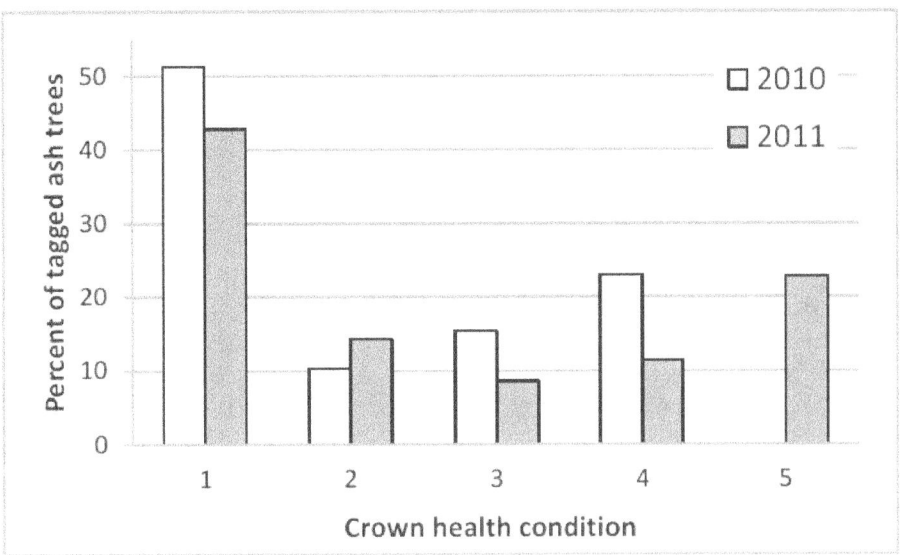

Figure 5—Ash tree health at Indian Springs.

Table 2a—Ash health transitions at Oak Openings

Health condition 2010	Health condition 2011				
	1	2	3	4	5
1	74[a]	18	3	5	0
2	11	40	26	14	9
3	0	0	11	41	48
4	0	0	0	8	92

[a] For each health class in 2010, the percent of trees that transitioned to each health class in 2011 is reported.

Table 2b—Ash health transitions at Indian Springs

Health condition 2010	Health condition 2011				
	1	2	3	4	5
1	78[a]	11	6	6	0
2	33	67	0	0	0
3	0	20	40	40	0
4	0	0	0	11	89

[a] For each health class in 2010, the percent of trees that transitioned to each health class in 2011 is reported.

Discussion

The study suggests that at these sites, a small proportion (approximately 1 percent at Oak Openings) of the ash trees remained healthy after EAB killed the vast majority of the trees. The living ash tree populations at the two sites exhibited remarkably similar population dynamics over time. At Oak Openings, 74 percent of the healthy trees remained healthy, while at Indian Springs, 78 percent of the healthy trees remained healthy. Declining trees were likely to continue declining or die. This suggests that the healthy trees observed at these sites have not recovered after initially declining, but rather have always been healthy. It is too early to determine the ultimate fate of these lingering ash as EAB populations continue to persist at low densities at both sites. However, it is possible that the surviving trees are tolerant to EAB. We will continue to monitor the surviving trees to understand the dynamics of potential EAB tolerance in this natural system.

Rare allopatric resistance or tolerance to EAB by North American ash species would not be surprising, as Asian ash species exhibit resistance and North American ash species have been shown to vary in attractiveness to EAB adults. Asian ash species have been shown to have greater resistance to EAB than North American ash cultivars in common garden studies in North America (Rebek et al. 2008) and plantations in China (Liu et al. 2007). Outbreaks of EAB in Asia appear to be infrequent and associated with stress in Asian ash trees (Gould et al. 2005, Liu et al. 2007). In studies of North American ash trees, blue ash is less preferred than other species in field (Anulewicz et al 2007) and laboratory (Pureswaran and Poland 2009) studies. Mechanisms underlying the differences in host selection may lie in volatile compounds that allow ovipositing females to locate hosts (Pureswaran et al. 2007, Rodriguez-Saona et al. 2006), while defensive secondary compounds in phloem tissue may play a role in host resistance in Asian ash species by decreasing larval growth and survival (Cipollini et al. 2011). Thus, nonpreference, antibiosis, compensatory growth (McNaughton 1983), or a combination of these mechanisms may play a role in the existence of lingering ash. We speculate that different mechanisms may be responsible for the healthy ash trees in our study that exhibited symptoms of EAB and the healthy ash trees that exhibited no symptoms of EAB. Alternatively, it is possible that previously infested trees are subsequently preferentially attacked, which could generate a similar pattern when EAB densities are low, at least in the short term.

Rare resistance or tolerance to nonnative pests and pathogens (allopatric resistance) has been commonly observed in many other tree species worldwide, and screening and breeding programs are underway for many of these species. Examples from eastern North America include American elm tolerant to Dutch elm disease (caused by *Ophiostoma novo-ulmi*) (Townsend et al. 2005) and beech (*Fagus grandifolia* Ehrh.) tolerant to beech bark disease (Houston 1983, Koch et al. 2010). The development of EAB-resistant ash trees is of interest for long-term reforestation and preservation of ash in natural and urban forests. Our observations that lingering ash can remain healthy over time suggest that they may be a source of resistance or tolerance to EAB. Alternatively, these surviving ash trees may represent the residual tail of the survivorship curve after EAB populations have declined to low density as their carrying capacity has crashed. Further study is needed including exposure of these genotypes to EAB infestations under controlled conditions. We are collaborating with Jennifer Koch (USDA Forest Service) to propagate lingering ash trees through grafting and seed collection. Through a larger collaborative program, the trees are then tested for resistance or tolerance to EAB and the potential mechanisms are studied (Koch et al., Breeding strategies for the development of Emerald Ash Borer resistant North American ash, this proceedings).

Acknowledgments

Helpful comments from Jennifer Koch and Mary Mason improved this manuscript. We thank the USDA Forest Service, and staff and students of The Ohio State University, for assistance with field data collection. We thank the Metroparks of the Toledo Area and the Huron-Clinton Metroparks for access to study sites. This research was supported by funding from the American Recovery and Reinvestment Act, USDA National Research Initiative, USDA Animal and Plant Health Inspection Service, USDA National Institute of Food and Agriculture, USDA Forest Service Northern Research Station, and state and federal appropriations to the Ohio Agricultural Research and Development Center and The Ohio State University.

Literature Cited

Anulewicz, A.C.; McCullough, D.G.; Cappaert, D.L. 2007. Emerald ash borer (*Agrilus planipennis*) density and crown dieback in three North American ash species. Arboriculture and Urban Forestry. 33(5): 338–349.

Brewer, L.G.; Vankat, J.L. 2004. Description of vegetation of the Oak Openings of Northwestern Ohio at the time of Euro-American settlement. Ohio Journal of Science. 104 (4): 76–85.

Cipollini, D.; Wang, Q.; Whitehill, J.G.A.; Powell, J.R.; Bonello, P.; Herms, D.A. 2011. Distinguishing defensive characteristics in the phloem of ash species resistant and susceptible to emerald ash borer. Journal of Chemical Ecology. 37: 450–459.

Easterly, N.W. 1976. Woody plants of the Oak Openings. Department of Biological Sciences, Bowling Green State University. Bowling Green, Ohio. 2, 4.

Gould, J.; Bauer, L.; Liu, H.; Williams, D.; Schaefer, P.; Reardon, D. 2005. Potential for biological control of the emerald ash borer. In: Gottschalk, K.W., ed. Proceedings. 16th U.S. Department of Agriculture interagency research forum on invasive species 2005. Gen. Tech. Rep. NE-337. Newtown Square, PA: U.S. Department of Agriculture, Forest Service, Northeastern Research Station: 22.

Herms, D.A.; Gandhi, K.J.K.; Smith, A.; Cardina, J.; Knight, K.S.; Herms, C.P.; Long, R.P.; McCullough, D. 2009. Ecological impacts of emerald ash borer in forests of southeast Michigan. In: McManus, K.A; Gottschalk, K.W., eds. Proceedings. 20th U.S. Department of Agriculture interagency research forum on invasive species 2009. . Gen. Tech. Rep. NRS-P-51. Newtown Square, PA: U.S. Department of Agriculture, Forest Service, Northern Research Station: 36–37.

Houston, D.R. 1983. American beech resistance to *Cryptococcus fagisuga*. In: Proceedings, IUFRO Beech Bark Disease Working Party Conference. Gen. Tech.Rep. WO-37. Washington, DC: U.S. Department of Agriculture, Forest Service: 38–41.

Knight, K.S.; Herms, D.A.; Cardina, J.; Long, R.P.; Rebbeck, J.; Gandhi, K.J.K.; Smith, A.; Klooster, W.S.; Herms, C.P. 2010. Emerald ash borer aftermath forests: the dynamics of ash mortality and the responses of other plant species. In: Michler, C.H.; Ginzel, M. D., eds. Proceedings of symposium on ash in North America. Gen. Tech. Rep. NRS-P-72. Newtown Square, PA: U.S. Department of Agriculture, Forest Service, Northern Research Station: 11.

Koch, J.L.; Mason, M.E.; Carey, D.W.; Nelson, C.D. 2010. Assessment of beech scale resistance in full and half-sibling American beech families. Canadian Journal of Forest Research. 40: 265–272.

Liu, H.; Bauer, L.S.; Miller, D.L.; Zhao, T.; Geo, R.; Song, L.; Luan, Q.; Jin, R.; Gao, C. 2007. Seasonal abundance of *Agrilus planipennis* (Coleoptera: Buprestidae) and its natural enemies *Oobius agrili* (Hymenoptera: Encyrtidae) and *Tetrastichus planipennisi* (Hymenoptera: Eulophidae) in China. Biological Control. 42(1): 61–71.

McNaughton, S.J. 1983. Compensatory plant growth as a response to herbivory. Oikos. 42: 329–336.

Poland, T.M.; McCullough, D.G. 2006. Emerald ash borer: invasion of urban forest and the threat to North America's ash resource. Journal of Forestry. 104:118–124.

Pureswaran, D.S.; Poland, T.M. 2009. Host selection and feeding preference of *Agrilus planipennis* (Coleoptera: Buprestidae) on ash (*Fraxinus* spp.). Environmental Entomology. 38(3): 757–765.

Pureswaran, D.S.; Poland, T.M.; Grant, G. 2007. Host selection by emerald ash borer: chemical ecology and behavioral studies. In: Mastro, V.; Lance, D.; Reardon, R.; Parra, G., comps. Emerald ash borer and Asian longhorned beetle research and development review meeting. FHTET 2007-04. Morgantown, WV: U.S. Department of Agriculture, Forest Service, Forest Health Technology Enterprise Team: 8.

Rebek, E.J.; Herms, D.A.; Smitley, D.R. 2008. Interspecific variation in resistance to emerald ash borer (Coleoptera: Buprestidae) among North American and Asian ash (*Fraxinus* spp.). Environmental Entomology. 37:242–246.

Rodriguez-Saona, C.; Poland, T.M.; Miller, J.R.; Stelinski, L.L.; Grant, G.G.; de Groot, P.; Buchan, L.; MacDonald, L. 2006. Behavioral and electrophysiological responses of the emerald ash borer, *Agrilus planipennis*, to induced volatiles of Manchurian ash, *Fraxinus mandshurica*. Chemoecology. 16: 75–86.

Smith, A. 2006. Effects of community structure on forest susceptibility and response to the emerald ash borer invasion of the Huron River watershed in southeast Michigan. Columbus, OH: The Ohio State University. M.S. thesis.

Townsend, A.M.; Bentz, S.E.; Douglass, L.W. 2005. Evaluation of 19 American elm clones for tolerance to Dutch elm disease. Journal of Environmental Horticulture. 23(1): 21–24.

Coast Live Oak Resistance to
Phytophthora ramorum

B.A. McPherson,[1] David L. Wood,[1] Sylvia R. Mori,[2] and Pierluigi Bonello[3]

Abstract

The oomycete *Phytophthora ramorum* is a plant pathogen with an unusually broad host range. Recognized in 2000 as a previously unknown and likely introduced species, this pathogen has become established in central and northern coastal California, southwestern Oregon, and Western Europe. Tree species that may be killed by stem cankers include true oaks (*Quercus agrifolia* Née, *Q. kelloggii* Newb., *Q. parvula* var. *shrevei* (C.H. Muller) Nixon, and *Q. chrysolepis* Liebm.), and tanoaks (*Notholithocarpus densiflorus* Hook. and Arn.), in North America; and Japanese larch (*Larix kaempferi* (Lam.) Carrière) in the United Kingdom. The disease, referred to as sudden oak death (SOD), is changing the composition of forests in California and potentially threatens forests worldwide. Coast live oak has been heavily-impacted by the epidemic, with infection and mortality rates in infested areas averaging 5 percent and 3 percent, per year, respectively, in forests of Marin County, California. Since this species is one of the dominant mast-producing trees in much of coastal California, the species composition and ecological integrity of many of these forests are threatened. Median survival of naturally infected coast live oaks in long-term disease progression plots established in 2000 was estimated as 9.7 years, using Weibull survival models. Beetle attacks in cankers reduced survival times by 65 to 80 percent. While coast live oak mortality has steadily increased since 2000, the infection rate in these sites has been declining. In heavily-affected areas, asymptomatic coast live oaks persist that have never exhibited the bleeding symptom of infection or that are in apparent remission from previously recorded bleeding.

Resistance to canker pathogens in trees can be assessed by measuring canker sizes induced by inoculation of the pathogen into mechanical wounds, which in resistant trees are not significantly different from wounds alone or are below a critical threshold. We inoculated a total of 80 asymptomatic mature coast live oaks with *P. ramorum* and mock-inoculated (controls; wounded without inoculation) 40 trees in two natural populations in Marin County in July 2002 and followed disease development to July 2009. By April 2003, 70 percent of the inoculated trees, and none of the controls, exhibited bleeding. We estimated the probability of survival to 2009 using a Logit model to regress on maximum external canker length measured 9 months after inoculation. Trees with external cankers < 21.2 cm (50 percent of the trees) had ≥ 80 percent probability of survival, while cankers < 6.6 cm (35 percent of the trees) predicted ≥ 90 percent probability of survival. The trees that died by 2009 (20 percent of the total inoculated with the pathogen) all had external cankers ≥ 40 cm in 2003. Because the study started in 2002, after the most susceptible individuals in the stands likely had already been infected or killed by *P. ramorum* infection, our data may overestimate the proportion of resistant trees in the pre-epidemic stands. Even so, our study shows that coast live oaks in northern California exhibit substantial resistance to *P. ramorum*. The distribution of canker lengths is consistent with quantitative multi-gene resistance to the pathogen.

---

[1] University of California, Department of Environmental Sciences, Policy and Management, Berkeley, CA 94720.
[2] USDA Forest Service, Pacific Southwest Research Station, Albany, CA 94710.
[3] Ohio State University, Columbus, OH 43210.
Corresponding author: bmcpherson@berkeley.edu.

Relationship Between Field Resistance to *Phytophthora ramorum* and Constitutive Phenolic Chemistry of Coast Live Oak

A.M. Nagle,[1] B.A. McPherson,[2] D.L. Wood,[2] M. Garbelotto,[2] A.O. Conrad,[1] S. Opiyo,[1] and P. Bonello[1]

Abstract

Sudden oak death, caused by *Phytophthora ramorum*, has resulted in high levels of coast live oak (*Quercus agrifolia* Nee (CLO) mortality. However, some CLO survive in areas with high disease pressure and may thus be resistant. We tested the hypothesis that such field resistant trees contain constitutively higher levels of phenolics than susceptible trees. Phloem was sampled from the trunks of two groups of trees (one previously inoculated, one naturally infected with *P. ramorum*) categorized over the course of several years as putatively resistant (PR, no symptoms), in remission (IR, showed symptoms but then recovered), and symptomatic (S). Individual and total soluble phenolics from these trees were quantified. There were no significant differences in individual or total soluble phenolics between groups of naturally infected trees. However, inoculated PR and IR trees were characterized by higher constitutive levels of total phenolics, as well as ellagic acid and tyrosol hexoside pentoside, than S trees. Threshold concentrations that predicted an individual tree's response to inoculation with *P. ramorum* were determined using logistic regression analysis for ellagic acid, tyrosol hexoside pentoside, and total phenolics. The identification of low molecular weight compounds (biomarkers) associated with resistance may lead to minimally invasive assays for assessing the response of individual coast live oaks or populations to *P. ramorum*. The ability to identify resistant trees prior to the arrival of the pathogen increases the options for managing threatened forests, e.g., by protecting highly resistant stands from logging, fire, and development.

[1] The Ohio State University, Columbus, OH 43210.
[2] University of California, Berkeley, CA 94720.
Corresponding author: bonello.2@osu.edu.

Modeling Elm Growth and Dutch Elm Disease Susceptibility

Alberto Santini[1] and Luisa Ghelardini[1]

Abstract

Elm susceptibility to Dutch elm disease (DED) displays strong seasonal variation. The period during which elms can become infected and express DED symptoms is generally restricted to several weeks after growth resumption in spring, although it can vary among species, provenances, and environmental conditions. The reason for this phenomenon is not understood, but the few studies correlating DED susceptibility with the host's rhythm of seasonal morphogenesis suggest that the seasonal variation in disease development depends on the pattern of growth. Susceptibility to DED is correlated to the date of bud burst in the European field elm, suggesting that a differentiation in spring phenology might cause an asynchrony between the period of susceptibility of the host and the phase of disease transmission by the insect vector allowing the tree to escape the disease.

In order to verify which conditions are determinant to express a susceptible response in elm, a thorough study of the time course of longitudinal growth, including reactivation of cambial activity and timing of bud burst, leaf area development, radial growth, wood ring anatomy, and their relations with DED susceptibility, assessed through repeated artificial inoculations from late winter to early summer, was conducted in an intermediately susceptible elm clone. Growth and seasonal variation in the response to DED infection were modeled in 2 consecutive years.

Three different patterns of shoot growth were observed at the same time in elm: predetermined growth, free growth, and growth for successive flushes. Each of the observed types of elongation growth had a specific spatial and temporal distribution, which corresponded to different anatomical patterns in the wood and different responses to DED inoculation.

The period of maximum susceptibility to DED coincided with a phase of initial and slow growth, during which reserves were rapidly exhausted, expanding leaves were behaving as energy sinks, and early wood was formed. The first decrement in DED susceptibility coincided with the transition to a subsequent phase of fast growth, when hefty energy was supplied by an increasing number of mature leaves able to efficiently photosynthesize, and a more compact late wood was formed.

The results fit the "Growth-Differentiation Balance Hypothesis" (Herms, D.A.; Mattson, W.J. 1992. The dilemma of plants - to grow or defend. Quarterly Review of Biology. 67 (4): 478.), which provides a framework for predicting possible allocation trade-offs in between differentiation-related and growth-related processes over a range of environmental conditions (Lorio, P.L. 1986. Growth-differentiation balance: a basis for understanding southern pine beetle tree interactions. Forest Ecology and Management. 14: 259–273.). Similarly to all other plants, elms are challenged by the highly unpleasant dilemma: to grow or to defend.

---

[1] Institute of Plant Protection, CNR, Via Madonna del Piano, 10, 50019 Sesto fiorentino, Firenze, Italy.
Corresponding author: a.santini@ipp.cnr.it.

Altered Distribution of Susceptibility Phenotypes Implies Environmental Modulation of Genetic Resistance

Thomas R. Gordon[1] and Neil McRoberts[1]

Resistance to disease is determined by the genetic capacity of a plant to recognize and respond to a pathogen, as modified to varying degrees by the environment in which the interaction occurs. Physical factors such as temperature and moisture can limit the ability of a pathogen to infect and cause disease, and may also influence the response of the host through effects on gene expression and/or by imposing constraints on physiological activities required to deliver an effective defense. Recent research has also drawn attention to the potential for the biotic environment to modulate susceptibility to disease. Thus, resistance may be enhanced by endophytic microbes and also by sub-lethal exposure to a plant pathogen. For example, studies under controlled conditions document that systemic-induced resistance (SIR) to pitch canker, caused by *Fusarium circinatum*, is operative in *Pinus radiata* D. Don (Monterey pine) (Bonello et al. 2001). Evidence for SIR in natural populations of *P. radiata* derives from studies showing that trees are more resistant to pitch canker in areas where the disease is of long residence than trees in areas where the disease is only recently established. Likewise, in a given stand, trees tend to become more resistant with time after establishment of pitch canker (Gordon et al. 2011). These observations suggest that susceptibility to a disease may be influenced as much by the history of exposure to a pathogen as by inherent genetic resistance.

To explore this possibility, we compared the distribution of virulence phenotypes in a native stand of *P. radiata* to a population of seedlings reared from seed collected from the same stand. Seedlings were maintained in a greenhouse and were not exposed to *F. circinatum.* At 1.5-years-of-age, each tree was inoculated once on the main stem, as described by Gordon et al. (1998). Three weeks later, the length of the lesion at the site of inoculation was measured. Lesion length was used as a proxy for susceptibility, with the more resistant trees sustaining shorter lesions than trees that are more susceptible. Lesion lengths on 614 trees were approximately normally distributed around a mean of 29.5 mm (fig. 1), which is consistent with resistance to pitch canker being a quantitatively inherited trait (Matheson et al. 2006). In contrast, lesion lengths in parent trees were not normally distributed, but instead were arrayed in a right skewed distribution (fig. 2).

The comparatively high proportion of short lesion lengths among parent trees cannot be attributed to a loss of susceptible trees due to pitch canker because the disease became established only after the sampled trees were mature, and no pitch canker caused mortality had occurred within that population. On the other hand, we cannot exclude the possibility that ontogenetic resistance contributed to the observed difference between progeny and parent trees. However, there is no evidence that susceptibility to pitch canker changes with the age of a tree. This is illustrated by results of an experiment in which 148 trees ranging in size from 3.5 to 77.5 cm were inoculated on each of three branches (fig. 3). Regression of lesion length on tree diameter (DBH) yields an R^2 of 0.006, indicating that DBH (as a surrogate for age) accounts for a negligible proportion of the observed variation.

---

[1] Department of Plant Pathology, University of California, Davis, CA 95616.
Corresponding author: trgordon@ucdavis.edu.

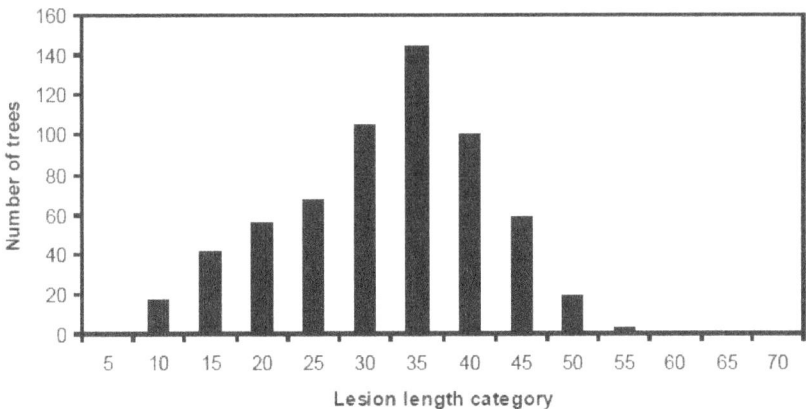

Figure 1—The number of trees corresponding to each lesion length category. Each category encompasses a range of 5mm, with the number on the X-axis representing the upper end of the range in mm.

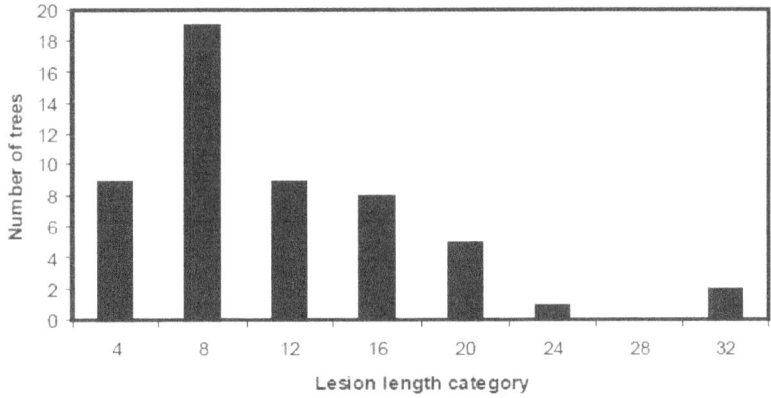

Figure 2—The number of trees corresponding to each lesion length category. Each category encompasses a range of 5mm, with the number on the X-axis representing the upper end of the range in mm.

An alternative explanation for a different distribution of lesion lengths between parent trees and their progeny is that environmental factors are influencing susceptibility, and more specifically, that exposure to parasitic microbes leads to a shift in the distribution of susceptibility phenotypes toward greater resistance. To test the merits of this proposition, we developed a simple model to simulate the transition from a normal distribution of lesion lengths (as occurs in unexposed seedlings) to the right-skewed distribution observed in the parent population. The model includes a stochastic contagious contact distribution between trees and the pathogen, which models exposure, and a host phenotypic response function that determines the impact of exposure events on lesion length. An outline of the model is shown in the schematic in fig. 4.

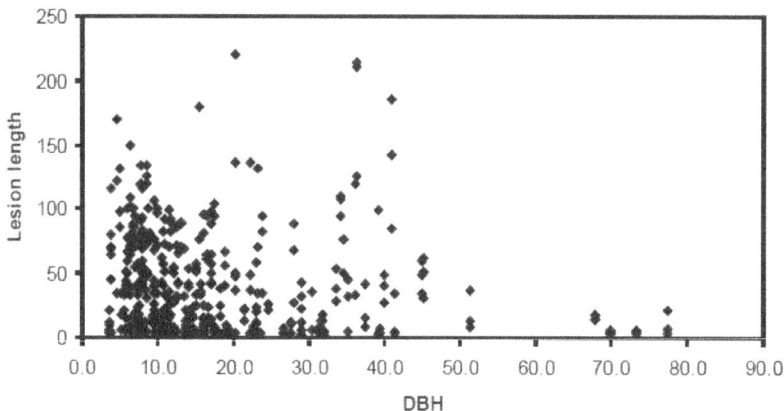

Figure 3—Each point corresponds to the length of a lesion on an inoculated branch (Y-axis) and the DBH (X-axis) of the tree. Each tree was inoculated on three branches and so is represented by three data points in this graph.

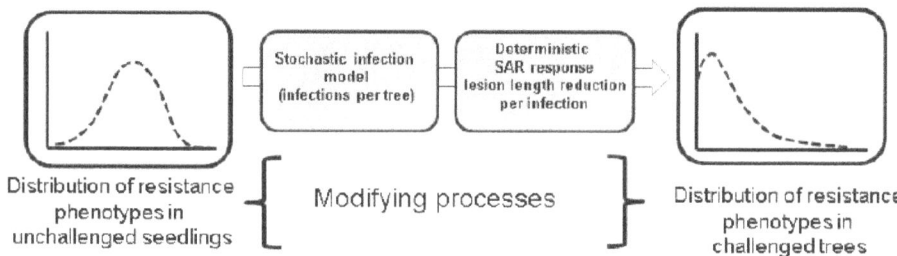

Figure 4—A schematic of the model used to simulate the transforming effect of induced resistance on the distribution of susceptibility phenotypes. (SAR = systemic acquired resistance).

Using parameters that are consistent with what we know about the epidemiology of pitch canker, the model effectively converts a normal distribution to one that resembles the pattern observed in nature. Experimental support for the operation of this process will be sought by establishing a population from seed and documenting that changes over time are associated with exposure to the pitch canker pathogen.

Literature Cited

Bonello, P.; Gordon, T.R.; Storer, A.J. 2001. Systemic induced resistance in Monterey pine. Forest Pathology. 31: 1–8.

Gordon, T.R.; Kirkpatrick, S.C.; Aegerter, B.J.; Fisher, A.J.; Storer, A.J.; Wood, D.L. 2011. Evidence for the natural occurrence of induced resistance to pitch canker, caused by *Gibberella circinata*, in populations of *Pinus radiata*. Forest Pathology. 41: 227–232.

Gordon, T.R.; Wikler, K.R.; Clark, S.L.; Okamoto, D.; Storer, A.J.; Bonello, P. 1998. Resistance to pitch canker disease, caused by *Fusarium subglutinans* f. sp. *pini*, in Monterey pine (*Pinus radiata*). Plant Pathology. 47: 706–711.

Matheson, A.C.; Devey, M.E.; Gordon, T.R.; Werner, W.; Vogler, D.R.; Balocchi, C.; Carson, M.J. 2006. Heritability of response to inoculation by pine pitch canker of seedlings of radiata pine. Australian Forestry Journal. 70: 101–106.

Latent Infection by *Fusarium circinatum* Influences Susceptibility of Monterey Pine Seedlings to Pitch Canker

Cassandra L. Swett[1] and Thomas R. Gordon[1]

Pitch canker, caused by *Fusarium circinatum*, is a serious disease affecting *Pinus radiata* D. Don (Monterey pine) in nurseries, landscapes, and native forests. A typical symptom of pitch canker is canopy dieback resulting from girdling lesions on terminal branches (Gordon et al. 2001). More extensive dieback can result from coalescing lesions on large branches or on the main stem of the tree. The severity of disease depends, in part, on susceptibility of the individual tree. Some will suffer no more than a few infected branch tips, whereas others sustain extensive damage and may ultimately die from the disease, often in conjunction with other forms of stress. However, some trees that become severely diseased eventually recover, with the absence of new infections attributed to systemic induced resistance (Gordon et al. 2011). To date, induced resistance in Monterey pine has been examined only in mature trees, but the disease can also affect seedlings, with potentially significant impacts on regeneration. Although the pitch canker pathogen can be a cause of mortality in seedlings, those that are not killed may remain infected without showing symptoms (Gordon et al. 2001, Storer et al. 2001). The present study was undertaken to determine if seedlings with symptomless infections manifest systemic-induced resistance to pitch canker.

To establish symptomless infected seedlings, seed was sown in sand infested with either 100 or 1,000 propagules per gram, referred to as the low and high inoculum treatments, respectively. Control seedlings were grown in non-infested sand. Six months after sowing, symptomless seedlings representative of each treatment were challenge inoculated by depositing a suspension of 1.25×10^4 spores per ml into a 1.0 mm diameter wound on the main stem. Susceptibility to pitch canker was quantified as the length of the lesion developing at the site of inoculation.

The results showed that resistance was significantly increased in seedlings previously exposed to the pathogen ($P < 0.001$). Stem lesions were 32 to 54 percent shorter than controls in the low inoculum induction treatment and 63 percent shorter in the high inoculum treatment (fig. 1). In addition, a greater proportion of plants appeared healthy in the high inoculum treatment, compared to untreated plants ($P = 0.033$) (fig. 2).

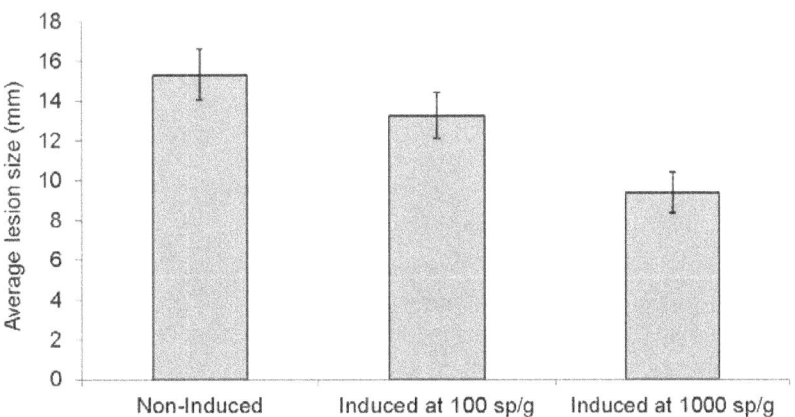

Figure 1—Lesion sizes on inoculated trees (n=60) 19 days after inoculations.

[1] Department of Plant Pathology, University of California, Davis, CA 95616.
Corresponding author: trgordon@ucdavis.edu.

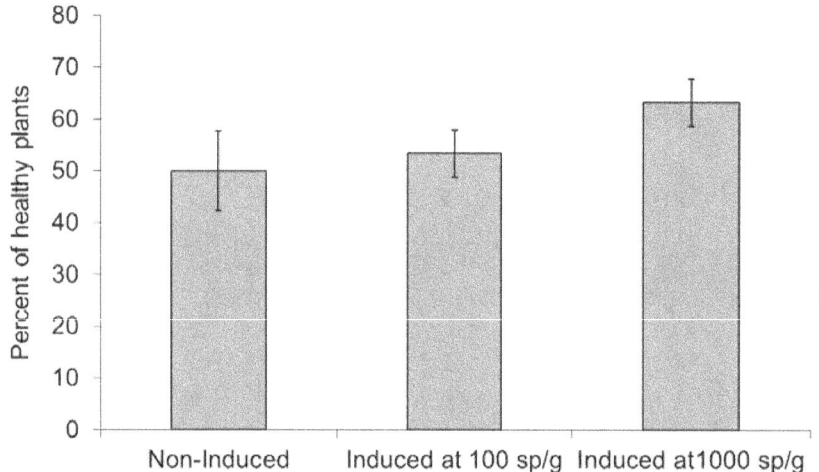

Figure 2—Percent of plants (n = 60) appearing healthy 19 days after inoculation.

Similar results were obtained in experiments using 18-month-old seedlings, suggesting that systemic-induced resistance can persist as seedlings mature. Together, these results indicate that symptomless root infections can induce systemic resistance in seedlings, potentially enhancing survival rates.

The growth-defense balance hypothesis predicts that increased expression of secondary metabolic pathways associated with disease resistance will decrease allocation of resources to growth. Contrary to this prediction, plant growth was not reduced in induced plants (fig. 3).

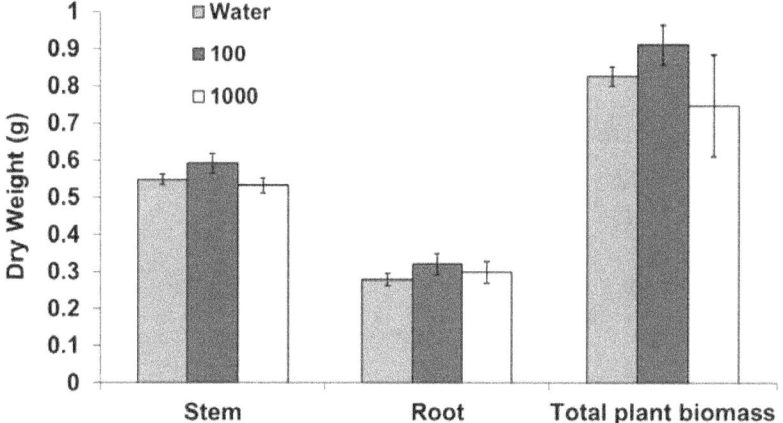

Figure 3—Effect of induced resistance on plant growth.

This is the first study to describe systemic-induced resistance in tree seedlings, and offers insight into the ecological role of *Fusarium circinatum* as an endophyte. If subsequent studies confirm these findings, we aim to determine if similar effects can be documented to occur under natural conditions. If so, it will be of interest to know what factors determine whether infections at the seedling stage result in death or a longer lasting association that may enhance resistance to subsequent challenge by the pitch canker pathogen.

Literature Cited

Gordon, T.R.; Kirkpatrick, S.C.; Aegerter, B.J.; Fisher, A.J.; Storer, A.J.; Wood, D.L. 2011. Evidence for the natural occurrence of induced resistance to pitch canker, caused by *Gibberella circinata*, in populations of *Pinus radiata*. Forest Pathology. 41: 227–232.

Gordon, T.R.; Storer, A.J.; Wood, D.L. 2001. The pitch canker epidemic in California. Plant Disease. 85: 1128–1139.

Storer, A.J.; Wood, D.L.; Gordon, T.R.; Libby, W.J. 2001. Restoring native Monterey pine forests in the presence of an exotic pathogen. Journal of Forestry. 99: 14–18.

Breeding for Resistance in Norway Spruce to the Root and Butt Rot Fungi *Heterobasidion* spp.

G. Swedjemark,[1] A.K. Borg-Karlson,[2] and B. Karlsson[1]

Abstract

Results from previous studies of resistance in Norway spruce (*Picea abies* (L.) Karst.) to the pathogens *Heterobasidion* spp. show significant genotypic variation in fungal growth and spore susceptibility among Norway spruce clones. The genetic variation and the heritability are large enough for practical breeding purposes and there is no adverse correlation between *Heterobasidion* infection and growth traits. There is an economic incentive to use plant materials which are more resistant than those used in reforestation today. Recent research on developing the methods for testing resistance in plant material have demonstrated that we need to identify new markers and early traits for screening young material before we can include resistance to the pathogen in existing breeding programs. In an ongoing project we are analyzing the differences in the chemical defense and the transcriptome of *Heterobasidion* spp.-infected *P. abies* clones with different susceptibility to *Heterobasidion* spp. infection. Preliminary results show that the quantity of certain substances involved in defense mechanisms is specific for resistant clones. For example, astringin may be a constitutive chemical marker for resistance.

Key words: *Heterobasidion* spp., Norway spruce, *Picea abies*, resistance breeding

Introduction

The root pathogens *Heterobasidion* spp. are able to infect living conifer roots of all ages (Asiegbu et al. 2005). The *Heterobasdion* species complex consists of five different species, of which two are common in Scandinavia: *Heterobasidion annosum* and *Heterobasidion parviporum* (Dahlman 2010). The complex causes serious damage to coniferous forests throughout the Northern Hemisphere and, under optimal conditions, can rapidly destroy a stand. The fungus spreads both by spores and by vegetative growth: spores land on recently exposed wood, such as freshly cut stumps, germinate, and form a mycelium, which colonizes the stump and its roots. It then infects healthy trees by growing via root contacts and grafts between stumps and trees and then extends through the roots and up into the stem.

Results from our previous studies (inoculation of differently aged clonal material and screening of naturally infected clone stands) of resistance in Norway spruce (*Picea abies* (L.) Karst.) to *Heterobasidion* spp. are promising. There is significant genetic variation in resistance to fungal growth and in spore susceptibility in Norway spruce. The results show the same pattern in inoculation experiments and in naturally-infected Norway spruce clone stands (Karlsson and Swedjemark 2006, Swedjemark 1995). The genetic variation and the heritability are large enough for practical breeding purposes and there is no adverse correlation between *Heterobasidion* infection and growth traits. The economic calculations show that losses due to root rot are significant; there is an economic incentive to use plant materials which are more resistant than those used today (Karlsson and Swedjemark 2006).

Genetic variation in Norway spruce has been detected for several traits such as growth capacity and wood density (Karlsson and Högberg 1998). Economic gain from using improved plant material could be even greater if resistance factors were included in selection programs. Previous results from *Heterobasidion* spp. inoculation experiments and inventories in field trials have shown that genetic variation in fungal extension and infection frequency is of the same magnitude as in other traits used in applied tree breeding. The genetic improvement was 15 percent less than the average

[1] Skogforsk, Ekebo 2250, SE-26890 Svalöv, Sweden.
[2] Ecological Chemistry Group, Department of Chemistry, KTH, Sweden.
Corresponding author: gunilla.swedjmark@skogforsk.se.

infection frequency when selecting the 10 percent top clones (Karlsson and Swedjemark 2006, Swedjemark 1995).

Inoculation experiments on twigs showed that the infection pattern is the same in twigs as in cuttings, which makes it possible to perform non-destructive inoculation experiments in field trials. In inoculation experiments on cuttings, a systemic induced resistance reaction was found up to 18 months after the first treatment with the pathogen (Swedjemark and Karlsson 2006, Swedjemark et al. 2007).

Being long-lived organisms, Norway spruce trees rely on both induced and constitutive defenses to restrict the spread of invading fungi and insects. The first line of defense in Norway spruce trees is the bark. The combination of the physical properties of lignified and suberized walls and the chemical properties of phenolics and terpenes makes bark a very efficient barrier against infection. Once an injury or an infection is recognized by the tree, induced defenses are activated, including cell wall re-enforcements, production of lytic enzymes, and secondary metabolites such as phenols, stilbenes, lignans, flavonoids, and terpenes (Keeling and Bohlmann 2006, Witzell and Martin 2008)

One generally debated hypothesis claims that the production of defense compounds depend on abiotic factors, e.g., the amount of nutrition available (Herms and Mattson 1992). In one of our studies on spruce, we have partly confirmed this hypothesis, as the induced amounts of monoterpenes were less in trees that obtained an excess nutrition. We also found that the absolute amounts of terpenes were positively correlated to the inoculated fungal performance (Danielsson et al. 2011).

The terpene chemistry in healthy *P. abies* is well documented, both within and between grafts, and in natural stands (Borg-Karlson et al. 1993, Persson et al.1996). Large variations between and within trees are found for the monoterpenes, and there also exists "chemo types" characterized by the occurrence of 3-carene. We have shown that only a few monoterpene enantiomers, including (+)-3-carene, are induced by fungi (Zhao et al. 2010) representing specific terpene synthases . With our technique, we can analyze the effects of stress elicitors in more detail, and we aim to show that individual changes in terpenes are highly dynamic and inducible.

The phenols stilbene, (*E*)-astringin and corresponding astringin dimers (piceasides), and a number of unknown phenolics, seem to be of major importance as resistant markers (Danielsson et al. 2011) and will be the focus of our further investigations. We have recently identified clones that produce enhanced amounts of astringin which is of interest in our search of resistant markers.

The aim of our research is to find the best constitutive or induced markers for resistance to be able to select parent clones to be included in existing breeding programs for Norway spruce. Knowledge of reliable resistance markers is essential for the production of future plant materials intended for selection of parent clones for the breeding population, and thus for commercial reforestation material.

Material and Methods

Plant Material

Since 1994, we have had access to Norway spruce plant and tree material included in the Swedish regional clonal forestry program at The Forest Research Institute in Sweden (Karlsson and Högberg 1998). During the years, we have tested ca 1,000 spruce clones for resistance to *Heterobasidion* spp., using artificial inoculation of plants, trees, twigs, stumps, and somatic embryos. In addition we have screened naturally infested clonal stands by felling trees, using a borer, or a root rot detector (Rotfinder©). Grafts of selected clones have been prepared and we have made controlled crossings between parents with known levels of resistance.

Methods for Artificial Inoculation

- Cuttings, roots, and twigs. Wounds are made aseptically in the bark to reach the xylem surface. Mycelium is attached to the wound. Incubation period is ca 3 weeks. At sampling, the stem is consecutively cut into 5 mm thick disks. The disks from each sample are incubated under humid conditions and are then checked for conidia of the fungi. The fungal extension is estimated for each sample.

- Artificial inoculation on stumps. The trees are felled, leaving stumps ca 50 cm high. Immediately after felling, the stumps are covered with a suspension of *Heterobasidion* spp. conidiospores (suspended in sterile water). After incubation (ca 3 months), the stumps are sliced into 1 cm thick discs, numbered, and stored in a plastic bag under humid conditions. After ca 10 days, the discs are checked for conidia development on the mycelia and the extension of fungal growth is measured.

Quantitative RT-PCR Analysis of PAL-Transcripts

The enzyme PAL (Phenylalanin Ammonia-Lyase) is central in the phenylpropanoid pathway and lignin biosynthesis, but also in production of stilbenes and flavonoids. Using quantitative real-time polymerase chain reaction (Quantitative RT-PCR) analysis of PAL transcript levels, the level of activation is measured in the tissues around the fungal growth. Small samples close to the fungi and at certain distances from the fungi are collected and frozen in -80 °C and processed according to Hietala et al. (2003).

Methods for Terpene and Phenol Analysis

Samples extracted in hexane, methanol, or by solid phase micro extraction (SPME) or thermal adsorption/desorption methods, are taken in order to measure the "metabolomics." We have well-established protocols for the extraction procedures and the separation of constituents in the complex mixtures is reliable. Sampling by solvent extraction gives information about the constitutive and induced resins, and the hexane extracts is analyzed by the two-dimensional GC-MS to separate the enantiomers of the chiral terpenes (Persson et al 1993). The dynamics of selected chiral monoterpenes α-pinene, β-pinene, and limonene and sesquiterpenes is analyzed in detail by SPME-GC-MS technique adsorption solvent or thermal desorption in 2D-GC-MS. Volatiles released by healthy and infested trees are collected and we localize the front of the mycelium by measuring the emission of specific de novo-produced stress compounds (methyl salicylate and α-and β-farnesenes).

The methanol/water extract rich in phenolic compounds is analyzed by using reversed phase-HPLC-MS[n]. Efforts to identify the unknown compounds is made by HPLC-prep-microprobe-NMR in cooperation with the NMR group at the Max Planck Institute of Chemical Ecology in Jena, Germany, a group already focusing in this area.

Recent Results and Discussion

A significant problem when studying resistance in forest ecosystems is the relevance of results from artificial trials in young material versus the natural situation. Are we really measuring actual resistance to the pathogen, and what will happen during a rotation period? The correlation between inoculation results is poor when comparing inoculation in the same clones from different propagation batches (Karlsson et al. 2008). Recent results indicate that it may be an environmental disturbance (stress) of the cuttings which triggers the induced resistance system, which may influence results from inoculation experiments. Induced resistance has showed to be a clone-dependent trait. A systemic-induced resistance reaction was found 18 months after the first treatment with *Heterobasidion* (Swedjemark et al. 2007). Inoculated twigs heavily attacked by *Sacchiphantes abietis* were more efficient in excluding the pathogen from the wood, indicating an induced resistance reaction (Swedjemark and Karlsson 2006). Plants infested with mites were tested for levels of α-and β-farnesenes (indicating stress); clones exposed to mite infection had high levels of volatiles and had a shorter extension of fungal growth when inoculated compared to unaffected control plants, indicating that the induced resistance reaction influenced the result. (Borg-Karlson and Swedjemark, unpublished data). Recent research has shown that induced stress affects tree resistance, where the least visually stressed trees were the most infested by blue stain fungi (Zhao et al. 2010). However, recent results show that the transcriptional regulation always shows the same pattern in the same spruce clones of different ages when inoculated with *Heterobasidion*.

(Danielsson et al. 2011) These findings make it possible to rely on inoculation studies if supplemented with analysis of transcriptional regulation.

Inoculations of *H. annosum* in roots of clones with high and low susceptibility show that the initial phenol composition differed between highly and less susceptible clones. Less susceptible clones were characterized by higher constitutive concentrations of the sesquiterpene α-longipinene, the stilbene (*E*)-astringin and astringin dimers (piceasides), and a number of unknown phenolics, possibly indicating further biochemical reactions downstream.

The levels of the flavonoid (+)-catechin showed a temporal variation; it accumulated between 5 and 15 days after inoculation (dpi) in response to *H. annosum* infection in the less susceptible genotypes. The transcriptome data suggested that the accumulation of free (+)-catechin was preceded by an induction of genes in the flavonoid and proanthocyanidin biosynthesis pathway such as leucoanthocyanidin reductase. Quantitative PCR analyses verified the induction of genes in the phenylpropanoid and flavonoid pathway. The qPCR data also highlighted genotype-dependent differences in the transcriptional regulation of these pathways.

It is obvious from our results that the transcriptional changes in responses to *H. annosum* or wounding treatments are substantially different between the two less susceptible genotypes. The pattern of extractable (+)-catechin in bark differ between the clones. The qPCR data also indicate differences between the clones; the PAL genes are down-regulated already at 15 dpi in wounded susceptible clones while they remain slightly up-regulated at 28 dpi irrespective of treatment in more resistant clones. The result indicates that the genotypes may perhaps depend on different successful defense strategies in the interaction with *Heterobasidion*. Clearly, an extended comparison between the chemistry and the transcriptional responses in the interaction with *Heterobasidion* between several independent genotypes is needed to catalogue the mechanisms of successful host defense strategies (Danielsson et al. 2011).

Conclusions

- There is significant genetic variation in resistance to fungal growth and in spore susceptibility in Norway spruce. Genetic variation and the heritability are large enough for practical breeding purposes and there is no adverse correlation between *Heterobasidion* infection and growth traits.

- Concentration of secondary metabolites in the tree differs between trees more or less susceptible to the pathogen: astringin could be a candidate as a constitutive marker for resistance.

- Concentration of specific phenols differs between trees more or less susceptible to the pathogen.

- Constitutive concentrations of terpenes do not seem to be specific for trees more or less resistant to *Heterobasidion*.

- The transcriptome always shows the same pattern in the same spruce clones when inoculated with *Heterobasidion*.

- Transcriptome data correlates with the chemical profile.

Literature Cited

Asiegbu, F.; Adomas, A.; Stenlid, J. 2005. Conifer root and butt rot caused by *Heterobasidion annosum* (Fr.) Bref. *s.l.* Molecular Plant Pathology. 6: 395–409.

Borg-Karlson, A.K.; Lindström, M.; Persson, M.; Norin, T.; Valterová, I. 1993. Enantiomeric composition of monoterpene hydrocarbons in different tissues of Norway spruce *Picea abies* (L.) Karst. A multidimensional gas chromatography study. Acta Chemica Scandinavica. 47: 138–144.

Dahlman, K. 2010. Heterobasidion root rot. Genetic mapping of virulence and evolutionary history. Uppsala: Swedish University of Agricultural Sciences. 67 p. Ph.D thesis Nr 2010:81.

Danielsson, M.; Lundén, K.; Arnerup, J.; Hu, J.; Zhao, T.; Swedjemark, G.; Elfstrand, M.; Borg-Karlson, A.K.; Stenlid, J. 2011. Chemical and transcriptional responses of Norway spruce clones with varying susceptibility to *Heterobasidion* spp. infection. BMC Plant Biology. doi:10.1186/1471-2229-11-154.

Herms, D.A.; Mattson, W. J. 1992. The dilemma of plants: to grow or defend. Quarterly Review of Biology. 67: 283–335

Hietala, A.M.; Eikenes, M.; Kvaalen, H.; Solheim, H.; Fossdal, C.M. 2003. Multiplex real-time PCR for monotoring *Heterobasidion annosum* colonization in Norway spruce clones that differ in disease resistance. Applied and Environmental Microbiology. 69: 4413–4420.

Karlsson, B.; Swedjemark, G. 2006. Genotypic variation in natural infection frequency of *Heterobasidion* sp. in a 20-year old clone trial of *Picea abies* (L.) Karst. in south Sweden. Scandinavian Journal of Forest Research. 21: 108–114.

Karlsson, B.; Högberg, K.A. 1998. Genotypic parameters and clone x site interaction in clone tests of Norway spruce (*Picea abies* (L.) Karst.). Forest Genetics. 5: 21–30.

Karlsson, B.; Tsopelas, P.; Zamponi, L.; Capretti, P.; Soulioti, N.; Swedjemark, G. 2008. Susceptibility to *Heterobasidion parviporum* in *Picea abies* clones grown in different environments. Forest Pathology. 38: 83–89.

Keeling, C.I.; Bohlmann, J. 2006. Genes, enzymes and chemicals of terpenoid diversity in the constitutive and induced defence of conifers against insects and pathogens. New Phytologist. 170: 657–675.

Persson, M.; Borg-Karlson, A.K.; Norin, T. 1993. Enantiomeric composition of the six main monoterpene hydrocarbons in different tissues of *Picea abies* (L.) Karst. Phytochemistry. 33: 303–307.

Persson, M.; Sjödin, K.; Borg-Karlson, A.K.; Norin, T.; Ekberg, I. 1996. Relative amounts and enantiomeric compositions of monoterpene hydrocarbons in xylem and needles of *Picea abies* (Pinaceae). Phytochemistry. 42: 1289–1297.

Swedjemark, G. 1995. *Heterobasidion annosum* root rot in *Picea abies*: variability and resistance. SLU Info/Repro, Uppsala: 1995 ISBN 91-576-5053-5. Ph.D. thesis.

Swedjemark, G.; Karlsson, B. 2006. Mycelial growth and exclusion of *Heterobasidion parviporum* inoculated in branches of 15-year old *Picea abies* clones. Forest Pathology. 36: 1–6.

Swedjemark, G.; Karlsson, B.; Stenlid, J. 2007. Exclusion of *Heterobasidion parviporum* from inoculated clones of *Picea abies* and evidence of systemic induced resistance. Scandinavian Journal of Forest Research. 22: 110–117.

Witzell, J.; Martin, J.A. 2008. Phenolic metabolites in the resistance of northern forest trees to pathogens - past experiences and future prospects. Canadian Journal of Forest Research-Revue Canadienne De Recherche Forestiere. 38: 2711–2727.

Zhao, T.; Krokene, P.; Björklund, N.; Långström, B.; Solheim, H.; Christiansen, E.; Borg-Karlson, A.K. 2010. The influence of *Ceratocystis polonica* inoculation and methyl jasmonate application on terpene chemistry and host resistance in Norway spruce, *Picea abies.* Phytochemistry. 71: 1332–1341.

Using Survival Analysis for Assessing Resistance to *Phytophthora lateralis* in Port-Orford-Cedar Families

Sylvia R. Mori,[1] Richard A. Sniezko,[2] Angelia Kegley,[2] and Jim Hamlin[3]

Abstract

In a greenhouse trial to examine genetic resistance among seedling families (half-sib, full-sib, and selfed) of Port-Orford-cedar (*Chamaecyparis lawsoniana* (A. Murr.) Parl.) to the root pathogen *Phytophthora lateralis*, the root tips of seedlings were inoculated, and the subsequent mortality was followed over a 3 year period. Mortality among families at the end of the trial varied from 0 to 100 percent, with continuing mortality for some families occurring throughout the trial period. A preliminary examination of mortality curves for the families indicated that some families were highly susceptible (100 percent mortality in less than 290 days), some appeared to have high survival putatively from a single major gene (0 to 50 percent mortality with little or no additional mortality after 180 days), and the majority of families appeared to show varying degrees of partial resistance, with different final levels of mortality and with the within-family mortality occurring at different rates. Here, we explore the use of survival analysis to examine the different patterns of mortality among the 125 families and place them into different resistance groups. To illustrate the usage of survival analysis, we applied some of these techniques to all families and others to a subsample of eight of the 125 seedling families. We used the Kaplan-Meier estimator to plot their survival function and compare them visually. One main objective was to discern how many of the 124 families were significantly different than the high susceptible control family (family 73), which in previous trials had reached 100 percent mortality in a relatively short time. We used the log-rank test (non-parametric approach) to compare groups of families with similar patterns. Using separate pairwise comparisons, this approach identified five (of the 124) families that were not significantly different from the susceptible control (family 73). In some other comparisons, the log-rank test did not separate them as well as anticipated based on the visual plots. This is mainly due to the small sample size and large variability. Only when survival curves looked extremely different from each other were there statistically significant differences. Therefore, the log-rank test should be used with caution, and as an exploratory tool. When possible, other techniques should be used such as Cox Proportional Hazard (PH, semi-parametric approach), and Weibull or Gamma regression models (parametric approach). The Cox PH model was used to compare a family's mortality risk with respect to another family; for example, high mortality family 73 had 4.4 times the risk of mortality than high mortality family 101. When possible, we also compared families and groups of families' survival patterns using the Gamma survival regression model (the 3-parameter Gamma survival curve fitted the data best) by comparing their estimated parameters or analyzing their quantile times (Q25, Q50 and Q75). In conclusion: (1) survival analysis is a useful tool for understanding the distribution of mortality responses, (2) small sample sizes and lack of homogeneity of the data can produce inconclusive results, (3) parametric models don't fit the data with long plateaus well, and (4) if parametric models fit well, they can be used to compare the mortality statistical distributions by means of their estimated parameters or estimated key quantile times.

[1] USDA Forest Service, Pacific Southwest Research Station, 800 Buchanan, Albany, CA 94710.
[2] USDA Forest Service, Dorena Genetic Resource Center, 34963 Shoreview Road, Cottage Grove, OR 97424.
[3] USDA Forest Service, USDA, Umpqua National Forest, Roseburg, OR 97471.
Corresponding author: smori@fs.fed.us.

Molecular and Genomics Tools in Resistance Programs

Port-Orford-cedar (*Chamaecyparis lawsoniana*) (a) *Phytophthora lateralis* mortality in Redwood National Park, (b) resistant parent 510015 surrounded by dead Port-Orford-cedar trees, (c) dead and dying Port-Orford-cedar along Highway 101 in southern Oregon, and (d) breeding Port-Orford-cedar for resistance in containerized orchard (Photos: R.Sniezko (a,c,d); C.Frank (b)).

Integrating Molecular Tools and Conventional Approaches in the Oregon State University Hazelnut Breeding Program

Shawn A. Mehlenbacher[1]

The Oregon State University (OSU) hazelnut breeding program, initiated in 1969, continues to develop new cultivars for the hazelnut industry that combine suitability to the blanched kernel market with resistance to eastern filbert blight (EFB) caused by *Anisogramma anomala*. Oregon's hazelnut growers support the program through the Oregon Hazelnut Commission. The need for improved disease-resistant cultivars and pollinizers is the program's driving force. About 5000 seedlings have been planted each year during the past 2 decades, and 10 cultivars and 10 pollinizers have been released. Oregon produces 99 percent of the United States crop, but only 3 to 5 percent of the of the world crop. Beginning in 2009, plantings have expanded from 12,000 ha by 1200 ha per year. Most new orchards are being planted to 'Jefferson,' increased by micropropagation.

Cultivars of European hazelnut (*Corylus avellana* L.) are highly heterozygous and clonally propagated. Hazelnuts were already being cultivated in Italy and Spain at the time of the Roman Empire as well as at an earlier date on the Black Sea coast of Turkey and in the Caucasus Mountains. All cultivars in these countries were selected from the local vegetation. *Corylus avellana* is native to most of Europe, Turkey, and the Caucasus republics were it grows as a small-stature, multi-stemmed shrub. Diverse germplasm has been imported as scions or seeds. The Corvallis collections contain ~900 accessions and include representatives of all 11 *Corylus* species and ~500 clones of *Corylus avellana*. Hazelnut is a model for the order Fagales and family Betulaceae. All *Corylus* species are diploid, have a small genome (0.48 pg/1C, 380 MB), and an estimated 35,000 genes. Morphology, phenology, and all marker types investigated to date have shown *C. avellana* to be highly polymorphic.

Objectives of the OSU hazelnut breeding program fall into two categories: suitability to the blanched kernel market and resistance to EFB. Some 93 percent of the world's hazelnuts are sold as kernels to chocolate makers and bakers; only 7 percent are sold in-shell for the table market. Kernel varieties should be resistant to bud mites (primarily *Phytoptus avellanae*), start to bear nuts at an early age, have consistent high nut yields, round nut shape, thin shells, easy pellicle removal, few nut and kernel defects, early nut maturity, and free-falling nuts. The process to develop varieties begins with 40 to 50 controlled pollinations each year. The hybrid seeds are harvested in late August and are soaked and placed in stratification in early November. The seedlings are grown in 4 L pots in the greenhouse in the first year and then transplanted 1 m apart in the field in October in rows that are 3 m apart. Most seedlings bear their first nuts in the fifth leaf. Evaluation of the seedlings in years 5 to 8 reduces their number to 25 to 40 selections, which are propagated by tie-off layerage. The layers are lined out in a nursery row for one season and then used to plant replicated yield trials. Data is collected from the trials in years 3 to 7. The breeding cycle from seed to seed is 8 years. New cultivars are released 16 to 17 years after the cross is made.

A few traits are controlled by single loci, including pollen-stigma incompatibility and some EFB resistance sources. Most of the program's breeding objectives involve quantitative traits for which heritability was estimated by regression (Mehlenbacher et al. 1993, Yao and Mehlenbacher 2000). Heritability is >50 percent for most traits we have investigated, so it is unlikely that marker-assisted selection will be more effective than phenotypic selection.

---

[1] Dept. of Horticulture, 4017 ALS Building, Oregon State University, Corvallis, OR 97331.
Corresponding author: mehlenbs@hort.oregonstate.edu.

Greenhouse inoculation with EFB is used to classify accessions as resistant or susceptible. Three trees per accession are grown in the greenhouse, inoculated with a spore suspension, and maintained under high humidity. The trees are placed outside where they go dormant, receive chilling, and then develop cankers 15 to 20 months after inoculation. Very high resistance has been identified in 23 accessions, which represent about 2 percent of those tested (Chen et al. 2007, Lunde et al. 2000, Sathuvalli et al. 2010b). Several resistant accessions have been used as parents in breeding. The resistance in 'Gasaway' is conferred by a dominant allele at a single locus which is carried by the recently released 'Yamhill' and 'Jefferson.' A very high level of resistance was detected in accessions imported as scions: the Spanish 'Ratoli' and 'Culpla,' Georgian OSU 759.010, Serbian 'Crvenje' and 'Uebov,' and eight selections from a forestry institute near Moscow, Russia. Seeds have been imported from several sources, and selected trees in these populations have been tested for EFB response. Highly resistant selections include OSU 408.040 from Minnesota; OSU 495.072 from Russia; and selections from southern Russia, Crimea (Ukraine), and the Republic of Georgia. DNA marker-assisted selection (MAS) has been practiced for 'Gasaway' resistance for more than 12 years. The MAS was initiated because of the pathogen's 2-year life cycle, a desire to select for resistance in the absence of the pathogen, and difficulties in determining disease response. Random Amplified Polymorphic DNA (RAPD) markers 152-800 and 268-580 flank the 'Gasaway' resistance locus, are robust and easy to score, and are useful in multiple populations (Mehlenbacher et al. 2004). Seedlings that carry one or both RAPD markers are planted in the field. Resistance from 'Ratoli,' OSU 408.040, and Georgian OSU 759.010 is also simply inherited, and linked DNA markers have been identified (Chen et al. 2005; Sathuvalli et al. 2010a, 2011).

A linkage map for hazelnut was constructed using RAPD markers (Mehlenbacher et al. 2006), and microsatellite markers were added to serve as anchors. EFB resistance from 'Gasaway' was assigned to linkage group 6 (LG6), from 'Ratoli' to LG 7, and from Georgian OSU 759.010 to LG 2. We will use DNA markers to pyramid different resistance genes. Microsatellite markers show transferability across genera in the Betulaceae (Gürcan and Mehlenbacher 2010), and have been used to fingerprint accessions and study genetic diversity.

Susceptible cultivars vary widely in level of susceptibility. To quantify susceptibility, cultivars and selections are propagated by tie-off layerage. The rooted layers are grown for 1 season in pots in the lathhouse. In the spring, 12 potted trees of each cultivar (including checks) are placed under a structure topped with diseased wood. Sprinklers keep the cankered branches wet, and spores rain down on the young shoot tips. After several weeks of exposure, the trees are planted in a nursery row where cankers are allowed to develop. Cankers are counted and measured 18 to 20 months after exposure. The total length of cankers is calculated for each tree, and a square root transformation used to reduce the relationship between mean and variance. Quantitative resistance, expressed as fewer and smaller cankers, is present in OSU releases 'Lewis,' 'Clark,' and 'Sacajawea'. In a set of nine progenies, the heritability estimate for proportion of wood diseased was 47 percent (Osterbauer et al. 1997).

Oregon State University has partnered with Rutgers University, the University of Nebraska-Lincoln, and the Arbor Day Foundation to form the Hybrid Hazelnut Research Consortium. The Consortium's goal is to develop *C. americana* × *C. avellana* hybrids with EFB resistance and adaptation to the climate of the eastern and Great Plains states. The high disease pressure in field plots at Rutgers University provides useful information.

With Todd Mockler and Illumina, the genome and transcriptome of 'Jefferson' hazelnut was sequenced, and seven accessions are being resequenced. The assembled sequences are being mined for microsatellites and single nucleotide polymorphisms (SNPs), with a special interest in markers for newly identified EFB resistance genes. Map-based cloning of the 'Gasaway' EFB resistance gene identified five candidate genes. A similar approach is in progress for the incompatibility locus. For use in marker-assisted selection with 4000 seedlings per year, markers must be high throughput, robust, and valid in different populations. For use with 400 selections per year, other markers types such as microsatellites are feasible. SNPs are abundant in the hazelnut genome (~1 in 50 bp). High

Resolution Melting (HRM) analysis using a LightScanner (Idaho Technology) is promising for cost-effective scoring of SNP markers. However, MAS is less useful for traits with high heritability, and most traits in hazelnut are highly heritable.

Literature Cited

Chen, H.; Mehlenbacher, S.A.; Smith, D.C. 2005. AFLP markers linked to eastern filbert blight resistance from OSU 408.040 hazelnut. Journal of the American Society for Horticultural Science. 130: 412–417.

Chen, H.; Mehlenbacher, S.A.; Smith, D.C. 2007. Hazelnut accessions provide new sources of resistance to eastern filbert blight. HortScience. 42: 466–469.

Gürcan, K.; Mehlenbacher, S.A. 2010. Transferability of microsatellite markers in the Betulaceae. Journal of the American Society for Horticultural Science. 135: 159–173.

Lunde, C.F.; Mehlenbacher, S.A.; Smith, D.C. 2000. Survey of hazelnut cultivars for response to eastern filbert blight inoculation. HortScience. 35: 729–731.

Mehlenbacher, S.A.; Brown, R.N.; Davis., J.W.; Chen, H.; Bassil, N.V.; Smith, D.C.; Kubisiak, T.L. 2004. RAPD markers linked to eastern filbert blight resistance in *Corylus avellana*. Theoretical and Applied Genetics. 108: 651–656.

Mehlenbacher, S.A.; Brown, R.N.; Nouhra, E.R.; Gokirmak, T.; Bassil, N.V.; Kubisiak, T.L. 2006. A genetic linkage map for hazelnut (*Corylus avellana* L.) based on RAPD and SSR markers. Genome. 49: 122–133.

Mehlenbacher, S.A.; Smith, D.C.; Brenner, L.K. 1993. Variance components and heritability of nut and kernel defects in hazelnut. Plant Breeding. 110: 144–152.

Osterbauer, N.K.; Johnson, K.B.; Mehlenbacher, S.A.; Sawyer, T.L. 1997. Analysis of resistance to eastern filbert blight in *Corylus avellana*. Plant Disease. 81: 388–394.

Sathuvalli, V.R.; Chen, H.L.; Mehlenbacher, S.A.; Smith, D.C. 2010a. DNA markers linked to eastern filbert blight resistance in 'Ratoli' hazelnut. Tree Genetics and Genomes. 7: 337–345.

Sathuvalli, V.R.; Mehlenbacher, S.A.; Smith, D.C. 2010b. Response of hazelnut accessions to greenhouse inoculation with *Anisogramma anomala*. HortScience. 45:1116–1119.

Sathuvalli, V.R.; Mehlenbacher, S.A.; Smith, D.C. 2011. DNA markers linked to eastern filbert blight resistance from a Georgian hazelnut accession. Journal of the American Society for Horticultural Science. 136: 350–357.

Yao, Q.; Mehlenbacher, S.A. 2000. Heritability, variance components and correlation of morphological and phenological traits in hazelnut. Plant Breeding. 119: 369–381.

High-Resolution Genetic and Physical Mapping of Eastern Filbert Blight Resistance in Hazelnut

Vidyasagar Sathuvalli[1] and Shawn A. Mehlenbacher[1]

Eastern filbert blight (EFB), caused by the pyrenomycete *Anisogramma anomala*, is a serious threat to the hazelnut (*Corylus avellana* L.) industry in the Pacific Northwest. A dominant allele at a single locus from the obsolete pollenizer 'Gasaway' confers a very high level of resistance, and has been extensively used in the hazelnut breeding program at Oregon State University. Several linked random amplified polymorphic DNA (RAPD) markers have been identified. Map-based cloning of the EFB resistance gene from 'Gasaway' was initiated by constructing a bacterial artificial chromosome (BAC) library for 'Jefferson' which is heterozygous for resistance (Sathuvalli and Mehlenbacher 2011). The BAC library was constructed using the cloning enzyme MboI and the vector pECBAC1 (BamHI site). The library consists of 39,936 clones arrayed in microtiter plates with an average insert size of 117 kb and estimated coverage of 12 genome equivalents.

A mapping population of 1,488 seedlings, which segregate for resistance, was developed and scored for flanking RAPD markers 152-800 and 268-580 to identify potential recombinants. Chromosome walking, initiated using primers designed from eight RAPD markers (Mehlenbacher et al. 2004, 2006) closely linked to resistance and extended with two further rounds of walking, identified a total of 93 BACs in the resistance region. The BAC library was screened using a PCR-based pooling and subpooling strategy (Sathuvalli and Mehlenbacher 2011). From the BACs, a total of 629 primers were designed, of which 63 pairs were polymorphic. Of these, we mapped 41 new markers to the resistance region. The new markers included 23 sequence-characterized amplified regions (SCARs), seven single-stranded conformational polymorphism (SSCP), seven high-resolution melting (HRM), and four simple-sequence repeat (SSR) markers. A high-resolution genetic map of the resistance region was created with 51 markers (41 from BACs, eight RAPD markers, and two SCAR markers derived from RAPDs) and the resistance phenotype in the mapping population using the program JoinMap v 4.0 (Van Ooijen 2006).

High-information content fingerprinting (HICF) was carried out on 93 BACs which were then assembled using the program FPC v 9.3 (Nelson and Soderlund 2009) into 22 contigs and 23 singletons. The combined maps (genetic and physical) identified a single contig that spans the EFB resistance locus. The 1,488 seedlings showed two recombination breakpoints within a single contig of three BACs (43F13, 66C22 and 85B7) and a physical distance of 135 kb. This region is the target for whole BAC sequencing and a search for disease resistance genes.

Whole BACs in the resistance region (< 1cM) were sequenced using an Illumina IIx genome analyzer, with multiplexing and barcoded adapters to reduce the cost, and paired-end reads to facilitate de novo sequence assembly. De novo assembly was carried out using the programs Velvet (Zerbino and Birney 2008) and SOPRA (Dayarian et al. 2010), and the resulting contigs were further aligned using CodonCode aligner software. The BAC sequencing and assembly generated contigs whose length ranged from 393 bp to 108,194 bp. Estimated coverage of the BACs ranged from 64 to 100 percent. The gene prediction program AUGUSTUS (Stanke et al. 2008) identified 233 genes from these sequences using *Arabidopsis* as the model. Of these, RNA-Seq data supported 32 genes at 100 percent support, of which five were in the contig that contains the resistance gene. The predicted gene sequences were compared with sequences in GenBank using a BLASTP search and identified two putative genes encoding a p-loop NTPase and F-box super family in the resistance region. Genes

[1] Department of Horticulture, 4017 ALS Building, Oregon State University, Corvallis, OR 97331. Corresponding author: vidyasas@hort.oregonstate.edu.

in these two superfamilies have defense response properties. Future expression, complementation, and mapping studies are essential to confirm which gene confers resistance.

Literature Cited

Dayarian, A.; Michael, T.P.; Sengupta, A.M. 2010. SOPRA: scaffolding algorithm for paired reads via statistical optimization. BMC Bioinformatics. 11: 345.

Mehlenbacher, S.A.; Brown, R.N.; Davis, J.W.; Chen, H.; Bassil, N.; Smith, D.C. 2004. RAPD markers linked to eastern filbert blight resistance in *Corylus avellana*. Theoretical and Applied Genetics. 108: 651–656.

Mehlenbacher, S.A.; Brown, R.N.; Nouhra, E.R.; Gökirmak, T.; Bassil, N.V.; Kubisiak, T.L. 2006. A genetic linkage map for hazelnut (*Corylus avellana* L.) based on RAPD and SSR markers. Genome. 49: 122–133.

Nelson, W.; Soderlund, C. 2009. Integrating sequence with FPC fingerprint maps. Nucleic Acids Research. 37(5): e36.

Sathuvalli, V.R.; Mehlenbacher, S.A. 2011. A bacterial artificial chromosome library for 'Jefferson' hazelnut: a resource for map-based cloning of eastern filbert blight resistance and pollen-stigma incompatibility genes. Genome. 54: 862–867.

Stanke, M.; Diekhans, M.; Baertsch, R.; Haussler, D. 2008. Using native and synthetically mapped cDNA alignments to improve de novo gene finding. Bioinformatics. 24: 637–644.

Van Ooijen, J.W. 2006. JoinMap 4.0, software for the calculation of genetic linkage maps. Wageningen, The Netherlands: Kyazama B.V.

Zerbino, D.R.; Birney, E. 2008. Velvet: algorithms for de novo short read assembly using de Bruijn graphs. Genome Research. 18: 821–829.

Molecular and Genetic Basis for Partial Resistance of Western White Pine against *Cronartium ribicola*

Jun-Jun Liu,[1] Arezoo Zamany,[1] and Richard Sniezko[2]

Abstract

Western white pine (*Pinus monticola* Douglas ex D. Don) is an important forest species in North America. Forest genetics programs have been breeding for durable genetic resistance against white pine blister rust (WPBR) caused by *Cronartium ribicola* in the past few decades. As various genetic resistance resources are screened and available from breeding programs, we are interested in understanding the genetic mechanisms at the molecular level. This will facilitate a breeding strategy of pyramiding several resistance mechanisms in white pine elite stocks, which would make durable resistance possible for effective and long-term WPBR management.

Both major gene resistance and quantitative partial resistance have been identified in *P. monticola* populations. In contrast to the *Cr2*-mediated major gene resistance that occurs on pine needles by the hypersensitive response (HR), quantitative partial resistance was observed in stems after *C. ribicola* infection as slow canker growth, or bark reaction. Quantitative stem resistance was displayed with various phenotypes in different seed families, ranging from complete susceptibility (rust dead) to complete stem resistance (stem symptom-free), including normal canker development, partial bark reaction with incomplete inhibition of fungal growth, complete bark reaction without fungal activity in the bark, delayed stem infection, fewer stem infections, or longer time to mortality as compared to susceptible controls. Partial resistance is believed to be a heritable and polygenic resistance trait that allows greater survivability of infected white pine trees. Based on phenotypic data collected yearly from western white pine seed families sowed in 2003 and inoculated with *C. ribicola* in 2004, partial resistance levels were analyzed and ranked for each seedling.

Using these plant materials, we used a candidate gene-based association study to reveal what genomic DNA variants underlie phenotypic variation of white pine partial resistance. A set of pathogenesis-related (PR) genes was selected as candidates, including defense-related genes encoding for ß-1,3-glucanases (PR2), chitinases (PR3), thaumatin-like proteins (PR5), cytosolic nuclease-like proteins (PR10), and anti-microbial proteins (AMPs). Genomic DNA sequences of these genes were determined in white pine trees. DNA sequence data of selected candidate genes showed rich single nucleotide polymorphisms (SNPs) in white pine seed families. We will report on the genetic variations of these genes. Development of DNA markers will be discussed for marker-assisted selection of partial resistance to speed up of white pine breeding programs.

Defense responses of white pine trees with partial resistance were also investigated by measuring PR protein accumulation post *C. ribicola* infection. Using Pm-AMP1 as a biochemical indicator, a few patterns were documented for protein regulation in white pine seed families. Our results revealed that different molecular mechanisms may be responsible for various phenotypes of partial resistance in white pine populations. Cross-pollination between seed families with different resistance mechanisms would produce progeny with more durable resistance against *C. ribicola*.

---

[1] Natural Resources Canada, Canadian Forest Service, Pacific Forestry Centre, 506 West Burnside Road, Victoria, British Columbia, V8Z 1M5, Canada.
[2] USDA Forest Service, Dorena Genetic Resource Center, 34963 Shoreview Road, Cottage Grove, OR 97424.
Corresponding author: Jun-Jun.Liu@NRCan-RNCan.gc.ca.

Mapping Resistance to *Phytophthora cinnamomi* in Chestnut (*Castanea* sp.)

Bode A. Olukolu,[1] C. Dana Nelson,[2] and Albert G. Abbott[1]

Abstract

Phytophthora cinnamomi (Phytophthora crown and root rot, or ink disease) is now known to infect several hundred plant species in the world and is especially linked to the widespread death of mature chestnut (*Castanea*) and evergreen oak (*Quercus ilex* L.) trees in southeast United States. With an expanding geographical distribution of *P. cinnamomi* in Northern America, and coupled with the chestnut blight disease (caused by *Cryphonectria parasitica*) that initially decimated the 4 billion-strong American chestnut population (about 30 percent of trees in the Appalachian mountains), *P. cinnamomi* is becoming a crucial limiting factor in natural regeneration and reforestation due to the high susceptibility of both young seedlings and mature trees. In this preliminary study, we report the use of various genomic resources for identifying quantitative trait loci (QTLs) and candidate genes (CGs) underlying resistance to root rot disease. The strategy involved the use of single nucleotide polymorphism (SNP) markers and a small segregating population (48 progenies) for the construction of a transcriptome-based map and identification of root rot disease resistance QTLs. Using a resistant Chinese chestnut and susceptible American chestnut parents, two major QTLs were detected on the chestnut linkage group E (64.8 cM map length) at a logarithm of the odds (LOD) of 4.42 and 5.39. These QTLs spanned 3 cM (12-15 cM) and 16 cM (42-62 cM), respectively and explained 34.6 ± 11 percent and 40.4 ± 10.9 percent of the total phenotypic variance, respectively. Following the alignment of this low resolution map (211 mapped SNP markers) against the high density consensus chestnut map, additional expressed sequence tag (EST)-based markers provided better marker saturation of the QTLs. Two of these EST-based markers within the QTLs reveal two plausible CGs that include CCR1 (Cinnamoyl CoA Reductase 1) and BAG1 (BCL-2-Associated Athanogene 1). Additionally, comparative analysis with the peach genome using the chestnut physical map revealed that the chestnut QTL regions correspond to homologous segments of the peach genome on chromosome 3 and 4. The homologous regions in peach identified three plausible CGs including RPH1 (resistance to *Phytophthora*), NPR3/NPR4 (non-expresser of pathogenesis-related genes 3/4) and BAG4 (BCL-2-Associated Athanogene 4). Following Southern hybridization on chestnut bacterial artificial chromosome (BAC) filters using overgo probes, the co-localization of the CGs with the QTLs was confirmed. For further validation based on gene expression, a larger mapping population, or an association mapping panel, is required. These results can provide functional markers for precise and accurate marker-assisted breeding for introgression of resistance genes into the American chestnut. Transgenic trees are currently also been developed in parallel based on cloned CGs.

[1] Genetics and Biochemistry Department, 100 Jordan Hall, Clemson University, Clemson, SC 29634.
[2] USDA Forest Service, Southern Research Station, Southern Institute of Forest Genetics, 23332 Success Road, Saucier, MS 39574.
Corresponding author: baolukol@ncsu.edu.

Evaluating Resistance

Testing six species of white pines (*Pinus albicaulis*, *P. aristata*, *P. flexilis*, *P. lambertiana*, *P. monticola*, *P. strobiformis*) for white pine blister rust resistance at Dorena Genetic Resource Center, Cottage Grove, OR.
(Photo: R. Sniezko)

Methods for Screening Port-Orford-Cedar for Resistance to *Phytophthora lateralis*

Everett M. Hansen,[1] Paul Reeser,[1] Wendy Sutton,[1] and Richard A. Sniezko[2]

Abstract

Port-Orford-cedar (*Chamaecyparis lawsoniana* (A. Murray) Parl.) (POC) is an economically and ecologically valuable tree in the forests of southwest Oregon and northern California and in the horticultural trade worldwide. *Phytophthora lateralis*, the aggressive, invasive cause of POC root disease, was introduced to the native range of POC about 1950, and has since killed trees along roads and streams throughout the forest area where the tree grows. The federal forest management agencies responded with an integrated disease management program designed to slow further spread of the pathogen in order to protect remaining POC and restore the species with planted resistant stock in impacted areas. Various short-term resistance screening methods have been used since the 1980s. Ultimately, in any resistance program, the screening assays have to be ground truthed using field trials and the screening methods updated and refined to assist in resistance evaluations. In this paper we describe and compare the various inoculation methods and screening tests we use to evaluate POC parents and their progenies for resistance and offer evolving insights on their utility. This should provide food for thought for other newer resistance programs working with other pathogens or insects.

Introduction

Port-Orford-cedar (*Chamaecyparis lawsoniana* (A. Murray) Parl.) (POC) is an economically and ecologically valuable tree in the forests of southwest Oregon and northern California and in the horticultural trade worldwide. *Phytophthora lateralis*, an exotic, invasive root pathogen, is the primary cause of POC mortality in southwest Oregon and northwest California (Betlejewski et al. 2011). The origin of *P. lateralis* is not known, although it was first described killing POC in horticultural nurseries in the 1920s (Hansen et al. 2000). Recently *P. lateralis* or a very close relative was reported from native *Chamaecyparis obtusa* (Siebold & Zucc.) Siebold & Zucc. ex Endl. forests in Taiwan (Brasier et al. 2010), suggesting that the pathogen originated in eastern Asia. In North America it spreads as sporangia and zoospores in streams and is transported by vehicles along roads in the forest (Hansen et al. 2000). Even in infested areas, however, occasional Port-Orford-cedars escape mortality by *P. lateralis*.

Phytophthora lateralis was introduced to the forest range of POC about 1950. It has since killed trees along roads and streams throughout the tree's range. The federal forest management agencies—U.S. Department of Agriculture, Forest Service (USFS) and U.S. Department of the Interior, Bureau of Land Management (BLM)—have responded with a disease management program integrated into forest plans (Betlejewski et al. 2003, USDA FS and USDI BLM 2004). Mandated actions are designed to slow further spread of the pathogen in order to protect remaining POC, and to restore the species with planted resistant stock in areas where the pathogen has eliminated POC. Since the late 1980s, the USFS and the BLM, in cooperation with Oregon State University (OSU), have conducted an intensive program to identify and test resistant trees from the field and propagate them in a seed orchard with the goal of providing resistant seedlings for regeneration (http://www.fs.fed.us/r6/dorena/poc/; Sniezko 2006, Sniezko et al. 2006; Sniezko et al., Operational program to develop *Phytophthora lateralis* resistant populations of Port-Orford-cedar (*Chamaecyparis lawsoniana*), these proceedings). In this paper we describe the various inoculation methods and screening tests we use to evaluate POC parents for resistance.

---

[1] Department of Botany and Plant Pathology, 2082 Cordley Hall, Oregon State University, Corvallis, OR 97331.
[2] USDA Forest Service, Dorena Genetic Resource Center, Cottage Grove, OR 97424.
Corresponding author: hansene@science.oregonstate.edu.

Most POC trees in the field are very susceptible, but genetic resistance to this pathogen has been demonstrated (Hansen et al. 1989, Sniezko 2006, Sniezko et al. 2006). Susceptible seedling families showed only 0 to 10 percent survival using a variety of inoculation techniques. Rooted cuttings of the most resistant parents were seldom killed, and seedling families of these parents exhibited 25 to 100 percent survival, depending on family and inoculation technique (Oh et al. 2006; Sniezko et al., Nine year survival of 16 *Phytophthora lateralis* resistant and susceptible Port-Orford-cedar families in a southern Oregon field trial, these proceedings). Symptom development on resistant trees, including reduced colonization and reisolation success, sunken lesions, and resinosis, was consistent with a hypersensitive reaction (Oh and Hansen 2007).

Methods
Screening Protocol
The USFS and BLM funded and soon led the effort to locate candidate resistant trees in the forest and to collect vegetative material and seeds for testing. Inoculations and resistance screening carried out at OSU have evolved through time to take advantage of the unique features of POC and to meet the changing needs of the program. Candidate parents from the field are initially challenged with a rapid stem dip zoospore inoculation test. "Winners" are then propagated as rooted cuttings, which are in turn exposed to zoospore inoculum in a root dip test. The best individuals are incorporated into containerized seed orchards at Dorena Genetic Resource Center (DGRC) in Cottage Grove, Oregon. Seedlings from cross or self pollination within the orchards are further challenged with the root dip test and by planting into infested soil for a 2-year exposure in outdoor raised beds. Finally, the most promising materials are included in long-term field tests on infested sites and maintained in the seed orchards by breeding zone. Over 10,000 field selections have been screened and over 1,100 trees have been chosen for further evaluation (Sniezko et al., Operational program to develop *Phytophthora lateralis* resistance populations of Port-Orford-cedar (*Chamaecyparis lawsoniana*), these proceedings).

Inoculum Production
Port-Orford-cedar cuttings, rooted cuttings, and seedlings are inoculated with zoospores. Two isolates of *P. lateralis*, collected from diseased POC trees in southern Oregon or northern California, were used. Isolates were grown on homemade corn meal agar amended with *B*-sitosterol (CMAB) (15 g Bacto agar, 50 ml corn steep, 20 mg *B*-sitosterol). Corn steep was made by mixing 100 g yellow corn meal in 650 ml de-ionized water at 60 °C for 1 hr. Solids were removed by pouring through eight layers of cheesecloth then filtering through Celite 545. Cultures were maintained in water storage in the culture collection at Oregon State University.

To produce zoospores, isolates were grown for one week on CMAB then three, 3 mm dia. plugs cut from the advancing edge of colonies were transferred to pea broth (150 g dry split peas per liter, autoclaved for 3 min and strained through a double layer of cheesecloth, then autoclaved for 60 min at 121 °C) and grown for 7 days. The culture medium was removed, plates were rinsed with de-ionized water, then filled with 10 ml filtered water from a local stream. After 24 hours, zoospore release was triggered, if needed, by chilling plates 1 hr at 5 °C then returning to room temperature.

Stem Dip Test
Initial screening of POC trees for resistance to *P. lateralis* is done on fresh cuttings from candidate trees. Six to 10 branch tips, each about 30 cm long, were clipped from each candidate tree, labeled, and transported cool and moist to the OSU lab for testing.

For zoospore inoculations, zoospores were produced as described above, and the water containing the colonies and zoospores was poured from plates into 1 L glass jars. Water and zoospores from one plate of each isolate, along with additional water to total 40 ml, were combined in each jar to an approximate depth of 1 cm.

Branches were freshly trimmed to 20 to 30 cm length, mixed among the candidate and control trees in two replications (three to five branches per parent per replication), and clustered in bundles of 10 then placed cut end down in each glass jar with zoospores, care being taken to insure that each cut end was immersed (fig. 1).

Figure 1—Stem dip test. Left: Branch tips with cut ends immersed in zoospore suspension. Right: Lesions on susceptible control (left) and resistant control (right) branches after three weeks.

Branches remain with cut ends in the zoospore suspension for 24 hours and then are transferred individually to plastic growth tubes filled with wet vermiculite. Racks of test cuttings are held in the greenhouse and watered regularly. After 3 weeks, they are scored. Each branch tip was removed from the vermiculite, rinsed, and scraped at the cut end to reveal the discolored lesion in the inner bark. Lesion length was recorded. The best 10 percent of all parent trees in each test, including all trees with average lesion lengths less than or equal to the resistant control, were declared "winners" and advanced to further testing.

Root Dip Test

Port-Orford-cedar for root dip inoculation trials was grown from cuttings from "winner" parent trees. Cuttings were rooted under mist and grown about 12 months. Rooted cuttings were grown in individual 3.7 cm top diameter, 20.6 cm length, 'supercell' plastic conical tubes (Cone-tainer™). Seedlings, mostly from controlled crosses at DGRC, were grown for about 9 months in supercells. Seedlings or rooted cuttings were grown until roots emerged from the bottom of the containers. Emergent roots were trimmed immediately prior to inoculation.

Seedlings or rooted cuttings were randomized and groups of six were clustered in each inoculation container. The lower 1 cm of the root system (in the growth tube) was immersed in a *P. lateralis* zoospore suspension (prepared as above) for 24 hours (fig. 2). The inoculated trees were then incubated in the greenhouse for up to 36 months, and symptom development was periodically recorded. At the first sign of yellowing or wilting (usually after about 6 months), a small slice in the bark at soil level was made and the stem examined for the characteristic necrotic lesion caused by *P. lateralis*. Mortality was recorded when the lesion reached the top of the growth tube. Mortality, evidenced by diagnostic lesion at the ground line, was noted regularly and the days from planting to mortality recorded.

Figure 2—Root dip test. Container grown seedlings and rooted cuttings, inoculated by immersing the bottom 1 cm of the container in zoospore suspension.

Port-Orford-cedar seedlings and rooted cuttings were also planted in infested soil in an outdoor raised bed (fig. 3). Two raised beds were established in 2000, each 1.5 x 10 m and 30 cm deep, and contained a soil mix comprised of 1/4 loam, 1/4 peat, 1/4 pumice, 1/4 fine bark, plus 1/2 kg gypsum/m^3, and 1 kg lime/m^3. The soil mix was infested with *P. lateralis* by mixing sporulating cultures and chopped roots of infected POC seedlings with the soil. Port-Orford-cedar trees were planted in family row plots in a replicated design and received regular summer irrigation. Mortality, evidenced by diagnostic lesion at the ground line, was noted regularly and the days from planting to mortality recorded.

Figure 3—Raised bed test. Seedlings and rooted cuttings planted in infested soil.

Outplanting Tests

Port-Orford-cedar seedlings and rooted cuttings were also planted in artificially or naturally infested soil at field sites. Some of the first selected families and clones were planted in 1989 and 1990 in a replicated block design at the OSU Botany and Plant Pathology Field Lab near Corvallis, Oregon (table 1). Parent trees other than parent id numbers CF1 and ESOC were initially collected by Professor L. F. Roth from forested areas in Coos County, Oregon, either because they were survivors in areas of widespread mortality or as unselected control trees from areas with no previous mortality. The 1/10 ha plot had been artificially infested with *P. lateralis* some years previously, and was initially used for screening different species of *Chamaecyparis* for resistance to *P. lateralis*. Mortality and cause of death were recorded annually to the present. Surviving trees are now 10 to 20 cm dbh. Additional long-term outplanting test sites were selected at forest sites where local concentrations of POC had been recently killed by *P. lateralis* (fig. 4).

Table 1—Survival of POC trees selected for resistance or as susceptible controls at the Oregon State University Botany Farm outplanting site

Parent tree	Year planted	Trees planted (n)	Trees alive July 2011 (%)
CF1-cuttings	1989	25	48.0
CF1-seedlings	1989	25	24.0
CF2	1989	20	80.0
CF3	1989	4	50.0
CF4	1989	20	15.0
ESOC	1990	30	3.3
CHECK10	1990	20	0.0
CB1	1989	20	40.0
CB2	1989	20	0.0
CB4	1989	18	5.6
CB5	1989	20	0.0
CHECK13	1989	20	0.0
CHECK14	1989	20	0.0

Figure 4—Forest outplanting site established on naturally infested ground within a mixed Douglas-fir-POC forest in Douglas County, Oregon.

Results

Sniezko et al. present extensive validation data for the screening tests, comparing greenhouse and raised bed rankings with outplanting test results elsewhere in this proceedings. Here we present two additional examples. The stem dip test reliably separated a small number of POC families with good survival at the Botany Farm planting from susceptible families with poor or no survival (table 2). Similarly, root dip test scores reliably predicted survival after 2 ½ years at an infested outplanting site (fig. 5).

Table 2—Stem dip lesion length scores for branch tips collected from susceptible and resistant trees from the Botany Farm outplanting site

Parent tree	Alive 2011 (%)	Stem dip score (mm)
Resistant control		9.2
CF1 (cuttings)	48	9.4
CF2	80	12.5
CB1	45	10.7
CB2	0	28.2
CB4	6	28.9
CB5	0	28.9
Susceptible control		32.7

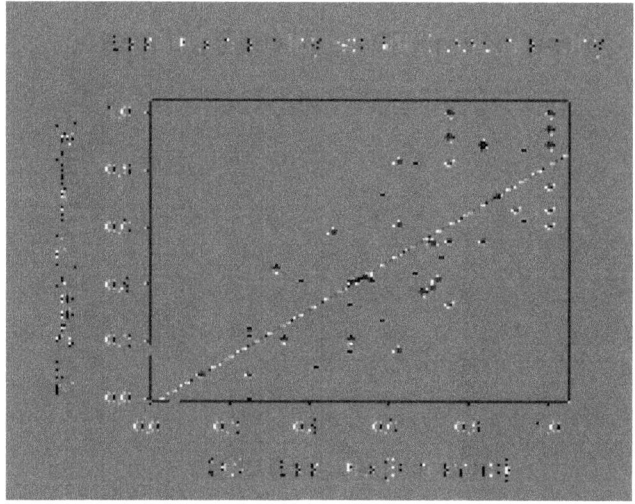

Figure 5—Root dip vs outplanting survival, Bill Creek test site. See Sniezko et al. 2006 for trial background.

Discussion

Short-term assays of resistance are a vital part of operational resistance programs. The four methods of short-term screening currently used for POC to discern *P. lateralis* resistance—(1) stem dip; (2) root dip using rooted cuttings; (3) root dip using seedlings; and (4) raised bed—all have potential advantages. The stem dip test can be done fastest and cheapest. The raised bed trial may mimic field conditions or could be monitored for three years or more for continued mortality or evolution of virulence. The root dip tests may allow evaluation of hundreds of families or clones at a time and provide very controlled conditions. However, ultimately the utility of these tests depends on how their results relate to field trials. At this point in time, the seedling root dip assay, and probably the raised bed trials, provide the best overall indication that there might be several types of resistance and information on the upper level of survival to expect under field conditions (Sniezko et al., Nine year survival of 16 *Phytophthora lateralis* resistant and susceptible Port-Orford-cedar families in a southern Oregon field trial, these proceedings; Sniezko and Savin, unpublished).

The POC resistance screening program is an evolving success. Resistant seed with demonstrated survival potential is available for regeneration programs in the most important POC seed zones. The program continues, screening additional forest trees as candidates are identified, and root dip testing a backlog of stem dip "winners" to add additional parents to the orchards. In addition, orchards are continuously rogued and upgraded as field testing results are available and through selection of resistant progeny from controlled crosses.

Each of the screening tests has advantages as well as limitations. The original intention of the stem dip test was to provide a quick first screen of candidate trees assuming most would prove susceptible and could be eliminated before costly propagation efforts are made. It is likely that such an indirect test can only select for one type of resistance. However, with the compilation of data from a large number of selections, a re-evaluation of the utility of the stem dip test is underway. The test identifies some of the parents with the highest and lowest levels of resistance, but has a low correlation with the root dip tests (Sniezko and Savin, unpublished). It is not sensitive enough to rank trees with intermediate levels of disease tolerance. There appear to be several types of resistance in POC (Sniezko 2006; Sniezko, unpublished), and more understanding of these mechanisms is needed to fully evaluate the limitations of the stem dip method. We hope to use other current existing data or selections to more fully investigate the utility of this method. Other 'indirect' methods (e.g., biochemical markers, or genetic markers) of selecting for different types of resistance could be useful in short-cutting the initial testing step.

Rankings from root dip testing correlate well with outplanting test results (Sniezko et al., Nine year survival of 16 *Phytophthora lateralis* resistant and susceptible Port-Orford-cedar families in a southern Oregon field trial, these proceedings). The infection pathway is more realistic and the longer test period allows at least preliminary identification of "slow to die" families. Seedlings outgrow their containers after 2 or 3 years, however, and rooted cuttings are often difficult to evaluate because they may be slow to develop a robust root system. In a recent comparison of rooting cuttings and seedling families, there was good agreement, but the seedling assay appeared more consistent (Sniezko and Savin, unpublished). The current seedling assay takes several years to complete; the seedlings are grown for 9 months and then followed for 1 to 3 years after inoculation. Now that we have well defined resistant and susceptible families, there may be merit to see if we can short-cut the process by utilizing much younger, smaller seedlings in smaller containers. If so, this could reduce some costs as well as speed evaluation.

The various outplanting trials, especially on high-hazard forest sites, provide the ultimate test of the program, but are also most difficult to establish and maintain. It is challenging to find sites of sufficient area with uniform inoculum and topography. Regular recording of mortality is often precluded by limited travel budgets, and other mortality agents confuse the analysis.

Lessons learned in the POC resistance program should be valuable in providing guidance to other programs. Blind faith in a single short-term seedling assay may lead to over- or under-estimation of the level and types of resistance or may preclude utilizing some types of resistance. Establishing some field trials early to help validate short-term screening methods is essential to helping maximize progress in the development of resistant populations. The development of new screening assays such as biomarkers or genetic markers could be a useful addition to any resistance program, provided they are validated with field trials.

Acknowledgments

We thank the USDA Forest Service and USDI Bureau of Land Management for their continuing support of the program. We also thank Dave Shaw and Douglas Savin for their reviews of an earlier version of this paper.

GENERAL TECHNICAL REPORT PSW-GTR-240

Literature Cited

Betlejewski, F.; Casavan, K.; Dawson, A.; Goheen, D.; Mastrofini, K.; Rose, D.; White, D. 2003. A Range-wide assessment of Port-Orford-cedar (*Chamaecyparis lawsoniana*) on federal lands. Oregon/Washington State Office, Portland, OR: U.S. Department of Agriculture, Forest Service, and U.S. Department of the Interior, Bureau of Land Management.
http://www fs.usda.gov/Internet/FSE_DOCUMENTS/stelprdb5316517.pdf 182 p. (13 March 2012).

Betlejewski, F.; Goheen, D.; Angwin, P.; Sniezko, R. 2011. Port-Orford-cedar root disease. Forest Insect and Disease Leaflet 131. Portland, Oregon: U.S. Department of Agriculture, Forest Service, Pacific Northwest Region. 12 p.

Brasier, C.M.; Vettraino, A.M.; Chang, T.T.; Vannini, A. 2010. *Phytophthora lateralis* discovered in an old growth *Chamaecyparis* forest in Taiwan. Plant Pathology. 59: 595–603.

Hansen, E.M.; Hamm, P.B.; Roth. L.F. 1989. Testing Port Orford cedar for resistance to *Phytophthora*. Plant Disease. 73:791–794.

Hansen, E.M.; Goheen, D.J.; Jules, E.; Ullian, B. 2000. Managing Port-Orford-cedar and the introduced pathogen *Phytophthora lateralis*. Plant Disease. 84: 4–14.

Oh, E.; Hansen, E.M.; Sniezko, R.A. 2006. Port-Orford-cedar resistant to *Phytophthora lateralis.* Forest Pathology. 36:385–394.

Oh, E.; Hansen E.M. 2007. Histopathology of infection and colonization of Port-Orford-cedar by *Phytophthora lateralis*. Phytopathology. 97: 684–693.

Sniezko, R.A. 2006. Resistance breeding against nonnative pathogens in forest trees — current successes in North America. Canadian Journal of Plant Pathology. 28: S270–S279.

Sniezko, R.A.; Kolpak, S.E.; Hansen, E.M.; Goheen, D.J.; Elliott, L.J.; Angwin, P.A. 2006. Field survival of *Phytophthora lateralis* resistant and susceptible Port-Orford-cedar families. In: Brasier, C.; Jung, T.; Osswald, W., eds. Progress in research on *Phytophthora* diseases of forest trees: Proceedings of the Third International IUFRO Working Party S07.02.09. Farnham, UK: Forest Research: 104–108.

USDA FS and USDI BLM 2004. Final supplemental environmental impact statement – management of Port-Orford-cedar in southwest Oregon, Portland OR: U.S. Department of Agriculture, Forest Service, Pacific Northwest Region. http://www fs.usda.gov/Internet/FSE_DOCUMENTS/stelprdb5316520.pdf . (06 June 2012).

188

Resistance to *Phytophthora cinnamomi* in the Genus *Abies*

John Frampton,[1] Fikret Isik,[1] Mike Benson,[2] Jaroslav Kobliha,[3] and Jan Stejskal[3]

Abstract

A major limiting factor for the culture of true firs as Christmas trees is their susceptibility to Oomycete species belonging to the genus *Phytophthora*. In North Carolina alone, the Fraser fir (*Abies fraseri* [Pursh] Poir.) Christmas tree industry loses 6 to 7 million dollars annually to root rot primarily caused by *Phytophthora cinnamomi*. Because no resistance has been found in Fraser fir, in 2003, the North Carolina State University (NCSU) Christmas Tree Genetics (CTG) Program conducted an extensive resistance screening of 32 *Abies* species (50 unique taxa) from around the world.

Overall mortality was high (88 percent), but was less frequent in two of the eight taxonomic sections of the genus evaluated: *Momi* (65.5 percent) and *Abies* (79.3 percent). Species mortality rates in all other sections exceeded 93 percent. Final species mortality ranged from 10.6 percent (*A. firma* Sieb. et Zucc.) to 100.0 percent (several species). Hierarchical cluster analysis was used to classify species into groups representing six levels of resistance, designated as very resistant (*A. firma*), resistant (*A. pindrow* [D.Don] Royle), moderately resistant (four species), intermediate (five species), susceptible (seven species), and very susceptible (17 species).

In the species screening trial, Turkish fir (*A. bornmuelleriana* Mattf.) and closely related Trojan fir (*A. equitrojani* Coode et Cullen) ranked third and tenth for resistance, but mortality in these species was relatively high. A systematic approach to understand and better use *Phytophthora* resistance within Turkish and Trojan fir was undertaken. Using seeds from a 2005 cone collection expedition to Turkey, greenhouse-grown seedlings from 105 open-pollinated families were inoculated with *P. cinnamomi*. Sixteen weeks after inoculation, overall seedling mortality was 56 percent for Trojan fir and 35 percent for Turkish fir. As a comparison, 97 percent of inoculated Fraser fir seedlings, but only 3 percent of inoculated momi fir seedlings, died. For Turkish and Trojan fir, there was a distinct relationship between mortality and geographic origin; mortality percentage decreased from west to east. Additionally, estimates of family mean heritabilities were extremely high for both Turkish (0.96+0.010) and Trojan (0.97+0.011) fir.

In another approach, hybrid firs are being developed through a collaborative effort between the NCSU CTG Program and researchers at the Czech University of Life Sciences (CULS) Prague. Researchers at CULS have utilized Toros fir (*A. cilicica* Carr.) from southern Turkey and Greek fir (*A. cephalonica* Loud.) in a long-term hybrid breeding effort aimed at developing a faster growing fir that is hardier to changing ecological conditions than the native European silver fir (*A. alba* Mill.). Toros and Greek fir were ranked fourth and eighth, respectively, in the species screening trial. Seedlings of F1, F2, and complex hybrids with Fraser fir are being assessed for *Phytophthora* resistance.

[1] Dept. of Forestry and Environmental Resources, N.C. State University, Raleigh, NC 27695.
[2] Dept. of Plant Pathology, N.C. State University, Raleigh, NC 27695.
[3] Dept. of Dendrology and Forest Tree Breeding, Faculty of Forestry and Wood Sciences, Czech University of Life Sciences, Prague, Kamýcká 1176, 165 21 Praha 6 – Suchdol, Czech Republic.
Corresponding author: frampton@ncsu.edu.

Host Resistance Screening for Balsam Woolly Adelgid: A Comparison of Seedlings from 12 Fir Species

Leslie Newton,[1] John Frampton,[2] and Fred Hain[1]

Introduction

The balsam woolly adelgid, *Adelges piceae* (Hemiptera: Adelgidae) (BWA), first reported on Fraser fir, *Abies fraseri* (Pursh) Poiret, on Mount Mitchell in 1955 (Amman 1966, Boyce 1955), is a major pest in Christmas tree plantations and in native stands. Nearly all Fraser fir Christmas trees produced in North Carolina need to be treated one or more times during their 5- to 10-year rotation to prevent or lessen damage caused by this adelgid. These chemical treatments cost the industry over 1.5 million dollars per year (Potter et al. 2005) and may compromise the effectiveness of integrated pest management systems. The development of BWA-resistant Fraser fir trees would be a relatively inexpensive solution to a difficult pest problem and would minimize adverse effects from management strategies.

The balsam woolly adelgid, specific to the genus *Abies*, reproduces through parthenogenesis and completes two or more generations per year (Arthur and Hain 1984, Balch 1952). The early phase of the first instar (crawler) is the only motile stage. Feeding sites are chosen for accessibility to parenchyma cells (Balch 1952) and, once settled, the adelgid remains fairly sessile for the remainder of its life. Susceptibility to BWA varies among *Abies* species. Host responses include gouting (abnormal cell growth resembling a gall) at the feeding site, loss of apical dominance, and the production of abnormal xylem ('redwood' or 'rotholtz').

In the 100+ years that BWA has been in North America, studies on its biology and interaction with host trees have been conducted in the Pacific Northwest, Canada, and the Southern Appalachians on multiple fir species of different ages, utilizing various sources of the adelgid. Three subspecies of BWA have been identified in North America (Foottit and Mackauer 1983). Our long-term objective is to develop BWA-resistant Fraser fir trees for the Christmas tree industry and native stand restoration. Our objective for this study was to screen for resistance across multiple fir species utilizing trees of equal age, grown under the same conditions and infested with BWA from the same source, and to observe the reactions of both host and insect.

Methods

A BWA resistance screening trial was established in a greenhouse at the Upper Mountain Research Station in Ashe County, North Carolina in August 2007, utilizing 4-year-old seedlings. The study included 12 fir species, 9 representing the range of known susceptibility and 3 representing unknown susceptibilities. Susceptible species included Fraser fir (three seed sources: Roan Mountain, Richland Balsam, Mount Mitchell), balsam fir (*A. balsamea*), West Virginia Canaan fir (*A. balsamea* var. *phanerolepis*), corkbark fir (*A. lasiocarpa* var. *arizonica*), and Korean fir (*A. koreana*). Moderately resistant or tolerant species included European silver fir (*A. alba*) and white fir (*A. concolor*). Resistant species included Veitch fir (*A. veitchii*) and Momi fir (*A. firma*). Species representing unknown susceptibility included Turkish fir (*A. bornmuellariana*), Trojan fir (*A. equi-trojani*), and West Himalayan or Pindrow fir (*A. pindrow*). The greenhouse was divided into four blocks, each

---

[1] North Carolina State University, Department of Entomology, Raleigh, NC 27695-7626.
[2] North Carolina State University, Department of Forestry and Environmental Resources, Raleigh, NC 27695.
Corresponding author: fred_hain@ncsu.edu.

containing two treatment plots representing seasonal effect (August/September). There were 48 trees per species in each of the 8 treatment plots, for a total of 672 trees. Trees were exposed to BWA by suspending logs of BWA-infested Fraser fir over each treatment plot. This technique (Newton et al., 2011) mimics natural dispersal, allowing crawlers to drop onto the trees.

In December 2007 one-half of the study was dismantled and in May 2008 the remaining half was dismantled. Data collected from the first group of trees included the number and location of settled first instars (neosistentes). Data from the second group included presence/absence of settled instars, an assessment of infestation (yes/no), the number of BWA adults with eggs, the number of eggs, fecundity (mean number of eggs per adult), evidence of early BWA development (yes/no), and presence/absence of gouting. A subsampling technique was developed; the most predictive scheme was to take the first three branches from the top of the tree with secondary or tertiary branching (i.e., the bushiest branches from the second and third whorls). Data were collected from branches and boles, but we report here only branch responses. Because there was a significant difference in height between the species, infestation levels are expressed as counts per cm of branch.

Results

From the first group of trees (December 2007), there were no significant differences among species in the number of settled neosistentes per branch. Least squares means ranged from 0.03 ($\pm$ 0.51) for *A. concolor* (white fir) to 2.09 ($\pm$ 0.59) for *A. lasiocarpa* 'arizonica' (corkbark fir). The susceptible species consistently ranked higher than the resistant and tolerant species. Crawlers settled at the base of the branches, at the nodes under old bud scales, at the base of leaves along the branch stem, and at the base of buds (both lateral and apical). They appeared to show a preference for the base of buds regardless of species.

From the second group of trees (May 2008), there were no differences among species in presence/absence of settled instars, with 81 to 100 percent of trees showing settled instars. Although one can consider trees with settled instars to be infested, here we consider 'infested' to mean that adults with egg clutches have developed on the tree. Differences in the proportion of infested trees (supporting adults with eggs) were highly significant (p < .0001) and, with few exceptions, the results were consistent with known susceptibility levels. Susceptible species generally showed higher proportions of infested trees than the tolerant or resistant species. Two of the unknowns, *A. equitrojani* (Trojan fir) and *A. bornmuelleriana* (Turkish fir), were at opposite ends of this range, with almost all (0.99) of the Trojan fir trees becoming infested and only about one-third (0.34) of the Turkish fir trees. In the number of adults and eggs per cm branch, Trojan fir ranked significantly higher than Korean, Turkish, and white firs.

Mean fecundity levels reflected significant (p = .0143) differences among species, ranging from 4.4 eggs per adult in *A. pindrow* to 16.8 in *A. alba*. Trojan fir ranked high, along with corkbark fir, Fraser fir, and balsam fir, species known to be very susceptible to BWA. Early BWA development was evident on approximately half of the trees from most species. Turkish fir appeared least likely to exhibit early development (0.16) and Trojan fir the most likely (0.63). Fraser fir (Roan Mountain) exhibited the highest proportion of trees with gouting. Gouting responses were highly significant (p < .0001) with susceptible species ranking highest, tolerant and resistant species lowest, and the unknowns in the middle – one notable exception is Korean fir, which showed the least amount of gouting (0.18).

Discussion

Data collected from the first group of trees, harvested before winter dormancy, provide evidence that the trees were exposed to a sufficient number of crawlers to complete development to the next generation. Although the differences among species were not statistically significant, the rankings were consistent with a priori resistance classifications – susceptible species ranked higher than resistant or tolerant species. This may reflect some constitutive defense that inhibits settling by the crawler. The preference for buds exhibited by the crawlers may indicate the presence of higher nutritive values in that region.

The second group of trees, when harvested, had gone through winter dormancy and entered into the growing season (although budbreak had not yet begun). Most trees from all species exhibited the presence of settled instars. At least some trees from each species were able to support the development of adults with eggs, but the differences in the proportion of trees that became fully infested suggest that this parameter alone (adults with eggs) may not be adequate for assessing resistance. Complete development took place on 89 percent of the *A. firma* fir trees, a species that exhibits resistance to BWA when mature (Mitchell 1966). One of the most interesting results revolves around the differences between two of the 'unknown' species, *A. equi-trojani* (Trojan fir) and *A. bornmuelleriana* (Turkish fir). Both are from the same global region, but here Trojan fir consistently suggests high susceptibility to BWA and Turkish fir consistently suggests resistance. This is observed in the proportion of trees that became fully infested, the numbers of adults with eggs, the number of eggs in general, the ability of BWA to complete development very early in the season, and, to a certain extent, fecundity. One important factor in the 'susceptibility status' of Trojan fir relates to the gouting response, generally considered detrimental to the health of the tree. While European silver fir can become infested with BWA, it suffers very little from BWA attack and here exhibited the highest fecundity levels (16.8 eggs per adult), but comparatively little gouting response (27 percent of the trees). Trojan fir appears to be highly susceptible, but it ranked with European silver fir in both fecundity levels and gouting responses. The other 'unknown,' Pindrow fir, generally ranked near the resistant and tolerant species. *Abies veitchii* (Veitch fir) consistently exhibited resistance and Fraser fir and the balsam firs consistently exhibited susceptibility. *Abies koreana* (Korean fir) is considered to be susceptible to BWA (Mitchell 1966); however, here its responses suggest resistance in the seedling class.

Acknowledgments

We gratefully acknowledge John Strider and the NC State Forest Entomology Lab, Anne Margaret Braham and the NC State Christmas Tree Genetics Program, Les Miller and the Upper Mountain Research Station for technical assistance, and the USDA Cooperative State Research, Education, and Extension Service (CSREES) and the NC State Department of Entomology for funding assistance.

Literature Cited

Amman, G.D. 1966. *Aphidecta obliterata* (Coleoptera: Coccinellidae) an introduced predator of the balsam woolly aphid, *Chermes piceae* (Homoptera: Chermidae), established in North Carolina. Journal of Economic Entomology. 59: 506–511.

Arthur, F.H.; Hain, F.P. 1984. Seasonal history of the balsam woolly adelgid (Homoptera: Adelgidae) in natural stands and plantations of Fraser fir. Journal of Economic Entomology. 77: 1154–1158.

Balch, R.E. 1952. Studies of the balsam woolly aphid, *Adelges piceae* (Ratz.) and its effect on balsam fir, *Abies balsamea* (L.) Mill. Publication 867. (place of publication unknown): Canadian Department of Agriculture. 76 p.

Boyce, J.S. 1955. Memorandum of October 7, 1955 to North Carolina National Forests, Toecane Ranger District, Burnsville, North Carolina. Asheville, NC: U.S. Department of Agriculture, Forest Service, Southeastern Forest Experiment Station. (As reported in Amman 1966.)

Foottit, R.G.; Mackauer, M. 1983. Subspecies of the balsam woolly aphid, *Adelges piceae* (Homoptera: Adelgidae), in North America. Annals of the Entomological Society of America. 7: 299–304.

Mitchell, R.G. 1966. Infestation characteristics of the balsam woolly aphid in the Pacific Northwest. Research Paper PNW-35. Portland, OR: U.S. Department of Agriculture, Forest Service, Pacific Northwest Forest and Range Experiment Station. 18 p.

Newton, L.; Frampton, J.; Monahan, J.; Goldfarb, B.; Hain, F. 2011. Two novel techniques to screen *Abies* seedlings for resistance to the balsam woolly adelgid, *Adelges piceae*. Journal of Insect Science. 11:158.

Potter, K.M.; Frampton, J.; Sidebottom, J. 2005. Impacts of balsam woolly adelgid on the southern Appalachian spruce-fir ecosystem and the North Carolina Christmas tree industry. In: Onken, B.; Reardon, R., eds. Proceedings, 3rd symposium on hemlock woolly adelgid in the eastern United States. FHTET-2005-01. Morgantown, WV: U.S. Department of Agriculture, Forest Service, Forest Health Technology Enterprise Team: 25–41.

Resistance to *Phytophthora cinnamomi* Among Seedlings From Backcross Families of Hybrid American Chestnut

Steven N. Jeffers,[1] **Inga M. Meadows,**[1] **Joseph B. James,**[2] **and Paul H. Sisco**[3]

American chestnut (*Castanea dentata* (Marsh.) Borkh.) once was a primary hardwood species in forests of the eastern United States. Sometime during the late 18th century, it is speculated that *Phytophthora cinnamomi*, which causes Phytophthora root rot (PRR) on many woody plant species, was introduced to the southeast region of the United States, and this pathogen spread as people moved inland from the coast (Zentmyer 1980). In the 1800s, PRR (also known as ink disease) caused extensive mortality to American chestnut trees in the southern portion of its range (Freinkel 2007, Zentmyer 1980). Then, in the early 1900s, chestnut blight, caused by *Cryphonectria parasitica*, almost eliminated American chestnut trees from eastern forests (Freinkel 2007). Since 1989, The American Chestnut Foundation (TACF) has been producing hybrid chestnut seedlings by crossing Chinese chestnut (*C. mollissima*), which is resistant to *C. parasitica*, with American chestnut and then backcrossing progeny to *C. dentata* to produce resistant American-type chestnut trees. Since 2000, hybrid seedlings planted in some locations in southeastern states have died from PRR before they could be challenged by naturally-occurring populations of *C. parasitica*. Therefore, we wanted to determine if any of the backcross trees selected for resistance to *C. parasitica* were resistant to *P. cinnamomi* as well because Chinese chestnut also is resistant to this pathogen.

Each year from 2004 to 2010, hybrid seeds from trees of known parentage were obtained from TACF cooperators, and seeds from *C. dentata* and *C. mollissima* were collected in the field. All seeds from a single cross were considered to be a family. Seeds were stratified and then planted outside in April in six or seven replicate 570 L plastic tubs filled with a soilless container mix at a field site in Oconee County, South Carolina. Each tub contained a sub-sample of seeds from each family. Inoculum consisted of two isolates of *P. cinnamomi* originally recovered from diseased chestnut seedlings growing at the study site. Isolates were grown on autoclaved rice grains or sterilized vermiculite moistened with V8 juice broth (Meadows et al. 2011, Roiger and Jeffers 1991). Seedlings were inoculated 12 to 14 weeks after planting. Inocula from the two isolates were combined, mixed thoroughly, and then evenly distributed in 1- to 3-cm-deep furrows between rows of seedlings. Seedlings were watered as needed throughout the study period, and the container mix in each tub was brought to saturation at least once while plants were actively growing to encourage disease development. Plants were evaluated in December when fully dormant. Each seedling was scored for mortality and PRR severity by examining the roots. A complete description of our methods was reported previously (Jeffers et al. 2009).

Each year, seedlings began to die approximately 3 weeks after inoculation and continued to die until the end of the growing season. *Castanea dentata* seedlings consistently were susceptible and died, and *C. mollissima* seedlings consistently were resistant and survived. In 7 years, we have tested 197 hybrid families from generations that ranged from F_1 to BC_4 (table 1). Families with seedlings resistant to *P. cinnamomi* occurred each year, but the number of resistant seedlings and PRR severity ratings varied considerably among families. Mean annual mortality for all hybrid seedling families combined was 83 percent over the 7-year period. The genes for resistance to *P. cinnamomi* and *C. parasitica* do not appear to be linked because most families were derived from backcross trees selected for blight resistance, but PRR resistance was infrequent. The pattern of inheritance of

---

[1]School of Agricultural, Forest, and Environmental Sciences, Clemson University; Clemson, SC 29634.
[2]Chestnut Return Farm; Seneca, SC 29678.
[3] The American Chestnut Foundation, Asheville, NC 28801.
Corresponding author: sjffrs@clemson.edu.

resistance to PRR was consistent with it being controlled by a single gene. This may facilitate introgression of PRR resistance into breeding populations of backcrossed American chestnut. The paper by Olukolu et al. in these proceedings (Genomics assisted breeding for resistance to *Phytophthora cinnamomi* in chestnut [*Castanea* sp.]) provides more detailed information on the genes controlling resistance to *P. cinnamomi* in hybrid chestnut seedlings.

Table 1—Numbers of hybrid American chestnut families screened for resistance to *Phytophthora cinnamomi* over 7 years: 2004 to 2010

Year	No. families	No. with resistance	Mortality (%)
2004	5	3	94
2005	20	9	90
2006	23	5	99
2007	41	5	80
2008	22	4	75
2009	32	8	68
2010	54	6	72

Screening of hybrid American chestnut seedlings continued in 2011 (48 families screened) and will be conducted each year for the foreseeable future as we search for resistance to PRR. In addition to hybrid seedlings, we also began to evaluate transgenic plants in 2011. These plants were developed for resistance to chestnut blight by colleagues at the State University of New York at Syracuse (College of Environmental Science and Forestry) and at the University of Georgia (Warnell School of Forestry and Natural Resources). It will be interesting to see if these plants have any resistance to *P. cinnamomi*.

Literature Cited

Freinkel, S. 2007. American chestnut – The life, death and rebirth of a perfect tree. Berkeley, CA: University of California Press. 284 p.

Jeffers, S.N.; James, J.B.; Sisco, P.H. 2009. Screening for resistance to *Phytophthora cinnamomi* in hybrid seedlings of American chestnut. In: Goheen, E.M.; Frankel, S.J., tech. coords. Proceedings of the fourth meeting of the International Union of Forest Research Organizations (IUFRO) working party S07.02.09: Phytophthoras in Forests & Natural Ecosystems. Gen. Tech. Rep. PSW-GTR-221. Albany, CA: U.S. Department of Agriculture, Forest Service, Pacific Southwest Research Station: 188–194.

Meadows, I.M.; Zwart, D.C.; Jeffers, S.N.; Waldrop, T.A.; Bridges, W.C., Jr. 2011. Effects of fuel reduction treatments on incidence of *Phytophthora* species in soil of a southern Appalachian Mountain forest. Plant Disease. 95: 811–820.

Roiger, D.J.; Jeffers, S.N. 1991. Evaluation of *Trichoderma* species for biological control of Phytophthora crown and root rot of apple seedlings. Phytopathology. 81: 910-917.

Zentmyer, G.A. 1980. *Phytophthora cinnamomi* and the diseases it causes. St. Paul, MN: APS Press. The American Phytopathological Society. 96 p.

Screening for Resistance to Beech Bark Disease: Improvements and Results From Seedlings and Grafted Field Selections

Jennifer L. Koch,[1] Mary E. Mason,[2] and David W. Carey[1]

Abstract

Beech bark disease (BBD) is an insect-disease complex that has been killing American beech (*Fagus grandifolia* Ehrh.) trees since the accidental introduction of the beech scale insect (*Cryptococcus fagisuga*) to Canada around 1890. Insect infestation is followed by infection with *Neonectria ditissima* or *N. faginata*. Mortality levels in the first wave of the disease can be as high as 50 percent, with consequent loss to stand health, merchantable timber, and many wildlife and ecosystem services. It is currently estimated that between 1 and 5 percent of the native American beech are resistant to beech bark disease, and resistance has been shown to be to the insect part of the complex.

Recent work has shown that artificial infestation techniques can be used to screen seedlings for scale resistance. Here we present results from additional beech insect resistance screening experiments, including additional seedling families, grafted parental ramets of seedlings, and nonnative beech species. Results further confirm the utility of the screen to allow selection of better performing individuals, even within families that perform poorly overall, and to rank families for overall performance. When full-sibling families using parents of known scale phenotype were screened, an enriched proportion of resistant progeny were observed only in families with two resistant parents.

Trees selected in the field can be grafted and the assay is useful to confirm the field-assessed scale resistant phenotype. We are currently identifying, grafting, and testing scale-resistant beech trees as part of a multi-state, multi-agency cooperative effort. Confirmed resistant genotypes will be used to establish seed orchards to supply regionally adapted disease-resistant beechnuts for use in restoration plantings and BBD management. The use of resistant parents is necessary to produce significant improvement over unselected seed lots.

Key words: beech bark disease, beech scale, *Cryptococcus fagisuga*, *Neonectria*, scale resistance

Introduction

Beech bark disease (BBD) was introduced into North America in Nova Scotia in the late 1890s and has been steadily spreading south and west over the last 120 years (Ehrlich 1934). Beech bark disease is caused by an insect-fungal complex. The beech scale insect (*Cryptococcus fagisuga*) is the insect component, and a canker-causing *Neonectria* (either *Neonectria ditissima* or *N. faginata* in North America) is the fungal component (Castlebury et al. 2006). Insect infestation appears first and is believed to predispose trees to fungal infection of insect-damaged bark (Ehrlich 1934). Many forests where American beech is the dominant component of stands are already heavily impacted, with mortality in the 'killing front' as high as 50 percent followed by significant additional damage due to beech snap (Miller-Weeks 1983, Papaik et al. 2005). Residual and regenerating stands may be dominated by susceptible beech, with susceptible beech root sprouts capable of forming thickets that prevent regeneration of resistant beech or other species, and offer no economic and severely reduced ecological value as beech bark disease continues to kill susceptible beech over time (Morin et al. 2007).

[1] USDA Forest Service, Northern Research Station, 359 Main Rd, Delaware, OH 43015.
[2] Dept. Entomology, Ohio Agricultural Research and Development Center, The Ohio State University, 1680 Madison Ave., Wooster, OH 44691.
Corresponding author: jkoch@fs.fed.us.

In native beech populations heavily infested with BBD, there are an estimated 1 to 5 percent of trees that remain healthy (Houston 1983). These apparently resistant beech trees are frequently found in clusters suggesting they may be clonal or related seedlings. Houston (Houston 1982) developed a scale infestation technique and used it to demonstrate that these healthy trees are actually resistant to the scale insect component of BBD. To investigate the genetic control of resistance to beech scale in American beech, its inheritance, and its potential for improvement through breeding, the U.S. Department of Agriculture, Forest Service (USDA FS) has been conducting beech scale resistance studies. Koch and Carey (2005) selected and tested scale-resistant American beech trees in the field (to determine if they were resistant to scale (R) or susceptible to scale (S)) and performed controlled cross pollinations that produced RxR and RxS seedling families (Koch et al. 2006). Houston's (Houston 1982) artificial infestation technique was adapted to screen the seedlings and significant family effects were found for scale resistance (Koch et al. 2010). In this paper, we present results from several experiments conducted over several years, including:

- Screening cultivars and seedlings.
- Screening grafted trees and improving the screen.
- Screening families of seedlings.
- Development of regional seed orchards for breeding resistant beech.

Methods and Materials

Plant Materials and Growth Conditions

Beech plants were grown in containers, either in a greenhouse or shaded outside growing areas, as previously described (Koch et al. 2010), and repotted to larger containers as needed. In general, seedlings were screened at 1 to 2 years of age and grafts were screened 1 to 2 years post-graft. The European beech seedlings and cultivars were purchased from Lawyer's nursery (Plains, Montana). Scion was grafted using either top (cleft) grafts or side-veneer grafts and utilizing a 'hot-callous' system to warm the graft union relative to the rootstock and scion (Koch et al. 2006). Rootstocks were grown from unselected seed collected in Ohio. Grafts were maintained in a greenhouse for the first year and received intensive aftercare (rewrapping grafting rubber, pruning rootstock, etc.). After the first year, plants were grown outside under shade (approximately 50 percent).

Grafted trees may produce flowers, either from mature scion in the year of grafting or after resuming normal cyclical flowering; these flowers were utilized in control pollinations. Flowering ramets used as female parents were isolated and emasculated to prevent rare self-pollination, then pollinated using camel hair brushes when receptive (Koch and Carey 2004). Flowering ramets used as male parents were isolated, and male flowers were collected when dehiscent. Pollen was collected and passed through fine mesh screen to remove any anthers or other debris, then stored at -80 °C over desiccant until use. Ramets carrying nuts were maintained in the greenhouse and protected from insect infestation.

Beech nuts were collected before being shed from the burrs. The burrs were allowed to dry and open in the laboratory, and the nuts were then separated and stratified 90 days in Banrot® wetted peat moss at 4 to 10 °C. When radicals began to emerge, nuts were transferred to soil-less media in the greenhouse to complete germination and begin growth.

Scale Screening

When grafted ramets and seedlings were of sufficient size to support the required number of scale screening pads, they were transferred to the screening facility at Holden Arboretum (Kirtland, Ohio). Scale pads were applied as previously described (Koch et al. 2010) including the use of Tyvek® covers to prevent excess moisture from reaching the foam pads. Field scale pads were established in a stand of susceptible beech trees at Holden Arboretum to provide a consistent supply of eggs for use in screening. One hundred eggs (through 2006) or 150 eggs (2007 and thereafter) were placed on each pad prior to the pad being affixed to the tree (seedling or grafted ramet). Viability assays were conducted on each batch of eggs prior to use for quality control. Scale pads were scored 52 weeks after application to maximize the number of scale adults and egg clusters and to minimize the number of mobile juvenile nymphs at the time of scoring due to the difficulty in counting them (Koch et al. 2010). Trees were overwintered with scale test pads affixed either in a 4 °C cold storage facility or a heated poly-house maintained just above freezing.

Scale pad data was examined for quality prior to further analysis and inclusion in statistical datasets. Multiple pads were reviewed for consistency and any obviously discordant pads were either discarded (for three or more pads total, leaving at least two), or the ramet or seedling was rescreened. For seedlings or ramets with only two pads, an additional quality control metric was calculated to confirm the two pads were consistent. The quality control metric is adjusted difference:
Adjusted difference = (pad 2 value – pad 1 value)/(pad value mean + 0.0001).

An adjusted difference of zero corresponds to two identical pads, while an adjusted difference of one corresponds to the difference between the two pads being equal to the mean. Ramets or seedlings with an adjusted difference greater than 1.5 were considered to be inconsistent and were rescreened. The cutoff value of 1.5 was originally chosen by graphing the adjusted difference values for the 2009 dataset, and observing that there was a break in the distribution of adjusted difference around 1.5, with approximately 90 percent of values below 1.5. Adjusted difference has been similarly distributed in later years.

Scale pads were scored resistant if they had zero (or occasional one small or unhealthy) scale adults and no egg clusters. Susceptible pads had both healthy scale adults and egg clusters, often in equal or greater number than the scale adults count indicating a robust and reproductive scale population. Pads were scored intermediate if they had only a few scale adults, or mainly unhealthy scale adults and no or only a few egg clusters (many less egg clusters than scale adults, e.g., a pad with 6 small adults and one egg cluster would be considered intermediate). Intermediate classification was less stringently defined, and when stringent classification was desired, these pads were classified as susceptible. Grafts or seedlings were scored resistant, intermediate, or susceptible based on the score of all the pads, with a resistant score being most conservative. A resistant genotype had only resistant pads. A genotype with a mix of resistant and intermediate pads was scored intermediate (or, more stringently, susceptible). A susceptible genotype had susceptible pads or a mix of susceptible and intermediate pads. Additional exploratory data analysis including calculation of summary statistics and graphing were carried out using Minitab®.

Statistical Analysis

Repeatability (for fig. 3, section titled Screening Grafted Trees and Improving the Screen) was estimated by r, the ratio of the variance attributed to genotype over the total variance. Minitab® was used to fit an analysis of variance (ANOVA) with model:
Scale adults = intercept + Genotype (Sample) + Error

Model fit was assessed by examination of residuals. The use of ANOVA was appropriate here because we were modeling the scale adults over the full experiment (essentially averaging), and the model fit was confirmed by examination of residuals. Variance components were reported for genotype, sample, error, and total, and used to compute r. Expected relative error variance was calculated using the relationship:
$E=(1-r)/n$.

For family analysis (for fig. 5, table 4, and section titled Screening of Families of Seedlings), SAS® was used to fit a generalized linear model using the GENMOD procedure. Model fit was assessed by examination of residuals and alternate models were compared using deviance/degrees of freedom, AIC, AICC, and BIC scores, and graphing of residuals supplied by GENMOD. Model variation was guided by exploratory data analysis and included models with different distribution and link function options as well as models with and without interactions and main effects. The best-fit model was selected and the differences of least square means computed and interpreted only for the best fit model. Actual p-values are reported rather than an a priori cutoff or adjustment. The current dataset contained many susceptible trees, so it was not as severely zero-inflated as data containing more highly resistant families. Therefore, the current data was sufficiently normalized by applying square root transformation prior to analysis. The best fit model was:

Square root (sum of adults) = intercept + family + scorer + year + error;

specifying tree (genotype within family) as the subject of repeat observations to correctly specify the covariance structure and account for repeated measure on individual seedlings. Replication in the model comes from evaluating multiple pads per genotype.

Results and Discussion

Screening Cultivars and Seedlings

Koch et al. (2010) described an artificial scale infestation technique and reported data from several families screened using one pad per seedling per year and combining analysis over 2 years to obtain statistically analyzable results. In this paper, we report data from several smaller groups of seedlings that were also screened using one pad per seedling per year. Table 1 shows a summary of the results of these screenings. Results are consistent with those reported in Koch et al. (2010) in that only families produced from crosses where both parents were scored resistant had an enriched number of resistant seedlings. Families with a beech scale susceptible parent and open-pollinated (all male parents presumed susceptible) families had only a few, if any, resistant progeny.

Table 1—Beech seedlings and families screened by USDA Forest Service

Entry	Type	Source[a]	No. R trees	No. S trees	Avg adults	Avg eggs	Year(s) screened
DSP1973xOP	seedling	open-pollinated family, S mother	0	6	25.5	25.6	2004, 2005
1505xOP	seedling	open-pollinated family, R mother	2	14	32.21	33.24	2008
1505xSebois23	seedling	control cross, RxR'	17	7	14.8	15.86	2008
1505xSebois85	seedling	control cross, RxR'	2	9	3.22	15.33	2008
1520xOP	seedling	open-pollinated family, S mother	0	21	45.71	52.95	2008
DNxOP	seedling	open-pollinated family, S mother	0	50	6.25	8.73	2005, 2006

[a] Source is either control-cross pollinated or open-pollinated family with parents field scored as R=resistant in field test, R'=field selected as healthy with no visible scale in post-aftermath forest, presumed scale resistant. S=susceptible in field test.

A number of exotic species and selections of beech are commercially available in the United States, and a sample of these were purchased and screened in 2005 and 2006 (table 2). Similar to observations with American beech (*Fagus grandifolia* Ehrh.), the additional species had both resistant and susceptible individuals. Several of the cultivars of European beech (*Fagus sylvatica* L.) appear to be resistant to beech scale. Also similar to the American beech data, susceptible trees of the different *Fagus* species showed a range in the size of the scale population they supported (fig. 1).

Table 2—Beech (*Fagus*) cultivars screened by USDA Forest Service

Entry	Type	Source	No. R trees	No. S trees	Avg adults[a]	Avg eggs[a]	Year(s) screened
F. orientalis[b]	Asian species	commercial horticulture	5	0	-	-	2006
F. sylatica v. *cristata*	European cultivar	commercial horticulture	6	0	-	-	2006
F. sylatica v. *rotundafolia*	European cultivar	commercial horticulture	9	0	-	-	2006
F. sylvatica v. *spaethiana*	European cultivar	commercial horticulture	6	4	0.7	3.0	2006
F.sylvatica v. *asplendafolia*	European cultivar	commercial horticulture	1	0	-	-	2006
F. purpurea	European sub-species	commercial horticulture	7	19	10.3	8.4	2008
F. sylvatica	European sub-species	commercial horticulture	15	19	24.0	27.8	2008

[a] Average of the susceptible trees only: reflects the relative degree of susceptibility of the S population. The value cannot be calculated (is undefined) if all trees are resistant.

[b] *F. orientalis*, *purpurea*, and *sylvatica* are species within *Fagus*. The other groups are horticultural selections or sub-species of *Fagus sylvatica*.

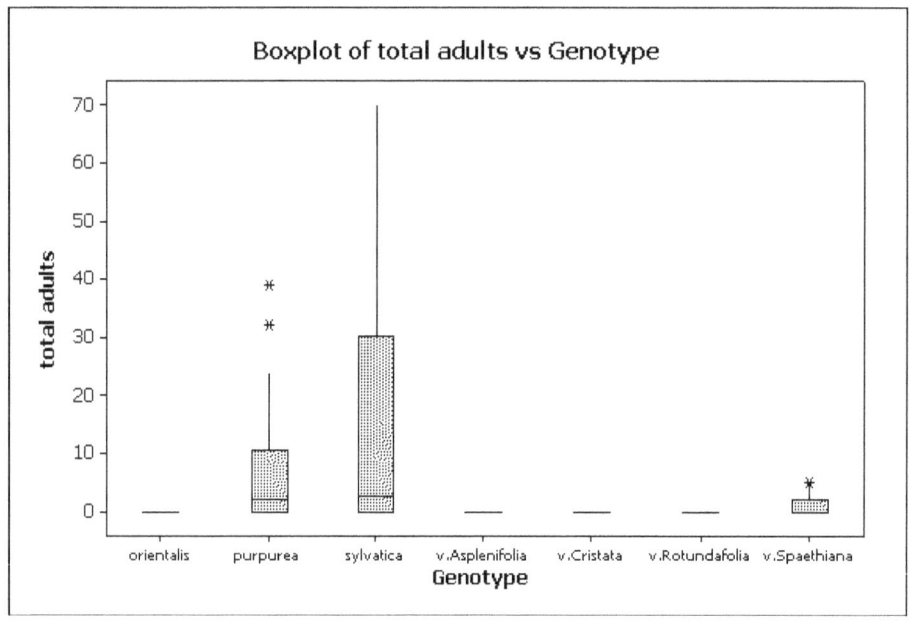

Figure 1—Boxplot of the distribution of beech scale adults count of several exotic species and cultivars of beech screened by the USDA Forest Service. Box: first to third quartile, line: median, 'whiskers:' upper (or lower) quartile plus (minus) 1.5 times the inter-quartile range, asterisks: outliers.

Screening Grafted Trees and Improving the Screen

Parent trees and other field selected trees were grafted, and ramets were screened to confirm the greenhouse screening with the field selection phenotypes. Early screens (2006) used one pad per ramet and relied on screening multiple ramets to determine screening result (R or S). This replication of the genotypes allows the reproducibility of the screen to be assessed. An examination of the screen data showed generally consistent results, but problems were identified as well (discordant ramets; table 3). Examination of the notes taken during scoring revealed several problems with early screens. Often small side branches needed to be pruned in order to place the screening pads and Tyvek® protectors on the tree. Scale insects appear to establish more readily on this freshly wounded tissue fig. 2A), sometimes even on normally resistant trees. To avoid the impact that pruning wounds have on scale tests, pads are now installed either away from the wound entirely or with the foam facing the unwounded side of the branch only. An additional problem in scoring was a concomitant infestation of oyster shell scale (fig. 2B), including adults and juveniles present on and under beech scale test pads. While the adult stage is not difficult to distinguish, the egg and juvenile phases of the two scale insects are much more similar in appearance and can be confused. It is unknown what impact the two scale infestations may have on each other, but oyster shell scale infestation appeared to cause seedling mortality at the infestation levels present in the experiment, so it was likely having a significant impact on overall tree health during the beech scale screen.

Table 3—Performance of grafted ramets of trees in different years with different numbers of pads

Genotype	Source	Year	Pads per ramet	No. R ramets	No. S ramets	No. discordant pads/total pads	Avg. adults	Avg. eggs
1503	selection	2006	1	6	1*	n/a	1	1
1504	selection	2006	1	2	3*	n/a	0.67	1
2179	unselected	2006	1	1	2	n/a	2.5	0
2189	unselected	2006	1	1	1	n/a	4	2
PA2691	selected	2006	1	3	2*	n/a	2	0.5
PA2692	selected	2006	1	6	1*	n/a	0	1
WV193	unselected	2006	1	0	1	n/a	7	2
WV963	unselected	2006	1	0	1	n/a	9	9
WV964	unselected	2006	1	1	2	n/a	7.5	5.5
WV966	unselected	2006	1	0	2	n/a	8	7.5
WV969	unselected	2006	1	0	2	n/a	8.5	2.5
WV970	unselected	2006	1	0	3	n/a	11.6	2
1504	selection	2009	1-2	3	0	1/5[a]	0	0
1505	selection	2009	2-3	5	0	1/13[b]	0	0
1506	selection	2009	1-3	0	4	1/8[c]	23.4	23.4
1520	selection	2009	2	0	1	0/2	15.5	23
DN00726	unselected	2009	2-3	0	5	1/13[c]	14.1	13.5
DN00740	unselected	2009	1-3	0	4	0/8	37.6	32.5
BEWL01	selected	2009	3	1	0	0/1	0	0

*discordant ramets likely mis-scored due to interfering conditions (insects, wounds, failed pad).

[a] One pad with five adults and six egg clusters.

[b] One pad with six adults and no egg clusters.

[c] One pad with no adults and no egg clusters.

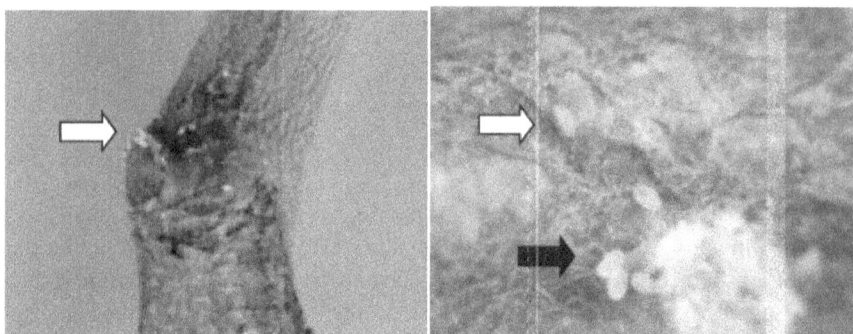

Figure 2—Beech scale infestation complications. Left (A): beech scale established around pruning wound (white arrow). Right (B): oyster shell scale adult and juvenile (white arrow) in area of beech scale juveniles and eggs (black arrow) on a tested tree. Note the very similar size and morphology of the juveniles.

The use of multiple pads per tree has made it possible to identify occasional discordant screening pads (pads inconsistent with the set of pads on the genotype). These discordant pads fall into two types: R pads on apparently S trees, and S or I pads on apparently R trees. The first conditions (R pad on S tree) can be considered a failed pad. A number of potential causes of pad failure have been identified including pads not receiving eggs and pads being placed backwards, or drying out before attachment to the tree during setup. Occasionally pads became loose over the duration of the experiment and/or the Tyvek® covers also became loose resulting in the pad being compromised. In the second case (S pad on R tree) the causes are potentially less clear, but a number of factors that impact tree health either locally or systemically can be supposed to compromise a score pad. Poor overall tree health or infection with other insects or fungi and damage or broken bark, especially fresh pruning wounds, are all noted on scoring sheets associated with discordant pads. Pads inadvertently placed below or straddling the graft union are an easily recognized case of S pads on R trees, and are discarded. With multiple pads per tree or ramet, discordant or failed pads can be easily detected and the data either carefully scrutinized for consistency or discarded.

Koch et al. (2010) used the relationship between expected relative error variance and number of pads (replicates) for a set of beech seedlings screened with only one pad from 2004 to 2006 to predict the number of pads that would improve control of error variance and improve the overall accuracy of the screen while maintaining a manageable workload. Increasing from one pad per tree to three to four pads per tree was estimated to give the best improvement of error variance. We calculated the same value for a set of grafted ramets screened in 2009 with multiple pads per ramet (fig. 3) and found a similar value of three to five pads per tree to give the optimal reduction in error variance (estimated by the inflection point of the curve, with pads above five giving only marginal improvement in error variance for each additional pad).

Based upon the 2006 results, and the predicted improvement based on increased replication, a new set of grafts was screened beginning in 2009 with a goal of screening three ramets with three to four scale pads each for a total of nine reps per genotype. The improvement in the ability to identify and discard discordant pads greatly improves the accuracy and confidence of the screen based phenotype (table 3). Figure 4 shows our standardized scale egg score pad attached to a tree (fig. 4A), a grafted ramet with the improved replication of three scale pads with Tyvek® covers (fig. 4B), and our improved scale screening facility at Holden Arboretum (fig. 4C) that provides consistent, quality, dedicated beech growing space. The new growing space is optimized for growing beech trees and isolation from other Holden Arboretum growing stock reduces insect problems. This screening intensity allows consistent phenotyping of selected genotypes in one year, even if there are problems with a particular pad or ramet. Seedlings are also now screened at higher replication of test pads, generally with two applied per seedling. After scoring the pads, we compute a pad consistency metric, adjusted difference, and rescreen any seedlings with values over a cutoff value of 1.5. Trees with only one pad scored due to a pad failure are also automatically rescreened. The improved screen replication, improved and consistent growing space, and adoption of quality control metrics combine to greatly improve the robustness and efficiency of the screening technique.

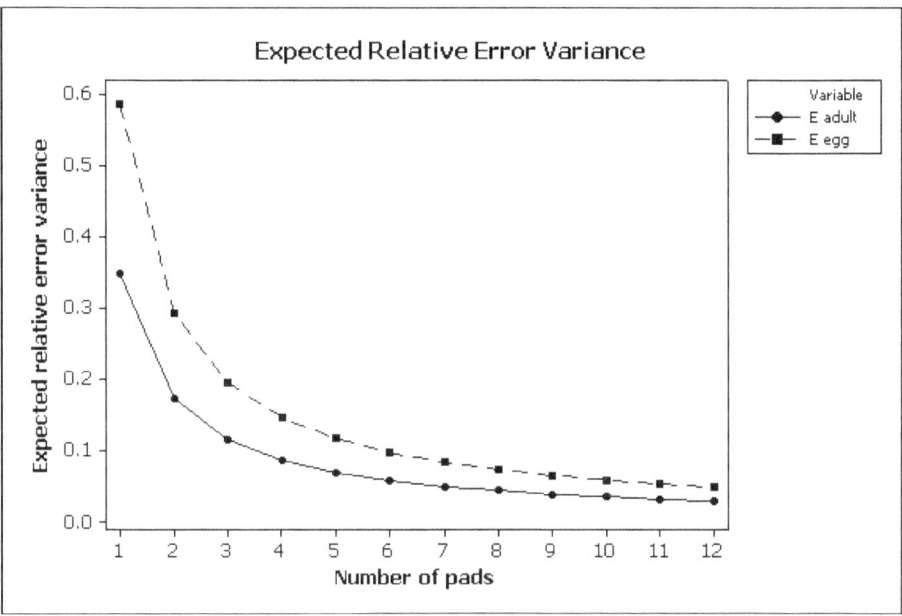

Figure 3—Expected relative error variance by number of pads screened. Expected relative error variance was calculated from the repeatability of grafts with two or more pads in 2009, based on the relationship E= (1-r)/n. Three to five pads is considered an optimal balance between the additional time and effort to add a pad and the reduction in expected relative error variance.

Screening Families of Seedlings

As field-selected trees are grafted for screening, grafted ramets occasionally flower. Any ramets that produce flowers are moved to the greenhouse and control pollinated to produce families of seedlings for screening. Ramets used as female parents are maintained in the greenhouse until nut collection, and this 'containerized seed orchard' approach is an efficient method to generate high quality controlled cross pollinated beechnuts (Koch et al. 2006). Ideally all trees grafted would flower and be used once or twice as a male parent and once or twice as a female parent to allow assessment of their suitability as R parents and to provide a source of improved seedlings for testing of planting requirements. A small group of five inter-related families were produced on flowering ramets in 2006 and the resulting seedlings were screened at the scale screening facility from 2008 to 2011.

The distribution of total scale adults per scoring pad is shown in figure 5 for all the pads on all the trees in the experiment and has the features typical of these datasets in all experiments. The zero 'spike' is typical for scale screen datasets and is more or less pronounced depending on how many trees in the dataset are resistant (in this case it is less pronounced). Due to the number of zeroes, the data are sometimes zero inflated relative to the distribution that accurately models the non-zero portion of the data, so zero-inflated models are considered in the analysis in addition to several transformations (either directly or by varying the distribution and link function in the generalized linear model specifications). Only the best fit model based on typical goodness of fit measures (e.g., deviance/df=1, or smallest AIC) is used to determine significance of effects and evaluate family rankings.

Figure 4—Scale screening pads and current improved screening facility. A: Foam pad with scale eggs is attached to the tree using wire ties. B: Several foam pads are placed on each tree and covered with Tyvek® to protect them from rain and irrigation water. C: Grafted ramets at the U.S. Department of Agriculture, Forest Service scale screening facility at Holden Arboretum.

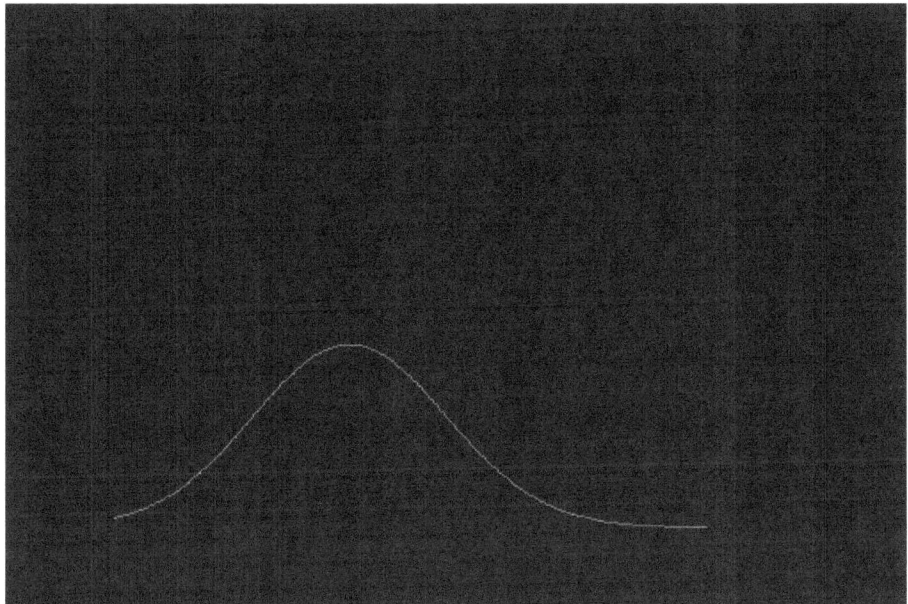

Figure 5—Histogram of scale adults per tree with normal curve. The normal curve based on the mean and standard deviation for the sample is superimposed over the histogram. Both the high proportion of zero counts and the lack of normality expected for count data can be seen in the chart. Depending on the proportion of zeroes in a given dataset, simple transformation may be insufficient to normalize the data and zero-inflated models should also be investigated.

For this experiment (dataset), the best model for the total scale adults per tree analyzed the square root of the total adults with main effects for family, year, and person scoring (scorer), and using a generalized linear model specifying the normal distribution, identity link function, and tree as the subject of repeated observations. Effects were tested using the Wald statistics. Family and year were significant (both p<0.0001), but scorer was not (p=0.2049). Least squares means were computed for family and year and are shown in table 4. Consistent with the previous results, only the RxR family had operationally reasonable numbers of resistant progeny (over half), while the SxR and SxS families were dominated by susceptible individuals. The scale population carried by the three groups of families (RxR, SxR, and SxS) differed in the expected way with fewer scale insects on families with both resistant parents. We also found that the least squares mean for SxR families is significantly (p<0.0001 for difference of LSM=0) less than those for SxS families. These families also had a small number of resistant progeny, consistent with estimates of resistance in natural stands. The YEAR effect was also significant. Relative rankings will probably be most robust if completed within a year and control trees or families should be screened each year for multi-year experiments (to allow differences in years to be estimated statistically). Five different individuals scored trees over the 3 years including the research scientist that developed the assay and summer interns. The lack of significance for scorer is reassuring that the screen and training is robust and should be transferable to other work groups or managers.

Development of Regional Seed Orchards for Resistant Beech

Early experiments (Koch et al. 2010) showed both the utility of the screen to identify beech scale resistant individuals and superior families and indicated that the degree of genetic determination of resistance to beech scale was sufficient to realize genetic gain through traditional tree breeding programs. However, these conclusions were based on the analysis of a small number of families. The findings presented here further support the conclusions of Koch et al. (2010) and Koch (2010), and

Table 4—Least squares means for family (A) and year (B)

A. Family	Field score of parents in cross	Proportion of resistant progeny	Least squares mean estimate for total adults	Significance
BEWL01x1504	R x R	0.607	1.4	A[a]
DNx1504	S x R	0.08	23.9	B
DNx1505	S x R	0.21	27.40	B
DNx1506	S x S	0	59.2	C
DNxDN	S x S	0	50.5	C

B. Year	Least squares mean estimate	Significance
2009	43.3	A
2010	15.0	B
2011	27.1	AB

[a] Means that share a letter are not significantly different (all significant differences had an unadjusted p<0.0001).

taken together provide the framework to develop a strategy for managing beech bark disease. A multi-state, multi-agency workgroup has been assembled to select, screen, and propagate beech scale-resistant American beech for use in the installation of regional seed orchards. The initial efforts have focused on both the Lower and Upper Peninsulas of Michigan, and central Pennsylvania. A number of beech trees have been selected, grafted, and screened (table 5). Resistant beech trees appear easier to detect during the killing front phase, and harder to detect in aftermath forest. Based on these early results, selected trees are being field tested before grafting.

Table 5—Regional seed orchard project (American beech trees were selected by local cooperators, then grafted and screened for beech scale resistance by U.S. Forest Service personnel at the screening facility at the Holden Arboretum)

Region	Beech bark disease status	Tree ID for screen result: resistant[a]	Tree ID for screen result: intermediate[b]	Tree ID for screen result: susceptible[c]
Michigan-Lower Peninsula	killing front	1503,1504,1505,1510		1506[d] 1520[d]
Michigan-Upper Peninsula	killing front	1201,1207,1208,1209,1210,1211,1213, 1214,1215,1217,1219,1220,1228,1229, 1230, 1231, 1301		1202 1216
Pennsylvania	aftermath	PA2661, PA2663, PA2665, PA2691, ANF4491304, ANF4491308, ANF4491321, ANF4693608, ANF4694223, ANF4693619, ANF4694209, ANF4714904, D-9-1, D-9-2	ANF4491304 ANF4694204 PA2692	PA2659 ANF4693615 ANF4693905 ANF4693622
West Virginia	killing front/ aftermath	MNF3839335 MNF3839557		
Ohio	uninfested			DN00726[d] DN00740[d]

[a] No more than 3 adults and/or one egg cluster.
[b] A few adult scale or mainly unhealthy adult scale, and only a few egg clusters.
[c] Robust scale infestation present with both adults and eggs.
[d] Originally selected as susceptible control.

Conclusions

We report results from screening several different sets of seedlings, including open-pollinated, controlled-pollinated, commercially available, and grafted ramets of American beech for resistance to the beech scale insect. Evaluation of these scale test results has guided improvement, quality control, and standardization (best practices) of the beech scale insect screening for both grafted trees and seedlings. These changes have also made the process of successfully scoring beech grafted trees and seedlings faster, more predictable, and more efficient. Analysis of family data continues to support the conclusions of Koch et al. (2010) that only families with two resistant parents have high numbers of resistant seedlings. Based on these finding, a pilot seed orchard project is being established where collaborators are identifying superior parents in their region for establishment in a seed orchard to supply resistant beech nuts for planting.

Acknowledgments

We would like to thank Kathleen Knight (NRS, USDA Forest Service), John Davis (University of Florida), Dana Nelson (SRS, USDA Forest Service), and John Stanovick (NRS, USDA Forest Service) for helpful comments on the manuscript. We thank the Holden Arboretum for partnership on the scale resistance screening facility. We thank our collaborators for the work and vision on the beech seed orchard project: Bob Heyd and Rich Mergener (Michigan Department of Natural Resources), Andrea Hille (Allegheny National Forest), Tom Hall (Pennsylvania Dept. of Conservation and Natural Resources), Dan Twardus (SPF, USDA Forest Service), Manfred Mielke (FHP, USDA Forest Service), Paul Berrang (Region 9, USDA Forest Service), and Glenn Juergans (Monangahela National Forest, retired). Funding for this work was supplied in part by the Evaluation Monitoring Program (NE-EM-B-11-03) and the Special Technology Development Program (NA-2009-01) of Forest Health Protection, USDA Forest Service.

Literature Cited

Castlebury, L.A.; Rossman, A.Y.; Hyten, A.S. 2006. Phylogentic relationships of *Neonectria/Cylindrocarpon* on *Fagus* in North America. Canadian Journal of Botany. 84: 1417–1433.

Ehrlich, J. 1934. The beech bark disease: a *Nectria* disease of *Fagus*, following *Cryptococcus fagi* (Baer.). Canadian Journal of Research. 10(6): 593–692.

Houston, D.R. 1982. A technique to artificially infest beech bark with the beech scale. *Cryptococcus fagisuga* (Lindinger). Res. Pap. NE-507. Broomhall, PA: U.S. Department of Agriculture, Forest Service, Northeastern Research Station. 8 p.

Houston, D.R. 1983. American beech resistance to *Cryptococcus fagisuga*. In: [Editors unknown]. Proceedings, IUFRO beech bark disease working party conference. Gen. Tech. Rep. WO-37. Washington, DC: U.S. Department of Agriculture, Forest Service, Northeastern Forest Experiment Station: 38–41.

Koch, J.L. 2010. Beech bark disease: The oldest "new" threat to American beech in the United States. Outlooks on Pest Management. April 2010: 64–68.

Koch, J.L.; Carey, D.W. 2004. Controlled cross-pollinations with American beech trees that are resistant to beech bark disease. In: Yaussy, D.; Hix, D.M.; Goebel, P.C.; Long, R.P., eds. Proceedings, 14th Central Hardwood Forest Conference. Gen. Tech. Rep. NE-316. Newtown Square, PA: U.S. Department of Agriculture, Forest Service, Northern Research Station: 358–364.

Koch, J.L.; Carey, D.W. 2005. The genetics of resistance of American beech to beech bark disease: knowledge through 2004. In: Evans, C.A.; Lucas, J.A.; Twery, M.J., eds. Proceedings of the beech bark disease symposium. Gen. Tech. Rep. NE-331. Newtown Square, PA: U.S. Department of Agriculture, Forest Service, Northeastern Research Station: 98–105.

Koch, J.L.; Mason, M.E.; Carey, D.W. 2006. Advances in breeding American beech for resistance to beech bark disease. In: Proceedings of the 3rd Northern Forest Genetics Association meeting. Staff Paper Series No. 194. St. Paul, MN: Dept. of Forest Resources, University of Minnesota: 22–28.

Koch, J.L.; Mason, M.E.; Carey, D.W.; Nelson, C.D. 2010. Assessment of beech scale resistance in full and half-sibling American beech families. Canadian Journal of Forest Research. 40: 265–272.

Miller-Weeks, M. 1983. Current status of beech bark disease in New England and New York. In: Proceedings, IUFRO beech bark disease working party conference. Gen. Tech. Rep. WO-37. Washington, DC: U.S. Department of Agriculture, Forest Service, Northeastern Forest Experiment Station: 21–23.

Morin, R.S.; Liebhold, A.M.; Tobin, P.C.; Gottschalk, K.W.; Luzader, E. 2007. Spread of beech bark disease in the eastern United States and its relationship to regional forest composition. Canadian Journal of Forest Research. 37: 726–736.

Papaik, M.J.; Canham, C.D.; Latty, E.F.; Woods, K.D. 2005. Effects of an introduced pathogen on resistance to natural disturbance: beech bark disease and windthrow. Canadian Journal of Forest Research. 35: 1832–1843.

Breeding Resistance to Butternut Canker Disease

James McKenna,[1] Keith Woeste[1] and Michael Ostry[2]

Abstract

Butternut (*Juglans cinerea* L.) is being killed throughout its native range by an exotic fungus *Ophiognomonia clavigignenti-juglandacearum* (*Ocj*). In recent years, many disease-free trees have been determined to be complex hybrids with an admixture of Japanese walnut (*J. ailantifolia*). Recently developed molecular and morphological characterizations allow us to accurately identify and separate hybrid and pure butternut progeny. Disease-free-trees, from across butternut's native range, are the basis of our breeding program in the Central Hardwood Region of the eastern United States. Our first clone banks and seed orchards were grafted and established in the 1990s and 2000s, and are now producing seed for resistance screening. In 2008, we challenged 5-year-old trees from our first two field progeny tests with *Ocj*.

The first test, planted in 2003, had 37 diverse families (n=319). Thirty-two of these seedling families were derived from a grafted orchard of putatively resistant selections. Five additional families were collected from healthy hybrid trees. In early fall of 2008, trees were inoculated with two isolates of *Ocj* obtained from branch cankers on trees in two locations in Indiana. The trees were scored 8, 12, 20, and 24 months after inoculation for canker incidence and severity. Native butternuts in the adjacent woods provided a source of inoculum whereby natural infections from *Ocj* began to occur in the third year. Cumulative natural canker incidence and severity were recorded at 5 and 7 years.

The second test, planted in 2004, had 12 pure butternut half-sib families collected from a woodlot with: four resistant, four moderately resistant, four susceptible, and one resistant hybrid families (n=213). Resistance ratings were based on the disease status of the mother trees in the stand when the seed was harvested in the fall of 2002. In early fall of 2008, trees were inoculated with the same two isolates of *Ocj* used in the first test. The trees were scored 8, 12, 20, and 24 months after inoculation for canker incidence and severity. There was no natural infection in the second test.

Hybrid butternut families were more resistant to natural infection than the pure butternut families. Eight months after inoculation, canker incidence and severity varied significantly among butternut hybrid families and *Ocj* isolate, but not among pure butternut families. After 12, 20, and 24 months, canker incidence and severity of pure butternut families changed. By 24 months, hybrid families in general have shown reduced canker expansion and a high level of resistance. Pure butternut families exhibit more variation from highly susceptible to resistant. Year-to-year variation in canker growth suggests that it may take several years to determine the resistance status of butternut with artificial stem inoculations.

[1] USDA Forest Service, Northern Research Station, Hardwood Tree Improvement and Regeneration Center at Purdue University, 715 West State St., Department of Forestry and Natural Resources, West Lafayette, IN 47907.
[2] USDA Forest Service, Northern Research Station, 1561 Lindig Ave, St. Paul, MN 55108.
Corresponding author: jrmckenn@purdue.edu.

Towards the Development of a Laurel Wilt Screening Program in Redbay (*Persea borbonia*)

Marc Hughes[1] and Jason Smith[2]

Abstract

Laurel wilt is a highly destructive disease of redbay (*Persea borbonia* (L.) Spreng.) and other Lauraceous natives in the southeastern United States. The disease and associated vector, the redbay ambrosia beetle (*Xyleborus glabratus*), has spread through the United States coastal plain. The presence of surviving and asymptomatic individuals in severely-affected stands illustrates the possibility of natural resistance by surviving redbays.

In 2008, a field survey was initiated to locate and identify healthy, asymptomatic redbays in areas of severe mortality. Six heavily-affected sites were chosen along the redbay-dense barrier islands of Florida, Georgia, and South Carolina. Over 80 trees with a 7.6 cm or larger diameter at breast height were selected as putatively resistant candidates. A 0.7 ha plot was then established around each candidate tree along with measurements of redbay plot disease severity and redbay ambrosia beetle activity, based on trapping studies. Branch cuttings were taken and used in novel experiments to investigate methods of redbay vegetative propagation and disease resistance screening. A mean of 25 percent rooting was achieved in the propagation experiment, although genotype had a large effect on rooting success. The vegetatively propagated clones of live parent trees are currently being tested for resistance/tolerance to the laurel wilt fungus by inoculation experiments. A preliminary study tested 10 clones; a single clone (FG-C1) has survived at 10 months post-inoculation, suggesting a possible tolerance response. Further testing of FG-C1, and over 50 new clones, is under way. Additional studies on the genetic/pathogenic variability of the pathogen and effects of inoculum concentration on symptom expression are underway.

---

[1] Department of Plant Pathology, University of Florida, Gainesville, FL 32611.
[2] School of Forest Resources and Conservation, University of Florida, Gainesville, FL 32611.
Corresponding author: mhughes741@ufl.edu.

Breeding *Eucalyptus* for Disease Resistance

Edival A.V. Zauza,[1] Acelino Couto Alfenas,[2] Lúcio Mauro da Silva Guimarães,[1] and João Flávio da Silva[1]

Abstract

Eucalyptus plantations cover about 1.5 percent of the agricultural area in Brazil, and contribute to 4 percent of GDP and 3 percent in exports of forest products. Technological and research advances in silviculture and genetic improvement have increased productivity up to 80 m^3 of wood/ha/year, with an average of 35 to 45 m^3/ha/year. The greatest challenge to the introduction and commercial use of exotic species is the adaptation of species to climatic conditions. Even when maladapted species are able to survive, they are subjected to continuous stress that limits the expression of their maximum genetic potential. The incidence of insects and diseases frequently represent another limiting factor, because the exotic tree species have not co-evolved with most of the local insect and pathogen pests. In recent decades, the expansion of *Eucalyptus* plantations in Brazil has been frequently associated with frequent disease outbreaks. Prominent diseases, such as Ceratocystis wilt, Ralstonia wilt, rust, and bacterial/fungal leaf blights, have limited the establishment and growth of plantations that contain susceptible species or clones in regions favorable to disease establishment. Plantations of hybrid clones or elite-resistant varieties represent the most efficient strategy for disease control. In general, fungicide application is restricted to control of nursery diseases, and rarely for rust control in the field. *Eucalyptus* clonal forests offer potential to establish homogeneous, disease-free stands of high yield. Currently, the hybrid clones of *E. urograndis* (*E. urophylla* S.T. Blake x *E. grandis* Hill ex Maiden) are among the most planted material in Brazil because of their high adaptability, wood quality for pulping, and resistance to Chrysoporthe canker. Other interspecific hybrids have been developed in an attempt to incorporate specific traits from other species, such as drought and frost tolerance, disease resistance, and high pulp yield. Primary breeding strategies are based on selecting species/provenances, coupled with individual genetic selection within populations, to capture the natural variability among and within populations. The recurrent selection method and its variants are applied to genetic improvement of *Eucalyptus* to obtain new clones of interspecific and intraspecific hybrids. Backcrosses, mutation induction, and polyploidy have also been applied to develop new genotypes. These strategies help ensure the sustainability of commercial plantations and the continual contributions from the improvement program through the selection in advanced generations and superior clones. With interspecific breeding to incorporate contrasting traits, it is usually necessary to make continued backcrosses to the species of interest as the recurrent donor to recover the desired forest features and industrial properties. For each breeding generation, it is essential to perform disease screening under controlled conditions to select disease-resistant genetic materials for commercial cloning or identifying sources of resistance for other crosses. For disease-resistance evaluations, reliable inoculation protocols are essential. In recent years, approximately 90 percent of elite-clones were susceptible to at least one of the main diseases tested using artificially inoculations under controlled conditions. Determining the genetic basis and the mode of inheritance of disease resistance is an essential step to obtain disease-resistant plant material for the breeding program. The breeding strategy varies according to the inheritance model. To reduce losses caused by rust (*Puccinia psidii*), efforts have been conducted to select and plant rust-resistant clones and determine the mode of inheritance. In *E. grandis*, the segregation pattern of resistance to rust is controlled by one locus with major effect, *Ppr*-1 (*P. psidii* resistance, gene 1), which is tightly linked to RAPD marker AT9-917. Controlled inoculations of other families allowed the identification of a homozygous, rust-resistant mother parent of *E. grandis*, currently used to obtain rust-resistant progenies, regardless of pollen source. Screen tests for resistance to Ceratocystis wilt (caused by *Ceratocystis fimbriata*) showed a continuous variation in resistance, ranging from highly susceptible to highly resistant, indicating a pattern typical of horizontal resistance. Additional studies are needed to determine the genetic basis, the new sources of resistance, and the inheritance patterns of resistance of *Eucalyptus* spp. to other diseases. Furthermore, a better understanding of the population genetic structure of pathogens is needed to determine the role of pathogen variability in disease resistance that is targeted by the breeding strategies.

[1] Suzano Papel e Celulose.
[2] Departamento de Fitopatologia/BIOAGRO, Universidade Federal de Viçosa (UFV), 36570-000, Viçosa, MG, Brazil. Corresponding author: edivalzauza@suzano.com.br.

Fusiform Rust Resistance - Southern Pines

Fusiform rust canker on loblolly pine.
(Photo: J. Bronson)

Identification of Pathogen Avirulence Genes in the Fusiform Rust Pathosystem

John M. Davis,[1,2] Katherine E. Smith,[2,3] Amanda Pendleton,[2] Jason A. Smith,[1] and C. Dana Nelson[3]

Abstract

The *Cronartium quercuum* f.sp. *fusiforme* (*Cqf*) whole genome sequencing project will enable identification of avirulence genes in the most devastating pine fungal pathogen in the southeastern United States. Amerson and colleagues (unpublished) have mapped nine fusiform rust resistance genes in loblolly pine, suggesting that at least nine corresponding avirulence genes likely exist in the fungus. Identification of these avirulence genes would greatly facilitate selection of resistant pine genotypes for deployment to forest plantations. Based on work in other rusts, we anticipate avirulence genes may encode secreted effector proteins that interact directly or indirectly with host resistance proteins. As a step toward testing this hypothesis, we genetically mapped the *Cqf* avirulence gene *Avr1*, which specifically interacts with the *Fr1* resistance gene, with the goal of integrating this map with the *Cqf* genome sequence assembly so that *Avr1* can be identified. Once *Avr1* is identified, we want to determine its allele frequency across geographically defined hazard maps for fusiform rust, to help guide genotype deployment by growers. We view identification of *Avr1* as our initial case study, guiding our strategy to efficiently identify additional avirulence genes in *Cqf* that in turn can be used to guide plantation deployment of all genotypes currently represented in southern pine breeding programs.

---

[1] School of Forest Resources and Conservation, University of Florida, Gainesville, FL 32611.
[2] Plant Molecular and Cellular Biology Program, University of Florida, Gainesville, FL 32611.
[3] Southern Institute of Forest Genetics, U.S. Forest Service, Saucier, MS 39574.
Corresponding author: jmdavis@ufl.edu.

Tandem Selection for Fusiform Rust Disease Resistance to Develop a Clonal Elite Breeding Population of Loblolly Pine

Steve McKeand,[1] Saul Garcia,[1] Josh Steiger,[1] Jim Grissom,[1] Ross Whetten,[1] and Fikret Isik[1]

Abstract

The elite breeding populations of loblolly pine (*Pinus taeda* L.) in the North Carolina State University Cooperative Tree Improvement Program are intensively managed for short-term genetic gain. Fusiform rust disease, caused by the fungus *Cronartium quercuum* f. sp. *fusiforme*, is the most economically important disease in pine plantations across the southeastern United States, causing multi-million dollar annual losses. In order to cull susceptible crosses and progeny prior to field testing, seedling progeny of 51 crosses were challenged with bulked inocula of the fusiform rust fungus at the U.S. Department of Agriculture Forest Service Resistance Screening Center in Ashville, North Carolina. We used a high spore load (50,000 spores/ml) of a broad-base field inoculum that covered the entire range of deployment for these pine genotypes. Through this culling, we eliminated genotypes that may be susceptible in the field to rust, and we are able to focus on selection for growth and quality traits in the remaining population. Overall mean disease incidence was 48 percent, which was ideal for assessing genetic variation for a binary trait. Family disease means ranged from 5 percent to 81 percent. We fit a generalized linear mixed model and logit link function to partition observed variance in the response variable (1=gall, 0=no gall) into causal (additive and dominance) components. The genetic control for disease incidence was very high, with family mean heritability of 0.95, and the individual tree narrow-sense heritability was 0.5. Substantial genetic gains can be achieved for fusiform rust disease incidence in loblolly pine in a relatively short time (6 months) using greenhouse screening protocols. Subsequent to the greenhouse screening, we cloned 2,442 full-sib progeny that were non-galled for field testing to carry out selection for growth and stem quality traits. Cloned progeny have been established in various locations in 2009 and 2010 using a resolvable alpha incomplete block design.

[1] North Carolina State University, Cooperative Tree Improvement Program, Raleigh, NC 27695-8002.
Corresponding author: Steve_McKeand@ncsu.edu.

Bulked Fusiform Rust Inocula and Fr Gene Interactions in Loblolly Pine

Fikret Isik,[1] Henry Amerson,[1] Saul Garcia,[1] Ross Whetten,[1] and Steve McKeand[1]

Abstract

Fusiform rust disease in loblolly (*Pinus taeda* L.) and slash (*Pinus elliottii* Engelm. var *elliottii*) pine plantations in the southern United States causes multi-million dollar annual losses. The disease is endemic to the region. The fusiform rust fungus (*Cronartium quercuum* sp. *fusiforme*) infects young pine trees and develops galls on stems and branches. Single pathogen gene and single host (pine) gene interactions can predict phenotype (disease expression) with high accuracy (Wilcox et al. 1996). There are nine known pathotype-specific Fr genes in seven loblolly pine families. The R alleles condition resistance to specific genotypes of the fungal pathogen while r alleles do not condition for resistance.

We investigated interactions of R genotypes (seedlings bearing R allele) and r genotypes (seedling bearing r allele) of seven families with 10 bulked inocula. Our specific objectives were to (i) understand the response of pine R and r genotypes to different bulked inocula and (ii) assess the level of virulence in the fungus population that are able to overcome resistance in pine families. Such results would have significant effect on the breeding and disease management in pine plantations. Half-sib progeny of seven loblolly pine families were challenged with 10 different bulked inocula of the fusiform rust fungus and assessed for disease incidence in greenhouse. Progeny of these families were genotyped to identify carriers of known alleles, "R" for resistance or "r" for lack of resistance/susceptibility.

Significant differences were detected among bulked inocula with regards to their ability to incite disease at the family level (F test Pr<0.001). Bulked inocula were also significantly different in virulence against R (Pr=0.002) and r genotypes (Pr=0.007). Across the inocula, disease levels differed significantly among half-sib families (Pr<0.001). Seedlings that carried only r alleles typically exhibited higher disease rates than did carriers of R alleles within each family. Interaction of bulked inocula with R genotypes from seven families was highly significant (<0.001), but it was not significant with r genotypes because regardless of inocula, r genotypes developed high levels of disease. However, the response of R genotypes varied across inocula. The magnitude of difference (odds ratio) between the R vs. r genotypes for disease incidence within each family varied from 1.0 times to 32 times. The results demonstrate that greenhouse assessments of pathogen virulence against known fusiform rust resistance alleles can detect virulence variation among inocula. Such virulence assessments should be effective guides for the field deployment of plants carrying specific R alleles to regions where inocula samples are observed to show low or no corresponding virulence.

Literature Cited

Wilcox, P.L.; Amerson, H.V.; Kuhlman, E.G.; Liu, B.H.; O'Malley, D.M.; Sederoff, R.R. 1996. Detection of a major gene for resistance to fusiform rust disease in loblolly pine by genomic mapping. Proceedings of the National Academy of Science USA. 93: 3859–3864.

---

[1] North Carolina State University, Cooperative Tree Improvement Program, Raleigh, NC 27695.
Corresponding author: fisik@ncsu.edu.

Selection of Loblolly Pine Varieties Resistant to Fusiform Rust for Commercial Deployment

Andy Benowicz[1] and Robert J. Weir[2]

Abstract

Commercial production of loblolly pine (*Pinus taeda* L.) varieties through somatic embryogenesis has been increasing significantly over the last several years. Large-scale operational plantations have been established since 2004 across the Southeastern United States, while the oldest field tests are now at mid-rotation. Extensive surveys of fusiform rust (*Cronartium quercuum* f.sp. *fusiforme*) infection rates in over 80 operational varietal plantations and demonstration plots were conducted in eight southeastern states. The surveyed stands were 3- to 9-years old. The operational data confirm that the selection program for rust resistance in loblolly pine varieties has been very successful. Genotypes characterized by fast growth rate and tentative resistance to fusiform rust are identified at a young age in several field test sites. Cryogenic tissue from the selected genotypes is used to produce seedlings for tests involving artificial inoculations. Artificial inoculation tests of CellFor-produced loblolly pine clones have been performed by the U.S. Department of Agriculture resistance screening center in Asheville, North Carolina over the last 8 years. A number of loblolly pine clones of Atlantic Coastal Plains and Western Gulf origin were exposed to high concentrations of fusiform rust inocula. The inocula were developed from aeciospores collected in three regions representing the eastern, central and western distribution range of loblolly pine. The inocula from the three regions were used in separate tests. Commercial varieties ranked as resistant or very resistant, based on field data and artificial inoculation tests, show less than 0.5 percent stem infection rates, based on all 56 surveyed operational plantations and demonstration plots they were present in.

---

[1] CellFor, 4-6772 Oldfield Road, Victoria, BC, V8M 2A3.
[2] CellFor, Portland, Maine.
Corresponding author: abenowicz@gmail.com.

Resistance Breeding Programs

Resistance to Ceratocystis wilt in eucalyptus, caused by *C. fimbriata* in a 5 year-old plantation, in Minas Geratis, Brazil. A resistant clone is on the left. On the right is a susceptible clone (*Eucalyptus grandis x urophylla* hybrid clones). (Photo: A.C. Alfenas)

The American Chestnut Foundation Breeding Program

F.V. Hebard[1]

Introduction

Chestnut blight, incited by *Cryphonectria parasistica*, devastated American chestnut (*Castanea dentata* (Borkh.) Marsh) in the first half of the 20th century, killing approximately 4 billion dominant and codominant trees. Millions of small sprouts still persist throughout the botanical range of *C. dentata*. Most are not infected and do not flower, except for short periods, before the shoot is killed by blight. Around the fringes of the botanical range, isolated trees can escape infection for prolonged periods, reaching diameters of about 50 cm at breast height (dbh). In the heart of the range, fewer than 20 large (>33 cm dbh) trees are known to persist that have survived blight infection for longer than 10 years (Griffin et al. 1983). Those trees are termed large, surviving American chestnut trees. Some have low levels of blight resistance, but not enough for very many of their progeny to persist. They currently are being bred for higher levels of blight resistance (Griffin 2000).

Without active control measures, such as breeding for resistance and introduction of hypoviruses, it generally has been assumed that American chestnut will become extinct in its native range due to blight and the paucity of reproduction. However, the rate of extinction is quite low and numerous sprouts persist throughout the range (Scrivani 2011). These often flower for short periods when exposed to high light levels and serve as a reservoir of germplasm. However, the persistence of this reservoir is not assured in the face of the changing environment, and continued monitoring is necessary. Increasing deer populations currently are a major threat to long-term survival of American chestnut sprout clumps (Burke and Wilber, unpublished [2]).

Breeding for blight resistance was initiated around 1930, but those early programs were abandoned as hopeless in the early 1960s because they had been unable to combine the forest competitiveness of American chestnut with the chosen sources of blight resistance, oriental chestnut species. However, the early breeding programs did identify species with blight resistance and develop methods for making crosses, cultivating seedlings, and screening them for blight resistance.

Charles Burnham (1981) first hypothesized that the blight resistance of Chinese chestnut, *C. mollissima* Blume, could be backcrossed into American chestnut. Backcrossing is the method of choice for introgressing a simply inherited trait into an otherwise acceptable cultivar. One of Burnham's assumptions in 1981 was that blight resistance is controlled by a single factor. Subsequently, in 1986, Burnham, French, and Rutter (Burnham et al. 1986) accepted Clapper's (1952) conjecture that blight resistance is controlled by two incompletely dominant factors. Burnham, French, and Rutter were the principals who started the American Chestnut Foundation (TACF) in 1983 to facilitate testing of the Burnham hypothesis.

Burnham recruited Lawrence Inman to help with design of the program. Inman (1987) proposed breeding populations of chestnut at multiple locations throughout the American chestnut range to preserve local adaptation and increase genetic diversity. He also proposed using multiple sources of blight resistance. Inman (1989) suggested restricting local collections to within a radius of 16 kilometers. Following Namkoong (1991), Hebard (1994) proposed breeding each source of blight resistance with 20 different American chestnut trees for each cycle of backcrossing; on average, 20 individuals would capture alleles occurring at frequencies greater than 0.05 (=1/20).

[1] The American Chestnut Foundation, 29010 Hawthorne Dr., Meadowview, VA 24361. Fred@acf.org
[2] Burke, K.L.; Wilbur, H.M. Unpublished. Effects of white-tailed deer on growth and mortality of *Castanea dentata* and *Acer pensylvanicum*.

Hebard (2006) specified that intercrossing after backcrossing, whose purpose is to restore true breeding by creating and identifying segregants homozygous for resistance alleles, should be restricted to single sources of blight resistance. It would be impossible to eliminate alleles for susceptibility at the F_2 stage if different donor trees had different loci with alleles for resistance.

Hebard (2006) presented results to date for the TACF breeding program, and discussed methods in depth. The purpose of the present report is to update the overall results and to discuss population management aspects of the program. While the TACF breeding program occurs in multiple locations, the most advanced crosses are located at our principal research facility in Meadowview, Virginia (fig.1). Results given below were gathered at Meadowview.

Figure 1—View of the American Chestnut Foundation's Price Research Farm from its Bryan Research Farm. The Foundation has four farms in Meadowview covering about 150 acres; the other two farms are B_3-F_2 seedling seed orchards of about 15 acres each.

Results and Discussion

Variation in Pathogenicity Between Virulent Strains of *Cryphonectria parasitica*

Blight resistance is evaluated using two strains of the blight fungus, both virulent, but one, SG2-3, of mild pathogenicity and one, Ep155, of high pathogenicity. Cankers incited by the highly pathogenic Ep155 differ in size most prominently between chestnut trees with high and intermediate levels of blight resistance; whereas cankers incited by the mildly pathogenic SG2-3 differ in size most prominently between trees with intermediate and non-existent levels of blight resistance (fig. 2). Thus, a wider range of resistance can be distinguished using both strains rather than just one alone.

The experiment summarized in fig. 2 employed a set of trees of various ages and levels of blight resistance that were planted in a randomized, complete-block design over several years and inoculated in 1 year, using Ep155 and SG2-3. The three main effects were highly significant (table 1).

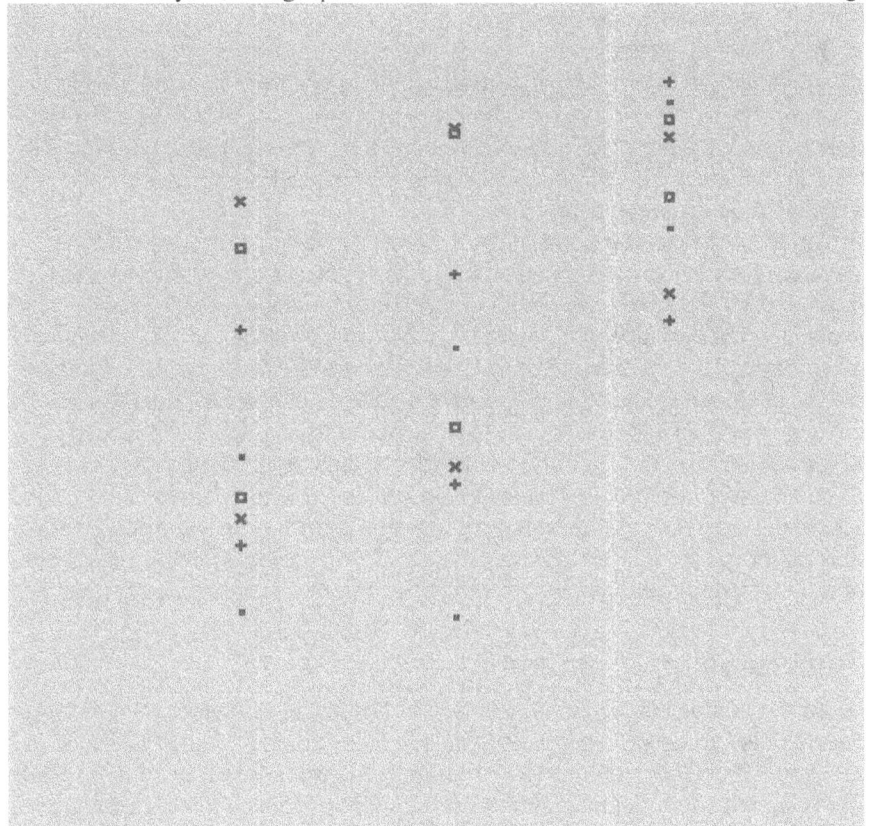

Figure 2—Mean canker length versus resistance for chestnut trees of different ages inoculated with two virulent strains of *Cryphonectria parasitica*, one highly pathogenic (Ep155) and the other slightly pathogenic (SG 2-3).

Table 1—Analysis of variance of chestnut blight canker length 2 months after inoculation, testing the effect of blight resistance (cross type), tree age, and inoculum pathogenicity

Source	DF	Sum of Squares	Mean Square	F Ratio	Prob > F
Block	5	45.99630	9.1993	3.9453	0.0026
Cross Type	2	286.67139	143.3357	61.4732	<.0001
Age	3	60.11460	20.0382	8.5939	<.0001
Cross Type*Age	6	39.19499	6.5325	2.8016	0.0144
Inoculum	1	346.72540	346.7254	148.7021	<.0001
Cross Type*Inoculum	2	19.39003	9.6950	4.1580	0.0183
Age*Inoculum	3	7.23204	2.4107	1.0339	0.3808
Cross Type*Age*Inoculum	6	14.61847	2.4364	1.0449	0.4007
Model	28	889.5520	31.7697	13.6253	
Error	105	244.8262	2.3317		
C. Total	133	1134.3782			<.0001

The effect of age in the experiment was confounded with shading of young trees by older trees. This occurred because spacing (3.0 m x 1.5 m) had not been set widely enough to avoid shading. So "age" was treated as a fixed effect in analysis of variance. Cross type and inoculum pathogenicity also were treated as fixed effects. Nevertheless, the "age" factor is an environmental effect, and illustrates (once again) that environment, broadly considered, has a major effect on expansion of chestnut blight cankers, and thus assessments of blight resistance.

The significant (p=0.014) interaction of cross type with age (table 1) occurred because age did not affect canker size on American chestnut as much as on Chinese chestnut and on their F_1 hybrid (fig. 2). In this experiment, canker sizes were closer overall to American rather than Chinese chestnut. The reverse occurred in another experiment conducted in another year (described below), again illustrating effects of environment on canker expansion.

Inoculum pathogenicity affected canker size more in the F_1s than the pure species (p=0.018), which is to be expected as rates of canker expansion reach lower and upper limits in Chinese and American chestnut, respectively. An idealized shape of canker expansion versus resistance is a sigmoid curve, where the plateaus are the upper and lower limits of canker expansion. Thus, even though rates of linear canker expansion have fairly uniform variances throughout their range, and are appropriate metrics for resistance, host variety x fungus strain interactions can occur (Huang et al. 1996); however, this is not host specificity associated with avirulence genes, which has not been detected yet for chestnut blight. Likewise, the overall non-linearity of canker size with resistance can also lead to association of quantitative trait loci (QTL) for blight resistance with only one strain of the blight fungus. For instance, in fig. 2, 3-year-old trees might show a resistance QTL with SG2-3 but not Ep155. That same locus might show a lack of "virulence" for SG2-3 but not Ep155 in 1-year-old trees. I conclude that care must be exercised in analyzing variety x strain interactions for chestnut blight.

Current Stage of Backcrossing Program

At Meadowview, we have almost completed advancing two sources of blight resistance, derived from the 'Clapper' and 'Graves' first backcrosses (Hebard 2006) into 30 B_3-F_2 lines each of American chestnut. We have planted about 58,600 such nuts in two seedling seed orchards; about 35,400 remain after rogueing (table 2). As selection and rogueing continue, these will be reduced to about 500 plants, which should occur within 3 to 5 years.

Hopefully we will be able to select for true breeding for blight resistance in these B_3-F_2 trees. Simulations based on patterns of inheritance of resistance in straight F_2s and B_1-F_2s indicate that it would be difficult to select for homozygous resistance to blight caused by two loci and impossible with three loci, due to overlap of phenotypic resistance classes. Analysis of those populations and others suggested that two or three loci control blight resistance in Chinese chestnut (Hebard 2006, Kubisiak et al. 1997). Three QTLs for blight resistance were found in the F_2 mapping population originally genotyped by Kubisiak et al. in 1997 when it was regenotyped with several thousand new markers (Kubisiak et al., unpublished[3]). Additional populations have been genotyped and phenotyped and data are being analyzed. Markers fairly close to these loci might facilitate identification of trees homozygous for blight resistance. In the meantime, the most blight-resistant individuals are being selected based on results from inoculation of their open-pollinated B_3-F_3 progeny in orchard settings, after initial selection in the parents, also based on inoculation. B_3-F_3 progeny additionally are being evaluated in wooded settings for forest performance. It currently is unclear whether those forest tests will contribute to selection of B_3-F_2 parents.

The Rationale of Screening B_3-F_2s for Blight Resistance

We use a gradual process to select for blight resistance in our B_3-F_2 seed orchards. A more rapid process would have to be more stringent, which would kill too many good trees.

---

[3] Kubisiak, T.L.; Nelson, C.D.; Staton, M.E.; Zhebentyayeva, T.; Smith, C.; Olukolu, B.A.; Fang, G.C.; Hebard, F.V.; Anagnostakis, S.; Wheeler, N.; Sisco, P.; Abbott, A.G.; Sederoff, R.R. Unpublished. A transcriptome-based genetic map of Chinese chestnut, (*Castanea mollissima*), and identification of regions of segmental homology with peach (*Prunus persica*).

We start by inoculating 2-year-old seedlings with the SG2-3 strain of the blight fungus and selecting those with small cankers. Although virulent and capable of killing American chestnut trees, the SG2-3 strain is considerably less pathogenic than the Ep155 strain, as shown above. Previous tests, including that summarized in fig. 2 and table 1 above, indicated that even 2-year-old Chinese chestnut trees are most likely killed by Ep155, whereas most 2-year-old trees survive inoculation with SG2-3 if they possess levels of blight resistance equal to or greater than that of F_1s between Chinese and American. Such F_1s typically are intermediate in blight resistance between the two parents. The results of the SG2-3 inoculations enable us to eliminate about 60 to 70 percent of the B_3-F_2s, depending on the size of the tested trees and the year.

We do not include controls such as Chinese chestnut in the B_3-F_2 seed orchards. The small SG2-3 cankers after the first season of canker expansion on the selections could not get any smaller on Chinese chestnut, so their inclusion as controls for that period would not be informative. Chinese chestnut trees could be informative in later years if left in the orchard, but would then start to produce undesired pollen. The B_3-F_2 orchards also are designed to produce seed with maximum genetic diversity over long periods by maximizing distance between sibs, and the design appropriate for that goal cannot provide statistically and experimentally sound evidence of blight resistance in the B_3-F_2s.

We make additional selections over the next few years following inoculation by examining cankers on the preliminary selections. However, as outlined above, we have been intending to make the final selections among the B_3-F_2 trees by testing the blight resistance and performance of their B_3-F_3 progeny in orchard and, possibly, forest settings.

Results of the First Season of Canker Expansion in an Orchard Test of Blight Resistance in B_3-F_3 Chestnut Trees Planted Using a Formal Experimental Design

In 2008, we harvested our first crop of B_3-F_3s large enough to test formally in both the orchard and forest using an experimental design and control plants. The orchard test was planted in 2009 using a completely randomized design. In retrospect, an incomplete block design would have enabled more accurate selection of superior parents, and we subsequently changed to that. In June 2011, we inoculated that first test planted in 2009 and measured canker lengths in December 2011, using methods described by Hebard (2006).

Table 3 shows statistics for cankers incited by both Ep155 and SG2-3 on the different cross types in the experiment. The controls for canker sizes, ranked from susceptible to resistant, were American, B_2, F_1 plus B_1-F_2, B_1xChinese, and Chinese. (The backcross controls are imperfect resistance standards, as mistakes in selection can lessen their resistance). We expected the B_3-F_2 selections in the seed orchard that produced these progeny to have blight resistance equal to or greater than that of F_1s and B_1-F_2s, since those B_3-F_2s had been screened only using strain SG2-3. If this first expectation were met, one would then expect their B_3-F_3 progeny from open pollination to have mean canker lengths intermediate between the F_1/B_1-F_2s and the B_1xCs. However, instead, cankers on the B_3-F_3s were similar to or slightly longer than those on B_1-F_2s. Reasons this may have occurred include that pollen is still being produced by unselected as well as selected B_3-F_2 parents in the seed orchards, that selection is not complete, and/or that there was some degradation of factors for blight resistance during backcrossing.

Out of 583 trees tested, there were 95 B_3-F_3s with small cankers for both strains Ep155 and SG2-3, where small cankers are those less than 5 cm in length. Normally, one would expect trees with such small cankers to have a high level of blight resistance. However, there was dominance toward small cankers in this test, leading to a higher frequency of trees with small cankers in the B_1-F_2 progenies than is observed in most tests of F2s. We observed 35 out of 171 B_1-F_2s with small cankers, where usually we would expect to observe about 10. We expect many of these small cankers on the B_1-F_2s to start expanding in 2012. How much that occurs also in the 95 B_3-F_3s with small Ep155 cankers will be interesting to follow.

The phenotypic dominance toward small cankers, after the first season of canker expansion in this test, also is reflected in the bimodal distribution of canker sizes. The bimodality is most evident for the Ep155 cankers in the B_3-F_3 and B_1-F_2 crosses in table 3, where there is a peak in the 0-5 cm class and another in the 10-15 cm class. The peak at 0-5 cm occurred because cankers in the 0-5 cm class cannot get any smaller, so their numbers pile up when phenotypic dominance is toward small cankers. There was even more clustering in the small canker class for the SG2-3 cankers, which is expected given its lesser pathogenicity. However, the ranking of mean canker size for cross type was the same for both strains.

The predominance of small cankers led to a significant fungus strain by cross type interaction, since the SG2-3 and Ep155 cankers on Chinese chestnut were similar in size, while in the other cross types, SG2-3 cankers were about 6-8 cm shorter than Ep155 cankers. There was no interaction between strain and families nested within cross type. Another effect of very small cankers was that the variance of canker length was reduced in Chinese chestnut compared to the other crosses, especially for strain SG2-3. The unequal variances (heteroscedasticity) for strain SG2-3 increased the likelihood that differences between cross types and families would be declared statistically significant, making declarations of significance suspect for SG2-3.

Table 4 shows canker length statistics for individual families within the various cross types. The Ep155 cankers yielded significant differences in canker size for the more resistant trees while the SG2-3 cankers yielded significant differences for the more susceptible trees (although, again, the significance of the SG2-3 differences is suspect). Twenty-one of 36 B_3-F_3 families had significantly ($p<0.05$) smaller SG2-3 cankers than the American chestnut family. The B_3-F_2 parents of the remaining 16 families are candidates for rogueing.

Discussion of B_3-F_3 Canker Results

This crop of B_3-F_3s was significantly more blight resistant than American chestnut, roughly comparable in resistance to Chinese x American F_1s or backcross F_2s, in the aggregate. None of the families had as high a level of blight resistance as Chinese chestnut, but many contained highly blight-resistant individuals as of the end of the first season of canker expansion. This is roughly in accord with expectation, given that selection is not finished in the B_3-F_2 orchards from which the nuts were harvested. The best families had resistance roughly comparable to that of crosses of selected straight backcrosses with Chinese chestnut, which is what we would expect in crosses of Chinese chestnut with the pollen being produced in the orchards. However, we have not eliminated the possibility that some of the blight resistance of Chinese chestnut has been lost during backcrossing.

Characterization of Breeding Populations

The effective population size, denoted N_e, is used commonly to estimate minimal sizes needed to maintain long-term viability of populations, such as species. Using quantitative genetic considerations, Franklin (1980) estimated that an N_e of 50 is needed to avoid immediate collapse of a population due to inbreeding depression, and an N_e of 500 is needed to offset loss of alleles by genetic drift with recruitment of new alleles by mutation. N_e can be estimated as the harmonic mean of population sizes, given the other assumptions of Hardy-Weinberg equilibrium.

To compute N_e as a harmonic mean, we need the number of individuals at each generation. The size of the original American chestnut population can be considered infinite for this computation; whereas, the population goes through a bottleneck at the straight backcross stage. The population size at straight backcross was set at 20 using Namkoong's considerations, as mentioned above in the introduction. Hebard (2002) estimated from first principles that obtaining nine F_2 progeny from a straight backcross mother tree gives a 95 percent chance of capturing all her alleles. Thus the size of the F_2 generation is nine multiplied by 20 American chestnut lines per source of blight resistance, or 180. The size of backcross F_3 and subsequent filial generations also can be considered infinite, but were limited to several thousand in simulations of inbreeding to be discussed momentarily. Using these numbers of individuals, the N_e of 20 lines of American chestnut, computed from the harmonic mean, is about 72. It would increase if more than one individual per line were retained as a parent of the backcross F_2 generation (fig. 3), which is generally the case.

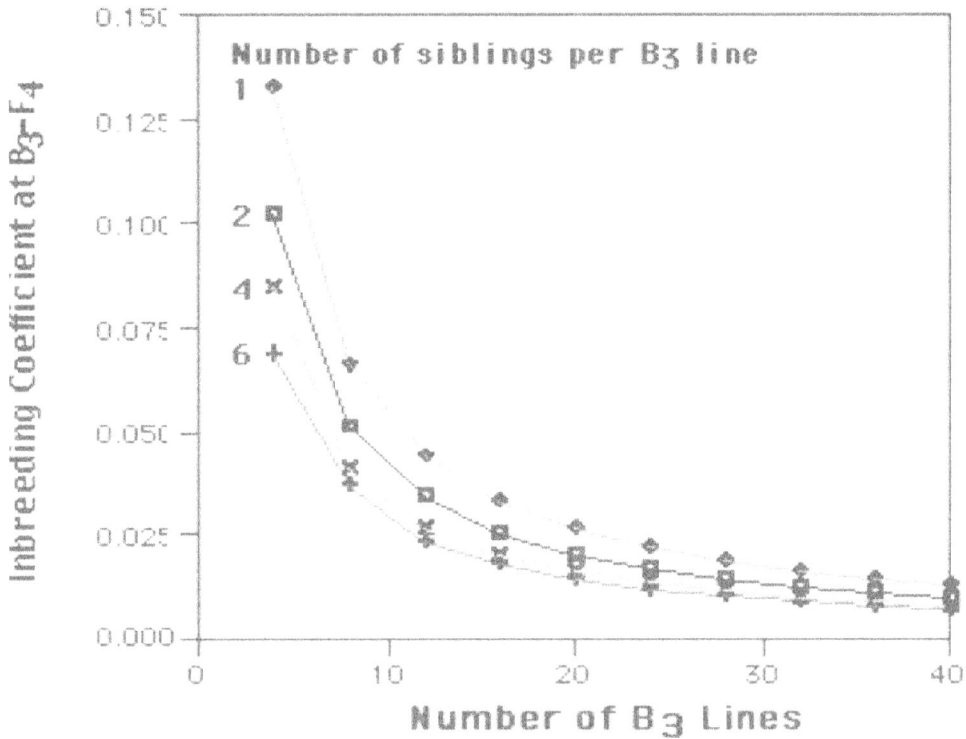

Figure 3—Effect of the number of siblings per B_3 line on the inbreeding coefficient at B_3-F_4 versus the number of American chestnut lines at B_3, for partial diallel mating at B_3 with four lines per diallel, ten B_3-F_2 offspring per line, and for random mating thereafter.

The inbreeding effective population size can be estimated independently using the inbreeding coefficient of a population. For some breeding scenarios, a harmonic mean cannot be used to compute N_e, but inbreeding coefficients can. Hebard (2002) computed inbreeding coefficients by 'brute force' simulation. The results of similar simulations are shown in table 5, which illustrate the effect of TACF's Chapter breeding program on the overall N_e of the breeding population at B_3-F_4 (each chapter has a goal of breeding 20 American lines for at least one source of blight resistance).

Two sources of blight resistance, derived from the 'Clapper' and 'Graves' trees, constitute most of the breeding stock in the TACF program. We probably will be able to breed at five locations for each source, which would make the N_e of the overall breeding stock about 500 (table 5). Of course, selection at loci for resistance will decrease N_e, as will other violations of Hardy-Weinberg assumptions, such as skewed numbers of progeny per parent. This degradation will be offset somewhat by the chapters using more advanced breeding stock than that simulated for table 5. We plan to measure N_e in the breeding stock to compare with these predictions and to guide further breeding. We have some baseline data from the native population of American chestnut from a rather thorough sampling of the species (Kubisiak and Roberds 2006). DNA from that sampling also is available for further probing.

A third source of blight resistance, derived from the Nanking cultivar of Chinese chestnut, is being advanced in 20 American lines at Meadowview and a few other chapters. This will increase the N_e of our breeding population. We also hope to expand other sources of blight resistance to an N_e of 72 at various chapters, as outlined by Hebard (2004).

The decision to introgress blight resistance into American chestnut from other species was based in part on the thought that no blight resistance existed in the native population. This does not appear to be the case (Griffin 2000). Burnham (1990) outlined a plan for utilizing this native resistance which we have been following in a breeding program at Meadowview separate from the backcrossing effort. Ironically, the relatively small progeny sizes required by the backcross method make it a more efficient means of generating a breeding population with large N_e than recurrent selection of large, surviving American chestnut trees after introgressing them into a broad enough base of American chestnut with no resistance to blight.

As the backcross breeding program has developed, we have come to realize that our goal is to enable the American chestnut to resume evolving on its own, as a wild species. Our B_3-F_3 'Restoration' chestnut trees should have sufficient blight resistance to produce numerous viable offspring in natural settings, although it is still unclear whether they will have levels of blight resistance similar to Chinese chestnut and whether even that level of blight resistance will enable them to be dominant forest trees. Their blight resistance could be increased further, if need be, by allowing them to intercross in forested settings with other sources of blight resistance, such as from additional backcross lines produced by TACF, from large, surviving American chestnut trees, or from other sources, such as transgenics or cisgenics. The intercrossing and further increase of progeny could be facilitated as needed by silvicultural interventions, but further intensive breeding in an orchard setting would not occur with the new base population, only with these supplemental populations. Hypovirulence may also play a role in re-establishing a self-sustaining breeding population, as Griffin (2000) and others have pointed out. The important point is that we are close to developing a self-sustaining breeding population of predominately American chestnut with a large enough N_e to constitute a viable species.

Table 2—Type and number of chestnut trees and planted nuts at TACF Meadowview Research Farms in May 2011, with the number of sources of blight resistance and the number of American chestnut lines in the breeding stock

Type of Tree	Number of		
	Nuts or Trees	Sources of Resistance	American Lines
American	1575		223
Chinese	1014	30	
Chinese x American: F_1	417	18	57
American x (Chinese x American): B_1	646	11	24
American x [American x (Chinese x American)]: B_2	1316	13	43
American x {American x [American x (Chinese x American)]}: B_3	2158	10	92
Am x (Am x {Am x [Am x (Ch x Am)]}): B_4	888	4	14
(Ch x Am) x (Ch x Am): F_2	213	5	5
[(Ch x Am) x (Ch x Am)] x [(Ch x Am) x (Ch x Am)]: F_3	5	1	1
[Am x (Ch x Am)] x [Am x (Ch x Am)]: B_1-F_2	625	7	10
{Am x [Am x (Ch x Am)]} x {Am x [Am x (Ch x Am)]}: B_2-F_2	667	9	12
B_2-F_3	31	1	1
(Am x {Am x [Am x (Ch x Am)]}) x (Am x {Am x [Am x (Ch x Am)]}): B_3-F_2	35394	2	51
B_3-F_3	3826	2	22
Clapper B_3 x Graves B_3: B_3-I_1	110	2	9
Chinese x [American x (Chinese x American)]: Chinese x B_1	167	3	7
Ch x {Am x [Am x (Ch x Am)]}: Chinese x B_2	72	1	2
Ch x (Am x {Am x [Am x (Ch x Am)]}): Chinese Test Suite x B_3	286	5	16
Chinese Test Suite x Chinese	1471	67	67
Chinese Test Suite x Japanese	46	2	2
Chinese Test Suite x European	43	1	1
Chinese Test Suite x Large, Surviving American	149	7	7
European x American: F_1	2	1	1
Japanese	3	1	1
Japanese x American: F_1	8	1	1
[(Japanese x American) x American]: B_1	5	1	1

(Table 2 continued)

Japanese x European	142	1	1
Japanese x Large, Surviving American	80	1	1
Castanea ozarkensis	27	5	5
Castanea pumila	21	1	2
Castanea seguinii	44	3	3
Seguin x American: F_1	48	3	3
[unclear]	54	2	2
Large Surviving American: F_1	486	12	37
Large Surviving American: B_1	506	8	14
Large Surviving American: B_2	72	3	4
Large Surviving American: B_3	161	1	1
Large Surviving American: F_2	266	13	11
Large Surviving American: F_3	270	1	2
Large Surviving American: I_1	1666	32	13
Large Surviving American: I_2	303	11	1
Large Surviving American: I_3	104	2	32
Large Surviving American advanced: F_1	804	12	25
Other	3		
Total	**56194**		

Table 3—Mean, standard deviation, and distribution of canker size classes (length in cm) for cankers incited by two strains of the blight fungus on cross types of American and Chinese chestnut in 2011

Cross Type	Fungus Strain	N	Least Squares Mean*	Standard Deviation	Length Class					
					0-5	5-10	10-15	15-20	20-25	25-
American	Ep155	20	17.4 A	3.4		1	4	11	4	
B₂	Ep155	44	14.5 AB	6.6	4	2	19	15	2	2
B₃-F₃	Ep155	583	11.7 BC	6.3	95	71	219	151	32	15
B₁-F₂	Ep155	171	10.9 BC	6.4	35	23	70	30	10	3
F₁	Ep155	8	10.0 ABCD	3.6		4	3	1		
B₁xC	Ep155	39	8.3 CD	5.0	12	9	16	2		
CxC	Ep155	38	3.2 D	2.3	27	11				
American	SG2-3	17	11.0 A	7.8	3	5	7		2	
B₂	SG2-3	45	5.3 B	5.6	32	5	6		2	
B₃-F₃	SG2-3	592	4.9 B	4.3	402	111	65	10	3	1
B₁-F₂	SG2-3	172	3.0 BC	3.9	126	26	18	2		
F₁	SG2-3	7	3.3 BC	1.7	6	1				
B₁xC	SG2-3	39	1.8 BC	2.6	35	3				
CxC	SG2-3	38	1.6 C	0.6	38		1			

* Means followed by the same letter are not significantly different at p<0.05 by a Tukey HSD test. The declarations are suspect for strain SG2-3 due to heteroscedasticity.

231

Table 4—Means for length (in cm) of cankers incited by two strains of the blight fungus on individual families of American and Chinese chestnut in 2011

Cross Type	Mother*	Father	Source of Resistance	N	Grand Mean	Least Square Means**	
						Strain Ep155	Strain SG2-3
American	PL1-08	op	none	16	14.4	17.4 A	11.4 A
B_3-F_3	D5-26-54	op	Clapper	14	12.5	17.0 AB	8.0 ABC
B_2	B2208	AN17	Nanking:none	5	11.7	16.4 ABCD	7.0 ABCD
B_3-F_3	D5-29-124	op	Clapper	1	11.2	12.1 ABCDE	10.4 ABCD
B_3-F_3	D3-28-10	op	Clapper	11	11.0	16.2 ABC	5.8 ABCD
B_2	TM474	A1530	Nanking:none	8	10.8	15.0 ABC	6.6 ABCD
B_3-F_3	D5-17-89	op	Clapper	20	10.6	13.8 ABC	7.5 AB
B_3-F_3	D5-19-72	op	Clapper	22	10.2	14.2 ABC	6.1 ABCD
B_3-F_3	D5-18-95	op	Clapper	7	10.0	11.4 ABCDE	8.6 ABCD
B_3-F_3	D5-18-50	op	Clapper	10	9.8	14.1 ABCD	5.4 ABCD
B_3-F_3	D5-27-108	op	Clapper	17	9.3	13.8 ABC	4.7 BCD
B_3-F_3	D5-27-101	op	Clapper	29	9.3	14.1 ABC	4.5 BCD
B_3-F_3	D5-26-131	op	Clapper	32	9.3	13.1 ABC	5.4 BCD
B_3-F_3	D5-29-50	op	Clapper	10	9.1	11.9 ABCDE	6.3 ABCD
B_2	B210	A1117	Nanking:none	15	9.1	13.4 ABC	4.9 BCD
B_3-F_3	D5-25-49	op	Clapper	18	9.1	12.2 ABCD	6.1 ABCD
B_3-F_3	D5-18-101	op	Clapper	12	8.9	14.1 ABC	3.8 BCD
B_3-F_3	D5-29-3	op	Clapper	23	8.9	13.5 ABC	4.2 BCD
B_1-F_2	TM538	TM158	Nanking:Nanking	7	8.8	14.8 ABCD	2.7 BCD
B_3-F_3	D5-22-17	op	Clapper	15	8.8	13.1 ABCD	4.5 BCD
B_3-F_3	D5-27-36	op	Clapper	24	8.8	13.0 ABC	4.6 BCD
B_3-F_3	D5-26-94	op	Clapper	28	8.6	13.0 ABC	4.2 BCD
B_3-F_3	D6-26-27	op	Clapper	37	8.6	12.9 ABC	4.3 BCD
B_3-F_3	D5-18-25	op	Clapper	26	8.4	13.0 ABC	3.7 BCD
B_3-F_3	D5-17-122	op	Clapper	1	8.2	10.4 ABCDE	6.0 ABCD
B_2	CY554	MB190	Nanking:none	16	8.0	13.1 ABC	2.8 BCD
B_3-F_3	D2-29-44	op	Clapper	24	8.0	11.6 ABCD	4.3 BCD
B_1-F_2	B2354	TM672	Nanking:Nanking	117	7.9	11.7 ABC	4.2 BCD
B_3-F_3	D5-30-24	op	Clapper	20	7.7	11.7 ABCD	3.6 BCD
B_3-F_3	D5-27-95	op	Clapper	32	7.4	11.7 ABCD	3.1 BCD
B_3-F_3	D4-28-31	op	Clapper	4	7.2	12.0 ABCDE	2.4 ABCD
B_1xC	JB478	MuChin1	MuChinX:MuChin1	1	7.1	13.3 ABCDE	0.8 ABCD
B_1-F_2	TM158	TM538	Nanking:Nanking	21	7.1	10.5 ABCDE	3.6 BCD
B_3-F_3	D2-26-72	op	Clapper	23	6.9	10.3 ABCDE	3.6 BCD
B_3-F_3	D1-27-25	op	Clapper	12	6.8	11.7 ABCDE	2.0 BCD
F_1	TA3	MB190	Kuling:none	1	6.7	9.5 ABCDE	3.8 ABCD
F_1	KY106	MB190	Meiling:none	6	6.7	10.5 ABCDE	2.9 BCD
B_3-F_3	D5-22-86	op	Clapper	17	6.7	11.2 ABCDE	2.2 BCD

(Table 4 continued)

B3-F3	D5-25-147	op	Clapper	11	6.6	ABCDE	9.9	3.4	BCD
B3-F3	D5-18-2	op	Clapper	7	6.5	ABCDE	9.1	3.8	ABCD
B3-F3	D5-30-11	op	Clapper	22	6.4	ABCDE	10.5	2.3	CD
B3-F3	D9-26-36	op	Clapper	3	5.9	ABCDE	7.4	4.4	ABCD
B1xC	TM672	GR119	Nanking:Nanking	18	5.7	ABCDE	9.1	2.4	BCD
B1-F2	B2275	B293	72-211:72-211	10	5.5	ABCDE	9.3	1.7	BCD
B1-F2	B2430	B2275	72-211:72-211	13	5.5	ABCDE	8.4	2.6	BCD
B3-F3	D2-28-76	op	Clapper	14	5.3	BCDE	7.9	2.8	BCD
B3-F3	D5-17-130	op	Clapper	9	5.2	ABCDE	7.9	2.5	BCD
B3-F3	D8-26-69	op	Clapper	16	5.2	CDE	8.0	2.4	BCD
B3-F3	D2-26-66	op	Clapper	3	5.0	ABCDE	8.2	1.7	ABCD
B3-F3	D2-28-52	op	Clapper	3	4.3	ABCDE	5.9	2.7	ABCD
B1xC	B2239	GR119	Nanking:Nanking	6	4.2	ABCDE	6.4	1.9	BCD
B1xC	JB5	MuChin1	MuChinX:MuChin1	3	4.1	ABCDE	5.9	2.3	ABCD
B1xC	B2426	GR119	Nanking:Nanking	10	4.1	CDE	6.8	1.4	BCD
CxC	GR119	SLR1T15	Nanking:Mahogany	20	2.6	E	3.7	1.5	D
CxC	KY106	op	Meiling:unknown	5	2.4	CDE	3.3	1.4	BCD
CxC	KY75	SLR1T15	Meiling:Mahogany	10	2.4	DE	3.2	1.6	BCD
CxC	TA3	op	Kuling:Unknown	3	2.2	ABCDE	2.8	1.7	ABCD

* The first letter of the code for the B3-F3 crosses identifies the farm containing its B3-F2 parent. The first number identifies the block of trees containing the B3-F2 parent. The middle number identifies the plot within a block, and corresponds to the American great, great grandparent of the B3-F2. The last number is the tree number within a plot, within a block. In this set of crosses, there is only one open-pollinated B3 grandparent of the B3-F3s in a plot, except that the B3 grandparent of D5-18-95 and D5-18-101 differs from the B3 grandparent of the other trees in plot 18.

** Within a column, means not followed by the same letter are significantly different at p<0.05 by a Tukey HSD test. The declarations are suspect for strain SG2-3 due to heteroseedasticity.

Table 5—Effect of adding sets of 20 B₃-F₂ progeny from the American Chestnut Foundation's Chapter breeding program on inbreeding and effective population size for the same source of blight resistance (inbreeding effective population size doubles with each additional chapter if different sources of blight resistance are used)

Number of Chapters	Inbreeding Coefficient	Inbreeding Effective Population Size
1	0.0207	72
2	0.0115	130
3	0.0085	176
4	0.0070	214
5	0.0060	248

233

Literature Cited

Burnham, C.R. 1981. Blight-resistant American chestnut: there's hope. Plant Disease. 65: 459–460.

Burnham, C.R. 1990. Evaluation and use of large American chestnut survivors in blight areas. Journal of the American Chestnut Foundation. 4:43-45.

Burnham, C.R.; Rutter, P.A.; French, D.W. 1986. Breeding blight-resistant chestnuts. Plant Breeding Reviews. 4: 347–397.

Clapper, R.B. 1952. Relative blight resistance of some chestnut species and hybrids. Journal of Forestry. 50(6): 453–455.

Franklin, I.R. 1980. Evolutionary change in small populations. In: Soule, M.E.; Wilcox, B.A., eds., Conservation biology: an evolutionary-ecological perspective. Sunderland, MA: Sinauer Associates: 135–140.

Griffin, G.J. 2000. Blight control and restoration of the American chestnut. Journal of Forestry. 98: 22–27.

Griffin, G.J.; Hebard, F.V.; Wendt, R.W.; Elkins, J.R. 1983. Survival of American chestnut trees: evaluation of blight resistance and hypovirulence in *Endothia parasitica*. Phytopathology. 73: 1084–1092.

Hebard, F.V. 1994. The American Chestnut Foundation breeding plan: beginning and intermediate steps. Journal of the American Chestnut Foundation. 8: 21–28.

Hebard, F.V. 2002. Meadowview Notes 2001-2002. Journal of the American Chestnut Foundation. 16: 7–18.

Hebard, F.V. 2004. Research objectives of the American Chestnut Foundation, 2004-2014. Summary of TACF's 10-year plan. Journal of the American Chestnut Foundation. 18: 13–19.

Hebard, F.V. 2006. The backcross breeding program of the American Chestnut Foundation. In: Steiner, K.C.; Carlson, J.E., eds. Restoration of American chestnut to forest lands, proceedings of a conference and workshop, May 4-6, 2004, The North Carolina Arboretum, Asheville. Natural Resources Report NPS/NCR/CUE/NRR – 2006/01. Washington, DC: National Park Service: 61–77.

Huang, H.; Carey, W.A.; Dane, F.; Norton, J.D. 1996. Evaluation of Chinese chestnut cultivars for resistance to *Cryphonectria parasitica*. Plant Disease. 80(1): 45–47.

Inman, L.I. 1987. Proposed strategies to preserve and restore the American chestnut. Journal of the American Chestnut Foundation. 2: 6–9.

Inman, L.I. 1989. Simultaneous breeding of the American chestnut for many traits. Journal of the American Chestnut Foundation. 4: 16–17.

Kubisiak, T.L.; Hebard, F.V.; Nelson, C.D.; Zhang, J.; Bernatzky, R.; Huang, H.; Anagnostakis, S.L.; Doudrick, R.L. 1997. Molecular mapping of resistance to blight in an interspecific cross in the genus *Castanea*. Phytopathology. 87: 751–759.

Kubisiak, T.L.; Roberds, J.H. 2006. In: Steiner, K.C.; Carlson, J.E., eds. Genetic structure of American chestnut populations based on neutral DNA markers. In: Restoration of American chestnut to forest lands, proceedings of a conference and workshop, May 4-6, 2004, The North Carolina Arboretum, Asheville. Natural Resources Report NPS/NCR/CUE/NRR – 2006/01Washington, DC: National Park Service: 109–122.

Namkoong, G. 1991. Maintaining genetic diversity in breeding for resistance in forest trees. Annual Review of Phytopathology. 29: 325–42.

Scrivani, J. 2011. Forest inventory and analysis. Journal of the American Chestnut Foundation. 25: 17–18.

Breeding Strategies for the Development of Emerald Ash Borer - Resistant North American Ash

Jennifer L. Koch,[1] David W. Carey,[1] Kathleen S. Knight,[1] Therese Poland,[2] Daniel A. Herms,[3] and Mary E. Mason[3]

Introduction

The emerald ash borer (*Agrilus plannipennis;* EAB) is a phloem-feeding beetle that is endemic to Asia. It was discovered in North America in 2002, found almost simultaneously near Detroit, Michigan and Windsor, Ontario, Canada. Adult beetles feed on ash (*Fraxinus* spp.) foliage, but larval feeding on phloem, cambium, and outer xylem is far more detrimental because it effectively girdles the tree, disrupting nutrient and water transport and ultimately killing the tree. As of 2007, it was estimated that 53 million ash trees had been killed by EAB in North America (Kovacs et al. 2010). Potentially, more than 8 billion ash trees could eventually be affected, or about 2.6 percent of the timber trees in the United States (Sydnor et al. 2007).

Breeding for pest resistance in forest trees is a proven approach for managing both native and non-native insects and diseases (FAO UN 2011). We initiated a breeding program that employs two strategies to incorporate EAB resistance into North American ash species: hybrid and traditional breeding. In the hybrid breeding approach, we are looking for EAB resistance in Asian species of ash from EAB's region of origin (sympatric resistance). Asian ashes resistant to EAB will be crossed with native North American species to create hybrids. The hybrids subsequently will be subjected to rounds of testing, selection, and backcrossing to the native species that will be repeated until only the resistance genes from the exotic species are carried into the native population while all of the traits of the native species are retained, similar to the breeding program of the American Chestnut Foundation (Hebard 2006). For a more traditional breeding approach, we are searching for rare native individuals with resistance or tolerance to EAB (allopatric resistance). The following is an overview of the current status of our program.

Hybrid Breeding

Contrary to the situation in North America, severe EAB outbreaks on ash species native to Asia are a rarity. These tree species, having co-evolved with EAB, are likely to have developed mechanisms of resistance. This hypothesis is supported by a recent common garden study that reports significantly less EAB-induced mortality in Manchurian ash (*F. mandshurica* Rupr.) compared to green (*F. pennsylvanica* Marsh.) and white (*F. americana* L.) ash (Rebek et al. 2008). Evidence for the EAB resistance of Korean ash (*F. chinensis* ssp. *rhynchophylla* (Hance) Hemsley) is described by Liu et al. (2007), who reported a mixed plantation of Korean ash and green ash where 95 percent of all green ash was found to be EAB infested while the Korean ash of similar size and in close proximity remained free of EAB. More recently, a study by Dian et al. (2010) reported that in both Manchurian and Korean ash, more than 75 percent of EAB larvae dissected from the trees had been killed through "host plant resistance," or the formation of callous by the host trees that encapsulated the larvae.

---

[1] USDA Forest Service, Northern Research Station, 359 Main Rd., Delaware, OH 43015.
[2] USDA Forest Service, Northern Research Station, 220 Nisbet Bldg., Michigan State University, East Lansing, MI 48823.
[3] The Department of Entomology, Ohio Agricultural Research and Development Center, The Ohio State University, 1680 Madison Ave., Wooster, OH 44691.
Corresponding author: jkoch@fs.fed.us.

To identify additional EAB-resistant species that may be used as parents in a hybrid breeding program, we have been accessioning Asian ash species across a wide geographical and ecological range. A summary of our current collections is outlined in table 1.

Table 1: Exotic ash (*Fraxinus*) collection, U.S. Department of Agriculture, Forest Service, NRS, Delaware, Ohio

Species	Origin	Unique accessions
F. aspertisuquamifera	Japan	1
F. angustifolia	Syria, Europe	2
F. chinensis	China, Korea	26*
F. excelsior	Europe	3
F. insularis	China	6*
F. lanuginosa	Japan	4*
F. longicuspis	China	1*
F. mandshurica	China, Korea, Russia, Japan	25*
F. ornus	Europe	3
F. paxiana	China	5*
F. sieboldiana	China, Korea, Japan	3
F. sogdiana	China	3
F. spaethiana	Japan	1
F. stylosa	China	4*

*Includes accessions from the Morton Arboretum including those from a recent North American Chinese Plant Exploration Consortium (NACPEC) collection.

Each accession is confirmed for proper species identity through the use of DNA-based technologies, including internal transcribed spacer (ITS) sequencing and amplified fragment length polymorphism (AFLPs). The ITS sequences were compared to published sequences for each species (Wallander 2008). The AFLP data was assessed for its utility in verifying species identities relative to control reference species previously confirmed with ITS data. Species confirmation is a critical step because currently there is no comprehensive global taxonomic key, and few traits are diagnostic between closely related but geographically isolated species. Our current exotic ash collection includes 85 independent accessions, including 11 Asian species and 3 European species. While confirming species identities, we uncovered seven different Asian ash accessions from reputable gardens and arboreta that were incorrectly identified, illustrating the difficulty of distinguishing *Fraxinus* species (table 2). Most of these errors were native North American green ash mislabeled as Asian species, but in a few cases, Asian species were misidentified as other Asian species, European species, and North American black ash. In addition, six different seed lots (representing both Asian and North American species) from two different commercial seed companies were found to be incorrectly identified as shown in table 3. To date, about 70 percent of all of the commercially obtained *Fraxinus* seed sources have been incorrectly identified at the species level and 15 percent of the Asian accessions.

After species identity is confirmed, the individual accessions are replicated through grafting and will be installed in a common garden study at the Ohio Agricultural Research and Development Center in Wooster, Ohio along with North American EAB-susceptible species. The long-term goal of this study is to assess EAB resistance as well other desired characteristics such as growth rate, form, color, tolerance to native pests and diseases, and site suitability.

Inter-specific hybridization of *Fraxinus* species has not been widely reported, with the exception of hybridization of *F. nigra* and *F. mandshurica* that resulted in the release of two horticultural cultivars, Northern Gem and Northern Treasure (Davidson 1999). To determine what species combinations may produce successful F1 hybrids, we performed controlled cross-pollinations using as many combinations as possible (dependent on the availability of viable male and female flowers). In 2010, 42 different species combinations were crossed and 15 successfully produced seed. Five of the species combinations have now produced seedlings, with family sizes ranging from 11 to 104.

236

Backcrosses were also performed between the commercially available F1 hybrid Northern Gem and both *F. mandshurica* and *F. nigra*. These crosses successfully produced seed, and the seed is beginning to germinate. These new germinants represent the most advanced *Fraxinus* interspecies pedigree, and demonstrate that F1 hybrids are reproductively competent providing evidence that the hybrid/backcross breeding approach has potential to be successful in ash. All resulting F1 and backcross seedlings will be screened for EAB resistance and their hybrid parentage confirmed using molecular techniques.

Table 2—Misidentified *Fraxinus* accessions from arboreta and botanical gardens

Species labeled as:	Number of incorrect accessions	Correct species IDs (based on ITS and/or AFLP)	Location of arboretum	Origin of accessions
F. chinensis	3	*F. pennsylvanica*	United States	Chinese Botanical Garden, Chinese Forest Preserve
F. chinensis var. *accuminata*	2	*F. pennsylvanica*	Europe	Chinese Botanical Garden
F. chinensis var. *rhyncophylla*	1	*F. mandshurica*	United States	China seed collection
F. mandshurica	6	*F. pennsylvanica, F. excelsior, F. nigra, and F. chinensis*	United States	China seed collection, US nursery, US university
F. sogdiana	1	*F. pennsylvanica*	United States	unknown

Table 3—Commercially obtained *Fraxinus* seed lots that were incorrectly identified at the species level

Distributed as:	Number of incorrect seed lots	Correct species ID (ITS and/or AFLP)	Number of commercial sources
F. bungeana	3	*F. pennsylvanica*	3
F. chinensis	3	*F. pennsylvanica*	2
F. chinensis var. *rhyncophylla*	1	*F. pennsylvanica*	1
F. nigra	2	*F. excelsior*	2

Traditional Breeding

Initial EAB infestations were in urban areas where a few ash cultivars were planted in high numbers. Although a large number of these trees were killed, they represented a small number of genotypes. As EAB moved into natural stands with greater genetic diversity, small numbers of surviving ash trees have been identified that persist in areas where more than 98 percent of the ash trees have been killed by EAB (Knight et al., these proceedings; Marshall et al. 2010). These "lingering ash" may be simply the last trees to die, or they may be trees with rare phenotypes that are less preferred by EAB or are tolerant or resistant to EAB infestation.

We have been working to identify such "lingering ash" and preserve and replicate them through grafting. Currently, we have 33 individual grafted lingering ash tree genotypes grafted (primarily green and white). Two of these genotypes flowered and controlled cross-pollinations were performed resulting in two small seedling families. In addition, 2011 was a good seed year for ash and we were able to collect open-pollinated seed from nine lingering ash located in the southeast Michigan survey site and seven lingering ash trees in the northwest Ohio survey site described by Knight et al. (these proceedings). Because of the high degree of ash mortality in these areas, the pollen donors are assumed to also be lingering ash, so these open-pollinated seed are likely the resulting progeny of two lingering ash parents. These families will be analyzed for segregation of EAB tolerance/resistance phenotypes and will give an indication of the potential for enhancing native resistance through breeding.

Currently, our work focuses on developing a screen to distinguish EAB-resistant and EAB-susceptible phenotypes in grafted lingering ash ramets and seedling families. Adult EABs are being reared at the East Lansing, Michigan, Northern Research Station laboratory. Adult EAB that emerge from naturally infested logs are placed along with ash foliage in plastic containers covered by a paper coffee filter. Groups of approximately 10 females and 4 males are placed in each container; adults mate and the females lay eggs on the coffee filters. Small sections of coffee filter with eggs attached are cut and then placed on each tree and wrapped with cheesecloth to prevent scavenging by predators (fig. 1A).

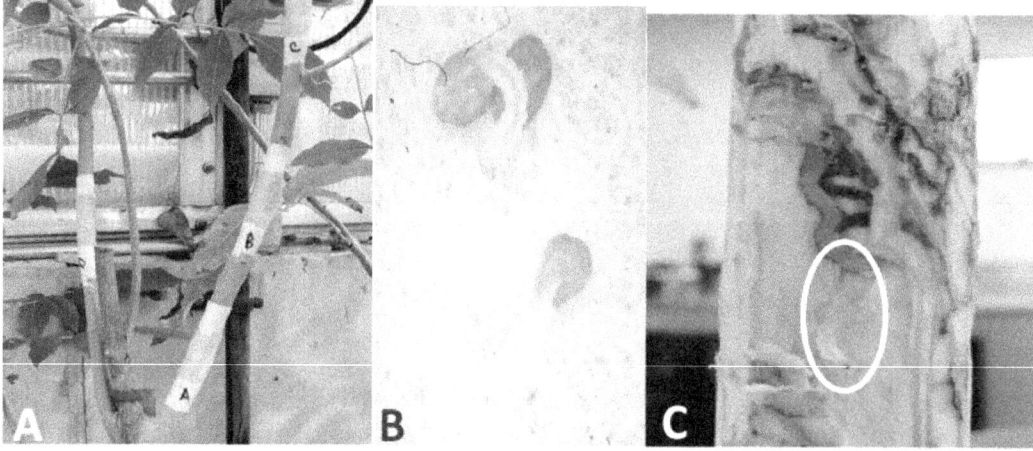

Figure 1—Development of emerald ash borer (EAB)-resistance screen. A. Coffee filters with EAB eggs are placed against the tree and covered with cheesecloth. B. Neonate larvae emerging from their eggs on the coffee filter. C. 3rd instar larva and gallery 6 weeks after egg hatch.

Approximately 8 to 10 weeks after the expected egg hatch date, the coffee filters will be removed and inspected to determine the number of eggs that successfully hatched. At each egg placement site, the bark will carefully be peeled back to dissect out larvae, recording the number of larvae, instar development, larval weight, and any evidence for host defense response such as callous formation. Data will be analyzed to discern any differences between lingering ash and controls regarding successful larval infestation.

Lingering ash grafted ramets and seedling families will also be installed in replicated field trials to assess differences in response to natural EAB infestation. Interestingly, the nursery growing area at the Delaware, Ohio, USDA Forest Service Laboratory was plagued by a naturally occurring EAB infestation in the summer of 2010. One of the infested nursery beds contained grafted lingering ash selections that remained uninfested while known susceptible grafted selections immediately adjacent to the lingering ash were infested, an observation that supports the hypothesis that lingering ash are less preferred by EAB.

Literature Cited

Davidson, C.G. 1999. 'Northern Treasure' and 'Northern Gem' hybrid ash. HortScience. 34: 151–152.

Dian, J.J.; Ulyshen, M.D.; Bauer, L.S.; Gould, J.; Van Driesche, R. 2010. Measuring the impact of biotic factors on populations of immature emerald ash borers (Coleoptera: Buprestidae). Environmental Entomology. 39(5): 1513–1522.

Food and Agriculture Organization of the United Nations [FAO UN]. 2011. Selection and breeding for insect and disease resistance. http://www.fao.org/forestry/26445/en/. (25 October 2011).

Hebard, F.V. 2006. The backcross breeding program of the American Chestnut Foundation. Journal of the American Chestnut Foundation. 19: 55–77.

Kovacs, K.F.; Haight, R.G.; McCullough, D.G.; Mercader R.J.; Siegert, N.W.; Liebhold, A.M. 2010. Cost of potential EAB damage in US communities, 2009-1019. Ecological Economics. 69: 569–578.

Liu, H.; Bauer, L.S.; Miller, D.L.; Zhao, T.; Gao, R.; Song, L.; Lusan, Q.; Jin, R.; Gao, C. 2007. Seasonal abundance of *Agrilus planipennis* (Coleoptera:Buprestidae) and its natural enemies *Oobius agrili* (Hymentoptera: Encyritidae) and *Tetrastichus planipennisi* (Hymenoptera: Eulophidae) in China. Biological Control. 42: 61–71.

Marshall, J.M.; Storer, A.J.; Mech, R.; Katovick, S.A. 2010. Prospects for long-term ash survival in the core emerald ash borer mortality zone. In: McManus, K.A.; Gottschalk, K.W., eds. Proceedings. 21st U.S. Department of Agriculture interagency symposium on invasive species. Gen. Tech. Rep. NRS-P-75. Newtown Square, PA: U.S. Department of Agriculture, Forest Service, Northern Research Station: 99.

Rebek, E.J.; Herms, D.A.; Smitley, D.R. 2008. Interspecific variation in resistance to emerald ash borer (Coleoptera: Buprestidae) among North American and Asian ash (*Fraxinus* spp.). Plant-Insect Interactions. 37: 242–246.

Sydnor, T.D.; Bumgardner, M.; Todd, A. 2007. The potential economic impacts of emerald ash borer (*Agrilus planipennis*) on Ohio, U.S., communities. Arboriculture & Urban Forestry. 33(1): 48–54.

Wallander, E. 2008. Systematics of *Fraxinus* (Oleaceae) and evolution of dioecy. Plant Systematics and Evolution. 273: 25–49.

Breeding for Disease Resistance in *Hevea* spp. - Status, Potential Threats, and Possible Strategies

Chaendaekattu Narayanan[1] and Kavitha K. Mydin[1]

Abstract

Hevea brasiliensis (Willd. ex A. Juss.) Müll. Arg., a forest tree native to the tropical rain forests of Central and South America, has only been recently domesticated outside its natural range of distribution. Almost all of the commercially cultivated clones of *H. brasiliensis* represent a very narrow genetic base since they originated through hybridization or selection from a few seedlings of so called Wickham germplasm. Hence, the commercial rubber cultivation, due to their genetic vulnerability, is under a constant threat of attack by native as well as exotic diseases and insects. Climate change, which is clearly felt in the traditional rubber growing regions of India, may possibly alter the host-pathogen interactions leading to epidemics of otherwise minor diseases.

Pathogenic fungal diseases including *Phytophthora*-caused abnormal leaf fall (ALF) and shoot rot, pink disease caused by *Corticium salmonicolor*, *Corynespora*-caused leaf disease, and powdery-mildew (*Oidium* sp.) are challenging diseases posing epidemic threats to rubber cultivation. South American leaf blight (SALB) is a devastating disease caused by *Microcyclus ulei* (=*Dothidella ulei*) which has prevented large-scale planting of rubber in Brazil due to epidemic outbreaks. The SALB is a looming threat to other rubber growing areas. Hence, it is essential that a global SALB resistance breeding program be implemented to tackle such future threats of epidemics. *Hevea* clones clearly exhibit variable levels of susceptibility to pathogenic diseases. *Hevea* clones have been tested for their capacity to produce phytoalexins; a strong correlation was observed between phytoalexin accumulation and clone resistance. More lignin accumulation was also often associated with clone resistance. Attempts have been made to identify possible disease resistance gene analogues in rubber. The role of *M13-1bn* marker (a putative quantitative trait locus) in screening for resistance to SALB had been investigated through genome mapping, but needs further validation. Earlier selection and breeding of *Hevea* clones resistant to *M. ulei* and *Phytophthora* sp. in Brazil led to screening of resistant clones. Most of the resistant material had been derived from *H. benthamiana* "F4542." Few other attempts for inter-specific hybridization have been made, particularly for SALB resistance (*H. camargoana* x FX 4098), but they did not follow large-scale evaluations for field resistance.

Many man hours of labor and enormous quantities of fungicidal chemicals are required every year for management of above diseases in vast areas of rubber plantations in India and other rubber growing countries. The cost of fungicides and their long-term effect on environment justify the need for breeding disease resistant trees. There are several theories for genetic basis for disease resistance (horizontal/vertical) in *Hevea*. Nevertheless, there is every possibility for breakdown of resistance due to ever-evolving pathogenic races coupled with climate change, which is exemplified by evolving SALB races. A multidisciplinary breeding program for development of disease resistant clones would have to continuously utilize Wickham resource as well as wild germplasm, in addition to other *Hevea* spp., in order to have sustainable rubber production.

Key words: *Hevea brasiliensis*, fungal diseases, South American leaf blight, *Microcyclus ulei*, disease resistance breeding

Introduction

Hevea brasiliensis (Willd. ex A. Juss.) Müll. Arg. (family, Euphorbiaceae; diploid, 2n=36), the Para rubber tree, is a forest species native to the tropical rain forests of Central and South America. Though the tree has only been recently domesticated outside its natural range of distribution, it has great commercial and socio-economic significance in many countries (Narayanan and Mydin 2011).

[1] Rubber Research Institute of India, Kottayam 686 009 Kerala, India.
Corresponding author: cnarayanan@rubberboard.org.in.

Hevea brasiliensis is monoecious, entomophilic, and predominantly out-crossing, and continues to be the major source of natural rubber in the entire plant kingdom. Latex (essentially cytoplasmic fluid) is collected from laticifer cells located in the bark tissue through systematic manual incision (the entire process referred to as 'tapping') for various uses. Most of the cultivated clones of *Hevea* have been derived either through selection or breeding among the few selected seedlings (or their progenies) which were reportedly collected from a small geographic location in Boim, near the Tapajos river in Brazil (Allen 1984, Schultes 1977, Wycherley 1968). Commercially cultivated clones of *H. brasiliensis* represent a very narrow genetic base possibly originating from few selected seedlings collected by Henry Wickham in 1876 (Baulkwill 1989).

Rubber cultivation is under a constant threat of attack by native as well as exotic pathogenic fungal diseases due to genetic vulnerability of the *Hevea* clones. Leaves, stems, and roots of *Hevea* are susceptible to fungal pathogens. Leaf diseases are caused by *Oidium heveae*, *Colletotrichum* spp., *Phytophthora* spp., *Corynespora cassiicola*, and *Microcyclus ulei*. The above pathogens cause abnormal leaf fall or leaf spot of young as well as mature leaves of *Hevea*. Among stem infections, pink disease, caused by *Corticium salmonicolor*, is the most important, capable of infecting young as well as mature trees. Dry rot caused by *Ustulina deusta*, patch canker caused by *Phytophthora palmivora*, and black stripe caused by *P. palmivora*, *P. meadii*, or *P. botryose*, are other important diseases affecting the stem. White root rot caused by *Rigidiporus lignosus*, brown rot caused by *Phellinus noxius*, and red rot caused by *Ganoderma philippii* are notable diseases of roots. Among the above diseases, South American leaf blight (SALB), caused by *M. ulei* (=*Dothidella ulei*), is the most devastating. This disease caused several serious epidemics, almost leading to cessation of planting of *Hevea* in Brazil.

The change in weather parameters due to the increasing trend in climate change, which is clearly felt in the traditional rubber growing regions of India, may possibly alter the host-pathogen interactions. This will possibly lead to epidemic outbreaks of otherwise minor diseases. Besides, there is every possibility that hitherto unreported exotic pathogens may be favored by the altered weather parameters. Emergence of leaf disease caused by *C. cassiicola* as a major pathogen is a classic example. This pathogen is rapidly progressing into new areas, thus highlighting the need for a stronger and advanced resistance breeding approach.

Clonal Variation and Breeding for Disease Resistance

Hevea breeding primarily aims at developing clones with potential to produce more latex. Introduction, ortet (plus tree) selection, and hybridization followed by clonal selection, are the major methods of crop improvement in rubber. During various stages of evaluation, observations are made on various pest and disease incidences (Mydin and Saraswathyamma 2005). Better growth vigor, smooth and thick bark, good bark renewal after tapping, and tolerance to major diseases are considered as good secondary characteristics (Varghese 1992, Varghese and Mydin 2000).

In *Hevea*, the breeding strategy follows the conventional method of cyclical 'generation-wise assortative mating' (GAM), where superior genotypes of one generation form parents for subsequent breeding programs (Simmonds 1989). Most of the cultivated clones have been developed through selection or hybridization from among few selected high-yielding popular clones. Since yield remained the primary trait for breeding, there had been limited selection for resistance genes and their transmission among the hybrid progenies, and hence, many of the *Hevea* clones exhibit variable levels of susceptibility to the pathogenic fungal diseases in the field.

Although systematic breeding in *Hevea* started in early 1900s, studies on genetic parameters were initiated after 1970 (Tan and Tan 1996). Studies on genetic parameters, however, aimed at major economic traits like yield and vigor and there were very limited attempts to understand the genetic basis of disease resistance in *Hevea*. Subsequent to major disease epidemic outbreaks of SALB, efforts were made to understand the genetic basis of disease resistance in *Hevea* and specific resistance breeding programs were implemented to identify and breed resistant clones.

Understanding the pattern of genetic inheritance of disease resistance is crucial for developing successful resistance breeding programs.

In a genetic analysis study, two populations viz. (i) 18 selected genotypes of various degrees of resistance, and (ii) 15 randomly selected progenies of a five-parent diallel cross, were screened for leaf disease resistance after artificial inoculation with *Colletotrichum* and natural infection of *Corynespora* and *Oidium* (Tan and Tan 1996). The results revealed that *Colletotrichum* and *Corynespora* resistance had higher heritability estimates than *Oidium* resistance. Hence, selection for genotypes with *Colletotrichum* and *Corynespora* would be more effective than the selection for *Oidium*-resistant genotypes. A considerable part of major genetic variation of *Colletotrichum* disease resistance was attributed to additive gene control; *Corynespora* and *Oidium* resistance was ascribed to non-additive gene control. There were high proportions of general combining ability (GCA) effects for the above three diseases. However, specific combining ability effect was significant only for *Corynespora* and *Oidium*. Earlier, degrees of resistance to *Colletotrichum*, *Corynespora,* and *Oidium*, and continuous form of variation, had indicated operation of polygenic inheritance of disease resistance in *Hevea* (Lim 1973, Tan et al. 1992, Wastie 1973). Since no adverse genetic associations have been found between disease resistance traits and latex yield or growth vigor, breeding for durable resistance contributed by polygenic inheritance has been recommended as the best resistance breeding strategy in *Hevea* (Ho 1986; Simmonds 1983, 1985, 1986, 1989, 1990; Tan 1987).

Oidium-Caused Leaf Disease

Leaf fall resulting from *Oidium* infection is capable of causing extensive defoliation, particularly when trees refoliate after wintering, leading to serious retardation of growth and considerable loss in yield (Liyanage and Jacob 1992). Although one low-yielding clone from Sri Lanka, LCB 870, has been reported to possess resistance to the disease, most of the high-yielding clones are susceptible to the disease. While clones PB 86, GT 1, GL 1, PR 107, PB 5/139, RRIM 703, RRII 208, and PB 310 show limited levels of resistance, other clones viz., Tjir 1, PB 5/51, and RRIM 605 are highly susceptible. RRII 105, the hybrid clone extensively cultivated for several years in India, PB 235, PB 280, as well as RRII 118 and RRII 300 are also susceptible to the disease. Interestingly, RRII 105 is a hybrid between Tjir 1 and Gl 1 and the male parent has been reported to show some level of resistance.

A study on *Oidium*-caused leaf fall sensitivity of 25 *Hevea* clones developed from India, Indonesia, China, Thailand, and Malaysia revealed that clones SCATC 93-114, RRIM 703, Haiken 1, RRII 208, RRII 5, and PB 310 had comparatively stable tolerance towards *Oidium*-caused leaf fall disease. These clones have been suggested for use in breeding for disease resistance (John et al. 2001, Rajalakshmy et al. 1997). In another study carried out in a plantation with 20 clones, PB 86, RRIC 52, AC/S/12 42/186, PR 261, RO/CM/10 44/7, RRIM 703, AC/S/12 42/59, and IAN 45-873 exhibited low levels of infection (John et al. 2000). High resistance in the wild genotypes viz., AC/S/12 42/59, AC/S/12 42/186, and RO/CM/10 44/7 has already been reported (Quiong 1993). Of the RRII 400 series clones developed by Rubber Research Institute of India (RRII), almost all recommended clones were affected by the disease. However, RRII 422 followed by RRII 414 showed comparatively less infection (Varghese et al. 2009).

Based on disease intensity in the field, 3,561 wild germplasm accessions of *Hevea* were screened for tolerance to *Oidium* leaf infection (Mydin et al. 2011). The above study, which was carried out for 3 consecutive years, identified two potential accessions which had less than 10 percent disease incidence. Such tolerant accessions could be used in future resistance breeding programs. Similar field screening studies carried out in Tripura (north east state of India) could identify seven wild accessions viz., MT 4859, MT 5136, RO 3794, RO 5055, RO 5087, RO 5160, and RO 5365 tolerant to *Oidium* leaf infection. Similarly, in another north east state of Assam (India), field screening revealed stable disease tolerance in three wild accessions viz., RO 1737, AC 587, and AC 5302 (Mydin et al. 2011).

Phytophthora Leaf Diseases

Although *Hevea* clones that evolved in various rubber growing regions show variable levels of susceptibility to abnormal leaf fall disease caused by *Phytophthora* spp., most of the high-yielding clones are susceptible. High yielding clones such as RRII 105, GT 1, Gl 1, PB 86, PB 217, PB 235, PB 260, PB 311, PB 28/59, RRIM 600, RRIM 628, RRIM 703, PR 255, PR 261, and Tjir 1 are reported to be affected by the disease. Some of the above clones showed higher leaf retention under prophylactic fungicidal spraying (Liyanage and Jacob 1992). Clones susceptible to abnormal leaf fall disease are also highly susceptible to shoot rot caused by *Phytophthora* spp. In India, among the RRII 400 series clones, RRII 414 and RRII 430 exhibited low incidences of abnormal leaf fall due to *Phytophthora* spp.

Two trials consisting of 13 clones each were assessed for tolerance to the disease under prophylactic fungicidal spray (Mushrif et al. 2004). High leaf retention was observed in RRII 105 and RRII 5. Clones RRIM 600, PB 260, and PB 280 along with RRIM 703 showed low leaf retention. It may be noted that RRIM 703 had been identified as a moderately tolerant clone in Malaysia (RRIM 1975). Interestingly, another clone, PR 255, showed significantly more leaf retention although its parents, namely Tjir 1 and PR 107, are susceptible. Since stomatal entry of the pathogen had been observed, attempts were made to identify anatomical factors, particularly petiolar stomata, influencing disease development in various clones (Premakumari et al. 1979, Premakumari and Panikkar 1984, Thankamma et al. 1975). Subsequent studies using various clones also indicated the frequency of petiolar stomata and the aperture index as potential criteria for selection of disease-resistant clones (Premakumari et al. 1988). The above study showed that 68 percent variation in leaf retention after the incidence of *Phytophthora*-caused leaf fall disease could be explained by the characteristics of petiolar stomata.

About 2,691 accessions of wild germplasm of *Hevea*, originally collected from provenances viz., Mato Grasso, Acre and Rondonia were assessed for field level abnormal leaf fall disease (Mydin et al. 2011). Based on percent leaf retention after infection, 257 accessions were found to retain more than 75 percent of leaves, while more than 1,900 accessions shed leaves indicating varying levels of disease resistance operating among the wild germplasm accessions. Detached leaves of more than 100 wild accessions were subjected to artificial laboratory inoculation using zoospore suspensions. Based on lesion size as an indicator of resistance, 18 accessions were rated as tolerant compared to check clone RRII 105. The tolerant accessions include one (RO 4423) from Rondonia, three (AC 2016, AC 3146, and AC 462) from Acre, and 14 (MT 1617, MT 4494, MT 1631, MT 4436, MT 1581, MT 1715, MT 2219, MT 2233, MT 3707, MT 4252, MT 1027, MT 900, MT 4702, and MT 4874) from Mato Grosso (Mydin et al. 2011).

Corynespora-Caused Leaf Disease

Leaf disease caused by *Corynespora* infection was first reported from India in seedling nurseries (Ramkrishnan and Pillay 1961). Subsequently, the disease has been reported from Malaysia, Nigeria, Indonesia, Sri Lanka, and Thailand. The disease has now spread to almost all rubber growing regions (Chee 1990). In Thailand, several cultivated clones were screened for disease resistance in the laboratory as well as the field using 24 isolates of *C. cassiicola* (Rodesuchit and Kajornchaiyakul 1996). For laboratory bioassay 10- to 12-day-old juvenile leaflets were used and for field assessment 1-year-old budwood were inoculated with virulent isolates. Based on the laboratory bioassay and field inoculations, the study grouped clones into three classes viz., highly susceptible to susceptible, moderate, and resistant to highly resistant. While clones GT 1, RRIM 600, and KRS 225 were rated susceptible to highly susceptible in laboratory and field assays, clone KRS 226 which was rated as resistant to highly resistant in the laboratory assay was found to be highly susceptible after field inoculation. Similarly, clone PR 261 which was rated as highly susceptible to susceptible after laboratory inoculations later proved to be resistant to highly resistant based on field inoculations. In Malaysia, high variability for resistance to *C. cassiicola* races have been reported in clones (Hashim 2011). Clones PB 260, PB 350, PB 359, RRIM 929, and RRIM 2025 were highly susceptible to race 2, but resistant to race 1. In contrary, clones RRIM 2009 and RRIM 2026 were resistant to race 2, but highly susceptible to race 1. It was also found that clone PB 355 was resistant to both the races. Also, clones RRIM 600, RRIM 928, and RRIM 2001 were highly susceptible to both the races. The above variability for resistance indicated possible operation of horizontal as well as vertical resistance in *Hevea*. While few other clones including RRIM 2024 and RRIM 2025 have been reported to be mildly infected by the pathogen (Murnita 2011), the disease reaction needs further long-term evaluation in multiple locations. These studies once again reiterate the need for a careful approach in breeding for disease resistance to *Corynespora* leaf infection in *Hevea* where laboratory assays should always be correlated with field-level resistance. In addition, multilocational field trials under different eco-climatic conditions are also needed before finally rating a clone as resistant or susceptible.

In Malaysia, more than 90 clones and 47 wild germplasm accessions were screened for resistance under laboratory and field conditions (Chee 1988). This and other studies (Othman et al. 1996, Tan et al., 1992) showed that clones which were earlier rated as resistant subsequently became susceptible, possibly due to more virulent pathotypes of the pathogen. Specifically, clone RRIM 600 which was relatively resistant to the disease eventually showed severe infection. Othman et al. (1996) hypothesized allelic heterozygosity for *Corynespora* leaf disease in *Hevea,* since controlled crosses between susceptible parents produced moderately or less susceptible progenies. Also, they observed that RRIM 600 (Tjir 1 x PB 86) was severely infected; however, both the parental clones of RRIM 600 were almost free from fungal infection.

In India, almost all clones were reported to be affected by the disease (Jacob 1997, Mathew 2006). While clone RRIC 103 has been reported to be highly susceptible, GT 1 is fairly tolerant. Sri Lankan clones viz., RRIC 104, RRIC 110, and RRIC 133 have been reported to be susceptible (Jayasinghe and Silva 1996). The disease has already been reported in many Malaysian clones including RRIM 600, PB 5/51, PB 235, and the Indonesian clone Tjir 1 (Tan 1990). AVROS 2037 (Indonesia), BPM 24 (Indonesia), and RRIC 100 (Sri Lanka) have been reported to show tolerance to the disease under Indonesian conditions (Azwer et al. 1993). In India, most of the high-yielding clones, including RRII 105, RRIM 600, PB 260, and PR 107 are susceptible (Jacob 1997). Among RRII 400 series clones developed by RRII, RRII 414, and RRII 430 have been found comparatively less infected by the pathogen under the assistance of prophylactic fungicidal spray (Varghese et al. 2009). In order to screen tolerant genotypes, wild germplasm accessions were artificially inoculated with spore suspensions and monitored for lesion development compared to GT 1 and RRII 105 (Mydin et al. 2011) and tolerant accessions were shortlisted for further evaluation.

Molecular techniques have been used to study genetic variability in *Corynespora* affecting *Hevea* (Atan and Hamid 2003, Darmano et al. 1996, Philip et al. 2004, Saha et al. 2000, Silva et al. 1998, Romruensukharom et al. 2005) using RAPD, rDNA-RFLP, etc. In general, studies revealed considerable levels of genetic variability among the isolates, which indicates the need for a molecular marker-assisted approach in breeding *Hevea* for resistance to *Corynespora*. Attempts have been made to develop *Hevea* clones resistant to the pathogen through genetic transformation techniques (Sunderasan et al. 2011) using anti-cassicolin-specific scFv gene.

Colletotrichum-Caused Leaf Disease

Studies have shown that cultivated clones viz. PB 86, RRII 5, RRII 105, RRII 118, RRII 208, and RRII 300 are susceptible to the disease. Clones PB 217, PB 260, and RRIM 600 have been shown to have comparatively more tolerance. Preliminary studies on intensity and severity of *Colletotrichum-*

caused leaf disease in wild germplasm accessions helped in identification of accessions with varying levels of disease reaction (Mydin et al. 2011). While 161 accessions were almost disease free, more than 700 accessions showed severe infection in the form of spots and leaf fall.

South American Leaf Blight

South American leaf blight (SALB), caused by *M. ulei*, is the most devastating disease of *Hevea* so far reported from the entire rubber growing region, capable of causing up to 90 percent loss in yield of rubber. The disease occurred in epidemic proportions in Brazil and adjacent regions leading to almost complete failure of rubber cultivation. The leaf blight is an obligate pathogen reported only in *Hevea* spp. and it occurs only in tropical America (Chee and Holliday 1986, Lieberei 2007). The pathogen has been recorded from four species of *Hevea* viz., *H. brasiliensis*, *H. benthamiana*, *H. guianensis*, and *H. spruceana*. Breeding for resistance to SALB is the only long-term strategy for disease management. Crown budding, a process where a resistant clone like FX 516 is budded on otherwise susceptible clone, has also been suggested as an interim strategy for management of the disease. Clones of *Hevea* have been screened for susceptibility to the SALB pathogen (Chee 1976). Several other trials are also underway in order to assess resistance of clones to SALB (Omokhafe 2011).

Hevea clones were tested for their capacity to produce a phytoalexin named scopoletin and to produce lignins in their infection sites (Garcia et al. 1999). A strong correlation was observed between scopoletin accumulation and clone resistance. Moreover, strong lignin accumulation was often associated with a longer stromatic generation period. These two physiological reactions could interfere by limiting fungal development in several clones. However, neither scopoletin nor lignin accumulation could individually explain the behavior of all clones (Garcia et al. 1999). Studies carried out in several accessions of wild germplasm using microsatellite markers indicated correlation between genetic resistance and geographical distribution (Guen 2011).

The earliest breeding program concentrated on breeding resistant genotypes using surviving trees identified from severely diseased plantations at Belterra and Fordlandia in Brazil (ANRPC 1995). The strategy involved crossing resistant genotypes like F 170, F 315, F 351, F 1425, and F 4542 with high-yielding clones viz., AVROS 49, AVROS 193, AVROS 363, PB 86, PB 186, and Tjir 1 imported from Indonesia and Malaysia. Later, resistance breeding was continued in Brazil by crossing clones, including RRIM 600 and RRIM 501 (introduced from Malaysia, Sri Lanka, and Indonesia) with the primary Ford clones and also progenies of the Ford crosses. Although there have been several other reports about breeding for SALB resistance, none of the reported clones have been found resistant to the pathogen, possibly due to rapidly evolving pathogenic races. Another collaborative breeding program carried led to development and selection of 13 CMS clones with promising horizontal resistance to SALB (Mattos 2011). The resistant clones viz., CD 1174, CDC 56, CDC 312, MDX 607, MDX 624, PMB 1, FDR 4575, FDR 5240, FDR 5283, FDR 5597, FDR 5665, FRD 5788, and FDR 5802 were tested in multi-regional trials in Brazil, Ecuador, Colombia, Guatemala, and Peru. The above clones were also found to possess putative resistance to selected isolates of *C. cassiicola* (Murnita et al. 2011). However, further studies are required to assess the *C. cassiicola* resistance of the above clones through large-scale field testing.

The mechanism of resistance of *Hevea* to *M. ulei* has not yet been fully understood, but two possible types of resistance viz., vertical (race specific) and horizontal (race non-specific), have been proposed (Hashim and Pereira 1989a, 1989b) based on field observations and laboratory assays. At least 11 physiological races of the pathogen have been reported so far. Hitherto, resistant clones were susceptible to new races of the pathogen. Among the species of *Hevea*, *H. benthamiana* clone F 4542 was found resistant to Race 1 (wild race) of *M. ulei*. However, most of the progenies of F 4542 were susceptible to Race 2 and Race 3.

Vertical resistance has been attributed to host cell death around the site of infection in clones which are resistant to some races of the pathogen. Breeding for vertical resistance led to clones which were resistant only to few races. Clones with vertical resistance subsequently succumbed to new races of the pathogen. Horizontal resistance has been suggested as more durable since it confers resistance to almost all races of the pathogen. Clones with horizontal resistance allowed fungal penetration, but prolonged the rate of spread, reduced the size of lesion, and minimized spore production. In order to simplify the field assessment method for SALB disease, Rivano et al. (2010) tested the resistance of eight rubber tree clones to *M. ulei* in Ecuador in a Fisher block design with four replicates per treatment and concluded that assessing the resistance of rubber tree clones to SALB in large-scale clone trials can be optimized to reduce the number of observation times by 50 percent.

In the lines of conventional breeding for disease resistance, intra- and inter-specific hybridizations were attempted for developing SALB resistance. While the initial intra-specific breeding utilized clones of *H. brasiliensis*, subsequent inter-specific hybridization involved another species, *H. benthamiana* (clone F 4542). Further search for resistance in other species led to the identification and use of *H. pauciflora* (clone P 10) since this species was free from SALB infection. Thus, *H. pauciflora* was hybridized with *H. brasiliensis* and *H. benthamiana* (Pinheiro and Libonati 1971). Subsequently, controlled crosses were also made between *H. camargoana* and *H. brasiliensis* (*H. camargoana* x Fx 4098); Fx 4098 is a hybrid of PB 86 x FB 74, both primary clones of *H. brasiliensis* (developed in Malaysia and Brazil, respectively) and the resultant hybrid progenies were selected for resistance to SALB (Goncalves et al. 1982). However, the resistant hybrids were apparently not high-yielding. As indicated in several studies using wild genotypes as well as cultivated clones, durable resistance is possibly present in wild accessions of *H. brasiliensis* as well as other allied species (Priyadarshan and Goncalves 2003).

Stem Diseases

Pink disease, caused by *C. salmonicolor*, mainly affects young trees, but of late, trees up to 7-years-old are also affected. Repeated infection of young branches lead to retardation of growth, thereby extending the period before the trees can be utilized for extraction of rubber through tapping. Clones PB 217, PB 311, and RRII 105 are highly susceptible to the disease. Among the other cultivated clones, Tjir 1, LCB 1320, RRIM 501, RRIM 701, etc., were also found affected. Another study indicated less susceptibility to the disease in clones viz., PB 86, RRIM 513, Gl 1, PR 107, GT 1, and PB 260 (Ramakrishnan and Pillay 1962, RRIM 1992). Among the RRII 400 series clones, RRII 430 is least affected while RRII 429 is highly susceptible (Varghese et al. 2009).

With regard to other minor stem diseases, clones RRIM 600, PB 235, PB 311, and PB 28/59 are severely affected by black stripe due to *Phytophthora* spp.; PB 217 is moderately affected. With reference to patch canker caused by *Phytophthora* spp., clone PB 260 is highly susceptible (Kothandaraman and Idicula 2000).

Disease Resistance Genes, Molecular Mapping, and Marker-Assisted Selection

Attempts have been made to identify markers linked to disease resistance in *Hevea*. Chen et al. (1994, 2003) used RAPD markers to identify *Oidium* leaf fall resistance gene and subsequently sequence one RAPD marker (OPV-10$_{390}$) possibly linked to gene conferring resistance to *Phytophthora*. Studies have been carried out to identify possible disease resistance gene analogues in rubber (Licy et al. 2000). Eighteen primers, designed based on homologies between known resistance genes, were used in various combinations to amplify sequences from rubber cultivar FX 516, which is resistant to *Phytophthora*-caused leaf fall disease and cultivar RRII 105, which is tolerant. Although none of the clones obtained had high homology to resistance gene sequences, the putative protein encoded by one sequence had some homology to *hem* N gene. Studies are being carried out at RRII on resistant gene analogues (RGAs) and their relationship with functional RGAs in response to *Corynespora* infection (Saha et al. 2010). Using degenerated primers based on conserved motifs of NBS domains of known *R*-genes, a PCR-based approach was followed. RGAs of NBS-LRR class were cloned from *H. brasiliensis* and *H. benthamiana* and 22 transcriptionally active diverged RT-RGAs were identified. Characterization of these RGAs is required for better understanding plant reaction to *Corynespora* infection.

Using a population of 192 progeny individuals derived from a cross between a resistant clone (RO 38; original name is FX3899, a low yielding inter-specific hybrid between *H. brasiliensis* and *H. benthamiana*) and a susceptible cultivated clone (PB 260), Guen et al. (2003) identified a major QTL named as *M13-1bn*, located on linkage group g13, that is responsible for 36 to 89 percent of the phenotypic variance of resistance. The role of *M13-1bn* in screening clones for resistance to SALB needs validation through large-scale multilocational field testing.

Discussion and Conclusion

Field evaluation through visual observation and laboratory assays through excised leaf inoculation have led to screening of putatively resistant Wickham clones and wild germplasm. However, laboratory bioassays are preliminary and may not ensure actual field-level resistance as observed for diseases of other forest trees. *Hevea* clones have also been tested for their capacity to produce phytoalexins; a strong correlation was observed between phytoalexin accumulation and clone resistance. More lignin accumulation was also often associated with clone resistance. With regard to wild germplasm, earlier studies indicated considerable variation in growth and disease resistance among and within genotypes collected from various provenances of Brazil.

Many man hours of labor and enormous quantities of fungicidal chemicals are required every year for management of the above diseases in vast areas of rubber plantations in India and other rubber growing countries. The cost of fungicides and their long-term effect on the environment justify the need for breeding disease-resistant trees. There are several theories for genetic basis for disease resistance (horizontal/vertical) in *Hevea*. Nevertheless, there is every possibility for breakdown of resistance due to ever-evolving pathogenic races coupled with climate change, which is exemplified by evolving SALB races. Multidisciplinary breeding programs for development of disease-resistant clones would have to continuously utilize the Wickham resource, as well as wild germplasm, in addition to other *Hevea* spp. in order to have sustainable rubber production. The present germplasm resource of *Hevea* is predominantly constituted by the domesticated clones and more than 4,000 wild germplasm accessions collected from Acre, Rondonia, and Mato Grosso.

Disease resistance in *Hevea*, like other forest trees, is apparently polygenic, as indicated by varying levels of resistance in domesticated and wild germplasm. Elaborate studies are needed to understand the molecular basis of resistance and mechanisms of inheritance of disease resistance in *Hevea*. Molecular markers, wherever feasible, should be integrated into breeding programs to accelerate selections. Once the germplasm accessions are characterized for disease resistance, association mapping strategies could be employed for identifying markers linked to resistance which would ultimately help in molecular-assisted selection/breeding (MAS/MAB) in *Hevea*.

Acknowledgments

The first author expresses his sincere thanks to: Chairman, Rubber Board, Government of India and Director, Rubber Research Institute of India, India, for granting sponsorship; Department of Science and Technology, Government of India, for the travel grant; Richard Sniezko, Geneticist and Workshop Chair, Dorena Genetic Resource Center, Oregon; Katie Palmieri and Janice Alexander, California Oak Mortality Task Force, University of California; and many others at the workshop for all their help.

Literature Cited

Allen, P.W. 1984. Fresh germplasm for natural rubber. Span. 27 (1): 7–8.

ANRPC [Association of Natural Rubber Producing Countries]. 1995. South American leaf blight (*Microcyclus ulei*) of rubber – a training manual. Kuala Lumpur: Association of Natural Rubber Producing Countries. 36 p.

Atan, S.; Hamid, N.H. 2003. Differentiating races of *Corynespora cassiicola* using RAPD and internal transcribed spacer markers. Malaysian Journal of Rubber Research. 6(1): 3.

Azwer, R.; Daslin, A.; Anzwar, R. 1993. Performance of 1974 multilateral exchange rubber clones at various locations in Indonesia. International Journal of Crop Science. 8(1): 11–22.

Baulkwill, W.J. 1989. The history of natural rubber production. In: Webster, C.C.; Baulkwill, W.J., eds. Rubber. Harlow, UK: Longman Scientific and Technical. 56 p.

Chee, K.H. 1976. Assessing susceptibility of *Hevea* clones to *Microcyclus ulei*. Annals of Applied Biology. 84 (2): 135–145.

Chee, K.H.; Holliday, P. 1986. South American leaf blight of *Hevea* rubber. Monograph No. 13. Kuala Lumpur: Malaysian Rubber Research and Development Board. 50 p.

Chee, K.H. 1988. Sporulation, pathogenicity and epidemiology of *C. cassiicola* on *Hevea* rubber. Journal of Natural Rubber Research. 3(1): 21–29.

Chee, K.H. 1990. Present status of rubber diseases and their control. Review of Plant Pathology. 69: 423–430.

Chen, S.; Shao, H.; Hu, D.; Lin, S.; Zheng, X. 1994. Identification of mildew resistance from *Hevea* tree by RAPD technique. Chinese Journal of Tropical Crops. 15(2): 26.

Chen, S.; Shao, H.; Hu, D.; Wu, K.; Zheng, X.F. 2003. Use of RAPD marker to screen mildew-resistance germplasm from *Hevea brasiliensis*. In: Chen, Q.; Zhou, J., eds. Proceedings of the IRRDB Rubber Conference, 1999. [Place of publication unknown]: [Publisher unknown]: 345–350.

Darmano, T.W.; Darussamin, A.; Pawirosoemardjo, S. 1996. Variation among isolates of *Corynespora cassiicola* associated with *Hevea brasiliensis* in Indonesia. In: Darussamin, A.; Pawirosoemardjo, S.; Basuki, Azwar, R.; and Sadaruddin. eds. Proceedings on the workshop on *Corynespora* leaf fall disease of *Hevea* rubber. Indonesian Rubber Research Institute, Indonesia: 79–91.

Garcia, D.; Troispoux,V.; Grange, N.; Rivano, F.; D'Auzac, J. 1999. Evaluation of the resistance of 36 *Hevea* clones to *Microcyclus ulei* and relation to their capacity to accumulate scopoletin and lignins. European Journal of Forest Pathology. 29 (5): 323–338.

Goncalves, P. de. S.; Fernando, D.M.; Rossetti, A.G. 1982. Interspecific crosses in the genus *Hevea*. Pesquisa Agropecuária Brasileira (Brasilia). 17(5): 775–781.

Guen, V.; Le Lespinasse, D.; Oliver, G.; Rodier-Goud, M.; Pinard, F.; Seguin, M. 2003. Molecular mapping of genes conferring field resistance to South American leaf blight (*Microcyclus ulei*) in rubber tree. Theoretical and Applied Genetics.108 (1): 160–167.

Guen, V. 2011. Characterization of genetic structure of Amazonian rubber tree populations with microsatellite markers. Paper presented at IRRDB-CIRAD plant breeders seminar, 4-7 April 2011. Bahia: Brazil.

Hashim, I.; Pereira, J.C.R. 1989a. Lesion size, latent period and sporulation on leaf discs as indicators of resistance of *Hevea* to *Microcyclus ulei*. Journal of Natural Rubber Research. 4: 56–65.

Hashim, I.; Pereira, J.C.R. 1989b. Influence of resistance of *Hevea* on development of *Microcyclus ulei*. Journal of Natural Rubber Research. 4: 212–218.

Hashim, I. 2011. South American leaf blight and *Corynespora* leaf fall: challenging diseases of *Hevea* rubber. Paper presented at IRRDB-CIRAD plant breeders seminar, 4-7 April 2011. Bahia: Brazil.

Ho, C.K. 1986. Rubber, *Hevea brasiliensis*. In: Breeding for durable resistance in perennial crops, FAO Plant Production and Protection Paper No. 70. Rome: FAO: 85–114.

Jacob, C.K. 1997. Diseases of potential threat to rubber in India. Planters Chronicle. 92: 451–461.

Jayasinghe, C.K.; Silva, W.P.K. 1996. Current status of *Corynespora* leaf fall in Sri Lanka. In: Darussamin, A.; Pawirosoemardjo, S.; Basuki, Azwar, R.; and Sadaruddin, eds. Proceedings of the workshop on *Corynespora* leaf fall disease of *Hevea* rubber. Indonesia. 3–5.

John, A.; Annakutty, J.; Meenakumari, T.; Saraswathyamma, C.K.; Varghese, Y.A. 2000. Clonal variation in the intensity of powdery mildew (*Oidium heveae* Steinm.) disease of *Hevea*. Indian Journal of Natural Rubber Research. 13 (1&2): 64–68.

John, A.; Nair, R.B.; Rajalakshmy, V.K.; Saraswathyamma, C.K.; Varghese, Y.A. 2001. Sensitivity relationship of *Hevea* clones to the stress of powdery mildew (*Oidium heveae* Steinm.). Indian Journal of Natural Rubber Research. 14 (2): 88–92.

Kothandaraman, R.; Idicula, S.P. 2000. Stem diseases. In: George, P.J.; Jacob, C.K., eds. Natural rubber: agromanagement and crop processing. Rubber Research Institute of India, India. 297–308 .

Licy, J.; Dickinson, M.J.; Bligh, F.J.; Power, B.J.; Saraswathyamma, C.K.; Davey, M.R. 2000. An approach to identify disease resistance gene analogues in *Hevea*. Indian Journal of Natural Rubber Research. 13 (1&2): 79–85.

Lieberei, R. 2007 South American leaf blight of the rubber tree (*Hevea* spp.): New steps in plant domestication using physiological features and molecular markers. Annals of Botany. 100 (6): 1125–1142.

Lim, T.M. 1973. A rapid laboratory method of assessing susceptibility of *Hevea* clones to *Oidium heveae*. Experimental Agriculture. 9: 275.

Liyanage, A.D.S.; Jacob, C.K. 1992. Disease of economic importance in rubber. In: Sethuraj, M.R.; Mathew, N.M. eds. Natural rubber: biology, cultivation and technology. Developments in Crop Science 23. The Netherlands: Elsevier Science Publishers: 324–369.

Mathew, J. 2006. Clonal resistance of *Hevea brasiliensis* to *Corynespora* leaf fall disease. In: Jacob, C.K.; Srinivas, P.; Roy C.B., eds. *Corynespora* leaf disease of *Hevea brasiliensis* - strategies for management. Rubber Research Institute of India: 83–101.

Mattos, C. 2011. CMB (CIRAD-MICHELIN-BRAZIL) Project for the genetic improvement of rubber trees in Brazil. Paper presented at IRRDB-CIRAD plant breeders seminar, 4-7 April 2011. Bahia: Brazil.

Murnita, M.M. 2011. Major leaf diseases distribution, severity and clonal susceptibility in peninsular Malaysia. Paper presented at IRRDB-CIRAD plant breeders seminar, 4-7 April 2011. Bahia: Brazil.

Murnita, M.M.; Nasaruddin, M.A; Othman, R. 2011. Susceptibility of South American leaf blight tolerant clones to *Corynespora cassiicola* infection. Paper presented at IRRDB-CIRAD plant breeders seminar, 4-7 April 2011. Bahia: Brazil.

Mushrif, S.K.; Joseph, A.; Johan, A.; Jacob, C.K. 2004. Evaluation of *Hevea brasiliensis* clones against abnormal leaf fall disease caused by *Phytophthora*. Natural Rubber Research. 17 (1): 74–78.

Mydin, K.K.; Saraswathyamma, C.K. 2005. A manual on breeding of *Hevea brasiliensis*. Rubber Research Institute of India. 97 p.

Mydin, K.K.; Jacob, J.; Reghu, C.P.; Sankariammal, L.; Nair, D.B.; Mercy, M.A.; Joseph, A.; Saha, T.; Das, K.; Sreelatha, S.; Mondal, G.C.; Das, G. 2011. Conservation, characterization, evaluation and utilization of the 1981 IRRDB wild *Hevea* germplasm collection in *Hevea*. Paper presented at IRRDB-CIRAD plant breeders seminar, 4-7 April 2011. Bahia: Brazil.

Narayanan, C.; Mydin, K.K. 2011. Heritability of yield and secondary traits in two populations of Para rubber tree (*Hevea brasiliensis*). Silvae Genetica. 60 (3-4): 132–139.

Omokhafe, K. 2011. Strategy for trials of the SALB resistant clones in *Hevea brasiliensis* in Nigeria. Paper presented at IRRDB-CIRAD plant breeders seminar, 4-7 April 2011. Bahia: Brazil.

Othman, R.; Benong, M.; Ong, S.H.; Hashim, I. 1996. Strategies and development of resistant *Hevea* clones against *Corynespora* leaf fall. In: Darussamin, A.; Pawirosoemardjo, S.; Basuki, Azwar, R.; and Sadaruddin. eds. Proceedings of the workshop on *Corynespora* leaf fall disease of *Hevea* rubber. Indonesian Rubber Research Institute, Indonesia: 177–193.

Philip, S.; Joseph, A.; Abraham, T.; Zacharia, C.A.; George, J.; Manju, M.J.; Jacob, C.K. 2004. ERIC PCR based genomic finger printing of *Corynespora cassiicola* isolates infecting rubber (*Hevea brasiliensis*) plantations. Journal of Plantation Crops. 32: 301–305.

Pinheiro, E.; Libonati, V.F. 1971. O emprego do *Hevea pauciflora* M.A. como fuente genetica de resistencia ao mal das folhas. Poliméros. 1:31–39.

Premakumari, D.; Annamma, Y.; Bhaskaran Nair, V.K. 1979. Clonal variability for stomatal characters and its application in *Hevea* breeding and selection. Indian Journal of Agricultural Sciences. 49 (6): 411–413.

Premakumari, D.; Panikkar, A.O.N. 1984. Organographic variability of stomatal characters in *Hevea brasiliensis* (Willd. ex A. Juss.) Müll. Arg. and it possible significance in clonal susceptibility to leaf fall disease. In: Proceeding of the International Rubber Conference. Sri Lanka: Rubber Research Institute of Sri Lanka: 317–324.

Premakumari, D.; Panikkar, A.O.N.; Sethuraj, M.R. 1988. Correlations of the characters of petiolar stomata with leaf retention after the incidence of *Phytophthora* leaf fall disease in *Hevea brasiliensis* (Willd. ex A. Juss.) Müll. Arg. Indian Journal of Natural Rubber Research. 1(1): 22–26.

Priyadarshan P.M.; Goncalves, P. de. S. 2003. *Hevea* gene pool for breeding. Genetic Resources and Crop Evolution. 50 (1): 101–114.

Quiong, H.D. 1993. Identification and evaluation by major characteristics of part of the 1981 Amazon collection of wild *Hevea* germplasm in China. In: Proceedings of the IIRDB Joint Meeting. Hartford, England: International Rubber Research and Development Board: 47–59 .

Rajalakshmy, V.K.; Annakutty, J.; Varghese, Y.A.; Kothandaraman, R. 1997. Evaluation of *Hevea* clones against powdery mildew caused by *Oidium heveae* Steinm. Indian Journal of Natural Rubber Research. 10 (1 and 2): 110–112.

Ramakrishnan, T.S.;. Pillay. P.N.R. 1961. Leaf spot of rubber caused by *Corynespora cassiicola* (Berk. & Curt.) Wei. Rubber Board Bulletin. 5: 52–53.

Ramkrishnan, T.S.; Pillay, R. 1962. Pink disease of rubber caused by *Pellicularia salmonicolor* (Berk. and Br.) Dastur (=*Corticium salmonicolor* Berk. and Br.). Rubber Board Bulletin. 5(3): 120–126.

Rivano, F.; Martinez, M.; Cevallos, V.; Cilas, C. 2010. Assessing resistance of rubber tree clones to *Microcyclus ulei* in large-scale clone trials in Ecuador: a less time-consuming field method. European Journal of Plant Pathology. 126(4): 541–552.

Rodesuchit, A.; Kajornchaiyakul, P. 1996. Screening *Corynespora* resistant clones of rubber in Thailand. In: Darussamin, A.; Pawirosoemardjo, S.; Basuki, Azwar, R.; and Sadaruddin, eds. Proceedings of the Workshop on *Corynespora* Leaf Fall Disease of *Hevea* Rubber. Indonesian Rubber Research Institute, Indonesia. 163–176.

Romruensukharom, P.; Tragoonrung, S.; Vanacichit, A.; Toojinda, T. 2005. Genetic variability of Corynespora *cassiicola* populations in Thailand. Malaysian Journal of Rubber Research. 8(1): 3.

RRIM [Rubber Research Institute of Malaysia]. 1975. Enviromax planting recommendations, 1975-1976. Planters' Bulletin. 137: 27–50.

RRIM [Rubber Research Institute of Malaysia]. 1992. Planting recommendations, 1992-1994. Planters' Bulletin 211: 31–50.

Saha, T.; Kumar, A.; Sreena, A.S.; Joseph, A.; Jacob, C.K.; Kothandaraman, R.; Nazeer, M. A. 2000. Genetic variability of *Corynespora cassiicola* infecting *Hevea brasiliensis* isolated from the traditional rubber growing areas in India. Indian Journal of Natural Rubber Research. 13(1and 2): 1–10.

Saha, T.; Roy, C.B.; Ravindran, M. 2010. Characterization of a family of disease resistant gene analogues (RGAs) in rubber (*Hevea brasiliensis*) and their relationship with functional RGAs in response to *Corynespora* infection. In: Proceedings of the national symposium on molecular approaches in management of fungal diseases of crop plants. Bangalore: Indian Institute of Horticultural Research. 101 p.

Schultes, R.E. 1977. Wild *Hevea* – an untapped source of germplasm. Journal of Rubber Research Institute of Sri Lanka. 54: 1–31.

Silva, W.P.K.; Deverall, B.J.; Lyon, B.R. 1998. Molecular, physiological and pathological characterization of *Corynespora* leaf spot fungi from rubber plantations in Sri Lanka. Plant Pathology. 47(3): 267–277.

Simmonds, N.W. 1983. Strategies for disease resistance breeding. FAO Plant Protection Bulletin v. 31(1): 2–10.

Simmonds, N.W. 1985. A plant breeder's perspective of durable resistance. FAO Plant Protection Bulletin. 33: 13–17.

Simmonds, N.W. 1986. Strategies for disease resistance breeding in tropical perennial crops. In: Breeding for durable resistance in perennial crops. FAO Plant Production and Protection Paper No. 70: 3–15.

Simmonds, N.W. 1989. Rubber Breeding. In: Webster, C.C.; Baulkwill, W.J., eds. Rubber. England: Longman Scientific and Technical: 85–124.

Simmonds, N.W. 1990. Breeding horizontal resistance to South American leaf blight of rubber. Journal of Natural Rubber Research. 5(2): 102–113.

Sunderasan, E; Kadir, R.A.; Valerie, P.R.; Malik, A.; Badarudin, B.E.; Yeang, H.Y.; Nathan, S. 2011. *Hevea* genetic transformation: A molecular approach to enhance resistance to *Corynespora* leaf disease. Paper presented at IRRDB-CIRAD plant breeders seminar, 4-7 April 2011. Bahia: Brazil.

Tan, H. 1987. Strategies in rubber tree breeding.. In: Abbott, A.J.; Atkin, R.K., eds. Improving vegetatively propagated crops. London: Academic Press. 27–62.

Tan, A.M. 1990. Survey of *Corynespora* leaf fall disease. Planters Bulletin. 204: 80–85.

Tan, A.M.; Loo, T.P.; Vadivel, G.; Bachik, M.R.; Yoon, K.F. 1992. Survey of major leaf disease of rubber in Peninsular Malaysia. Planters Bulletin. 211: 51–62.

Tan, H.; Tan, A.M. 1996. Genetic studies of leaf resistance in *Hevea*. Journal of Natural Rubber Research. 11(2): 108–114.

Thankamma, L.; Rajalakshmy, V.K.; Radhakrishna Pillai, P.N. 1975. Mode of entry of *Phytophthora* in *Hevea brasiliensis*. In: Proceedings of the International Conference, vol. III. Kuala Lumpur: Rubber Research Institute of Malaysia: 213–216.

Varghese, Y.A. 1992. Germplasm resources and genetic improvement. In: Sethuraj, M.R.; Mathew, N.M. eds. Natural rubber: biology, cultivation and technology. Developments in Crop Science 23. The Netherlands: Elsevier Science Publishers: 88–115.

Varghese, Y.A.; Mydin, K.K.; Meenakumari, T. 2009. Performance of the RRII 400 series and certain Prang Besar (PB) clones in various locations in India. Rubber Research Institute of India, India. 63 p.

Varghese, Y.A.; Mydin, K.K. 2000. Genetic improvement. In: George, P.J.; Jacob, C.K., eds. Natural rubber: agromanagement and crop processing. Rubber Research Institute of India: 297–308.

Wastie, R.L. 1973. Nursery screening of *Hevea* for resistance to *Gleosporium* leaf disease. Journal of Rubber Research institute of Malaya. 23 (5): 339.

Wycherley, P.R. 1968. Introduction of *Hevea* to the Orient. Planter (Kuala Lumpur). 44: 1–11.

Developing a Disease Resistance Research Program for Tanoaks

Katherine J. Hayden,[1] Jessica W. Wright,[2] Richard S. Dodd,[1] and Matteo Garbelotto[1]

Abstract

The introduced pathogen *Phtyophthora ramorum* has had a devastating impact on populations of tanoak (*Notholithocarpus densiflorus* (Hook. & Arn.) Manos, Cannon & S.H.Oh) in California and Oregon, where it causes the disease known as sudden oak death. Tanoaks are a keystone species ecologically, and one of the few species that are both killed by *P. ramorum* and contributes to its spread. While ecologically important, tanoaks were little studied prior to the onset of the sudden oak death epidemic, resulting in few intellectual or material resources on which to base a disease resistance research program.

We report on progress to date on a project funded since 2006 by the U.S. Department of Agriculture, Forest Service, Pacific Southwest Research Station, with the goal to collect the information required to understand what role resistance might play in the disease dynamics and/or management of tanoak populations. A common garden population of open-pollinated tanoak seed families has been established. These trees have been evaluated for variation in neutral genetic markers, growth and morphology, and quantitative resistance to laboratory inoculations. Simultaneously, a field disease trial, using the same families of trees, was initiated to validate and expand on laboratory observations, under natural disease pressures.

The work thus far has resulted in a significant expansion of the understanding of tanoak phylogeography and population genetics, the discovery of heritable quantitative resistance to disease in the lab, and potential links between morphology and disease resistance in the lab and field. Here, we tie together the investigations, presenting 3 years of data from laboratory and field resistance trials, along with their correlations with growth traits, in light of the understanding of tanoak population dynamics generated from neutral markers. We show the relevance of laboratory studies to field outcomes, and discuss the potential for disease resistance in driving the management or evolution of the species in response to this considerable threat.

[1] University of California, Berkeley, Environmental Science, Policy, and Management, Berkeley, CA 94702.
[2] USDA Forest Service, Pacific Southwest Research Station, Davis, CA.
Corresponding author: khayden@berkeley.edu.

Genetic Variation in Resistance to Pine Pitch Canker and Western Gall Rust in Monterey Pine (*Pinus radiata* D. Don): Results From a Three-Country Collaborative Field Trial

A.C. Matheson,[1] W.R. Mark,[2] G. Stovold,[3] C. Balocchi,[4] N Smith,[2] and C. Brassey[2]

In 1998, Australia, Chile, and New Zealand agreed to work together in a program designed to test their elite breeding lines and to test for the genetics of resistance to pitch canker (causative organism *Fusarium circinatum*). Pitch canker was first discovered in the United States in 1946 and in California in 1986. The first discoveries in California were in ornamental plantings, and the disease was first found in native stands of Monterey pine (*Pinus radiata* D. Don) in 1992. By 1997, pitch canker was found in 22 counties in California, and the Board of Forestry established a "Zone of Infestation." Early estimates of resistance levels were as low as 3 percent. Pitch canker is also found in Spain, South Africa, Chile, Haiti, Mexico, Portugal, and Chile. The pathogen has not been found in Australia or New Zealand, and its introduction could result in an economic disaster to the respective softwood forest industries. Due to the widespread use of Monterey pine around the world (table 1), there was interest in assessing the risk of forest plantations outside the United States for pitch canker.

Table 1—Estimated land area used for Monterey pine plantations worldwide in 1999 (adapted from Balocchi, et al. 1999)

Country	Area (000 ha)	Production (1000m^3/yr)
Chile	1 380	18 548
Australia	1 338	17 000
New Zealand	642	10 400
Spain	237	2 000
South Africa	66	486
Other	100	NA
Totals	3 763	48 434

The first step was a conference (called IMPACT Monterey) held at Monterey, California to bring together present knowledge of the disease, its epidemiology, known vectors, as well as host responses. Proceedings were published by the Australia Commonwealth Scientific and Industrial Research Organization (CSIRO) (Devey et al. 1999). The planned effort included collaboration in California for greenhouse trials and field trials of greenhouse screened lines.

Phase 1 of the IMPACT Project, a greenhouse trial, was conducted at Pebble Beach, California, comparing the responses of more than 500 open- or control-pollinated families to inoculation by *F. circinatum*. Results using a t-test showed there were significant differences between families for the length of the lesion developed 6 weeks following inoculation (Matheson et al. 2006). Estimates of heritability, using the statistical software package ASReml, in the different populations are presented in table 2. There were also significant differences between male parents, but apparently not between female parents (table 3). The next step was to test the

[1] CSIRO, Kingston, Australia.
[2] California Polytechnic State University, San Luis Obispo, CA, USA.
[3] Scion, Rotorua, New Zealand.
[4] Bioforest, SA, Concepcion, Chile.
Corresponding author: wmark@calpoly.edu.

same families in the field to see if the family rankings would match those obtained in the greenhouse.

Table 2—Individual tree heritability in the analysis of lesion length (adapted from Matheson et al. 2006)

Population	Heritability	SE (Heritability)	Residual variance
Chile CP	0.34	0.06	192
Año Nuevo	0.78	0.29	206
Monterey	0.46	0.26	169
Australian crosses	0.34	0.05	162
NZ OP	0.49	0.08	158

Table 3—Heritability estimates for lesion length separated by parent sex (adapted from Matheson et al. 2006)

Term	Variance component	Standard error of variance component	Heritability estimate	Standard error of heritability estimate
Female	1.9	3.7	0.04	0.08
Male	16.8	6	0.38	0.12
Combined female X male	11.4	5.4	0.21	0.07

In 2005, Phase 2 of the IMPACT Project, a field trial was set up at Davenport, California at the Swanton Pacific Ranch, owned by California Polytechnic State University. A total of 264 seedlots were available to test disease scores in the same environment as a disease-affected natural stand of the species. Seedlots from Chile were selected from among those tested in Phase 1, so as to cover the range of response; those from New Zealand were selected from among the better performing families in Phase 1. New seedlots were included from Australia to include reciprocal pairs of controlled pollinations, but also included seedlots with a range of performance from Phase 1. The trial was designed to be removed before pollen from the trial would materially affect the gene pool of the native stand nearby. Environmental factors, including wet areas in the planting site and deer damage, were analyzed to eliminate those factors from the analysis. The analysis of the deer damage showed that the damage was associated with replicate (location in the planting site) and height of the trees at the time they were damaged. High mortality following the planting in 2005 resulted in the mapped wet areas.

The field trial was assessed annually for disease symptoms until the final assessment in February 2011, after which the trial was removed. Apparent quite early in the life of the trial were galls produced by the western gall rust (causative organism *Endocronartium harknessii*), acquired both at the Institute of Forest Genetics at Placerville, where many of the trial seedlings overwintered, as well as at Swanton, following planting. Other disease symptoms included those caused by *Diplodia pinea*, particularly in the 2009 assessment. Pitch canker was confirmed present in the trial in 2009, and became more severe in 2010 and 2011.

Western gall rust findings were analyzed to look for differences among families (seedlots) in resistance. A mixed model, treating seedlots and replicates as fixed rows and columns (random), was used to obtain an estimate of the statistical significance of the differences between families. The differences between seedlots using a logarithmic transformation are highly statistically significant ($P<0.001$). The fact that the difference between families is so strong suggests that the heritability will be high. A proper genetic analysis is not done yet, so no estimate for the heritability is available at this time.

Diplodia blight outbreaks in Monterey pine in the United States have not been considered significant, but have caused significant damage in Monterey pine plantations in the Southern Hemisphere (Peterson 1981). The native population has extensive pycnidia presence, but no other symptoms. The plantation suffered extensive tip mortality, resulting in stunting, excessive branching and forked tops. Little, if any, mortality was recorded due to Diplodia blight. In this experiment, symptomatic trees were found to have a significantly clustered distribution, which is consistent with rain splash being the primary mechanism of spore dispersal in *D. pinea*.

Preliminary analysis of the pitch canker data used only the blocking structures (replicates, rows, and columns) provided for in the original design and included the tree height as a covariate. Replicates were treated as fixed effects, the rows and columns as random effects. A binomial model with a logistic link function rather than models using normal distribution suggests the heritability is 15.21 percent ± 9.44 percent (or 0.1521 ± 0.0944). A fitted individual-tree mixed model in ASReml was utilized to get the BLUP (Best Linear Unbiased Predicted) breeding values for the parents of the trees involved in the trial. The correlation with the greenhouse results is 0.284, using the Chilean and New Zealand families only.

Some potential explanations of poor correlation with greenhouse results are as follows: 1) Presence-absence data collected in the field versus measured values for lesion lengths in the greenhouse; 2) Artificial inoculation in the greenhouse versus natural infection from vectors or wounds in the field trial; 3) Escape of susceptible individuals in the field trial; and 4) Difficulty in accurate assessment of large trees in the field.

Work on a complete analysis of the heritability of resistance to western gall rust and pitch canker is continuing.

Acknowledgments

Funding for this study came from The Agricultural Research Initiative, California State University; CSIRO, Australia; Scion, New Zealand; and Bioforest SA, Chile. Thanks to Swanton Pacific Ranch, California Polytechnic Corporation for land use, equipment, and personnel.

Literature Cited

Balocchi, C.; Ahumada, R.; Ramirez, O. 1999. Present and future of radiata pine in Chile. In: Devey, M.; Matheson, C.; Gordon, T.R., eds. Current and potential impacts of pitch canker in radiata pine. Proc. IMPACT Monterey Workshop. Tech. Rep. No 112. Canberra, Australia: CSIRO, Forestry and Forest Products: 1–4.

Devey, M.E.; Matheson, A.C.; Gordon, T.R., eds. 1999. Current and potential impacts of pitch canker in radiata pine. Proc. IMPACT Monterey Workshop. Tech. Rep. No 112. Canberra, Australia: CSIRO, Forestry and Forest Products. 120 p.

Matheson, A.C.; Devey, M.E.; Gordon, T.R.; Balocchi, C.; Carson, M.J.; Werner, W. 2006. The genetics of response to inoculation by pine pitch canker (*Fusarium circinatum* Nirenberg and O'Donnell) infection by seedlings of radiata pine (*Pinus radiata* D. Don). Australian Forestry. 69(2): 101–106.

Peterson, G. 1981. Diplodia blight of pines. Forest insect and disease leaflet 161. Washington, DC: U.S. Department of Agriculture, Forest Service, Rocky Mountain Forest and Range Experiment Station. 8 p.

Genetic Selection in Coastal Douglas-fir for Tolerance to Swiss Needle Cast Disease

Keith J.S. Jayawickrama,[1] David Shaw,[2] and Terrance Z. Ye[1]

Introduction

Swiss needle cast (SNC) of Douglas-fir (*Pseudotsuga menziesii* (Mirb.) Franco), caused by the ascomycete fungus *Phaeocryptopus gaeumannii*, is associated with significant volume growth losses (20 to 50 percent) along the Oregon Coast. Although the pathogen is endemic, disease symptoms have intensified in coastal forests of Oregon and Washington since the early 1990s, reaching a peak of 177,691 symptomatic hectares detected in the 2011 aerial survey of western Oregon (fig. 1). This symptom expression is the highest in 16 years of survey, despite the conversion of tens of thousands of pure Douglas-fir plantations to mixed or alternate species over that period. Regular surveys have not been done in Washington State in the same way, but in 1999 and 2000, about 75,000 ha with visible symptoms were detected, and the disease continues to affect stands.

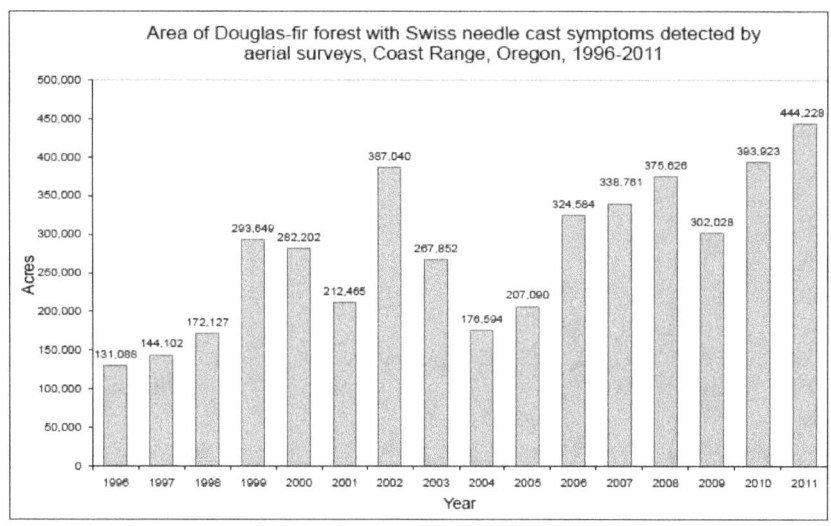

Figure 1—Area of Douglas-fir forest in western Oregon with symptoms of Swiss needle cast detected during aerial surveys conducted from April-June, 1996-2011. (Figure from Alan Kanaskie and Mike McWilliams, Oregon Department of Forestry)

Coastal Douglas-fir is an enormously important timber species for Oregon; consequently, there has been considerable interest and investment in understanding the disease, quantifying its impact, finding silvicultural and management solutions, and developing seed sources suitable for this zone. The Swiss Needle Cast Cooperative (SNCC) based at Oregon State University (OSU) and several breeding and testing cooperatives (supported by the Northwest Tree Improvement Cooperative also based at OSU) are working toward these goals.

---

[1] Department of Forest Ecosystems and Society, Oregon State University (OSU), Corvallis, Oregon.
[2] Department of Forest Engineering, Resources, and Management, OSU.
Corresponding author: jayawickrama@oregonstate.edu.

Douglas-fir everywhere are naturally infected with *P. gaeumannii*, yet the disease only develops in certain geographic settings where pseudothecia are produced on 1- and 2-year-old needles. Needle retention (NR) is directly related to tree productivity. Trees with less than 2 years NR are significantly less productive than normal NR (3 years or more). Severely infected trees have <1 year foliage retention. Fungal infection and needle colonization occur passively, through needle stomata and the needle apoplast, respectively, and neither process requires physical or enzymatic penetration of host tissue that might trigger a host defense response. Climatic conditions near the Oregon coast are often conducive to SNC disease development. Mild winter temperatures and spring/summer leaf wetness are key.

There are no known resistance mechanisms, as all foliage and all trees are susceptible given the right climatic conditions during spore dispersal and colonization. No significant differences were found between families in fungal DNA content (Temel 2002). Nonetheless, tolerance to the disease has been well documented, with some families continuing to grow well in the presence of SNC, and adequate family-mean narrow-sense heritabilities for foliage traits are present.

Work in First Generation Programs

Several studies have centered on the Nehalem progeny trial series of 400 first-generation families established on 10 sites in the northern Oregon coast range in 1986 and subject to moderate to heavy SNC disease pressure. This series was measured for the fourth time in summer 2010, and age-26 diameter growth (DBH) from 200 families on five sites were obtained. Data have also been collected from other first-generation programs near the coast. Some key conclusions from Nehalem and other first-generation programs are as follows:

(1) Foliage traits are heritable (individual $h^2 \approx 0.10$ to 0.23), but less heritable than growth traits ($h^2 \approx 0.3$) (table 1). This could be from foliage traits being subjectively scored.

(2) Crown density was seen as a better indicator of genetic tolerance than NR (Johnson 2002), but due to extensive use of NR by the SNCC it has been adopted in tree improvement programs as well.

(3) Growth after age-11 was more strongly associated with age-11 tree size (type-B correlations ≈ 0.7) than with foliage traits (type B correlations ≈ 0.2 to 0.5). However, rank changes have taken place for DBH between age-11 and age-26.

(4) Usable gains for DBH were seen even at age-26. The top 10 percent of parents for DBH-26 had predicted gains of 18.2 percent over population mean, and predicted gains of 23.7 percent over population mean for DBH-18 to -26 increments.

(5) In areas with >2 years of foliage, gains from selection for DBH should be adequate to offset volume growth losses from SNC and keep Douglas-fir as a viable plantation species.

(6) Selecting on an index of age-11 crown density + age-11 DBH (≈ 13.8 percent gain) was only slightly better than age-11 DBH alone (≈ 13.4 percent gain) in improving age-26 DBH.

(7) Selecting for NR alone, foliage color or crown density at age-11 gave little to modest (≈ 1 percent, 2.2 percent, and 5.7 percent) gains in age-26 DBH.

Table 1—Heritabilities obtained from the Nehalem first-generation Douglas-fir program

Trait	Across sites	
	Individual	Family mean
Height 11	0.30	0.81
Volume index 11	0.29	0.80
DBH 11	0.27	0.79
DBH 17/18	0.35	0.82
DBH 26	0.36	0.70
DBH increment (age-11 to 17/18)	0.32	0.80
Needle retention: 1993 secondary laterals	0.23	0.77
Crown density	0.18	0.71
Foliage color	0.11	0.59

Second-Cycle Trials

One second-cycle program has been established in Washington (Washington coast), and four on the Oregon coast:

(1) South Central Coast (SCC) in the south, with the mainline in the core Douglas-fir area, and a smaller satellite program in the zone most affected by SNC.

(2) Plum Creek's CL98 program adjacent to South Central Coast.

(3) Trask in the north, with a coast program (moderately affected by SNC), and an inland program (little affected by SNC).

(4) Plum Creek's Toledo program in the same geographic area as Trask coast.

These five programs have 40 progeny test sites planted between 1997 and 2008. Key points about the second-cycle work to date:

(1) Needle retention is being assessed at age-7 and age-12 and DBH is being assessed at age-7 and age-12 so that an age-7 to age-12 DBH increment can be calculated. There may be additional (later) DBH assessments to confirm continued growth in DBH.

(2) Ability to maintain height and diameter growth, and good needle retention scores, will be the primary selection criteria within these trials.

(3) Relative heritability patterns for growth traits vs. NR are similar to the first-generation (NR is less heritable than growth).

(4) No molecular marker work has been done to date or is currently planned. It is speculated that the ability to grow in the presence of SNC is controlled by many small-effect genes.

(5) A cloned breeding population might provide additional gains compared to a seedling breeding population, but due to the difficulty of rooting Douglas-fir, it would be expensive.

(6) No early (e.g., age-2) testing has been implemented. Research done by Temel et al. (2005) indicated that such testing would provide gains in foliage traits, but little in the way of growth gains even at age-10.

(7) Tested 2nd-cycle families have shown large realized gains in growth over unimproved Douglas-Fir in the SNC zone. In SCC, the tested families had 39.9 percent age-7 volume index (DBH^2 x height) gains over unimproved controls (on SNC sites) and 2.8 percent gains for NR. For Trask, the corresponding numbers for the top 50 families were 48.2 percent and 5.7 percent.

Seed Orchards and Deployment

Orchard blocks (such as Georgia-Pacific's Toledo block, the Forest Service's Hebo block, and the Nehalem block at the Schroeder seed orchard complex near St Paul, Oregon) serving the northern Oregon coast were established between the 1970s and 1990s. The Oregon Department of Forestry (ODF) had a strong commitment to growing a proportion of Douglas-fir on the coast, and a large area under timber management. The ODF saw tree improvement as the main viable tool to counteract SNC and continue growing Douglas-fir, and took the lead in developing a "needlecast-tolerant" orchard block around 2002 built around the Nehalem orchard block.

This orchard incorporated elite selections from the Nehalem and other coastal breeding units on the Oregon coast. The orchard is 2.4 ha in extent, and other cooperators have subsequently joined. Other blocks are being established, and ability to grow in the presence of SNC will remain a priority as selections are added from the 2nd-cycle and beyond. Tree-form, wind-pollinated orchards are likely to be the predominant engine for producing tolerant seed. Mixtures of family lots are used. The goal is to develop seed sources capable of acceptable growth rates on sites averaging ≥2 years of needle retention.

Alternate Species

In areas with higher disease pressure and foliage retention ≤2 years, it may be prudent to use alternate timber species such as western hemlock, western red cedar, red alder, western white pine, and Sitka spruce. Many forest owners have been making this switch during the past 10 to15 years. Either through complete replacement as described above or through mixed species plantings with a component of Douglas-fir (in moderate SNC areas); pure Douglas-fir stands are gradually being replaced. One consequence of SNC infection has been strong support for cooperative genetic improvement of western hemlock (Jayawickrama 2003) which is now entering into a third cycle of breeding and testing.

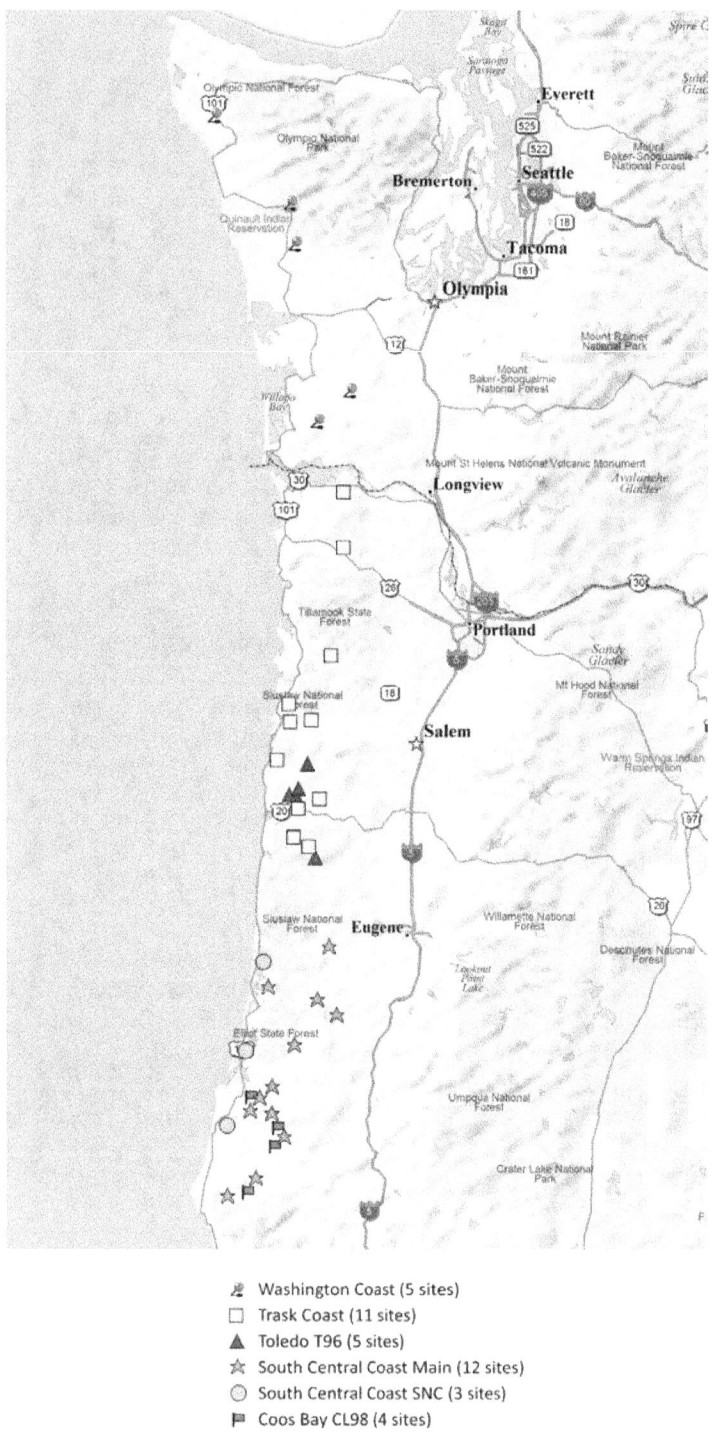

Washington Coast (5 sites)
Trask Coast (11 sites)
Toledo T96 (5 sites)
South Central Coast Main (12 sites)
South Central Coast SNC (3 sites)
Coos Bay CL98 (4 sites)

Figure 2—Second-cycle Douglas-fir test sites established on the Oregon and Washington coasts.

Literature Cited

Jayawickrama, K.J.S. 2003. Genetic improvement and deployment of western hemlock in Oregon and Washington: review and future prospects. Silvae Genetica. 52: 25–36.

Johnson, G.R. 2002. Genetic variation in tolerance of Douglas-fir to Swiss needle cast as assessed by symptom expression. Silvae Genetica. 51: 80–86.

Temel, F. 2002. Early testing of Douglas-fir (*Pseudotsuga menziesii* var. *menziesii* (Mirb.) Franco) for Swiss needle cast tolerance. Corvallis, OR: Oregon State University. 177 p. Ph.D thesis.

Temel, F.; Johnson, G.R.; Adams, W.T. 2005. Early genetic testing of coastal Douglas-fir for Swiss needle cast tolerance. Canadian Journal of Forest Research. 35: 521–529.

White Pine Blister Rust Resistance in *Pinus monticola* and *P. albicaulis* in the Pacific Northwest U.S. – A Tale of Two Species

Richard A. Sniezko,[1] Angelia Kegley,[1] and Robert Danchok[1]

Western white pine (*Pinus monticola* Dougl. ex D. Don) and whitebark pine (*P. albicaulis* Engelm.) are white pine species with similar latitudinal and longitudinal geographic ranges in Oregon and Washington (figs. 1 and 2). Throughout these areas, whitebark pine generally occurs at higher elevations than western white pine. Both of these long-lived forest tree species are highly susceptible to white pine blister rust, caused by the non-native fungus *Cronartium ribicola*, and both have suffered extensive mortality in many parts of their range (Aubry et al. 2008, Fins et al. 2001, Geils et al. 2010, Schwandt et al. 2010). The high susceptibility of these two species to blister rust has limited their use in reforestation and restoration. In July 2011, due to multiple threats, including blister rust, whitebark pine was added as a candidate species eligible for protection under the United States Endangered Species Act and assigned a listing priority number of 2, which means the threats are of high magnitude and are imminent (U.S. Fish and Wildlife Service 2011). Gene conservation efforts with whitebark pine are underway (Mangold 2011; Sniezko et al. 2011b).

Genetic diversity and genetic resistance to pathogens and insects are a species' primary defense and avenue to evolving in the face of threats such as blister rust and climate change. Several operational programs in forest tree species to utilize this natural genetic resistance to help mitigate the impacts of invasive pathogens are well underway (Sniezko 2006; Sniezko et al. 2011a). Active research and management to identify and utilize the low frequency of genetic resistance to blister rust within western white pine and whitebark pine populations offers the best potential for successful long-term reforestation or restoration. Planting resistant seedlings will likely be necessary to retain these white pine species as viable components in many ecosystems (Fins et al. 2001, Harvey et al. 2008, Keane and Schoettle 2011) and to help increase the frequency of the resistance genes throughout the range. In the Pacific Northwest, an operational program to find and utilize naturally occurring genetic resistance in western white pine has been ongoing for more than 50 years, while the program for whitebark pine has been in progress for only a decade (Kegley and Sniezko 2004; King et al. 2010; McDonald et al. 2004; Sniezko et al. 2007, 2011a). However, the program for whitebark pine has benefited greatly from the existence of facilities and expertise in use for the western white pine program.

For both species, parent trees are rated for resistance based on performance of their seedling progeny in artificial inoculation trials. In the first cycle of selection and testing, using wind-pollinated seed from selections in the forest, progeny of over 4,200 parent trees of western white pine have been evaluated for resistance, and progeny of 360 parent trees of whitebark pine have been evaluated or are currently in testing. Resistance screening of hundreds of additional whitebark pine seedling families is anticipated in the next 5 years. After inoculation, seedlings are assessed annually for up to 5 years to examine genetic variation in a range of resistance types, including number of needle lesions ('spots'), type of needle spots (normal or hypersensitive-like response, HR), number of stem symptoms, type of stem symptoms (normal cankers or bark reactions), timing of stem symptom appearance, and severity of infection (Kegley and Sniezko 2004; Sniezko et al. 2007, 2011a).

---

[1] USDA Forest Service, Dorena Genetic Resource Center, Cottage Grove, Oregon, USA.
Corresponding author: rsniezko@fs.fed.us.

Although western white pine and whitebark pine inhabit similar geographic distributions in the Oregon and Washington portions of their geographic ranges, there are both similarities and differences in their resistance to blister rust. Nearly 100 percent of the seedlings of both species develop needle spots in artificial inoculation trials at the U.S. Department of Agriculture, Forest Service's Dorena Genetic Resource Center (DGRC) in Cottage Grove, Oregon. Ninety to 100 percent of the seedlings in the most susceptible families develop stem infections, usually within 8 to 24 months after inoculation (Kegley and Sniezko 2004; Sniezko et al. 2007, 2011a). Progeny of a small percentage of western white pine parents from western Oregon show signs of a hypersensitive-like response in the needles (HR) (Kinloch et al. 1999, 2003), but no whitebark pine with HR have been noted to date (Sniezko, unpublished data[2]). In western white pine, HR appears to be present only in western Oregon and in parts of California, and virulence to this resistance has been documented in parts of the range (Kinloch et al. 2003, 2004).

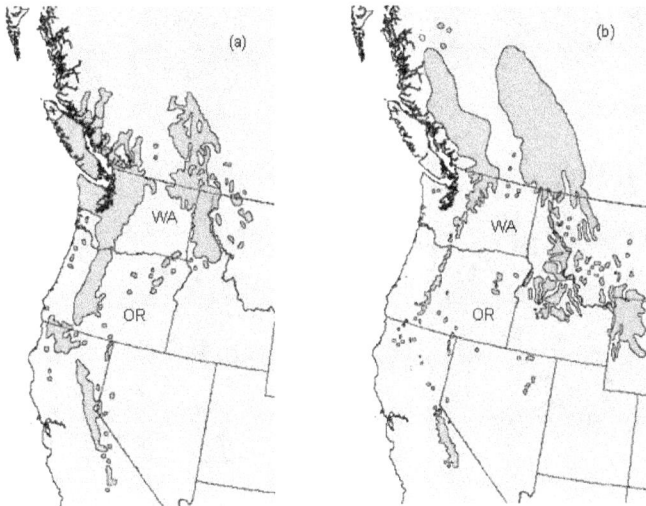

Figure 1—Range maps for (a) western white pine (*Pinus monticola*) and (b) whitebark pine (*P. albicaulis*) (adapted from U.S. Geological Survey 1999).

Moderate levels of other types of resistance, such as canker-free (and not HR) and bark reaction, are relatively rare in wind-pollinated seedling families of western white pine from parents selected in Pacific Northwest forests (Kegley and Sniezko 2004). Only a few non-HR families of western white pine show canker-free levels of >30 percent in the seedling testing at DGRC (Kegley and Sniezko 2004, Sniezko 2006; Sniezko and Kegley 2003a, 2003b). This is in contrast to whitebark pine, which appears to have a higher frequency of progenies with moderate levels of canker-free seedlings (Kegley et al., Blister rust resistance among 20 families of whitebark pine, *Pinus albicaulis*, from Oregon and Washington – early results from an artificial inoculation trial, these proceedings; Sniezko et al. 2007, 2011a). Preliminary summary of the early trials of whitebark pine families indicate that the highest frequency of parents with moderate levels of canker-free seedlings occur in the Cascade Range from central Oregon to central Washington, with a much lower frequency of resistance in eastern Oregon (Kegley et al., Blister rust resistance among 20 families of whitebark pine, *Pinus albicaulis*, from Oregon and Washington – early results from an artificial inoculation trial, these proceedings; Sniezko et al. 2007, 2011a). In some of these areas, many of the families tested have 20 to 50 percent (or more) canker-free seedlings (Sniezko, unpublished, see footnote 2). The highest resistant (and non-HR) families of both species show several common resistance attributes including

[2] Unpublished data from blister rust testing at Dorena GRC – 2004 and 2007 trials. On file: USDA Forest Service, Dorena Genetic Resource Center, Cottage Grove, OR 97424.

a lower frequency of seedlings with cankers, more latent infections, more bark reactions, and longer time to mortality (Sniezko and Kegley 2003a, Sniezko et al. 2007). Only a small number of seedlots of whitebark pine from outside Oregon and Washington have been tested at DGRC and none of these seedlots show the level of resistance exhibited by many of the seedlots from the Cascade Range (Sniezko et al. 2011a; Sniezko, unpublished, see footnote 2).

Figure 2—(a) whitebark pine (WBP) at Crater Lake National Park, (CRLA), (b) western white pine (WWP) at CRLA, (c) WBP in eastern Oregon, (d) WBP with blister rust at CRLA, (e) blister rust susceptible and resistant WBP seedling families in rows in rust resistance testing, (f) dead WWP with >100 rust cankers, directly adjacent to WWP field trial in southern Oregon. (Photo credits: Richard Sniezko: a, b, d, e, f; Chris Jensen: c)

It is encouraging that both western white pine and whitebark pine show family variation in resistance to *C. ribicola*. For both species, more information is needed on the number of resistant mechanisms and their inheritance as well as their expected efficacy and durability in the presence of an evolving pathogen and a changing climate. For western white pine, breeding zones are established, seed orchards are producing seed, breeding to increase resistance is underway, and a large number of field trials have been established (see Sniezko et al., White pine blister rust resistance of 12 western white pine families at three field sites in the Pacific Northwest, these proceedings, for results from some field trials). For whitebark pine, seed zones have been established (Aubry et al. 2008) and land managers will be notified about which parent trees show resistance to facilitate additional seed collection for restoration; a few small field trials have recently been established. For both species, the field trials will serve to help validate the results of artificial inoculation trials, to provide land managers with updated information on efficacy of rust resistance over a range of sites, and to monitor for changes in durability of resistance or changes in general health of the species with changing climate. The parent trees selected previously in the field will be rated for resistance based on their progeny rust resistance, and they can serve as valuable long-term monitors of changes in efficacy of resistance over time or changes in virulence of the pathogen.

Literature Cited

Aubry, C.; Goheen, D.; Shoal, R.; Ohlson, T.; Lorenz, T.; Bower, A.; Mehmel, C.; Sniezko, R. 2008. Whitebark pine restoration strategy for the Pacific Northwest Region 2009-2013. Portland, OR: U.S. Department of Agriculture, Forest Service, Pacific Northwest Region. 212 p. http://www.fs.usda.gov/detail/r6/landmanagement/resourcemanagement/?cid=stelprdb5278980. (02 January 2012).

Fins, L.; Byler, J.; Ferguson, D.; Harvey, A.; Mahalovich, M.F.; McDonald, G.; Miller, D.; Schwandt, J.; Zach, A. 2001. Return of the giants: restoring white pine ecosystems by breeding and aggressive planting of blister rust-resistant white pines. Station Bulletin 72. Moscow, ID: University of Idaho, College of Natural Resources. 20 p. http://www.fs.fed.us/rm/pubs_other/rmrs_2001_fins_l001.pdf . (02 January 2012).

Geils, B.W.; Hummer, K.E.; Hunt, R.S. 2010. White pines, *Ribes*, and blister rust; a review and synthesis. Forest Pathology. 40: 147–185.

Harvey, A.E.; Byler, J.W.; McDonald, G.I.; Neuenschwander, L.F.; Tonn, J.R. 2008. Death of an ecosystem: perspectives on western white pine ecosystems of North America at the end of the twentieth century. Gen.Tech. Rep. RMRS-GTR-208. Fort Collins, CO: U.S. Department of Agriculture, Forest Service, Rocky Mountain Research Station. 10 p. http://www.fs.usda.gov/Internet/FSE_DOCUMENTS/fsm9_018495.pdf. (02 January 2012).

Keane, R.E.; Schoettle, A.W. 2011. Strategies, tools, and challenges for sustaining and restoring high elevation five-needle white pine forests in western North America. In: Keane, R.E.; Tomback, D.F.; Murray, M.P.; Smith, C.M., eds. 2011. The future of high-elevation, five-needle white pines in western North America: Proceedings of the high five symposium. Proceedings RMRS-P-63. Fort Collins, CO: U.S. Department of Agriculture, Forest Service, Rocky Mountain Research Station: 276–294. http://www.fs.fed.us/rm/pubs/rmrs_p063/rmrs_p063_276_294.pdf. (02 January 2012).

Kegley, A.; Sniezko, R.A. 2004. Variation in blister rust resistance among 226 *Pinus monticola* and 217 *P. lambertiana* seedling families in the Pacific Northwest. In: Sniezko, R.A.; Samman, S.; Schlarbaum, S.E.; Kriebel, H.B., eds. Breeding and genetic resources of five-needle pines: growth, adaptability, and pest resistance. Proceedings RMRS-P-32. Fort Collins, CO: U.S. Department of Agriculture, Forest Service, Rocky Mountain Research Station: 209–226. http://www.fs.fed.us/rm/pubs/rmrs_p032/rmrs_p032_209_226.pdf. (01 January 2012).

King, J.N.; Noshad, D.A.; Smith, J. 2010. A review of genetic approaches to the management of blister rust in white pines. Forest Pathology. 40: 292–313.

Kinloch, B.B., Jr.; Sniezko R.A.; Barnes, G.D.; Greathouse, T.E. 1999. A major gene for resistance to white pine blister rust in western white pine from the western Cascade Range. Phytopathology. 89(10): 861–867.

Kinloch, B.B., Jr.; Sniezko, R.A.; Dupper, G.E. 2003. Origin and distribution of Cr2, a gene for resistance to white pine blister rust in natural populations of western white pine. Phytopathology. 93(6): 691–694.

Kinloch, B.B., Jr.; Sniezko, R.A.; Dupper, G.E. 2004. Virulence gene distribution and dynamics of the white pine blister rust pathogen in western North America. Phytopathology 94(7): 751–758.

Mangold, R.D. 2011. The U.S. Forest Service's renewed focus on gene conservation of five-needle pine species. In: Keane, R.E.; Tomback, D.F.; Murray, M.P.; Smith, C.M., eds. 2011. The future of high-elevation, five-needle white pines in western North America: Proceedings of the high five symposium.

Proceedings RMRS-P-63. Fort Collins, CO: U.S. Department of Agriculture, Forest Service, Rocky Mountain Research Station: 151. http://www.fs.fed.us/rm/pubs/rmrs_p063/rmrs_p063_151.pdf. (02 January 2012).

McDonald, G.I.; Zambino, P.J.; Sniezko, R.A. 2004. Breeding rust-resistant five-needled pines in the western United States: lessons from the past and a look to the future. In: Sniezko, R.A.; Samman, S.; Schlarbaum, S.E.; Kriebel, H.B., eds. Breeding and genetic resources of five-needle pines: growth, adaptability and pest resistance. IUFRO Working Party 2.02.15. Proceedings RMRS-P-32. Fort Collins, CO: U.S. Department of Agriculture, Forest Service, Rocky Mountain Research Station: 28–50. http://www.fs.fed.us/rm/pubs/rmrs_p032.html. (02 January 2012).

Schwandt, J.W.; Lockman, I.B.; Kliejunas, J.T.; Muir, J.A. 2010. Current health issues and management strategies for white pines in the western United States and Canada. Forest Pathology. 40: 226–250.

Sniezko, R.A. 2006. Resistance breeding against nonnative pathogens in forest trees—current successes in North America. Canadian Journal of Plant Pathology. 28: S270–S279.

Sniezko, R.A.; Kegley A. 2003a. Blister rust resistance experiences in Oregon and Washington: evolving perspectives. In: Stone, J.; Maffei, H., comps. Proceedings of the 50th Western International Forest Disease Work Conference. Bend, OR: U.S. Department of Agriculture, Forest Service, Central Oregon Service Center: 111–117.

Sniezko, R.A.; Kegley, A.J. 2003b. Blister rust resistance of five-needle pines in Oregon and Washington. In: Xu, M.; Walla, J.; Zhao, W., eds. Proceedings of the second IUFRO rusts of forest trees working party conference. Forest Research. 16 (Suppl.): 101–112.

Sniezko, R.A.; Kegley, A.J.; Danchok, R.S.; Long, S. 2007. Variation in resistance to white pine blister rust among 43 whitebark pine families from Oregon and Washington—early results and implications for conservation. In: Goheen, E.M.; Sniezko, R.A., tech. coords. Proceedings of the conference whitebark pine: Whitebark pine: a Pacific Coast perspective; R6-NR-FHP-2007-01. Portland, OR: U.S. Department of Agriculture, Forest Service, Pacific Northwest Region: 82–97. http://www.fs.fed.us/r6/nr/fid/wbpine/papers/2007-wbp-wpbr-resist-sniezko.pdf. (01 January 2012).

Sniezko, R.A.; Mahalovich, M.F.; Schoettle, A.W.; Vogler, D.R. 2011a. Past and current investigations of the genetic resistance to *Cronartium ribicola* in high-elevation five-needle pines. In: Keane, R.E.; Tomback, D.F.; Murray, M.P.; Smith, C.M., eds. 2011. The future of high-elevation, five-needle white pines in western North America: Proceedings of the high five symposium. Proceedings RMRS-P-63. Fort Collins, CO: U.S. Department of Agriculture, Forest Service, Rocky Mountain Research Station: 246–264. http://www.fs.fed.us/rm/pubs/rmrs_p063/rmrs_p063_246_264.pdf. (01 January 2012).

Sniezko, R.A.; Schoettle, A.; Dunlap, J.; Vogler, D.; Conklin, D.; Bower, A.; Jensen, C.; Mangold, R.; Daoust, D.; Man, G. 2011b. Ex situ gene conservation in high elevation white pine species in the United States: a beginning. In: Keane, R.E.; Tomback, D.F.; Murray, M.P.; Smith, C.M., eds. 2011. The future of high-elevation, five-needle white pines in western North America: Proceedings of the high five symposium. Proceedings RMRS-P-63. Fort Collins, CO: U.S. Department of Agriculture, Forest Service, Rocky Mountain Research Station: 147–149. http://www.fs.fed.us/rm/pubs/rmrs_p063/rmrs_p063_147_149.pdf. (02 January 2012).

U.S. Fish and Wildlife Service. 2011. Endangered species: whitebark pine. http://www.fws.gov/mountain-prairie/species/plants/whitebarkpine/. (01 January 2012).

U.S. Geological Survey. 1999. Digital representation of Atlas of United States trees, by Elbert L. Little Jr.; http://esp.cr.usgs.gov/data/atlas/little/. (01 January 2012).

Shoot Winter Injury and Nut Cold Tolerance: Possible Limitations for American Chestnut Restoration in Cold Environments?

Thomas M. Saielli,[1] Paul G. Schaberg,[2] Gary J. Hawley,[3] Joshua M. Halman,[3] and Kendra M. Gurney[4]

Abstract

Approximately 100 years ago, American chestnut (*Castanea dentata* (Marsh.) Borkh.) was rapidly removed as an overstory tree by the fungal pathogen *Cryphonectria parasitica* (the causal agent of chestnut blight). Currently, the most effective method of restoration involves the hybridization of American chestnut with the highly blight-resistant Chinese chestnut (*Castanea mollissima* Blume), with subsequent backcrossing of resistant stock to American chestnut sources. However, preliminary evidence suggests that backcross material may not have the cold hardiness needed for restoration in the north. Two factors that can significantly influence cold tolerance are plant genetics and environmental parameters (e.g., cold exposure of plant tissues). Also, the cold tolerance of nuts is of concern because reproductive tissues are particularly sensitive to freezing damage. To contribute to the successful restoration of American chestnut in the north, the focus of this research was to analyze the cold tolerance of American chestnut through 1) an assessment of first-year growth and shoot winter injury of a range of American and Chinese chestnut and red oak (*Quercus rubra* L., a native competitor) seedlings under three silvicultural treatments (open, partial, and closed canopies) in the Green Mountain National Forest, Vermont, and 2) the comprehensive evaluation of nut cold tolerance for a range of American and Chinese chestnut nuts and red oak acorns. We examined American chestnut sources by temperature zones (warm, moderate, or cold) that differentiated sources based on winter low temperatures in the areas where they originated.

Seedlings grown under open canopies exhibited greater growth than seedlings grown under partial and closed canopies, but also experienced increased shoot winter injury. Chinese chestnut seedlings had significantly greater growth, but also experienced greater winter injury than American chestnut and red oak seedlings. Among American chestnut sources, seedlings from sources from warmer, low-elevation southern and central locations grew more, but experienced greater winter injury than seedlings from sources from the colder north. Additionally, nuts of Chinese chestnut were significantly less cold-tolerant than either American chestnut nuts or red oak acorns. Among American chestnut sources, nuts from warm and moderate temperature zones exhibited similar levels of cold tolerance, but were significantly less cold tolerant than nuts from the cold temperature zone. There were significant differences among sources within the warm and moderate temperature zones, but not among sources within the cold temperature zone. We believe that the temperature zone index may provide a reliable guide for targeting sources with lower winter shoot injury and greater nut cold tolerance. Our results suggest that both silvicultural treatment and genetic selection can influence growth and winter injury of American chestnut at the northern limit of its range. There was also a strong correlation between nut cold tolerance and winter shoot injury, suggesting that nut cold tolerance measurements (that can be obtained in weeks rather than years) may be a reasonable screening tool for identifying sources with greater shoot hardiness.

[1] The American Chestnut Foundation, 160 Zillicoa Street, Suite D, Asheville, NC 28801.

[2] U.S. Department of Agriculture, Forest Service, Northern Research Station, 705 Spear Street, South Burlington, VT 05403.

[3] University of Vermont, Rubenstein School of Environment and Natural Resources, 105 Carrigan Drive, Burlington, VT 05405.

[4] The American Chestnut Foundation, 705 Spear Street, South Burlington, VT 05403.

Corresponding author: tom@acf.org.

Posters

White Pine Blister Rust Testing at Dorena Genetic Resource Center - 5 host pines shown – with needle spots and stem infections (cankers & bark reactions)

(Photo credit: R.Sniezko)

Screening Sitka Spruce for Resistance to Weevil Damage in British Columbia

René I. Alfaro[1] and John N. King[2]

Abstract

The white pine weevil, *Pissodes strobi* (Coleoptera, Curculionidae), has serious impacts on Sitka (*Picea sitchensis* (Bong.) Carrière), Engelmann (*P. engelmannii* Parry ex Engelm.), and white spruce (*P. glauca* (Moench) Voss) plantations in British Columbia (BC), Canada. This weevil attacks the terminal leader of the tree, causing significant growth loss and deformities. Genetic resistance to this insect was demonstrated in early provenance trials in BC. This encouraged us to initiate a systematic search for resistant trees to confirm this resistance and to improve parent source selections, especially in the Sitka spruce breeding program. Test plantations were initiated and, to accelerate the screening process and create a uniform weevil pressure, insect populations were artificially augmented at many of these trial sites. Artificial infestation provided quick and effective screening and allowed us to proceed with the construction of an F-1 population, and to understand the mechanisms and heritability of resistance. Seed orchards have been established and weevil resistant seedlings are now available for operational planting.

Key words: spruce, weevil, genetic resistance, tree improvement, pest management

Introduction

The white pine weevil, *Pissodes strobi* (Colepoptera, Curculionidae), is an important native pest that limits Sitka (*Picea sitchensis* (Bong.) Carrière), Engelmann (*P. engelmannii* Parry ex Engelm.), and white spruce (*P. glauca* (Moench) Voss) reforestation in western Canada. This insect lays its eggs on the uppermost shoot or leader of the tree. Upon hatching, the larvae mine under the leader bark, causing the destruction of the leader. Although this insect does not destroy the entire tree, a weevil attack leads to deformity and a reduction of growth, thereby making the tree economically unsuitable as a timber resource. By preventing restocking with spruce, the natural species for certain sites, the weevil also affects non-timber values such as biodiversity.

In order to find a natural solution to the problem, we searched for trees that are naturally resistant to the weevil. Several spruce provenances and genotypes with heritable resistance were found and are now included in seed orchards and reforestation programs in British Columbia (BC). To further understand the inheritance of resistance, we investigated resistance of progeny from selected crosses (F1) from parents with different levels of resistance. We also conducted studies aimed at understanding the basis for the observed resistance.

Materials and Methods

Sources Tested for Resistance

Seed was collected by BC Ministry of Forests and Range personnel from potentially resistant trees throughout the range of Sitka spruce in Coastal BC and the United States in Alaska, Washington, Oregon, and California. Seedlings produced from the collected seed were planted and tested in field trials (fig. 1) located in BC and Oregon and screened by Canadian Forest Service personnel. Plantations included block and family replication to allow statistical comparisons and heritability calculations.

[1] Canadian Forest Service, Pacific Forestry Centre, Victoria, BC, Canada.
[2] BC Ministry of Forests and Range (retired), Victoria, BC, Canada.
Corresponding author: ralfaro@pfc.forestry.ca.

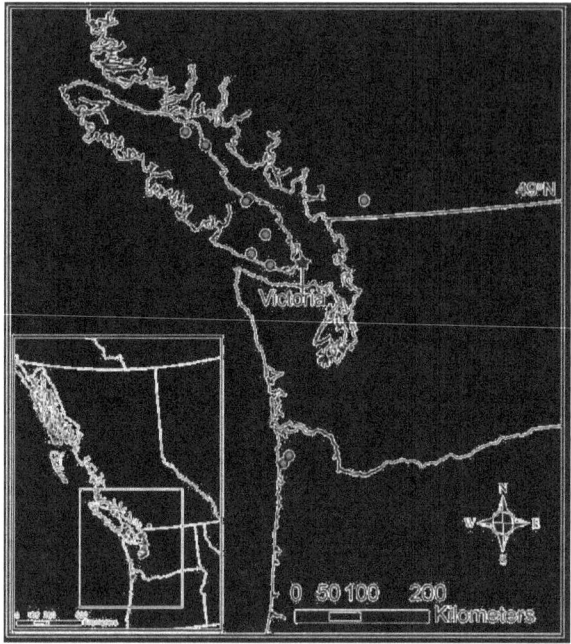

Figure 1—Locations of Sitka spruce screening trials on the west coast of North America.

Screening Methods

Screening of over 29,000 trees was conducted by artificially releasing laboratory-reared weevils (fig. 2) into the test plantations (for methods, see Alfaro et al. 2008) and then conducting annual evaluations of attack rates on the tested genotypes. Statistical analysis determined if particular families were resistant to attack and the heritability statistics.

Figure 2—Weevil release in Sitka spruce screening trial to screen genotypes for resistance to white pine weevil.

Results

Our trials indicated significant provenance variation in weevil resistance (fig. 3), with some open-pollinated parents consistently producing offspring with statistically demonstrable resistance to *P. strobi* (Alfaro et al. 2008). These parents are now in seed orchards and producing resistant seed for reforestation. We have also determined that resistance is both heritable and stable.

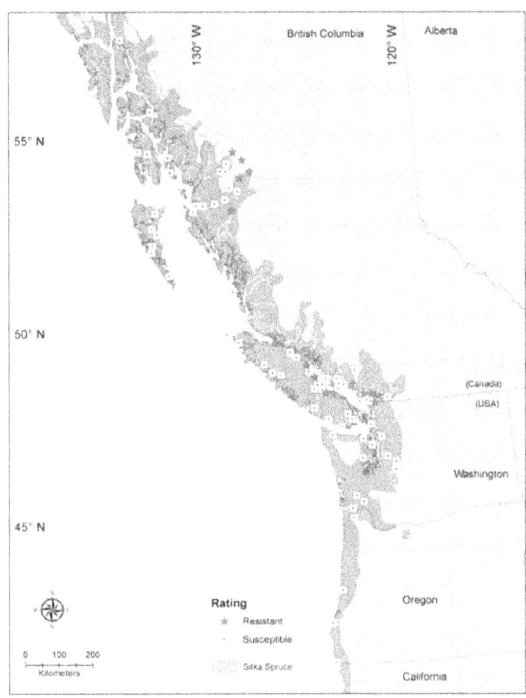

Figure 3—Range of Sitka spruce in western North America (green). Dots indicate sources tested for genetic resistance to weevil damage. Red dots indicate sources found to consistently produce progeny with resistance.

Artificial infestations allowed us to quickly and effectively proceed with the construction of an F1 population, to determine the heritability of resistance, and to further our understanding of the mechanisms that underlie weevil resistance. This F1 population is now screened (Moreira et al. 2011) using the same methodology as is used for the parent populations. Weevil resistance in the F1 spruce progeny demonstrated that progeny from resistant parents (R × R progeny) sustained significantly fewer weevil attacks than progeny from susceptible parents (S × S progeny) or progeny with one resistant and one susceptible parent (R × S progeny). Individual and family heritability estimates of the weevil resistance were 0.5 and 0.9, respectively. We also related the level of resistance in the F1 crosses to two constitutive mechanisms of resistance: the density of cortical resin canals and the amount of sclereid cells in the leader cortex (Moreira et al. 2011). Constitutive defenses were significantly higher in R × R progeny than in R × S or S × S progeny. We observed a negative correlation between the percentage of trees attacked in each cross and the average density of the resin canals or sclereid cells for each cross.

Our results indicated that effective screening for weevil resistance can be accomplished by using artificial weevil infestation. At the time of weevil release, trees need to be of susceptible height, i.e., outplanted for approximately 3 to 4 years in coastal BC. Once plantations are artificially infested, they should be monitored for at least 4 years to ensure that resistance is stable, i.e., that the selected genotypes sustain consistently low attack rates. This is a fairly quick turnaround time for studying resistance of forest trees from temperate regions. This is a promising result, which should encourage resistance studies for other regeneration pests.

Production and Deployment of Resistant Trees

The resistant genotypes identified through this program now form the basis for the successful establishment of Sitka spruce plantations in BC. Using our selections of weevil resistant parents, seed orchards have been established and are producing regeneration material for operational planting (seeds and seedlings) (fig. 4).

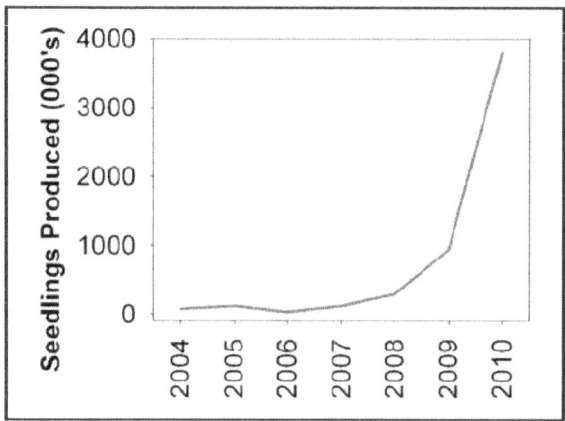

Figure 4—Annual amount resistant seedlings produced in British Columbia at Western Forest Products nursery in Saanich, BC.

While in the past, BC provincial coastal reforestation guidelines for high weevil hazard areas have recommended exclusion or limited planting of spruce, current guidelines indicate that up to half of the stand could be planted with Sitka spruce in moderate- or high-hazard areas if "A+" seed (from selected orchard-grown, weevil-resistant trees [R+87]) is used, and about a third if "B+" seed is used (from naturally resistant stands [R+64]) (Heppner and Turner 2006).

Conclusions

- The screening of putative parents for weevil resistance has been successfully completed (over 29,000 trees screened).
- Resistant Sitka spruce parents have been selected.
- Resistance is heritable and stable.
- An F1 progeny test was produced from control crosses of Resistant x Resistant, Resistant x Susceptible, and Susceptible x Susceptible parents.
- Breeding for resistance: Individual and family heritability estimates of weevil resistance were 0.5 and 0.9, respectively.
- Seed orchards are now producing the first generation of resistant seed for BC's next forest crop.

Acknowledgments

We thank George Brown, Forest Technician, Canadian Forest Service (retired) for the detailed assessment of the Sitka spruce test plantations over more than a decade.

Literature Cited

Alfaro, R.I.; King, J.N.; Brown, R.G.; Buddingh, S.M. 2008. Screening of Sitka spruce genotypes for resistance to the white pine weevil using artificial infestations. Forest Ecology and Management. 255: 1749–1758.

Heppner, D.; Turner, J. 2006. British Columbia's coastal forests: spruce weevil and western spruce budworm forest health stand establishment decision aids. BC Journal of Ecosystems and Management .7(3):45–49. http://www.forrex.org/publications/jem/ISS38/vol7_no3_art6.pdf. (29 January 2012).

Moreira, Xoaquín; Alfaro, R.I.; King, J.N. 2011. Constitutive defenses and damage in Sitka spruce progeny obtained from crosses between white pine weevil resistant and susceptible parents. Forestry. doi:10.1093/forestry/cpr060.

Developing Clones of *Eucalyptus cloeziana* Resistant to Rust (*Puccinia psidii*)

Rafael F. Alfenas,[1] Marcelo M. Coutinho,[2] Camila S. Freitas,[1] Rodrigo G. Freitas,[1] and Acelino C. Alfenas[1]

Abstract

Besides its high resistance to *Chrysoporthe cubensis* canker, *Eucalyptus cloeziana* F. Muell. is a highly valuable tree species for wood production. It can be used for furniture, electric poles, fence posts, and charcoal. Nevertheless, it is highly susceptible to the rust caused by *Puccinia psidii*, which limits its growth in areas favorable to infection. Since *E. cloeziana* does not interbreed naturally with other *Eucalyptus* species, its seedling plantations in Brazil are relatively uniform. Thus, the selection and multiplication of rust- resistant genotypes could constitute the best strategy for rust control. However, it is recalcitrant to rooting, which limits its large-scale clonal multiplication of resistant genotypes for planting, as has been done with *E. grandis* Hill ex Maiden, *E. urophylla* S.T. Blake and their hybrids. Aiming to obtain the greatest possible number of rust-resistant genotypes for cloning, about 3,500 seedlings of several seed lots of different origins were spray-inoculated with an inoculum suspension of 2×10^4 urediniospores/ml of the single pustule isolate (EUBA-1, race 4) of *P. psidii* according to the standard procedures used in our laboratory. The assessment of disease severity on each seedling was performed 12 and 20 days after inoculation using the rust severity scale of Junghans et al. (2003, Fitpatologia Brasileira. 28: 261–265). *Eucalyptus grandis* x *E. urophylla* hybrid clones C1179 (resistant) and C1183 (susceptible) were used as controls. Only about 2 percent of the inoculated seedlings were resistant and clonable. Attempts to multiply all 69 resistant clones are being made in order to have enough plants for clonal trials to evaluate their silvicultural performance and wood properties.

[1] Departamento de Fitopatologia, Universidade Federal de Viçosa, Viçosa, MG 36570-000, Brasil.
[2] Clonar Resistência a Doenças Florestais, Viçosa, MG 36570-000, Brasil.
Corresponding author: aalfenas@ufv.br.

Screening for Resistance to Fusiform Rust in Southern United States Forest Trees

Josh Bronson[1]

Abstract

The Resistance Screening Center (RSC) is operated by the Forest Health Protection unit of the U.S. Department of Agriculture, Forest Service, Southern Region, State and Private Forestry. The RSC is located at the Bent Creek Experimental Forest near Asheville, North Carolina. The center evaluates seedlings for resistance to disease, primarily fusiform rust (caused by *Cronartium quercuum* f. sp. *fusiforme*) and pitch canker (caused by *Fusarium circinatum*) as a service to tree improvement specialists, seed orchard managers, scientists, government agencies, research institutions, universities, and private industry. Testing enables clients to obtain information on the relative resistance of their materials in much less time than is possible in field progeny tests. The RSC has the flexibility to modify current screening procedures to accommodate specialized requests, such as unique species or inoculation procedures. This allows researchers to use the RSC as an additional experimental tool. In a research assistance capacity, the RSC has played an important role in newly developed understanding of genetic interactions in the pine-fusiform rust pathosystem, and will continue to do so in the foreseeable future. By using information from the resistance screening center tests, trees producing resistant progeny can be identified, or questions may be answered, concerning such things as the nature of pathogen variation or the effectiveness of fungicides. The RSC remains open to service screening work or research endeavors in an effort to improve forest health.

[1] USDA Forest Service, Resistance Screening Center, 1579 Brevard Road, Asheville, NC 28805.
Corresponding author: jjbronson@fs.fed.us.

Variation in the Development of Current Season Needle Necrosis on Noble, Nordmann, and Turkish Fir Christmas Trees in the United States Pacific Northwest

Gary A. Chastagner,[1] Kathy Riley,[1] and Chal Landgren[2]

Introduction

Current season needle necrosis (CSNN) is a poorly understood disease that affects a number of *Abies* spp. that are grown as Christmas trees (fig. 1). The disease has been reported on noble (*A. procera* Rehder), Nordmann (*A. nordmanniana* (Steven) Spach), and grand fir (*A. grandis* (Douglas ex D. Don) Lindl.) in Europe and these species, plus Turkish fir (*A. bornmuelleriana* Mattf.), in the United States Pacific Northwest (Chastagner 1997, Chastagner et al. 1990, Talgø et al. 2010). The development of CSNN varies by site and there is tremendous tree-to-tree variation in susceptibility to this disease (Chastagner and Landgren 1998; Chastagner et al. 1990, 2008). In an effort to determine year-to-year variation in the development of CSNN and identify sources of trees with resistance to this disease, data have been collected from a series of genetic trials at Washington State University (WSU), Puyallup.

Figure 1—Current season needle necrosis (CSNN) symptoms on a noble fir Christmas tree at Washington State University (WSU), Puyallup.

Methods

In 2002 and 2004, a series of replicated genetic field trials were established at the WSU Research Center in Puyallup, Washington. This is a low elevation site that is very conducive to the development of CSNN. These trials contain 91 sources of noble fir, 15 sources of Nordmann fir, and 4 sources of Turkish fir. Over a 4- to 6-year-period, symptom severity was rated on a scale of 0 to 10 during late summer/early fall.

Results and Discussion

There was significant yearly variation in the overall average CSNN ratings for the trees in these trials. Over 6 years, ratings for the 37 sources of noble fir in the 2002 planting ranged from an average low of 1.5 in 2009 to an average high of 3.4 in 2006. Over 5 years, the yearly overall average rating for

[1] Washington State University, Research and Extension Center, 2606 West Pioneer, Puyallup, WA 98731.
[2] Oregon State University, North Willamette Research and Extension Center, 15210 NE Miley Rd, Aurora, OR 97002. Corresponding author: chastag@wsu.edu.

the 54 sources of noble fir in the 2004 trial ranged from a low of about 1.1 in 2005 to a high of 3.3 in 2008. Compared to the noble fir, limited CSNN developed on the Nordmann and Turkish fir trees. Over 4 years, the average ratings for the sources of Nordmann and Turkish fir ranged from 0.3 to 0.9.

In the 2002 noble fir plot, the percentage of trees that were resistant to CSNN ranged from 5 to 80 percent depending on the source (fig. 2). In the 2004 noble fir plot, the range was 4 to 65 percent. No CSNN developed on over 80 percent of the trees from seven of the sources of Nordmann/Turkish fir. Although there was significant yearly variation in the severity of CSNN, Spearman rank order correlation analysis indicated that there was a highly significant correlation between the yearly susceptibility rankings of the noble, Nordmann, and Turkish fir sources in each of these plots.

Figure 2—Five trees from a resistant source of trees
in the 2002 noble fir trial at WSU, Puyallup.

The effect of the site on CSNN development was examined by comparing the severity of CSNN development on trees in the 2004 noble fir genetic test plot at Puyallup to the same sources at Silver Mountain Christmas Trees near Sublimity, Oregon in 2009. The overall plot CSNN rating for the trees at Silver Mountain was much lower than Puyallup. Over 94 percent of the trees at Silver Mountain had no CSNN, compared to only 23 percent at Puyallup. Even though much less CSNN developed at Silver Mountain, Spearman rank order analysis indicated that there was a highly significant correlation in susceptibility rankings of the sources at both sites. Regression analysis of CSNN ratings from Nordmann and Turkish fir planted in a "valley" and "hill" at Puyallup also indicated that there was a highly significant correlation between the 4-year-average ratings of the individual sources at the valley and hill sites.

These results indicate that there is considerable variation in the susceptibility of different sources of noble, Nordmann, and Turkish fir to CSNN and that the relative susceptibility of different sources of trees to CSNN can be determined after 1 or 2 years at conducive sites.

Literature Cited

Chastagner, G.A., ed. 1997. Christmas tree diseases, insects, and disorders in the Pacific Northwest: identification and management. Cooperative Ext. Publication MISC0186. Pullman: Washington State University. 154 p.

Chastagner, G.A.; Landgren, C. 1998. Genetic variation and the influence of fertilization on the development of current season needle necrosis on noble fir Christmas trees. In: Leflamme, G.; Berube, J.A.; Hamelin, R.C., eds. Foliage, shoot and stem diseases of trees. Quebec: Natural Resources Canada, Canadian Forest Service: 219–226.

Chastagner, G.A.; Riley, K.L.; Landgren, C. 2008. Variation in the susceptibility of noble fir to current season needle necrosis. In: Thomsen, I.M.; Rasmussen, H.N.; Sørensen, J.M., eds. Proceedings of the 8th international Christmas tree research and extension conference. Hørsholm, Denmark: University of Copenhagen: 87–88. www.ps-xmastree.dk and www.iufro.org. (29 January 2012).

Chastagner, G.A.; Staley, J.M.; Riley, K.L. 1990. Current season needle necrosis: a needle disorder of unknown etiology on noble and grand fir Christmas trees in the Pacific Northwest. In: Merrill, W.; Ostry, M.E., eds. Recent research on foliar diseases. Gen. Tech. Rept. WO-56. Washington, DC: U.S. Department of Agriculture, Forest Service: 38–42.

Talgø, V.; Chastagner, G.A.; Thomsen, I.M.; Cech, T.; Riley, K.L.; Lange, K.; Klemsdal, S.S.; Stensvand, A. 2010. *Sydowia polyspora* associated with current season needle necrosis (CSNN) on true fir (*Abies* spp.). Fungal Biology. 114: 545–554.

Frequency of Hypersensitive-Like Reaction and Stem Infections in a Large Full-Sib Family of *Pinus monticola*

Robert S. Danchok,[1] R.A. Sniezko,[1] S. Long,[1] A. Kegley,[1] D. Savin,[1] J.B. Mayo,[1] J.J. Liu,[2] and J. Hill[3]

Introduction

Western white pine (WWP) (*Pinus monticola* Douglas ex D. Don) is a long-lived forest tree species with a large native range in western North America. The tree species is highly susceptible to the non-native fungal pathogen, *Cronartium ribicola*, the causative agent of white pine blister rust (WPBR).

Several types of genetic resistance to WPBR are present in WWP, of which the best documented is a hypersensitive-like reaction (HR) in the needles that conveys complete resistance (generally no stem infection) and is conditioned by a single dominant gene (*Cr2*). The HR resistance is rare, and its occurrence is geographically limited (Kinloch et al. 1999, 2003). Virulence to *Cr2* in the rust (*vcr2*) is known (Kinloch et al. 2004). Most screening trials examine relatively few seedlings for any one family for HR. We report on the frequency of HR (using needle phenotypes) in a large full-sib family (3,592 individuals) in a cross between two putative *Cr2* heterozygotes (this is part of a larger genetic study to map *Cr2*); the frequency of stem symptoms and mortality in HR and non-HR seedlings; and the number of stem symptoms per seedling for HR and non-HR phenotypes.

Materials and Methods

Western white pine (WWP) seed of a single full-sib family (15045-862 x 15045-837) was stratified for 120 days and then sown in June 2010. The 3,592 seedlings from this 1991 seed collection were grown in a greenhouse at Dorena Genetic Resource Center (DGRC), Cottage Grove, Oregon in the summer of 2010 (fig. 1). Both parents are heterozygotes (*Cr2cr2*) for HR resistance and originated from the Champion Mine area on the Cottage Grove Ranger District, Umpqua National Forest in Oregon. This stand had previously been noted for having the highest incidence of parents with *Cr2* of any areas tested (Kinloch et al. 1999, 2003). Seedlings had both primary needles and cotyledons present at inoculation (only a few seedlings displayed any secondary needles). Seedlings were inoculated with *C. ribicola* in September 2010 using standard DGRC protocols (Danchok et al. 2004). For artificial inoculation, infected *Ribes* spp. leaves (the alternate host of *C. ribicola*) from geographical areas outside of the areas of known occurrence of *vcr2* were collected and suspended above the pines under optimal conditions for spore drop and germination. Inoculum density for the trial averaged 6,805 basidiospores/cm^2, and spore germination averaged 89 percent. After inoculation, seedlings were placed in an unheated greenhouse for nursery culture and subsequent development of rust symptoms.

Seedlings were assessed at periodic intervals when needle spots and stem symptoms were evident. The assessments for spot type included rating each seedling for whether all spots were susceptible (code 1) or whether all spots were HR type (code 4). Seedlings with a combination of HR and susceptible spots (or some of the seedlings with HR-like spots, but stem symptoms at the early assessments) were initially assigned a separate category (code 2), as were seedlings where the spot phenotype was ambiguous (code

[1] USDA Forest Service, Dorena Genetic Resource Center, Cottage Grove, Oregon, USA.
[2] Natural Resources Canada, Canadian Forest Service, Pacific Forestry Centre, Victoria, British Columbia, Canada.
[3] National Park Service, Southeast Utah Group, Moab, Utah, USA.
Corresponding author: rsniezko@fs.fed.us.

3). The presence of stem symptoms was also recorded, and in March and April 2011, a count of stem symptoms was made. Mortality was also recorded. In June 2011, the spot type was re-evaluated on the 33 seedlings coded as '3' to classify into type 1, 2, or 4. A subset of 150 seedlings was examined for type of stem symptoms in July 2010.

Results

The artificial inoculation was very successful, with most seedlings having dozens to hundreds of needle spots (fig. 1). All seedlings were ultimately classified as having type 1, 2, or 4 spots. All 3,592 seedlings showed needle spots by April 2011, and 36 percent had only susceptible (S), non-HR spots (fig. 1). The 64:36 ratio (HR spots: S spots) differed significantly from the expected 3:1 ratio (Chi-square p-value < 0.0001) and also from a 1:1 ratio (p-value < 0.0001).

Figure 1—March 2011 photos (6 months after inoculation): (a) overview of *P. monticola* trial; (b) hundreds of needle spots (HR) on inoculated *P. monticola* seedling; (c) resistant (HR) and susceptible (S) spots on *P. monticola*; note many infections per needle, (d) needles with S and HR spots (note incomplete development at this point of HR spots on one needle).

By April 2011, 94.4 percent of the category 1 (S) seedlings had stem symptoms, versus 29.5 percent for the HR seedlings (groups 2 and 4) (57.4 percent and 13.8 percent of the category 2 and 4 (HR) seedlings, respectively) (figs. 1 to 3). By November 2011, stem symptoms had increased to 97.5 and 53.1 percent for S and HR seedlings, respectively. The non-HR (S) seedlings averaged 4.6 stem symptoms per infected tree in April, while the HR seedlings averaged 1.6 (type 2 and 4 seedlings averaged 1.7 and 1.4 stem symptoms per infected tree, respectively (fig. 4)). This difference was significant (two-sided p-value < 0.0001 from a likelihood ratio test); the mean number of stem symptoms per infected tree is estimated to be 2.9 times greater for S seedlings than HR seedlings (95 percent confidence interval from 2.7 to 3.1 times greater) (figs. 2 and 4). Stem symptoms generally appeared earlier on non-HR than on the HR seedlings: 77.9 percent of non-HR had SS in March, while only 14.1 percent and 3.1 percent of the HR seedlings in categories 2 and 4, respectively, had SS (fig. 3).

Overall mortality (seedlings with and without stem symptoms) by November 2011 was 92.2 and 72.6 percent for S and HR seedlings, respectively; the odds of mortality for S seedlings were estimated to be 3.6 times to 5.6 times as large as the odds of mortality for HR seedlings (approximate 95 percent confidence interval). The mortality for the subset of seedlings with stem symptoms was 92.2 and 77.0 percent for S and HR seedlings, respectively. For seedlings with no visible stem symptoms, mortality was also high: 90.9 and 67.5 percent for the S and HR groups.

Discussion

Based on the needle phenotypes following artificial inoculation, the ratio of HR:non-HR seedlings (64:36) was less than the 75:25 ratio anticipated in a cross of two *Cr2* heterozygotes. In a previous trial, progenies of some of the parents from the Champion Mine stand have showed reduced penetrance of *Cr2*– expressed by altered Mendelian ratios (mostly less-than-expected resistant phenotypes) in specific combinations of certain parents, indicating the potential presence of modifier genes with effects that ranged from mild to almost complete suppression of *Cr2* (Kinloch et al. 1999). This may explain the

Figure 2—Stem infections observed on seedlings with S spots (a, c, and e) and on seedlings with HR spots (b and d).

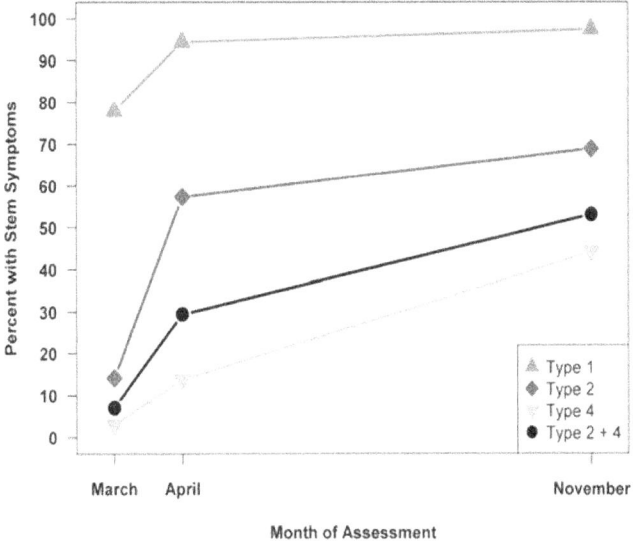

Figure 3—Percentage of *Pinus monticola* seedlings with stem symptoms by assessment date for the three needle spot types: 1: all susceptible (S) spots, 2: at least one resistant (HR) spot, 4: all (HR) spots.

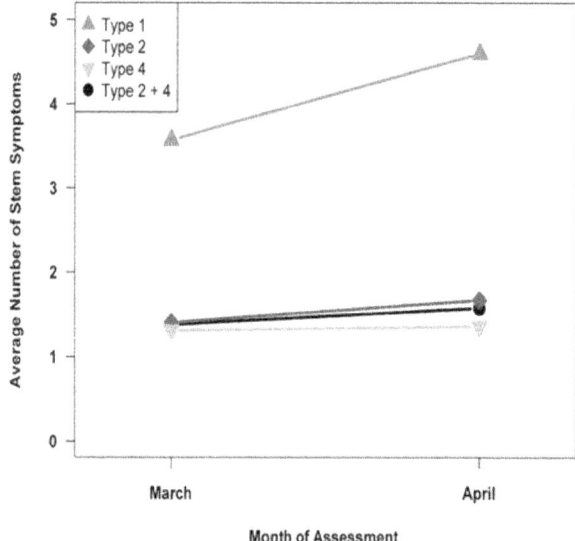

Figure 4—Mean number of stem symptoms (per infected tree) by assessment date for the three needle phenotype category types: 1: all susceptible (S) spots, 2: at least one HR spot, 4: all HR spots.

slightly lower than expected frequency of HR phenotypes in this full-sib family. Previous tests in 2002 and 2008 using this full-sib family from five different seed collection years (1974, 1980, 1988, 1989, 1991) showed similar results, with ratios in all tests exhibiting <75 percent HR type spots (unpublished data). There was no evidence of a difference in the ratio of HR:non-HR seedlings for any of the five different seed collection years (p-value = 0.14 from a likelihood ratio test). This suggests that inadvertent contamination of this full-sib seedlot by other pollens or seedlots is unlikely, but further investigation is needed to discern whether this is a possibility. Other possible explanations are discussed below.

The number of HR seedlings with stem symptoms was unexpected. In previous trials, including the 2002 and 2008 trials with this same family, few or no seedlings of WWP with HR had stem symptoms in the absence of known *vcr2* sources of rust. The reason for the high incidence of stem infection of HR seedlings in this trial is unknown, but it is possible that a very low frequency of *vcr2* was present in the inoculum and coupled with a very large number of needle infections per seedling resulted in stem infections on some seedlings. Another possible explanation is that there could be 'leakage' in the HR, at least under this high-effective infection level and some environments. Many seedlings had several hundred needle spots with some individual needles having more than 15 needle spots (fig.1). It was observed that the timing of development of the necrotic bands around the yellow spots could vary even within a seedling and that on several seedlings the necrotic band did not fully encircle the spot, suggesting that HR was sometimes only partially effective. Some of these seedlings showed stem symptoms at the base of such needles. The HR in some plant pathosystems is a temperature-dependent trait (Goodman and Novacky 1994, Wang et al. 2009) and that may have had some influence here, but investigations of the temperature sensitivity of HR in WWP (and other white pines) have not been done. However, relatively high levels of stem symptoms of HR seedlings are not unprecedented. Kinloch and Comstock (1980) reported that about 32 percent of sugar pine (*P. lambertiana* Dougl.) seedlings with HR showed evidence of stem symptoms, and that this infection was generally only apparent on seedlings with primary needles (versus cotyledons or secondary needles). In sugar pine HR seedlings, the stem infections were abnormal and never sporulated.

The latency in stem symptom development observed on HR seedlings in this WWP trial is similar to that reported on HR seedlings in sugar pine by Kinloch and Littlefield (1977). They reported that 27 percent of HR ('fleck') phenotypes developed atypical bark symptoms from primary needle infection. The bark symptoms resulting from primary needle infection on fleck phenotypes of sugar pine developed at a slower rate and were always incompatible and healed by the second year after inoculation. It was hypothesized that primary needles may react differently or have a somewhat lower resistance than secondary needles (Kinloch and Comstock 1980). Primary needles were the predominant needles present on the WWP in this study. In this study, in contrast to S seedlings, the HR seedlings with stem symptoms tended to show SSs later, had fewer SSs, and had lower mortality of both seedlings with SSs and those showing no SSs. This trial had a very high number of needle spots on the primary needles and a high level of stem symptoms on HR seedlings, as well as an unexpected and relatively high mortality of seedlings with no stem symptoms (reason unknown). In the earlier 2002 and 2008 trials of this full-sib family, very few of the HR seedlings developed stem symptoms and there was little mortality of HR seedlings. Thus, if very young WWP seedlings are used, needle spot type would generally be a more reliable indicator of presence or absence of HR in WWP than relying on whether stem symptoms are present.

The nature of the resistance for seedlings showing an HR-like needle spot is still unknown. Some recent histological investigations indicate that it is not the classic, very rapid, hypersensitive response that often occurs within hours of infection; further histological work is underway to further characterize the nature of this needle resistance in WWP (Sweeney et al., Are needle reactions in resistance to *Cronartium ribicola* a hypersensitivity response?, these proceedings). Tissue from the seedlings in this WWP study will be used by Dr. Liu's group for molecular characterization by RNA-seq for discovery of single nucleotide polymorphisms (SNPs) between phenotypic groups, with some future work using high throughput SNP genotyping technique to find functional genes tightly linked to *Cr2* in this full-sib family for positional characterization of *Cr2*.

Acknowledgments

We thank Brian Luis for assistance with assessments and Bohun B. Kinloch Jr. for review of an earlier version of this paper.

Literature Cited

Danchok, R.; Sharpe, J.; Bates, K.; Fitzgerald, K.; Kegley, A.; Long, S.; Sniezko, R; Danielson, J.; Spence, R. 2004. Operational manual for white pine blister rust inoculation at Dorena Genetic Resource Center. 31 p. On file with: USDA Forest Service, Dorena Genetic Resource Center, Cottage Grove, Oregon.

Goodman, R.N.; Novacky, A.J. 1994. The hypersensitive reaction in plants to pathogens—a resistance phenomenon. St. Paul, MN: APS Press. 244 p.

Kinloch, B.B., Jr.; Comstock, M. 1980. Cotyledon test for major gene resistance to white pine blister rust in sugar pine. Canadian Journal of Botany. 58: 1912–1914.

Kinloch, B.B., Jr.; Littlefield, J.L. 1977. White pine blister rust: hypersensitive resistance in sugar pine. Canadian Journal of Botany. 55: 1148–1154.

Kinloch, B.B. ,Jr.; Sniezko, R.A.; Barnes, G.D.; Greathouse, T.E. 1999. A major gene for resistance to white pine blister rust in western white pine from the western Cascade Range. Phytopathology. 89(10): 861–867.

Kinloch, B.B., Jr.; Sniezko, R.A.; Dupper, G.E. 2003. Origin and distribution of Cr2, a gene for resistance to white pine blister rust in natural populations of western white pine. Phytopathology. 93(6): 691–694.

Kinloch, B.B. ,Jr.; Sniezko, R.A.; Dupper, G.E. 2004. Virulence gene distribution and dynamics of the white pine blister rust pathogen in western North America. Phytopathology. 94(7): 751–758.

Wang, Y.; Bao, Z.; Zhu, Y.; Hua, J. 2009. Analysis of temperature modulation of plant defense against biotropic microbes. Molecular Plant-Microbe Interactions. 22(5): 498–505.

Operational Disease Screening Program for Resistance to Wilt in *Acacia koa* in Hawaii[1]

Nick Dudley,[2] Robert James,[3] Richard Sniezko,[4] Phil Cannon,[5] Aileen Yeh,[2] Tyler Jones,[2] and Michael Kaufmann[2]

Introduction

In Hawaii, koa (*Acacia koa* A. Gray) is a valuable tree species economically, ecologically, and culturally. With significant land use change and declines in sugarcane, pineapple, and cattle production, there is an opportunity and keen interest in utilizing native koa in reforestation and restoration efforts. However, moderate to high mortality rates in many of the low to moderate elevation plantings have impeded past efforts (fig. 1). The primary cause for this mortality, particularly in young plantings, is thought to be koa wilt, caused by *Fusarium oxysporum* f. sp. *koae* (FOXY) (Gardner 1980). *Fusarium oxysporum* is a relatively common agricultural and nursery fungus, but the origin of strains of FOXY virulent to koa in Hawaii is unknown.

Figure 1—Koa stand killed by *Fusarium oxysporum* f. sp. *koae* (FOXY).

[1] With the exception of minor word changes and the addition of photos, this paper was previously published in the Hawaii Forestry Association August 29 2009 issue of the Association Newsletter.
[2] Hawaii Agriculture Research Center, Forestry, Honolulu, HI, USA.
[3] Plant Disease Consulting Northwest, Vancouver, WA, USA.
[4] USDA Forest Service, Dorena Genetic Resource Center, Cottage Grove, OR, USA.
[5] USDA Forest Service, Forest Health Protection, Vallejo, CA, USA.
Corresponding author: ndudley@harc-hspa.com.

Solution

Identifying and developing koa populations that are genetically resistant to virulent strains of FOXY may be the key to successful koa restoration and reforestation (Sniezko 2006). Great differences in mortality among seed sources in young koa field trials planted in the 1990s were the impetus for developing a seedling screening test and investigating genetic resistance to FOXY (Sniezko 2003).

Status of Resistance Breeding Program

A statewide survey was conducted to determine distribution of koa wilt/dieback disease across the four main Hawaiian Islands: Kauai, Maui, Oahu, and Hawaii (fig. 2). A total of 386 samples were taken at 46 different sites covering approximately 5,597 ha of natural and planted koa forest. Koa trees and seedlings infected by *F. oxysporum* were found on all of the major islands in forest tree seedling nurseries and in natural and plantation forests. From these samples, more than 500 isolates of *F. oxysporum* were obtained. Of these, 160 isolates have been tested for virulence on koa seedlings in controlled greenhouse inoculation tests. From isolate screening tests, 10 highly virulent isolates have been identified for use in screening selected koa families for disease resistance (Dudley et al. 2007).

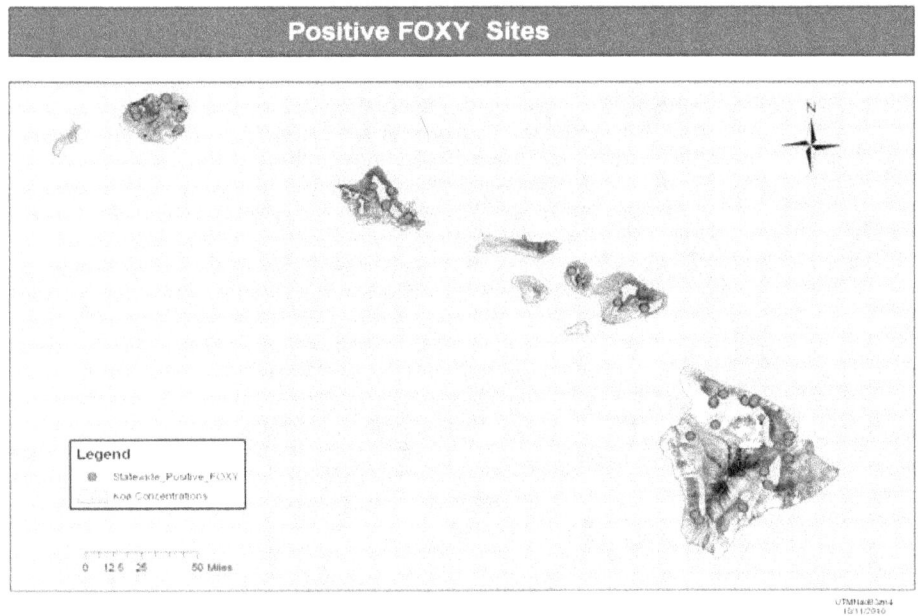

Figure 2—Koa concentrations and sites with *Fusarium oxysporum* f. sp. *koae* (FOXY) in Hawaii.

Between 2006 and 2011, more than 270 koa families were evaluated for their potential FOXY resistance in greenhouse tests (fig. 3). Most of the seed lots came from wild populations. However, several seed lots were from survivors of family level progeny trials at the Hawaii Agriculture Research Center's (HARC) Maunawili Field Station (fig. 4). All seed lots were open-pollinated. A composite of five virulent isolates of FOXY were used for inoculation (Dudley et al. 2007). Seedling wilting and mortality in the greenhouse was monitored over a 90-day period for each test. Seedling mortality among seed lots varied widely (4 to 100 percent) and averaged 60 percent (Dudley et al. 2009). These initial results indicate that natural resistance to FOXY is low within native koa populations.

Figure 3—Koa disease screening trial at the Hawaii Agriculture Research Center (HARC).

Figure 4—Koa seed orchard at the Hawaii Agriculture Research Center (HARC).

Continued screening of additional koa families for pathogen resistance, retesting putative resistant families, and developing koa seed orchards with disease-resistant stock are either ongoing or planned.

Literature Cited

Dudley, N.S.; James R.L.; Sniezko R.A.; Yeh A. 2007. Investigating koa wilt and dieback in Hawai`i-pathogenicity of *Fusarium* species on *Acacia koa* seedlings. Native Plants. : 259–266.

Dudley, N.S.; Sniezko, R.A.; James, R.L.; Cannon, P.; Jones, T.; Yeh, A.; Kaufman M. 2009. Developing resistant koa-early results from survey to seedlings resistance testing in Hawaii. In: Cram, M.M., ed. Proceedings of the 7th meeting of IUFRO Working Party 7.03.04. Diseases and insects in forest nurseries. Forest Health Protection Report 10-01-01. Atlanta, GA: U.S. Department of Agriculture, Forest Service, Southern Region: 39–47.

Gardner, D.E. 1980. *Acacia koa* seedling wilt caused by *Fusarium oxysporum*. Phytopathology. 70: 594–597.

Sniezko, R.A. 2003. Potential for selecting for genetic resistance to *F. oxysporum* (koa wilt) in koa for conservation, restoration and utilization in Hawaii. Trip report (8/23/2003). Cottage Grove, OR: U.S. Department of Agriculture, Forest Service, Dorena Genetic Resource Center. 13 p.

Sniezko, R.A. 2006. Resistance breeding against nonnative pathogens in forest trees–current successes in North America. Canadian Journal of Plant Pathology. 28: S270–S279.

A First Look at Genetic Variation in Resistance to the Root Pathogen *Phytophthora cinnamomi* using a Range-wide Collection of Pacific Madrone (*Arbutus menziesii*)

Marianne Elliott,[1] Gary A. Chastagner,[1] Annie DeBauw,[1] Gil Dermott,[1] and Richard A. Sniezko[2]

Introduction

Phytophthora cinnamomi (Oomycetes) causes root disease and basal canker on a number of hardwood and conifer hosts, including Pacific madrone (*Arbutus menziesii* Pursh) (figs. 1, 2), a broadleaf evergreen species whose range extends from coastal British Columbia to southern California (Reeves 2007). Increasing mortality of Pacific madrone and the related shrub species manzanita (*Arctostaphylos* spp.) has been seen in California forests (Fichtner et al. 2009) in recent years.

Considered to be one of the world's most invasive species, *P. cinnamomi* is thought to have originated in southeast Asia and spread worldwide, causing decline in Australian eucalypt forests, crop losses on avocado in California and Europe, and on Christmas tree plantations in the southeast United States. It has a wide host range and infects many ornamental trees and shrubs in landscape plantings. In this situation, it is thought that the pathogen moves in contaminated soil on nursery stock (Smith 1988).

Materials and Methods

Between 2006 and 2008, Pacific madrone (*Arbutus menziesii* Pursh) fruit was collected from 237 trees at various sites throughout its natural distribution range in British Columbia, California, Oregon, and Washington and extracted seed was added to the Washington State University (WSU) Puyallup madrone seed collection. From this collection, seedlings were grown from 34 families representing seven ecoregions for the study (table 1). One to five families per geographic location within one or two locations in each ecoregion were sampled. Twelve one-year-old seedlings per family were arranged randomly in rows on the greenhouse benches. Six seedlings per family were inoculated with an isolate of *P. cinnamomi* collected from madrone roots in Sonoma County, California, and the remaining six were not inoculated. After inoculation, all plant pots were placed in 946 ml plastic cups which were then flooded with water. Plants remained submerged in water for 2 days.

Seedlings were then observed for wilting and browning symptoms (fig. 3) over a 6- week period after which roots and stems of inoculated and check plants were sampled for dry weight (table 2). Principal components analysis was performed on mean values of all variables arranged by seedlot (family) after standardization (z-score). Non-parametric ANOVA (Kruskal-Wallis test) was performed on the original variables grouped by site and ecoregion, and Dunn's post-hoc test was performed if the differences were significant at $P = 0.05$.

[1] Washington State University, Research and Extension Center, 2606 West Pioneer, Puyallup, WA 98731.
[2] USDA Forest Service, Dorena Genetic Resource Center, 34963 Shoreview Road, Cottage Grove, OR 97424.
Corresponding author: melliott2@wsu.edu.

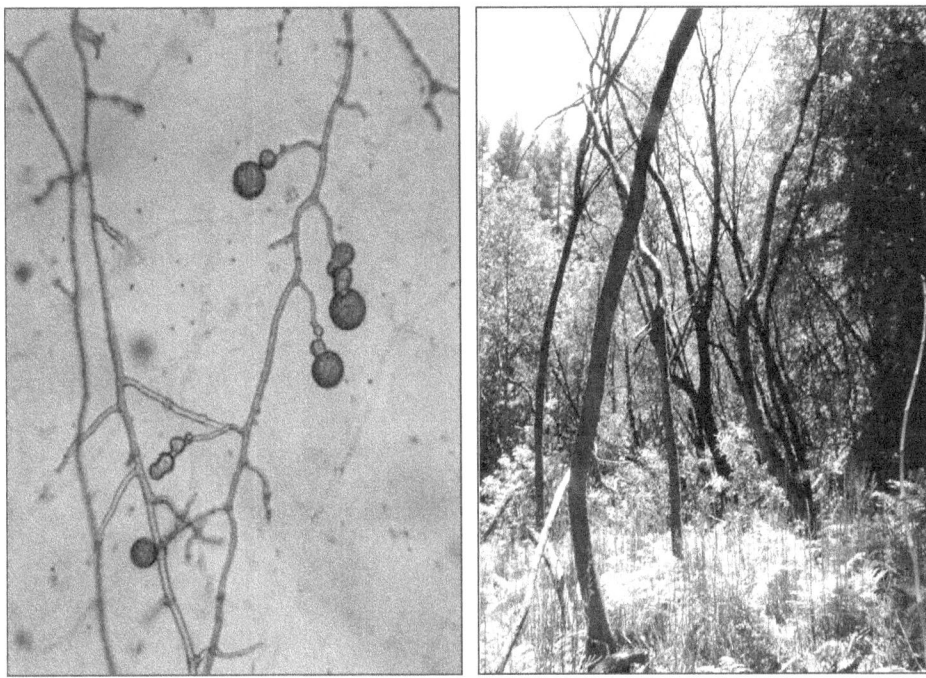

Figure 1 (left)—*Phytophthora cinnamomi* in V8 culture The organism can be identified by clusters of chlamydospores and coralloid hyphae. (Photo: Jeff Kepley)

Figure 2 (right)—Madrones in Soquel State Demonstration Forest, California. These trees have symptoms of crown dieback and general decline. *Phytophthora cinnamomi* was baited out of soil from this area. Horsetail (*Equisetum* spp.) is growing on the site, which is near the bottom of a slope, and is indicative of a wet site.

Table 1—Sites and ecoregions in western North America where Pacific madrone seed sources used in this experiment originated

Site	Ecoregion	Number of seed sources
BC16	Coastal western hemlock/Sitka spruce	1
BC14	Pacific and Nass ranges	1
FB, FW	Strait of Georgia, Puget lowland	10
WV	Willamette Valley	2
CP, KL	Klamath mountains	10
PL	Sierra Nevada	5
CC, SC	California coastal sage, chaparral, and oak woodlands	5

Figure 3—Madrone seedlings in greenhouse 21 days after inoculation. Some variability in symptom expression can be seen. The seedling on the left is dead where the seedling on the right is relatively healthy.

Table 2—Data collected on Pacific madrone seedlings inoculated with *Phytophthora cinnamomi* in the greenhouse trial

Variable	Description
BR	Disease severity - 0-10: 0 = 0% brown foliage, 1= 1-10% brown, 2=11-20% brown, 10= 91-100% brown, dead plant.
WR	Wilt rating - 0-4: 0 = no disease, 1= slight disease, 2 = Moderate disease, 3 = severe, 4= dead plant.
RR	Root ball size rating - 1-5: 1 = smallest, 5 = largest
RDW	Root dry wt, grams
SDW	Stem dry wt, grams

Results and Discussion

Variability within seed sources was high for root dry weight in both inoculated and check treatments and lower for other variables. *Phytophthora cinnamomi* was isolated from the roots of all inoculated plants and not from the roots of check plants.

No relationship between ecoregion and any of the variables was observed. There were significant differences in disease severity on inoculated plants among sites, with the least disease seen on seedlings obtained from parent trees at Fidalgo Bay, Washington (fig. 4). There was no significant difference in disease severity among families when considered separately; however, agglomerative hierarchical clustering produced three groups with low, intermediate, and high disease severity (table 3).

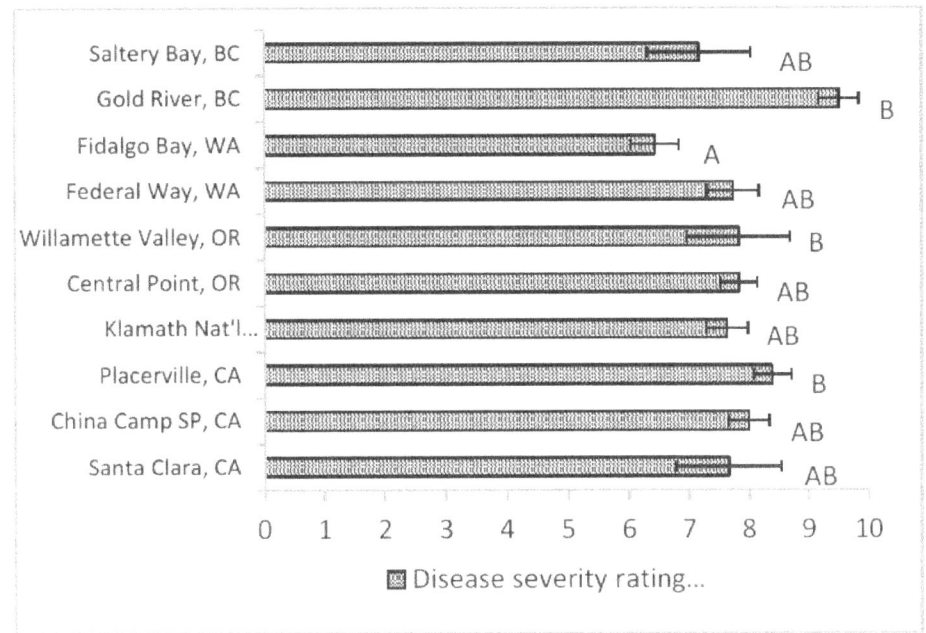

Figure 4—Severity of browning and wilting symptoms on madrone seedlings from seed collected at 10 sites. (Kruskal-Wallis test with Dunn's multiple comparisons. Bars with different letters are significantly different at p = 0.05).

Table 3—Groupings of families by severity of browning symptoms on plants inoculated with *Phytophthora cinnamomi* using agglomerative hierarchical clustering (AHC)

Class	Disease severity rating[a]	Families
1	6.0	FB3, FB5, FB8, FW10, KL8
2	7.5	BC14, CC2, CC3, CC7, CP18, CP21, CP23, CP24, FB1, FB6, FW5, FW7, FW9, KL1, KL2, PL11, PL4, SC9, WV2
3	8.9	BC16, CC1, CP11, FW3, KL10, KL7, PL3, PL5, PL9, WV5

[a] Disease severity rating is given as the class centroid for each group.

Root ball size rating (RR) and root dry weight (RDW) of inoculated plants were negatively correlated with the disease severity rating (r = -0.459 RR, -0.424 RDW). The root dry weight, stem dry weight, and root ball size rating on check plants showed no relationship with disease ratings on inoculated plants from the same seed sources. The first two principal components accounted for 63% of the variation in the data set (Figure 5). The first principal component was related to root and shoot weights and root ball rating (inoculated and check plants), and the second to disease severity (inoculated plants). Thus, plant size was not a predictor of disease development in this experiment.

This initial study indicated that while madrones from some seed sources had less severe symptoms than others, there was no significant relationship of disease severity with plant characteristics measured, such as root ball size and stem dry weight. To confirm these results, this experiment was repeated in fall 2011 using seedlings from the same seedlots. Results from 2011 were similar to those from 2010.

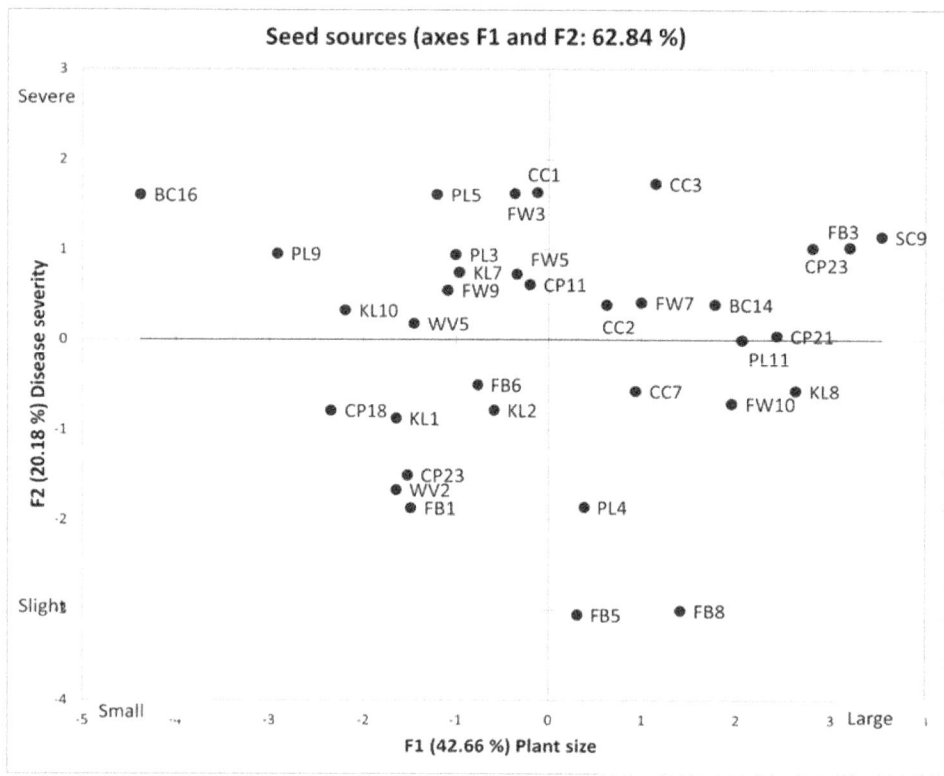

Figure 5—Scatter plot showing results of principal components analysis on the variables measured in this study. Individual seed sources are labeled by site and tree number.

Literature Cited

Fichtner, E.J.; Rizzo, D.M.; Swiecki, T.J.; Bernhardt, E.A. 2009. Emergence of *Phytophthora cinnamomi* in a sudden oak death-impacted forest. In: Frankel, Susan J.; Kliejunas, John T.; Palmieri, Katharine M. 2010. Proceedings of the sudden oak death fourth science symposium. Gen. Tech. Rep. PSW-GTR-229. Albany, CA: U.S. Department of Agriculture, Forest Service, Pacific Southwest Research Station. 378 p.

Reeves, S.L. 2007. *Arbutus menziesii.* In: Fire effects information system, [online]. U.S. Department of Agriculture, Forest Service, Rocky Mountain Research Station, Fire Sciences Laboratory (Producer). http://www fs.fed.us/database/feis/. (06 October 2011).

Smith, P.M. 1988. *Phytophthora cinnamomi.* In: Smith, I.M.; Dunez, J.; Lelliott, R.A.; Phillips, D.H.; Archer, S.A., eds. European handbook of plant diseases. Oxford, UK: Blackwell Scientific Publications: 213–215.

Range-wide Genetic Variability in Pacific Madrone (*Arbutus menziesii*): Examining Disease Resistance, Growth, and Survival in a Common Garden Study

Marianne Elliott,[1] Gary A. Chastagner,[1] Gil Dermott,[1] Alan Kanaskie,[2] Richard A. Sniezko,[3] and Jim Hamlin[4]

Introduction

Pacific madrone (*Arbutus menziesii* Pursh, Ericaceae) is an important evergreen hardwood species in Pacific Northwest (PNW) forests that provides food and habitat for wildlife and has high value in urban environments. Reeves (2007) indicates that Pacific madrone provides habitat for numerous wildlife species, especially cavity-nesting birds. Its evergreen foliage provides browse, especially in the winter, for a number of animals. The berries are an important food for deer, birds, and other small mammals because they are produced in large quantities and may persist on the tree in winter when alternative food sources are limited (Dayton 1931). Reeves (2007) also indicates that it provides excellent erosion control and slope stabilization and is highly prized as an ornamental species for its crooked beauty, colorful bark, showy flowers, and brightly colored fruits. Pacific madrone is relatively drought tolerant, which makes it desirable in urban habitats. Native American tribes have also used various portions of this tree for food, utensils, and medicinal purposes (Arno et al. 1977, Dayton 1931).

The species has been in decline for several decades due to a combination of factors such as climate change, forest management, and several endemic fungal pathogens. Several diseases affect the health of Pacific madrone throughout its range from southern British Columbia (lat. 50 °N) to southern California (lat. 33 °N). These include the endemic canker disease caused by species of *Fusicoccum* (*F. arbuti* and *F. aesculi*), numerous foliar pathogens, and introduced diseases such as *Phytophthora ramorum* and *P. cinnamomi*. Changes in climate over the past 100 years as well as the introduction of *P. ramorum* have resulted in an increase in disease incidence and tree mortality in western North American forests. *Phytophthora ramorum*, *F. arbuti*, and *Phacidiopycnis washingtonensis*, a newly identified potential foliar pathogen, are cool-temperature organisms, having optimum temperatures for growth below 25 °C (Farr et al. 2005, Werres et al. 2001, Xiao et al. 2005). Damage from foliar blight attributed to *P. washingtonensis* was especially severe in 2010, which was a strong La Niña year resulting in extended periods of cool, wet weather in the Pacific Northwest.

Many foliar and canker diseases are more severe during periods of increased wetness and warm temperatures. An example of increased foliar disease due to climate change is the Dothistroma needle blight outbreak on lodgepole pine in Canada (Woods et al. 2005). The higher incidence of observed foliar disease and new canker infections on Pacific madrone may be attributed to the increased frequency of warmer, wetter spring weather during the last half of the 20th century. *Phytophthora cinnamomi*, which causes root disease, is favored by high soil temperatures and has increased in incidence in California forests. The incidence and severity of these diseases is likely to be affected by

[1] Washington State University, Research and Extension Center, 2606 West Pioneer, Puyallup, WA 98731.
[2] Oregon Department of Forestry, 2600 State Street, Salem, OR 97310.
[3] USDA Forest Service, Dorena Genetic Resource Center, 34963 Shoreview Road, Cottage Grove, OR 97424.
[4] USDA Forest Service, Umpqua National Forest, 2900 NW Stewart Parkway, Roseburg, OR 97471.
Corresponding author: melliott2@wsu.edu.

changes in temperature and precipitation and may cause certain populations of Pacific madrone to go extinct under predicted climate change scenarios. A better understanding of the epidemiology of these pathogens on Pacific madrone and the level of genetic resistance among different seed sources is needed to assess this risk.

Very little is known about the range of genetic variability in Pacific madrone. A Canadian study found that genetic diversity was low within populations in the northern part of the range (Beland et al. 2005), and we believe this will be the first common garden study of the species. Establishing field provenance trials of this species over multiple sites will give baseline information on the genetic variation in a range of adaptive traits and will provide guidance for its management under changing climate.

Project Description and Objectives

This project will use a range-wide collection of Pacific madrone to examine genetic variability in a range of traits. Using material from the Washington State University Pacific madrone seed collection (seed collected from 2006 to 2010), common garden plantings consisting of 105 families collected from seven ecoregions were planted in five locations in California, Oregon, and Washington during fall 2011 and winter 2012 (fig. 1). A separate sowing is planned for a planting site in British Columbia. Smaller demonstration plantings with a few trees taken from a range of widely different geographic seed sources, and including other *Arbutus* species from the western states, are planned at other locations to be determined.

Specific objectives include:
1) Screen for resistance to multiple pathogens such as *P. ramorum*, *P. cinnamomi*, and endemic canker and foliar pathogens.
2) Examine variation in growth and adaptive traits in the nursery and at multiple field sites.
3) Identify seed sources or populations that may contain individuals that are best adapted to climate change and for urban and restoration plantings.

Seedling Production

Seed from 125 families of Pacific madrone representing seven ecoregions were cleaned and weighed in lots of 100 seed each prior to sowing in plug trays. Plug trays were watered and placed into a 1.1 °C cooler for stratification in February 2011. Trays were removed from the cooler in April 2011 and placed in a greenhouse. Fertilizer was applied twice a week at the rate of 200 ppm N with Technigro 20-9-20 soluble. Seedling germination data was collected in June 2011. No significant relationship between seed weight and percent germination was seen.

Plugs were transplanted into Treepots with media consisting of 50 percent Specialty Soils standard greenhouse mix + 50 percent fine fir bark + 3 kg/m slow release Plantacote 14-9-15. The seedlings were grown outside until planting (fig. 2). Common garden sites in the United States were planted in fall 2011/winter 2012. Seed was shipped to British Columbia for sowing and planting in fall 2012/winter 2013.

Data collected on these seedlings prior to planting included height, stem diameter, leaf area, and leaf color (fig. 3). Preliminary data collected on a subset of the seedlings in August 2011 and on seedlings from a 2008 sowing of some of the same families indicates that there is some variability in these traits within and among families.

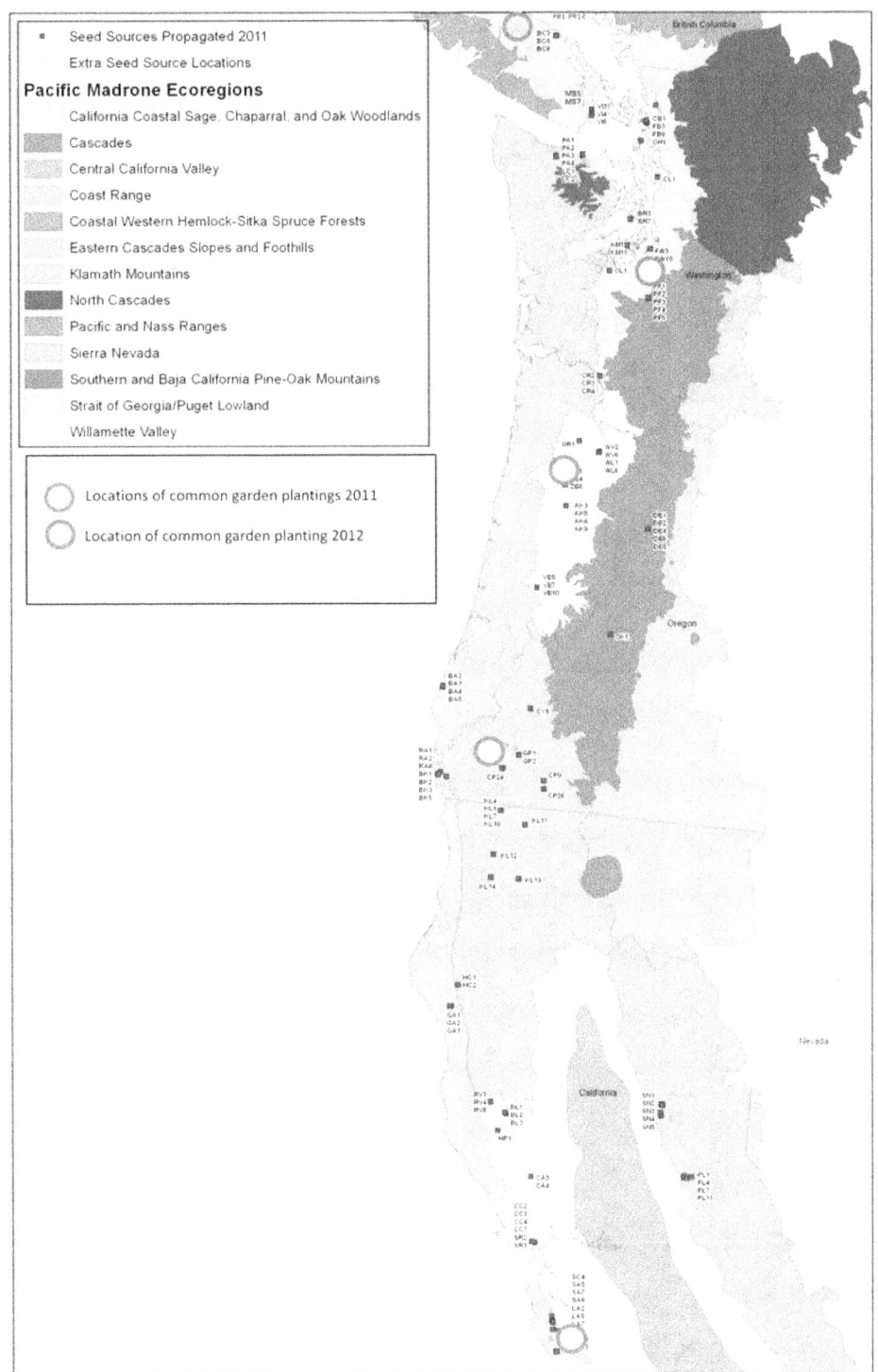

Figure 1—Map showing Pacific madrone range, ecoregions, seed collection sites, and locations for common garden plantings in western North America. The range of Pacific madrone extends to San Diego County, California, but the species occurs rarely in the far southern portion of the range.

Figure 2—Madrone seedlings in the container nursery at WSU-Puyallup after transplanting from plug trays. These seedlings were planted in the common garden sites in the United States in winter 2011.

Figure 3—Differences in leaf color in Pacific madrone seedlings. The seedlings on the left have more red pigment than those on the right. Quantitative differences in color were measured using a Minolta CR200b Chroma Meter.

Transplanting Madrone Seedlings

Pacific madrone has a reputation for being difficult to transplant since its roots react poorly to disturbance. Before transplanting into the common garden sites, a study was undertaken to determine the best methods for planting madrone seedlings. Two-year-old seedlings from three families were subjected to five treatments based on methods used in Hummel et al. (2008) and planted in December 2010. Seedlings were examined in May 2011. Treatments that involved washing the roots resulted in the most seedling mortality (fig. 4). Seedling mortality was between 5 and 10 percent in the unwashed treatments and 30 to 50 percent in the two treatments that involved washing the roots. Resprouting was observed on some seedlings that had died back, indicating that the root system may still be functioning. Total mortality and final measurements of height, stem diameter, and dry weight will be taken after two growing seasons.

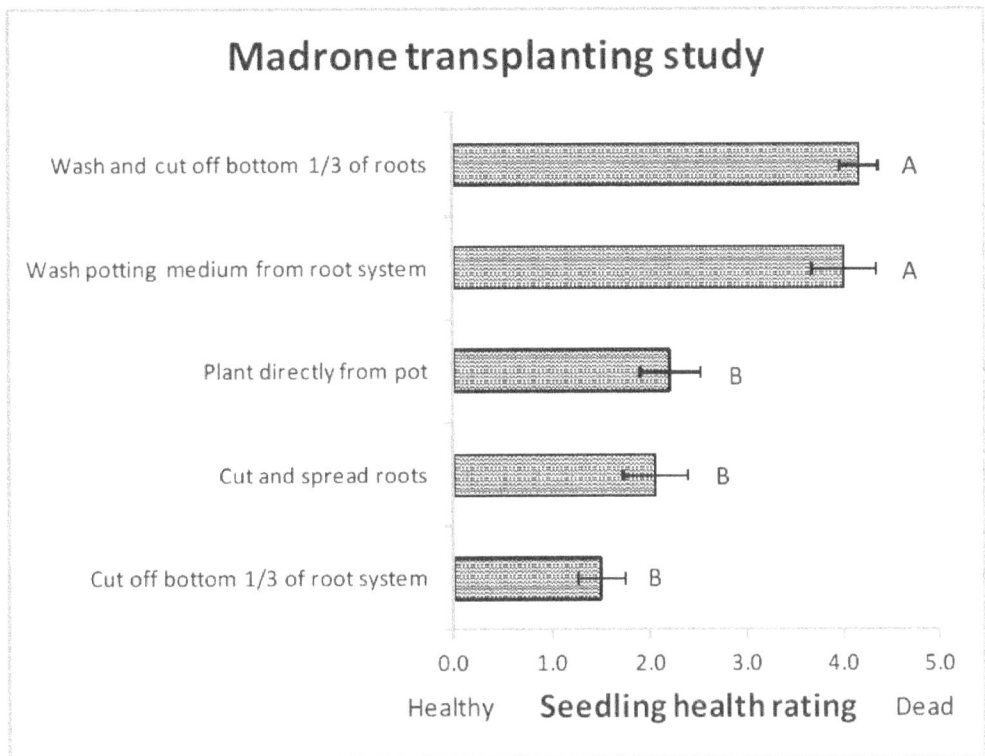

Figure 4—Effects of several transplanting methods on the growth of two-year-old Pacific madrone seedlings. Bars with different letters are significantly different at p = 0.05, Kruskal-Wallis test with Dunn's multiple comparisons.

Summary

We believe this project represents the first common garden study involving a range-wide collection of Pacific madrone. This project will provide baseline information on the genetic variation in a range of adaptive traits and will provide guidance for the management of this species under changing climatic conditions. Preliminary data on the seedlings grown for the common garden study indicates that variability is present in a number of plant characteristics. Other studies to assess the range of resistance to various pathogens, such as *P. cinnamomi* and *P. ramorum*, have been conducted in the greenhouse and biocontainment facilities at WSU Puyallup.

In addition to the common garden field plots, a series of long-term disease monitoring plots in naturally occurring stands of Pacific madrone near the common garden test sites are planned to determine which pathogens are present near these sites. These plots will be monitored at several intervals to observe changes in pathogen populations and disease severity due to fluctuations in climate or other factors. For example, it is known that *P. ramorum* and *P. cinnamomi* have been detected in the vicinity of the California site. Damage attributed to the foliar pathogen *P. washingtonensis* and others has been observed throughout the range of the species. This provides an opportunity to formally document portions of the range and the incidence of these pathogens and to study field resistance to several important pathogens of Pacific madrone.

The potential for many projects including molecular phylogenetic studies of Pacific madrone exists and we invite other scientists with an interest in working on special assessments from these tests to contact us. More information and updates on the project will be available on the website: http://www.puyallup.wsu.edu/ppo/madrone/.

Acknowledgments

The authors wish to thank everyone who helped to collect seed, identify, plant, and provide possible sites for the common garden and demonstration plantings (B.C. Ministry of Forests, BLM, Starker Forests, CalFire, WSU, Willamette University), and with growing and maintaining the seedlings. Funding for this project was provided by the USDA Forest Service, Forest Health Protection.

Literature Cited

Arno, S.F.; Hammerly, R.P. 1977. Northwest trees. Identifying and understanding the region's native trees. Seattle, WA: The Mountaineers. 222 p.

Dayton, W.A. 1931. Important western browse plants. Misc. Publ. No. 101. Washington, DC: U.S. Department of Agriculture. 214 p.

Beland, J.D.; Krakowski, J.; Ritland, C.E.; Ritland, K.; El-Kassaby, Y.A. 2005. Genetic structure and mating system of northern *Arbutus menziesii* (Ericaceae) populations. Canadian Journal of Botany. 83: 1581–1589.

Farr, D.F.; Elliott, M.; Rossman, A.Y.; Edmonds, R.L. 2005. *Fusicoccum arbuti* sp. nov. causing cankers on Pacific madrone in western North America with notes on *Fusicoccum dimidiatum*, the correct name for *Scytalidium dimidatum* and *Nattrassia mangiferae*. Mycologia. 97(3): 730–741.

Hummel, R.L.; Evans, E.; Riley, R. 2008. Effect of mechanical root disruption at transplant on short- and longer-term growth and survival of Scotch pine (*Pinus sylvestris*) and shore pine (*Pinus contorta* var. *contorta*). In: Watson, G.; Costello, L.; Scharenbroch, B.; Gilman, E., eds. The landscape below ground III. Proceedings of an international workshop on tree root development in urban soils. Champaign, IL; ISA: 211–221.

Reeves, S.L. 2007. *Arbutus menziesii*. In: Fire effects information system. [Online]. U.S. Department of Agriculture, Forest Service, Rocky Mountain Research Station, Fire Sciences Laboratory (Producer). http://www fs.fed.us/database/feis/. (06 October 2011).

Werres, S.; Marwitz, R.; Man in 't Veld, W.A.; De Cock, A.W.; Bonants, P.J.M.; De Weerdt, M.; Themann, K.; Ilieva, E.; Baayen, R.P. 2001. *Phytophthora ramorum* sp. nov: a new pathogen on *Rhododendron* and *Viburnum*. Mycological Research. 105(10): 1155–1165.

Woods, A.; Coates, K.D.; Hamann, A. 2005. Is an unprecedented Dothistroma needle blight epidemic related to climate change? BioScience. 55(9): 761–769.

Xiao, C.L.; Rogers, J.D.; Kim, Y.K.; Liu, Q. 2005. *Phacidiopycnis washingtonensis* – a new species associated with pome fruits from Washington State. Mycologia. 97(2): 464–473.

Development of Screening Trials to Rank *Pinus radiata* Genotypes for Resistance to Defoliation by Monterey Pine Aphid (*Essigella californica*)

Stephen Elms,[1] Peter Ades,[2] and Nick Collet[3]

Abstract

The Monterey pine aphid (*Essigella californica*) is a recent arrival in Australia, having first been detected in 1998. It quickly spread throughout the national radiata pine (*Pinus radiata* D. Don) plantation estate, causing seasonal defoliation and compromising tree growth in many areas. Selection of resistant radiata pine for deployment commenced in 2002, based on heritable defoliation in mature progeny trials. Further development of the breeding program requires efficient methods for screening later generation germplasm.

Glasshouse and nursery-based screening trials, involving infestation of potted radiata pine plants with aphids, were used to develop guidelines for operational scale screening of defoliation resistance. Three types of plant material were tested: physiologically aged clonal cuttings (10 to 30 years); 1-year-old clones derived from somatic embryogenesis; and 1-year-old seedling families. All of the plant types examined supported dramatic increases in aphid populations under suitable environmental conditions. Variability between plants within clones and between clones was high. For example, over a period of 28 days, one m tall aged cuttings infested with 30 aphids yielded between 26 and 3,804 aphids (mean 584). Significant and repeatable differences in aphid population counts among different radiata pine genotypes and families were obtained using trial durations of 18 to 35 days.

Treatment options, including environmental conditions, initial infestation levels, and replication requirements, were examined. Specific attention needs to be paid to managing peak aphid production levels by infestation level and experiment duration in order to minimize alate initiation.

Glasshouse screening results were tested by counting aphids on 1-year-old clonal cuttings in the field, and on 1-year-old stool beds. Both showed good correlation with glasshouse trial results (r=0.45 and 0.93). Damage to foliage and eventual loss of foliage, was observed where aphid counts were high, suggesting that identification and deployment of genetic material which does not support rapid aphid population buildup is likely to result in reduced defoliation and reduced growth losses in plantations due to *Essigella* activity.

---

[1] HVP Plantations, PO Box 385, Churchill, Victoria, Australia 3842.
[2] University of Melbourne, Victoria, Australia 3010.
[3] DPI Victoria, Melbourne, Victoria, Australia.
Corresponding author: selms@hvp.com.au.

Tree-Mediated Interactions Between the Jack Pine Budworm and a Mountain Pine Beetle Fungal Associate

Nadir Erbilgin[1] and Jessie Colgan[1]

Abstract

Coniferous trees deploy a combination of constitutive (pre-existing) and induced (post-invasion) structural and biochemical defenses against invaders. Induced responses can also alter host suitability for other organisms sharing the same host, which may result in indirect, plant-mediated, interactions between different species of attacking organisms. Current range and host expansion of the mountain pine beetle (*Dendroctonus ponderosae*, MPB) from lodgepole pine (*Pinus contorta* Douglas ex Loudon)-dominated forests to the jack pine (*Pinus banksiana* Lamb.)-dominated boreal forests provides a unique opportunity to investigate whether the colonization of jack pine by MPB will be affected by induced responses of jack pine to a native herbaceous insect species, the jack pine budworm (*Choristoneura pinus pinus*, JPBW). We simulated MPB attacks with one of its fungal associates, *Grosmannia clavigera*, and tested induction of either herbivory by JPBW or inoculation with the fungus followed by a challenge treatment with the other organism on jack pine seedlings and measured and compared monoterpene responses in needle. There was clear evidence of an increase in jack pine resistance to *G. clavigera* with prior herbivory, indicated by smaller lesions in response to fungal inoculations. In contrast, although needle monoterpenes greatly increased after *G. clavigera* inoculation and continued to increase during the herbivory challenge, JPBW growth was not affected. However, JPBW increased feeding rate to possibly compensate for altered host quality. Jack pine responses varied greatly and depended on whether seedlings were treated with single or multiple organisms, and their order of damage.

---

[1] University of Alberta, 4-42 ESB, Edmonton, Alberta, Canada T6G2E3.
Corresponding author: erbilgin@ualberta.ca.

The Chapter Breeding Program of the American Chestnut Foundation

Sara Fitzsimmons,[1] Kendra Gurney,[2] William White,[3] and Katy McCune[4]

Abstract

A unique feature of the American Chestnut Foundation breeding program is the use of volunteers to conduct most of the regional breeding that will help increase genetic diversity and preserve local adaptation in the products of our program. This effort is coordinated by the four authors of this abstract, who are employees of the Foundation. The Foundation has 16 state chapters spread over almost the entire range of the American chestnut (*Castanea dentata* (Marsh.) Borkh.). Fourteen chapters have active breeding programs. The chapter with the most advanced program, Pennsylvania, has been planting a B3-F2 seedling seed orchard for a number of years, and is starting to harvest B3-F3 seed from the selections. The stages of breeding at other chapters range from making B3 crosses, to making selections, to beginning to plant B3-F2 orchards.

The chapters make one backcross onto local American chestnut trees using pollen from B2 and B3 trees at the Foundation's professionally operated Meadowview facilities. Most chapters have been using the 'Graves' and 'Clapper' sources of blight resistance, since these exist in about 30 unique American backgrounds each. The chapters endeavor to cross pollen from 20 backgrounds onto 20 local chestnut trees; 20 backgrounds yields a reasonable prospect of avoiding population collapse from inbreeding depression, with an inbreeding effective population size of about 72. Collectively across all units, the inbreeding Ne (effective breeding number) for 'Graves' and 'Clapper' combined exceeds 500.

Full recovery of local adaptation may not occur with only one cross onto local trees, but may enable that adaptation to be recovered by natural selection. As the number of regional science coordinators has increased, and the collective knowledge of the chapters has increased, the ability of chapters to embark on more complex breeding endeavors has increased. Increasing additional sources of resistance into 20 American backgrounds with two cycles of backcrossing should be possible.

The regional science coordinators also are developing a curriculum to train volunteers to plant and monitor forest test plantings. This will need to be a focused, long-term, effort should the performance of the trees be sufficient. It should be an interesting process, hopefully increasing awareness of the forest as well as producing valuable data.

[1] 206 Forest Resources Lab, Pennsylvania State University, University Park, PA 16802.
[2] U.S. Forest Service, Northern Research Station, 705 Spear St., South Burlington, VT 05403.
[3] Department of Biology and Environmental Science, University of Tennessee - Chattanooga, 615 McCallie Ave., Chattanooga, TN 37403.
[4] Virginia Department of Forestry Central Office, 900 Natural Resources Dr., Charlottesville, VA 22903.
Corresponding author: Fred@acf.org.

Needle Terpenoid Composition of *Pinus halepensis* (Mill.) Trees Infested by the Scale Insect *Marchalina hellenica* (Genn.) in Greece

Athanassios Gallis,[1] Carlos Arrabal,[2] Aristotle C. Papageorgiou,[3] and Maria C. Garcia-Vallejo[4]

Abstract

Needle terpenoid composition was determined by using GLC-MS in *Pinus halepensis* (Mill.) trees that were infested and not infested by the scale insect *Marchalina hellenica*. The study area was within the Forest National Park of the Cape Sounion, southern Attica region, Greece. A total of 43 compounds, 32 of which were identified, were detected, including monoterpenes, sesquiterpenes, and neutral diterpenes. The healthy trees showed higher mean concentration for the monoterpenes fraction as well as for the diterpene fraction than the mean concentration of infested trees; whereas, the concentration for the sesquiterpene fraction was more or less similar in infested and non-infested trees. The statistical analysis of terpene data showed the existence of quantitative differences between healthy and infested trees mainly for the components β-caryophyllene, neoabietal, α- humulene, cembrene, and neoabietol. A Ward cluster analysis based on selected major compounds classified all trees in two chemotypes, with the majority of healthy trees belonging to one chemotype and most of the infested trees belonging to the second.

Key words: *Pinus halepensis*, *Marchalina hellenica*, needle terpenoids

Introduction

Marchalina hellenica is a scale insect which in Greece infests mainly *Pinus halepensis* (Mill.) and *Pinus brutia* (Ten.) (Avtzis 1985). The insect attack results in the production of honeydew, which is used as a feeding substrate by honeybees and converted into honey (Erlinghagen 2001, Gounari 2006). During the mid-1990s, *M. hellenica* was artificially introduced into the pinewoods of the Attica region in Greece in order to increase the total honey yield. The artificial infestations resulted in an ecological imbalance in the ecosystems of regional Aleppo pine. Current field observations show the overpopulated occurrence of the insect in the pinewoods of the area (Gallis 2007). Terpene composition in conifers is usually strongly inherited, not greatly affected by environmental conditions, and offers a valuable tool to study several scientific problems such as: hybrid identification, introgression, tree resistance to insect attacks and diseases, and others (Hannover 1992, Squillace 1987). The objectives of this study are: a) to determine the qualitative and quantitative terpenoid composition in the needles of Aleppo pine trees that are infested and not infested by the scale insect *M. hellenica*, and b) to investigate if the needle terpenoid composition could be used to study the parasitism of the scale insect to Aleppo pine trees.

Materials and Methods

All trees investigated were sampled from two natural stands of Aleppo pine: the "Markati" and "Agia Triada" in the area of the National Park of Cape Sounion, southern Attica region, Greece. A total of

[1] Decentralized Administration of Macedonia and Thrace, 11, Professor Rossidis Street, GR-54008, Thessaloniki, Greece.
[2] Departamento de Ingenieria Forestal, ETSI Montes, Universidad Polytechnica de Madrid, Cuidad Universitaria, 28040, Madrid, Spain.
[3] Department of Forestry, Environment and Natural Resources, Democritus University of Thrace, P.O. Box 129, Pantazidou 193, GR – 68200, Orestiada, Greece.
[4] Departamento de Industrias Forestalaes, INIA-CIFOR, Apartado 8188, 28080, Madrid, Spain.
Corresponding author: tgallis@hotmail.com.

22 trees, including 11 trees infested by *M. hellenica* and 11 healthy trees (not infested), were sampled in late March 2006. The sampling of the infested trees in the field depended on the macroscopic evaluation of the insect's attack on the tree as described in the literature (Erlinghagen 2001, Gounari 2006), including: white cottonish secretions, the degree of tree desiccation, and the existence and the extent of drained needles. The trees were of similar age (over 30 years old) in both stands, have been subjected to the same silvicultural treatments, and so far have been protected effectively from forest fires. As mentioned above, healthy and infested Aleppo pine trees occurred in the same area in both sampled stands in our study. Gounari (2006) states that it is normal that both infested and non-infested Aleppo pine trees occur in the same area. This differentiation is due to phenol-immunity phenomenon. The differentiation could also be permanent or temporary and periodic, with permanent immunity controlled genetically (Smirnoff and Valero 1975).

From each tree, 1-year-old needles were collected from the upper 1/3 part of the crown and from the same side to avoid any epigenetic variation in terpene composition due to tissue age, crown position, grown conditions, etc. After collection, the samples were put in plastic bags and stored in a refrigerator at -20 °C for about 2 months. The needle samples were transferred into a portable ultra low freezer with CO_2 (dry ice) and transported the same day by plane to Spain. Chemical analysis was conducted by the Department of Forestry Engineering, Escuela Tecnica Superior de Ingenieros (ETSI), Montes, Polytechnic University of Madrid, Spain.

The needles were cut into small pieces (2 to 4 mm). A known weight of needles (3 g approx.) was extracted with 5 ml petroleum ether/diethyl ether (1:1) for 24 hours at 4 °C. Isobuthylbencene (60 µg/ml), heptadecane (60 µg/ml), and heptadecanoic acid (60 µg/ml) were used as internal standards. One µl of the mixture was injected into a gas chromatograph. The samples were analyzed with an HP5890A gas chromatograph and connected to an HP 5971 mass detector (EI, 70 eV). The following temperature program was used: the oven temperature was initially at 60 °C, increasing at a rate of 4 °C/minutes to a final temperature of 270° C, and was held for 10 min. The injector's temperature was set at 260 °C and the detector's temperature was set at 300 °C. A DB-5 capillary column, 30 m x 0.25 mm (0.25 µm film thickness), was used for component separation. Helium was used as a carrier gas with 15 psi column head pressure and a split ratio of 1:50. For quantitative measurements, by the internal standard method, additional injections of replicate samples were made using a flame ionization detector under the same working conditions. All compounds were identified on the basis of their retention time and their electron impact (EI) mass spectra by comparing them with those in the database and literature. Hewlett Packard Chemstation software was used for peaks integration. Components were quantified as a percentage contribution of each peak to the total terpenoids found in the chromatogram, i.e. total oleoresin basis. The concentration of each terpenoid fraction (monoterpenes, sesquiterpenes, and neutral diterpenes) was also calculated, using the internal standard method. For statistical analysis, a Statistical Packages for Social Sciences statistical package (SPSS/PC) was used. Thirteen components were selected due to their presence in amounts more than 2 percent in most samples. To separate the infested and healthy pine trees, a cluster analysis (Ward, squared Euclidian distance) on the basis of the percentage amounts of the selected components was used. A discriminate analysis was performed to see which components have the largest effect in classifying trees as healthy or infested. The percentages of the components were transformed into arcsine - square root functions (Kung 1988) before statistical analysis.

Results

A total of 43 compounds were detected in current year needles of Aleppo pine trees analyzed by Gas Liquid Chromatography Mass Spectrometry (GLC-MS), including monoterpenes, sesquiterpenes, and neutral diterpenes (table 1).

Table 1—Terpenoid composition (total oleoresin basis) in *Pinus halepensis* needles

		Components	Healthy Trees % mean	Trees std	Wounded % mean	Trees std
1		α-thujene	0.13	0.19	0.19	0.15
2	•[a]	α-pinene	5.30	1.96	4.52	2.25
3		camphene	0.95	1.03	0.01	0.02
4	•	sabinene	2.41	4.19	2.01	1.04
5		β-pinene	0.78	0.69	0.47	0.26
6	•	myrcene	4.87	4.68	5.88	4.43
7		3-δ-carene	0.31	0.55	0.62	0.57
8		α-terpinene	0.20	0.23	0.10	0.22
9		limonene+phellandrene	0.51	0.79	0.31	0.21
10		trans-β-ocimene	0.15	0.21	0.17	0.18
11		γ-terpinene	0.13	0.19	0.14	0.14
12	•	terpinolene	2.47	2.82	2.03	0.97
13		terpine-4-ol	0.05	0.12	0.02	0.04
14		α-terpineol	0.01	0.04	0.03	0.10
15		bornyl acetate	0.02	0.05	0.11	0.20
16		α-copaene	0.24	0.12	0.22	0.22
17	•	β-caryophyllene	11.89	1.96	14.01	2.42
18	•	α-humulene *	2.03	0.32	2.39	0.41
19		germacrene-D	1.23	1.05	0.96	0.32
20	•	phenylethyl isovaleranate	3.99	1.33	3.31	1.59
21		α-Muurolene	0.31	0.20	0.19	0.14
22		δ- cadinene	0.39	0.25	0.49	0.19
23		β-cadinene	0.22	0.18	0.17	0.19
24		α-bisalolene	0.17	0.09	0.13	0.12
25		β-elemene	0.25	0.13	0.08	0.07
26		M+220	0.24	0.13	0.21	0.19
27		M+222	0.30	0.20	0.33	0.15
28		M+222	0.26	0.16	0.26	0.05
29	•	cembrene	33.03	11.27	24.69	9.22
30		M+286 (Diterpenic aldehyde)	1.09	1.21	0.90	0.35
31		dehydroabietal	1.23	0.92	1.38	0.48
32	•	methyl levopimarate	1.88	1.52	3.72	3.45
33	•	methyl dehydroabietate	1.81	1.31	2.28	0.90
34	•	neoabietal	1.43	1.05	2.77	1.82
35	•	methyl 8.13(15) abietadien 18 oate	2.57	1.77	2.78	1.36
36	•	neoabietol	2.10	1.42	3.79	2.31
37		M+332	0.92	0.64	1.71	1.19
38		M+ 314	1.91	1.07	1.66	1.35
39		M+330	1.35	0.69	1.60	1.24
40		M+332	0.83	0.49	1.53	1.03
41		M+330 ($C_{21}H_{30}O_3$)	1.12	1.16	1.81	1.00
42		M+316	0.74	0.55	1.43	0.83
43		M+406	0.62	0.63	1.16	0.58
		% monoterpenes total	19.68		19.41	
		% sesquiterpenes total	23.31		23.76	
		% diterpenes total	57.01		56.82	
		Mean concentration monoterpenes (mg g^{-1})	1.25		1.10	
		Mean concentration sesquiterpenes (mg g^{-1})	1.50		1.55	
		Mean concentration diterpenes (mg g^{-1})	1.27		0.89	

[a] Components selected for further evaluation.

The components α-pinene, sabinene, myrcene, and terpinolene were the major constituents in the monoterpenes fraction of all the samples analyzed. The sesquiterpene fraction is characterized by the high amounts of β-caryophyllene found to be in higher levels (14.01 percent) in infested trees compared with those (11.89 percent) in healthy trees. The macrocyclic diterpene cembrene is the major component among all the samples analyzed in our investigation. Cembrene is found with higher amounts (33.03 percent) in healthy trees than in infested trees (24.69 percent). The mean (mg g^{-1} dry weight of needles) concentration of monoterpene, sesquiterpene, and diterpene fractions for infested and healthy trees was also calculated too (table 1). The healthy trees showed higher mean concentration (1.25 mg g^{-1}) for the monoterpenes fraction in comparison to mean concentration (1.10 mg g^{-1}) of infested trees. The concentration of the sesquiterpene fraction was similar in infested (1.55 mg g^{-1}) and in healthy trees (1.50 mg g^{-1}). Concerning the diterpene fraction, the differences between healthy (1.27 mg g^{-1}) and infested (0.89 mg g^{-1}) trees are larger.

Compounds selected for statistical analysis were α-pinene, sabinene, myrcene, terpinolene, β-caryophyllene, α-humulene, phenylethyl isovaleranate, cembrene, methyl 8, 13 (15) abietadien 18 oate, neoabietol, methyl levopimarate, methyl dehydroabietate, and neoabietal. The last three compounds were present in amounts less than 2 percent in healthy trees, but were also included because they occurred in amounts more than 2 percent in infested trees. The dendrogram produced by hierarchical cluster analysis revealed the classification of all Aleppo pine trees in two major clusters (clusters A and B). Cluster A contains 12 trees in total (54.54 percent), while cluster B contains 10 pine trees in total (45.45 percent). The frequencies of clusters in each group of trees differ significantly. A total of 81.81 percent of the infested trees (nine trees) included in our analysis belong to cluster A, and 72.72 percent of the healthy trees (8 trees) belong to cluster B (table 2). The two

Table 2—Mean (percent) terpene composition of clusters, distribution, and percent frequency in healthy and wounded Aleppo pine trees

	Components	Cluster A (mean %)	Cluster B (mean %)
1	α-pinene	7,28	5,69
2	sabinene	2,89	3,08
3	myrcene	6,28	8,26
4	terpinolene	3,76	2,15
5	β-caryophyllene	19,86	14,36
6	α-humulene	3,40	2,44
7	phenylethyl isovaleranate	4,94	6,46
8	cembrene	29,35	48,51
9	methyl levopimarate	5,04	2,22
10	methyl dehydroabietate	3,61	1,70
11	neoabietal	4,14	1,37
12	methyl 8, 13 (15) abietadien 18 oate	3,74	3,43
13	neoabietol	5,67	1,99
	Total trees	12	10
	% total frequency	54,54	45,45
	Healthy trees	3	8
	% frequency of healthy trees	27,27	72,72
	Wounded trees	9	2
	% frequency of wounded trees	81,81	18,18

clusters (A and B) differ in the amounts of the most components. The components: β-caryophyllene, α-humulene, neoabietal, cembrene, and neoabietol showed differences between clusters. Results of discriminate analysis showed that the above mentioned five compounds have the largest discriminate ability between healthy and wounded trees. The quantitative terpene composition of clusters expressed as percent contribution on the basis of the total area of 13 components is shown in table 2.

Discussion

The literature concerning the relation of terpenes in *P. halepensis* with an attack by *M. hellenica* are rather rare. Mitta et al. (2002) analyzed cortical oleoresin terpenes in Aleppo pine trees infested by the insect from Crete Island, Greece. The authors reported that sensitivity of the pine to attack by *M. hellenica* was significantly correlated with high levels of α- pinene and low levels of limonene and α-terpinyl acetate. In our study, statistically significant differences in quantitative terpene composition between infested and non-infested trees were found for β-caryophyllene, α-humulene, neoabietal, cembrene, and neoabietol. A Ward cluster analysis, based on relative (percent) quantity of 13 selected components, revealed that arrangement of all trees into two clusters occurred at different frequencies. The quantitative terpene composition of cluster A is characterized by high amounts of β-caryophyllene (19.86 percent) and the composition of cluster B by very high amounts (48.51 percent) of cembrene (table 2). With respect to the limited number of trees analyzed from our results, it could be suggested that the presence of cluster A indicates infested trees, while the presence of cluster B indicates healthy ones. To conclude, the needle terpenoid analysis by gas chromatography seems to be a valuable tool to help the scientists study the parasitism of *M. hellenica* to Aleppo pine. However, further research will be required, with analysis of a larger number of samples by GLC-MS, including trees from different seasons of the year as well from several locations around the area, to clarify the influence of *M. hellenica* on terpenoid content and composition of *P. halepensis* in order to study the interaction between insect and pine tree as well the parameters involved in this complicated phenomenon.

Acknowledgments

The authors thank Dr. Paz Andres for performing the laboratory preparation of needle samples and Dr. Sofia Gounari for supplying valuable literature. Special thanks to Mr. Konstantinos Priftis for his great assistance during field sampling. The study was conducted under a short-term official educational license of the first author by the Authority of the Region of Attica, Greece, which also funded the travel expenses.

Literature Cited

Avtzis, N. 1985. *Marchalina hellenica* (*Monophlebus hellenicus*) Genn. Greece's most important honey-bearing-insect. Forestry Research. 6 (1): 51–64 (in Greek).

Erlinghagen, F. 2001. Portrait of an insect: *Marchalina hellenica* (Genn). (Sternorrhyncha: Coccina: Margarodidae), important producer of honeydew in Greece. Apiacta. 36: 131–137.

Gallis, A.T. 2007. Evaluation of the damage by insect *Marchalina hellenica* (Genn.) in eastern Attica, Greece. Conclusions for sustainable management of forest ecosystems. In: (eds unknown). Proceedings of the 10th international conference on environmental science and technology, (place of publication unknown): G-NEST and University of Aegean: B191–B196.

Gounari, S. 2006. Studies on the phenology of *Marchalina hellenica* (Hemiptera: Coccoidea, Margarodidae) in relation to honeydew flow. Journal of Apicultural Research. 45(1): 8–12.

Hanover, J.W. 1992. Applications of terpene analysis in forest genetics. New Forests. 6: 159–178.

Kung, F.H. 1988. Application of data transformation in forest genetics. Silvae Genetica. 37(2):45–49.

Mitta, E.; Tsitsimpikou, C.; Tsiveleka, L.; Petrakis, P.; Ortiz, A.; Vagias, C.; Roussis, V. 2002. Seasonal variation of oleoresin terpenoids from *Pinus halepensis* and *Pinus pinea* and host selection of the scale insect *Marchalina hellenica* (Homoptera, Coccoidea, Margarodidae, Coelostonidiinae). Holzforschung. 56: 572–578.

Squillace, A.E. 1987. Monoterpene composition in forest genetics research. Naval Stores Review. 97(1): 12–15.

Smirnoff, W.A.; Valero, L. 1975. Effects au moyen de la fertilization par ure ou par potassium sur *Pinus nanksiana L.* et le comportment de ses insects devastateurs: tel que *Neodiprion swainei et Toumeyella numismaticum.* Canadian Journal Forest Research. 5: 236–244.

Genetic Variation of Piperidine Alkaloids in *Pinus ponderosa* From a Common Garden

Elizabeth A. Gerson,[1] Rick G. Kelsey,[1] and J. Bradley St. Clair[1]

Abstract

Most species of pine and spruce synthesize and accumulate variable quantities of alkaloids in their tissues. These compounds express numerous types of biological activities in bioassay and could potentially offer resistance against enemies, although this function has never been confirmed for any known enemies of pine or spruce under natural conditions. The present study takes a complementary, and intensive, common garden approach to examine genetic variation in *Pinus ponderosa* Lawson & C. Lawson var. *ponderosa* C. Lawson alkaloid production. It also investigates the potential trade-off between seedling growth and alkaloid production, and associations between topographic/climatic variables and alkaloid production. Piperidine alkaloids were quantified in foliage of 501 nursery seedlings grown from seed sources in west-central Washington, Oregon, and California, roughly covering the western half of the native range of ponderosa pine. A nested mixed model was used to test differences among broad-scale regions and among families within regions. Alkaloid concentrations were regressed on seedling growth measurements to test metabolite allocation theory. Likewise, climate characteristics at the seed sources were also considered as explanatory variables.

Qualitative variation in alkaloid profiles was low. However, quantitative variation from seedling to seedling was high, and regional variation exceeded variation among families. Regions along the western margin of the species range exhibited the highest alkaloid concentrations, while those further east had relatively low alkaloid levels. All measures of seedling growth related negatively to alkaloid concentrations on a natural log (ln) scale; however, coefficients of determination were low. At best, annual height increment explained 19.4 percent of the variation in ln(total alkaloids). Among the climate variables, temperature range showed a negative, linear association that explained 41.8 percent of the variation. Given the wide geographic scope of the seed sources and the uniformity of resources in the seedlings' environment, observed differences in alkaloid concentrations are evidence for genetic regulation of alkaloid secondary metabolism in ponderosa pine. The theoretical trade-off with seedling growth appeared to be real, however slight. The climate variables provided little evidence for adaptive alkaloid variation, especially within regions. This study has been published in full (Gerson, E.A.; Kelsey, R.G.; St Clair, J.B. 2009. Genetic variation of piperidine alkaloids in *Pinus ponderosa*: a common garden study. Annals of Botany. 103: 447–457.).

[1] USDA Forest Service, PNW Research Station, 3200 Jefferson Way, Corvallis, OR 97331.
Corresponding author: rkelsey@fs.fed.us.

Gene Expression in the Tanoak-*Phytophthora ramorum* Interaction

Katherine J. Hayden,[1] Matteo Garbelotto,[1] Hardeep Rai,[2] Brian Knaus,[3] Richard Cronn,[3] and Jessica W. Wright[4]

Abstract

Disease processes are dynamic, involving a suite of gene expression changes in both the host and the pathogen, all within a single tissue. As such, they lend themselves well to transcriptomic analysis. Here we focus on a generalist invasive pathogen (*Phytophthora ramorum*) and its most susceptible California Floristic Province native host, tanoak (*Notholithocarpus densiflorus* (Hook. & Arn.) Manos, Cannon & S.H. Oh). The advent of new sequencing technologies has made the study of non-model systems possible at a scale never before possible. We argue that this non-model system is ideal for studying the interactions between host and pathogen using massively parallel mRNA sequencing, in part because the *P. ramorum* genome has been fully sequenced.

We present early data in a project developed to elucidate the molecular genetic interactions between these two species. We used the Illumina Genetic Analyzer system to sequence all mRNA present in a single tanoak genotype after inoculation with *P. ramorum*, and from a non-inoculated control. We separated sequences from the dataset that originated from the pathogen, or from highly conserved regions, by aligning the reads to the *P. ramorum* genome; this first set includes the genes expressed in vivo by the pathogen. The remaining sequences were used to generate a de novo reference transcriptome for tanoak, and then to subsequently pinpoint gene regions of interest with increased or decreased expression after infection. Each of the three outcomes—the set of expressed *P. ramorum* gene regions, the tanoak gene regions showing changes in expression, and the tanoak transcriptome reference itself—are an important step in understanding the interactions of forest pathogens and their hosts at the molecular level.

---

[1] University of California, Berkeley, Environmental Science, Policy, and Management, 137 Mulford Hall, Berkeley, CA 94720.
[2] Utah State University, Logan, UT.
[3] USDA Forest Service, Pacific Northwest Research Station, Corvallis, OR.
[4] USDA Forest Service, Pacific Southwest Research Station, Davis, CA.
Corresponding author: khayden@berkeley.edu.

Blister Rust Resistance Among 19 Families of Whitebark Pine, *Pinus albicaulis*, From Oregon and Washington – Early Results From an Artificial Inoculation Trial

Angelia Kegley,[1] Richard A. Sniezko,[1] Robert Danchok,[1] and Douglas P. Savin[1]

Whitebark pine is considered one of the most susceptible white pine species to white pine blister rust, the disease caused by the non-native pathogen *Cronartium ribicola*. High mortality from blister rust and other factors in much of the range in the United States and Canada have raised serious concerns about the future viability of this high-elevation forest tree species (USFWS 2011). A major effort is now underway to collect seed for gene conservation, to evaluate trees for genetic resistance to blister rust, and to establish restoration plantings (Aubry et al. 2008, Mangold 2011; Sniezko et al. 2011a, 2011b).

Seed collected from 19 whitebark pine parent trees at four locations in Oregon and Washington were sown in 2005 (fig. 1). The number of families represented in this study varied by geographic source: eight from Mt. Rainier National Park, three from the Colville National Forest, two from the Deschutes National Forest, and six from the Fremont National Forest. The number of seedlings available per family for blister rust inoculations ranged from 21 to 60.

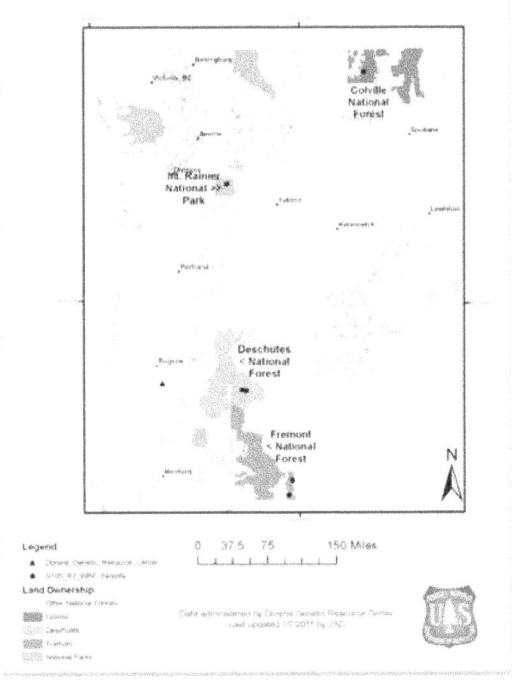

Figure 1—Parent tree locations for 19 whitebark pine families sown in 2005 for a white pine blister rust resistance screening trial.

[1] USDA Forest Service, Dorena Genetic Resource Center, Cottage Grove, Oregon, USA.
Corresponding author: rsniezko@fs.fed.us.

A randomized complete block design was used, with each of the 19 families distributed randomly in row plots in six blocks. Within each family, the number of seedlings in each row plot was made as equal as possible between the blocks, but varied between families (from 3 to 10). Seedlings were inoculated with *C. ribicola* twice, initially in 2006, and again in 2009, using the well-established protocols at Dorena Genetic Resource Center (DGRC), Cottage Grove, Oregon. The first inoculation was very effective in producing needle spots (on >99 percent of the seedlings), but, unexpectedly, less than 10 percent of the seedlings later developed cankers. The second inoculation was also very effective in producing needle spots (on >99 percent of the seedlings), and subsequently led to the expected high levels of stem infection (fig. 2). This second inoculation will be particularly interesting to follow; the trees were 5 years old and much larger than any whitebark pine previously subjected to artificial inoculation at DGRC.

Figure 2—(a) Seedlings of whitebark pine in April 2010 (following September 2009 inoculation); (b) needle lesions in June 2010 from blister rust inoculation; (c) and (d) many stem infections on seedlings in early November 2010. (Photo credits: Richard Sniezko)

As of November 2010, 76.6 percent of trees had stem symptoms (SSp). The Deschutes and Fremont locations from eastern Oregon averaged 97 percent and 96 percent SSp, respectively; the Colville location (northeastern Washington) averaged 71 percent SSp, and the Mt. Rainier location (west-central Washington) averaged 58 percent SSp. Family means ranged from 46.9 percent (a Mt. Rainier family) to 100 percent (four families, all in the Fremont population).

The number of stem symptoms per infected tree (excludes trees with needle spots, but no stem symptoms) at the November 2010 assessment averaged 16.4, with family mean number of stem symptoms per infected tree ranging from 7.3 (a Mt. Rainier family) to 28.3 (also a Mt. Rainier family). One individual seedling had 90 stem symptoms. In addition to normal cankers, some bark reactions (complete and partial) were apparent; families from the Colville and Mt. Rainier locations had the highest levels of bark reaction.

To estimate the effect of geographic source (population) and family within a source on tree resistance, analyses of variance (ANOVAs) were conducted on row plot means using SAS PROC GLIMMIX (SAS 2008). For these analyses, population and family within population were considered fixed effects, while block and associated interactions were treated as random effects.

The first response examined was the presence or absence of stem symptoms. A binomial model with logit link was applied to the data. In cases where the proportion of trees with a stem symptom was 0 or 1 in a row plot, an adjustment of +0.01 or -0.01 was applied to the row plot mean, respectively. The analysis indicates that there is strong evidence of an association between the odds of getting a stem symptom and the geographic source of the family parent ($p<0.0001$, fig. 3). In addition, within a source there is suggestive evidence of a family difference in the odds of getting a stem symptom ($p=0.055$). It is estimated that the odds of getting a stem symptom for seedlings with parents in the Deschutes and Fremont National Forests are 19.6 and 30.7 times higher (respectively) than for seedlings with parents in Mt. Rainier National Park; the 95 percent confidence intervals with Tukey-Kramer adjustment are from 3.9 times higher to 99.2 times higher and from 7.0 times higher to 134.3 times higher for Deschutes and Fremont, respectively.

The second response examined was the number of stem symptoms per infected tree. A negative binomial model with log link was applied to the data. There is suggestive but inconclusive evidence of an association between the number of stem symptoms on an infected tree and the geographic source of origin of the family parent ($p=0.057$, fig. 3). However, within sources, there is convincing evidence of family differences in the mean number of stem symptoms per infected tree ($p<0.0001$). If all trees (including those with no stem symptoms at this stage) are included in the analysis, then the evidence of an association between the number of stem symptoms and the geographic source of origin is highly significant ($p=0.0002$), with families from the two northern sources generally having much lower means than those from the Deschutes and Fremont National Forests.

The early results for this trial show similar trends to those observed from previous inoculation trials at DGRC. Families from Mt. Rainier were highest in resistance: all families from Mt. Rainier showed fewer seedlings with stem symptoms and tended to have fewer stem symptoms than those from Deschutes and Fremont. The two northern-most sources (of the four tested here), Mt. Rainier and Colville, in this trial have the highest level of resistance. Other recent trials have suggested possible geographic trends in the percentage of seedlings developing stem symptoms (Sniezko et al. 2007; Sniezko, unpublished).

This trial included relatively few families from each of the four populations, but the trends for SSp observed in this trial are consistent with population results from other trials at DGRC (Sniezko, unpublished). However, screening of more families from each population will likely identify families with some level of resistance even amongst populations such as Deschutes and Fremont that have very high SSp in this trial.

At this stage of the trial, there are differences in both the percent of trees with stem symptoms (between populations and between families within populations) as well as in the number of stem symptoms per tree (between families). Both of these traits may have utility in selecting parents that will be most resistant to blister rust in the field. The first field trials for whitebark pine have recently been established and will serve to help validate seedling resistance screening as well as monitor the durability of rust resistance.

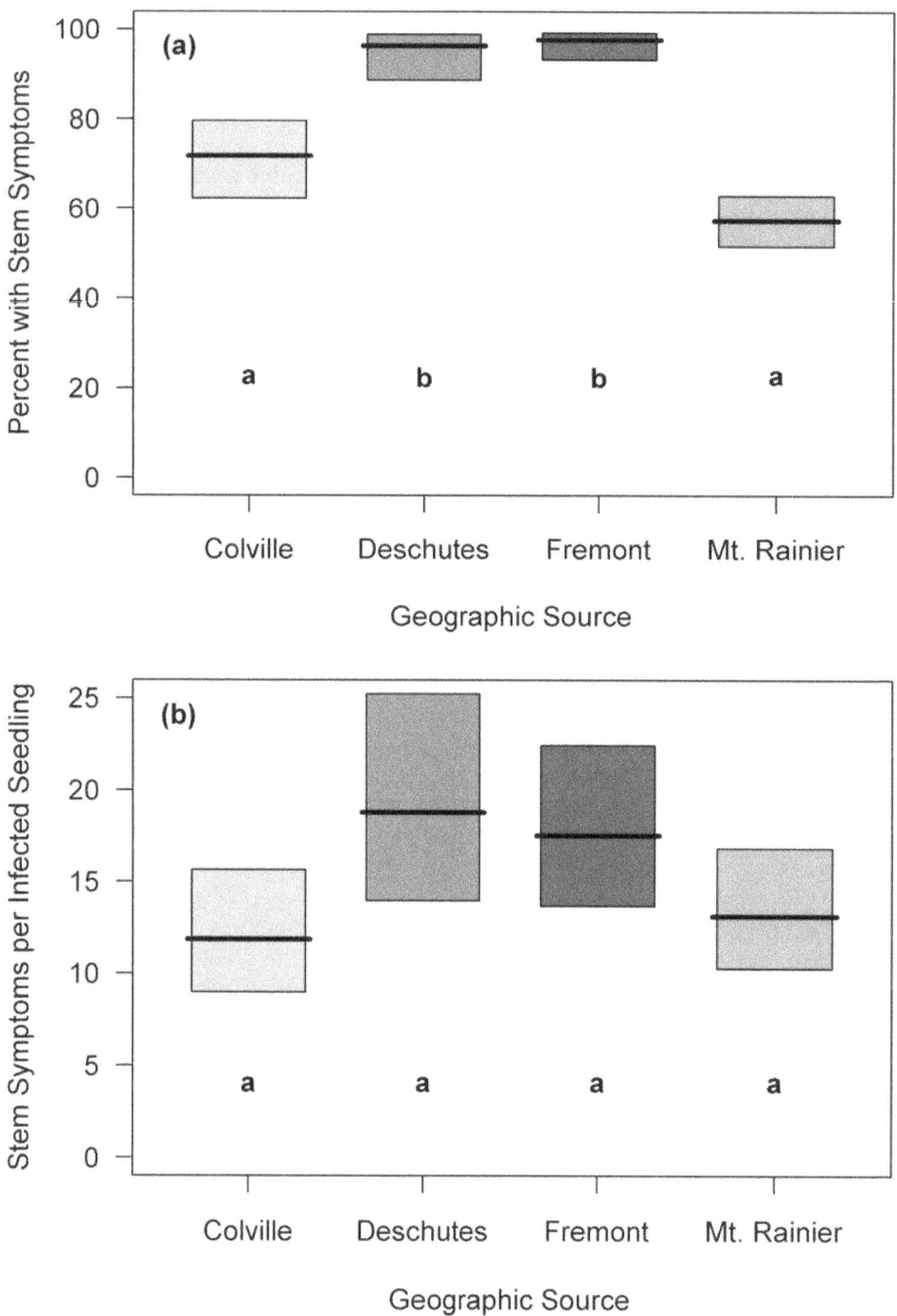

Figure 3—Least squares means and 95 percent confidence intervals for (a) the percent of seedlings with stem symptoms, and (b) the number of stem symptoms per infected seedling for each source using the final models described in the text. Locations sharing the same letter indicate no significant difference at the α=0.05 level after Tukey-Kramer adjustment.

Canker severity is currently low (3 on a 9 point scale), but is expected to increase dramatically over the next year. Mortality from blister rust is currently low (3.7 percent), but is expected to continue, with very high mortality expected over the next 2 years. Seedlings will be assessed annually over the next several years for additional stem symptom development and mortality. The high levels of canker-free seedlings in some families at this stage are encouraging, but at least one additional year of assessments will be needed to discern latent stem symptoms. The parents identified with genetic resistance to blister rust in seedling screening trials will be a key component to successful restoration of whitebark pine. Seedlings from top families can be grafted for gene conservation, and land managers will be contacted concerning the potential to collect seed from the top parents to use for restoration.

Acknowledgments

We would like to acknowledge the USDI National Park Service (NPS), Mt. Rainier National Park, and USDA Forest Service, Pacific Northwest Region (Region 6), particularly the Genetic Resources and Forest Health Programs, which provided funding for this project; also the USDI NPS, Region 6 Geneticists and Tree Improvement personnel for tree selection and cone collection; DGRC technicians and staff for inoculating the seedlings with blister rust, providing nursery culture after inoculation, and assessing the seedlings. We would also like to thank Jim Hamlin for invaluable assistance with the analysis and reviewing of a previous version of this manuscript.

Literature Cited

Aubry, C.; Goheen, D.; Shoal, R.; Ohlson, T.; Lorenz, T.; Bower, A.; Mehmel, C.; Sniezko, R. 2008. Whitebark pine restoration strategy for the Pacific Northwest Region 2009-2013. Portland, OR: U.S. Department of Agriculture, Forest Service, Pacific Northwest Region. 212 p. http://www.fs.usda.gov/detail/r6/landmanagement/resourcemanagement/?cid=stelprdb5278980 (22 March 2012).

Mangold, R.D. 2011. The U.S. Forest Service's renewed focus on gene conservation of five-needle pine species. In: Keane, R.E.; Tomback, D.F.; Murray, M.P.; Smith, C.M., eds. The future of high-elevation, five-needle white pines in western North America: proceedings of the high five symposium. Proceedings RMRS-P-63. Fort Collins, CO: U.S. Department of Agriculture, Forest Service, Rocky Mountain Research Station: 151.

SAS Institute Inc. 2008. SAS® Component Language 9.2: Reference. Cary, NC: SAS Institute Inc.

Sniezko, R.A.; Kegley, A.J.; Danchok, R.S.; Long, S. 2007. Variation in resistance to white pine blister rust among 43 whitebark pine families from Oregon and Washington—early results and implications for conservation. In: Goheen, E.M.; Sniezko, R.A., tech. coords. Proceedings of the conference whitebark pine: whitebark pine: a Pacific Coast perspective; R6-NR-FHP-2007-01. Portland, OR: U.S. Department of Agriculture, Forest Service, Pacific Northwest Region: 82–97. (22 March 2012).

Sniezko, R.A.; Mahalovich, M.F.; Schoettle, A.W.; Vogler, D.R. 2011a. Past and current investigations of the genetic resistance to *Cronartium ribicola* in high-elevation five-needle pines. In: Keane, R.E.; Tomback, D.F.; Murray, M.P.; and Smith, C.M., eds. The future of high-elevation, five-needle white pines in western North America: proceedings of the high five symposium. Proceedings RMRS-P-63. Fort Collins, CO: U.S. Department of Agriculture, Forest Service, Rocky Mountain Research Station: 246–264.

Sniezko, R.A.; Schoettle, A.; Dunlap, J.; Vogler, D.; Conklin, D.; Bower, A.; Jensen, C.; Mangold, R.; Daoust, D.; Man, G. 2011b. Ex situ gene conservation in high elevation white pine species in the United States: a beginning. In: Keane, R.E.; Tomback, D.F.; Murray, M.P.; Smith, C.M., eds. The future of high-elevation, five-needle white pines in western North America: proceedings of the high five symposium. Proceedings RMRS-P-63. Fort Collins, CO: U.S. Department of Agriculture, Forest Service, Rocky Mountain Research Station: 147–179.

U.S. Fish and Wildlife Service. 2011. Endangered species: whitebark pine. http://www.fws.gov/mountain-prairie/species/plants/whitebarkpine/. (22 March 2012).

Interaction of an Invasive Bark Beetle with a Native Forest Pathogen: Potential Effect of Dwarf Mistletoe on Range Expansion of Mountain Pine Beetle in Jack Pine Forests

Jennifer Klutsch[1] and Nadir Erbilgin[1]

Abstract

In recent decades, climate change has facilitated shifts in species ranges that have the potential to significantly affect ecosystem dynamics and resilience. Mountain pine beetle (*Dendroctonus ponderosae*) is expanding east from British Columbia, where it has killed millions of pine trees, primarily lodgepole pine (*Pinus contorta* Douglas ex Loudon) over the last 10 years. In Alberta, mountain pine beetle is in portions of the lodgepole pine x jack pine hybrid zone and was recently intercepted at the western edge of jack pine (*P. banksiana* Lamb.) forests. There is a potential threat that mountain pine beetle will expand into the naïve host, jack pine, which extends from Alberta into eastern Canada and the Great Lakes Region in the United States. A successful invasion of jack pine by mountain pine beetle could generate serious ecological and economic problems throughout the boreal forest. Therefore, studies conducted during this initial establishment of mountain pine beetle in jack pine forests, and their applied implications for controlling the invasion, are highly relevant for the rest of jack pine and eastern pine forests. If done proactively, such studies may identify jack pine stands susceptible to mountain pine beetle and help forge pre-emptive management strategies prior to mountain pine beetle arrival. The further easterly expansion of mountain pine beetle might be constrained by low winter temperatures, by the amount of weakened or stressed trees, and by low, endemic, beetle populations. The native parasitic plant, dwarf mistletoe (*Arceuthobium americanum*), induces stress in jack pine and causes extensive damage throughout its range. In this study, we will investigate whether infection of jack pine by the dwarf mistletoe will influence jack pine susceptibility to mountain pine beetle. The work that started in 2011 will evaluate how dwarf mistletoe-induced chemical and physiological changes in jack pine affect growth and development of mountain pine beetle and its associated fungi. Interactions between dwarf mistletoe and mountain pine beetle on jack pine will be identified by addressing a number of research objectives, focusing primarily on how changes in jack pine defenses mediate mountain pine beetle-dwarf mistletoe interactions. These investigations are important because the eastward expanding wave of mountain pine beetle will likely first encounter, and colonize, these highly abundant dwarf mistletoe-infected jack pine trees.

[1] University of Alberta, Department of Renewable Resources, ESB 442, Edmonton, Alberta T6G 2E3. Corresponding author: klutsch@ualberta.ca.

Using Dutch Elm Disease-Tolerant Elm to Restore Floodplains Impacted by Emerald Ash Borer

Kathleen S. Knight,[1] James M. Slavicek,[1] Rachel Kappler,[2] Elizabeth Pisarczyk,[2] Bernadette Wiggin,[2] and Karen Menard[2]

Abstract

American elm (*Ulmus Americana* L.) was a dominant species in floodplains and swamps of the Midwest before Dutch elm disease (DED) (*Ophiostoma ulmi* and *O. novo-ulmi*) reduced its populations. In many areas, ash (*Fraxinus* spp.) became dominant in these ecosystems. Emerald ash borer (EAB) (*Agrilus planipennis*), an introduced insect, is now spreading through the Midwest and killing up to 99 percent of ash trees in infested areas. In spring 2011, we began a restoration experiment to study reforestation of ash-dominated floodplains impacted by EAB through plantings of native tree species, including DED-tolerant American elm, sycamore (*Platanus occidentalis* L.), and pin oak (*Quercus palustris* Münch.). We are testing the effect of planting trees before, during, or after ash mortality by planting in sites across a gradient of EAB infestation duration. Initial causes of seedling damage differed among sites. At sites that experienced flooding, many seedlings had wilted leaves. However, at the site that did not experience flooding, most seedlings had insect herbivory. Initial seedling mortality was low and differed among sites and species. American elm seedlings tolerant to DED performed as well as or better than the pin oak and sycamore seedlings planted in this experiment. Future results of this experiment will provide recommendations to managers for methods to restore EAB-impacted floodplain forests with DED-tolerant American elm and other tree species.

Key words: American elm, Dutch elm disease, emerald ash borer, floodplain restoration

Introduction

Dutch elm disease (DED) is caused by two nonnative fungal pathogens (*Ophiostoma ulmi* and *O. novo-ulmi*) of elm trees (*Ulmus* spp.) (Brasier 1991), which are spread by elm bark beetle species (primarily *Scolytus multistriatus* and *Hylurgopinus rufipes*) in North America (Schreiber and Peacock 1979). The first epidemic of *O. ulmi* was noticed in North America in the 1930s (Schreiber and Peacock 1979), and the second, more aggressive epidemic of *O. novo-ulmi* probably spread during the 1940s. The two epidemics decimated populations of American elm (*Ulmus americana*) (Gibbs 1978). While it was a popular street tree, American elm also was an important tree species in many riparian areas and swamps (Barnes 1976). The disease killed almost all of the large American elm trees, restricting elm populations to small diameter trees, while ash (*Fraxinus* spp.) and a few other tree species replaced American elm as dominant canopy species in these habitats (Barnes 1976).

Emerald ash borer (EAB) (*Agrilus planipennis*), an introduced insect pest, has killed millions of ash trees in the midwestern United States and adjacent Canada and is spreading rapidly (Cappaert et al. 2005). The impact of EAB is greatest in riparian areas and swamps where ash is the most abundant tree genus, sometimes making up 50 percent or more of the basal area of these stands (Knight, unpublished data). As the ash trees are killed, large canopy gaps provide an opportunity for both native plants and invasive plants to respond to the increased light in the understory (Knight et al. 2010). In turn, these changes reverberate through the ecosystem, affecting other organisms and ecosystem processes. In some areas, there is very little regeneration of native tree species. Invasive plants such as reed canary grass (*Phalaris arundinacea* L.) and common buckthorn (*Rhamnus*

[1] USDA Forest Service, Northern Research Station, Delaware, OH.
[2] Metroparks of the Toledo Area, Toledo, OH.
Corresponding author: ksknight@fs.fed.us.

cathartica L.), which inhabit these ash-dominated areas (Knight, unpublished data), may inhibit future tree establishment.

Restoration strategies for ash-dominated riparian and swamp habitats are needed. Ongoing work to develop DED-tolerant American elm trees has generated several genotypes of DED-tolerant American elm trees from large-scale screening operations (Smalley and Guries 1993; Townsend and Douglas 2001; Townsend et al. 1995, 2005). Ash mortality provides an opportunity to introduce DED-tolerant American elm into these areas, re-establishing a canopy tree species that had been lost from these forests. This is also an important opportunity to diversify these forests by planting other native forest tree species, with a long-term restoration goal of creating resilient, functional floodplain forests.

We are conducting a restoration experiment to understand tree seedling growth and survival in floodplains, to study the performance of planted DED-tolerant elms, and to determine optimal restoration techniques for these ecosystems. Our long-term research is focused on two main questions:

- What factors affect the growth and survival of planted tree seedlings in Ohio floodplains impacted by EAB?
- What factors affect DED incidence and survival of planted elms?

These questions will be answered over several years. However, for the initial spring planting, we have examined the following questions:

- What are the major causes of initial damage or mortality for the planted tree seedlings?
- Does damage or mortality differ among species, sites, and sizes of planted tree seedlings?

Methods

Three riparian sites in Ohio were selected for this study (fig. 1). The Swan Creek floodplain in Oak Openings Preserve Metropark in northwest Ohio has been infested by EAB for the longest time period. The first EAB exit holes were observed in 2005 and 97 percent of the mature ash trees were dead by 2009. Green ash (*F. pennsylvanica* Marsh.) was the most abundant tree species in the floodplain, followed by American elm, boxelder (*Acer negundo* L.), and silver maple (*A. saccharinum* L.). The Tuscawaras River floodplain in the Clinton Conservation Area in northeast Ohio is currently uninfested by EAB (no exit holes have been observed), and the majority of the ash trees are healthy. Green ash is the most abundant tree species in this floodplain, followed by silver maple, red maple (*A. rubrum* L.), and boxelder. The Spring Creek floodplain in Sharon Woods Metro Park in central Ohio has been recently infested by EAB. The first

Figure 1—Restoration planting sites in Ohio, USA.

EAB exit holes were observed in 2009 and 33 percent ash mortality in the floodplain was recorded in 2011. White ash (*F. americana* L.) is the most abundant species in the floodplain, followed by American elm, sugar maple (*A. saccharum* L.), and blue ash (*F. quadrangulata* Michx.).

Pin oak (*Quercus palustris* Münchh.) and sycamore (*Platanus occidentalis* L.) seedlings grown from seeds collected in Ohio were purchased from Riverside Native Trees (Delaware, Ohio). American elm seedlings were produced by the USDA Forest Service from crosses between Valley

Forge and R18-2, two cultivars with known tolerance to DED. Valley Forge is a selection from a chemical test that showed high levels of DED tolerance that was identified by Alden Townsend and Lawrence Schreiber. R18-2 is one of 17 survivors out of 21,000 seedlings screened for DED tolerance by Cornell University and the Boyce Thompson Institute. The geographic origin of these trees is unknown. Crosses between these disease-tolerant cultivars have been shown to have high levels of tolerance to DED (Slavicek and Knight, Generation of American elm trees with tolerance to Dutch elm disease through controlled crosses and selection, these proceedings).

At each site, plots were located in ash-dominated areas that were easily accessible. Three "large tree plots" were planted at each site with containerized seedlings 0.5 to 2.5 m tall on a 6 x 7 m grid (fig. 2). Two sites—Oak Openings Preserve Metropark and Clinton Conservation Area—also had three "small tree plots" planted with containerized seedlings 0.3 to 1 m tall on a 2.5 x 2.5 m grid. American elm, pin oak, and sycamore containerized tree seedlings were planted in random order on a grid pattern at each plot with half of the trees planted in spring 2011 (late May and early June) and the other half in fall 2011 (September) (fig. 2). Half of the large trees received cages to prevent deer browsing and rubbing. The DED-tolerant cultivars Valley Forge (VF), Princeton (PRN), and New Harmony (NH) were obtained from JLPN Inc. (Salem, OR) as bare-root stock, grown for 3 weeks in containers, and then planted in rows outside of each plot (fig. 2). These known DED-tolerant cultivars were planted to compare their survival to those elms from the USDA Forest Service crosses.

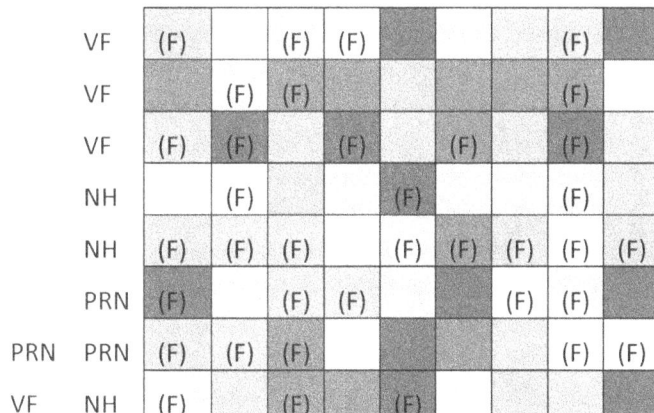

Figure 2—Planting design for one of the large tree plots, with trees planted on a 6 x 7 m grid. Valley Forge (VF), Princeton (PRN), and New Harmony (NH) are the Dutch elm disease-tolerant cultivars planted outside the plot. (F) represents cages randomly assigned to half of the trees.

One to 2 days after spring planting, Oak Openings Preserve Metropark and Clinton Conservation Area experienced heavy flooding. Trees were submerged for 1 to 4 days. The duration and depth of flooding was not measured, but appeared to be greater at Clinton Conservation Area. Approximately 2 weeks to 1 month after spring planting, we measured the following variables for each planted seedling: initial damage, survival, diameter of the stem at 2.5 cm height, seedling stem height to highest live leaf or bud, and canopy openness using a concave spherical densiometer.

A general linear multivariate mixed model using a binomial logit distribution was used to analyze mortality and the incidence of wilting, deer browsing, and insect herbivory. The main effects of site, tree size class (small seedlings or large seedlings), and species (elm, oak, sycamore) were tested. Analyses comparing tree size classes included both small tree and large tree plots at Oak Openings Preserve Metropark and Clinton Conservation Area. Sharon Woods Metropark data was analyzed in separate analyses using only large trees for all three sites, because only large trees were planted at Sharon Woods. These results were similar to the results of the first analyses and are not reported here. Post-hoc Tukey tests were used to determine differences among class variables.

Results

Damage

Leaves that were submerged during flooding wilted and died, then the seedlings sprouted new leaves (fig. 3) or died. Tall seedlings often exhibited wilted lower leaves and healthy upper leaves, probably because the upper leaves were not submerged long enough to kill them. Wilting differed among sites (p<0.0001) and species (p<0.0001). Wilting was most common at Clinton Conservation Area, with >50 percent of the trees of all species exhibiting wilting (fig. 4). Wilting was also observed at Oak Openings Preserve Metropark, but was uncommon at Sharon Woods Metropark. The incidence of wilting was similar for small and large trees (p>0.05). Differences among species were inconsistent between sites and size classes, but in general, sycamore seedlings exhibited more wilting than oak seedlings.

Insect herbivory differed among sites (p=0.006) and was most common at Sharon Woods Metropark, where almost 100 percent of the trees exhibited some herbivory (fig. 5). Herbivory was more common on large trees than small trees (p=0.0003) and was less common on elms than other species (p<0.0001). Browsing by deer was uncommon at all sites during the spring when the data was collected (fig. 6), but differed significantly among sites (p<0.0001) and species (p=0.0004). However, browsing was more common in the fall (data not shown), and may have a greater impact than the initial results suggest. Raccoons or groundhogs dug up or destroyed some of the small seedlings planted at Oak Openings Metropark and Clinton Conservation Area; seedlings that survived this disturbance were replanted.

Figure 3—Elm with wilted lower leaves; re-sprouting new upper leaves (left). Elm with dead lower leaves that fell off, surviving upper leaves (center). Sycamore with dead lower leaves and surviving upper leaves (right).

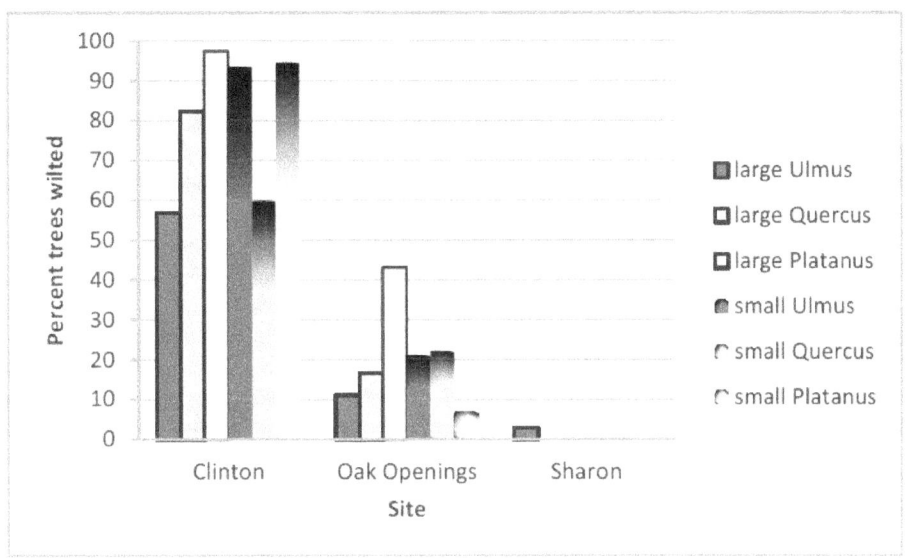

Figure 4—Wilting differed among sites and species.

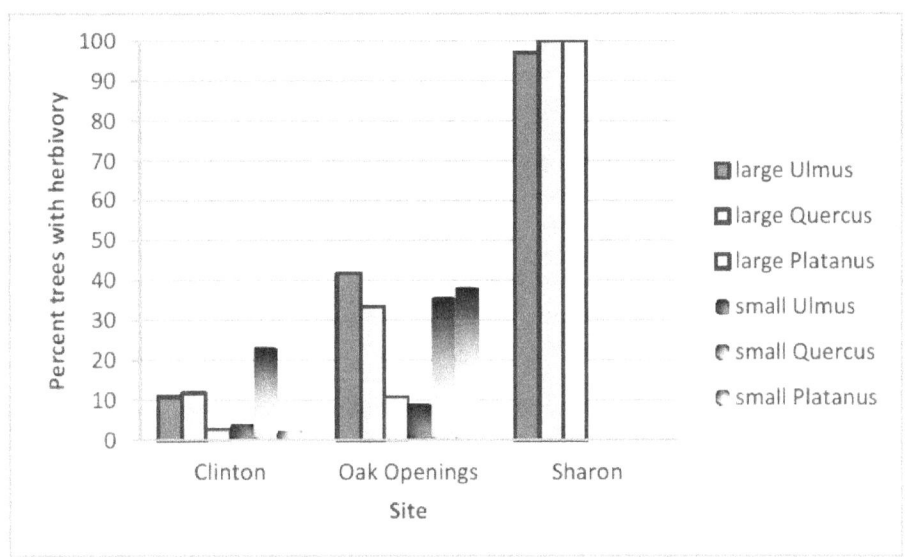

Figure 5—Insect herbivory differed among sites and species.

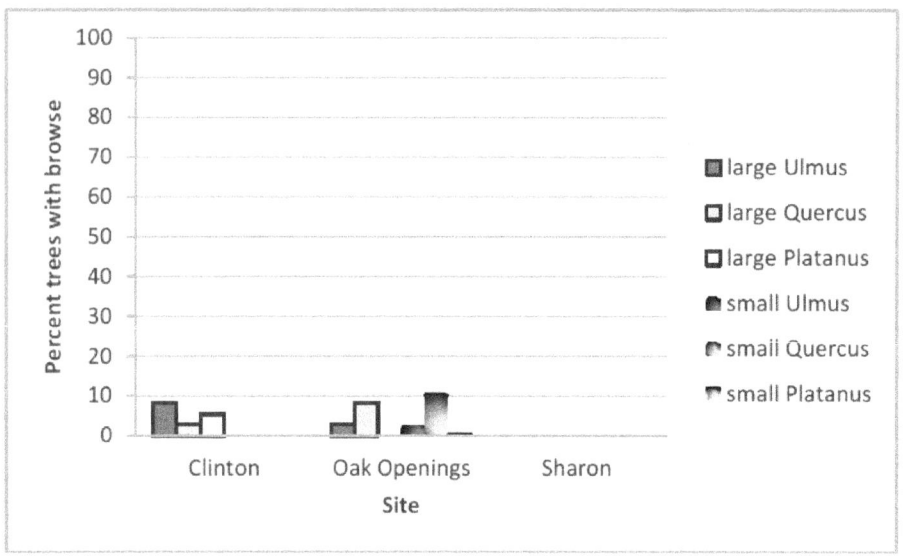

Figure 6—Browsing by deer was uncommon.

Mortality

Initial mortality was greater for small seedlings than large seedlings (p<0.0001), and differed among species and sites (p<0.0001) (fig. 7). Small sycamore seedlings exhibited the greatest mortality. Initial mortality was greatest at Oak Openings Preserve Metropark, and there was no initial mortality at Sharon Woods Metropark. It was difficult to determine the cause of mortality among seedlings. Some seedlings may have died from submergence under water at the flooded sites. During the fall planting, additional mortality, especially of small sycamore seedlings at Clinton Conservation Area, was recorded (data not shown). A second flood in July at Clinton Conservation Area may have caused the additional mortality.

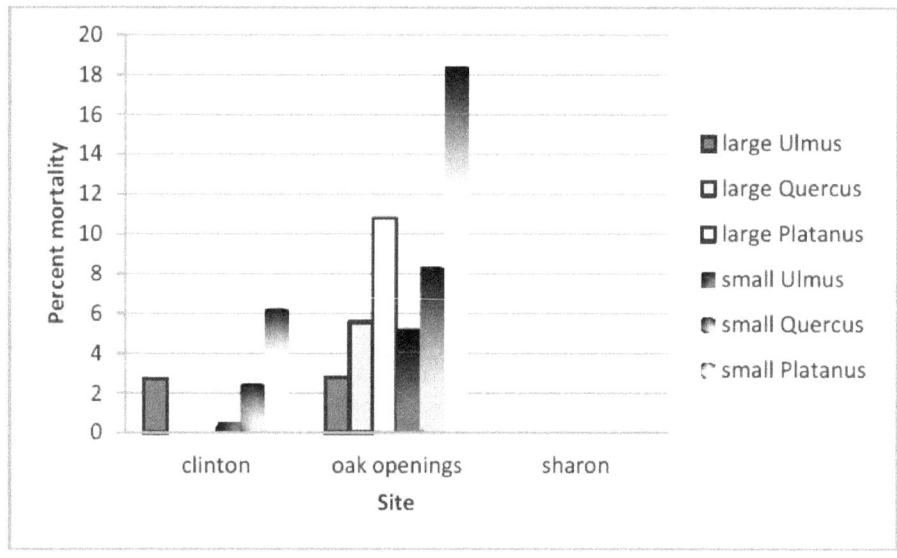

Figure 7—Mortality differed among sites, species, and size classes.

Discussion

Mixed plantings of DED-tolerant American elm, sycamore, and pin oak showed good initial survival. Damage for all three species was mostly due to wilting from flooded conditions or herbivory at the site that was not flooded. The incidence of wilting seems to reflect the severity of flooding with >50 percent of the seedlings wilted at the site with the greatest depth and duration of flood waters. However, many of the wilted seedlings resprouted. At the site that did not experience flooding, herbivory by insects was common. It is possible that insect populations are greater at that site or that herbivory was inhibited by flooding. DED-tolerant elm seedlings (VF x R18-2) performed as well as or better than the other two floodplain tree species, which is a promising result for the use of DED-tolerant elm in restoration. We will continue to monitor the survival and growth of the planted seedlings. The future results of this study will allow us to make recommendations to managers for restoration of EAB-impacted floodplains using DED-tolerant American elm and other tree species.

Acknowledgments

We thank the Metroparks of the Toledo Area, MetroParks Serving Summit County, and Columbus Metro Parks for their collaboration in establishing the restoration experiment at their parks. The American Recovery and Reinvestment Act and the USDA Forest Service provided funding to support this research. Kyle Costilow, Charles Flower, Stephanie Fluke, Stephanie Smith, and Lawrence Long helped establish the plots and collect the data. Eileen Sawyer, Reid Plumb, and Daniel Spalink helped to collect data on tree composition at Oak Openings. John Stanovick assisted with statistical analysis. Suggestions from Shivanand Hiremath and Linda Haugen improved this manuscript.

Literature Cited

Barnes, B.V. 1976. Succession in deciduous swamp communities of southeastern Michigan formerly dominated by American elm. Canadian Journal of Botany. 54: 19–24.

Brasier, C.M. 1991. *Ophiostoma novo-ul*mi sp. nov., causative agent of current Dutch elm disease pandemics. Mycopathologia. 115: 151–161.

Cappaert, D.; McCullough, D.G.; Poland, T.M.; Siegert, N.W. 2005. Emerald ash borer in North America: a research and regulatory challenge. American Entomologist. 51: 152–165.

Gibbs, J.N. 1978. Intercontinental epidemiology of Dutch elm disease. Annual Review of Phytopathology. 16: 287–307.

Knight, K.S.; Herms, D.A.; Cardina, J.; Long, R.P.; Rebbeck, J.; Gandhi, K.J.K.; Smith, A.; Klooster, W.S.; Herms, C.P.; Royo, A.A. 2010. EAB aftermath forests: the dynamics of ash mortality and the responses of other plant species. In: Michler, C.H.; Ginzel, M.D., eds. Proceedings of the symposium on ash in North America. Gen. Tech. Rep. NRS-P-72. Newtown Square, PA. U.S. Department of Agriculture, Forest Service, Northern Research Station: 11.

Schreiber, R. R.; Peacock, J.W. 1979. Dutch elm disease and its control. Agriculture Information Bulletin No. 193. Washington, DC: U.S. Department of Agriculture, Forest Service.

Smalley, E.B.; Guries, R.P. 1993. Breeding elms for resistance to Dutch elm disease. Annual Review of Phytopathology. 31: 325–352.

Townsend, A.M.; Bentz, S.E.; Douglass, L.W. 2005. Evaluation of 19 American elm clones for tolerance to Dutch elm disease. Journal of Environmental Horticulture. 23(1): 21–24.

Townsend, A.M.; Bentz, S.E.; Johnson, G.R. 1995. Variation in response of selected American elm clones to *Ophiostoma ulmi*. Journal of Environmental Horticulture.13: 126–128.

Townsend, A.M.; Douglass, L.W. 2001. Variation among American elm clones in long-term dieback, growth, and survival following *Ophiostoma* inoculation. Journal of Environmental Horticulture. 19(2): 100–103.

Quantitative Trait Loci for Resistance to Two Fungal Pathogens in *Quercus robur*

Cécile Robin,[1] Amira Mougou-Hamdane,[1] Jean-Marc Gion,[1] Antoine Kremer,[1] and Marie-Laure Desprez-Loustau[1]

Abstract

Powdery mildew, caused by *Erysiphe alphitoides* (Ascomycete), is the most frequent disease of oaks, which are also known to be host plants for *Phytophthora cinnamomi* (Oomycete), the causal agent of ink disease. Components of genetic resistance to these two pathogens, infecting either leaves or root and collar, were investigated in a full-sib family of *Quercus robur* L, that was vegetatively propagated by cuttings.

Resistance to powdery mildew was assessed by two methods. First, inoculations with *E. alphitoides* were performed under controlled conditions on excised leaves removed from cuttings grown in the greenhouse. The level of host-pathogen compatibility was assessed by recording infection success and mycelial growth. Second, the progeny, planted in a comparative test, were assessed for susceptibility to powdery mildew using field evaluation under natural infection conditions over 3 years. Resistance to ink disease was estimated by inoculating *P. cinnamomi* on stems of 2-year-old cuttings grown in the glasshouse, and by measuring the length of the induced lesion in two experiments.

Preliminary results showed that quantitative trait loci (QTL) associated with the response to both pathogens were located on the genetic linkage maps available for the two parents of the F1 family. However we could not identify QTL involved in both diseases.

Although the genetic architecture of resistance to *E. alphitoides* varied between years and infection conditions, stable QTL were detected. Because infection by this fungus is strongly dependent on the phenological status of its host, co-locations between QTL for resistance and QTL for phenology were studied.

[1] INRA, UMR 1202 BIOGECO, INRA-Université Bordeaux 1, 69 route d'Arcachon, 33612 Cestas, France.
Corresponding author: robin@bordeaux.inra.fr.

Testing Resistance to Chestnut Blight of Hybrid Chestnuts

Cécile Robin,[1] Xavier Capdevielle,[1] Gilles Saint-Jean,[1] and Teresa Barreneche[2]

Abstract

Castanea sativa Mill. is an ecologically and economically important species in Europe, not only as a forest tree, but also as a fruit tree. It is dramatically threatened by ink disease caused by *Phytophthora* spp., introduced during the nineteenth century. To limit its impact, *C. mollissima* and *C. crenata*, which proved to be tolerant species, were imported from China and Japan to Europe at the beginning of the twentieth century, together with the agent of chestnut blight (*Cryphonectria parasitica*) which is now spreading throughout Europe. A clonal selection has resulted in the use of a few inter-specific hybrids as rootstocks tolerant to ink disease, and onto which fruit cultivars are grafted, as fruit cultivars for the fruit quality and as forest clones selected for growth characteristics. New chestnut forest plantations are clonal in Spain, but not yet in France. However, with the threat of increasing loss due to ink disease and chestnut blight, hybrid clones are seen as a promise by some foresters. Our aim was to test the resistance to chestnut blight of hybrid chestnuts which are used as rootstocks or grafted varieties for fruit production, or inter-specific full sib families used for building chestnut maps. Field testing revealed significant differences among genotypes: some fruit cultivars being less susceptible than the large majority, in agreement with field observations. With excised stem assays, a large phenotypic variation within the F1 progeny was observed.

[1] INRA, UMR 1202 BIOGECO, INRA-Université Bordeaux 1, 69 route d'Arcachon, 33612 Cestas, France.
[2] INRA, UREF INRA UREF, 71, Avenue Edouard-Bourlaux, B.P.81- 33883 Villenave d'Ornon Cédex, France.
Corresponding author: robin@bordeaux.inra.fr.

The Italian Elm Breeding Program for Dutch Elm Disease Resistance

Alberto Santini,[1] Francesco Pecori,[1] and Luisa Ghelardini[1]

Abstract

In the 20th century, elms across Europe and North America were devastated by two pandemics of Dutch elm disease (DED), caused by the introduction of two fungal pathogens: *Ophiostoma ulmi*, followed by *O. novo-ulmi*. At the end of 1920s, research into a resistance to DED began in Europe and then in the United States. No worthwhile resistance was ever found within the native European or American elms. The Dutch team resorted to hybridizing European elms, from which the first cultivars exhibiting a resistance were obtained during the 1930s, but these clones did not have sufficient resistance to the second pandemic. It was the use of Asian species, with their higher resistance to DED, which accelerated progress on both sides of the Atlantic. Eventually a number of second-generation resistant clones derived from hybrids of native and Asian species were released to commerce.

Many efforts were dedicated to control the disease, such as the elm breeding program started in Italy in 1975 by the Institute of Plant Protection (IPP). This program was born of a conviction that the Mediterranean environment would demand its own selections. In Italy, the favorable adaptation of species such as the Siberian elm (*U. pumila* L.), and the unsuitability of the Dutch selections to the more arid regions, encouraged the wider assessment of the Asian elms. The purpose was twofold: to examine more fully adaptability to the climate and to broaden the genetic base of the native species.

Selection of superior genotypes ostensibly reduces genetic variation in cultivated species. However, when breeding is designed for obtaining plants adapted to different environmental conditions and for different uses, the outcome can actually result in increased variation. The case of elm breeding for resistance to DED is paradigmatic. The uses of elm are in fact manifold. For this reason, breeding for resistance is not enough. Many other features are required, including fast growth, and aesthetic factors such as attractive shape and foliage. To satisfy all these needs, whilst maintaining enough genetic variability to buffer the effects of climate change and possible arrival of new strains of DED or other diseases, it was decided to undertake a fundamental broadening of genetic resources, or, as it will be called later, "incorporation." A base of native elms with enough good characters to act as parents was hybridized with those disease-resistant Asian species able to acclimatize.

This program has produced DED-resistant elm varieties able to adapt to arid conditions, yet endowed with some remarkable ornamental characteristics. Five of these clones have already been patented and released to commerce: 'San Zanobi,' 'Plinio,' 'Arno,' 'Fiorente,' and, more recently, 'Morfeo.' 'Morfeo' is a robust, attractive tree that is extremely resistant to DED. It is also fast-growing and tolerant of both summer drought and winter floods, thus proving as well adapted to the climate of northwestern Europe as that of the Mediterranean. Indeed, following trials in England, 'Morfeo' is now considered potentially the most important cultivar in the conservation of several invertebrates there endangered by the consequences of DED.

Key words: Dutch elm disease, *Ophiostoma*, Italian elm breeding program

Introduction

In the 20th century, elms across Europe and North America were devastated by two pandemics of Dutch Elm Disease (DED), caused by the introduction of two fungal pathogens with very different aggressiveness: *Ophiostoma ulmi* circa 1910, followed 60 years later by the three times more lethal

---

[1] Institute of Plant Protection – C.N.R Via Madonna del Piano, 10, 50019 Sesto fiorentino, Italy.
Corresponding author: a.santini@ipp.cnr.it .

O. novo-ulmi (Brasier 2000). The gravity and impressiveness of the damages caused by the disease stirred up the interest of researchers and public opinion, such as to necessitate a solution to the problem. The elm is, in fact, a plant of great beauty, has significant historic and artistic value, and adapts exceptionally well to stress and to difficult sites, such as those occurring in cities, alongside roads, and in windswept coastal areas. Thanks to these features, the elm is an important and characteristic component of the cities' tree-lined roads and of the rural landscape in several European and North American countries.

The idea of searching for resistance to DED through breeding arose in 1928 at the Willie Commelin Scholten Phytopathological Laboratorium in Baarn (The Netherlands). There, the first studies were performed on the etiology of the disease that had been killing elms in western Europe since the end of World War I. The causal fungus was firstly isolated by Dina Spierenburg (Buisman 1921), then described and named by Marie B. Schwarz (Schwarz 1922); later followed by the development of a reliable inoculation method by Christine Buisman (Westerdijk et al. 1931). The path-breaking research conducted by the two latter scientists—both of whom were working at the aforesaid Laboratorium—constituted the fundamental requisite for starting up a breeding program (Holmes 1993).

At the beginning, research focused on selecting resistant individuals within the native species. During this phase, a couple of clones were selected into the species of field elm (*Ulmus minor* Miller) and named 'Christine Buisman' (1936) and 'Bea Schwarz' (1947). However, these proved disappointing because of their slow growth, poor shape, and susceptibility to a branch canker caused by the *Nectria cinnabarina* fungus. In order to combine resistance mechanisms of different species and enhance the growth rate, Dutch researchers started crossing different elm species. In addition to resistance to DED, the long-term goals of the program were resistance to coral spot (caused by *N. cinnabarina*), to frost, and to wind. Fast growth, good form, decorative leaves, and valuable timber were also considered. The first two releases, the 'Commelin' (1960) and 'Groeneveld' (1963) clones, were first-generation hybrids between European elm species. Initially, they proved to be a great success. However, the arrival in the late 1960s of the new, more aggressive species, *O. novo-ulmi*, to which 'Commelin' was particularly susceptible, inflicted a hard blow on the Dutch breeding program. Although decades of breeding have shown that it was possible to slowly accumulate resistance in second or third generation clones of purely European elms (Heybroek, personal communication), complete DED resistance was not found in European nor in American native elms, but individuals highly resistant to DED have nevertheless been identified (Townsend et al. 2005). At that time, it was noticed that the most resistant clones were second generation hybrids which contained one grandparent of Asian provenance.

Therefore, since then, Asian DED-resistant elm species have generally been crossed to native elms to speed up the selection of resistant trees. A base of native elms with desirable characteristics was bred with Asian elms species that, besides a fair level of DED resistance, showed the ability to adapt to a range of climatic conditions and environments. This artificial base broadening of the genetic resources, or "incorporation" (Simmonds 1993), was planned in order to satisfy all traditional elm uses, so taking into account not only DED resistance, but also fast growth, tree silhouette, leaf and bark color, leaf shape, and overall tree size. The resulting progeny were expected to combine the DED resistance of Asian species with the superior growth, ornamental value, and environmental adaptability of European elms.

The risk of adopting this kind of strategy was to go toward a genetic bottle-neck, since selection of superior genotypes reduces genetic variation (Simmonds 1993, Tanksley and McCouch 1997). However, when breeding, as in this case, is designed to obtain plants adapted to different environmental conditions and for different uses, the outcome could result in an increase of variability (Cox and Wood 1999).

The case of elm breeding for resistance to DED is, therefore, paradigmatic. The uses of elm are manifold: from wood to fodder, from medicine to urban silviculture, and many others. For this reason, breeding for resistance is not enough; many other features are requested as tree silhouette, fast growth, leaf and bark color, and leaf shape and dimensions. In order to satisfy all these needs, maintaining at the same time enough genetic variability to buffer the rising of possible new stresses, such as new forms of the disease or other diseases and climate change, we decided to initiate a base broadening of the genetic resources, or, as it will be called later, "incorporation" (Simmonds 1993).

The Italian Program

A second elm breeding program in Europe was initiated in the late 1970s in Florence by the Institute of Plant Protection (IPP), part of the Italian National Research Council (C.N.R.), when the second more destructive DED pandemic incited by *O. novo-ulmi* reached Italy. The goal of the Italian elm breeding program was the selection of elm cultivars resistant to DED, but suited to the Mediterranean climate, unlike the Dutch selections intended for northern Europe. European elm species and selections with desirable morphological and physiological characteristics were hybridized with DED-resistant Asian species (Smalley and Guries 1993) that had thrived in the Mediterranean climate, broadening genetic resources (Simmonds 1993). The breeding strategy program is reported in figure 1.

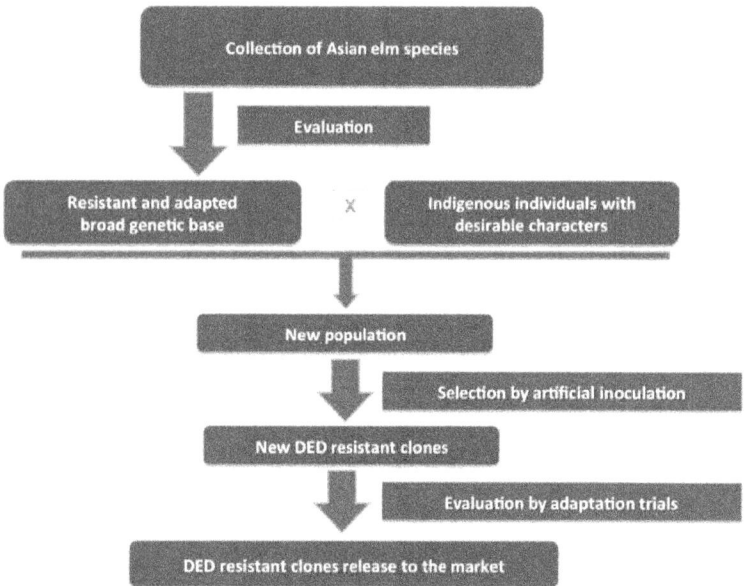

Figure 1—Italian elm breeding strategy program.

The Italian program is indebted to the work of the Dutch researchers for the breeding strategy and for much of the material used in the crossings. Other materials came from native species and from extant plantations of Siberian elm, as well as through exchanges with Americans and other research Institutes. The inoculation and crossing techniques used in Florence were also derived from the Dutch experience, with the introduction of a few improvements, such as the realization of pollination without having to lift the isolation sack, by blowing the pollen into the sack (Mittempergher and La Porta 1991).

Material and Methods

Collection of Material

In late 1970s, a wide collection of elm species and provenances from all over the world with a particular preference for Asian species, generally more resistant to DED (Smalley and Guries 1993), was set up. Collections were established with two aims:

1)   to check adaptation to a new environment, constituted by the Mediterranean climate and by all the biotic and abiotic damage agents that may affect introduced species under these conditions, and, as a consequence the new hybrid clones; and

2)   to obtain adult plants for breeding work.

Hybridization Studies

Crossability among elm species which involved the use of several European and Asian species of different taxonomic sections was checked under Mediterranean climatic conditions (Mittempergher and La Porta 1991). Pollen of the desired species was obtained from cut branchlets held in vases with water during the pollen dispersal phase. Different species and individuals were kept in separate rooms of a greenhouse to avoid contamination. The collected pollens were conserved at 3° to 4°C and dehydrated at 10 percent relative humidity (RH) when used within a short period of time (few days or weeks). When pollen had to be stored for 6 months (Asian Autumn flowering species), or for about 1 year (to cross the later pollen donor with the earlier spring flowering species), it was conserved at -20 °C and 10 percent RH. Pollen vitality was checked before pollination by using the Fluoro-chromatic Reaction technique (Heslop-Harrison and Heslop-Harrison 1970, Heslop-Harrison et al. 1984).

Flower pollination was carried out by injecting pollen into the pollination bags with forced air. At least three bags were used for each single cross, and, at least three control bags on each mother tree did not receive foreign pollen in order to check the selfing for each mother tree. Matured seeds were harvested and sown in open air nursery beds, monitoring germination. The seedlings were checked morphologically during the first and second growing season in order to ascertain their hybrid nature. The percent of viable seedlings from full seeds sown was scored at the end of the first growing season.

Screening Disease Resistance

The seedlings were evaluated for DED resistance. Selection for resistance was operated following a two-step protocol:

1)   Mass inoculation. Three-year-old elm seedlings obtained by controlled crosses were grown in the IPP nursery and planted in the field. The following year, during the third week of May, which is the time of beetle flight in the area of Florence, trees were inoculated. Inoculation was performed with a single wound per plant, using a knife blade carrying two drops of a 0.2 ml of a $1 \times 10^6 \, ml^{-1}$ yeast phase cells, consisting of two tester isolates of the subsp. *novo-ulmi* and subsp. *americana* of *O. novo-ulmi* (Brasier and Kirk 2001), so that the inoculum would be absorbed by the tree's rising sap. Symptoms of disease (percent of defoliation and percent of dieback) were observed after 4 weeks and at 3 and 8 months from inoculation date and assessed by three independent assessors.

2)   Selection. Seedlings with less than 10 percent dieback were vegetatively propagated by hardwood cuttings and planted out the following year in a randomized complete block design. Clones showing less than 25 percent dieback were considered resistant, and were evaluated for other characters. Twelve rooted cuttings per clone, divided into three blocks, were used. Inoculations and disease evaluations were performed 2 years after, as described above, and the symptoms were compared with those expressed by clones having known DED responses acting as controls, generally the Dutch clones 'Commelin' and 'Lobel', highly susceptible and intermediately resistant, respectively.

Adaptation Trials

In order to check the possible effect of phenotypic plasticity and to determine the best environmental condition for growth of each, a series of traits were evaluated in different ecological conditions. Several field trials were planted in different climates in Italy. In each trial, a randomized complete block design was used with generally three blocks of four ramets for each clone. Traits were measured each year and a final evaluation was performed at the end of the trial, generally after 6 to10 years.

Clones showing DED resistance were also evaluated for:

1)   leaf shape: length, breadth, and slenderness, with the favorite shape being that of *U. minor* leaves which are rounder than Asian elms.

2)   leaf color: dark green was considered preferable for being similar to the native field elm.

3)   shape of the crown: columnar with a monocormic straight trunk and slender branches is the favorite shape.

4)   height and diameter growth.

Clones were ranked for these traits and resistance according to a 5-step scale by three independent observers. This datum is reported together with the clone code as a variable number of marks. The scale goes from no marks = not an eligible clone, to four marks = clone that accomplishes all the requested characteristics: resistance, adaptation, leaf color, trunk and crown shape.

Results and Discussion

More than 50,000 hybrid seedlings have been raised and tested, of which circa 80 individuals totaled a very high score. A wide range of resistant elm clones with different parentage and valuable characters are going to be released. This should help further safeguard against the appearance of new and even more aggressive strains of the pathogen, as occurred in the 1970s when the *O. novo-ulmi* appeared in Europe, or against different unpredictable risks (Santini et al. 2008).

Five DED-resistant elm clones have been patented and released to the market. 'San Zanobi' (Pat. n. RM97NV0006) and 'Plinio' (Pat. n. RM97NV0005) (Santini et al. 2002), both obtained by a controlled crossing of the Dutch hybrid 'Plantijn' with two different individuals of *U. pumila*, were released in 1997. The resistance levels of the clones were significantly higher than the resistance levels of 'Lobel' and other reference clones.

'San Zanobi' is monocormic and shows exceptionally rapid growth on fertile soils and in temperate climates, suggesting that it could be used also for production of construction timber (Santini et al. 2002, 2010). Its habit is cone-shaped with pronounced apical dominance, resulting in limited lateral branching on the developing shoots of the current season's growth (fig. 2). The crown is therefore narrow and columnar. Apical dominance is so marked that seedlings rarely need pruning or training. The wood characteristics of this clone are not different from those known for European field elm (*Ulmus minor* Mill.) (Santini et al. 2004).

'Plinio' grows rapidly, although slightly slower than 'San Zanobi,' roughly similar to that of fast-growing benchmark 'Lobel.' 'Plinio' can be used as an ornamental shade tree (fig. 2). The crown is vase shaped. In isolated trees, the width of the crown can be up to 70 percent of its height. The trunk is straight, at times slightly sinuous and short.

Ulmus 'San Zanobi   *Ulmus* 'Plinio'

Figure 2—Characteristics of two Dutch elm disease-resistant clones.

In 2006, 'Arno' (Community Plant Variety Right n. 27598) and 'Fiorente' (Community Plant Variety Right n. 27599) (Santini et al. 2007) were released. The first is a full sib of 'Plinio,' while the second is a first generation hybrid between a *U. pumila* with a *U. minor* that originated in Italy. The resistance levels of the clones are comparable to that of 'Lobel.'

'Arno' is single stemmed (monocormic), with erect habit, ascending branches, and an upright oval crown (fig. 3). Field trials indicate that 'Arno,' although slower than 'Fiorente,' is among the fastest growers ever tested. The trunk is straight, branching at a height of 3 m. The wood characteristics of this clone are not different from those known for field elm (Santini et al. 2004).

'Fiorente' is monocormic and shows exceptionally rapid growth, significantly greater than the other cultivars planted at the same site, suggesting that it could also be used for timber production. Its habit is conical with pronounced apical dominance, a result of the limited lateral branching on the developing shoots of the current season's growth (fig. 3). The crown is therefore slender and columnar. The trunk is straight and long.

Ulmus 'Arno'   *Ulmus* 'Fiorente'

Figure 3—Characteristics of two Dutch elm disease-resistant clones.

In 2010, the Italian elm breeding program raised a new variety by crossing a specimen of *U. chenmoui* W. C. Cheng with the Dutch hybrid clone '405.' This new release, named 'Morfeo' (Community Plant Variety n. 2011/0223) (Santini et al. 2011), is extremely resistant to DED and has an attractive form and foliage. It is also fast-growing, able to free stand at a very early age, and tolerant of drought and soils waterlogged in winter (fig. 4). Therefore, it is proving well adapted to the maritime, wet winter climate, where temperatures are moderated by the gulfstream of northwestern Europe, as well as the Mediterranean climate. Following trials in England, Morfeo' is considered of potential importance in the conservation of several invertebrates endangered by the consequences of DED.

Ulmus 'Morfeo'

Figure 4—Characteristics of the Dutch elm disease resistant clone 'Morfeo'.

Regarding genotype x environment interaction (GxE), results show that some DED-resistant elm clones showed superior growth at all experimental sites. These clones are likely suitable for successful planting in a range of different environments. In addition, several resistant clones showed a more marked GxE interaction having high-growth parameters at a particular site (Santini et al. 2010). Results deriving from biometric studies strongly support our belief that these elm clones can be successfully used for timber and biomass production.

The introduction of non-native elm species from different continents is one of the main features of the elm breeding program for DED resistance. It may involve the risk that local parasites of minor importance toward native species might cause some damage to new the hosts. For instance, a disease named 'Elm Yellows' caused by phytoplasmas, which until 1985 had been regarded of American origin, was found to be harmful and even deadly for a number of Asian elm species resistant to DED and for their hybrids (Mittempergher 2000). This disease commonly kills the American elm (*U. americana* L.); therefore, its outcome in this case does not differ from the results of DED. Yet in Europe, Elm Yellows is tolerated by the populations of native elms, with only a few individuals showing symptoms of yellowing, witches' brooms, growth retardation, or a general decline (Mittempergher 2000) and sometimes death.

Numerous insects are also known to damage European elms. Among these, the elm leaf beetle (*Xantogalerucha luteola*) and the goat moth (*Cossus cossus*) have to be mentioned. The various Asian elm species used in breeding programs because of their resistance to DED show varying susceptibility to these insects. For example, in our experience, the Chinese species *U. laciniata* (Trautv.) Mayr is so susceptible to leaf beetle that it is very difficult to raise it in central Italy without chemical control, whereas *U. parvifolia* Jacq. and *U. wilsoniana* Schneid., are scarcely damaged. The IPP has thus set up a rating program to assess the extent to which the commonly used Asian species may be susceptible to Elm Yellows and to the elm leaf beetle.

Multiple resistances to all of these different threats is taken into account when the clones are in adaptation trial fields by scoring their natural susceptibility. It is very conceivable that the climate could play a primary role in the build-up of insect populations and to phytoplasma infection, which is vectored by some species of insects belonging to phloem-feeding Hemiptera.

Moreover, the strategy adopted for elm genetic improvement had produced a new population that has a high proportion of unique, exotic-derived alleles that indeed broaden the elm genetic base, so that variance will be enhanced (Simmonds 1993). The gain in genetic richness and variability should encompass the strong bottleneck that, for the use of exotic species, even if hybridized with endogenous germplasm, is represented by adaptation to new environments. In conclusion, these results open the possibility for elms to overcome the condition of shrubs to which DED seemed to have destined these magnificent trees, and to be cultivated again for providing us not only with beauty, but also with new and different possible uses.

Acknowledgments

The authors wish to thank Prof. Lorenzo Mittempergher, who lead the Italian elm breeding program until 1999; Mr. Fabio Ferrini, Mr. Alberto Fagnani, and Mr. Abdellah Dahmani, without whom the results of this program would not be achieved.

Literature Cited

Brasier, C.M. 2000. Intercontinental spread and continuing evolution of the Dutch elm disease pathogens. In: Dunn, C.P., ed. The elms: breeding, conservation, and disease management. Boston: Kluwer Academic Publishers: 61–72.

Brasier, C.M.; Kirk, S.A. 2001. Designation of the EAN and NAN races of *Ophiostoma ulmi* as subspecies. Mycological Research. 105: 547–554.

Buisman, C. 1931. Overzicht van de soorten van iepen, in verband met het iepenziekteonderzoek. Tijdschrift Over Plantenziekten. 37: 111–116.

Cox, T.S.; Wood, D. 1999. The nature and role of crop biodiversity. In: Wood, D.; Lenne, J.M., eds. Agrobiodiversity: characterization, utilization, and management. Wallingford, UK: CABI Publishing: 35–57.

Heslop-Harrison, J.; Heslop-Harrison, Y. 1970. Evaluation of pollen viability by enzymatically induced fluorescence; intracellular hydrolysis of fluorescein diacetate. Stain Technology. 45: 115–120.

Heslop-Harrison, J.; Heslop-Harrison, Y.; Shivanna, K.R. 1984. The evaluation of pollen quality and a further appraisal of the fluorochromatic (FCR) test procedure. Theoretical and Applied Genetics. 67: 367–379.

Holmes, F.W. 1993. Seven Dutch women scientists whose early research is basic to our knowledge of the "Dutch elm disease". In: Sticklen, M.B.; Sherald, J.L., eds. Dutch elm disease research: cellular and molecular approaches. New York: Springer-Verlag: 9–15.

Mittempergher, L. 2000. Elm yellows in Europe. In: Dunn, C.P., ed. The elms: breeding, conservation, and disease management. Boston: Kluwer Academic Publishers: 103–119.

Mittempergher, L.; La Porta, N. 1991. Hybridization studies in the Eurasian species of elm (*Ulmus* sp.). Silvae Genetica. 40: 237–243.

Santini, A.; Fagnani, A.; Ferrini, F.; Ghelardini, L.; Mittempergher, L. 2007. 'Fiorente' and 'Arno' Elm trees. Hortscience. 42: 712–714.

Santini, A.; Fagnani, A.; Ferrini, F.; Mittempergher, L. 2002. San Zanobi and Plinio elm trees. Hortscience. 37: 1139–1141.

Santini, A.; Fagnani, A.; Ferrini, F.; Mittempergher, L.; Brunetti, M.; Crivellaro, A.; Macchioni, N. 2004. Elm breeding for DED resistance, the Italian clones and their wood properties. Investigación Agraria: Sistemas y Recursos Forestales. 13: 179–184.

Santini, A.; La Porta, N.; Ghelardini, L.; Mittempergher, L. 2008. Breeding against Dutch elm disease adapted to the Mediterranean climate. Euphytica. 163: 45–56.

Santini, A.; Pecori, F.; Pepori, A.L.; Ferrini, F.; Ghelardini, L. 2010. Genotype×environment interaction and growth stability of several elm clones resistant to Dutch elm disease. Forest Ecology and Management. 260: 1017–1025.

Santini, A.; Pecori, F.; Pepori, A.; Brookes, A. 2011. 'Morfeo' elm: a new variety resistant to Dutch elm disease. Forest Pathology. doi: 10.1111/j.1439-0329.2011.00737.

Schwarz, M.B. 1922. Das zweigsterben der ulmen, trauerweiden und pfirsichbaume. Utrecht, The Netherlands: University of Utrecht.73 p. Ph.D thesis.

Simmonds, N.W. 1993. Introgression and incorporation. Strategies for the use of crop genetic resources. Biological Reviews. 68: 539–562.

Smalley, E.B.; Guries, R.P. 1993. Breeding elms for resistance to Dutch elm disease. Annual Review of Phytopathology. 31: 325–352.

Spierenburg, D. 1921. Een onbekende ziekte in de iepen. Tijdschrift Over Plantenziekten. 18: 53–61.

Tanksley, S.D.; McCouch, S.R. 1997. Seed banks and molecular maps: unlocking genetic potential from the wild. Science. 277: 1063–1066.

Townsend, A.M.; Bentz, S.E.; Douglass, L.W. 2005. Evaluation of 19 American elm clones for tolerance to Dutch elm disease. Journal of Environmental Horticulture. 23: 21–24.

Westerdijk, J.; Ledeboer, M.; Went, J. 1931. Mededeelingen omtrent gevoeligheidsproeven van iepen voor graphium ulmi Schwarz, Gedurende 1929 en 1930. Tijdschrift Over Plantenziekten. 37: 105–110.

Patterns of Resistance to *Cronartium ribicola* in *Pinus aristata*, Rocky Mountain Bristlecone Pine

A.W. Schoettle,[1] R.A. Sniezko,[2] A. Kegley,[2] R. Danchok,[2] and K.S. Burns[3]

Abstract

The core distribution of Rocky Mountain bristlecone pine, *Pinus aristata* Engelm., extends from central Colorado into northern New Mexico, with a disjunct population on the San Francisco Peaks in northern Arizona. Populations are primarily at high elevations and often define the alpine treeline; however, the species can also be found in open mixed conifer stands with ponderosa (*Pinus ponderosa* Lawson & C. Lawson) and/or pinyon (*Pinus edulis* Engelm.) pines in some locations. On dry, exposed sites the stands are open and sparse and Rocky Mountain bristlecone (hereafter referred to as bristlecone) is commonly the only species present. The combination of the pine's adaptive traits with infrequent disturbance has enabled trees on these sites to attain ages of over 2,500 years. These same traits and conditions, which contribute to a long generation time, will inevitably hinder the ability of bristlecone pine to adapt to novel anthropogenic stresses such as climate change and infection by the non-native pathogen (*Cronartium ribicola*) that causes the lethal disease white pine blister rust (WPBR). Infection of bristlecone pine by *C. ribicola* was first documented in the field in 2003 in south-central Colorado. Rapid climate warming and the associated increase in mountain pine beetle activity are also affecting these high elevation ecosystems. These threats and the species' unique aesthetic and ecological roles make bristlecone pine a species of conservation interest. Blister rust invasion is relatively recent compared to the generation time of bristlecone pine, thus we still have a window of opportunity to gain and utilize new knowledge of this species and their ecosystems under natural conditions and develop proactive conservation strategies.

Genetic resistance to WPBR is a key factor that will affect the trajectory of bristlecone pine populations in the future. Preliminary results of studies to identify and quantify rust resistance in bristlecone pine families are reported here. Seeds collected in 2001 from 184 individual trees across 11 sites along the full latitudinal gradient in Colorado were sown in 2002. The 3-year-old seedlings were inoculated with *C. ribicola* at Dorena Genetic Resource Center in 2005. Seeds for an additional smaller test, also conducted at Dorena Genetic Resources Center, were sown in April 2009 and seedlings inoculated with *C. ribicola* in September 2009. Needle infection lesions (spots) were easily identified on needles of the seedlings inoculated at a young age (2009 trial), but were less obvious on needles of the seedlings inoculated at an older age (2005 trial). However, WPBR stem symptoms did develop on many of the older seedlings in the 2005 trial for which infection spots were not observed, suggesting that needle lesions are not a good early measure of infection in older bristlecone pine seedlings. Multiple WPBR resistant phenotypes are expressed by bristlecone pine including canker-free seedlings, seedlings with partial bark reactions, and seedlings developing stem infections later or showing longer survival with stem infections. Survivorship of seedlings in the large study, 5 years post-inoculation, range from 0 percent to 92 percent among families, and 17 percent to 60 percent among geographic areas.

[1] USDA Forest Service, Rocky Mountain Research Station, Ft. Collins, CO.
[2] USDA Forest Service, Dorena Genetic Resource Center, Cottage Grove, OR.
[3] USDA Forest Service, Forest Health Management, Lakewood, CO.
Corresponding author: aschoettle@fs.fed.us.

Development of Methods for the Restoration of the American Elm in Forested Landscapes

James M. Slavicek[1]

Abstract

A project was initiated in 2003 to establish test sites to develop methods to reintroduce the American elm (*Ulmus americana* L.) in forested landscapes. American elm tree strains with high levels of tolerance to Dutch elm disease (DED) were established in areas where the trees can naturally regenerate and spread. The process of regeneration will allow the American elm to co-evolve with the DED fungal pathogen to ensure this valuable tree species will not be lost from the landscape. This effort in Ohio is being carried out in partnership with the Ohio Department of Natural Resources-Division of Forestry, Franklin County Metro Parks, Worthington City Parks, and The Wilds. The project was expanded in 2005 by establishment of restoration sites in Iowa; Wisconsin; and Minnesota in partnership with the USDA Forest Service Northern Area State and Private Forestry; Luther College, Iowa; the U.S. Army Corps of Engineers; and the Carpenter St. Croix Valley Nature Center in Minnesota. In 2007, a site was established at Dago Slough near Cassville, Wisconsin in partnership with the U.S. Department of the Interior, Fish and Wildlife Service, and a test planting was established at the Bad River Indian Reservation in Wisconsin to assess tree cold hardiness. The restoration effort was expanded in 2010 in partnership with The Nature Conservancy through establishment of three sites in Vermont. To date, 12 American elm restoration test sites have been established in five states.

Key words: Dutch elm disease, American elm, restoration

Introduction

The American elm (*Ulmus americana* L.) was once widely distributed throughout the eastern United States and was a preferred tree for use along city streets and in the yards of many homeowners. The Dutch elm disease (DED) fungal pathogen *Ophiostoma ulmi* was introduced into the United States in 1930 and *O. novo-ulmi* in the early 1940s (Brasier 2000). In the subsequent years, these pathogens have destroyed millions of American elm trees in the United States and Canada. By 1976, only 34 million of the estimated 77 million elms present in the urban landscape before the introduction of the DED pathogen remained, and far fewer are still present today.

One line of research on the American elm from the 1970s to the present focused on the identification of American elm isolates that could withstand the DED pathogen. Over 100,000 American elm trees were tested for resistance to DED. No trees were found that were resistant; however, a few were identified that exhibited high levels of tolerance (approximately 60 to 96 percent survival after fungal inoculation) to the disease (Sherald 1993, Smalley and Guries 1993). Out of over 100,000 American elm trees screened for DED resistance, a very small number of trees (about seven) were identified that exhibit the necessary levels of DED tolerance to withstand the disease. Five of these selections include trees that have been released to the nursery industry: Valley Forge, Princeton, and New Harmony, and two other selections, the R18-2 and Delaware 2 (Smalley et al. 1993, Townsend et al. 1995, Townsend and Douglass 2001, Townsend et al. 2005). These five selections were planted at experimental test plots to assess fitness for selected sites and to develop methods for restoration of the American elm.

[1] Northern Research Station, Forestry Sciences Laboratory, 359 Main Road, Delaware, OH 43015.
Corresponding author: jslavicek@fs.fed.us.

Materials and Methods

The origin of the following American elm selections used in the test plots are:

- Princeton: A cultivar originating from Princeton, NJ that exhibits high tolerance to DED identified in 1922.
- R18-2: One of 17 survivors out of 21,000 seedlings screened for DED tolerance by Cornell University and the Boyce Thompson Institute reported in 1993.
- Delaware 2: One of the two most DED-tolerant trees identified in a screen of 35,000 seedlings by the U.S. Department of Agriculture, Bureau of Plant Industry selected in the 1940s.
- New Harmony: A clone of an ancient tree near Springfield, Ohio that was identified by Denny Townsend and Larry Schreiber in 1975 and exhibits high DED tolerance .
- Valley Forge: A selection out of hundreds that was identified by Denny Townsend and Larry Schreiber in 1975 and showed high levels of DED tolerance .
- Valley Forge x New Harmony seedling trees.

Additional selections will be added to the test sites as they become available. Test sites established to date are listed in table 1.

Table 1. Test sites established as of June 2012

Site	Location	Year established	Site description
Highbanks Metro Park	Delaware County, OH	2003	Upland, heavy clay
Mohican Memorial State Forest	Ashland County, OH	2003	Upland, loam
The Wilds	Muskingum County, OH	2003	Reclaimed coal mine
Maumee State Forest	Fulton County, OH	2004	Lowland, sand
Glacier Ridge Metro Park	Union County, OH	2004	Upland, heavy clay
Carpenter St. Croix Valley Nature Center	Hastings, MN	2005	Lowland, loam
Eagle Island	Stoddard Islands, WI	2005	Island within the Mississippi River
Luther College	Decorah, IA	2005	Upland, loam
Dago Slough	Cassville, WI	2007	Mississippi River floodplain
Olentangy River Park	Worthington, OH	2009	Olentangy River floodplain
Otter Creek	Cornwall, VT	2010	Otter Creek floodplain
Connecticut River	Maidstone, VT	2010	Connecticut River floodplain
LaPlatte River	Shelburne, VT	2010	LaPlatte River floodplain

American elm selections were propagated by vegetative cuttings, grown in 7.6 L pots for 2 years, and were about 2 m in height at planting. Valley Forge x New Harmony seedlings were generated by controlled pollinations, the seedlings were grown in 7.6 L pots for 1 year, and were about 1.3 m in height at planting. A 0.9 m diameter space was cleared of vegetation, 400 cm^3 of 10-10-10 fertilizer and 20 cm^3 of trace elements was added to the bottom of the planting hole, the trees were planted, and watered if the soil was dry. Mulch was added to the base around the trees with the exception of trees planted in 2003 where weed barriers of recycled plastic were used. Wire enclosures 0.76 m in diameter were constructed of poultry wire, 12 gauge woven wire, or plastic deer fencing and were placed around the trees to prevent deer browse and deer rub. A variety of site types were selected including upland, lowland, floodplain, and island sites as indicated in table 1 above. Trees were planted in a grid pattern or in clusters with spacing of individual trees from approximately 8 to 11 m apart. Annual measurements of trunk diameter at 1.2 m in height and height were made in early spring before leaf expansion. Instances of mortality were noted and the cause determined when possible.

Results and Discussion

All deer exclusion methods employed were effective; however, the wire enclosures made of 12 gauge woven wire were the most durable and needed no attention after placement. Mulching the base of trees provided effective weed/plant control for about 2 to 3 years after planting. Weed barrier mats provided long-term effective weed/plant control; however, they also provided nesting cover for mice which fed on bark during winter causing the loss of a few trees. The mats were removed in the spring of 2005.

At the Mohican Memorial State Forest site, average yearly growth ranged from 0.3 to 1.02 m in height for the clonally propagated selections, and from 0.25 to 0.9 m for Valley Forge x New Harmony seedling trees (fig. 1). Cumulative growth to date resulted in an average height of 6.2 m for the clonal selections and 3.5 m for the seedling trees (fig. 2). Average yearly growth ranged from 7.5 to 15 mm in stem diameter of the clonally propagated selections, and from 0.25 to 14.5 mm of Valley Forge x New Harmony seedling trees (fig. 3). Cumulative stem growth to date resulted in an average stem diameter of 80 mm for the clonal selections and 30 mm for the seedling trees (fig. 4).

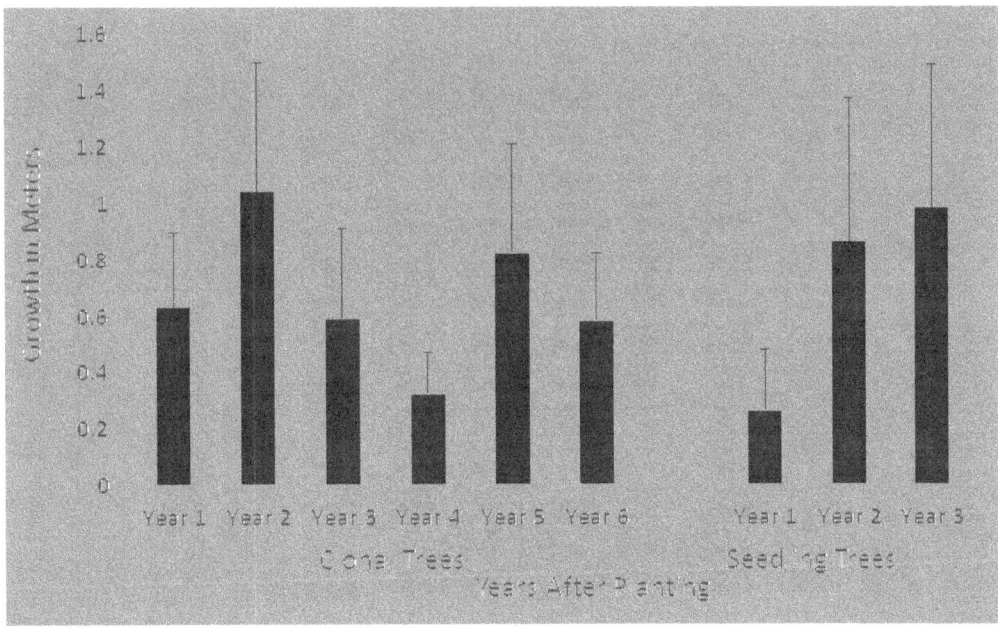

Figure 1—Average growth in American elm tree height of trees planted in 2003 at the Mohican Memorial State Forest in Ohio. The average growth plus the standard deviation for each year is shown.

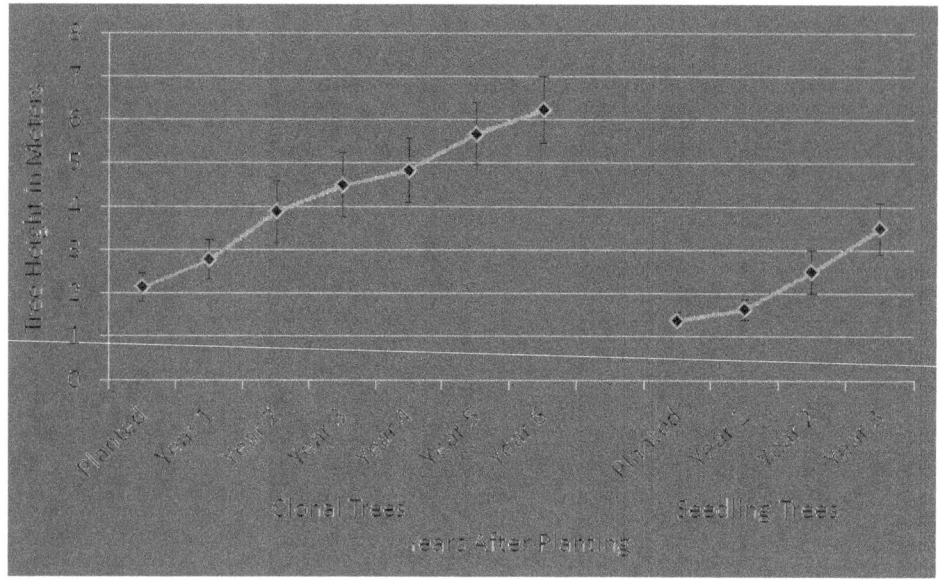

Figure 2—Cumulative growth in American elm tree height of trees planted at the Mohican Memorial State Forest in Ohio. The average cumulative height +/- the standard deviation for each year is shown.

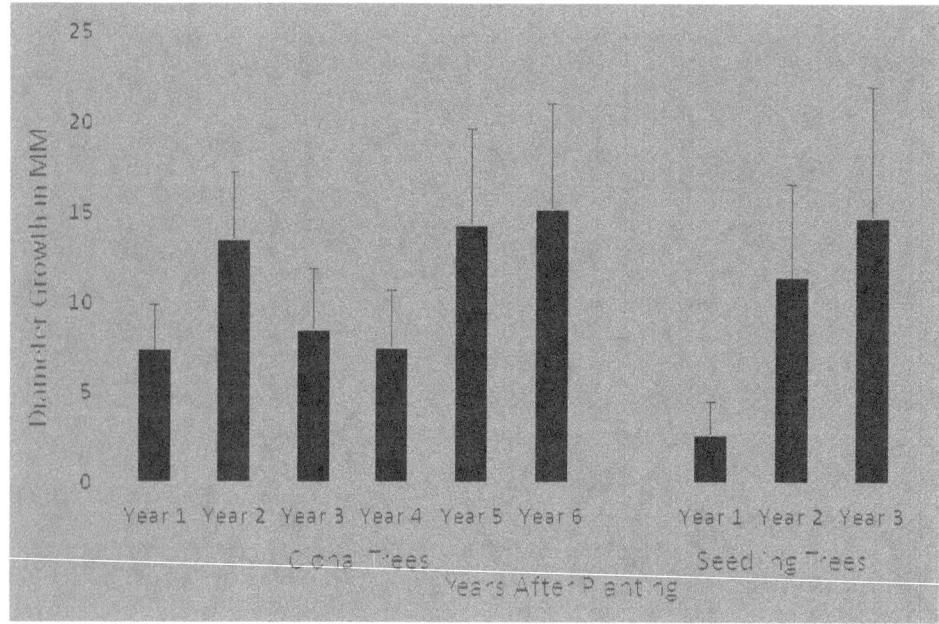

Figure 3—Average growth in American elm tree trunk diameter at 1.2 m in height of trees planted in 2003 at the Mohican Memorial State Forest in Ohio. The average growth plus the standard deviation for each year is shown.

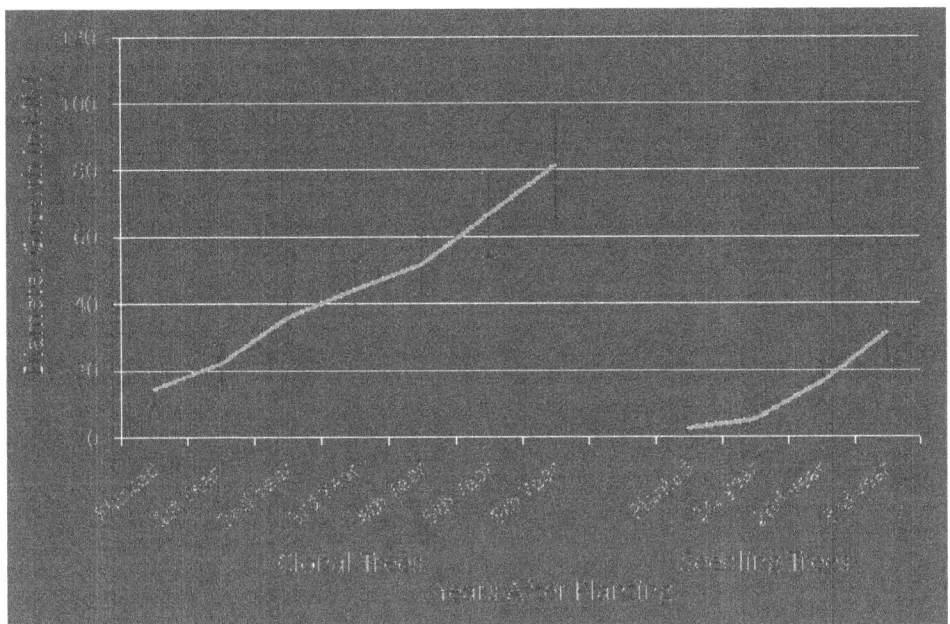

Figure 4—Cumulative growth in American elm tree trunk diameter at 1.2 m in height of trees planted in 2003 at the Mohican Memorial State Forest in Ohio. The average cumulative growth +/- the standard deviation for each year is shown.

Literature Cited

Brasier, C.M. 2000. Intercontinental spread and continuing evolution of the Dutch elm disease pathogens. In: Dunn, C.P., ed. The elms: breeding, conservation and disease management. Boston: Kluwer Academic Publishers: 61–72.

Sherald, J.L. 1993. Demands and opportunities for selecting disease-resistant elms. In: Sticklen, M.B.; Sherald, J.L., eds. Dutch elm disease research: cellular and molecular approaches. New York: Springer-Verlag: 60–68.

Smalley, E.B.; Guries, R.P. 1993. Breeding elms for resistance to Dutch elm disease. Annual Review of Phytopathology. 31: 325–352.

Smalley, E.B.; Guries, R.P.; Lester, D.T. 1993. American Liberty elms and beyond: going from the impossible to the difficult. In: Sticklen, M.B., Sherald, J.L., eds. Dutch elm disease research: cellular and molecular approaches. New York: Springer-Verlag: 26-45.

Townsend, A.M.; Bentz, S.E.; Douglass, L.W. 2005. Evaluation of 19 American elm clones for tolerance to Dutch elm disease. Journal of Environmental Horticulture. 23: 21–24.

Townsend, A.M.; Bentz, S.E.; Johnson, G.R. 1995. Variation in response of selected American elm clones to Ophiostoma ulmi. Journal of Environmental Horticulture. 13: 126–128.

Townsend, A.M.; Douglass, L.W. 2001. Variation among American elm clones in long-term dieback, growth, and survival following *Ophiostoma* inoculation. Journal of Environmental Horticulture. 19(2): 100–103.

Generation of American Elm Trees with Tolerance to Dutch Elm Disease Through Controlled Crosses and Selection

James M. Slavicek[1] and Kathleen S. Knight[1]

Abstract

The goal of our research and development efforts is to generate new and/or improved selections of the American elm (*Ulmus americana* L.) with tolerance/resistance to Dutch elm disease (DED). The approaches we are taking for this effort include: 1) controlled breeding using known DED -tolerant selections, 2) controlled breeding using DED-tolerant selections and local escape/survivor trees from specific geographic areas to generate site-adapted and DED-tolerant selections, 3) screening of escape/survivor trees for tolerance to DED, and 4) identification of additional American elm escape/survivor trees across its range. Our efforts in these areas are described. Progeny trees generated from crosses of Delaware 2 x New Harmony, Valley Forge x New Harmony, R18-2 x New Harmony, and Valley Forge x R18-2 exhibited a significantly lower mean of foliar symptoms at 8 to 9 weeks compared to the susceptible control.

Key words: American elm, *Ulmus americana*, Dutch elm disease resistance, tolerance

Introduction

Dutch elm disease (DED) has devastated North American species of elm, nearly eliminating the use of American elm (*Ulmus americana* L.) as an urban shade tree. There is a need for multiple, genetically diverse, American elm cultivars with superior tolerance to DED to be used by arborists and nurseries for urban plantings as shade trees and for the restoration of the American elm in forests. A few American elm selections have been identified and released to the nursery industry. The Princeton cultivar is the most sold cultivar by far in the United States (Sherald 1993, Smalley et al. 1993, Townsend and Douglass 2001, Townsend et al. 1995, Townsend et al. 2005).

Previous attempts at selective breeding of American elm resulted in low levels of resistance (Lester 1969a, 1969b). In Wisconsin, a group led by Smalley and Guries (1993) crossed 29 trees yielding more than 3,000 progeny. After inoculation screenings of vigorous individuals multiplied for clonal trials, six trees were selected to comprise the American Liberty Multiclone and one of these was patented as the Independence elm. Unfortunately, the DED tolerance of American Liberty has subsequently been extensively tested and found to be unexceptional (Townsend and Douglass 2001, Townsend et al.1995, Townsend et al. 2005).

Several American elm clones have tested with higher DED tolerance than the American Liberty. Valley Forge showed the best tolerance of all clones, but significant tolerance was also measured for New Harmony, Princeton, R18-2, and Delaware 2 (Townsend and Douglass 2001, Townsend et al. 1995, Townsend et al. 2005). The different levels of foliar symptoms and crown dieback may suggest that multiple distinct genes are involved in conferring tolerance to DED. If complementary DED tolerance genes from both parental trees were placed in a progeny tree through crossing, the progeny could exhibit greater tolerance to DED than the parents.

There have been about 80 years of DED pressure on American elms in the landscape. Consequently, there is an increasing likelihood that the remaining large trees (0.9 to 1.2 m diameter at breast height) have tolerance to DED and the screening of these trees could be fruitful.

[1] Northern Research Station, Forestry Sciences Laboratory, 359 Main Road, Delaware, OH 43015. Corresponding author: jslavicek@fs.fed.us.

Materials and Methods

Controlled breeding was carried out in the laboratory with cut branches and/or with field-planted trees. The selections listed in table 1 have been used to date.

Table 1—DED tolerant, escape/survivor, and elm yellow escape/survivor selections used

Known DED tolerant	Escape/survivor trees on the Chippewa NF	Escape/survivor trees in Massachusetts & Connecticut
Princeton (Pr)	Black Duck (BD)	Hadley (HA)
Valley Forge (VF)	SO 1	Rainbow Bridge 1 (RB1)
New Harmony (NH)	SO 2	Goff (GF)
Delaware 2 (Del2)	Walker (WR)	Rainbow Bridge 2 (RB2)
R18-2 (18-2) 8630 (elm yellows survivor)		

Pollination bags were placed on branches on trees in the field prior to flower bud opening. Branches from trees were collected, brought into the laboratory, and pollen was collected after pollen drop. Pollen was used to pollinate flowers within bagged branches on trees in the field and flowers on branches in the laboratory. The controlled pollinations performed to date include:

VF ♀ x 18-2 ♂, 18-2 ♀ x VF ♂, VF ♀ x SO 2 ♂, 18-2 ♀ x SO 2 ♂, 18-2 ♀ x GF ♂
VF ♀ x NH ♂, NH ♀ x Del2 ♂, VF ♀ x WR ♂, Del 2 ♀ x BD ♂, 18-2 ♀ x RB 2 ♂
R18-2 ♀ x NH ♂, VF ♀ x 8630 ♂, 18-2 ♀ x SO 1 ♂, Pr ♀ x SO 2 ♂, VF ♀ x HA ♂
Del2 ♀ x NH ♂, VF ♀ x BD ♂, 18-2 ♀ x WR ♂, 18-2 ♀ x HA ♂, VF ♀ x RB 1 ♂
Pr ♀ x VF ♂, VF ♀ x SO 1 ♂, 18-2 ♀ x BD ♂, 18-2 ♀ x RB 1 ♂, VF ♀ x GF ♂
VF ♀ x Pr ♂, VF ♀ x RB 2 ♂, Pr ♀ x RB 1 ♂, Pr ♀ x HA ♂, Pr ♀ x GF ♂
Pr ♀ x RB 2 ♂

Progeny generated from controlled pollinations of Del2 x NH, VF x NH, R18-2 x NH, and VF x R18-2 were established in field plots at the Delaware, Ohio Forestry Sciences Laboratory, Northern Research Station, using a randomized complete block design. The plot design consists of 10 blocks of 3.05 m x 3.05 m plantings with a total of 100 progeny of each of the four crosses; ramets of each parent and a susceptible clone, NA57845; and unselected seedlings (total n = 720). When trees reached 5 to 7 years old, each was inoculated with *O. novo-ulmi* strains PMP1 and H961, and the *O. ulmi* strain PG442, using a mixed inoculum consisting of equal counts of conidia of the three strains. The mixed inoculum resolves degrees of tolerance among American elm clones better than a single strain inoculum (Townsend, ARS, US National Arboretum, retired, personal communication). An aliquot of approximately 0.15 ml of an aqueous stock suspension with a concentration of 4 million spores/ml was applied to a hole drilled with a 0.2 cm diameter bit to a 2.54 cm depth in the lower third of the trunk, and the hole was wrapped with parafilm. Foliar symptoms of DED include wilting, chlorosis, and necrosis. For each tree, the combined percentage of the crown exhibiting wilting, chlorosis, or necrosis was visually estimated (consensus rating by a pair of evaluators) to the nearest 5 percent at 8 to 9 weeks, 1 year, and 2 years after inoculation. In addition to the 5 percent intervals, an additional interval of < 5 percent was used to indicate trace symptoms that were significantly less than 5 percent.

Results and Discussion

Controlled Crosses of Chippewa National Forest, Connecticut, and Massachusetts Escape/Survivor American Elms

The results of field pollinations performed in 2011 are shown in table 2. The number of seeds generated per flower ranged from 2.1 to 19.0. The control bags produced essentially no viable seeds. The germination rate of seed from the crosses ranged from 70 to 85 percent.

Table 2—Results of controlled pollinations performed in 2011

Cross	Seeds/Flower Bud	Cross	Seeds/Flower Bud
18-2 ♀ x HA ♂	7.2, 8.9, 6.0	Pr ♀ x HA ♂	10.1
18-2 ♀ x RB 1♂	3.2, 8.0, 2.2	Pr ♀ x RB 1♂	8.5, 11.4
18-2 ♀ x GF ♂	7.4, 6.4, 4.6	Pr ♀ x GF ♂	8.7
18-2 ♀ x RB 2 ♂	4.6, 6.9, 2.1	Pr ♀ x RB 2 ♂	10.5
VF ♀ x HA ♂	2.1	18-2 ♀ control	0, 0, 0.3, 0
VF ♀ x RB 1♂	13.4, 12.2	VF ♀ control	0.1, 0, 0, 0
VF ♀ x GF ♂	10.0, 8.8	Pr ♀ x 18-2 ♂	10.2
VF ♀ x RB 2 ♂	3.0	18-2 ♀ x VF ♂	9.9, 19.0

Seedlings generated from crosses between known DED-tolerant and Chippewa National Forest elm trees, and known DED-tolerant and Massachusetts and Connecticut trees, have been planted in test sites at the Chippewa National Forest and in Connecticut. When the trees are approximately 5 to 7 years old they will be inoculated with *O. ulmi* and *O. novo-ulmi* to test for DED tolerance.

DED Testing of Progeny Trees From Controlled Crosses of DED Tolerant Selections

The Del 2 x NH, VF x NH, R18-2 x NH, and VF x R18-2 crosses yielded seedlings with lower-mean foliar symptoms at 8-9 weeks compared to the susceptible control. The distributions of symptom severity for the progeny trees of the VF x R18-2 cross and the clonally propagated DED susceptible control (NA54845) are shown in fig. 1. The progeny trees from the other crosses exhibited a similar symptom response and distribution compared to the progeny trees from the VF x R18-2 cross (data not shown). Valley Forge x R18-2 yielded the highest number of individuals with few to no symptoms compared to the other crosses (data not shown). The crosses showed no correlation between tree height or caliper and foliar symptoms (data not shown). These results show that it may be possible to generate new American elm clones with high levels of DED tolerance using these selected crossings. Fifteen progeny trees that showed little or no DED symptoms were clonally propagated, the clones were established in field plots, and the trees will be challenged with *O. novo-ulmi* as described above in 2 to 3 years.

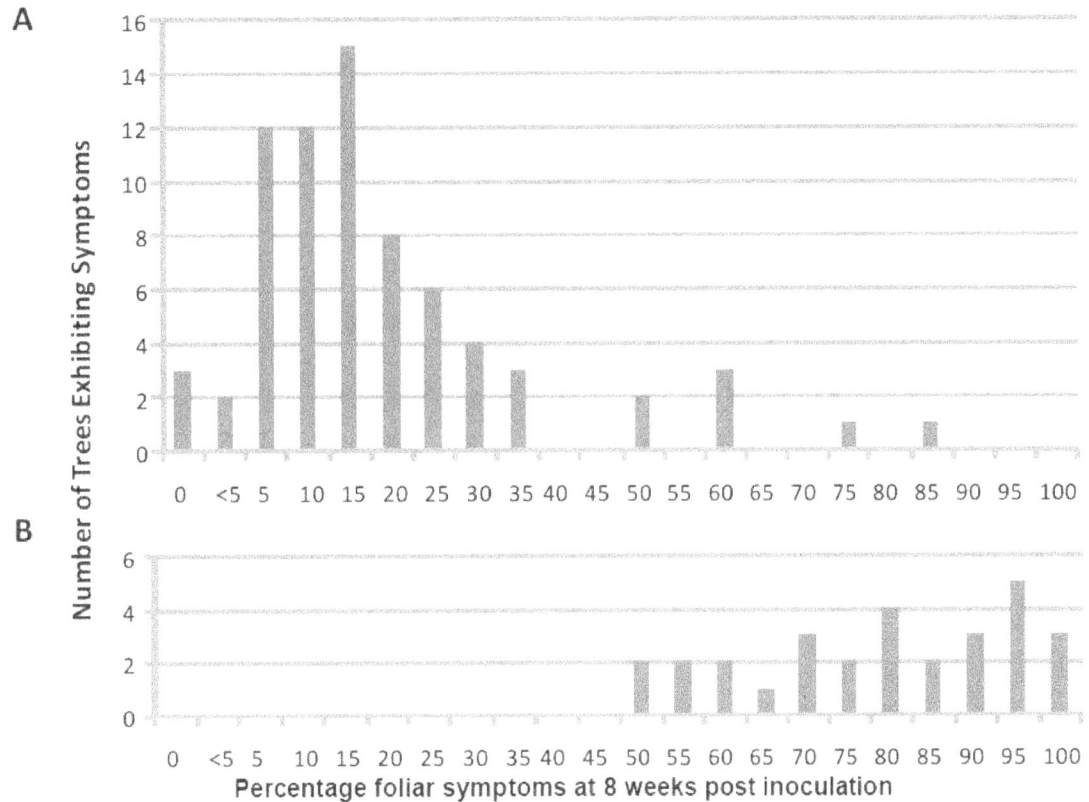

Figure 1—(A) Dutch elm disease symptoms on progeny trees from the R18-2 x Valley Forge cross, and (B) on clonally propagated susceptible control NA54845.

Identification of Large American Elm Escape/Survivor Trees

Twenty-five large escape/survivor American elms have been identified in Michigan, Ohio, Indiana, and Illinois. These trees were clonally propagated, established in replicate blocks at Delaware, Ohio, and will be tested for DED tolerance in 2 to 3 years. Additional escape/survivor trees are being identified with the help of interested foresters and others as discussed below.

A new effort was initiated to identify additional large surviving American elms through the generation of a website where information on these trees can be submitted (http://nrs.fs.fed.us/SurvivorElms). Approximately 605 elm trees throughout the region have been submitted as of June 5, 2012. We are asking for the help of state foresters, park employees, and the interested public to identify large American elm trees on their landscapes.

Potential DED-tolerant elm trees identified by cooperators (fig. 2) will be compiled in a database and prioritized for sampling. When funding becomes available, scion wood will be collected from the identified high-priority trees and used to clonally propagate these trees initially through bud grafts and then vegetative cuttings. When the trees reach susceptible size, they will be screened for DED tolerance, and selections with tolerance will be released to state tree nurseries for generation of elm seed orchards and to the commercial nursery trade. In addition, seed collected from the seed orchards created at the Delaware, Ohio Forest Service laboratory will be used in landscape restoration efforts.

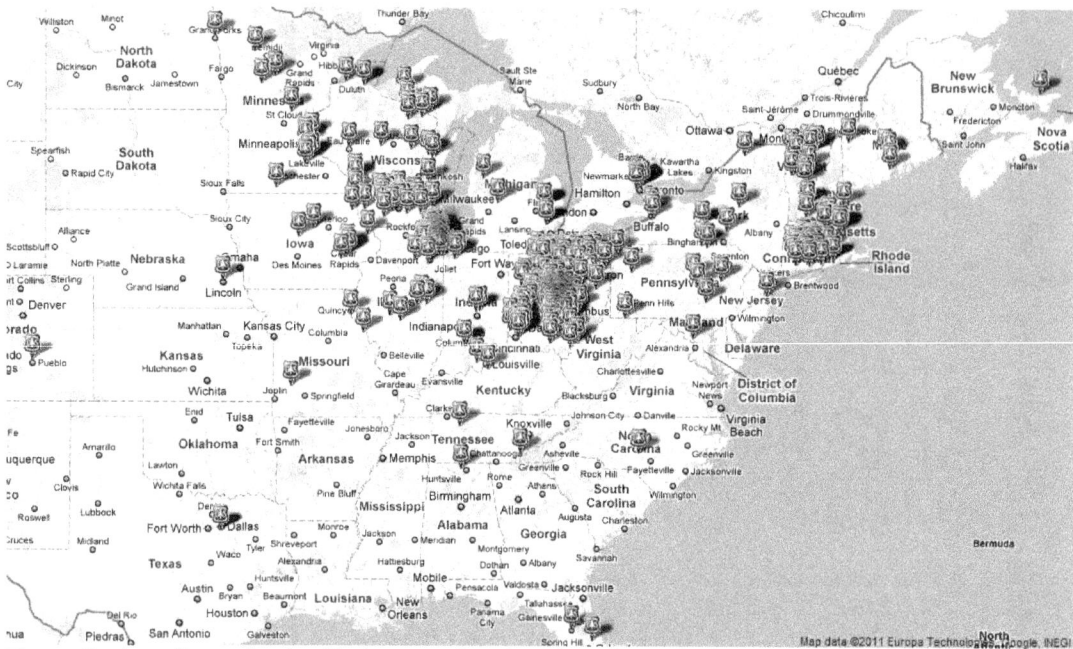

Figure 2—Locations of submitted escape/survivor American elm trees as of August 17, 2011.

Literature Cited

Lester, D.T. 1969a. Genetics and breeding of American elm. In: Proceeding of the 16th northeastern forest tree improvement conference. Ottawa: Canada Department of Forestry: 9–13.

Lester, D.T. 1969b. Self-compatibility and inbreeding depression in American elm. Forest Science. 17: 321–322.

Sherald, J.L. 1993. Demands and opportunities for selecting disease-resistant elms. In: Sticklen, M.B.; Sherald, J.L., eds. Dutch elm disease research: cellular and molecular approaches. New York: Springer-Verlag: 60–68.

Smalley, E.B.; Guries, R.P. 1993. Breeding elms for resistance to Dutch elm disease. Annual Review of Phytopathology 31: 325–352.

Smalley, E.B.; Guries, R.P.; Lester, D.T. 1993. American Liberty elms and beyond: going from the impossible to the difficult. In: Sticklen, M.B.; Sherald, J.L., eds. Dutch elm disease research: cellular and molecular approaches. New York: Springer-Verlag: 26–45.

Townsend, A.M.; Bentz, S.E.; Johnson, G.R. 1995. Variation in response of selected American elm clones to *Ophiostoma ulmi*. Journal of Environmental Horticulture. 13: 126–128.

Townsend, A.M.; Bentz, S.E.; Douglass, L.W. 2005. Evaluation of 19 American elm clones for tolerance to Dutch elm disease. Journal of Environmental Horticulture. 23: 21–24.

Townsend, A.M.; Douglass, L.W. 2001. Variation among American elm clones in long-term dieback, growth, and survival following *Ophiostoma* inoculation. Journal of Environmental Horticulture. 19: 100–103.

Breeding for Resistance to Adelgids in *Abies fraseri*, *Tsuga canadensis*, and *T. caroliniana*

Ben Smith,[1] Fred Hain,[2] and John Frampton[2]

Abstract

The balsam woolly adelgid (BWA; *Adelges piceae*) and hemlock woolly adelgid (HWA; *Adelges tsugae*) have had a tremendous impact on native ecosystems with Fraser fir (*Abies fraseri* (Pursh) Poir), eastern hemlock (*Tsuga canadensis* (L.) Carrière), and Carolina hemlock (*T. caroliniana* Engelm.) in the eastern United States since their introduction from Asia. They have also caused serious economic damage in Christmas tree plantations and nurseries. The Alliance for Saving Threatened Forests is engaged in research to complement other methods of adelgid control through the development of genetically resistant Fraser fir and hemlocks. The approach focuses on the identification, testing, and breeding of resistance or tolerance found within natural populations. In addition, development of interspecific hybrids is underway, incorporating both traditional breeding techniques and somatic embryogenesis.

[1] North Carolina State University, Alliance for Saving Threatened Forests, 239 Test Farm Rd., Waynesville, NC 28786.
[2] North Carolina State University, Raleigh, NC.
Corresponding author: threatenedforests@ncsu.edu.

Nine Year Survival of 16 *Phytophthora lateralis* Resistant and Susceptible Port-Orford-Cedar Families in a Southern Oregon Field Trial

Richard A. Sniezko,[1] Jim Hamlin,[2] Everett M. Hansen,[3] and Sunny Lucas[1]

Abstract

Port-Orford-cedar (*Chamaecyparis lawsoniana*) has suffered high mortality from the pathogen *Phytophthora lateralis* in portions of its natural range in southwest Oregon and northwest California, as well as in horticultural plantings in North America, and more recently in Europe. A program to develop genetically resistant populations of Port-Orford-cedar is underway. This operational program began in 1996 and utilizes artificial inoculation of the roots of young seedlings (or rooted cuttings) to rate parent trees for resistance. A key step to any such program is to establish field trials: to validate the results of artificial inoculation trials; to examine resistance at a range of sites and environments conducive to the pathogen; and to monitor the durability of resistance. The field trial ('Foggy Eden' site) examined here consists of 16 Port-Orford-cedar families established in southern Oregon in 2002 at a site on the Rogue River-Siskiyou National Forest. The Foggy Eden (FE-02) site was chosen because of the notable recent heavy *P. lateralis* related mortality of the natural Port-Orford-cedar trees in the immediate vicinity. Sixteen families had been selected to cover a range from highly susceptible (100 percent mortality) to highly resistant (0 percent mortality) in a previous short-term greenhouse artificial inoculation ('root dip,' RD) trial. Some of the families were also included in two short-term raised bed (RB) trials, where the raised bed had been previously infested with *P. lateralis*. By summer 2010, overall mortality at FE was 42.7 percent (263 of 616 trees). Most of the mortality occurred by 2006 (244 trees). Family variation in survival ranges from 20.8 to 93.8 percent. The top three families for survival involve a common parent and all have less than 11 percent mortality. The comparison of the results from FE-02 with the short-term 'root dip' and raised bed tests showed a strong relationship between these trials. The results are encouraging at this point, but the trial needs to be followed longer, and the results from the additional trials in other environments conducive to *P. lateralis* need to be examined to determine the efficacy of resistance in different environments. Resistant seed from wind-pollinated orchards is now available to aid restoration and reforestation.

Key words: Port-Orford-cedar, *Chamaecyparis lawsoniana*, *Phytophthora lateralis*, genetic resistance, field trials

Introduction

Port-Orford-cedar (POC) (*Chamaecyparis lawsoniana* (A. Murr.) Parl.), a long-lived conifer, has experienced high mortality from the non-native root pathogen *Phytophthora lateralis* (Tucker and Milbrath) in portions of its natural range in southwest Oregon and northwest California (USDA FS and USDI BLM 2004), as well as in horticultural plantings in North America and Europe. The use of growing stock with genetic resistance is key to restoration of POC in these areas as well as in general reforestation and horticultural plantings where *P. lateralis* may be problematic. An applied program to develop genetically resistant populations of POC is underway (Sniezko 2006, Sniezko et al. 2009; Sniezko et al., Operational program to develop *Phytophthora lateralis* resistant populations of Port-Orford-cedar (*Chamaecyparis lawsoniana*), these proceedings). This resistance program utilizes several methods of short-term testing to rapidly evaluate hundreds of field selections for resistance. However, there are few reports detailing differential survival of resistant and susceptible POC

[1] USDA Forest Service, Dorena Genetic Resource Center, Cottage Grove, Oregon, USA.
[2] USDA Forest Service, Umpqua National Forest, Roseburg, Oregon, USA.
[3] Department of Botany and Plant Pathology, Oregon State University, Corvallis, Oregon, USA.
Corresponding author: rsniezko@fs.fed.us.

families in field tests or the correspondence between genetic resistance in short-term seedling tests and field tests (Sniezko et al. 2006).

In this paper, we examine field survival 9 years after the planting of 16 POC families at a site where *P. lateralis* mortality of the existing POC in the forest stand had been moderately high. We also examine the relationship between field mortality in this trial with seedling mortality in four short-term greenhouse and raised bed trials.

Materials and Methods

Seedlings for all trials were grown for 1 year in 164 ml tubes using a soilless nursery medium (mixture of peat, vermiculite, composted fir bark, perlite, and pumice) in a greenhouse at Dorena Genetic Resource Center (DGRC) in Cottage Grove, Oregon. The 'Foggy Eden' field site (42° 48.195' N, 123° 53.340' W, 731 m elevation; fig. 1) on the Powers Ranger District of the Rogue River-Siskiyou National Forest was planted at 1.83 m x 1.83 m spacing on April 5th and 6th 2002 using 616 1-year- old seedlings from 16 families (representing 20 parents). Seedlings were planted in family row plots with 4 to 12 trees per family in each of the four blocks of the randomized complete block design. The parent trees were forest selections from within varying parts of the natural range in Oregon and California. The nine open-pollinated (wind-pollinated seed lots from a clone bank at DGRC) and six full-sib families had been chosen to represent a wide range of resistance (0 to 100 percent survival) based on a previous short-term (7 month) seedling test (RD-00, see below). The Foggy Eden site (FE-02) was chosen due to the presence of recent mortality from *P. lateralis* of approximately 75 percent of the POC in the overstory and surrounding area. For each of the seven assessments since the 2002 planting, seedlings were rated as alive, 'fading,' or dead. We report on the cumulative mortality of POC through the July 2010 assessment.

Figure 1—Port-Orford-cedar *Phytophthora lateralis* resistance trial planted in 2002 in understory of forest canopy at Foggy Eden (FE-02) site on Siskiyou National Forest in Oregon. (Photo credit: Eric Martz)

Subsets of the 16 families planted in FE-02 were also tested as part of four short-term (7-month to 2-year duration) greenhouse or raised bed trials (table 1) at Oregon State University in 2000 and

2002. The two greenhouse trials (RD-00, RD-02) utilized the 'root dip' technique where roots that had emerged from the bottom of the 164 ml tubes were clipped and the bottom 1 cm of the upright tubes were immersed in a zoospore suspension for 48 hours. The suspension was a mix of two standard *P. lateralis* isolates, '366' and '368.' The seedlings remained in the greenhouse for monitoring and assessments over the subsequent 5 to 7 months (table 1; fig. 2). In the raised bed trials (RB-00, RB-02), seedlings were planted in a raised bed (fig. 3) in which the soil had been previously infested with the same two isolates of *P. lateralis*. Mortality in all four seedling trials was recorded over the ensuing 5 to 18 months as seedling foliage began to wilt or turn chlorotic (table 1). At each assessment, fading seedlings were scraped at the root collar to check for the presence of the characteristic cinnamon-colored stain (fig. 3). *Phytophthora lateralis* was also confirmed on a small subset of seedlings using a combination of culture and PCR techniques. Selective culture and PCR methods were adapted from Winton and Hansen (2001). Further details are discussed elsewhere (Oh et al. 2006). Further details on methods for root dip and raised bed testing are reported by Hansen et al., Methods for screening Port-Orford-cedar for resistance to *Phytophthora lateralis*, these proceedings.

Figure 2—Port-Orford-cedar seedlings in greenhouse following 'root dip' inoculation with *Phytophthora lateralis*. (Photo credit: Richard Sniezko)

Figure 3—Raised bed trial of Port-Orford-cedar for *Phytophthora lateralis* resistance and seedling showing brown lesion from *P. lateralis* at root collar. (Photo credit: Richard Sniezko)

The design for all trials was a randomized complete block, with the number of seedlings per family in each block varying by trial (table 1). The 2000 trials (RD-00 and RB-02) had relatively few seedlings per family compared to the other trials (table 1). Survival in all trials was analyzed with blocks considered random and families as fixed effects using SAS (SAS Institute Inc., V9.2, 2008).

Survival at the termination of the four short-term trials (RD-00, RD-02, RB-00, RB-02) and field survival through summer 2010 for FE-02 (9 years after planting) were used for all analyses. Family differences in survival were analyzed using family-plot means in Proc Glimmix (binomial distribution); plot means were adjusted by 0.01 for those values of 1.0 (adjusted to 0.99) and 0.0 (adjusted to 0.01) in order to avoid the non-convergence issue in Proc Glimmix when numerous values of 1 or 0 are encountered in the dataset. Proc Corr (product moment correlation) was used to examine family mean correlations among the respective experiments, and Proc Reg (regression) was used to plot the family mean survival among experiments. All statistical analyses were conducted using SAS (SAS Institute Inc., V9.2, 2008).

Table 1—Background information on five *Phytophthora lateralis* resistance trials: field trial (FE-02), raised bed trials (RB-00, RB-02), and root dip trials (RD-00, RD-02)

Trial	No. Families (F)	No. Blocks (B)	No. Seedlings/F/B	First Assessment	Final Assessment	No. of Assessments
FE-02	16	4	4 to 12	2002	2010	7
RD-00	15	6	1 to 6	04/2000	01/2001	22
RD-02	9	4	6 to 12	04/2002	09/2002	5
RB-00	15	6	1 to 4	04/2000	01/2001	20
RB-02	9	4	6 to 12	05/2002	11/2003	8

Results

Overall survival of POC was 57.3 percent through summer 2010 at FE-02. Most of the mortality occurred within 4 years of planting (fig. 4). Visual symptoms (cinnamon-colored staining of the phloem tissue at the base of the tree after scraping away the bark) or DNA testing using PCR indicated that *P. lateralis* was the probable cause of mortality, but because the field site was only assessed periodically, definitive confirmation of cause of death for some seedlings was not possible. A few seedlings in the 2003 examination showed the lesion only at ground level (not downward into the roots) indicating that there may have been overland water flow infecting the seedlings right at the soil line, and not through the root tips, thus, potentially bypassing some resistances.

Significant differences ($p<.05$) among families were found at FE-02 with survival varying from 20.8 to 93.8 percent (fig. 4; table 2). The three families involving parent 117490 and the two families involving CF1 (both resistant parent controls) had high survival at FE-02 (table 2). Significant differences were also found among families in all of the raised bed and root dip trials (RB-00, RB-02, RD-00, RD-02). There was a moderate to high correlation between trials for the five tests, with only the correlations of RB-00 with RB-02 and RD-02 being non-significant (table 3; fig. 5). Families involving parents 117490, CF1, 117486, 510015, and 510005 generally ranked high for survival in the trials, although a few of these families showed higher mortality in the raised bed trials (table 2). In contrast, families involving relatively susceptible female parents 118463, D-70013, D-70103, and D-70119 have low survival across all tests. The remaining six families generally showed intermediate survival across the tests (table 2).

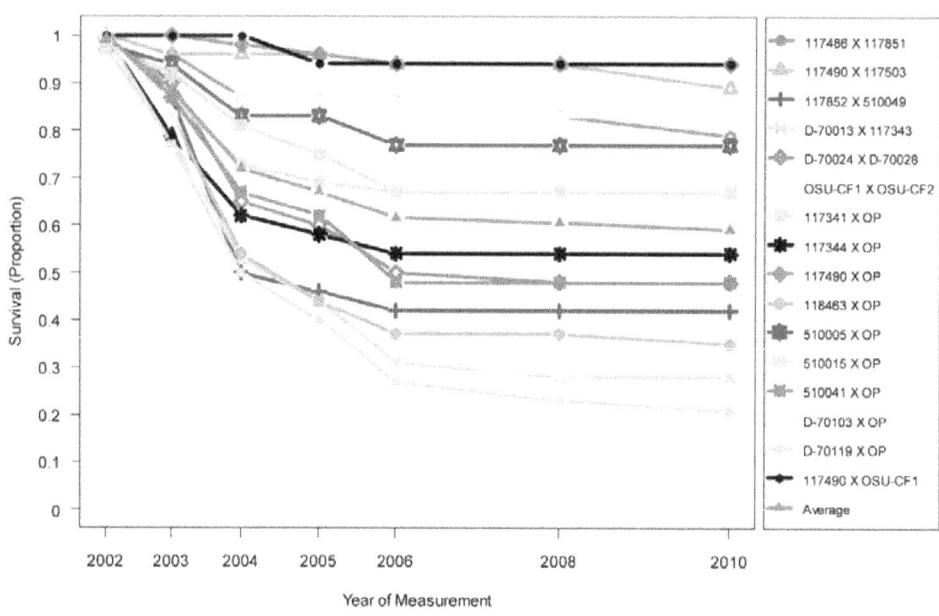

Figure 4—Survival from 2002 to 2010 for 16 Port-Orford-cedar families in Foggy Eden 2002 (FE-02) *Phytophthora lateralis* resistance planting.

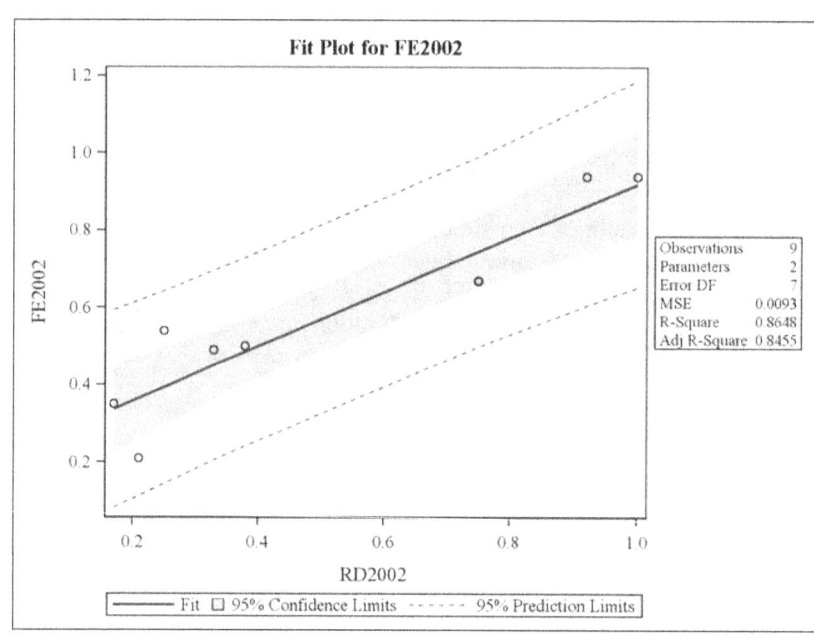

Figure 5—Regression plot between family mean survival in Foggy Eden field test (FE2002) and survival in 2002 root dip test (RD2002) for *Phytophthora lateralis* resistance (using eight common families).

Discussion

After 9 years in the field, we found very large differences in survival among the 16 families in the FE-02 trial. Visual examination or PCR testing confirmed the likelihood of *P. lateralis* as the causative agent of mortality and no other apparent cause of mortality was noted at this site. Little mortality has occurred in the last 5 years, suggesting that the genetic resistance present may be

Table 2—Mean survival proportions (and number of seedlings tested) by family for five trials: field test (FE-02), two raised bed tests (RB-00, RB-02), and two root dip tests (RD-00, RD-02)

Family	Test				
	FE-02	RB-00	RB-02	RD-00	RD-02
117490 x CF1	0.94 (16)	nt	0.77 (47)	nt	1.00 (48)
117490 x w	0.94 (48)	0.33 (6)	0.50 (48)	1.00 (6)	0.92 (24)
117490 x 117503	0.90 (48)	0.72 (18)	nt	1.00 (18)	nt
CF1 x CF2	0.83 (24)	0.67 (12)	nt	0.83 (12)	nt
117486 x 117851	0.79 (24)	0.92 (12)	nt	0.92 (12)	nt
510005 x w	0.77 (48)	0.67 (12)	nt	0.75 (12)	nt
510015 x w	0.67 (36)	0.29 (24)	0.21 (18)	0.58 (12)	0.75 (48)
117341 x w	0.67 (48)	0.44 (18)	0.33 (48)	0.50 (18)	0.75 (48)
117344 x w	0.54 (24)	0.25 (12)	0.23 (48)	0.50 (12)	0.25 (24)
510041 x w	0.50 (48)	0.33 (6)	0.17 (48)	0.60 (6)	0.38 (48)
70024 x 70028	0.49 (49)	0.33 (6)	0 (48)	0 (6)	0.33 (48)
117852 x 510049	0.42 (24)	0.39 (22)	nt	0.58 (24)	nt
118463 x w	0.35 (48)	0 (12)	0.02 (48)	0 (12)	0.17 (48)
70013 x 117343	0.28 (36)	0.12 (24)	nt	0.08 (24)	nt
70103 x w	0.21 (47)	0 (12)	0.04 (24)	0 (12)	0.21 (24)
70119 x w	0.21 (48)	0 (12)	nt	0 (12)	nt

Note: nt = not tested; w= wind-pollinated.

Table 3—Family mean correlations (number of families; significance value) for survival between five tests for *Phytophthora lateralis* resistance: Foggy Eden field trial (FE-02), two raised bed trials (RB-00, RB-02), and two root dip trials (RD-00, RD-02)

	RB-00	RB-02	RD-00	RD-02
FE-02	0.81 (15; <0.001)	0.89 (9; 0.001)	0.91 (15; 0.001)	0.93 (9; <0.001)
RB-00		0.60 (8; 0.118)	0.82 (15; <0.001)	0.68 (8; 0.066)
RB-02			0.93 (8; <0.001)	0.87 (9; 0.002)
RD-00				0.79 (8; 0.019)

durable or that the environmental conditions present now are less conducive to further infection and impact by *P. lateralis*. None of the families, including those with 100 percent mortality in some of the earlier seedling screening trials, have reached 100 percent mortality at FE-02 suggesting that micro-site or other factors may at least temporarily reduce the impacts by *P. lateralis* in this area. This site will continue to be monitored for changes in status of the remaining trees, and especially the more resistant families.

In many resistance programs, short-term testing of seedlings is a common procedure for evaluating resistance of parent trees or their progenies. However, verification of seedling test results in field trials is essential to confirm the relationship with seedling tests and to examine durability of resistance. In this series of tests examining genetic variation in *P. lateralis* resistance, there is generally good correspondence between survivals in the four short-term tests with that in the FE-02 field trial through the 2010 assessment. Similar results have also been found in early assessments from several other field trials and these seedling trials (Sniezko et al. 2006). The somewhat higher than expected mortality of a few resistant families in the two raised bed trials warrants further examination. These families were selected from among the first tests of *P. lateralis* resistance, and more recent trials will be examined to further evaluate resistance in the different trial types. Future updates from FE-02 and the earlier reported trials (Sniezko et al. 2006) will also be of interest.

The seedlings planted at FE-02 are in the understory of an existing forest stand and are growing slowly. Although this may be somewhat typical for some stands with POC, and the survival results are very encouraging, data from additional field sites are needed to more fully examine the effectiveness of *P. lateralis* resistance under a wider range of growing conditions. Several other field trials were planted in Oregon in 2002 using a subset of these 16 families, and they show little or no mortality from *P. lateralis* at this point (Harrington et al. 2012), indicating that many sites may be free of *P. lateralis*, at least initially. Classification of sites for *P. lateralis* hazard (low, moderate, high, and extremely high) would be helpful in establishing any further locations or interpreting results from current field trials as well as in making recommendations to land managers on the use of resistant POC seed. Additional field trials have been established in areas where *P. lateralis* is known to be active, and results from these trials should greatly expand the scope of reference regarding effectiveness of *P. lateralis* resistance.

Resistant POC seed is now available from seed orchards for several breeding zones and is in use by several organizations. Resistant seed lots are generally bulk collections and would be expected to give some intermediate level of field survival in the presence of *P. lateralis* as opposed to the high survival shown by the top families in the FE-02 trial. Further testing of these bulk open-pollinated seed orchard lots at multiple sites is needed to define the level of survival to be expected for general restoration and reforestation. Breeding work in POC has begun and further increases in resistance are expected in future seed orchard populations.

A genetic resistance program offers a natural method of coping with major pathogen and insect problems in forest trees. The POC program is one of the few resistance programs for non-native pathogens or insects in forest trees to reach the level of producing seed for operational use (FAO 2008, Sniezko 2006). However, as discussed at this conference, there is more need and interest than ever in using this approach. Existing programs such as the one for POC can provide insights to help increase the efficiency of efforts in other species. Regional centers of expertise and facilities can also facilitate efficient development of resistance in multiple species. Sustained support is essential to help ensure success in resistance programs.

Acknowledgments

Eric Martz, Holly Looney, Leslie Elliott, Scott Kolpak, Don Goheen, and other USDA Forest Service personnel for help in planning, planting, or assessments of FE-02; OSU personnel for inoculation and assessments of the short-term tests; and Douglas Savin for assistance with generating graphs. Funding from the USDA Forest Service and USDI Bureau of Land Management and the help of Dorena Genetic Resource Center personnel are gratefully acknowledged. We thank Dave Shaw, Phil Cannon, Tom Blush, and Arnaldo Ferreira for their reviews of an earlier version of this paper.

Literature Cited

FAO. 2008. Selection and breeding for insect and disease resistance. http://www fao.org/forestry/26445. (30 December 2011).

Harrington, C.A.; Sniezko, R.; Gould, P. 2012. Growth and survival of Port-Orford-cedar families on three sites on the south Oregon coast. Western Journal of Applied Forestry, 27:156-158.

Oh, E.; Hansen, E.M.; Sniezko, R.A. 2006. Port-Orford-cedar resistant to *Phytophthora lateralis*. Forest Pathology. 36: 385–394.

Sniezko, R.A. 2006. Resistance breeding against nonnative pathogens in forest trees — current successes in North America. Canadian Journal of Plant Pathology. 28: S270–S279.

Sniezko, R.A.; Elliott, L.E.; Hansen, E.M.; Betlejewski, F.; Goheen, D.J.; Casavan, K.; Kolpak, S.E.; Frank, C.L.; Angwin, P.A.; Hamlin, J. 2009. Operational program to develop resistance to *P. lateralis* in

Port-Orford-cedar (*Chamaecyparis lawsoniana*): the first ten years. In: Goheen, E.M.; Frankel, S.J., tech. coords. *Phytophthoras* in forests and natural ecosystems: Proceedings of the fourth meeting of the International Union of Forest Research Organizations (IUFRO) Working Party S07.02.09. Gen. Tech. Rep. PSW-G-TR-221. Albany, CA: U.S. Department of Agriculture, Forest Service, Pacific Southwest Research Station: 158–160.

Sniezko, R.A.; Kolpak, S.E.; Hansen, E.M.; Goheen, D.J.; Elliott, L.J.; Angwin, P.A. 2006. Field survival of *Phytophthora lateralis* resistant and susceptible Port-Orford-cedar families. In: Brasier, C.; Jung, T.; Osswald, W., eds. Progress in research on *Phytophthora* diseases of forest trees: Proceedings of the third international IUFRO working party S07.02.09. Farnham, UK: Forest Research: 104–108.

U.S. Department of Agriculture, Forest Service; U.S. Department of Interior, Bureau of Land Management [USDA FS and USDI BLM]. 2004. Management of Port-Orford-cedar in southwest Oregon: final supplemental environmental impact statement. BLM/OR/WA/PL-04/005-1792, Portland, OR, USA. http://www.fs.usda.gov/detail/rogue-siskiyou/landmanagement/resourcemanagement/?cid=stelprdb5316256. (31 December 2011).

Winton, L.M.; Hansen, E.M. 2001. Molecular diagnosis of *Phytophthora lateralis* in trees, water, and foliage baits using multiplex polymerase chain reaction. Forest Pathology. 31: 275–283.

White Pine Blister Rust Resistance of 12 Western White Pine Families at Three Field Sites in the Pacific Northwest

Richard A. Sniezko,[1] Robert Danchok,[1] Jim Hamlin,[2] Angelia Kegley,[1] Sally Long,[1] and James Mayo[1]

Abstract

Western white pine (*Pinus monticola* Douglas ex D. Don) is highly susceptible to the non-native, invasive pathogen *Cronartium ribicola*, the causative agent of white pine blister rust. The susceptibility of western white pine to blister rust has limited its use in restoration and reforestation throughout much of western North America. Fortunately, some genetic resistance to blister rust exists in western white pine, and several operational programs to select for resistance and develop orchards to produce resistant seed exist. These programs, such as that of the U.S. Department of Agriculture, Forest Service (USDA FS) Pacific Northwest Region, utilize short-term artificial inoculation trials of seedlings to evaluate resistance. However, until recently, there have been very few multi-site field trials to examine resistance closely. In this paper, we report on 12 western white pine families common to three field trials in western Oregon and northern California. The sites have been assessed for white pine blister rust infection and mortality at multiple ages since they were planted from 1996 to 2003. The 12 families had been selected based on results in previous artificial inoculation trials of seedlings of more than 4,000 parent trees at Dorena Genetic Resource Center (DGRC). Most of the families were from wind-pollinated seedlots from forest stands and represent some of the top ranked families from a first round of selection. Timing and frequency of field trial assessments varied to coincide with the appearance and development of rust infection at the three sites. By 2010, all three sites had moderate to high levels of blister rust infection, and moderate levels of mortality were present at some sites. The susceptible control family had 92 to 100 percent of trees with stem symptoms at the three sites, while only 29 to 43 percent of the trees in the top resistant family showed stem symptoms in those trials. The high level of stem symptoms in the two families with the Cr2 gene, which conditions a hypersensitive-like reaction (HR) in the needles, suggests that it is likely that a virulent *vcr2* strain of rust is present at all three sites. A wide range in family variation is present at all three sites for the proportion of trees with stem symptoms. Mortality lags behind stem infection, and more time is needed to assess the full impact of current stem infections. Infected trees in families with putative partial resistance traits such as bark reaction noted in previous screening trials will continue to be followed to examine their subsequent survival under field conditions. In general, moderate to high correlations were found between current levels of resistance at the three sites and seedling screening results from DGRC, providing some of the first field validation of results of short-term testing. These current results and future assessments will provide valuable information on the level of rust resistance and survival that land managers can expect over a range of sites. Long-term monitoring of these sites will be essential to evaluate durability of the various resistance types. Ongoing breeding efforts are aimed at increasing the levels of resistance to provide greater opportunities for successful reforestation and restoration use.

Key words: *Pinus monticola*, *Cronartium ribicola*, rust resistance, field trials, operational program

Introduction

Western white pine, *Pinus monticola* Dougl. ex D. Don, a wide ranging forest tree species in western North America, is highly susceptible to the non-native, invasive pathogen *Cronartium ribicola*, the fungus causing white pine blister rust (Geils et al. 2010). Fortunately, some natural genetic resistance

---

[1] USDA Forest Service, Dorena Genetic Resource Center, Cottage Grove, Oregon, USA.
[2] USDA Forest Service, Umpqua National Forest, Roseburg, Oregon, USA.
Corresponding author: rsniezko@fs.fed.us.

exists in white pine populations (Bingham 1983, Kegley and Sniezko 2004, King et al. 2010, Kinloch et al. 1999, Sniezko 2006). The development of populations of white pine with genetic resistance to white pine blister rust offers an invaluable management tool to restore this species and its utilization in managed forests. In the Pacific Northwest (Oregon and Washington), the U.S. Department of Agriculture, Forest Service (USDA FS) has a regional program at Dorena Genetic Resource Center (DGRC) in Oregon to develop genetically resistant populations of western white pine to blister rust. Resistance is identified through artificial inoculation of 2-year-old seedlings and subsequent assessments, using seed collected from parent trees selected in the forest or from control crosses among selected parents. Thousands of parent trees have been evaluated since the 1960s and several types of complete and partial resistance have been documented in these seedling tests (Kegley and Sniezko 2004; Kinloch et al. 1999, 2003; Sniezko and Kegley 2003a, 2003b; Sniezko 2006).

Western white pine is a long-lived conifer, and in many environments it will be exposed to *C. ribicola* for decades or even hundreds of years. Field testing is essential to validate the results of short-term rust resistance screening by artificial inoculation on very young seedlings and to monitor the durability of blister rust resistance. There are few summaries of field trials that examine white pine blister rust resistance in individual families of western white pine in the Pacific Northwest, and generally these reports encompass only one field site or have a more limited range of resistance types available (Hunt 2002, Kinloch et al. 2008, King et al. 2010, Kolpak et al. 2008; Sniezko et al. 2000, 2004a, 2004b). Until relatively recently, there were few multi-site field trials that closely monitored the field performance of families with the different types of putative resistance observed in artificial inoculation trials of seedlings. However, a series of field trials have been established in the Pacific Northwest since 1996 to examine the effectiveness and durability of resistance under field conditions. In this paper, we examine the incidence of blister rust stem symptoms and mortality in a common set of 12 western white pine families established in three field trials between 1996 and 2003 in western Oregon and northern California. These trials include families from diverse geographic and resistance backgrounds. We also examine the correlation of field performance to seedling test results following artificial inoculation at DGRC.

Materials and Methods

Seed from western white pine parents with varying types and levels of resistance observed in previous seedling artificial inoculation trials at DGRC were used to establish a series of field trials since 1996. We examine the subset of 12 families that are common to three trials in northern California and western Oregon. The seedlots include 11 half-sib families from wind pollination of parent trees in natural stands from a wide range of geographic areas in Oregon and Washington (10 families), or in an orchard at DGRC (one family); the remaining family is a full-sib from a control cross between two parent trees in an orchard at DGRC (table 1). The families were chosen to represent varying levels and types of complete and partial resistance identified in seedling screening, and include a susceptible control (family 4) that showed little or no resistance in previous testing at DGRC. In addition, two of the 12 families (families 11 and 12) have R gene resistance conveyed from the *Cr2* gene, which imparts complete resistance (from a hypersensitive-type reaction in the needles, HR) in the absence of a strain of rust with corresponding virulence gene, *vcr2* (Kinloch et al. 1999, 2003, 2004). The inheritance of HR resistance is due to a single dominant gene and, based on results from a previous artificial inoculation trial at DGRC, these families would be expected to have 75 percent or more of their progeny canker free in the absence of a virulent strain of rust (Sniezko et al. 2004b). The remaining nine families had previously displayed varying types and levels of partial resistance in seedling tests at DGRC (see Kegley and Sniezko 2004, Sniezko et al. 2004a; Sniezko and Kegley 2003a, 2003b). Seedlings with partial resistance often develop stem symptoms, but not to the degree of the most susceptible seedlings. In the seedling trials at DGRC most wind-pollinated families with partial resistance show high levels of stem symptoms (70 to 100 percent of seedlings), but in contrast to the high-susceptible families, partial-resistance families often have fewer stem symptoms per seedling, more of the stem symptoms appear at a later assessment (latent), more stem symptoms manifest as bark reactions (complete or partial bark reactions) rather than normal cankers, and there is longer survival of seedlings with stem symptoms. More information is needed on the underlying basis of partial resistance(s) and its inheritance. Family 6 displays many of the partial resistant traits, but in the seedling testing it also has a relatively high level of seedlings with no stem symptoms (Sniezko et al. 2004a; Sniezko and Kegley 2003a, 2003b).

Table 1—Family identities, origin, and resistance type for 12 western white pine families: 11 wind-pollinated and one control crossed

Family code	Family	Parent origin	Resistance[a]
1	11053-552 x w	OR	pr
2	03023-509 x w	WA	pr
3	03024-510 x w	WA	pr
4	03024-532 x w	WA	susceptible control
5	03024-793 x w	WA	pr
6	05081-003 x w	WA	high canker free, non-HR
7	06023-521 x w	OR	pr
8	18034-140 x w	OR	pr
9	18035-150 x w	OR	pr
10	21105-052 x w	WA	high bark reaction
11	(15045-816 x 15045-841) x w_{so}	OR	HR
12	15045-823 x 15045-840	OR	HR

w= wind pollinated (in forest stand); w_{so} =wind pollinated in orchard; OR=Oregon, WA=Washington; HR= hypersensitive-like reaction in needles; pr= low levels of partial resistance (Sniezko et al. 2004a).
[a] Based on previous screening trials at Dorena Genetic Resource Center.

Periodic visits to each field site were made, but formal assessments began only after blister rust infection was noted in each trial (figs. 1 and 2). Trees were assessed in multiple years for growth as well as number of stem symptoms (on main bole or branches), types of stem symptoms (incipient infections that appear as small orange circles at the base of some infected needles, normal cankers, bark reactions, partial bark reactions), severity of infection, and mortality. For this paper, we report on family variation, 8 to 11 years after planting (depending on site), only on the proportion of trees (1) with stem symptoms from blister rust and (2) surviving. Analyses of the other traits such as number of stem symptoms are pending. We report on cumulative proportion of stem symptoms, since some stem symptoms present in 1 year may not be seen in some future years (e.g., the tree may outgrow small bark reactions or branches with stem symptoms may self prune).

Happy Camp (HC)

The site is located on the Happy Camp Ranger District on the Klamath National Forest in northern California (N41° 53' 08.51'; W123° 24 09.82', 777 m elevation). This location is the main field test site for sugar pine (*Pinus lambertiana* Dougl.) for the USDA FS, Pacific Southwest Region's blister rust resistance program, but western white pine has also previously been tested on the site (Kinloch et al. 2008). Seedlings from the spring 1995 sowing of 12 sugar pine and 13 western white pine families were planted in April 1996 in a randomized complete block (RCB) design with 12 blocks and up to four trees per family per block in row plots. Trees were planted at 0.60 x 0.75 m spacing. *Ribes sanguineum*, an alternate host to *C. ribicola*, was inter-planted among the pines to augment existing sources of rust spores and to help ensure uniform exposure to rust infection. Assessments of blister rust stem symptoms, mortality, and growth were done annually from 1999 to 2003, and also in 2005 and 2007. Additional background and earlier results are presented elsewhere (Sniezko et al. 2000, 2004a).

Kerbluey (K)

The site is located on the Cottage Grove Ranger District (CGRD). Umpqua National Forest. in southern Oregon (N 43°39.765', W 122° 39.711', 974 m elevation). Western white pine occurs naturally as well as in reforestation areas. *Ribes* species are present in the area. and white pine blister rust had previously been documented in the area. The parents for the two families with HR resistance were selected during the 1950s on CGRD. Seedlings sown in 1995 for the same 25 families used for HC were planted in June 1997 (blocks 1 to 4) and October 1997 (blocks 5 to 8) in a RCB design: a few trees that died in blocks 1 to 4 were replaced in October 1997. In most cases. there were four trees in each family row plot per block (varied from two to five). Eleven families are included in all eight blocks. and one of the 12 families is included only in four blocks. Trees are planted at 3 x 3 m spacing. Assessments of blister rust infection and mortality were done in 1999. 2001 to 2005. and 2008.

Figure 1—Western white pine trial at Coast Plum site in 2010/2011: (a) overview, (b) incipient stem symptom with the 'point-of-entry' needle still alive in the center, (c) expanding canker, (d) older canker with aecia and girdling stem, (e) partial bark reaction, (f) partial bark reaction. (Photo credits: Richard Sniezko (a to e), Robert Danchok (f))

Coast Plum (CP)

The site is located on Plum Creek Corporation land in the Coast Range of Oregon (N 44° 49.966'. W 123° 44.790'. 533 m elevation). One-year-old seedlings of 28 western white pine families. sown in early March 2002. grown in containers at Plum Creek Corporation's nursery in Cottage Grove. Oregon were planted in early February 2003 in a RCB design with nine blocks. Nine of the 12 families are included in all nine blocks, one family is included in seven blocks, and two families are included in six blocks. Seedlings were planted in family row plots with generally five trees per family plot (varied from three to six trees per family row plot). Trees were planted at 1.8 x 3 m spacing. Blister rust incidence was very low until the first assessment in 2010 (figs. 1 and 2); the trial was also assessed in 2011. There is little or no other known western white pine in the general vicinity, but abundant *R. sanguineum*, an alternate host to *C. ribicola*, was noted in the surrounding areas.

DGRC Seedling Artificial Inoculation Trial (DGRC1995)

All 12 families had previously been evaluated for rust screening in various seedling trials at DGRC, and 10 of the families are included in a common test sown in 1995 (inoculated in 1996). Two-year-old seedlings are used in the artificial inoculation trials, and these seedlings often have primary needles as well as secondary needles. Kegley and Sniezko (2004) provide detailed information on seedling screening trials at DGRC. We use the results from the 1995 test to examine the relationship between short-term seedling screening and field results at the three sites (Sniezko et al. 2004a). The two families with HR resistance are not included in the 1995 seedling test. The three variables used in this paper from the screening trial results include needle lesion mean (NLC), proportion of trees with stem symptoms (SSp), and proportion of trees dead from rust (RMORT) 5 years after inoculation. NLC is based upon number of needle lesions or "spots" on all secondary needles, and ranges from 0 to 4 for individual seedlings. Generally, the scale is setup, after examining a subset of seedlings, to have approximately 25 percent of the seedlings in each needle lesion class; seedlings with no needle lesions are usually rare and are assigned to class 0. The NLC and a preliminary estimate of SSp were used in an earlier summary of early mortality at the Happy Camp site (Sniezko et al. 2004a).

Statistical analysis procedures were conducted using SAS (SAS Institute Inc., V 9.2, 2008) where the trials were analyzed as a RCB. Family differences in survival (and proportion of trees with stem symptoms) were analyzed using family-plot means in Proc Glimmix (binomial distribution); plot means were adjusted by 0.01 for those values of 1.0 (adjusted to 0.99) and 0.0 (adjusted to 0.01) in order to avoid the non-convergence issue in Proc Glimmix when numerous values of 1 or 0 are encountered in the dataset. Site, family, and site x family interaction were considered as fixed effects in the model. Proc Corr (product moment correlation) was used to examine family mean correlations among the respective field trials as well as between these three field trials and the 1995 seedling screening trial at DGRC.

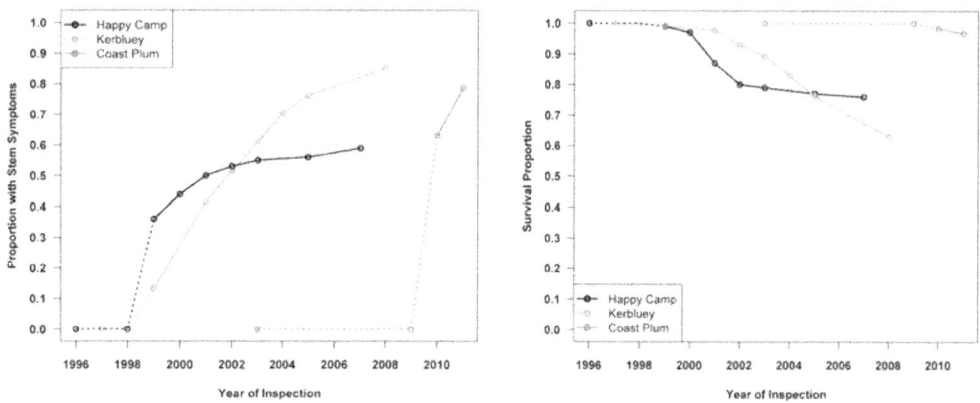

Figure 2—Time trend for proportion of white pines with (a) stem symptoms and (b) surviving, at three sites: Happy Camp (planted 1996), Kerbluey (planted 1997), and Coast Plum (planted 2003).

Results

A moderate (0.60 at HC) to high proportion (0.78 at CP and 0.84 at K) of trees displayed stem symptoms (SSp) by the latest assessment (fig. 2; table 2) at the three sites. The temporal dynamics of blister rust infection varied among the three sites. For the 1996 HC trial, over 35 percent of trees had stem symptoms by 1999, but there has been only a gradual increase in infection through 2007; for the 1997 K planting, over 35 percent of trees had stem symptoms by 2001 and there has been a continued steady increase in infection through the last assessment (2008); for the 2003 CP planting, over 60 percent of trees had infection by the first assessment in 2010 and a further jump in infection was recorded in 2011 (fig. 2). The severity codes associated with the first assessments at each site indicated that only 7 (of 311) trees at K, and 14 (of 556) trees at HC had larger and presumably older active cankers at their first assessments, while 105 trees (of 465) at CP had relatively large active cankers at that site's first assessment (fig. 1). Most of the symptoms noted at CP in 2010 were on the 2007 and 2008 portions of the main stem or branches. At their first assessment, 2, 6, and 8 trees were dead from blister rust at K, HC, and CP, respectively. The number of stem symptoms per living tree varied by site and year from a maximum of 0.60 at HC to 7.18 at K, and 9.53 at CP (table 3).

Table 2—Overall site means (and range in variation among the 12 families) for proportion of trees with blister rust stem symptoms and survival at three field sites

Site	Stem symptom	Survival
Coast Plum (CP)	.78 (.37 to 1.0)	.95 (.90 to 1.0)
Kerbluey (K)	.84 (.43 to 1.0)	.64 (.19 to .94)
Happy Camp (HC)	.60 (.29 to. 92)	.75 (.43 to 1.0)

Highly significant differences (p < .0001) existed among sites and families in the inter-site analysis for SSp. In addition, there was a significant site x family interaction (p = .0001). This interaction appears to be influenced by the relatively low proportion of trees in families 11 and 12 with stem symptoms at HC relative to that at CP and K (fig. 3). When these two families with HR resistance are excluded from the inter-site analysis, the site x family interaction is not significant for SSp (p = .056). A wide range of family variation in SSp was evident at all three sites (table 2, fig. 3).

Table 3—Number of stem symptoms (SS) per living tree at several assessments for three western white pine blister rust resistance trials

Site	Year	Number of living trees	Mean number of stem symptoms (SS) per living tree	Range in SS per tree
Happy Camp	1999	551	0.60	0 to 9
Happy Camp	2003	438	0.15*	0 to 4
Kerbluey	2001	305	1.08	0 to 11
Kerbluey	2005	244	2.39	0 to 20
Kerbluey	2008	192	7.18	0 to 48
Coast Plum	2010	457	4.95	0 to 91
Coast Plum	2011	449	9.53	0 to 80

Happy Camp planted in 1996; Kerbluey in 1997; Coast Plum in 2002.
*Decrease in SS at HC reflects mortality of many of the trees with early stem symptoms.

SSp for the susceptible control (family 4) was very high (0.92 to 1.0) at all sites (fig. 3; table 2). At HC, the difference in SSp between the susceptible family and the other 11 families was particularly notable (fig. 3). At K, four families showed 100 percent stem symptoms, including the susceptible control (family 4), the two families with HR resistance (families 11 and 12), and family 2. Family 2 was the only one to have 100 percent stem symptoms at CP, which was slightly higher than the 98 percent for the susceptible control (fig. 3). Family 6 had the lowest proportion of trees with stem symptoms (0.29 to 0.43) at all three sites (fig. 3). At K, the two families (11 and 12) with HR resistance showed delayed, but then rapid, steady increase in infection over time (fig. 4).

Despite the moderate to high level of stem infection, the proportion of trees surviving (SURV) was moderate (0.64 at K, 0.75 at HC) to high (0.95 at CP) at the three sites (table 2, fig. 3), with family survival varying from 0.19 to 1.0 (table 2, fig. 3). Through the latest assessments, mortality has just begun at CP, it has nearly plateaued at HC, and it appears to be steadily increasing at K (fig. 2). There were significant differences among both sites and families (p < .0001), but the site x family interaction for SURV was not significant (p=.50). The susceptible control (family 4) has the lowest survival at all sites (fig. 3). Family 6 had the highest survival at CP and K, and second highest at survival HC (fig. 3).

Survival of the 12 families was significantly correlated among the three sites (0.64 to 0.81), but for SSp, only the family mean correlation between CP and K (0.92) was significant (table 4). SSp at HC

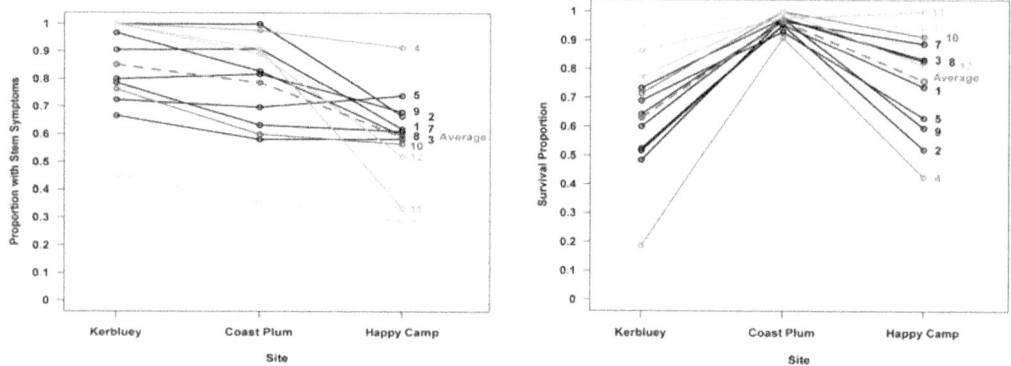

Figure 3—Family means at last assessment over three sites for 12 families for (a) proportion of trees with stem symptoms and (b) proportion of trees surviving.

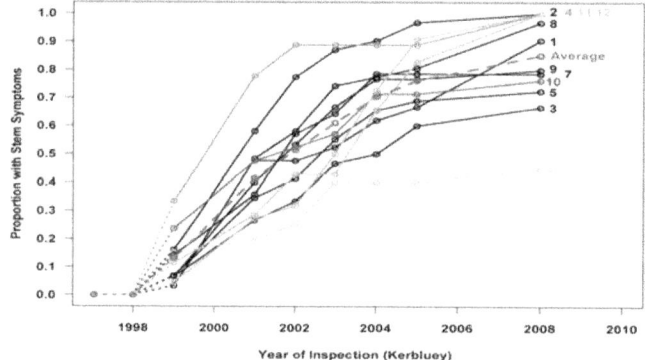

Figure 4—Time trend for 12 western white pine families for 1997 Kerbluey planting for proportion of trees with stem symptoms from blister rust infection (first assessment in 1999).

was significantly correlated with survival at all three sites (-0.78 to -0.88); there was a moderate family mean correlation of SSp at CP with survival at both K (- 0.59, p = .04) and HC (-0.56, p = .06); there was a moderate, but non-significant correlation of SSp and survival at K (-0.51, p = .09) (table 3, fig. 4)). At K, the majority of the stem symptoms on families 11 and 12, the two families with HR resistance, appear much later than other families, but reached 100 percent by 2008 (fig. 4). When families 11 and 12 are excluded (n=10), many of the family mean correlations for SURV and SSp were higher and additional ones were significant (14 of the 15 correlations ranged from 0.59 to 0.92, with only SSp at K with Surv at CP being somewhat lower (-0.40)).

For the 10 families included in the DGRC artificial inoculation trial, there were significant moderate- to high-family mean correlations (0.60 to 0.87) of SSp and RMORT at DGRC with both SSp and SURV at each of the three field trials (table 5, fig. 5). The correlations of seedling results at DGRC (SSp and RMORT) were slightly higher for SSp (0.82 to 0.87) at the field sites than for SURV (-0.60 to -0.78) (table 4). The correlations of seedling needle lesion class (NLC_DGRC) with SSp and SURV in the field were only low to moderate, and were non-significant (table 5).

Table 4— Family mean correlations (p-values) between three field trials for proportion of trees with white pine blister rust stem symptoms (SSp) and survival (Surv)

	Surv_CP	SSp_K	Surv_K	SSp_HC	Surv_HC
SSp_CP	-0.42 (0.178)	0.92 (0.0001)	-0.59 (0.044)	0.45 (0.138)	-0.56 (0.059)
Surv_CP		-0.19 (0.546)	0.64 (0.025)	-0.78 (0.0028)	0.76 (0.004)
SSp_K			-0.51 (0.088)	0.34 (0.271)	-0.31 (0.329)
Surv_K				-0.88 (0.0001)	0.81 (0.0015)
SSp_HC					-0.85 (0.0005)

Based on 12 families.

HC, K, and CP field trials assessed through 2007, 2008, and 2011, respectively.

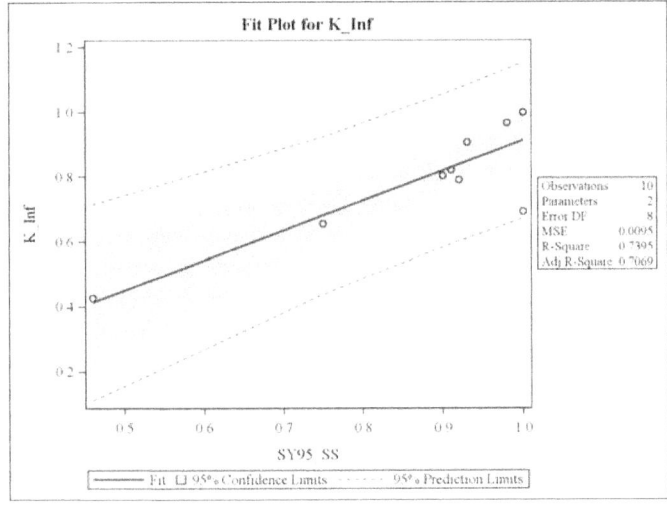

Figure 5—Relationship between proportion of seedlings with stem symptoms in artificial inoculation trial at DGRC (SY95_SS) and proportion of trees with stem symptoms at Kerbluey field trial (K_Inf) for 10 western white pine families (excludes two families with HR resistance).

Table 5—Family mean correlations (p-values) between results from the 1995 artificial inoculation test of seedlings at DGRC and proportion of trees with white pine blister rust stem symptoms (SSp) and survival (Surv) at three field trials

	SSp_CP	Surv_CP	SSp_K	Surv_K	SSp_HC	Surv_HC
NLC_DGRC	0.34 (.338)	-0.33 (.346)	0.46 (.185)	-0.59 (.074)	0.48 (.157)	-0.35 (.318)
SSp_DGRC	0.82 (.004)	-0.61 (.059)	0.86 (.001)	-0.72 (.019)	0.84 (.002)	-0.60 (.067)
MORT_DGRC	0.87 (.001)	-0.72 (.018)	0.83 (.003)	-0.78 (.008)	0.84 (.002)	-0.68 (.029)

10 families included (excludes the two families with HR resistance, refer to text for details).

NLC = needle lesion rating after artificial inoculation (see text for details). MORT=mortality proportion 5 years after inoculation.

Discussion

As evidenced by the high proportion of stem symptoms on the susceptible control (family 4), all three sites have had moderate to heavy exposure to blister rust infection. The incidence of rust at the Coast Plum 2003 planting was low until the first assessment in 2010. From the early data, CP would have appeared to be a low rust hazard, but the abundance of *Ribes* spp., the alternate host of blister rust, and favorable climate eventually led to a large jump in stem symptoms by 2010 and again in 2011. The rust hazard of this site likely increased since 2003 as tree harvest operations in the surrounding areas removed the forest canopy, permitting more abundant natural regeneration of *Ribes*, the alternate host. The levels of infection and family variation in proportion of trees with stem symptoms in these trials appears to be somewhat comparable to results from other field trials with mostly different families (at Happy Camp and in Idaho) discussed by Kinloch et al. (2008), in British Columbia (Hunt 2002), and somewhat lower than the 0.93 (six years after planting) for another trial on CGRD (Kolpak et al. 2008). It will be important to monitor these sites over time since western white pine is a long-lived tree species and exposure to blister rust infection will continue to occur at periodic intervals.

There are large differences in blister rust resistance among the 12 families tested. In the absence of the *vcr2* strain of rust, families 11 and 12, with HR resistance, were expected to show little or no incidence of stem symptoms. The moderate to high incidence of stem symptoms on families 11 and 12 confirms the presence of the *vcr2* strain of rust at all three sites. Several other trials on CGRD also show a very high incidence of stem symptoms on families with HR resistance (Kolpak et al. 2008, Sniezko et al. 2004b). Previous monitoring has indicated that a low to high frequency of this strain of rust is present in much of western Oregon, as well as at HC (Kinloch et al. 2004). At two of the three sites, K and CP, the proportion of trees with stem symptoms for these two families is now very similar to that of the susceptible control. At the third site, HC, the level of stem symptoms in these two families has increased since the last report (Sniezko et al. 2004a). At this stage, the survival of the two families with HR resistance is relatively high, but this may be at least partially a function of the more recent infection at CP and the relatively recent increase in incidence of *vcr2* at K. Future monitoring of these families at these sites will indicate whether they have any resistance beyond HR. The airborne spread of rust spores and the current geographic distribution of *vcr2* will limit the utility of HR resistance in many areas of western Oregon. At some sites where *vcr2* is not yet present, HR resistance may offer utility in delaying stem infections until trees are larger which may benefit overall survival. Combining HR resistance with partial resistances would offer an attractive option and has been implemented in the design of current seed orchards.

The other nine families are thought to have varying levels of partial resistance. Two of these, families 6 (05081-003 x w) and 10 (21105-052 x w), have been tested many times and have repeatedly shown moderate to high resistance in artificial inoculation trials of seedlings at DGRC (Kegley and Sniezko 2004; Sniezko and Kegley 2003a, 2003b). In the DGRC trials, these two families have been among the most outstanding for partial resistances. These two wind-pollinated families are probably in the top 1 percent for partial resistance of the thousands of forest selections evaluated in seedling testing. In these three field trials, these two families are also among the top for rust resistance. In seedling testing at DGRC, these two families show a higher incidence of seedlings free of stem symptoms and seedlings with bark reactions than do many other families (Kegley and Sniezko 2004; Sniezko and Kegley 2003a, 2003b). They also show comparable or higher levels of resistance in rust screening at DGRC to the full-sib checklots from the Interior West rust resistance program based in Idaho (see Table 5 in Kegley and Sniezko 2004) and higher resistance in the field at the CP site than the full-sib seedlots from the British Columbia program (Sniezko et al. 2010). Progeny of these parents have been grafted into orchards, and clone banks, pollinations made with them, and other clones will help increase resistance and help us understand more about inheritance of some of the mechanisms involved.

The significant correlations among some resistance traits at DGRC and those in the field are encouraging, and validate short-term testing. Only a low, non-significant correlation of the needle spot class trait (at DGRC) with the proportion of trees infected or dead was found in this study; a somewhat similar result has been found elsewhere (Hunt 2002). However, in another study, needle spot class correlated with number of stem symptoms in the field (Kolpak et al. 2008). Data analyses for the relationship between needle lesion mean (at DGRC) and number of stem symptoms at these three field sites has not yet been done. A significant amount of additional data to examine this relationship will also be available in the near future as assessments on many other field trials are completed and analyzed.

Continued observations from these field trials will help confirm the type of resistances and their effectiveness on larger trees under repeated exposure to *C. ribicola* infection. Of particular interest will be what level of bark reaction in these families is manifested in the field and whether it contributes significantly to survival. Some further discussion of possible resistances and their inheritance in western white pine is reported for an older trial at HC (Kinloch et al. 2008) and from the early results from another trial on CGRD (Kolpak et al. 2008). However, more research is needed into the underlying mechanisms and the inheritance of partial resistance.

Mortality from blister rust usually lags at least several years behind stem infection, so future assessments will be needed to provide a more definitive indication of the full impact of blister rust infection. Most infections at CP were observed for the first time in 2010 or 2011, 7 and 8 years after planting, and it is expected to be several years before these larger, older trees show much mortality. Coast Plum showed a relatively large jump in stem symptoms from 2010 to 2011, probably due to some latent infections not being visible during the February 2010 assessment on trees with partial resistance as well as new infections from what now appears to be a fairly high-hazard site for rust. The incidence of stem symptoms and mortality at HC has been relatively static between 2002 and 2007, and many of the previous infections appear to be inactive. At CP and K, the incidence of stem symptoms has been increasing and a commensurate increase in mortality may occur depending on the effectiveness of the partial resistances.

Somewhat surprisingly, blister rust mortality is only low to moderate at HC and K. The susceptible control shows the highest mortality of the 12 families, but only at one of the three sites is its mortality greater than 60 percent. The effectiveness of partial resistance may depend on several factors, including the size and age of the seedlings when infection occurs and the rust hazard of the site. In the three trials reported here, there is a moderate to high level proportion of trees with stem symptoms and a low to moderate number of stem symptoms per tree, but most of the symptoms occur several years or more after planting. On an extreme high-hazard site, there may be high incidence of infection events and a much higher number of stem infections per tree. Experience with 2-year-old seedlings in artificial inoculation trials at DGRC shows much higher mortality in most families, usually within 2 to 4 years of appearance of stem symptoms. Small seedlings in the field that are repeatedly infected or trees with dozens to hundreds of stem symptoms may not survive. Rating sites for rust hazard is still problematic in many cases, and more information is needed to provide land managers rust hazard ratings for lands being considered for planting western white pine.

These trials are the first tests in the Pacific Northwest to closely follow field performance of specific families at multiple sites. Results from short-term screening using artificial inoculation of 2-year-old seedlings correlates well with field performance at these three sites. However, the field sites need to be monitored over the long term to evaluate the impacts of continued new exposures to infection by *C. ribicola*, as well as the subsequent impact from existing stem symptoms. Additional field trials have been established in Oregon and Washington, including some with control crossed progenies as well as seedlots from the Interior West and British Columbia blister rust resistance programs. This set of trials will provide baseline information on the utility of current levels of blister rust resistance under a wide range of site conditions and the adaptability of the species under changing climatic conditions. The data from these trials will provide key information to allow land managers to utilize resistant western white pine. Long-term monitoring of these sites will be essential to evaluate durability of the various resistance types.

Most of the families represented here are wind-pollinated progenies from original field selections. The top parents or some of their progeny surviving rust testing at DGRC have been grafted into orchards managed by several groups, including the USDA FS; U.S. Department of the Interior, Bureau of Land Management; Washington Department of Natural Resources; Quinault Indian Nation; and British Columbia Ministry of Forests. Many of these orchards for the breeding zones in the Pacific Northwest have reached reproductive age and bulked seedlots to use in reforestation and restoration have been collected and are in use for some of them. Some of these orchard seedlots are now in testing at DGRC and in field trials. The level of resistance expected from the first cycle of orchards developed will depend on several factors, but will be less than that of the top families in these trials. Control crossing between orchard selections is ongoing. It is anticipated that the breeding and subsequent selections from artificial inoculation trials will supply higher levels of resistance from advanced-generation orchards. These anticipated levels and combinations of resistances in future orchards should provide land managers with higher levels of success in restoration and reforestation plantings.

Acknowledgments

The authors thank the USDA Forest Service for funding and personnel for the many phases of this work. We thank Jim Smith and Plum Creek Corporation for establishment of Coast Plum site, and Jerry Hill for his work on all these trials; and Douglas Savin for providing some of the graphs. We also acknowledge the help of Deems Burton and Dean Davis with many aspects of the Happy Camp trial. We thank Holly Kearns, Amy Kroll, Michael Murray, and Tom DeSpain for their reviews of an earlier version of this paper.

Literature Cited

Bingham, R.T. 1983. Blister rust resistant western white pine for the Inland Empire: the story of the first 25 years of the research and development program. Gen. Tech. Rep. INT-146. Ogden, UT: U.S. Department of Agriculture, Forest Service, Intermountain Forest and Range Experiment Station. 45 p.

Geils, B.W.; Hummer, K.E.; Hunt, R.S. 2010. White pines, *Ribes*, and blister rust; a review and synthesis. Forest Pathology. 40: 147–185.

Hunt, R.S. 2002. Relationship between early family-selection traits and natural blister rust cankering in western white pine families. Canadian Journal of Plant Pathology. 24: 200–204.

Kegley, A.; Sniezko, R.A. 2004. Variation in blister rust resistance among 226 *Pinus monticola* and 217 *P. lambertiana* seedling families in the Pacific Northwest. In: Sniezko, R.A.; Samman, S.; Schlarbaum, S.E.; Kriebel, H.B., eds. Breeding and genetic resources of five-needle pines: growth, adaptability, and pest resistance; IUFRO Working Party 2.02.15. Proceedings RMRS-P-32. Fort Collins, CO: U.S. Department of Agriculture, Forest Service, Rocky Mountain Research Station: 209–226. http://www fs.fed.us/rm/pubs/rmrs_p032/rmrs_p032_209_226.pdf. (14 January 2012).

King, J.N.; Noshad, D.A.; Smith, J. 2010. A review of genetic approaches to the management of blister rust in white pines. Forest Pathology. 40: 292–313.

Kinloch, B.B., Jr.; Davis, D.A.; Burton, D. 2008. Resistance and virulence interactions between two white pine species and blister rust in a 30-year field trial. Tree Genetics and Genomes. 4: 65–74.

Kinloch, B.B., Jr.; Sniezko, R.A.; Barnes, G.D.; Greathouse, T.E. 1999. A major gene for resistance to white pine blister rust in western white pine from the western Cascade Range. Phytopathology. 89(10): 861–867.

Kinloch, B.B., Jr.; Sniezko, R.A.; Dupper, G.E. 2003. Origin and distribution of Cr2, a gene for resistance to white pine blister rust in natural populations of western white pine. Phytopathology. 93(6): 691–694.

Kinloch, B.B., Jr.; Sniezko, R.A.; Dupper, G.E. 2004. Virulence gene distribution and dynamics of the white pine blister rust pathogen in western North America. Phytopathology. 94(7): 751–758.

Kolpak, S.E.; Sniezko, R.A.; Kegley, A.J. 2008. Rust infection and survival of 49 *Pinus monticola* families at a field site six years after planting. In: Blada, I.; King, J.; Sniezko, R., eds., 2008: Proceedings of the IUFRO Working Party 2.02.15 Breeding and genetic resources of five-needle pines conference. Annals of Forest Research. 51: 67–80. http://www.editurasilvica ro/afr/51/1/kolpak_1.pdf. (19 January 2012).

Sniezko, R.A. 2006. Resistance breeding against nonnative pathogens in forest trees — current successes in North America. Canadian Journal of Plant Pathology. 28: S270–S279.

Sniezko, R.A.; Bower, A.; Danielson, J. 2000. A comparison of early field results of white pine blister rust resistance of sugar pine and western white pine. HortTechnology. 10 (3): 519–522.

Sniezko, R.A.; Bower, A.; Kegley, A. 2004a. Variation in *Cronartium ribicola* field resistance among *Pinus monticola* and 12 *P. lambertiana* families: early results from Happy Camp. In: Sniezko, R.A.; Samman, S.; Schlarbaum, S.E.; Kriebel, H.B., eds. Breeding and genetic resources of five-needle pines: growth, adaptability, and pest resistance; IUFRO Working Party 2.02.15. Proceedings RMRS-P-32. Fort Collins, CO: U.S. Department of Agriculture, Forest Service, Rocky Mountain Research Station: 203–208. http://www.fs.fed.us/rm/pubs/rmrs_p032/rmrs_p032_203_208.pdf. (15 January 2012).

Sniezko, R.A.; Hill, J.; Danchok, R.; Kegley, A.; Long, S.; Mayo, J.; Smith, J. 2010. White pine blister rust resistance in a seven year old field trial of 28 western white pine (*Pinus monticola*) families in the Coast Range of Oregon. [Poster]. In: American phytopathology society meeting; 2010 August, Charlotte, NC.

Sniezko, R.A.; Kegley, A. 2003a. Blister rust resistance experiences in Oregon and Washington: evolving perspectives. In: Stone J.; Maffei, H., comps. Proceedings of the 50th Western International Forest Disease Work Conference. Bend, OR: U.S. Department of Agriculture, Forest Service, Central Oregon Service Center: 111–117. http://www.fs.usda.gov/Internet/FSE_DOCUMENTS/stelprdb5280665.pdf .(15 January 2012).

Sniezko, R.A.;Kegley, A.J. 2003b. Blister rust resistance of five-needle pines in Oregon and Washington. In: Xu, M.; Walla, J.; Zhao, W., eds. Proceedings of the second IUFRO rusts of forest trees working party conference. Forest Research. 16 (Suppl.): 101–112. http://www.fs.usda.gov/Internet/FSE_DOCUMENTS/stelprdb5280720.pdf. (15 January 2012).

Sniezko, R.A.; Kinloch, B.B., Jr.; Bower, A.D.; Danchok, R.S.; Linn, J.M.; Kegley, A.J. 2004b. Field resistance to *Cronartium ribicola* in full-sib families of *Pinus monticola* in Oregon. In: Sniezko, R.A.; Samman, S.; Schlarbaum, S.E.; Kriebel, H.B., eds. Breeding and genetic resources of five-needle pines: growth, adaptability, and pest resistance; IUFRO Working Party 2.02.15. Proceedings RMRS-P-32. Fort Collins, CO: U.S. Department of Agriculture, Forest Service, Rocky Mountain Research Station: 243–249. http://www.fs.fed.us/rm/pubs/rmrs_p032/rmrs_p032_243_249.pdf. (15 January 2012).

Are Needle Reactions in Resistance to *Cronartium ribicola* a Hypersensitivity Response?

Katarina Sweeney,[1] Jeffrey Stone,[1] Kathy Cook,[1] Richard A. Sniezko,[2] Angelia Kegley,[2] and Anna W. Schoettle[3]

White pine blister rust (WPBR) is caused by the fungal pathogen *Cronartium ribicola*. The pathogen is native to Eurasia and was introduced to North America early in the 20th century and is still spreading destructively throughout the range of native western white pines (Douglas ex D. Don) (McDonald and Hoff 2001). All of the North American five-needle (white) pines are susceptible to the pathogen and the disease is currently present in native populations of each species, except *Pinus longaeva* D.K. Bailey (Schwandt et al. 2010, Sniezko et al. 2011).

Naturally occurring, heritable resistance to blister rust has been detected in populations of North American five-needle pine species and has provided the basis for operational resistance breeding programs for *P. monticola* Douglas ex D. Don and *P. lambertiana* Douglas for several decades (Sniezko et al. 2011) and more recently restoration and proactive management programs for the other species (Keane and Schoettle 2011, Schoettle and Sniezko 2007). One type of resistance to *C. ribicola* has been attributed to major gene resistance (MGR) and has been described as a classical hypersensitivity response (HR) in infected needles and is conferred through a dominant allele at loci designated Cr1, Cr2, and Cr3 in *P. lambertiana*, *P. monticola*, and *P. strobiformis* Engelm., respectively (Kinloch and Dupper 2002; Kinloch and Littlefield 1977; Kinloch et al. 1970, 1999). Basidiospores germinate on the needle surface and hyphae penetrate into the needle via the stomata. In Cr1, Cr2, and Cr3 genotypes, it has been presumed that HR-mediated cell death near the point of *C. ribicola* entry confines fungal growth and prevents colonization of the mesophyll and ultimately the vascular cylinder (see fig. 1).

Localized cell death, or HR, is one of the major components of defense responses in plants against pathogen attack (Dangl and Jones 2001). It is generally characterized by rapid death of cells surrounding the infected tissues via vacuolar lysis, degrading of cellular machinery and complete cellular collapse. Generally, HR phenotypes are visible as yellow or brown necrotic lesions at the site of pathogen entry (Heath 2000, Morel and Dangl 1997). The HR constitutes coordinated plant responses to pathogen colonization, which involve oxidative burst with accumulation of reactive oxygen species (ROS), calcium ion fluxes, changes to the host cell wall, expression of **pathogenesis-related** (PR) proteins and localized host cell death (Innes 1998, Liu and Ekramoddoullah 2003, van Doorn 2011). These are key components of HR, which usually occur within hours of attack by pathogens (Lamb and Dixon 1997). This autolytic cell death is a means to eliminate infected cells, which will simultaneously restrict flow of nutrients to the invading pathogen hyphae and delimit fungal spread.

The HR is triggered by the interaction of disease resistance (R) genes of host plants and corresponding avirulence (AVR) genes in pathogens (Hammond-Kosack and Jones 1997, Staskawiecz et al. 2001). The AVR genes in the pathogen code for elicitor molecules that activate R genes in the host. Hence, host and pathogen recognize each other by their gene products and activate signal transduction cascades which orchestrate defense responses (Gilchrist 1998, Innes 1998). The complementary relationship between host and pathogen was first described as the gene-for-gene

[1] Dept. of Botany and Plant Pathology, Oregon State University, Corvallis, OR 97331.
[2] USDA Forest Service, Dorena Genetic Resource Center, Cottage Grove, OR 97424.
[3] USDA Forest Service, Rocky Mountain Research Center, Fort Collins, CO 80526.
Corresponding author: sweeneka@science.oregonstate.edu.

hypothesis by Flor (1942, 1955). This system is highly specific, as only pathogens with AVR genes are detected by the host and subsequently induce the HR response in host tissues. Accordingly, genotypes of *C. ribicola* virulent to Cr1 *P. lambertiana* and Cr2 *P. monticola* have been termed vcr1 and vcr2, respectively (Kinloch and Dupper 2002). Complementary virulence, avirulence, and resistance genes in *C. ribicola* and white pine host species appears to conform to the Flor gene-for-gene model (Kinloch and Dupper 2002).

In the *C. ribicola* pathosystem, the HR paradigm was described for the Cr1 phenotype in *P. lambertiana* and the Cr2 phenotype in *P. monticola*. Individuals resistant to *C. ribicola* were reported as having cell degeneration and necrosis leading to localized cell death at the site of fungal infection sufficient to stop pathogen growth. Kinloch and Littlefield (1977) noted that the onset of HR in resistant pines differs from that in classical HR; the onset of needle lesions in *P. lambertiana* is not observed until several weeks or even months after initial entry of *C. ribicola*. This observation suggests that the resistance mechanisms expressed by Cr1 or Cr2 may differ from the pattern of HR responses seen in most incompatible host reactions.

To further evaluate the apparent HR response in this pathosystem, we undertook structural analyses of early *C. ribicola* colonization in susceptible and resistant *P. monticola* and *P. lambertiana*. Resistant and susceptible *P. albicaulis* Engelm. and *P. flexilis* James phenotypes are also being compared to the reactions seen in susceptible and Cr1 and Cr2 seedlings. Secondary needles were harvested from 2-year-old seedlings grown and inoculated at the U.S. Department of Agriculture, Forest Service, Dorena Genetic Resource Center (DGRC) in Cottage Grove, Oregon. The histopathology of infection in resistant *P. monticola* and *P. lambertiana* suggests that the symptoms associated with HR phenotypes and their underlying physiology are fundamentally different from the typical HR described in other host-pathogen systems (fig. 2). We observed extensive proliferation of fungal hyphae in the host and penetration of the needle endodermis and vascular tissue by the pathogen prior to the onset of cell necrosis. Furthermore, preliminary results suggest the amount of fungal tissue present and its growth may be similar for both resistant and susceptible white pines (fig. 2).

Our results suggest that although resistance to WPBR in *P. monticola* and *P. lambertiana* conforms to the genetic model of HR, the mechanism of resistance may differ from that of typical HR. Histological examination of infected needles from Cr1 and Cr2 seedlings suggest that the blister rust pathogen proliferates within the host rapidly after inoculation and several weeks before the onset of typical macroscopic needle lesion symptoms or microscopic signs of autolytic cell death or tissue necrosis. Analyses of infection in resistant and susceptible *P. albicaulis* and *P. flexilis* phenotypes will provide additional insights. Resulting information will be used to help interpret resistance mechanisms in the species and provide baseline information useful for resistance breeding and disease management.

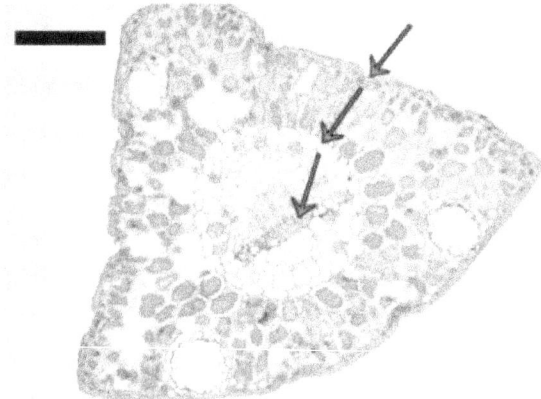

Figure 1—Cross section from a non-inoculated *Pinus monticola* secondary needle embedded with methacrylate and stained with toluidine blue. Arrows indicate the infection pathway. Pathogen enters through the stoma and grows within the mesophyll. The endodermis forms a barrier between mesophyll and vascular tissue. Crossing the endodermal layer and entrance into the vascular tissues allows the pathogen to spread into stem. Scale bar = 100µm. (Image: K. Cook)

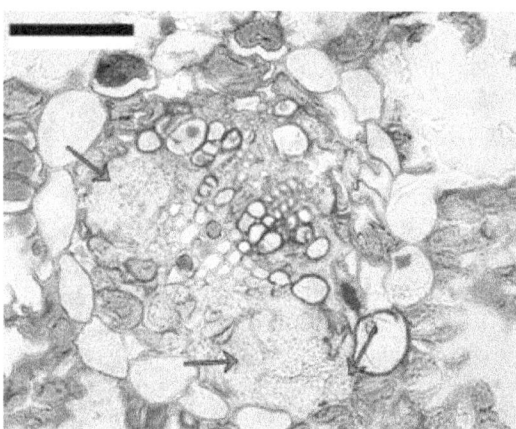

Figure 2—Cross section from resistant (Cr1) *Pinus lambertiana* secondary needle embedded with methacrylate and stained with toluidine blue. Sample taken from 2-year-old seedling, 6 weeks after inoculation with wild-type rust. Arrows point to *Cronartium ribicola* invading vascular tissues and endodermal cells. Scale bar = 100um. (Image: K. Cook)

Literature Cited

Dangl, J.L.; Jones, J.D. 2001. Plant pathogens and integrated defence responses to infection. Nature. 411: 826–833.

Flor, H.H. 1942. Inheritance of pathogenicity in *Melampsora lini*. Phytopathology. 32: 653–669.

Flor, H.H. 1955. Host-parasite interaction in flax rust - its genetics and other implications. Phytopathology. 45: 680–685.

Gilchrist, D.G. 1998. Programmed cell death in plant disease: the purpose and promise of cellular suicide. Annual Review of Phytopathology. 36: 393–414.

Hammond-Kosack, K.E.; Jones, J.D.G. 1997. Plant disease resistance genes. Annual Review of Plant Physiology and Plant Molecular Biology. 48: 575–607.

Heath, M.C. 2000. Hypersensitive response-related death. Plant Molecular Biology. 44: 321–334.

Innes, R.W. 1998. Genetic dissection of R gene signal transduction pathways. Current Opinion in Plant Biology. 1: 299–304.

Keane, R.E.; Schoettle, A.W. 2011. Strategies, tools, and challenges for sustaining and restoring high elevation five-needle white pine forests in western North America. In: Keane, R.E.; Tomback, D.F.; Murray, M.P.; Smith, C.M., eds. The future of high-elevation, five-needle white pines in western North America: proceedings of the high five symposium. Proc. RMRS-P-63. Ft. Collins, CO: U.S. Department of Agriculture, Forest Service, Rocky Mountain Research Station: 276–294.

Kinloch, B.B. Jr.; Littlefield, J.L. 1977. White pine blister rust: hypersensitive resistance in sugar pine. Canadian Journal of Botany. 55:1148–1155.

Kinloch, B.B. Jr.; Parks, G.K.; Fowler, C.W. 1970. White pine blister rust: simple inherited resistance in sugar pine. Science. 167:193–195.

Kinloch, B.B. Jr.; Sniezko, R.A.; Barnes, G.D.; Greathouse, T.E. 1999. A major gene for resistance to white pine blister rust in western white pine from the western Cascade Range. Phytopathology. 89: 861–867.

Kinloch, B.B. Jr.; Dupper, G.E. 2002. Genetic specificity in the white pine/blister rust pathosystem. Phytopathology. 92: 278–280.

Lamb, C.; Dixon, R.A. 1997. The oxidative burst in plant disease resistance. Annual Review of Plant Physiology and Plant Molecular Biology. 48: 251–275.

Liu, J.J.; Ekramoddoullah, A.K.M. 2003. Isolation, genetic variation and expression of TIR-NBS-LRR resistance gene analogs from western white pine (*Pinus monticola* Dougl. Ex. D. Don.). Molecular Genetics and Genomics. 270: 432–441.

McDonald, G.I.; Hoff, R.J. 2001. Blister rust: an introduced plague. In: Tomback, D.F.; Arno, S.F.; Keane, R.E., eds. Whitebark pine communities: ecology and restoration. Washington, DC: Island Press: 193–220.

Morel, J.B.; Dangl, J.L. 1997. The hypersensitive response and the induction of cell death in plants. Cell Death and Differentiation. 4: 671–683.

Schoettle, A.W.; Sniezko, R.A. 2007. Preparing the landscape for invasion – proactive intervention to mitigate impacts of a non-native pathogen. Journal of Forest Research. 12: 327–336.

Schwandt, J.W.; Lochman, I.B.; Kliejunas, J.T.; Muir, J.A. 2010. Current health issues and management strategies for white pines in the western United States and Canada. Forest Pathology. 40: 226–250.

Sniezko, R.A.; Mahalovich, M.F.; Schoettle, A.W.; Vogler, D.R. 2011. Plenary paper: past and current investigations of the genetic resistance to *Cronartium ribicola* .in Keane, R.E.; Tomback, D.F.; Murray, M.P.; Smith, C.M., eds. The future of high-elevation, five-needle white pines in western North America: proceedings of the high five symposium. Proc. RMRS-P-63. Ft. Collins, CO: U.S. Department of Agriculture, Forest Service, Rocky Mountain Research Station: 246–264.

Staskawicz, B.J.; Mudgett, M.B.; Dangl, J.L.; Galan, J.E. 2001. Common and contrasting themes of plant and animal diseases. Science. 292: 2285–2289.

van Doorn, W.G. 2011. Classes of programmed cell death in plants, compared to those in animals. The Journal of Experimental Botany. 62: 4749–4761.

The Potential of Breeding for Enhanced Inducibility in *Pinus pinaster* and *Pinus radiata*

Rafael Zas,[1] Alejandro Solla,[2] Xoaquin Moreira,[3] and Luis Sampedro[3]

Abstract

Most resistance mechanisms against pests and pathogens in pine trees involve the production of chemical defenses. These defenses are not cost free and the production of secondary metabolisms is generally inversely related with other plant fitness correlates, such as growth. The existence of these negative genetic correlations imposes an important obstacle for breeding for resistance and productivity simultaneously. Increased susceptibility to pests and diseases is, indeed, a common side-effect of enhancing productivity in many tree breeding programs. In a companion communication (Sampedro et al., these proceedings), we have reported negative correlation between constitutive resistance and growth potential of pine trees.

Pines are able to respond to insect and fungus attacks eliciting a wide array of responses. Induced defenses, i.e., those that are activated after biotic damage, are assumed to have evolved as a cost-saving strategy, as costs of induced resistance materialize only when strictly necessary. Despite the fact that breeding for resistance is emerging as an important tool to diminish the impact of forest pests and diseases on managed forests, to date no attention has been paid to the possibility of improving forest resistance through breeding for improving inducibility, i.e., the ability to respond to biotic damage eliciting induced defenses. Such a breeding strategy could likely integrate the benefits of both resistance and productivity, as inducible defensive strategies are cost saving. The very first step to explore whether inducibility can be increased through breeding is to determine whether these phenotypically plastic responses are under genetic control. Here we show that inducibility of chemical defenses in *Pinus pinaster* Aiton and *P. radiata* D. Don, two main forest tree species in southwestern Europe and other temperate regions, is genetically variable within populations.

We performed two greenhouse experiments with half-sib families of the two pine species. Plant material was a random selection of the actual breeding populations of these species in northwest Spain. We simulated biotic damage by spraying a solution of methyl jasmonate (MJ), a plant phytohormone that is known to be involved in the signalling and triggering of induced defenses, and when exogenously applied, elicit similar responses as real herbivory. Fifteen days after MJ application, we measured the concentration of diterpenes in the stem, total polyphenolics, and condensed tannins in the needles as measures of quantitative chemical defenses.

We found large genetic variation in all the defensive traits studied, but more interestingly, we also found additive genetic variation in the inducibility of the stem diterpenes in both species, as revealed by the significant family × MJ interaction. Although family × MJ interaction was not significant for phenolics, the different levels of genetic variation observed in control and MJ-induced plants, with significant differences among families found only in the MJ-induced treatment, does show the existence of genetic variation in the inducibility in this trait, too. Results indicate the existence of additive genetic variation for the inducibility of the three studied defensive traits in the two pine species, and the possibility of improving resistance of managed forests by artificially selecting for high inducibility potential, thus minimizing the possible undesired side-effects of enhancing productivity.

[1] Misión Biológica de Galicia, CSIC, Apdo. 28, 36080 Pontevedra, Spain.
[2] Universidad de Extremadura, Virgen del Puerto 2, 10600 Plasencia, Spain.
[3] Centro de Investigación Forestal de Lourizán, Apdo 127, 36080 Pontevedra, Spain.
Corresponding author: lsampe@uvigo.es.

www.ingramcontent.com/pod-product-compliance
Lightning Source LLC
Chambersburg PA
CBHW081204280526
45787CB00006B/2324